D0793275

MODERN JAPANESE WRITERS

MODERN JAPANESE WRITERS

JAY RUBIN
EDITOR

Charles Scribner's Sons
an imprint of the Gale Group
New York • Detroit • San Francisco • London • Boston • Woodbridge, CT

Charles Scribner's Sons
1633 Broadway
New York, NY 10019

Gale Group
27500 Drake Road
Farmington Hills, MI 48331

Library of Congress Cataloging-in-Publication Data

Modern Japanese writers / Jay Rubin, editor in chief
      p. cm.
      Includes bibliographical references and index.
      ISBN 0-684-80598-7
      1. Authors, Japanese—20th century—Biography. 2. Japanese literature—20th century—History and criticism. I. Rubin, Jay, 1941–
PL723 .M563 2000
895.6'090044—dc21
[B]

00-063505

1 2 3 4 5 6 7 8 9 10

Printed in the United States of America

EDITORIAL STAFF

CONTENTS

INTRODUCTION

THIS NEWEST ADDITION to the acclaimed Scribner Writers Series is its first foray into Japanese literature and a handy one-volume reference work on the most important modern Japanese authors. Most readers of this volume will be looking for background material on one particular author, but anyone who reads further will almost certainly be surprised at the richness, variety, and originality of modern Japanese literature in general. I like to think that these pages represent the triumph of diversity over stereotype, and that anyone searching for "the modern Japanese novel" or "the Japanese mind" will be pleasantly frustrated by the essays presented here.

Eleven of the twenty-four subjects selected for this volume are absolutely indispensable in any survey of the most important modern Japanese writers: Natsume Sōseki, Mori Ōgai, Shimazaki Tōson, Kawabata Yasunari, Tanizaki Jun'ichirō, Shiga Naoya, Futabatei Shimei, Akutagawa Ryūnosuke, Izumi Kyōka, Nagai Kafū, and Higuchi Ichiyō. All have assured places in the history of the development of modern Japanese literature, with massive academic studies in each case. Unfortunately, being dead is a great plus in such a ranking, the test of time being undeniable evidence of importance. Most writers of such stature have attracted the attention of translators, but the sheer existence of English translations (which, after all, could be merely a reflection of the pressures of the marketplace) was not one of our top criteria for inclusion. Similar backing exists for seven additional authors in this work, on whom opinions might diverge somewhat: Dazai Osamu, Nakagami Kenji, Nishiwaki Junzaburō, Sakaguchi Ango, Abe Kōbō, Enchi Fumiko, and Mishima Yukio.

None of the writers of the atomic bomb has individually attained such status, but it was my conviction that as a phenomenon unique to Japan, atomic bomb literature had been ignored far too long. The appearance of translations and major studies of the field in recent years also seemed to demand attention. As a student who has spent several years studying the subject, Karen Thornber was more than ready to share her expertise in the essay Atomic Bomb Writers.

INTRODUCTION

Another important essay is the piece on Narushima Ryūhoku, a writer I long ago hoped to study more deeply as I rushed past his period to focus on a later stage of the history of literary censorship in Japan. Ryūhoku is an absolute original in the closely related fields of literature and journalism, and though virtually untranslated, is such a vivid embodiment of the deep traditional (and Chinese) roots of modern Japanese literature that I leaped at the chance to have Matthew Fraleigh do a compact version of his forthcoming doctoral dissertation for the volume. Ryūhoku is the one writer in the book who will not be searched out by students reading him in translation, but I would strongly urge any reader wishing for background on one of the Meiji giants or with an interest in the early history of Japan's modern literature to read this essay in combination with the one(s) of primary interest.

This leaves us with only four writers to be argued over. 1994 Nobel prizewinner Ōe Kenzaburō has certainly earned a major place in literary and intellectual history but he is still very much alive, as are Kōno Taeko, Kurahashi Yumiko, and the enormously popular Murakami Haruki. Though none has (fortunately) stood the test of time, each has clearly emerged as a distinctive voice in his or her own time and each has inspired a good deal of scholarly exploration, though translators have been less uniformly attracted to them. As a translator of Murakami, I believe I see qualities in his work that are similar to that of Sōseki, the one writer at the head of anyone's list, but this will be for later generations to judge.

The following sampling should provide some idea of the range and variety to be found in modern Japanese literature.

Ōe Kenzaburō is gripped by a powerful historical awareness of belonging to a generation disfigured by the twin forces of modernization and war guilt.

Probably no other modern Japanese writer has been as intensely loved—and loathed—by as many readers as **Dazai Osamu.**

Depending where one looks, one can find in **Kawabata Yasunari**'s writing all-embracing cosmopolitanism or xenophobic nationalism, the demand for constant revolution or deep reverence for the past.

Nakagami Kenji rose to fame in the mid-1970s for vivid and powerful stories of a clan scarred by violence and poverty on the underside of Japan's economic miracle. His fiction burst apart stereotypes of a serene and homogenous Japan, presenting a clear view of oppression and discrimination.

In time **Murakami Haruki** came to feel that, whereas jazz might have supplied the energy for the clipped beat of his earlier works, the sustained power of his later style owed much to his long-distance running.

The first thing a foreign student of Japanese notices when he or she picks up one of **Shiga Naoya**'s works is how easy it is to read. The sentences are short, the language concrete. There is even something childish about the style.

Kōno Taeko usually writes about everyday events, focusing on the minutest details with obsessive intensity and incorporating glimpses of an extraordinary level of violence lying hidden beneath the quotidian surface.

INTRODUCTION

Writers of the atomic bomb frequently examine both the memories and the guilt that plague survivors and often comment on the discrimination that confronts them daily in a society that would prefer to forget.

Enchi Fumiko's writing is known especially for its depiction of the way women suffered, often silently, under the Japanese *ie*, or household system, as well as for its evocation of female eroticism and mystery. Above all, Enchi's work is known for its frequent incorporation of themes and texts from the classical Japanese canon.

Nishiwaki Junzaburō had been writing poetry in English and French quite freely long before he began writing poetry in Japanese. Herein lies the enigmatic core of his work: the new poetic language Nishiwaki invented was not an authentically Japanese one but rather a language of translation.

Kurahashi Yumiko looms as an inconvenient figure in modern Japanese literature, undoing perceptions of a field conventionally described as sentimental, confessional, transparent, and structureless. Her writing, in contrast, is logical, parodic, rhetorical, and well plotted.

Particularly challenging is **Abe Kōbō**'s combination of what might be called "sense" and "nonsense." Even within a single novel, some parts are inevitably characterized by close reasoning, intricate plotting, and rigorous logic, while other sections veer into seemingly uncontrolled and unresolved fantasy.

Akutagawa Ryūnosuke's brilliant success ended with the shock of his suicide in 1927, an event that has been viewed as symbolic of the failure of Japan's progress toward socialist ideals and democratic freedoms in the early twentieth century.

Starting out as a literary aesthete, **Mishima Yukio** transformed himself into a boxer, a bodybuilder, and a martial arts devotee. He acted in films and plays and assumed the guise of cultural critic lamenting the state of postwar Japanese society. He eventually became a political ideologue who created his own private military group devoted to a return to rule by the emperor.

Narushima Ryūhoku's mockery of those in power often landed him in serious trouble, both before and after the Meiji Restoration, but Ryūhoku never lost his sense of humor.

The bold strokes of **Shimazaki Tōson**'s early career gave way to a literature of self that foregrounded the author as struggling youth, beleaguered family member, tortured soul, spiritual seeker, and—finally—literary patriarch.

At the same moment Lafcadio Hearn was introducing Western readers to a new world he had fallen in love with, through such works as *A Japanese Miscellany: Strange Stories, Folklore Gleanings, and Studies Here & There* (1900), **Tanizaki Jun'ichirō** was a child growing up embedded in that very culture.

The change in period label from "Tokugawa" to "Meiji" did nothing to modify the ingrained habits of calculation that remained vital in Japanese interpersonal relations into the twenty-first century. **Natsume Sōseki**'s novels deal with questions that transcend nationality, but they portray some of the darkest aspects of human exchange the world over by capturing this open secret of Japanese society.

Higuchi Ichiyō wrote about adolescent love, lust, and identity before it was fashionable even to recognize youth as a time of significant social, emotional, and physical change.

Izumi Kyōka's famous depictions of the uncanny resulted from his own emotional need for literary ritual and a language that could address the sense of loss and profound fear—of death, of disease, of dogs, of thunder—that plagued him throughout his life.

From the outset, there was a fundamental division in **Futabatei Shimei**'s view of literature that manifested itself as an ambivalent attitude about his place as a transitional figure—an attitude that exemplified the divided sensibility of a generation that had undertaken radical cultural modernization.

Sakaguchi Ango lived his life at an almost primal, instinctual level, and this attitude was reflected in his work. Known to wear nothing but a loincloth for days on end, Ango struggled to peel the unnecessary in his writing as well: he shunned the literary conventions of the day and portrayed a human condition devoid of the rules of polite society.

While **Nagai Kafū** is remembered largely for his elegiac depictions of the vanishing culture of the Edo period, these portraits are often filtered through his fascination with French literature, a combination that has interested and confounded critics of his work.

Deeply concerned about the moral and philosophical ramifications of the modern condition, **Mori Ōgai** contributed to the formation of that very condition as a public intellectual and literary craftsman of the highest calibre. Together with his great contemporary, Natsume Sōseki, Ōgai may be credited with laying the foundation not only for a modern literature in Japan but for a modern Japan itself.

The majority of the writers covered in this volume have received Japan's highest literary honors. Japan's high-powered literary establishment (or *bundan*) is driven by prizes, usually sponsored by literary magazines, and the reader will find any number of them mentioned in these pages. The Akutagawa Prize, named after the writer Akutagawa Ryūnosuke, who killed himself in 1927, is considered the one most important boost for a writer on the rise. Some few writers (such as Dazai Osamu and Murakami Haruki) have managed to flourish quite handily without this certificate of authenticity from the literary establishment so frequently mentioned in these pages, and many writers have failed to live up to the promise the prize suggests. It is, after all, awarded twice annually, and the number of literary geniuses appearing in any country in a six-month period has to be limited.

It is important to note that some of the most important contemporary writers in Japan, both at the center of the literary establishment, and on the fringes, are women. Young readers, especially, may respond to this statement with a healthy "So what?" It should be pointed out that the current state of sexual equality in letters has not always been the case, and that after World War II, especially, there was a long transitional period when women writers were said to belong to the "women's school" *(joryū),* as if their writing were necessarily qualitatively different from (and, of course, inferior to) men's. They were singled out for encouragement through the awarding of various women's literature prizes. The essays and bibliographical material on Enchi Fumiko and Kōno Taeko would be good places to start reading about this phenomenon.

The contributors to this volume are as diverse as the authors they have written about; they write in distinctly different styles and take very different approaches to their subjects' lives and works. Although a relatively uniform framework has been adopted so as to provide much "hard" information, and scholarly standards are uniformly high, the reader will not find here a homogenized series of neutral-toned encyclopedia entries, but rather a deep sense of personal engagement of the contributors with their subjects. If the increase in enthusiasm means a loss of apparent objectivity, that is all to the good (within reason). The subject here is literature, after all, texts composed to stir people's blood, and unless some sense of that comes through, there is not much point in subjecting it to scholarly analysis. This is, in other words, a rather old-fashioned book, but that very fact seems to have stimulated the contributors, several of whom expressed to me their pleasure in the course of working on the volume at being able to get away from critical jargon and write for real people about books and authors they care about.

The contributors' varied purposes and interests are another source of the enthusiasm that can be sensed in these pages. We have two advanced graduate students here, still flush with the excitement of discovery, and many of the entries are the products of brand new Ph.D.s, who take very little that their predecessors have written for granted. The more seasoned contributors, on the other hand, are mostly writing about new loves of middle age, authors they have come to enjoy on their own, without the pressures of the academic mill, or to whom they have returned for a fresh look after years of working on other things.

All contributors to this volume are scholars of Japanese literature and write of the works under consideration based on their readings of the original Japanese texts. (For that reason, a character named Yoko or Toru in a published translation will show up as Yōko or Tōru here.) For the convenience of the reader without access to Japanese, all quoted passages cite published translations when those are available. When the contributor is satisfied with the published work, the citation refers simply to "tr." with page numbers. If the contributor has felt the need to revise the published translation slightly, the citation will specify that it has been "revised from" that source. Where the translation is judged to be based on a different or mistaken interpretation, the contributor will provide an original translation and "cf." the published translation. When no published translations are available, the translations of cited passages have been done by the contributors themselves.

Readers may note that none of the essays says anything about the vagueness or inherent untranslatability of the Japanese language. These are simply myths. A great deal of nonsense still clings to the notion of Japanese, which indeed has structures and vocabulary that make it very different from English, but Japanese is a language much like any other, with rules to be learned and with its own special areas of richness and poverty. Ted Goossen's essay on Shiga Naoya provides some fresh insights into one way in which the Japanese language can be different from English in its expression of "autonomous psychological phenomena." Translation itself is a central theme of Hosea Hirata's essay on Nishiwaki Junzaburō.

Let me return to the subject of the great variety in modern Japanese literature that makes generalizing about the modern Japanese novel next to impossible. For all the narrowly focused, autobiographical novels that may constitute the mainstream, there are plenty of others that have broad historical sweep and richly imagined imagery and incident. For those evidencing an Eastern serenity in nature, there are plenty of wildly crazy, violent, and frenzied works. In the supposed modern Japanese novel, we find obsessive sexuality and prudish restraint, transcendent beauty and degrading filth, deep pessimism, wide-eyed optimism and everything in between, stolid factuality and vivid fantasy, formless lyricism and tight-knit storytelling, unrelieved gloom and hilarious comedy.

All of the authors treated here are modern writers, which is to say that when they employ motifs or themes from Japan's classical literature, they do so by conscious choice. Writers like Tanizaki, Enchi, Akutagawa, and Kawabata—and especially Dazai—mine the classics for effect. Even Higuchi Ichiyō, perhaps the closest thing to an innocent writing within the tradition, was borrowing from the eleventh and seventeenth centuries as she consorted with her nearly twentieth-century colleagues. The reader of Japan's modern literature luxuriates amid the cherry blossoms, geisha, and Mt. Fuji only by turning a blind eye to the writers' critical purposes. Abe Kōbō "links the emotions associated with cherry blossoms to unthinking cultural pride and the rise of nationalism, and even the specter of renewed Japanese military expansion."

Which is not to say that all of Japan's modern writers cut their ties with the past, as demonstrated by the longing for a *furusato*, one's "old village" or "roots in the countryside," seen in several writers. We find this most purely in Shimazaki Tōson, whose "*furusato*-based traditionalism strongly resonates with current nativist thinking in Japan, which plays upon the theme of Japanese uniqueness." Sakaguchi Ango turned the concept on its head even during the wartime hysteria of the late thirties and early forties, making of it a place of "an unmediated, authentic engagement with our most primal needs and desires." The cosmopolitan Abe Kōbō gave up any hope of connecting with roots and declared, "I am a person without a home town," which he saw as the only way to remain free. Nakagami Kenji later lamented his lack of a place of belonging, but perhaps the problem is endemic to all writers of any age who must stand back and watch in order to write.

In pursuing the question of what is modern and Japanese about modern Japanese literature, the reader would do well to begin with Marvin Marcus' essay on Shimazaki Tōson, whose career is "regarded as emblematic of *kindai no seishin*—the spirit of modern Japan in the prewar period. *Kindai* may be defined simply as 'modern' or 'modern age,' but in the context of literary history the term has come to possess rich layers of meaning. The transformational *kindai* epoch holds a particular fascination for Japanese, and the lives of its representative writers have been 'read' inseparably from their literary texts." Marcus' piece on Mori Ōgai examines other facets of *kindai* literature.

An Overview of Historical Periods

Historical periods play a critical role in any study of Japanese literature. The two past literary epochs most frequently referred to in these essays are the Heian period (794–1185) and the Edo or Tokugawa Period (c.1600–1868). In the Heian period, the imperial court in Kyoto was the center of power and cultural creativity, and women connected with the court wrote the great literary works (most notably Murasaki Shikibu and her *The Tale of Genji*). Commercial comic fiction, by men, flourished during the long period when the capital shifted eastward to Edo (modern Tokyo) and the Tokugawa Shōguns ruled the country. The emperor was theoretically restored to power in the Meiji Restoration of 1868. Most Meiji references to Edo literature have to do with overcoming the benighted past, though a few Meiji writers adopted Edo humor in their works.

The essays on Narushima Ryūhoku and Natsume Sōseki provide information on the transition from Edo to the period called Meiji, when the practice was adopted of making the name of the period coincide with the reign of the current emperor (and then naming the emperor posthumously after the period over which he had presided). The death of the emperor who had been enthroned in 1868 marked the end of the Meiji period in 1912. The subsequent imperial reigns have been Taishō (1912–1926), Shōwa (1926–1989), and Heisei (1989–present), and although literary periods are not of course determined by the life spans of individual rulers, these labels are handy for outlining certain trends.

Narushima Ryūhoku (1837–1884) straddled the Edo and Meiji periods, holding a high post in the Tokugawa government and acting as a gadfly to both the shogunate and the supposedly more enlightened government that replaced it. His writing is a good example of the adaptation of traditional literary styles to meet the modern situation. Japan's first modern novel combines some of those early comic styles with Russian literary practice, as outlined in the article on Futabatei Shimei (1864–1909). The work of Higuchi Ichiyō (1872–1896) illustrates the continuing influence of a classical style even as writers experimented with a more neutral narrative medium that would combine the spoken and written styles *(genbun-itchi)*.

Russian (and French) influence was decisive again as a flood of translation followed the Russo-Japanese War of 1904–1905. Somber portraits of life among the masses and equally somber self-portraits of writers struggling with their sexuality and with the crushing weight of the traditional family system characterized the naturalist school that came to dominate the publishing world during the last few years of Meiji. By that time classical language and literary conventions were essentially dead, but Nagai Kafū (1879–1959) and Izumi Kyōka (1873–1939) both rejected naturalism and sought to recreate the mood and language of Edo in very different ways. Shimazaki Tōson is the writer in this collection most closely identified with the naturalist school. He was also one of the most successful writers of new-style verse, which rejected such traditional short forms as *waka* and *haiku* in favor of long, romantic songs heavily influenced by Christian hymns.

The rise of naturalism—which is to say, the maturation of the modern Japanese novel—spurred the Meiji government to mobilize its censorship and educational systems in the name of wholesome traditional values, and the pressure that had long been exerted on leftist writing began to be felt by individualistic writers. Leftist politics and writing entered their winter years following a severe crackdown in 1910–1911, and Japan moved decisively toward empire-building, most notably with the annexation of Korea.

One writer who came to share many of the concerns of the naturalists but whose deep knowledge of English literature, psychology, and philosophy helped him bring an unmatched philosophical depth to his work was Natsume Sōseki (1867–1916). Sōseki was born when samurai still wandered the streets with swords and topknots, but the intensity with which he captured the pain of the modern experience was as fresh at the opening of the twenty-first century as it had been early in the twentieth. The German-trained Mori Ōgai (1862–1922) was the other Meiji giant who stood apart from the naturalists and created probing studies of the struggles between traditional hearts and modern minds. The greatest works of both Sōseki and Ōgai were actually written in the Taishō period and reflected the wrenching changes produced by Meiji and by Meiji's coming to an end.

A certain diminishment of scale seemed to characterize the writing of the Taishō period, when technical polish, self-examination, and the pursuit of idiosyncratic visions came to replace the large sense of history that characterized the best of Meiji writing. The year 1910 marked the end of naturalism as a school and the simultaneous beginnings of the careers of Tanizaki Jun'ichirō (1886–1965) and Shiga Naoya (1883–1971). A new mood of cosmopolitanism followed the end of World War I, and leftist writings began to appear again. "Taishō democracy" is a phrase often applied to this period. The roaring twenties roared just as loudly in Japan as in the West. The Taishō writer par excellence was Akutagawa Ryūnosuke (1892–1927), whose suicide in 1927 seemed to confirm that bourgeois fiction had indeed come to a dead end. The long years of experimentation in free verse forms began to bear fruit in 1917 in the poetry of Hagiwara Sakutarō (1886–1942), who in turn influenced Nishiwaki Junzaburō (1894–1982), whose career flourished in the Shōwa period (see the Nishiwaki piece for Hagiwara).

Meiji inflicted psychic scars with Japan's national struggle to join the ranks of the so-called first-class powers, but the leaders' decision to seek empire along with its new peers made of the record-long Shōwa period a heady, horrifying roller-coaster ride. From flappers, gin, and jazz in the 1920s, the country moved quickly to a repressive junta rule in the thirties and forties, which was marked by enslavement of other Asian peoples, millions dead and cities in ruins on the continent and at home, nuclear weapons unleashed on the world, and Japan's first occupation by a foreign power. Kawabata Yasunari (1899–1972) saw all this, and witnessed, too, Japan's amazing rebirth, and the success of Japan's economic imperialism where the military version had failed. Although he did not live to see the opening of Tokyo Disneyland, he saw the almost equally freakish attempt by his younger colleague, Mishima Yukio (1925–1970), to rouse the constitutionally questionable Self Defense Forces in the name of the emperor.

While such atomic bomb survivors as Hara Tamiki (1905–1951), Hayashi Kyōko (1930–), Kurihara Sadako (1913–), Ōta Yōko (1903–1963), and Tōge Sankichi (1917–1963) struggled to convey the atrocity in words, Ibuse Masuji (1898–1993), who did not himself experience the bombing, is often credited with having written the most successful novel on Hiroshima. (See the section on Ibuse in the article Atomic Bomb Writers.)

Literature of the immediate postwar period, however, often seemed less earnest than outrageous. The decadent Sakaguchi Ango (1906–1955) helped his countrymen snap out of their postwar malaise by explaining to them why they had so loved the war and why they must reject the worship of the emperor and other false gods. Dazai Osamu (1909–1948) parodied the rush to democracy and turned to drugs and death.

Abe Kōbō (1924–1993), who had been raised in Manchukuo, Japan's puppet state in Manchuria, returned to his war-ravaged country to explore his sense of alienation by creating science-fiction fantasy worlds. Enchi Fumiko (1905–1986) mined the Japanese classics for material to throw back at the Japanese patriarchy. Kōno Taeko (1926–) survived forced war labor, hunger, and illness to create a sado-masochistic narrative critiquing Japanese male-dominated society. Ōe Kenzaburō (1935–) stood out as a critic of the imperial institution and of the United States for its use of nuclear weapons. Nakagami Kenji (1946–1992) demanded an end to silence surrounding the plight of the outcastes in Japan.

The emperor who almost dragged his people to destruction never squarely voiced his or the country's responsibility for Japan's depredations in Asia, but his death in 1989 seemed to free people to begin asking these questions. One of the writers who faced this most squarely in his fiction was the popular novelist Murakami Haruki (1949–), who was able to convey to his generally young readership some of the horror that he and they had missed by being born in an affluent Japan. In fiction and nonfiction, he has helped to make the Heisei era a time of re-evaluation of the Shōwa nightmare.

Little has been said about Christianity in the essays other than to point out how one or another Meiji or Taishō period writer embraced it briefly only to reject it. In general, the Japanese have a great respect for piety and are only too willing to bow their heads in any religious context without questioning the nature of the deity or religious principles being honored. When doctrines begin to demand exclusive devotion, however, the Japanese tend to balk. They see that each religion has its charming story of how the world came into being and how human life fits into the overall scheme of things, but recognize that each is just a story, which is nothing worth killing or dying for. As bloody as the country's political history has been, therefore, sectarian warfare of the kind we enjoy in the West is all but unknown in Japan.

Imagine, however, growing up in a society in which a person's worth is judged entirely according to how closely that person fits the models held up for prescribed social roles—lord, vassal, husband, wife, father, mother, son, daughter. Then imagine the shock of a person accustomed to living in such a society after being told that he or she is valuable as an individual simply by virtue of the fact that he or she exists as a human being separate from all the other human beings. This was the message of Christianity that thrilled some of the most sensitive and intelligent souls when Japan was opened to the West. Without Christianity, the Meiji-Taishō project of the discovery of the self would have been far slower to develop, and Japan's literature would have taken far longer to begin looking modern. Most writers, however, were not ready to restrain their sex drives or to curtail their lifestyles in the name of what they saw to be just another story. See the essay on Shiga Naoya as an example of the role Christianity played in one writer's spiritual quest.

Japanese Names and Overall Organization

Modern Japanese Writers is organized in alphabetical order and uses the names that a Japanese reader would find most natural, which in most cases means the surname, but in others, particularly those of authors who flourished around the turn of the twentieth century, means a traditional literary personal name or sobriquet (*gō* or *gagō*) composed of two Chinese characters containing images from classical Chinese or Japanese literature. The *gō* best known in the West dates from the seventeenth century: *Bashō*, meaning "banana (or plantain) leaf," an image of fragility and delicacy that identified the haiku poet Matsuo Bashō with the long Japanese tradition of poetry on the fleeting seasons and the transience of human life. (The young woman novelist Yoshimoto Banana had the same image in mind when she debuted with her cool, Western-sounding pen name in the late 1980s.)

Most of the authors with *gō* are known by those, and not by their family names. An author like Nagai Kafū is immediately recognized as Kafū, whereas Nagai has no such ready literary associations. Even this rule has one exception, Futabatei Shimei, which is entirely pseudonymous; the writer is often referred to as Shimei, but his surname is more commonly used. Sakaguchi Ango is another kind of exception. He flourished in the 1940s, half a century after most people stopped making up *gō* for themselves, but he took one and it caught on. Two other noteworthy cases are Dazai Osamu and Mishima Yukio. Both of these names are entirely made up, but neither uses a *gō*, and so the authors are known by their pseudonymous surnames. Readers wishing to familiarize themselves with the early development of modern Japanese literature would be well advised to read about those writers with *gō:* Narushima Ryūhoku, Futabatei Shimei, Higuchi Ichiyō, Mori Ōgai, Natsume Sōseki, Shimazaki Tōson, Izumi Kyōka, and Nagai Kafū.

Pronunciation of Japanese

Anyone familiar with names and words such as Toyota, Mitsubishi, Honda, Nissan, Tokyo, Hiroshima, Nagasaki, Nomo, Yoko Ono, Seiji Ozawa, sushi, and tsunami can safely pronounce Japanese words the way they look. A few familiar terms tend to be mangled, though: karaoke (kah-rah-OH-keh, not carry-okey), geisha (gay-shah, not geesha), sake (SAH-keh, not sacky), Isuzu (ee-SOO-zoo, not ee-ZOO-zoo). The Nagano Olympics should have been called something closer to "NAH-ga-no" rather than the "Nuh-GAH-no" more often heard on TV, but no great harm was done.

INTRODUCTION

We have tried to be consistent with the long marks (macrons) that differentiate long and short vowels in Japanese, but the practice of using such marks is inconsistent to begin with. Tokyo (a two-syllable word) should be written Tōkyō, but to insist on this would be the height of pedantry, and the only thing that the long mark on James Clavell's *Shōgun* accomplished was to heighten its exotic appeal. Although they can indicate crucial differences in meaning (ō=large, o=small), macrons are of interest only to people familiar with the language; the general reader can ignore them.

JAY RUBIN

ABE KŌBŌ
1924–1993

CHRISTOPHER BOLTON

ABE KŌBŌ played a key role in the Japanese literary avant-garde after World War II and remained on the cutting edge of letters for most of the next forty years. While he probed certain themes—including the relationship of the often-alienated individual to the community and society—consistently throughout his career, in other ways Abe continually reinvented himself and his work. Although he was best known for a series of brilliant novels, his interests and accomplishments also ranged from medicine to music, theater, photography, and film.

Abe's eclecticism has made it difficult for some readers and critics to come to terms with his work. Neither Abe nor his texts fits neatly into the usual categories, and the twists and turns one encounters going from one work to another can be baffling. Particularly challenging is Abe's combination of what might be called "sense" and "nonsense." Even within a single novel, some parts are inevitably characterized by close reasoning, intricate plotting, and rigorous logic, while other sections veer into seemingly uncontrolled and unresolved fantasy.

The divided personality of Abe's writing can sometimes hamper understanding of his works. But, in fact, the competition of these different ideas or styles—some sensible and some nonsensical—is a key aspect of Abe's fiction and his career. Abe spoke and thought in many registers, and so does his fiction. Both the author and his characters are formed by the harmony of these different voices.

Origins

The preoccupation with crises of identity and belonging in Abe's work, as well as the author's unique perspective, have sometimes been traced to the experiences of his youth, which was spent largely outside Japan, in Japanese-controlled Manchuria.

Abe's family registry was in Hokkaido, where both his parents grew up and where his grandparents had settled as pioneers in the Meiji era (1868–1912). Perhaps in the same spirit of frontier expansion, Abe's father, Asakichi, left Hokkaido to attend school at the medical college in Mukden, Manchuria. Asakichi later served on the faculty at the college and eventually opened a medical practice in the city. Like many other Japanese settlers, Asakichi was drawn to Manchuria by Japanese development and expansion in the region during the years leading up to Japan's full-scale military takeover in 1932.

Abe's mother, Yorimi, was a writer with an interest in proletarian literature. She and Abe's

1

father were married in Tokyo, where Abe was born on March 7, 1924. The first of four children, he was named Kimifusa but later changed the reading of the characters in his given name to "Kōbō." In 1925 Abe's father brought the family to Manchuria, and it was there that Abe Kōbō spent most of his early childhood.

Abe traveled to Tokyo to attend high school and, after graduating in 1943, entered the medical department of the prestigious Tokyo Imperial University. He went back to Manchuria a year later, though, when he realized Japan's defeat by the Allied Forces in World War II was imminent. By 1946, when Abe returned to Japan with his family, his entire world had been transformed: his father had died treating a typhus outbreak; Japan's defeat had brought about the end of the Manchurian puppet state which had been Abe's home; and drastic changes were in store for the Japanese nation that was his homeland.

When called on to produce a brief chronology of his life, Abe noted this confusing discrepancy between his place of birth, his place of origin, and his family registry, concluding: "Fundamentally you might say I am a person without a home town. Maybe the deep hostility that I feel toward the home town traces itself to my background. I am hurt by anything that attaches value to being settled" ("Ryaku nenpyō," in *Abe Kōbō zenshū [AKZ]*, vol. 20, p. 92). Taking their cue from this frequently quoted passage, many critics have traced Abe's preoccupation with identity and lost identity to these early events in his life, drawing a connection between Abe's lost homeland and the feelings of isolation, alienation, or loss experienced by his characters.

Abe's literary debut, *Owarishi michi no shirube ni* (1948, 1965; On the sign at the end of the road), is a work that draws on the author's wartime experiences. Set in Manchuria at the end of the war, it takes the form of a series of notebooks written by its opium addict narrator, who tells his own story of flight and imprisonment as he considers the nature of home and homeland.

A few of Abe's later works were explicitly grounded in these childhood and wartime experiences, but in contrast to the relentlessly personal and experiential writing of many of Abe's contemporaries, who wrote in the mode of naturalism, proletarian realism, or the I-novel, Abe moved away from straightforward autobiographical elements in his later writing. Nevertheless, even the dreamlike avant-garde stories which established his early reputation often revolve around the same images of identity and alienation, or home and escape.

For example, in "Akai mayu" (1950; "The Red Cocoon," 1986), a homeless man longing for a place to rest pulls on a thread emerging from his foot and finds that as he pulls on it, his body begins to unravel. Meanwhile the unraveling thread weaves itself around him in a cocoon, until finally his body disappears completely and only the empty casing of the cocoon remains. The question of home is no less central than in *Owarishi michi no shirube ni*, but now it is treated through this ambiguous image.

A detail from Abe's story *S. Karuma shi no hanzai* (1951; *The Crime of S. Karma*, 1991) suggests how images and experiences from Abe's personal experience undergo fantastic transformations in his later work. *Owarishi michi no shirube ni* begins with the image of a forgotten wall in the middle of a wide Manchurian plain. *The Crime of S. Karma* concludes with same image; this time, however, the empty plain is located not in Manchuria or in the author's memory, but literally inside the narrator: as a sign of the emptiness of Mr. S. Karma's life, he has fallen victim to a strange condition which transforms his chest cavity into an expanse of deserted grassy dunes.

As these striking transformations suggest, Abe's early life may be a starting point for understanding the issues of belonging in his work, but it would be risky to regard them as a map. It is tempting to draw a straight line between Abe's loss of homeland and the issues of alienation, isolation, and belonging evident in his work, but in the absurd or surreal landscape of Abe's fiction, identity and belonging—

like Abe's characters themselves—inevitably undergo fantastic metamorphoses. The issue of home is thus linked to the balance between sense and nonsense in Abe's writing. The problems that Abe probes in his work—of identity and belonging, or individual, society, and nation—are all pressingly real, but Abe often chooses to investigate them in the realm of fantasy. A possible connection between these issues of fantasy and homeland is suggested by a description of Manchuria at the end of the war. This passage, which is taken from another autobiographical chronology, may be even more revealing than Abe's comment about lacking a homeland. The entry for 1946 reads: "In August, abruptly, the war ended. Suddenly the world was bathed in light, and I felt as if every kind of possibility had materialized at once. The conditions which followed, without any government, were harsh; but along with fear and unease, the absence of government also planted something else in me—a dream" ("Nenpyō," in *AKZ*, vol. 12, p. 464).

Abe goes on to discuss the freedom imparted by the disintegration of the Japanese Empire and even his father's death. With this in mind, another way to view the issue of homeland is in this broader context of sense or meaning (including the meanings and values imposed by communities like family, society, or the state) and the need for the destruction of an old meaning before the possibility of a new one can arise. Abe regarded nationality or nationalism as but one species of this communal "sense" or "order" that art must struggle to overcome. "I feel nothing but repugnance for the pseudo-culture which tries to legitimize the walls surrounding nations," Abe wrote ("Chikyū," in *AKZ*, vol. 25, p. 360; tr. p. 43).

Instead of viewing Abe as caught between the twin homelands of Japan and Manchuria, it may be more interesting to see him as figuratively suspended between the relative freedom and imagination of the literary world (perhaps represented by his mother) and the world of logic, science, and medicine represented by his father the doctor.

In the second of the chronologies cited above, Abe wrote that his father's passing freed him from the obligation to continue with medicine. After returning to Japan, he did re-enter medical school and resume the studies which had been interrupted by the end of the war. But the poverty he had experienced since the war's end and his father's death apparently left him with little time or energy for his medical studies. And, perhaps more importantly, his growing literary success soon began to compete with medicine for his attention.

In 1947, before he had even finished medical school, Abe published a mimeographed poetry collection, *Mumeishū* (1947; The nameless collection). He had the work printed at his own expense, but by that time a part of *Owarishi michi no shirube ni* had already been accepted for publication in the literary journal *Kosei*, where it appeared early the following year.

When Abe graduated from medical school in 1948, his literary career was already launched. Instead of doing a residency, he pursued his budding career as a writer and over the course of the next year published a steady stream of poetry, fiction, essays, and criticism—the beginning of four decades of literary output.

But Abe never abandoned his earlier scientific training, nor his love of mathematics, which had been his strong suit since high school. Even through his most experimental or surreal works, there runs a strong undercurrent of logic and rationality. He makes frequent and very precise use of scientific and mathematical language, for example, as well as images and metaphors borrowed from a wide range of scientific disciplines.

Abe's scientific inclinations are examined in more detail later in this essay. For now it will suffice to say that one can see Abe's work as balanced between two poles: the logic and rationality of science on the one hand, and the surreal, sometimes irrational, fantastic possibilities of fiction on the other. These are two of the voices that Abe harmonized within his writing, and the striking combination of these two worlds is a trademark of Abe's work.

3

Early Works and the Avant-garde

Owarishi michi no shirube ni was accepted for publication in the journal *Kosei* on the recommendation of the avant-garde novelist and critic Haniya Yutaka. This was the beginning of Abe's involvement with a group of people, literary circles, and journals that constituted Japan's postwar avant-garde, a movement in which Abe would play an increasingly important role.

Abe was particularly influenced by the theorist Hanada Kiyoteru and was active in Hanada's circle, the Yoru no Kai (The Night Group), from the time it was launched in 1948. Abe was a junior member in this coterie of more established writers and intellectuals, but he was apparently an energetic participant in the circle's activities. In 1948–1949 he formed his own group, the Seiki no Kai (The Century Group), for younger writers and artists.

Like Hanada and many of the other figures in these movements, Abe associated progressive art with leftist politics. He was a member of the Communist Party in the 1950s and was active in a number of groups and publications that had close party ties, including *Jinmin bungaku* (People's literature) and *Shin Nihon bungaku* (New Japanese literature).

In principle, the avant-garde sought to go beyond Western modernism, but at the same time it drew inspiration from a number of modernist aesthetic movements. Since his youth, Abe had been drawn to Western authors (particularly the German poet Rainer Maria Rilke and the Russian novelist Fyodor Dostoyevsky), and now he was lecturing at literary meetings on such topics as Franz Kafka and surrealism. In his later writing, Abe's references range from Jean-Jacques Rousseau to Ray Bradbury.

These Western literary interests and influences, combined with Abe's unique background and, later, his growing fame abroad, have caused some to regard him as disconnected from the Japanese literary tradition. It is true that Abe seldom draws on premodern Japanese literature or "traditional" culture in

the way Tanizaki Jun'ichirō and Kawabata Yasunari do. But Abe's early association with like-minded Japanese artists in the avant-garde suggests that he was also part of a new Japanese literary tradition, a changing one that drew from an ever widening sphere of influences.

In the postscript *(atogaki)* to a collection of his criticism from the early and mid-1950s titled *Mōjū no kokoro ni keisanki no te o* (1957; The hand of a computer and the heart of a beast), Abe describes the essays as progressing from existentialism to surrealism, and then to communism. This convenient formula is often cited to explain the change in Abe's fiction as well, from the philosophical examination of individual existence in *Owarishi michi no shirube ni* to the more fantastic and indeterminate images of "The Red Cocoon," one of many works from the 1950s that turn on metamorphosis, distorted realities, and absurd situations.

Early on, Abe forged a distinctive voice with works like "The Red Cocoon" and "Dendorokakariya" (1949, 1952; "Dendrocacalia," 1991), which centers on a man's transformation into a plant. The protagonist, whose name is "Common," experiences attacks in which he finds himself turning into a type of flowering tree from whose Latin name the story takes its title. Common is pursued by a shady botanist who wants to put him on permanent display in a greenhouse. In the story's concluding scene, Common goes to the greenhouse intent on killing the botanist but ends up permanently transformed into a plant.

The attitude of the story toward Common's transformation is somewhat ambiguous. Life as a Dendrocacalia hardly sounds fulfilling, but compared with the lonely existence Common is leading at the outset of the story, it is not clear that he is any worse off as a plant. Does his metamorphosis then represent the degeneration forced upon him by society, or is it his own creative response to loneliness, an ecstatic escape from the workaday world?

In Hanada Kiyoteru's theory of avant-garde art, the transformation of human into nonhuman could be an image which allowed the artist to go beyond naively sentimental or romantic visions of individuality and see humanity and the individual in a new light. But whether the new vision of humanity revealed by Common's transformation is a positive or negative one, and whether he is in fact protected or imprisoned in the greenhouse at the end—these are questions the story does not resolve.

Whatever one's final conclusion, "Dendrocacalia" seems to describe the trade-offs between freedom and belonging. Common faces a dilemma that plagues many of Abe's characters: he can choose to remain outside, lonely and alienated but ultimately free, or he can join society and accept the restrictions of its obligations and expectations as well as its established way of understanding the world and its common (as opposed to "Common") sense. Common's transformation into a plant seems to be a concrete sign of his loss of freedom and free thinking. For Common, this is the price of entry into the greenhouse—a place of safety, or at least stability—just as the unraveling protagonist of "The Red Cocoon" gained a home at the price of literally losing himself. Much of Abe's work is characterized by this tension between community and its common sense versus a lonely independence and freedom of thought.

The desire for independence even at the cost of isolation that we see in a work like "Dendrocacalia" may seem at odds with Abe's involvement in the Communist Party. Likewise there was some potential tension between Abe's dream of an accessible, egalitarian, popular literature and his interest in the difficult styles of surrealism and high modernism. Like other Japanese artists at the time (and like the European avant-garde before them), Abe invested considerable effort in synthesizing or reconciling the demands of progressive art with those of progressive politics.

Abe began to gravitate toward the ideas of communism in the 1950s. He joined the Japan Communist Party (JCP) and was involved with *Jinmin bungaku*, a journal with close party ties formed to focus on proletarian writing. In a variety of activities and organizations he demonstrated a commitment to the idea of art for the common people, organizing literary circles among factory workers, for example, and showing an interest in new genres like reportage (a potential alternative to proletarian realism) and popular media. Throughout the 1950s he wrote a great deal of material for popular media like radio and television, including some children's programs, and he even experimented with musical theater.

In 1956 Abe traveled to Eastern Europe for the Congress of the Czechoslovak Writer's Union, touring the Balkans and East Germany in the process. An account of his trip is recorded in *Tōō ni iku* (1957; Going to Eastern Europe). Parts of Abe's account, like his support for the anti-Soviet, anti-Communist demonstrations wracking Poland at the time, were not entirely to the Party's liking. And, like many party intellectuals, Abe eventually began to chafe under the restrictions the JCP attempted to impose on its literary members.

In the late 1950s Abe was among the authors who criticized the policies of the JCP in the pages of *Shin Nihon bungaku*, a literary journal with party associations that had become a center of writers' discontent. Finally, in 1962, the Party expelled Abe and a number of other writers associated with these protests.

Abe's expulsion may have been an inevitable result of the tension in his artistic politics between revolutionary idealism on the one hand and resistance to either critical or political dogma on the other. This is evident in one of his earliest works from the 1950s, *The Crime of S. Karma*, a novel which brought Abe a new level of recognition by winning him the important Akutagawa prize for new writers in 1951.

The work begins with the protagonist waking up one morning to realize that his name is missing. Not only can he not remember it, but it has disappeared from his ID, his mail, and his belongings. Even the monograms are gone from his clothing. When he goes to his office to try and find out who he is, he discovers that his name ("Mr. S. Karma") has been stolen, and the culprit is none other than his own business card. A giant, walking version of the card is masquerading as its owner, parading about the office, conducting business, and flirting with his typist Miss Y.

In fact, the business card is just the leader of a group of revolutionaries comprised of all of the objects in Karma's life, including his clothing, glasses, wristwatch, and fountain pen. Tired of being exploited, they have banded together under the slogan: "Down with dead organic matter! Power to living inorganic matter!" (*AKZ*, vol. 2, p. 411). They plan to stage a general strike against their owner long enough for the business card to steal away the attractive Miss Y.

This story was written at the time of Abe's involvement with the Communist Party. In the essay "Ano asa no kioku" (1959; My memory of that morning), Abe noted that he learned about winning the Akutagawa prize by hearing the news broadcast on a radio playing in the factory district where he was organizing literary activities. But Abe's *Crime of S. Karma* puts the notion of artistic and social revolution inside comical quotation marks. The objects' complaints of exploitation gently parody the rhetoric of class revolution: the fountain pen, for example, grumbles that his ink reservoir is never full, so that he is forced to write on an empty stomach. The objects' slogan "Power to living inorganic matter!" is borrowed from Hanada Kiyoteru's ideas about viewing human and object on the same level; when spoken by Karma's belt or spectacles, though, the manifesto takes on a ridiculous air.

In fact, Abe's story is a mad tour in which the protagonist encounters one ideologue after another—jurists, philosophers, a mathematician, a doctor, a professor of urban studies, and others with specialties far more bizarre. Each of these specialists is limited by his narrow rationality, and each struggles to impose his own slogans and his own limited understanding of the world on the protagonist. And one can recognize among the targets of the parody the very groups vying for control of Abe's writing—aesthetic and political progressives.

The Crime of S. Karma can also be read in the same way as "Dendrocacalia": as Karma finds himself pitted against these successive ideologues, he faces a choice between accepting their logic in order to be accepted by them, or staying free and alone. In the end he refuses to be roped into any of these languages or rationalities, which makes him arguably the most heroic of all Abe's protagonists.

In one sense, the dilemma of characters like Karma is the dilemma Abe himself faced: through his early Communist Party activities Abe tried to connect his art to everyday political reality and to the world he shared with common people around him. But he also struggled to remain free from the narrow dogmatism which he saw hiding not only in political rhetoric but in what often passes for everyday common sense. Cognizant of this dilemma and of Abe's origins, critics have often given him the benefit of the doubt, endeavoring to find a progressive social message even in the most chaotic, dark, and violent of Abe's works.

Science and Science Fiction

The chaos in *The Crime of S. Karma* results from the collision between the ideas and voices of the different ideologues, but to portray that chaos convincingly Abe had to write each individual voice with an ear to accuracy and plausibility. Whether he is portraying a medical examination or a judicial proceeding, Abe is adept at creating and manipulating these technical dialects. He is able to unfold a scientific or philosophical argument so systematically and with such convincing logic that the reader does not notice that the argument is moving toward nonsense until it has already arrived there.

This contest between sense and nonsense is seldom more striking than in Abe's appropriation of science, which makes an appearance in many of his works but often yields fantastic or unexpected results. Abe's medical background has already been touched on, but the scientific elements in his work go well beyond medicine. His texts contain images, characters, plot elements, and highly technical language drawn from fields as diverse as geometry and geology, physics and physiology, optics and electronics.

Technology, too, plays a huge role in Abe's stories, which often include intricate descriptions of machines or inventions that the author devised. *Dai yon kanpyōki* (1958–1959; Inter Ice Age 4, 1970) contains illustrated plans for an underwater bicycle; *Mikkai* (1977; *Secret Rendezvous*, 1979) describes a design for a computer-controlled electronic surveillance system. In 1985 Abe even won an international inventor's award for designing and building a new kind of snow chain for tires.

Nor was Abe hesitant to apply new technologies to his art. He experimented with electronic music in the days of early patch-cord synthesizers, writing the scores for some of his stage productions. And he was among the first Japanese authors to make the transition to writing on a computer. In 1984 he completed his novel *Hakobune Sakura maru* (1984; *The Ark Sakura*, 1988) on an early NEC word processor. At the time personal computers were enough of a novelty that the slipcover of the novel featured a picture of Abe seated at the machine.

Abe lavished attention on the scientific details in his writing to make them accurate and consistent. But he also believed that science held its own surprises, something expressed in all his work. The idea that science and scientific thinking move forward in a logical way but nevertheless lead to unexpected destinations is a hallmark of the genre of science fiction, and some of Abe's work certainly belongs in this category. Abe's works from the late 1950s played an important role in the founding of this genre in Japan.

Although fantasy had a long and rich tradition in Japan, as late as the 1950s the genre of science fiction was still a new one dominated by foreign authors. During this time Abe published a number of short stories with plots involving such things as robotics ("R62 gō no hatsumei," 1953; The invention of R62), suspended animation ("Namari no tamago," 1957; The leaden egg), and alien visitation ("Shisha," 1958; "The Special Envoy," 1991). But a turn-

ing point for the genre came in 1958–1959 with the publication of Abe's *Inter Ice Age 4*, which Okuno Takeo identifies as "Japan's first real full-length science fiction novel" (p. 483).

Some readers and critics were not sure exactly what to make of *Inter Ice Age 4* when it originally appeared, serialized in the journal of art and politics *Sekai* (The world). But the novel helped pave the way for science-fiction publishing ventures like *SF magajin* (SF magazine), which started publication the following year. In one of the first issues, Abe's words of congratulation appeared alongside contributions by Isaac Asimov and Robert Heinlein. Over thirty years later, in an obituary for Abe, the magazine noted that the author's "strong declarations of support played an immeasurable role in the establishment and development of the genre" (Kawamata, p. 172).

Inter Ice Age 4 is the story of a computer scientist, Dr. Katsumi, who invents a computer that can predict the future. But when rogue researchers dare to ask the machine about the long-term future of humanity, it predicts a frightening world where a rise in sea levels has submerged the continents, and humans have been replaced by a new race of water breathing "aquans," who are even now being bred from aborted human fetuses in secret labs run by a vast conspiracy.

As if that were not bad enough, at the instant Katsumi learns of this, members of the conspiracy planted in his own lab inform him that they have been observing him and secretly using the computer to predict his actions and his reaction. They tell him that he will never be able to accept the new world he has been shown, and, based on his predicted resistance, they condemn him to death in order to protect their plot and their own version of future events.

At a time when even the word "computer" was unfamiliar to much of Abe's audience, the story contained intricate scientific descriptions of programming methods and genetic manipulation that put it far ahead of its time. Critics praised "its scientific and technical logic, and the accuracy and precision of its descriptions" (Okuno, p. 486). But Abe managed to direct this science toward a result—the prospect of gilled humans living on the sea floor—that was just as fantastic as his avant-garde work.

In a postscript to the novel, Abe criticized Katsumi as a character unable to transcend the narrow common sense of his everyday experience to face the changes in technology, society, and philosophy that the future brings. This became one of the best-known statements of Abe's idea about the necessity and the difficulty of breaking out of hardened patterns of thinking grounded in our limited everyday experience—what Abe called *nichijō* (the everyday). "Just living in the present does not provide us what we need to understand the future," Abe wrote. "We must open our eyes to the crime of this quotidian order we call the everyday" (*AKZ*, vol. 11, p. 141; revised from tr. p. 227).

Like Katsumi, the scientists, pseudoscientists, and rationalists who inhabit Abe's works are often limited by their own myopic reasoning, and a number of critics have focused on the failure or frustration of these inflexible, idiosyncratic rationalities in Abe's work. (See David Pollack's reading of Abe for a compelling example.)

But it is also important to note that science for Abe had a creative, unpredictable side, a side represented in *Inter Ice Age 4* by the rationally fantastic technology of the aquans and the perverse but inescapable logic of Katsumi's fate. Abe suggests elsewhere that true science often demands precisely the talent Katsumi lacks, of departing from conventional thinking to arrive at an unexpected new hypothesis. So science becomes a fitting image or impetus for creative thought.

As an example of this creativity, Abe once compared the creative process of writing to the task of solving a geometry problem. In his essay "Masuku no hakken" (1957; Discovery of the mask) Abe describes how a geometry diagram locks the viewer into a fixed way of seeing the figure, until he or she figures out where to draw a single additional line that reveals a new relationship between the elements and discloses the solution.

Inter Ice Age 4 pulls this unexpected rabbit from the hat of logic by juxtaposing two rational but very different kinds of language and reason. The many different dialects heard in *The Crime of S. Karma* are here pared down to two: the cool, dry logic and mathematical terminology of Katsumi's computer room, and the wet, vital language and technology of the biology lab where the aquans are engineered. Each of these technical worlds is rational within itself, but they are ultimately incompatible. The novel never departs from the path of reason. But when the unfamiliar logic of biology invades Katsumi's cool world and the computer begins to store and shuffle not just data but human lives, the result is an instability that drives the story toward its unexpected conclusion.

This technique of following logical assumptions to arrive at an entertaining paradox is a method *Inter Ice Age 4* shares with a great deal of conventional science fiction. But Abe's later, most celebrated novels depart from this pattern. In several of them Abe lays out scientific scenarios with the same painstaking care, only to break the rules or pull the rug out from under the reader halfway through by twisting the world of the story into something wholly unscientific, dreamlike, or strange. Unlike *Inter Ice Age 4* (and unlike the bulk of contemporary science fiction), many of Abe's later works happily overturn the rational premises or promises upon which the story initially seemed to be founded.

Mature Fiction

In the early 1960s Abe published his novel *Suna no onna* (1962; *The Woman in the Dunes*, 1964), a carefully reasoned fantasy about a man who escapes to an isolated stretch of the coast on holiday and falls victim to a band of villagers who kidnap him and imprison him in a house at the bottom of a deep sand pit. There he is made to live with a woman from the village and help her shovel sand to reinforce the perpetually collapsing walls of the hole. This evocative scenario, absurd but laden with unspoken meaning, is balanced by meticulously detailed descriptions of the sand: its geology, its ecology, its physics, and more.

The Woman in the Dunes was followed by a series of novels in a similar vein, including *Tanin no kao* (1964; *The Face of Another*, 1966) and *Moetsukita chizu* (1967; *The Ruined Map*, 1969). It is in these novels that Abe's characteristic balance between reason and fantasy is most carefully maintained.

Taken together, these novels from the 1960s represent some of Abe's most acclaimed work. They have attracted the largest share of attention from the author's Japanese interpreters, and translations of these works have also earned Abe a considerable reputation in the West, not just in America but throughout Europe and Russia as well.

Soon after its publication in Japan, *The Woman in the Dunes* was translated into English—and later into two dozen other languages, from Czech to Norwegian. Adding to Abe's international reputation was the recognition received by the film version of this novel: scripted by Abe and directed by Teshigahara Hiroshi, it won a special jury prize at the Cannes Film Festival in 1964.

Abe was also supported by a loyal and eminent group of foreign scholars and translators during his career. In 1975 he was awarded an honorary doctoral degree from Columbia University, and the university recognized him again in 1996 with a commemorative symposium that attracted the participation of writers, actors, journalists, and leading academics from almost a dozen different countries. Up until his death, it was widely speculated that Abe, with his strong international support, might become the second Japanese author ever to receive the Nobel prize in literature. (The first was Kawabata Yasunari, in 1968.) As it turned out, the prize, which is given only to living writers, went to the Japanese novelist Ōe Kenzaburō in 1994, the year after Abe died.

The Woman in the Dunes, The Face of Another, and *The Ruined Map* each take a slightly different approach to the struggle between escape and obligation that is suggested by the first novel's famous epigraph: "Without the threat of punishment, there is no joy in flight." All three novels feature lonely or alienated city-dwellers as their protagonists, men who skirt the edges of society, pulled between freedom and belonging. They are all trying to hold their worlds together with their own fragile logic, which they will have to open up or change if they hope to rejoin society.

The man in *The Woman in the Dunes* is an insect collector who does not look beyond his tiny specimens until he becomes trapped like a bug himself. In *The Face of Another*, a chemist with a scarred face believes he can restore his lost identity through technology, by constructing an elaborate latex mask. And in *The Ruined Map*, the protagonist is a detective charged with tracking down a woman's missing husband. In the absence of any useful clues, he is forced to rely on his own eccentric deductions and his feeling of jealousy and kinship toward the man who has escaped society without a trace.

As in Abe's other works, the conflict common to all these novels is whether the lonely, alienated protagonist will surrender his freedom and his logic in order to make peace with a world that to him seems topsy-turvy. But since each of these novels is narrated from the protagonist's own maladjusted perspective, the distortions produced by this character's peculiar logic make it difficult to determine whether it is the outside world or the protagonist's inside world that is really out of balance. The reader is never quite sure whether the entomologist, the chemist, and the detective are islands of sanity in a world gone crazy (like S. Karma), or whether they have retreated into their own delusions because they cannot face normal everyday reality.

Abe achieves this uncertainty by taking the dialogue of different voices and styles that was present in works like *The Crime of S. Karma* or *Inter Ice Age 4* and compressing it into a single long conversation that the protagonist has with himself, or a phantom partner, or an alter ego. One such partner is the latex mask in *The Face of Another*, which gradually takes on a voice and personality of its own and threatens to usurp control from its wearer.

The other "phantom partner" in each of these three novels is a woman. The tension between individual and society is focused on a female figure (like the woman in the dunes or the detective's alluring client), who comes to represent the boundary between society and the narrator's lonely no-man's-land. It is she who tempts him to rejoin the community and don the mantle of responsibility and everyday common sense. But because she embodies the choice between the protagonist's own personal reality and society's reality (and because the novels never reveal which of these is the more sane), the woman represents a point of stability and instability at the same time. The protagonist never knows whether she will lead him out of his madness or lure him farther down the rabbit hole.

Inevitably these women come to embody all the projected fears and hopes of the male characters, and readers may have difficulty finding much more in the women, because we learn about them only through the male characters' highly distorted accounts and impressions. Some might fault Abe for these incomplete or objectified female characters. But Abe's approach in this regard is an important aspect of portraying the male protagonists as people unable to make any meaningful connections with others, men who have only outlines of the other that they fill in with their own imaginings.

What is the eventual fate of these men? The balance of forces and the ambiguous status of reality in these novels allow a variety of interpretations, so that readers and critics can frequently see what they want in these works. An extreme example is *The Face of Another*, which ends with the narrator standing in a dark alley, clutching a loaded pistol, listening for a woman's approaching footsteps. Even this unsettling conclusion is interpreted positively by some critics, as a political allegory in which the narrator overcomes indecision and takes action (Ōe Kenzaburō), or as a heroic blow against the hypocrisy of modern social relationships (Muramatsu Takeshi).

Even those who find the conclusion pessimistic can lay the blame where they like: with the individual narrator, with modern society at large, or with human nature. And finally readers may elect to disregard the implied violence of the scene altogether, taking a hint from the narrator's parting question: "What was I doing this for? Was it only play acting to test myself, or was I plotting something in earnest?" (*AKZ*, vol. 18, p. 495; tr. p. 237). No doubt the ambiguity of the pessimism (or optimism) in these stories is one of the secrets of their popularity and success.

Visual Art and Drama

In the 1970s Abe turned his attention to drama in an intensive way with a new project, the Abe Kōbō Studio. The studio was an experimental theater troupe he founded and directed from 1971 to 1979, during which time he developed a unique brand of theater that focused closely on sense impressions and visual effects.

The studio was Abe's most ambitious foray into dramatic and visual art, but certainly not his first. As noted above, he had been writing for television, theater, and even musical theater since the early 1950s. For the avant-garde and for Abe in particular, these genres represented an effort to bridge the gap between the written and the visual, as well as between fine art and popular media, thereby broadening literature and making it accessible to a wider range of people.

Abe's wife, Machi, who married him soon after the end of the war, was a stage designer and visual artist, and she gave several of Abe's texts an added visual dimension by supplying unusual illustrations. In *Inter Ice Age 4*, for example, Machi depicted the complex machines and inventions of Abe's science-fiction story in the macabre style of expressionist woodcuts, deftly capturing the tension between the novel's detailed technology and its bizarre results.

Abe also had experience writing for the theater. *Bō ni natta otoko* (1969; *The Man Who Turned into a Stick*, 1975) marked his directorial debut, and his play *Tomodachi* (1967; *Friends*, 1969) has been translated and performed around the world. *Friends* was a reworking of Abe's story "Chinnyūsha" (1951; "Intruders," 1991), which the author had earlier rewritten as a television script. This was one of many examples of the way Abe constantly modified his texts for different media, frequently adapting his novels and short stories for radio, television, film, and the stage.

Because of this crossover, the themes in many of these earlier plays are similar to the themes of Abe's fiction. *Friends*, for example, examines the notion of community with the story of a man whose life is suddenly invaded by an unwanted family. They move into his apartment without his permission, adopt him against his will, and eventually do far worse things in the name of friendship.

Abe's film screenplays include adaptations of *The Woman in the Dunes* (in 1964), *The Face of Another* (in 1966), and *The Ruined Map* (in 1968). All were collaborations with the artist and director Teshigahara Hiroshi and the noted avant-garde composer Takemitsu Tōru, but *The Woman in the Dunes* was the most successful of the three. The involved internal dialogues and claustrophobic psychology of *The Face of Another* do not easily make the transition to film, even with Abe supplying the script. But in *The Woman in the Dunes*, Abe's use of landscape to highlight the relationship between the individual and his environment is captured dramatically in Teshigahara's stark images and Takemitsu's lonely, ominous score. And while the novel is narrated from the perspective of the man, Abe's script and Teshigahara's camera are more neutral, allowing Kishida Kyōko to imbue the woman with a presence that gives the film added interest.

Abe's involvement in visual art also extended to photography, and during his life he produced a great deal of distinctive photographic work. His camera was often drawn to the forgotten details of the urban landscape, and the resulting photographs exhibit a kind of detached interest or sympathy toward things like litter, the expression on a stranger's face, or someone sleeping on a city street. In 1974 Abe told the American interviewer Alan Levy "Human waste I can only watch through the camera eye—and dimly—because I couldn't stand it on my own."

One novel which combines Abe's writing and photographic work is *Hako otoko* (1973; *The Box Man*, 1974), the story of a man who lives in a cardboard box that he carries on his back like a snail shell. The invisible status of the homeless is indicated by the design of the box, whose specially shuttered openings allow the box man to see out but no one else to see in. However, the box is also an allegorical camera, and the box man's forgotten status confers a voyeuristic freedom. Scattered through the book are Abe's own photographs of scenes and objects that bear no direct relationship to the story but that seem to represent what a box man might see or where he might be hiding.

Abe apparently inherited his love of photography from his father, and the family's interest seems to have generated many pictures of Abe himself. In most of them he gazes toward the camera with a look of contented intensity, his eyes framed by his thick black hair and thick black glasses. In a striking touch, a number of these photos of Abe throughout his life have been used to line the insides of the slipcover boxes for the volumes of the *Abe Kōbō zenshū* (1997–2000; Complete works of Abe Kōbō; abbreviated as *AKZ*). The photos are partially visible through openings cut in the slipcovers, so that countless incarnations of Abe seems to peer out, half concealed, like box men themselves.

Abe built on his past experience for his work with the Abe Kōbō Studio. He not only wrote and directed the productions, but worked full time recruiting and training the actors in the special methods he required. In later productions Abe even composed the electronic music that accompanied the scenes. Abe's wife, Machi, designed the elaborate sets, costumes, and props.

The company produced over a dozen works

in its nine-year life, most of them shown at the Seibu Theater on the ninth floor of Shibuya's Parco department store, which was run by Tsutsumi Seiji, a businessman, writer, and friend of Abe's. The studio productions included some of Abe's older plays, like *Friends* and *The Man Who Turned into a Stick,* but also several new works in a wholly different style, written especially for the company to advance Abe's new ideas about drama. The more experimental plays included a crucial visual component that is hard to grasp from the texts alone. But English-language readers can get a sense of the plays and the process of their production from Nancy Shields's *Fake Fish,* an inside account of goings-on at the studio.

Abe was apparently intent on breaking down normal sequences of meaning in order to short-circuit conventional understandings and provide the audience a more direct, creative kind of experience. Shields describes how the productions and the elaborate games and exercises that led up to them often emphasized individual words or sounds over dialogue, discrete motions or postures over continuous dramatic action, and isolated images over story and plot. Abe emphasized the nonsequential aspects of the plays by referring to several of them as "exhibitions of images."

One such piece was the studio's final production, *Kozō wa shinda: ime iji no tenrankai III* (1979; The little elephant is dead: exhibition of images III). In this and some of the studio's other productions, parts of the action took place under a gigantic white drop cloth on the stage floor, with the audience observing not the actors but the bulges and undulations their movements produced in the fabric. This production included a grand finale to the studio's long run: before the final curtain fell in Japan, the company traveled to the United States and performed the play in five American cities to enthusiastic reviews.

Later Fiction

The Abe Kōbō Studio occupied Abe's time and energy during the 1970s, but even after the studio closed, Abe's fiction writing did not regain its earlier momentum. Between the publication of *The Box Man* in 1973 and Abe's death twenty years later, he published only three major novels: *Secret Rendezvous, The Ark Sakura,* and *Kangarū nōto* (1991; *Kangaroo Notebook,* 1996). A fourth novel in progress, *Tobu otoko* (1993; The flying man), was published posthumously after being discovered on floppy disks in Abe's study.

Whether this slowdown was due to writer's block, declining health, or simply other preoccupations is uncertain, but there is a sense of the labored about the later works. With longer and longer gaps between novels (up to seven years), they were preceded by great anticipation but not always greeted with enthusiasm. John Lewell, impatient with Abe's later writing, referred in his *Modern Japanese Novelists* to the interval after *Secret Rendezvous* as "a merciful silence." Even Abe's more charitable critics have generally chosen to focus on the author's earlier works instead of dealing with these difficult later ones.

Compared with Abe's later novels (from *The Box Man* onward), his works from the 1960s are more like controlled experiments. Only a few things are altered, and these subtly. Either the main character or the world he inhabits is slightly out of kilter, throwing his relationships off balance in a way that casts our own relationships and our own reality in a new light. But in Abe's later novels, the main character wanders through a world which is almost unrecognizable, a carnival of wild symbols. At the same time, the character's own understanding and narrative account are equally skewed. For all the chaos in *The Crime of S. Karma,* the implacability of the title character provides a sense of stability and a kind of perspective. In contrast, the interestingly unbalanced characters in *Secret Rendezvous* or *The Ark Sakura* do little to help the reader grasp the novel's parade of images and events.

For example, in *Secret Rendezvous* the narrator wanders lost through the tunnels and corridors of a surreal hospital searching for a missing patient (his wife). In the course of his journey he meets a man with a horse's body, a girl who is dissolving, and a host of other freakish characters who are the victims of strange illnesses and even stranger cures. Eventually he joins the hospital staff and gains an intimate knowledge of the institution's workings, but this only exacerbates his (and our) confusion. He and his wife remain lost.

In this way, perhaps, the novel resembles the "image exhibitions" that were a specialty of the Abe Kōbō Studio. Several reviewers of *Secret Rendezvous* were unable to come to terms with the novel in any way except by repeating its gallery of strange scenes. Describing this sequence of unrelated events, the Japanese reviewer Morota Kazuharu said that "readers must burn each page behind them as they read, their thirst for answers unsatisfied" (p. 5). More substantive criticism has been slow in coming. The single evocative transformation of a story like "Dendrocacalia" or "The Red Cocoon" is now replaced by a flood of images so fast and furious that the reader has little time to consider them except as a literary kaleidoscope.

Viewed as a union of sense and nonsense, Abe's later novels may appear to have lost their balance when compared with works like *The Woman in the Dunes*. But seen from the perspective of the competition between voices, works like *The Box Man* and *Secret Rendezvous* are part of Abe's exploration of the different voices and languages that combine to constitute the self.

Abe's earlier works trace the counterpoint between these different voices inside and outside the protagonist. They may be the voices of science and fantasy, or of biology and computer science, or of the self and the mask, but in every work the protagonist must combine or reconcile them to produce a whole, balanced identity. The later works show what happens when those voices multiply to the point where the narrator cannot put them together or even distinguish one from the other.

The text of *The Box Man* is ostensibly taken from contents of the box man's notebook, but these are composed of scraps and fragments by multiple narrators (and photographers) who vie for control of the narrative, arguing over who is the "real" box man and who really owns the notebook. Periodic annotations (by someone) indicate where there are telltale changes in the kind of paper or the color of the ink—indications that the narrator has changed in midstream, ambiguous clues as to which parts of the box man's narrative are authentic.

Ironically, Abe's own notebooks were later subjected to similar treatment. The notes in the back of the *Abe Kōbō zenshū* lovingly offer a physical description of the volumes that contained some of Abe's original drafts: the type of notebook ("Tōsei Brand, horizontal ruled"), the layout ("Fourth page: blank"), and even key erasures in the text (*AKZ*, vol. 1, p. 271n).

Secret Rendezvous is a virtual collage along the same lines, not of text but of sound. The hospital is covered with a sophisticated audio surveillance system that records sounds from everywhere on the grounds onto a series of tapes. When the narrator gains access to these, he is hopeful they will reveal the secrets of the hospital and the whereabouts of his wife. But the system's efficient technology gathers every snatch of noise until the resulting cacophony becomes unintelligible. Far from ordering his world, the microphones break it apart. Listening to tapes of himself, he finds he has been "torn into fragments of tongue-clucking, throat-clearing, off-key humming, chewing, entreaties, hollow obsequious laughter, belches, sniffling, timid excuses" (*AKZ*, vol. 26, p. 12; tr. p. 6).

Secret Rendezvous suggests that the increasing proliferation of language, accelerated by modern technology, has rendered it difficult to assemble a coherent self or experience from the fragments of language rushing around us. The process of interpreting Abe's novel recreates the difficult task we face every day as we try to make sense out of the chorus or cacophony of voices that surrounds us. Today these voices include not only the multiplying styles of art and literature, but the increasingly complex dialects of contemporary science, and a ceaseless torrent of language from advertising and the mass media. Even our most intimate conversations are now mediated and amplified by technologies from the telephone to the Internet.

Throughout his career Abe remained cognizant of the implications and possibilities of popular media and media technology, so he was not an author to let himself be overtaken by their advance or evolution. But there is a cautionary tone to *Secret Rendezvous* that casts Abe's early enthusiasm for popular media in a new light. As we become surrounded by more and more language, the process of writing our own narratives grows more complex.

In fact, there was an inkling of this back in 1951, when Abe won the Akutagawa prize for *The Crime of S. Karma.* Recall that, in his essay "Ano asa no kioku," Abe describes how he heard the news that he had won the prize: from a news broadcast rather than from officials of the prize committee. The essay emphasizes the image of an author more concerned with spreading literature to wider audiences than with prizes, so much so that he hears the news of his own prize unexpectedly on the radio.

But this piece also includes a prophetic comment, almost parenthetical, to the effect that it was odd that the news media received the information before Abe: "It was the early morning news, I believe, but no matter how early the news is, I think there is something strange about their knowing this even earlier than I did" (*AKZ*, vol. 9, p. 429). Twenty-five years later, this situation was amplified in the world of *Secret Rendezvous*, where information about the narrator travels the circuits of the surveillance network so fast that when he listens he cannot figure out what to believe about himself.

Abe's Voices

The image of an author trying to outrun his own news, maybe his own language, seems appropriate for Abe, who for more than forty-five years continually reinvented his own work, keeping readers and critics guessing. This chase finally ended with Abe's death on January 22, 1993, at the age of 68. Newspapers reported the cause of death as heart failure, following on the heels of a stroke the month before. His wife, Machi, died later that same year, in September. They left behind a daughter, Manō Neri, a physician.

While Abe's death at a relatively young age is a loss to the literary world, with it comes an opportunity to take critical stock of his works. Compared with other Japanese authors who achieved international stature, Abe has received relatively little attention from Japanese scholars. But there are signs that the conclusion of Abe's career will afford critics the opportunity to look at him anew and perhaps come to terms with his large and varied output. An important first step is the publication of Abe's complete works beginning in 1997.

While Abe's long novels, films, and some of his earlier plays have been examined closely by critics, there is still work to be done in other areas: his photography, his additional dramatic work (both for radio and television and for the Abe Kōbō Studio), and finally a substantial body of essays and criticism. The essays in particular represent a rich vein of Abe's work that is still largely untapped by Western audiences and scholars, who now have very few of Abe's pieces available in translation.

Abe published several essay collections, including *Mōjū no kokoro ni keisanki no te o, Sabaku no shisō* (1965; Desert thoughts), and *Uchi naru henkyō* (1971; The frontier within), whose title essay is one of the few essays by Abe that have been translated. The essays are written in a voice that is different from the voices of Abe's characters, but the two do have something in common: both Abe in the essays and the characters in his fiction are trying to reconcile or combine imagination and independent thinking with concrete reality and common sense. The essays show off Abe's combination of imagination and rigor to good advantage. Meticulously argued and organized, these pieces often center on a single powerful metaphor or image, which is explored with Abe's characteristic discipline and attention to technical detail until it unfolds its meaning in an entirely unexpected direction.

An example readily available in English is "Sakura wa itan shinmonkan no monshō," an essay written for the *Washington Post* and published there as "The Dark Side of the Cherry Blossoms" (1981). The essay uses this traditional floral image of Japan to discuss the state of Japanese art and politics. Weaving in references that range from Dostoyevsky to paint chemistry, "The Dark Side" threads a careful course between analytic and imagistic writing. Abe begins by confessing that he is sometimes prone to overanalyze things, but he also indicts images like cherry blossoms for their appeal to a level of emotion that short-circuits reason. He links the emotions associated with cherry blossoms to unthinking cultural pride, the rise of nationalism, and even the specter of renewed Japanese military expansion.

But Abe's essay also touches the reader's feelings with its own set of images. With a photographer's eye for light, Abe begins from the guidebook image of cherry blossoms illuminated at night in parks across Japan. Then he inquires into the nature of that illumination and takes the essay through a series of light metaphors that cleverly advances his argument. From stage lights and the ideological contradictions of contemporary theater, he moves to the torches of the inquisition, representing the imposed orthodoxies of nationalism and fanaticism. "No matter how beautifully the cherry blossoms have glowed in the light of the torches held up by the inquisitors," he says, "it has only been because of the intensity of the darkness around them" (*AKZ*, vol. 27, pp. 92–93; tr. p. 15). The essay concludes with an evocation of atomic fires, the potential outcome of Japan's rearmament.

This combination of careful argument, passionate conviction, and poetic imagery lives up to the metaphor set forth in the title essay of Abe's first essay collection, *Mōjū no kokoro ni keisanki no te o*, which ironically characterized the effective writer as someone with "the heart of a beast" and "the hand of a computer."

In his last essay collection, *Warau tsuki* (1975; Laughing moon), Abe blends the evocative and the analytical even more thoroughly by structuring the work as a dream journal. Selecting from pieces that he published in the journal *Nami* (Waves) between 1971 and 1975, the author combines dream accounts, reflections on dreams, and memories in a series of texts that frequently cross the lines between essay, fiction, and memoir. The title essay (1975) sets the stage with a metaphor drawn from physiology: stargazers know that very dim stars are sometimes visible only when they fall in one's peripheral vision; they disappear when stared at directly because the outer edges of the retina are more sensitive to dim light. In the same way, dreams reveal things that are invisible in daylight, precisely because they are free from the restrictions of daytime logic.

The rest of the pieces in the collection explore dreams and remembrances in a way that captures each poetic image and interrogates it thoroughly, but without destroying its inner dream logic. "Sora tobu otoko" (1972; The man who flew) is an account of a conversation with a flying man who drifts past the window one morning and then argues vigorously with the narrator that he is not a dream. Probing into the nature of a fantastic medicine composed of wood lice, "Waragenkō" (1974; Liceprin considered) describes the almost surreal state of medicine in Manchuria—though these reminiscences acknowledge that the fictional quality of Abe's life in Manchuria is partly a by-product of remembering and narrating that time. "Hassō no shushi" (1974; Seeds of an idea) opens up an old notebook where we can read the written fragments and a newspaper clipping that Abe eventually developed into *The Ruined Map* and *The Box Man*. The notebook shows Abe sifting and sorting the language around him in order to construct the collage-like text of the latter novel.

Warau tsuki is a fitting final collection for Abe—and an appropriate place to end this survey—because it ties together many of the themes of Abe's career. The pieces express the complex relationship between autobiography and fiction, as well as the delicate balance

15

between the technical and the fantastic, or sense and nonsense. The collection also addresses the connection between creativity and writing: not only do we see the writer mining his own dreams for creative ideas, but in the pieces that discuss the interrelationship of writing and memory, we also see the role that the act of writing plays for Abe in creating or authoring his own identity. After witnessing the characters in Abe's novels trying to order the voices around them into a coherent story about themselves or their world, the reader of *Warau tsuki* finally gets an intriguing glimpse of the author, Abe Kōbō, doing the same thing: marshaling language in order to form his fiction, express his ideas, record his own history, and write himself.

Abe has left a similar task for scholars, who now have the job of listening to the author's many voices and making literary sense of them—or at least of fashioning a good critical story about this important writer.

Selected Bibliography

PRIMARY WORKS

The editions of Abe's texts cited in this essay are those in *Abe Kōbō zenshū*. Volume and page references for each work follow the notation *AKZ*. Publication information for the first book printing of each work *(shokanbon)* is provided here for reference.

COLLECTIONS

Abe Kōbō zensakuhin. 15 vols. Tokyo: Shinchōsha, 1972–1973.
Four Stories by Kobo Abe/Abe Kōbō tanpenshū. Trans. by Andrew Horvat. In *Gendai Nihon bungaku eiyaku senshū.* Vol. 12. Tokyo: Hara Shobō, 1973. (Bilingual edition. Includes an essay on Abe.)
Beyond the Curve. Trans. by Juliet Winters Carpenter. New York: Kodansha America, 1991.
Three plays by Kōbō Abe. Trans. by Donald Keene. New York: Columbia University Press, 1993.
Abe Kōbō zenshū. 27 vols. Edited by Donald Keene. Tokyo: Shinchōsha, 1997– .

LONG FICTION

Owarishi michi no shirube ni. Tokyo: Shinzenbisha, 1948. Reprinted in *AKZ* 1:271–390. (Revised in 1965.)
S. Karuma shi no hanzai. In *Kabe.* Tokyo: Getsuyō

Shobō, 1951. Reprinted in *AKZ* 2:378–451. Excerpted and trans. by Juliet Winters Carpenter as *The Crime of S. Karma.* In *Beyond the Curve.* New York: Kodansha America, 1991. Pp. 35–42.
Kemonotachi wa kokyō o mezasu. Tokyo: Kōdansha, 1957. Reprinted in *AKZ* 6:301–451.
Dai yon kanpyōki. Tokyo: Kōdansha, 1959. Reprinted in *AKZ* 9:9–174, 11:141–142. Trans. by E. Dale Saunders as *Inter Ice Age 4.* New York: Knopf, 1970.
Suna no onna. Tokyo: Shinchōsha, 1962. Reprinted in *AKZ* 16:115–250. Trans. by E. Dale Saunders as *The Woman in the Dunes.* New York: Knopf, 1964.
Tanin no kao. Tokyo: Kōdansha, 1964. Reprinted in *AKZ* 18:321–495. Trans. by E. Dale Saunders as *The Face of Another.* New York: Knopf, 1966.
Enomoto Buyō. Tokyo: Chūō Kōronsha, 1965. Reprinted in *AKZ* 18:7–193.
Moetsukita chizu. Tokyo: Shinchōsha, 1967. Reprinted in *AKZ* 21:113–311. Trans. by E. Dale Saunders as *The Ruined Map.* New York: Knopf, 1969.
Hako otoko. Tokyo: Shinchōsha, 1973. Reprinted in *AKZ* 24:9–141. Trans. by E. Dale Saunders as *The Box Man.* New York, Knopf, 1974.
Mikkai. Tokyo: Shinchōsha, 1977. Reprinted in *AKZ* 26:7–140. Trans. by Juliet Winters Carpenter as *Secret Rendezvous.* New York: Knopf, 1979.
Hakobune Sakura maru. Tokyo: Shinchōsha, 1984. Reprinted in *AKZ* 27:247–469. Trans by Juliet Winters Carpenter as *The Ark Sakura.* New York: Knopf, 1988.
Kangarū nōto. Tokyo: Shinchōsha, 1991. Trans. by Maryellen Toman Mori as *Kangaroo Notebook.* New York: Knopf, 1996.
Tobu otoko. Tokyo: Shinchōsha, 1994.

SHORT FICTION

"Akai mayu," 1950. In *Kabe.* Tokyo: Getsuyō Shobō, 1951. Reprinted in *AKZ* 2:492–494. Trans. by Lane Dunlop as "The Red Cocoon." In *A Late Chrysanthemum: Twenty-one Stories from the Japanese.* San Francisco: North Point Press, 1986. Pp. 159–162.
"Chinnyūsha," 1951. In *Chinnyūsha.* Tokyo: Miraisha, 1952. Reprinted in *AKZ* 3:107–131. Trans. by Juliet Winters Carpenter as "Intruders." In *Beyond the Curve.* New York: Kodansha America, 1991. Pp. 101–134.
"Dendorokakariya." In *Ueta hifu.* Tokyo: Shoshi Yuri-ika, 1952. Reprinted in *AKZ* 3:349–365. Trans. by Juliet Winters Carpenter as "Dendrocacalia." In *Beyond the Curve.* New York: Kodansha America, 1991. Pp. 43–64. (Substantially revised from the original 1949 version.)
"R62 gō no hatsumei," 1953. In *R62 gō no hatsumei.* Yamauchi Shoten, 1956. Reprinted in *AKZ* 3:409–433.
"Namari no tamago," 1957. In *Suichū toshi.* Tokyo: Tōgensha, 1964. Reprinted in *AKZ* 7:411–433.
"Shisha," 1958. In *Mukankei na shi.* Tokyo:

Shinchōsha, 1964. Reprinted in *AKZ* 9:295–309. Trans. by Juliet Winters Carpenter as "The Special Envoy." In *Beyond the Curve*. New York: Kodansha America, 1991. Pp. 151–166.

DRAMA

Tomodachi. In *Gikyoku Tomodachi, Enomoto Buyō*. Tokyo: Kawade Shobō, 1967. Reprinted in *AKZ* 20:425–486. Trans. by Donald Keene as *Friends*. New York: Grove Press, 1969. (Revised in 1974.)

Bō ni natta otoko. Tokyo: Shinchōsha, 1969. Reprinted in *AKZ* 22:357–399. Trans. by Donald Keene as *The Man Who Turned into a Stick: Three Related Plays*. Tokyo: University of Tokyo Press, 1975.

Kozō wa shinda. *Shinchō* 76, no. 3 (March 1979). Reprinted in *AKZ* 26:353–368.

ESSAYS

"Masuku no hakken," 1957. In *Mōjū no kokoro ni keisanki no te o*. Tokyo: Heibonsha, 1957. Reprinted in *AKZ* 7:322–323.

"Atogaki." In *Mōjū no kokoro ni keisanki no te o*. Tokyo: Heibonsha, 1957. Reprinted in *AKZ* 7:476.

"Ano asa no kioku." *Bungakukai* 13, no. 3 (March 1959). Reprinted in *AKZ* 9:429–430.

Sabaku no shisō. Tokyo: Kōdansha, 1965.

"Uchi naru henkyō," 1968. In *Uchi naru henkyō*. Tokyo: Chūō Kōronsha, 1971. Reprinted in *AKZ* 22:205–228. Trans. by Andrew Horvat as "The Frontier Within." *Japan Quarterly* 22, nos. 2–3:135–143, 255–265 (April–August 1975).

"Sora tobu otoko," "Waragenkō," "Hassō no shushi," "Warau tsuki," 1972–1975. In *Warau tsuki*. Tokyo: Shinchōsha, 1975. Reprinted in *AKZ* 23:333–336, 24:494–496, 25:26–29, 362–364.

"Chikyū no mushikui ana e no tabi." *Asahi Shinbun*, 16 June 1975. Reprinted in *AKZ* 25:359–360. Trans. by Donald Keene as "Journey through a Wormhole in the Earth." *New York Times*, 11 June 1975, p. 43. (First published in English.)

"Sakura wa itan shinmonkan no monshō," 1981. In *Shiniisogu kujiratachi*. Tokyo: Shinchōsha, 1986. Reprinted in *AKZ* 27:91–93. Trans. by Donald Keene as "The Dark Side of the Cherry Blossoms." *Washington Post Book World*, 1 November 1981, p. 15. (First published in English.)

SCREENPLAYS AND TELEPLAYS

Chinnyūsha. *Sōsaku Gekijō*. Osaka: NHK Ōsaka, 23 February 1963. Reprinted in *AKZ* 17:73–97.

Suna no onna. Directed by Teshigahara Hiroshi. Teshigahara Purodakushon, 1964. Reprinted in *AKZ* 18:195–233.

Tanin no kao. Directed by Teshigahara Hiroshi. Tōkyō Eiga, Teshigahara Purodakushon, 1966. Reprinted in *AKZ* 20:95–127.

Moetsukita chizu. Directed by Teshigahara Hiroshi. Katsu Purodakushon, 1968. Reprinted in *AKZ* 22:53–99.

OTHER WORKS

Mumeishū. Tokyo: Self-published, 1947. Reprinted in *AKZ* 1:221–266.

Tōō ni iku. Tokyo: Kōdansha, 1957. Reprinted in *AKZ* 7:27–107.

"Nenpyō." In *Shin'ei bungaku sōsho*. Vol. 2. Tokyo: Chikuma Shobō, 1960. Reprinted in *AKZ* 12:464–467.

"Ryaku nenpyō." In *Warera no bungaku*. Vol. 7. Tokyo: Kōdansha, 1966. Reprinted in *AKZ* 20:92–93.

SECONDARY WORKS

CRITICAL AND BIOGRAPHICAL STUDIES

Currie, William. *Metaphors of Alienation: The Fiction of Abe, Beckett and Kafka*. Ann Arbor, Michigan: University Microfilms, 1973.

Kawamata Chiaki. "Tsuitō Abe Kōbō." *SF Magajin* 34, no. 4:172 (April 1993).

Levy, Alan. "The Box Man Cometh." *New York Times Magazine*, 17 November 1974, pp. 36, 64–74, 78–82.

Lewell, John. "Abe Kobo." In his *Modern Japanese Novelists: A Biographical Dictionary*. New York: Kodansha America, 1993. Pp. 12–23. (Includes a list of Abe's works available in translation.)

Lidin, Olof G. "Abe Kobo's Internationalism." In vol. 1 of *Rethinking Japan*. Edited by Adriana Boscaro, Franco Gatti, and Massimo Raveri. New York: St. Martin's Press, 1991. Pp. 2–9.

Morota Kazuharu. "Dokusha no genjitsu kankaku o tsukikuzusu." Review of *Mikkai*, by Abe Kōbō. *Nihon Dokusho Shinbun*, 23 January 1978, p. 5.

Motoyama Mutsuko. "The Literature and Politics of Abe Kōbō: Farewell to Communism in *Suna no Onna*." *Monumenta Nipponica* 50, no. 3:305–323 (fall 1995).

Muramatsu Takeshi. "Tanin no kao ni tsuite." *Kokubungaku: kaishaku to kanshō* 36, no. 1:163–165 (January 1971).

Ōe Kenzaburō. Kaisetsu (commentary) to *Tanin no kao*, by Abe Kōbō. Bunkobon edition. Tokyo: Shinchōsha, 1968. Pp. 285–290.

Okaniwa Noboru. *Hanada Kiyoteru to Abe Kōbō no sekai: avan garudo bungaku no saisei no tame ni*. Tokyo: Daisanbunmeisha, 1980.

Okuno Takeo. "Abe Kōbō—sono hito to sakuhin." Kaisetsu (commentary) to *Sekai SF zenshū*. Vol. 27. Tokyo: Hayakawa Shobō, 1974. Pp. 483–493.

Pollack, David. "The Ideology of Science: Kōbō Abe's *Woman in the Dunes*." In his *Reading against Culture: Ideology and Narrative in the Japanese Novel*. Ithaca, N.Y.: Cornell University Press, 1992. Pp. 121–135.

Shields, Nancy K. *Fake Fish: The Theater of Kobo Abe*. New York: Weatherhill, 1996. (Includes numerous photographs.)

Takano Toshimi. *Abe Kōbō ron*. Rev. ed. Tokyo: Kashinsha, 1979.

Tani Shinsuke. *Abe Kōbō retorikku jiten*. Tokyo: Shinchōsha, 1994. (Contains an annotated chronology of Abe's life and an extensive bibliography of critical articles.)

Van Wert, William F. "Levels of Sexuality in the Novels of Kobo Abe." *The International Fiction Review* 6, no. 2:129–132 (summer 1979).

Watanabe Hiroshi. *Abe Kōbō.* Tokyo: Shinbisha, 1976.

Williams, Philip. "Abe Kobo and Symbols of Absurdity." In vol. 1 of *Studies on Japanese Culture.* Edited by Ōta Saburō and Fukuda Rikutarō. Tokyo: Japan P.E.N. Club, 1973. Pp. 477–482.

Yamamoto Fumiko. "Metamorphosis in Abe Kōbō's Works." *Journal of the Association of Teachers of Japanese* 15, no. 2:179–184 (November 1980).

Yamanouchi Hisaaki. "Abe Kōbō and Ōe Kenzaburō: The Search for Identity in Contemporary Japanese Literature." In *Modern Japan: Aspects of History, Literature and Society.* Edited by W. G. Beasley. Berkeley, California: University of California Press, 1975. Pp. 166–184.

INTERVIEWS AND DISCUSSIONS

Interview by Nancy S. Hardin. *Contemporary Literature* 15, no. 4:439–456 (fall 1974). (Same author as Nancy Shields, above.)

Hassō no shūhen. Tokyo: Shinchōsha, 1974. (*Taidan* [discussion] collection.)

AKUTAGAWA RYŪNOSUKE

1892–1927

HOWARD HIBBETT

AKUTAGAWA RYŪNOSUKE is the most renowned short story writer in modern Japanese literature, and his brief career made him one of the major figures of the Taishō era (1912–1926). He also excelled as a poet in the haiku form and as an essayist, with a tendency toward the aphoristic. His taste for brevity was combined with a stylistic perfectionism in sharp contrast to the naturalistic fiction of his day, and his approximately one hundred fifty stories continue to be read widely in Japan. Most have been translated into English and other languages.

Akutagawa's brilliant success ended with the shock of his suicide in 1927, an event that has been viewed as symbolic of the failure of Japan's progress toward socialist ideals and democratic freedoms in the early twentieth century. Neither as spectacular as the suicide of Mishima Yukio in 1970 nor as quiet as that of Kawabata Yasunari in 1972, the death of Akutagawa appeared to many in Japan to mark the end of an era, foreshadowing the militarism and disasters to come. Critics have interpreted his works as reflecting bourgeois traditionalism, disintegrating modernism, and a disturbing combination of both. These works range from simple children's stories to complex portraits of psychotic suffering. Akutagawa expressed his poetic vision in many forms and in a variety of styles.

A Tokyo Education

Akutagawa Ryūnosuke was born on 1 March 1892, an auspicious Year of the Dragon, in the Tsukiji district of Tokyo near the harbor. His home was in a foreign settlement, where his father, Niihara Toshizō, operated a dairy business, supplying milk (still a rather exotic beverage to the Meiji-era Japanese) along with ice cream, bananas, and other novelties. Less than eight months after Ryūnosuke's birth, his mother, Fuku, became insane, and Ryūnosuke was brought up in the otherwise childless household of his uncle, Akutagawa Dōshō; Dōshō's wife, Tomo, and sister Fuki; and two maids. Ryūnosuke's mother remained in a psychotic state and was hidden upstairs in the Niihara house until her death ten years later.

Although not formally adopted until he was twelve years old, Ryūnosuke took the Akutagawa surname and was cared for chiefly by his unmarried aunt Fuki, who was old enough to be his grandmother. A shy, thin boy, Akutagawa seems to have grown up with little affection from his foster parents and with a sense of being different from his aggressive, enterprising father. In his reminiscences of childhood he recalls thinking of himself as physically weak because he had never been nurtured by his mother's milk, only by the cow's milk that was his father's stock-in-trade. Fuyu, his mother's younger sister, kept house for Ryūnosuke's vigorous father, had a son by him in 1899, and married him in 1904. Neither this half brother Tokuji nor an older sister Hisako became close to Akutagawa, but his position as first son gave him a lifelong responsibility for their welfare. The possessive love of his aunt Fuki remained a strong and often bitter tie throughout his life.

Occasional visits by Akutagawa to his father's home were uncomfortable at best. There was the specter of his silent, ashen-faced mother upstairs. (He recalled that once she unexpectedly hit him on the head with her long-stemmed pipe.) And Toshizō himself was alternately irascible and ingratiating toward his son, sometimes trying to persuade him to come back to his own family. From the time he began to go to school at the age of six—along with private lessons in calligraphy, Chinese, and English—Akutagawa was an outstanding student.

Life in the family of his uncle, which was of minor samurai background, was one of cultivated, genteel poverty. Until 1910 the family had lived in Honjo, a part of Tokyo that had not changed much since the Tokugawa days when the city was still called Edo. The family ancestors had long served as "tea-masters" to the shoguns. Dōshō's father was said to have been among those who received the emperor's troops when they arrived to take over Edo castle. Dōshō was an official in the Tokyo Public Works Department, then became a businessman, though not a successful one, after his retirement. He and his wife took pride in "the frugality of the warrior," but often lived beyond their means. Keeping up appearances became a strain, especially since the family continued to indulge in Kabuki-going, singing, painting, and other traditional Edo arts. The house was well stocked with books, including the haiku of Bashō and Buson, Japanese adaptations of Chinese novels, and many of the gaudy, violent, illustrated tales of the late Tokugawa years. Ryūnosuke became a voracious reader and once declared that books were

his sole entry into life. They were also an escape, however temporary, from the shadow of his mother's tragic fate. He was especially attracted to the macabre and supernatural element in a richly decadent vein of Edo fiction, and in the stories told to him at night by his aunt Fuki and by a nursemaid who related her personal experiences as well as the standard repertoire of tales of revengeful spirits. His own frail, stricken mother, who drew pictures of people with fox-faces, was thought to be possessed by the spirit of a malicious fox.

Ghost stories and grotesque imagery invaded Akutagawa's dreams, in keeping with the lingering Edo atmosphere of their Honjo neighborhood. Akutagawa himself believed that on his way to an evening lesson he had encountered wily, supernatural badgers, one of the famous "Seven Mysteries of Honjo." Even a railway construction worker had been known to faint at the sight of a neighborhood ghost, and his own foster father had been pushed into a canal by what he took to be a fox in the guise of a young samurai.

Later, during his years at the Third Middle School and the even more prestigious First Higher School, Akutagawa hated the rigid discipline and dreary factuality but thrived on the elite Westernized curriculum. Consoled by a few friends and many books—including Turgenev, Maupassant, and Anatole France in English translations, along with modern Japanese writers who were also steeped in European literature—he had no difficulty in gaining admission to the English Department of the Imperial University in Tokyo, where he began his studies in September 1913.

Studying, however, was clearly secondary to his own writing. He had already written an impressionistic essay entitled "Ōkawa" (1911; The great river), lyrically evoking the emotions aroused in him by the Sumida flowing past Honjo and by the urban landscape—nature breathing weakly—around his childhood home. Unhappiness inspired by a frustrated "first love" led him to write a set of ambiguous verses in a classical Japanese verse form, but he had no desire to express his feelings more directly. Literature was an abundant source of images and emotions with which to satisfy his own inner needs.

Entry into the Literary World

In 1914 at the University, Akutagawa and his classmates revived a literary magazine called *Shinshichō* (The new tide). Only a few years earlier the magazine had enabled Tanizaki Jun'ichirō (1886–1965) to launch his writing career, which began to attract a widening public (and the attention of the censors) after he left Tokyo University in 1911. Akutagawa's first contributions to *Shinshichō* were Japanese versions of Anatole France's exotic tale "Balthasar et la Reine Balkis" (from its English translation) and selections from W. B. Yeats's *Celtic Twilight*. Translation offered a natural apprenticeship to writing, a product of his study of literature but also a protective technique, a mask by means of which he could write without exposing himself through the thinner veil of fiction. His own first story, "Rōnen" (Old age), appeared in the May 1914 issue. In this story the budding young author portrays a foolish old man who has squandered his money and his life in the pleasure quarters, where he is now barely tolerated. Fusa-san, a shabby relic of Edo high life, can only expect to be humiliated when he revisits a Yanagibashi restaurant where geisha are practicing their plaintive songs. Yet from a shadowy corner he is heard whispering as flirtatiously as ever—to a cat.

Akutagawa's next story, "Hyottoko" (1915; "Hyottoko," 1969), has a more cheerful setting: a pleasure boat on excursion down the Sumida at cherry blossom time. Another aging, eccentric man is revealed to be a compulsive liar who courts humiliation to gain the favor of others. Dissolving his inhibitions in sake, which, after two heart attacks, he has been warned to avoid, he tries to amuse his fellow passengers by putting on a comically distorted clown's mask *(hyottoko)* and going into a wild solo dance that is broken off by his sudden death. A Japanese biographer of Akuta-

gawa compared him to this sad hero, who ended his life still masked.

In November 1915 Akutagawa published "Rashōmon" ("Rashomon," 1952), the most famous of his early short stories and, six months later, the title piece of his first collection. The setting is the desolate Rashomon gate in medieval Kyoto. There, among a heap of abandoned corpses, described in repellent detail, a desperate man finds an old crone who is busily plucking out the hair of the dead to sell to wig-makers. Out of sudden disgust, he robs her of her own ragged clothes and kicks her over among the corpses. Revulsion has driven him to his first criminal act in a life of crime.

In 1950 the director Kurosawa Akira used this story, combining it with Akutagawa's "Yabu no naka" (1922; "In a Grove," 1952) to make the film *Rashomon*, which brought Japanese cinema its first worldwide success. Both stories drew on the twelfth-century collection of short, vivid tales called *Konjaku monogatari* (*Tales of Times Now Past*, 1979), in which Akutagawa discovered a fascinating "brutality." His subtle psychological development of these stories of deceit and humiliation, further developed by Kurosawa, presents conflicting accounts of the same grisly event—a wife is raped before her husband's eyes, and he is murdered (or commits suicide?)—set against the backdrop of Kyoto, the ancient capital, at a violent, lawless time. Later Akutagawa explained that he used historical settings to make his lurid themes plausible. But he did not acknowledge his own attraction to such themes.

For "Hana" (1916; "The Nose," 1961) Akutagawa again drew on *Konjaku monogatari*, among other sources. He transformed the little tale of a priest with a long, dangling nose into a sadistically comic account of the priest's embarrassment and his strenuous efforts to shorten his nose. Obsessed with noses, the priest sees only this feature in other people, not one of whom has a nose as long as his. He tries every useless remedy from drinking snake-gourd tea to rubbing his nose with mouse urine. But once the priest has accomplished his aim—by a regime of soaking his nose in boiling water and having a colleague trample on it—he finds that people now laugh at him more than ever. He feels a certain relief when his nose grows back to its original length.

Akutagawa's story "Imogayu" (1916; "Yam Gruel," 1952) is another elegantly sadistic fable. It tells the story of a lowly samurai, a victim of crude practical jokes, who loses his appetite when forced to gorge himself on a dish he had once enjoyed.

Around this time, Akutagawa had been introduced to Natsume Sōseki, who had already written many of the finest novels in modern Japanese literature and was recognized as the dominant literary figure of his time. Sōseki praised Akutagawa's work and encouraged the publication of "The Nose" in *Shin-shōsetsu* (The new novel), a major literary magazine, which not only paid Akutagawa a small fee but asked him to contribute another story. By then he had at last completed a thesis on the nineteenth-century artist, artisan, and socialist William Morris. (Originally intended to cover Morris's entire life and works, the thesis had been reduced to dealing only with Morris's early career, and friends suggested it might dwindle to "Morris as an Infant.") Akutagawa graduated from Tokyo University in July 1916. Unlike Tanizaki, he lacked the self-confidence to disregard the safety of academic credentials and a possible teaching career.

Akutagawa's "Hankechi" (1916; "The Handkerchief," 1964) was published by the influential magazine *Chūō Kōron* (The central review) and confirmed his position as a versatile young writer. This story offers a contemporary portrait of a stiff, self-satisfied professor—modeled on Nitobe Inazō, the author of *Bushidō* (*The Way of the Warrior*) and principal of the First Higher School when Akutagawa was a student there—who is an ardent advocate of samurai ideals. The professor is impressed by the stoicism of a woman who calmly tells him of her son's death. On further reflection, he suspects that he has been swayed by a glimpse of the woman wringing her hand-

kerchief as if suppressing her grief. Perhaps even her calm smile is simply a mannerism. A touch of cynical irony undermines the values in which he takes so much pride.

Akutagawa used a number of different historical settings to achieve the distance he wanted from his more bizarre subjects. "Shuchū" (1916; "The Wine Worm," 1930), set in China, was another unappetizing anecdote. A wealthy gentleman named Liu is afflicted by a wine-guzzling worm in his belly. Liu's suffering is graphically described, and his treatment consists of lying naked in the scorching sun, next to an open wine jar. Liu feels something creeping up his throat. But when the worm emerges and plops into the jar, he is sickened again by seeing it swim about happily in the wine. A choice of moral judgments is offered, but merely, so the author informs the readers, in imitation of the didacticism of Chinese tale-tellers. Akutagawa's ironic interpretation satisfactorily rounds out a sophisticated parable in which images of physical and psychic revulsion reflect instinctual fears.

Early Japanese Christianity was a subject that Akutagawa sometimes used in mock-scholarly accounts of history and legend. His own addiction to cigarettes figured in "Tabako to akuma" (1916; "Tobacco and the Devil," 1930). According to the logic of this story, tobacco may have been introduced to Japan by the Devil, rather than by the "Southern Barbarians," since the sixteenth-century Portuguese Jesuits must have brought their Devil along with their God. Both were expelled by the Tokugawa shoguns, but both—not just the Christian God—must have returned in the Meiji era.

Another mock-scholarly story was "Hō-kyōnin no shi" (1918; "The Martyr," 1952), collected in *Rashomon and Other Stories*. The "martyrdom" in this case is another death by fire—a fiery crucifixion not unrealistic in the period of early Japanese Christianity, related in a prose style modeled on the Jesuits' publications in vernacular Japanese. But the martyr turns out to be the sweetly effeminate young Lorenzo—protected by the sturdy Brother

Simeon, but accused by the umbrella maker's daughter of having caused her pregnancy, and revealed at last to be a girl: "The eyes of all followed theirs to two soft, pure breasts, which stood out among the rags of the chest of the angel, now lying silently at the gate of Santa Lucia, bathed in the light of the fire red as the blood of Jesus Christ at his crucifixion" (*Akutagawa Ryūnosuke zenshū [ARZ]*, vol. 2, p. 278; tr. p. 85).

Unknown to all, not only to his critics but also to the dignified scholars and collectors who were deceived by Akutagawa's hoax, the plot was for once entirely his own invention, not derived from the dryly and meticulously described "book in my collection entitled *Legenda Aurea* which was published by the Nagasaki Church" (*ARZ*, vol. 2, p. 279; tr. p. 87). Books of this kind were in demand as the incunabula of Japanese printing, and a number of inquiries came to Akutagawa from persons intrigued by the description of this hitherto unknown work:

On the title-page of Volume I, the Latin title is written crosswise, and under the title are written two vertical Chinese lines, "Printed at the beginning of March, the year of Grace 1596." At either side of the date is a picture of an angel blowing a trumpet. It is technically very crude but has a charm of its own. . . . For publication, I ventured to add some literary embellishment to "The Martyr." I hope that the simple and refined style of the original has not been impaired.

(*ARZ*, vol. 2, p. 279; tr. pp. 88–89)

By the end of 1916 Akutagawa had begun teaching English at the Naval Engineering School in Yokosuka, commuting by train from lodgings in Kamakura, and was mourning the death of his revered master Sōseki. He wrote to a friend that he had never known such sorrow. Still he continued to be an active though meagerly paid writer, and in 1917 he saw the publication of a second collection of short stories. One of the finest of these short stories was "Gesaku zanmai" (1917; "Absorbed in Let-

ters," 1964). The story describes a long day in the life of Takizawa Bakin, an early nineteenth-century novelist who almost succeeded in lifting "frivolous writing" *(gesaku)* to the level of respectability. The day begins at a public bathhouse. Physically, Bakin is sketched with rough accuracy as a sturdy, half-blind old man, somehow still resisting the decline of his vigor. In terms of emotion and personality, he is tired and dejected, and his notorious pride and touchiness are apparent. Such qualities seem at last to compose a self-portrait of Akutagawa as a harried artist, rather than provide a faithful depiction of the great Edo novelist. Bakin is annoyed by a flattering reader who assures him that his current serial is beyond criticism but who agrees too readily that the master has no special aptitude for haiku; afterward, Bakin happens to overhear some harshly abusive criticism. Like Akutagawa, he has been accused of merely embroidering old stories. His reaction is to analyze himself:

As Bakin strolled along the street under the autumn sun, those derogatory comments he had heard in the bath recurred to him one by one, and he dissected them minutely. Examining each point, he was at once able to establish in his mind how foolish and valueless were the man's views. In spite of this, however, his feelings had been aroused, and they were not easily subdued. . . . "Why am I irked by such ridiculous remarks which hold me up to ridicule?"

(*ARZ*, vol. 2, p. 52; tr. *Exotic Japanese Stories*, p. 315)

At home Bakin finds an oily, coercive publisher awaiting him, eager to press him for another manuscript. That night, when he has composed himself and settled down at the desk in his quiet study, inspiration floods back again. Absorbed in writing, he ends the day in single-minded devotion to his lonely art.

In February 1918 Akutagawa married Tsukamoto Fumiko, the eighteen-year-old daughter of a naval officer who had died at sea during the Russo-Japanese War. His first year of marriage was a tranquil and productive interlude in his life, although his stern aunt Fuki came along to live with them in their new home in Kamakura, and required that he convey her many criticisms of his young bride. Stories in various historical settings appeared in magazines almost every month. In April, for example, Akutagawa published "Kesa to Moritō" ("Kesa and Morito," 1952), a startling reinterpretation of a famous story from classical Japanese literature. Two monologues cast a chilling light on the psychology of Kesa, a supposedly model wife who sacrifices her life to her lover, Morito, with whom she has conspired to murder her husband, Wataru. Morito soliloquizes about their faded love affair, her lost beauty (the lusterless skin, the dark rings around her eyes), the shameful motives that led him to suggest killing Wataru. But Kesa is about to take Wataru's place as victim. She has chosen to die out of a selfish desire to preserve her pride and take revenge on the man she now hates—and still loves.

In the following month, one of Akutagawa's most unforgettable stories appeared simultaneously in a Tokyo newspaper and in the *Ōsaka Mainichi Shinbun.* "Jigokuhen" ("Hell Screen," 1961) is a gorgeously colored parable of an artist's dedication to his work. But Yoshihide, another hero developed from a tale in *Konjaku monogatari,* is ugly, obscurely evil, and monomaniacal in his obsession with painting the horrors of the Buddhist hells. The Lord of Horikawa, whose advances have been rejected by Yoshihide's beautiful daughter, forces her to be the living model for her father's magnificent screen painting of a woman descending to one of the lower hells in a flaming carriage. Akutagawa was extraordinarily vivid in his descriptions of graphic art, as if he felt freest to portray scenes through a doubly refracting medium, and the images of the Hell Screen are conjured up as effectively as those of the burning carriage that contains Yoshihide's daughter. Torn between his devotion to art and the loss of his one human companion, Yoshihide finishes the painting and commits suicide.

"Hell Screen" is perhaps the longest work in which Akutagawa achieved the controlled intensity that he had long ago discovered in the hallucinatory stories of Edgar Allan Poe. (His last public lecture, given in Niigata two months before his death, was entitled "An Aspect of Poe," referring to that artist's craftsmanship.) Later in 1918 he attempted a sequel to "Hell Screen," entitled "Jashūmon" ("Heresy," 1964), a serialized novel about a conflict between the young son of the cruel Lord of Horikawa and a priest of the new "Mary Religion." Lacking the confidence to complete a full-scale novel, Akutagawa abandoned "Heresy," though already a third longer than "Hell Screen," at the moment of the confrontation between the son and the priest. This left Akutagawa's newspaper readers in some doubt as to what exactly was the announced subject of "the one strange event in the life of the Young Lord."

In October 1918 Akutagawa published a story on a more sympathetic subject: the death of the poet Bashō. Its title, "Karenoshō" ("Withered Fields," 1964), was derived from Bashō's haiku "Sick on a journey, / my dreams wander on / over withered fields," which had been written as a death verse. The story dwells on the mixed emotions of the poet's followers gathered around his deathbed. These introspective young literary men are more preoccupied with themselves than with their dying master. Their hidden feelings—indifference, self-interest, a revulsion even stronger than sorrow—are ironically different from the feelings that they see fit to express. Akutagawa was perhaps recalling his own grief at the death of Sōseki as well as his suspicious thoughts regarding Sōseki's other "disciples" gathered at the wake. In November, when Akutagawa fell ill during the worldwide epidemic of influenza, he wrote a death verse of his own: "One last look / at chrysanthemums glowing in a mountain village / in the fine autumn weather." During the spring of 1919 Akutagawa was again felled by the flu around the time that his father died from the same illness, seventeen years after Akutagawa's mother's death.

A Writing Life

In April 1919, shortly after his father's death, Akutagawa Ryūnosuke resigned his teaching position at the Naval Engineering School in the hope of making a living entirely from his writing. He signed a contract to publish all of his newspaper work in the *Ōsaka Mainichi Shinbun* and went with his wife and aunt to live with his foster parents in the quiet wooded suburb of Tabata, beyond Tokyo University. Within the next six years the household was enlarged by the birth of three sons: Hiroshi and Yasushi, who would have distinguished careers as an actor and a composer, respectively, and Takashi, who would be killed in Burma shortly before the end of World War II.

As a popular writer, Akutagawa was now able to engage in various travels—several times to Nagasaki, a site of both Chinese and Christian contacts—and to associate freely with his literary friends. Granting interviews and attending roundtable discussions was unpleasant, but traveling to give lectures was even more onerous, although it was necessary for his always precarious livelihood. Writing, however, seemed more difficult than ever, in the second floor study where he was supposed to be shielded from visitors except on the Sundays allotted to them. Efforts to write longer historical tales were greeted coldly by the public, and he turned increasingly to writing sketches based closely on his own experience.

These often slight pieces crystallized moods and minor epiphanies through the use of vivid imagery. One of the first, "Mikan" (1919; "The Tangerines," 1961), begins with the narrator, a weary, bored man, sitting unaccountably alone in a second-class car of the train to Yokosuka and waiting for it to leave the station. Even the platform is empty. Just as the train begins to move, a young girl dashes in, distracting him only briefly from his depressing newspaper. He is annoyed when she opens a window and smoke pours in as the train goes through a tunnel. But then, as she leans out the window, she showers a bag of bright, sunshine-colored tangerines over the heads of three small boys—a

surprise for her frantically waving little brothers, who had waited at the crossing to see her off—perhaps to a new life. The tired narrator feels new life welling up in himself.

Akutagawa wrote a number of stories about a similar lonely figure, whom he called Horikawa Yasukichi, an impoverished writer endlessly commuting to his dreary teaching job in Yokosuka. Akutagawa declared that all his writings were in fact more or less confessions but that he did not wish to disrobe in public, nor to win approval by exposing himself and his private life more daringly, so these stories were far from being as autobiographical as those written in the confessional style dominant at the time. (His reticence was criticized even by Kume Masao, one of his closest friends, a leading writer of the so-called I-novel.) Later Akutagawa began another quasi-autobiographical work called "Daidōji Shinsuke no hansei" (1925; The early life of Daidōji Shinsuke) but broke off his account after six episodes at the uneventful beginning college days of this character. His most painful memories were revealed in the dark family history "Tenkibo" (1926; Necrology) and in the elliptical, fragmentary writings left at his death.

In March 1921 Akutagawa went to China as a special correspondent for the *Ōsaka Mainichi*, one of his few congenial assignments under a contract that he had come to regret. He was supposed to write about the "new China" as well as the traditional culture that had enriched his literary imagination. During four months abroad he saw many of the famous sights, met many leading Chinese writers and intellectuals, and was generally lionized as a visiting celebrity of the literary world. But the trip began badly, with three weeks in a Shanghai hospital where he was treated for pleurisy. Other long-standing complaints—indigestion, insomnia, and attacks of "bad nerves"—were exacerbated by the stress of travel. He was unable to finish any reports for the newspaper until after he returned to Tokyo in July.

In spite of declining health, Akutagawa struggled to fulfill his commitments to write stories for the 1922 New Year issues of important magazines. In "Shōgun" ("The General," 1948) he dared to portray General Nogi, the hero of the Russo-Japanese War who committed ritual suicide after the death of the emperor Meiji, as a self-righteous patriot who sent his own men to certain death as readily as he ordered the execution of captured Chinese spies. "Yabu no naka" (1922; "In a Grove," 1952) marked a return to the medieval world of "Rashomon." Its multiple narrators, speaking from beyond the grave, reveal conflicting accounts of their roles in an appalling crime. In Akutagawa's last year of life he also began writing about his own darkest secrets, his hidden feelings and inner conflicts, embodied in despairing characters closely modeled after himself.

Pressed for manuscripts and always in need of money, Akutagawa found it more and more difficult to write. In January 1923 his friend Kikuchi Kan established a new magazine called *Bungei Shunjū* (Literary annals), but Akutagawa contributed only a series of cynical aphorisms to it. Efforts to write in the simple "pure" style of Shiga Naoya, whom he admired, led him to explore the poignant vein of the Yasukichi stories. Literary friends as different as Kume and Tanizaki agreed that he should try to find a new direction for his writing.

After the disastrous Tokyo earthquake of September 1923, Akutagawa even attempted an ambitious story about a farmer's struggling widow, a subject that might have suited a member of the rising school of proletarian fiction. "Ikkai no tsuchi," (1924; "A Clod of Soil," 1961) depicts the woman's tenacious work to save her precious land for her young son despite impending death from typhoid fever and the long-standing hostility of her mother-in-law. The subject was perfectly proletarian, but the psychological analysis of the characters was typical of Akutagawa.

In 1924 he wrote half a dozen more stories about Horikawa Yasukichi and his life of quiet desperation. That summer—always susceptible to new literary, if not political, movements—he began reading Marx and other socialist authors. His last work, "Aru ahō no isshō" (1927; "A Fool's Life," 1968), presents a personality divided between conventional bourgeois sin and socialist idealism:

You attack the present social system, why?

Because I see the evils born of capitalism.

Evils? I didn't think you discriminated between good and evil. In that case, how about your own life?

(*ARZ*, vol. 9, p. 331; tr. *The Essential Akutagawa*, pp. 196–197)

Interrogated by an angel in a silk hat, a capitalist at heaven's gate, the defensive Fool has no answer. He had been claiming a Nietzschean vantage point beyond good and evil, but has long since lost that worldview.

Last Years

For the January 1925 issue of *Chūō Kōron* Akutagawa began the melancholy but nostalgic "Life of Daidōji Shinsuke," his only major work of that year. Though the installments had been favorably received, he put an end to the project in June with a note to his readers, promising to expand the story to three or four times its present length. By then he was suffering from numerous physical symptoms, especially insomnia, and from many irksome responsibilities, such as the editing of a five-volume anthology of modern Japanese literature, which was followed by accusations of failure to secure permissions and distribute the minuscule royalties.

Family duties as husband, father, and especially as eldest son and so head of a difficult extended family weighed on him heavily. Besides his wife and children he was responsible for the support of his aunt Fuki, his foster parents, a brother-in-law ill with tuberculosis, a younger half brother unable to launch his own literary career successfully, and a sister whose second husband, a lawyer under suspicion of arson, had killed himself by jumping in front of a train. Also, having served as matchmaker for the marriage of a friend to the sister of another friend, Akutagawa was obliged within a year to see them through the complexities of their divorce.

In January 1926, after managing to provide a story with a Chinese setting for the New Year *Chūō Kōron*, he spent almost two months writing and convalescing at a hot-spring inn in Yugawara. In April he began publishing a series of brief sketches in *Bungei Shunjū* under the title *Tsuioku* (Reminiscences), his last writings before an extraordinary recovery of creative vigor later that year.

In April, Akutagawa and his wife, along with their youngest son (Yasushi, not yet a year old), went to live in her native village of Kugenuma, located on the ocean about a two-hour train ride from Tokyo. This move amounted to a sad renewal of their marriage, a peaceful time overshadowed by Akutagawa's worsening physical and mental symptoms and by his growing fear of having inherited his mother's insanity. By late summer he had decided to commit suicide. Then he began the most productive writing period of his life, sending a final message to all his survivors—friends, family, critics, rivals, readers. The short, somber necrology which appeared in October opened with the exposure of his mother's madness and ended with a quiet scene in the family burial plot, where the protagonist is reminded of a haiku by a follower of Bashō: "The shimmering haze! / Only for this moment / I live outside the grave." The year ended in the new Shōwa era, the Taishō emperor having died on Christmas Day, and the day after the New Year Akutagawa and his wife and child returned to the Tabata house in Tokyo.

In the January and February issues of *Chūō Kōron* Akutagawa published the grimly powerful "Genkaku sanbō" ("Genkaku-Sanbo," 1961). Within the handsome walls of his secluded villa the final scenes in the life of Horikoshi Genkaku, an old man dying of tuberculosis, are played out in the claustrophobic atmosphere of an oppressive household. Other characters include his sick wife, their daughter, a sensitive but seemingly indifferent son-in-law, a grandson, a maidservant, and the sinister nurse Mrs. Kōno. For a while the group includes Oyoshi, a former maid who had been Genkaku's mistress and the little boy who is their child.

Only the nurse takes any satisfaction from the situation:

She seemed rather to enjoy her role as spectator. She was a woman with a dark past. With her sick husband and her intimacies with hospital doctors, she had many times thought of taking a dose of potassium cyanide. Her past implanted in her mind a morbid interest in the sufferings of others.

(*ARZ*, vol. 8, p. 248; tr. *Japanese Short Stories*, p. 158)

Contemptuous of the entire family, Mrs. Kōno takes a singular pleasure in unobtrusively stirring up trouble. As Genkaku weakens, he reflects on the youthful charms of Oyoshi and on the fleeting happiness of the time when he had first made his fortune, though never without anxiety caused by the envy of his friends and by his own fear that he might lose it. But the pleasant memories fade away too easily. Awake, he wants only to forget his shameful life; asleep, he is subject to horrifying nightmares. His funeral is a "grand and imposing ceremony attended by a large number of mourners," but most of them leave their sadness behind as they depart through the splendid gate: " 'He must have lived a happy life,' all the mourners declared. 'Anyway he had a young mistress and made a sizable fortune, you know.' " (*ARZ*, vol. 8, p. 257; tr. pp. 168–169)

In March Akutagawa published two works: "Shinkirō" ("Mirage," 1965), an ominous, hallucinatory sketch of walking along the beach at Kugenuma, and *Kappa* (*Kappa*, 1977), a satirical novella that stands in vivid contrast to the impressionistic autobiographical style he often used in this period of his life. *Kappa*, however, begins and ends in madness, framing a Gulliveresque account of a visit to the land of Kappa: fabulous, troublesome water creatures that are greenish and frog-like but here exhibit all the familiar human occupations and vices. Indeed, Akutagawa often drew himself as an ink-black *kappa*, and the society he describes is a grotesquely comic exaggeration of early Shōwa Japan.

The tale is narrated by Patient No. 23 in a lunatic asylum. Seventeen short chapters recount his life among the *kappa*: his gradual familiarization with their language, their odd manners and customs, and their rather cramped and meager civilization. In some respects their practices are notably humane, especially that of calling in to the fetus to ask if it wishes to be born. In other respects, though, they are either ferociously efficient and rational (unemployment is solved by killing and eating surplus workers) or merely somewhat in advance of Japanese practices. Censorship, for example, is confined to musical performances, since anyone can see more or less clearly what is expressed in a painting or literary work—they are no longer a problem—but guardians of the public morals are on uneasy ground with music.

Closest to Akutagawa's graphic emblem of himself as a *kappa* is the philandering, pessimistic, tobacco-reeking minor poet Tok. Vain and supercilious, Tok is highly critical of *kappa* society, especially its absurd family system. Still, the self-indulgent life of the poet and his friends palls on him, and his wit turns increasingly morose. One day the visitor from Japan finds Tok in a desperate state, suffering from insomnia and delusions. Even his young student friend Lap behaves rather oddly. Suddenly Lap goes out to the middle of the street and bends over almost to the ground, watching between his legs the stream of cars and passersby. Lap explains that he wanted to try a different view of the world but found the upside-down view just as depressing.

Tok solves his problem by putting a bullet through his head. His suicide is attributed to chronic dyspepsia by the doctor and to the exhaustion of his poetical genius, his last poem having been cribbed from Goethe. There is general agreement about his selfishness and the misfortune of being a member of his family. One night his spirit turns up at a séance, as self-centered and vain as ever and inclined to mock his questioners.

QUESTION: Is a spirit's span of life eternal?

ANSWER: The various theories built round our life span are so confused and contradictory that it is hard to put any credence in any of them. You should not forget, of course, that in our midst, also, there are all manner of faiths—Christianity, Buddhism, Moslemism, Parseeism and so on.

QUESTION: How about yourself—what is your faith?

ANSWER: As ever, I am a skeptic.

QUESTION: Even so, I presume that you feel no skepticism about the existence of the spirit, at least, do you?

ANSWER: Well, I find I am unable to hold the same strong conviction about it that you all have.

(*ARZ*, vol. 8, p. 363; tr. p. 129)

In April Akutagawa began to publish a series of critical essays under the title *Bungeiteki na, amari ni bungeiteki na* (Literary, all too literary). Its title, parodying Nietzsche's *Human, All Too Human*, became the self-mocking epitaph for his own art, but had been intended to be an allusion to the novels of his friend Tanizaki. This began a lengthy but diffuse exchange in which Tanizaki took exception to the view that Japanese fiction needed more of its traditional poetic quality to reflect the acute sensibilities of "the observant eye" and "the sensitive heart." On the contrary, Tanizaki asserted, what it most needed was the architectonic strength of a firmly plotted tale; and he was unkind enough to suggest that Akutagawa lacked creative energy. The physical differences between them, he said, might have something to do with their differing views on art.

Characteristically, Akutagawa tried to mollify his friend. In distributing some of his most prized books, part of his preparation for death, he sent Tanizaki a French volume on Buddhist sculpture and an English translation of Prosper Mérimée's *Colomba*, which Tanizaki had said he liked.

On the morning of 24 July 1927, at home in Tabata, Akutagawa Ryūnosuke took a fatal dose of barbiturates. Among the manuscripts at his bedside was a long letter to Kume Masao describing his vague motives but meticulous plans for suicide. (Drowning was rejected, since he could swim; and jumping in front of a train seemed the most abhorrent method of all. After deciding on using drugs, he had read a great deal about toxicology.) He asked that the letter be kept from the public a few years, but its formal title "Aru kyūyū e okuru shuki" ("A Note to a Certain Old Friend," 1972) may have persuaded Kume to release it to the eager press later the same day.

Other posthumous works by Akutagawa appeared in leading magazines before the end of the year. "Saihō no hito" (The man of the West) was a collection of aphoristic comments on "My Christ," a poet of genius whose journalism had commanded the highest market price at the time of his crucifixion. Akutagawa's Christ was above all "the universal mirror" in which he discovered himself. In that mirror he saw not only extraordinary suffering but an all too human weakness: for Akutagawa, the greatest contradiction of Christ's life was that no matter how well he understood human beings, he could not understand himself.

The finest and most harrowing of these manuscripts were two brilliantly composed autobiographical attempts. *A Fool's Life*, a nearly surrealistic sequence of fifty fragmentary but moving scenes, opened with his youthful discovery of *fin-de-siècle* Western literature from a perch on a ladder placed against the shelves of the Maruzen bookshop in Tokyo. But the second section, "Mother," is a lacerating memory occasioned by a visit to a mental hospital to gather material for a story. Other bittersweet memories of family life, friends, and romantic attachments follow, but a sense of menace hangs over all of them. Most of his crucial experiences occur when he is alone: he finds the beauty of nature and a nostalgic past in the blossoming cherry trees along the Sumida; he mourns the death of Sōseki and becomes aware of his own mortality; besides seeing life through books, he discovers Van Gogh and the power of painting. An intense friendship with a painter begins when he sees one of his ink drawings in a magazine. Women he has loved are evoked by an image: one face looks as if it is in moonlight; another looks like the morning sun shining on thin ice; his parting from a "madwoman" he has both loved and hated is like scraping frosted, glittering snow from the trunk of a tree.

Long before, another image had revealed to him his own vocation to express the terror and the transient beauty of life through art. One rainy evening as he walks along in the downpour, he sees sparks flying from an overhead trolley power line:

> Strangely he was moved. Tucked away in his jacket pocket, meant for publication in the group magazine, was his manuscript. Walking on in the rain, once more he looked back at the line.
>
> Unremittingly it emitted its prickly sparks. Though he considered all of human existence, there was nothing special worth having. But those violet blossoms of fire— those awesome fireworks in the sky, to hold them, he would give his life.

> (*ARZ*, vol. 9, p. 315; tr. p. 182)

In one of the last sections Akutagawa ends with an image of his final despair:

> Stuffed Swan
>
> Draining what strength remained, he attempted an autobiography. It was harder than he had imagined. Self-importance and skepticism and calculation of advantages or disadvantages were all in him. He despised this self of his. At the same time he couldn't help thinking, "Remove a layer of skin and everybody is alike." . . . After completing *A Fool's Life* he happened to see in a junk shop a stuffed swan. It stood with its neck held erect, its wings yellowed, motheaten. Recalling his whole life, he felt a sudden onrush of tears and cold laughter. In front of him was either madness or suicide. In the twilight he walked the street alone, deter-

mined, patiently, to wait for his fate—for slowly approaching destruction.

(ARZ, vol. 9, p. 336; tr. p. 201)

Perhaps the swan reminded him of the "stuffed pheasant" once given to him as a school graduation gift.

"Haguruma" ("Cogwheels," 1987) was Akutagawa's last short story. It has the familiar subject of a few days in the life of an author, mostly alone at a hotel trying to write. Akutagawa not only writes in the first person but focuses his I-novel on the persona of Mr. A, the author of "Hell Screen." Sinister females turn up—his dead mother, a vengeful lover—but he also meets his own double and is tortured by hallucinations in the form of translucent cogwheels that gradually multiply to crowd his field of vision.

His world is full of threatening images. A worm wriggles on the edge of his plate at dinner. Sunlight is frightening; a yellow airplane zooms close overhead; taxis and even book jackets are in the dangerous color yellow, rather than in a soothing green. The nights are especially bad (Akutagawa had originally intended to call his story "Night," or "Tokyo Night"). After Mr. A goes back to rejoin his family at a small resort town on the ocean, his terror mounts even while he is walking home along a lonely path. Silhouetted against the gray sea is the empty frame for a swing, which reminds him of a gallows. He feels that something is pursuing him—and then he sees the cogwheels beginning to multiply, revolving faster and faster before his eyes. The tangled branches of pine trees along his path become as transparent as fine cut glass. Heart pounding, head held erect like the stuffed swan, he struggles on as if someone is pushing him from behind. . . .

"Cogwheels" ends with A's "most frightening experience," which occurs when his wife runs upstairs, thinking he has committed suicide. Its author, the celebrated young writer Akutagawa Ryūnosuke, less than half a year past his thirty-fifth birthday, had closed his short career with what some critics consider his masterpiece.

Selected Bibliography

PRIMARY WORKS
COLLECTED WORKS

Akutagawa Ryūnosuke zenshū. 9 vols. Tokyo: Chikuma Shobō, 1971.
Akutagawa Ryūnosuke zenshū. 12 vols. Tokyo: Iwanami Shoten, 1978. (Abbreviated as *ARZ* in citations.)
Akutagawa Ryūnosuke zenshū sōsakuin. Tokyo: Iwanami Shoten, 1993.

TRANSLATIONS

Tales Grotesque and Curious. Trans. by Glen W. Shaw. Tokyo: Hokuseidō, 1930.
Hell Screen and Other Stories. Trans. by W. H. H. Norman. Tokyo: Hokuseidō, 1948.
Rashomon and Other Stories. Trans. by Takashi Kojima. New York: Liveright, 1952.
Japanese Short Stories. Trans. by Takashi Kojima. New York: Liveright, 1961.
Exotic Japanese Stories. Trans. by Takashi Kojima and John McVittie. New York: Liveright, 1964.
Kappa. Trans. by Geoffrey Bownas. Tokyo: Tuttle, 1971.
The Essential Akutagawa. Edited by Seiji Lippit. New York: Marsilio, 1999.

SECONDARY WORKS
CRITICAL AND BIOGRAPHICAL STUDIES

Gerow, A. A. "The Self Seen As Other: Akutagawa and Film." *Literature/Film Quarterly* 23, no. 3:197–203 (1995).
Hibbett, Howard S. "Akutagawa Ryūnosuke and the Negative Ideal." In *Personality in Japanese History.* Edited by Albert M. Craig and Donald H. Shively. Berkeley: University of California Press, 1970.
Keene, Donald. *Dawn to the West: Japanese Literature of the Modern Era.* New York: Holt, Rinehart and Winston, 1984.
Kikuchi Hiroshi, Kubota Yoshitarō, and Sakaguchi Yasuyoshi, eds. *Akutagawa Ryūnosuke jiten.* Tokyo: Meiji Shoin, 1985.
Lippit, Seiji M. "The Disintegrating Machinery of the Modern: Akutagawa Ryūnosuke's Late Writings." *Journal of Asian Studies* 58, no. 1:27–50 (1999).
Morimoto Osamu. *Shinkō Akutagawa Ryūnosuke Den.* Kitazawa Tosho Shuppan. 1971.
Tsuruta, Kinya. "Akutagawa Ryūnosuke and I-Novelists." *Monumenta Nipponica* 25, no. 1–2:13–27 (1970).
Yu, Beongcheon. *Akutagawa: An Introduction.* Detroit, Mich.: Wayne State University Press, 1972.

FILM BASED ON THE WORKS OF AKUTAGAWA RYŪNOSUKE

Rashōmon. Directed by Kurosawa Akira. 1950.

Ango
(Sakaguchi Ango)
1906–1955

James Dorsey

It was probably the long history of "priors" that sealed fifteen-year-old Sakaguchi Ango's fate one September day in 1922. A notorious truant, he had already been required to repeat a grade once, and all indications were that it would be happening again soon. There had also been one memorable February morning when teachers had arrived at school to find a two-meter-high snow phallus erected in the yard. Though culpability was never fully established, rumor suggested that Ango had been responsible. Then came the straw that broke the camel's back: Ango punched one of the teachers, and he was expelled. Ango's father, a politician who spent most of his time in Japan's capital, promptly ripped his wayward son from his comfortable life in rural Niigata and dragged him off to Tokyo in hopes that strict parental supervision and the good influence of his eldest son, Kenkichi, would change Ango's behavior for the better. Shortly thereafter, Ango's former classmates flipped open the top of his desk and found a prediction he had left carved right into the wood: "I shall be the grand delinquent, rising again one day in the annals of history."

Ango made good on his word. Without missing a beat, he began cutting classes at his new school in Tokyo to hear the comedians in Asakusa or sneak a smoke behind Gokokuji Temple. By his early thirties he was a heavy drinker, once single-handedly emptying a dozen bottles of whiskey in a three-day binge. In the years immediately after World War II, when Ango's career was at its peak, he began taking philopon, a drug originally designed to keep pilots awake. A slow writer, Ango used the stimulant to boost production, injecting enough to keep him writing without sleep for as many as four days straight when deadlines were pressing. Then, after the manuscripts had been submitted, he needed something to help him relax. Adorm, a sleep-inducing drug, often washed down with whiskey, suited his need, and Ango was soon addicted to both in an insane cycle that produced hallucinations and violent outbursts. He was in jail for just such an outburst in 1953 when his only child was born.

Ango's first "serious" relationship was with Tomiko, the married older woman who operated one of his favorite drinking establishments. Her cleaver-wielding, jealous husband prompted the lovers to spend a lot of time in inns far from Tokyo. Next was a nameless clerk from a pie shop. During the extensive Allied bombing raids on Tokyo in 1945, Ango spent many an amorous night with her in his temporary home—a friend's bomb shelter. After the war Ango was embroiled in two very public scandals: a mudslinging match with tax officials and accusations of a betting scam at a local bicycle racetrack. Such indiscretions were regularly featured in newspapers and magazines as Ango, one of the first Japanese writers to achieve celebrity status, was watched carefully. He was indeed "the grand delinquent."

Ango lived his life at an almost primal, instinctual level, and this attitude was reflected in his work. Known to wear nothing but a loincloth for days on end, Ango struggled to peel away the unnecessary in his writing as well: he shunned the literary conventions of the day and portrayed a human condition devoid of the rules of polite society. It all struck a chord with his audience, particularly during the tumultuous early postwar period. His most famous work, "Darakuron" (1946; "Discourse on Decadence," 1986), is a call for disillusioned individuals and the defeated nation to continue their fall from the "heights" of the wartime regime. Salvation rests, he insisted, in a decadence wherein man embraces the deeper, and often ugly, truths of the human condition. This essay, it has been said, had an impact on the Japanese people equal to Emperor Hirohito's declaration of surrender at the end of World War II.

Since this initial splash in the immediate postwar years, Ango has enjoyed a number of revivals. The first was fueled by the student movement of late 1960s and early 1970s, which found inspiration in Ango's iconoclasm and anti-authoritarian stance. A paperback edition of "Discourse on Decadence," once on the verge of going out of print, was catapulted to the bestseller list, and the media was soon trumpeting an "Ango revival." This coincided with the publication of Ango's collected works and the literary studies that would lead to his canonization, in both senses of the word.

A similar phenomenon emerged in the 1990s. In 1991 an eighteen-volume paperback edition of his collected works was released, attesting to Ango's popularity with an entirely new, financially-challenged younger audience. A new hardcover set also became available,

published by Chikuma Shobō and complete with commentaries by the prominent critic and philosopher Karatani Kōjin. The annual gathering of Ango fans held in his hometown of Niigata continues to draw attention, with attendance having topped five hundred in the 1990s. Quite clearly, the title of award-winning novelist Ogino Anna's 1994 book, *I Love Ango*, expresses the sentiments of many. The prophesy has been fulfilled: Ango is the "grand delinquent," and he has indeed risen time and again in at least the literary history of postwar Japan.

Life in the Hometown

Ango's formative years in his native Niigata left such an indelible mark on his personality that the idea of a *furusato*, a "hometown" or "origin," runs through many of his works. (As the unifying theme of this essay, the Japanese term, rather than the English, will appear most often, since it carries a broader range of meaning than do individual English terms that translate the word only for specific situations.) He was born Sakaguchi Heigo on 20 October 1906, the eleventh of thirteen children. His father, Jin'ichirō, was the first son of a village mayor and forty-seven years old at the time of Ango's birth. A humorless man, Jin'ichirō had been married at the age of fifteen and was a typical overachieving firstborn son: in addition to establishing a reputation for poetry in the Chinese style, he also served as the chairman of a rice and grain brokerage, as the president of a local newspaper company, and as a representative in the lower house of the national assembly. Living in the shadow of such ambition and industry, it is only natural that when Ango turned to delinquency he did so with such gusto.

Ango relates his earliest childhood memories in "Ishi no omoi" (1946; The thoughts of a stone). Of his father, he writes:

Our relationship consisted of me being summoned once a month to prepare his ink. I would see the sour look on his face, get snapped at for something, lose my temper, and withdraw—and that was that. The 'fatherly love' that people talk about is just a joke to me, something foreign. Fortunately when I was in elementary school we didn't have anything like today's children's stories of happy families. Instead I read nothing but books about ninja masters and great heroes . . . so there was nothing, not a thing, to make me think about fatherly love.

(Teihon Sakaguchi Ango zenshū [SAZ], vol. 3, pp. 93–94)

Later, as a young man living with his father in Tokyo, Ango came to see Jin'ichirō's naive honesty and industry, his incessant sublimation of his own desires in an effort to serve and be liked by others, as evidence of an unforgivable mediocrity. Ango's aversion to this bourgeois temperance was so strong that in "Ishi no omoi"—written twenty-three years after his father's death—Ango is still vehemently insisting that he shares none of his father's personality traits.

Ango's mother, Asa, was Jin'ichirō's second wife, the first having died soon after giving birth to a third daughter. Asa bore her husband an additional nine children in the course of seventeen years, accepted the adoption of the thirteenth child (born to Jin'ichirō's mistress), and endured the resentment of the daughters from the first marriage, two of whom once tried to poison her. It is understandable that she was prone to fits of hysteria and did not shower Ango with the love he so desperately desired. Ango claims their relationship was antagonistic from the very start: the birth was an exceedingly difficult one, pushing his mother to the brink of death. Asa exacted revenge. As a child coming home late from his rounds of terrorizing the neighborhood, Ango would find she had locked him out. When he risked his life in the rough seas to gather clams as she had requested, Ango found her silent and unappreciative. So strained was the relationship between the two that when she told an eight-year-old Ango that he was not really her child, he actually felt relieved and would drift off to sleep at night with dreams of his

"real" mother dancing in his head. With all of this, Ango writes in "Ishi no omoi," "my twisted self was, as a matter of course, further twisted" *(SAZ, vol. 3, p. 100)*.

Ango's disdain of formal education developed early. His insecurities were further exacerbated by his mother's absorption with the newly born twelfth child, and Ango could not bring himself to actually attend the kindergarten in which he had been enrolled. Though only four at the time, Ango would aimlessly roam the streets instead. The truancy continued into his teens: Ango would spend sunny days alone on the seashore and rainy days playing cards above a bakery near the school. He would, however, show up in time for judo practice. It was around this time that he acquired the name he was to make famous. His classical Chinese teacher, so disappointed in this son of an aficionado, exploded on one of the few days that Ango was actually in class. Punning on the given name of Heigo, with the character "hei" meaning "bright" or "clear," the teacher screamed, "You're not deserving of the name. Being so in the dark concerning who you are, you will hereafter be known as 'Ango,' " and he wrote the character for "dark" (pronounced "an") on the blackboard. Taking a perverse pride in this dubious recognition, Ango adopted the name, albeit with an orthographic adjustment.

This rebellious romp from childhood to adolescence, including his tense relationship with his parents and expulsion from school, gave birth to Ango's conception of the *furusato*. While many literary men of the previous generation left wealthy, stable (though sometimes stifling) families in the hinterlands to further promising academic careers in the finest institutions in Tokyo, Ango left an economically strained, alienating family environment in order to play hooky from second rate schools he was enrolled in only as a last ditch effort to save him from certain ruin. So, while many in the urban population envisioned their rural roots as a lyrical, romantic web of family histories and personal interdependencies, Ango associated his *furusato* with the cold, bound-

33

less ocean he had once stared at from the desolate shore and the angry winds blowing off the water. Ango's experience of this *furusato* would serve as the touchstone for his essays and fiction in the years to come.

Flight from the Hometown

Ango never expressed homesickness or longing for Niigata after he moved to Tokyo in 1922, and initially the change of scenery did little to affect his behavior. He was still skipping school regularly to enjoy the varied distractions of the big city, and in his fondness for sports over books he added track and field, swimming, and baseball to his practice of judo. Perhaps Ango was able to continue his antics because his father, diagnosed with stomach cancer, was not physically able to discipline his son. Nor did the fact that Jin'ichirō spent most of his time in bed warm the relationship: when the plaster started shaking off the walls during the Great Kantō Earthquake of 1923, Ango made sure to get himself out of the house to safety immediately. Only later did he remember his bedridden father and return to find Jin'ichirō supporting with both hands a fallen crossbeam that had almost crushed his skull. Two months later Jin'ichirō was dead (though to date nobody has suggested the cause was related to Ango's negligence).

Slowly, through the influence of his brother and a menagerie of eccentric friends, Ango began to read fiction as well as books on religion and the natural sciences. He even tried his hand at composing Japanese *waka*, the traditional thirty-one-syllable poem, and occasionally visited a Zen temple to practice meditation. Ango was immediately drawn to the connection between matters of the spirit and the literary arts, writing to a friend: "Isn't the glory of true poetry the fact that a person breaks free from the self and quietly, objectively, contemplates his place in the universe? Isn't it precisely through this contemplative life that our suffering is relieved and the unseemly made sacred?" (*SAZ*, vol. 13, p. 381). Though he would later turn from poetry to fic-

tion and essays, and the religious element would shift from this romanticism to a grittier, more carnal understanding, the link between literary practice and religious concerns would run through Ango's life.

In April 1925 Ango, then eighteen, graduated from high school and faced decisions about his future. The pressure from debts left by his father prompted him to forgo his astonishing first choice, more schooling, in favor of an equally shocking second choice: a temporary job as an elementary school teacher in an as-yet undeveloped area of Tokyo. Anecdotes from this period, combined with thoughts on children and their education and an expression of his deepening interest in religion, are all included in "Kaze to hikari to hatachi no watashi" (1947; The wind, the light, and me at twenty. The title is confusing. Ango is calculating his age by calendar year, as was the custom, rather than by birthdate. Thus, though he speaks of being twenty, by Western reckoning he was eighteen when he began the job and nineteen when he quit.)

This fictionalized recreation of events that had occurred more than twenty years earlier probably says more about the world of Ango at forty than it does about the eighteen-year-old teacher. The school and environs, for example, are populated by the fictional characters familiar from other Ango works: a woman whose mental deficiencies render her an incarnation of physical desire, a madonna-like figure deified by her inaccessibility, and a crass man ultimately endearing for his authenticity. Still, though some of the characters come from the imagination, it is an imagination shaped by the actual people Ango encountered at that time. The relationship is dialectical: the experience shapes the mind that then writes the experience.

Therefore, though perhaps not factual, there is still some truth in the description of why the protagonist of this story, Ango's alter ego, chooses to leave his job after only a year. He is portrayed as saintly in his attention to the children, selfless in his attitude toward material possessions, and without desire for worldly pleasures. He describes himself as "a completely self-realized layman, my mind made up to feel no anger, no sadness, no resentment, and no joy—in short, I was trying to live in perfect sync with my surroundings, like the clouds floating through the sky and the water flowing in the river" (*SAZ*, vol. 3, p. 224). This sounds very much like the enlightened individual of Buddhist lore, and the protagonist seems primed for a sedate, spiritually full life. Voices in his head, however, insist that "unhappiness and suffering are the hometown *[furusato]* of the human spirit" (*SAZ*, vol. 3, p. 227). At the end of the school year he resigns his post in order to struggle with the study of Buddhism on his way to becoming a monk, all the while fully aware of the paradox in leaving a monk-like existence in pursuit of becoming a monk.

This turn of events in the story, and in Ango's life, is most certainly Buddhist inspired, for it plays out according to one of the most central patterns in that spiritual quest: having first left the world of impermanence by eradicating the desires which cause all suffering, the truly enlightened will immediately return to it lest they elevate that new "enlightened" existence into an obsession all its own. In this model, spiritual enlightenment is a process rather than a sustainable state. This spiritual trajectory has informed many works of Japanese literature, from Kamo no Chōmei's medieval classic *Hōjōki* (ca. 1212; *An Account of My Hut*, 1955) to Ihara Saikaku's *Kōshoku ichidai onna* (1686; *The Life of an Amorous Woman*, 1963), and it is revived here in both Sakaguchi Ango's story and his life. Rather than cling to the comforts of an established position, that position is thrust aside to engage the world anew. This accounts for Ango's constant changing of residence and domestic partners as well as the jumble of genres he explored: farce, literary criticism, autobiographical fiction, folktales, social criticism, mystery, historical novels, and journalism. The constant, volitional exposure of the self to both professional and personal risk was part of Ango's lifelong spiritual quest; it was how he maintained an authentic engagement with the human condition.

Ango's return to the "floating world" from his sanctuary as an isolated schoolteacher took the form of enrollment in the Department of Indian Philosophy at Tōyō University in April 1926. There, he subjected himself to the most rigorous self-discipline, poring over Buddhist texts and primers for Pali and Sanskrit. Ango is said to have slept for no more than four hours a day during this period, dousing himself with cold water when sleep threatened to interrupt his studies. Needless to say, this did not last long, and Ango began to suffer from nervous exhaustion. A concussion in an accident and his shock at the suicide of writer Akutagawa Ryūnosuke made things worse. His one comfort during this time was his study of languages, Pali and Sanskrit at school and French, which he took up at the private academy Athénée Français. Attempting to add French writers such as Henri-René Lenormand, Molière, and Voltaire to his readings of Uno Kōji, Kasai Zenzō, and Arishima Takeo meant that Ango spent a lot of time with his dictionaries. In his constantly agitated state, he found the endless process of looking up unfamiliar words strangely soothing.

This state of affairs continued until he graduated from university in April 1930 at the age of twenty-three. Unsure about what to do next, Ango applied for a job as a café manager and for a position with a traveling circus before dedicating himself to the production of a literary magazine, *Kotoba* (Words), with like-minded youths from Athénée Français. After just two issues the magazine was renamed *Aoi Uma* (The blue horse) and placed under the auspices of the prestigious Iwanami publishing company. This sponsorship did not result from Iwanami's recognition of the literary potential of Ango and associates but rather from a bit of blackmail: one of the group just happened to be the nephew of Akutagawa Ryūnosuke, and as the executor of Akutagawa's literary assets, he leveraged an Iwanami sponsorship for his magazine.

Most of Ango's early contributions to these magazines were in the form of hack translations of French literature. As he tells it in "Yo ni deru made" (1955; Until taking my place in the world), the editor would appear at Ango's door the night before a deadline and demand that he translate something for the next issue. Ango would spend the night frantically churning something out, often skipping the parts with too many unfamiliar words. The French novelist Marcel Proust's descriptions of sumptuous meals, for example, "were full of names for meats, vegetables, and fish that I had never heard of so I skipped most of them. As a result I served up some pretty meager meals. It was a terrible thing to do to both Proust and the readers . . ." (*SAZ*, vol. 8, p. 520). Ango published a few original works in these magazines as well, and these are what launched him into the literary limelight.

Forging a Literary Home

Broadly speaking, Ango's first original compositions were of two very different types: lyrical works set in the countryside and those in, or about, the genre of farce. The first category includes "Kurodani mura" (1931; The village of Kurodani), the story of a young man's simultaneous awakening to both religious and carnal desires in an isolated village, and the lesser known "Furusato ni yosuru sanka" (1931; Ode to my hometown). In both, Ango wrestled with the literary styles and tropes of the time in an attempt to carve out a niche of his own.

In "Furusato ni yosuru sanka" Ango adopts the first-person narrative voice and the rural setting so popular with the I-novelists and naturalists but combines these with the disorienting and defamiliarizing techniques of the infinitely urban Neoperceptionists Yokomitsu Riichi and Kawabata Yasunari. The "I" figures prominently, the pronoun repeated an inordinate number of times in the short story. This "I," however, is fragmented and emptied, as we see in these lines describing the trip back home to the country: "I was tired. There was no self in this me. I thought of nothing. As the scenery flowed past, that scenery was me" (*SAZ*, vol. 1, p. 20). The hometown to which the protagonist returns is equally disorienting, almost dreamlike. His family home is gone and

his romantic search for the girl he once spoke with as a child proves unsuccessful, the very memory of her disintegrating during the visit. His sister lies dying in a hospital but the situation causes him nothing but irritation. He decides to return to Tokyo, where at least he can feel that his pain and suffering are real.

Though the modernist techniques and surreal atmosphere found here were not to be pillars of Ango's later fiction, this story was an early attempt by Ango to fashion an understanding of an origin or *furusato* along lines consistent with his own unique experience of it. By presenting an absent self encountering a chimera of a hometown, Ango is rejecting the conventional understanding of a *furusato* as the fountainhead of the self and the place in which one confronts the past for an understanding of the present. In fact, the "hometown" that is really paid tribute to here is the harsh existence that is life in urban Tokyo—a life to which the protagonist returns, but now without a romantic image of rural roots to comfort him. In the literary *furusato* that Ango is forging, one is not afforded the luxury of idealized visions.

During the same period Ango published a number of works exploring the genre of farce. His first published original work was "Kogarashi no sakagura kara" (1931; From a sake warehouse in the winter's wind), which appeared in the second (and final issue) of *Kotoba*. Most of the story is given over to the monologue of a "pasty-faced lunatic" who bears a striking resemblance to the Ango-like protagonist. In a word, the story is about the lunatic's battle with the bottle. Try as he might to give it up in pursuit of spiritual enlightenment, the cold winter wind constantly drives him back to the sake warehouse, where a spiritual mentor awaits, drunk, to taunt him. It is a silly, slapstick story playing on a variation of the Buddhist paradox outlined above: the obsession with abstaining from drink can be a bigger obstacle to spiritual growth than imbibing freely.

Ango's second, and marginally more interesting, farce is "Kaze hakase" (1931; Professor

Blowhard), published in the more widely circulated *Aoi Uma*. The story, inspired by works of Edgar Allan Poe, relates the "suicide" of Professor Blowhard through two equally unreliable and outrageous narrative voices: that of the professor (in the form of his suicide note), and that of his student, who tries to persuade the reader that the note and suicide are real. Ango uses the wind in this story as well: the title might be rendered more literally as "Professor Wind," and this blustery pedagogue ends up as just that, blowing out of his home in a rage of resentment and infecting his nemesis with influenza. The story can be read in many ways: as a piece of slapstick, as a spoof on academics, as a mystery novel (or spoof on them), or as an exercise in twisted logic. What is perhaps most significant about this story (and "Kogarashi no sakagura kara" as well) is its bold departure from the proletarian literature and Marxist criticism that formed the mainstream of Japanese literature at the time. In these wild romps of fantasy and humor, too, Ango was attempting to break new ground.

More integral to Ango's career are the ideas and techniques found in his essay on the genre. In "FARCE ni tsuite" (1932; On farce) Ango rails against the repressive hegemony of literary realism. Though realism focuses attention on the concrete world, and language plays merely a supporting role by representing this world in recognizable ways, the tool of language is woefully inadequate for the task. After all, Ango writes, the only way to capture this complex world of ours realistically would be to stick the earth itself between the covers of a book! Far better, according to Ango, is the genre of farce, for it employs language in its purest form—to create or present rather than represent. Not limited by the conventions of the concrete world, farce becomes a "wild rampage" affirming

> all sides of man, completely and without leaving a single thing behind. Whether it be fantasies, dreams, death, rage, contradiction, absurdity, or ambiguity, farce attempts to affirm every last thing that is connected to human reality. Farce affirms negations, it affirms affirmations, and then it affirms this. In the end it tries to take everything related to man and forever, for eternity, and in perpetuity affirm, affirm, affirm and never stop.
>
> (*SAZ*, vol. 7, p. 19)

In Ango's mind, the glory of farce is that everything goes and there are no holds barred.

There is, of course, something ironic in seriously championing, of all things, farce as the finest of genres. Ango recognizes this irony and revels in it. In addition to the gross exaggeration evident in the quote above, he also incorporates the qualities of the genre in his rhetorical stance.

> First of all, right up front, I must confess that I don't know much, and in writing this piece I haven't consulted a single authoritative source by my predecessors. So, it is impossible for me to add even a gratuitous remark to the conventional understanding of the genre or its origins. But I've racked my brains and come up with an argument that just might let me pull one over on you . . . If you would do me the favor of taking this essay as itself a product of the farcical spirit, well, silly old me just might be so overwhelmed with gratitude that my heart stops and I keel over in a faint.
>
> (*SAZ*, vol. 7, pp. 13–14)

The essay is performative, making a farce out of a discourse on farce in its attempt to open the literary realm to any and all possibilities. While lacking the rhetorical power of his later essays, this one on farce already exhibits that playful attitude toward serious topics that would make Ango famous. We also see the beginnings of the eclectic style, the mixing of serious assertions with ridiculous examples, that eventually works so well for Ango. The best description of his style comes in his own *Furenzoku satsujin jiken* (1948; A case of nonserial murder), where a character claims that Ango's writings are like "a cross between some cheesy vaudeville act and the *Analects* of Confucius" (*SAZ*, vol. 10, p. 88).

Nearly ten years would go by before Ango returned to the question of literary genres in "Bungaku no furusato" (1941; The birthplace of literature). Comparing this later piece with Ango's work on farce foregrounds an important shift in Ango's thought that occurred between his literary debut and the works that would secure his reputation. While in the earlier essay the enemy had been realism, and the solution was the "wild rampage" of affirmations, in the latter essay Ango broadens his attack to include all static intellectual constructs and finds liberation in the short-circuiting of these conventional modes of apprehension.

At the heart of "Bungaku no furusato" are four anecdotes which capture literature in its most primal state. Three of these share a sudden deployment of violence and death that confounds all attempts at rational explanation. The most striking presents Akutagawa Ryūnosuke reading a poor farmer's manuscript describing infanticide. When Akutagawa questions whether such a terrifying story could possibly be true, the farmer admits that the story is a record of his very own actions. The farmer defensively dares Akutagawa to pass judgment, and "this talented man, who always had something to say about everything, was unable to answer" (*SAZ*, vol. 7, p. 113). The primal power of these stories—their ability to leave even Akutagawa, the quintessential intellectual, speechless—makes them the root, the *furusato*, of literature as Ango saw it.

Ango insists that the only moral in such stories is that there is no moral. They set us drifting on a dark, desolate plain with no hope of any salvation, no comfort other than the satisfaction of knowing that one is living authentically engaged with the harsh realities of the world. Without recourse to an intellectual understanding or rationalization, one lives life at ground zero. This was the stance that Ango was to adopt in many of his later works. While he had first sought freedom from reality in the flights of fancy made possible by farce, around the time of this essay, 1941, he began to yearn for an unmediated experience of reality, rejecting anything which muted its harsh cruelties.

The Hard Years, the War, and Ango at His Peak

Though his early stories and essays were unpolished, Ango's antagonistic stance toward the established literary community was enough to gain him the attention of Makino Shin'ichi, an established writer who was also trying to break new literary ground. Some critics have suggested that the praise Makino quite unexpectedly showered on "Kaze hakase" (Professor Blowhard) was motivated not so much by the story's innate qualities as by the part it could play in his larger literary agenda. Regardless, this recognition gained Ango a brief moment in the sun as some of his earlier works gained wider circulation and requests came in from prestigious publishers.

The fame, however, was premature, and it was to be ten years before Ango's next literary coup. These were hard years personally as well as professionally. In 1932 Ango met the beautiful woman writer Yada Tsuseko, also a media darling, and was immediately attracted to her. Though they saw each other socially, it did not evolve into the full-blown romance that Ango had hoped for. He continued to have feelings for her, and in some of his fiction transformed her into an almost madonna-like figure. All communication between the two came to a sudden halt in 1936.

In the autobiographical story "Sanjussai" (1948; Thirty) Ango dramatically recalls his realization, after their first kiss, that the relationship was not meant to be. He is up most of the night writing, and early the next day the letter severing their relationship "was mailed, express. The streets were covered in snow. The day: 26 February 1936. I remember that on the streets there was as yet no discernible sign of the bloody 26 February Incident. They were quiet, snow-covered streets" (*SAZ*, vol. 4, p. 158). While most agree that this scene is pure fabrication, the legend of Ango is better for it. In mailing the letter on that snowy morning, Ango was rejecting the myth of romantic love, just as he had once discarded the utopian vision of a rural hometown. Meanwhile, across town, 1,400 soldiers, most of them young officers of Ango's age, persisted in clinging to a different sort of myth—that of the nation—and were instigating the 26 February coup d'état in its name. On the one hand, Ango's concerns seem small in comparison with the soldiers' surrender of self in the name of nation. On the other hand, though, Ango's refusal to sublimate intimate, personal concerns to such grandiose abstractions also strikes us as more authentically human—and certainly less dangerous: the 26 February mutiny failed, and fourteen of those young soldiers would be executed in its aftermath. Ango's painfully unsuccessful relationship with Yada was instrumental in bringing him closer to his vision of man as properly alone in the world, without the comforts of true love or fanatical patriotism, both of which Mishima Yukio writes into his account of the 26 February Incident ("Yūkoku," 1961; "Patriotism," 1971).

Meanwhile, on top of his breakup with Yada, the death of a dear friend, and the pressure to live up to the media's expectations pushed Ango into a fragile emotional state. He was drinking heavily and was soon involved in the messy relationship with Tomiko mentioned earlier. Deciding that drastic measures were called for in ending his personal and professional slump, Ango set out for Kyoto, where he planned to write the full-length novel that would heal his soul. Ango stayed in Kyoto for a year and a half (January 1937 to July 1938), completing the first seven hundred pages of *Fubuki monogatari* (1938; Tale of a blizzard) in the first six months and spending the following year playing the Japanese board game *go* and drinking. This was the first of many attempts to compose a longer work, and it set the pattern: each time Ango would find himself incapable of the sustained effort and—on the rare occasion such a project was completed—the results would be mixed. When *Fubuki monogatari* came out in 1938, it was poorly received and Ango's depression deepened.

It was not until Ango was invited to join the coterie magazine *Gendai bungaku* in 1940 that things began to turn around. The politically aware, left-wing thinkers in the group (Ara Masahito, Hirano Ken, Honda Shūgo, Sasaki Kiichi, and Odagiri Hideo) had their attention focused on the war and on the increasingly intrusive social policies that the government was employing in order to sustain it. Censorship, in particular, was an issue for the group, as authorities prevented the publication of anything that might divide or "confuse" the people in this time of crisis. The company and concerns of this group opened Ango's eyes to a larger world, a political world, and his works began to take on a sharper edge.

In the war years Ango came fully into his own. Turning his attention to the horrible conditions under which the Japanese people were living, Ango soon focused on the growing gap between the wartime ideological constructions and the cold, hard realities of everyday life in 1940s Japan. This was exactly the type of inauthenticity that he despised, and he soon got to work delineating the *furusato* beneath all the demagoguery. The first piece into which Ango worked his wild rampage on the war and its ideologies was "Nihon bunka shikan" (1942; A personal view of Japanese culture). Responding in detail to a portrait of Japan, its people, and its culture that had most recently been popularized in a series of bestsellers by the German architect Bruno Taut (1880–1938), Ango deals with a multitude of Japanese cultural icons, many of which were being evoked in the militaristic wartime propaganda. In each and every case he rejects those ideologically charged symbols in favor of things that satisfy the everyday needs and plebeian desires of the common man.

In the opening paragraph Ango states his qualifications for giving his opinions on Japanese culture, and they have nothing to do with that traditional practice that had come to represent both the sum total of Japanese aesthetics and even the soul of the Japanese people themselves. Ango writes: "I know none of the formalities of the tea ceremony, but I am an expert on getting rip-roaring drunk" (*SAZ*, vol. 7, p. 122). On the precious architectural heritage that Taut and others saw as so central to Japan's national identity, Ango asserts: "I couldn't care less if both Hōryūji and Byōdōin burned to the ground. If the need should arise, we'd do well to tear down Hōryūji and put up a parking lot" (*SAZ*, vol. 7, p. 141), and later, "The destruction of Kyoto's temples or Nara's Buddhist statues wouldn't bother us in the least, but we'd be in real trouble if the streetcars stopped running" (*SAZ*, vol. 7, p. 124). Ango also mounts an attack from the other side of the issue, defending the Westernized lifestyle of his contemporaries by writing:

What is the nature of the "Japanese spirit"? We, of all people, do not need to theorize on that. . . . We yank trousers over our stubby bowlegs, deck ourselves out in Western clothes, waddle about, dance the jitterbug, toss out the tatami and strike affected poses amidst tacky chairs and tables. That this appears completely absurd to the Western eye has absolutely no bearing on the fact that we ourselves are satisfied with the convenience of it all.

(*SAZ*, vol. 7, p. 125)

In these bombastic, iconoclastic statements, Ango takes the sacred concept of the Japanese nation so dear to the wartime ideologues and drags it into the realm of the profane.

But Ango's rampage does not stop there. The essay makes constant reference to the ancient capital of Kyoto—home to some of the oldest and finest temples, shrines, and institutions of Japan—and it completely transforms the tenor of the city. Though he visits the famous temples of Arashiyama and the still oft-photographed stone garden at Ryōanji, Ango argues that these are cold and lifeless. Instead, his Kyoto is represented by the Kurumazaki Shrine and the Arashiyama Theatre, two locations in which people dive beneath the niceties of convention and decorum to indulge the desires, usually seamy, which make them human.

At the Kurumazaki Shrine people do not offer the typical prayers for academic success or world peace; rather, on stones left on the shrine grounds they scribble petitions to the gods for cold hard cash, and in very specific amounts. As Ango notes, though the shrine is "supposedly dedicated to the memory of somebody-or-other Kiyohara, a scholar it seems, the real object of veneration is quite obviously the almighty yen" (*SAZ*, vol. 7, p. 128). The second "shrine" in Ango's Kyoto, the Arashiyama Theatre, is a run-down old shack on the edge of town which hosts traveling performers, often farmers moonlighting during the slow winter months. The acts—some magic tricks, a few skits, and a dancing girl rolling up her kimono to bare her bottom—are all hopelessly amateurish, and the stench from the urine-splashed toilets is overwhelming. Still, Ango appreciates the site for its authenticity, its acceptance of its vulgar nature as a place to satisfy the everyday, understandable need for sexual titillation and entertainment (not to mention urination). Needless to say, this was not the quintessentially Japanese city of Kyoto, the symbol of a homeland for which young men were willing to die in battle.

This sustained critique of the symbols of nationhood has led many critics to champion this essay as one of the precious few acts of subversion on the part of intellectuals during the war. A good example is Okuno Takeo, the critic who edited the first collected works of Ango in the late 1960s and published an influential critical biography in 1972. Okuno read "Nihon bunka shikan" as an unambiguous critique not only of the ideology of cultural uniqueness, but of the ultra-nationalists and cultural conservatives as well. This is the standard interpretation of Ango, and it is not mistaken. A subversive voice Sakaguchi Ango most certainly is, as his continuing popularity among university students attests. His quest to expose the hard, cold, and often sordid realities of the human condition obscured and sterilized by conventions and rationalizations makes him a natural choice for those wanting to radically question the status quo.

Still, this is really only half of the story. Though the full implications have yet to be fully explicated, critics Isoda Kōichi, Ueno Takashi, and Suzuki Sadami have hinted at an ambivalence inherent in Ango's message. In his obsession with a spiritual authenticity defined as living true to one's desires, Ango seemed to open the door to other types of oppression. One of the authentic individuals appearing in "Nihon bunka shikan" is Toyotomi Hideyoshi, a man of humble origins who clawed his way up to the position of shogun. Hideyoshi's authenticity is attested to by the fact that he never tempered his will to power by dressing it in the ancient, refined, courtly elegance co-opted by so many of his predecessors. Instead, Hideyoshi remained true to his desire for power and influence, and the architecture that he commissioned shows it: Hideyoshi's name is linked to his gaudy, gold-flaked, collapsible tea room and some of the largest buildings ever erected in premodern Japan. To Hideyoshi "producing art and taking a shit were alike: both were endeavors born of the most vulgar intentions . . . There is no evidence of hesitation, no trace of even the slightest restraint" (*SAZ*, vol. 7, pp. 134–135). This is the authenticity that Ango longed for.

Though Ango does not explicitly mention them, there are other expressions of Hideyoshi's spiritual authenticity: in keeping with his unmediated assertion of power, Hideyoshi attempted not one but two bloody invasions of the Korean peninsula. The Japan of 1942 had completed that colonization of Korea and was attempting a Hideyoshi-like conquest of China as well, two facts that would not have escaped Ango's attention as he wrote this essay. In short, Ango's radically subversive worldview is undiscriminating in its targets: in addition to undermining the repressive ideology of nationalism within Japan, it also challenges the status quo of the world community, in which Japan was perceived as a second-class citizen. In this sense Ango's unmediated assertion of desires, functioning at the level of the nation, can be taken as a justification of Japan's desire for colonies (China,

Korea, Taiwan) and its unbridled aggression towards the Allied Forces.

The same dynamic is at work in the story "Shinjū" (1942; "Pearls"), in which Ango juxtaposes the selfless sacrifice of the U-boat pilots who died in the attack on Pearl Harbor with the dissolute life of his acquaintance, the sign painter nicknamed "Garandō." A media frenzy arose around the U-boat pilots when the details of their participation in the attack were released in March 1942. Ango takes the title of the story from a death poem composed by one of these "Nine War Gods": "Marching forth when the moment arrives / Over barriers and landmines / Striking, and as if a pearl / The jewel is shattered" (Kamiya, p. 122). The image of a shattered jewel *(gyokusai)* became in wartime propaganda a euphemism for the glorious war dead who chose an honorable death in battle over defeat and surrender. In both the poem and Ango's story, the image of the pearl carries this implication while also pointing to the destruction of Pearl Harbor.

Ango marvels at these "shattered jewels" who trained for the mission and carried it out, knowing all the while that they would not return alive. The manner in which they throw away thought, responsibilities, beliefs, and finally their lives, remaining true to this selflessness even when staring death in the face, makes them almost superhuman. What is more, Japan's glorious victories in the Greater East Asian War attest to the fact that they are indeed the ultimate warriors. What Ango admires most about them, however, is their arrival in a realm where they no longer need to see their fate in terms of military glory or some grand destiny: before boarding the U-boats, the men choose to wear their comfortable, stained work clothes rather than their uniforms, and they self-deprecatingly speak of their mission as an *ensoku*, a child's school "excursion."

In addition to being a paean to these heroes, "Shinjū" recounts Ango's life at the time of the Pearl Harbor attack. He is out of Tokyo, in Odawara, and scrambles for whatever information he can get, hungrily reading a news flyer and listening to the radio report. He is deeply moved: "The tears flowed. The time when words are no longer needed has arrived. If need be, I must give my life. We must not let the enemy, not even a single soldier, set foot on our land" (*SAZ*, vol. 2, p. 389). In stark contrast to Ango's excitement is the indifference of his friend Garandō, who tells jokes during the radio news and is intent only on securing some fresh fish. To this end he drags Ango from one village to the next, pausing only when there is moonshine to chug or an opportunity to add to his pottery collection.

Since its publication critics have struggled to reconcile the enormous gap between Ango's tribute to these "shattered jewels" and his endearing portrait of the indifferent Garandō. Most eventually conclude that by tempering the media's unmitigated glorification of U-boat pilots, Ango is subtly problematizing the romantic image of dying in the service of one's country. This reading, however, does not satisfactorily account for the genuine awe and admiration he expresses for the "Nine War Gods." In the end, these two seemingly incompatible types of hero are best read as sharing residence in Ango's *furusato*. The U-boat pilots have transcended the myth of nation—with its ideology of military glory—and have faced the harsh reality of death without rationalizing it in terms of these myths; Garandō has also transcended the myth of nation—with its ideology of both active and passive citizen support for any war effort—and has faced his world of privation without rationalizing it in such terms. In this sense, both sides have successfully cut through the static of ideologies to take life at face value, to live it without intellectual mediation. As different as they seem, there is something impenetrable and heroic about each, and Ango's emotional reaction to the war and his feelings of guilt over his self-centered pursuit of fish seem pathetic in comparison.

The third essay from this period is "Darakuron" (1946; "Discourse on Decadence," 1986), perhaps Ango's most famous work. The rhetoric of the essay is similar to that employed in "Nihon bunka shikan" (A personal view of Japanese culture), but the

icons which he smashes here are intimately linked to the landscape of the defeated, postwar Japan. Taking his cue from the debates raging in the newspapers, Ango applies his unique measuring rod to the war widows, the spared kamikaze pilots, the emperor system, Japan's warrior tradition, and wartime morals. He sets the tone in the opening lines:

> The world has changed in the last six months. "We, the humble shield of our Sovereign Lord, march forth, resigned to die at his side without looking back." These young kamikaze pilots died, scattering like cherry blossoms, but those who escaped with their lives are now black marketeers. "We do not hope for long lives together but we swear ourselves to you, his Majesty's humble shields." These women, who saw their men off so bravely, are six months later kneeling only mechanically before their husbands' mortuary tablets and it won't be long before they've got their eye on somebody new. Man hasn't changed; he's been like this from the very start. What has changed is just the surface of things.

> (*SAZ*, vol. 7, p. 197; cf. tr. p. 1)

Ango portrays the collapse of the ideological structures which held the country together during the war, and he insists that this fallen state is man's true condition.

Ango also works his iconoclasm on the emperor, the most sacred of topics during the war. Rather than a spiritual center arising out of a uniquely Japanese character and experience, Ango portrays the emperor system as the product and pawn of astute, opportunistic politicians who recognized and took advantage of the people's need for an ideology to which they could surrender themselves. That ideology could have been anything—Confucius, Gautama the Buddha, or even Lenin. Humanity's insatiable desire to tie its sense of self to something grander makes any of them possible.

In the disillusioned hand-to-mouth existence in the burned-out ruins of occupied Japan, Ango sees a golden opportunity to escape this pattern of warping the human condition to conform to some formalized system. This is the moment for a "complete fall" to that place beneath all ideological castles in the air. Human beings always have craved and always will crave systems that counter the pull of their most primal urges, but in the end salvation lies only in an embrace of those urges. The moment is now. "Man lives, man falls. There is no convenient shortcut to salvation that exists outside of this. . . . Like man, Japan, too, must fall. It must redeem itself by falling to the very depths and there finding itself. Redemption through politics is but a surface phenomenon, and of no value at all" (*SAZ*, vol. 7, pp. 203–204; cf. tr. p. 5).

Though the words have changed somewhat, the fall into decadence which Ango calls for here reverberates with the ideas he had advanced in "Bungaku no furusato" (The birthplace of literature) and "Nihon bunka shikan" (A personal view of Japanese culture). In all these places the objective is to dive beneath the contrived intellectual constructs by which we order our world, and live instead in the *furusato* of an unmediated, authentic engagement with our most primal needs and desires. This dive means leaving the ready-made worldview of the wartime ideologues, ultimately disastrous but also wonderfully comforting in the unity, sense of purpose, and identity it provided the Japanese people in a confusing world. The sincerity with which "Discourse on Decadence" acknowledges the joy and empowerment felt under the wartime regime while ultimately exposing and denouncing the tenuous, specious intellectual manipulations of its foundations has rightly made it a classic of the postwar era.

Idiots and Bandits: Two Postwar Stories

The three essays discussed above made the immediate postwar years good ones for Ango. The publishing industry was trying desperately to meet the demands of a public hungry for lit-erature which would shed light on the confusing experience of the war and the equally disorienting occupation period. This was Ango's forte, and under pressure from so many magazines he began churning out essays and stories at an incredible pace. While the quality of his work is uneven, there are a number of stories which brilliantly capture elements of human nature that few besides Ango were willing to acknowledge.

Coming on the heels of "Discourse on Decadence" was "Hakuchi" (1946; "The Idiot," 1962), long a favorite of Ango fans. Set in Tokyo during the extensive bombing raids at the end of the war, the story captures both the chaos and the vitality of life in times of crisis. The protagonist is a young man named Izawa, who feels stifled by a monotonous job in an unimaginative, repressive work environment. His residence and neighborhood, however, seem to be worlds away, an almost junglelike realm where anything goes. The area is covered with tenements populated by incestuous families, mercenaries, kept women, and prostitutes from all points on the price spectrum. Izawa's quarters themselves are almost a barnyard. "Various species lived in the house: human beings, a pig, a dog, a hen, a duck. But actually there was hardly any difference in their style of lodging or in the food they ate. . . . The room that Izawa rented was in a hut detached from the main house. . . . Even if it had been assigned to a consumptive pig, the hut could hardly have been considered extravagant" (*SAZ*, vol. 2, p. 447; tr. p. 384).

The frustrated, repressed Izawa's transformation begins when he returns to his room one night to find it occupied by the idiot wife of an insane neighbor. The woman, who is never named, has the appearance of good breeding but is unable to perform any of the duties expected of a wife. She is also hardly able to speak. Having been abused at home, she throws herself on the mercy of Izawa, whom she imagines has feelings for her. Unable to reason with her, he simply comforts her and puts her to bed. An affinity quickly blossoms and soon Izawa's mood of disdain turns completely around:

"What I've needed more than anything is a heart like this idiot's—a heart childlike and innocent. I had forgotten it somewhere and was now stained by the harried thoughts of man. I had done nothing but exhaust myself in chasing these shadowy illusions." Then, stroking the woman's hair to comfort her, Izawa continues, "The ultimate home for all men is their birthplace [*furusato*], and you, it would seem, have already taken up residence there . . ." (*SAZ*, vol. 2, p. 455; cf. tr. p. 396).

During the bombing of Tokyo in March 1945, which took the lives of more than 120,000 people, Izawa flees with the idiot woman. In the process he surrenders himself fully to the primal urges that have long reigned in his run-down neighborhood—urges that he has resisted for his life in polite society. The new Izawa will not take shelter in the elementary school as a policeman advises, but wanders, with the "pig" at his side, in search of a roost. He has left the realm of the "harried thoughts of man" and joined the woman in that "hometown." The success of "The Idiot" lies in its creation of an atmosphere wherein an animal-like existence is rendered appealing for its immediacy.

A second story from this period is "Sakura no mori no mankai no shita" (1947; "In the Forest, under Cherries in Full Bloom," 1997). Though it was overshadowed at the time of its publication by the immensely popular "Discourse on Decadence" and "The Idiot," critics have been poring over it since its rediscovery after Ango's death in 1955. Along with "Murasaki dainagon" (1939; Councillor Murasaki) and "Yonaga hime to mimio" (1952; Princess longnight and the ear man), it is one of a number of Ango stories that are evocative of *setsuwa*, the classical folktales of the oral tradition. Like many *setsuwa*, these stories by Ango shock and disorient the reader.

Set sometime long, long ago, "In the Forest, under Cherries in Full Bloom" is the story of a mountain bandit bewitched by a beautiful woman he takes captive. Unlike his seven other wives, this one is demanding, and she inspires in him a fear and uncertainty that he has previously only experienced in the forest, under cherries in full bloom. She makes him kill six of the seven wives, leaving only the ugliest cripple alive to serve her. In time she lures him into a life in the capital city, where she sends him out nightly to collect human heads. She spends all her time using these severed heads to reenact scenarios reminiscent of the affairs of Heian period courtiers. The description of her games is striking:

> Both the princess head and the councilor head had long since lost their hair. Their flesh was rotten and crawling with maggots, the bone showing through in places. The two heads would drink through the night and indulge in love play, biting each other, teeth chattering against bone, gobs of rotten flesh squashing and sticking, noses collapsing, eyeballs dropping out.
>
> The woman loved it when the faces would stick together and then fall apart. The sight would send her into peals of uncontrollable laughter.

(*SAZ*, vol. 3, p. 361; tr. p. 197)

The flat, matter-of-fact narration just adds to the eerie, disturbing atmosphere of the story. The story ends with the bandit bringing his beautiful wife back to the mountains, carrying her on his back. In his eagerness to get back to his alpine home, he decides to cut through the blooming cherry forest which had always frightened him. As he enters deeper into the forest, the woman on his back turns into a purple-skinned demon (or is he imagining it?). As he strangles her, she becomes human again (or does she?). Then, buried in the petals of the cherry blossoms, she begins to disappear. Reaching for her receding form, the bandit, too, vanishes.

Is the woman the embodiment of the cherry blossoms, and do these things represent some malignant spirit of nature? Does the story narrate the process of the bandit becoming human? Does Ango use the cherry blossoms, that most Japanese of flowers, as a metaphor

Selected Bibliography

PRIMARY WORKS

COLLECTIONS

Teihon Sakaguchi Ango zenshū (hereafter *SAZ*). Edited by Okuno Takeo. 13 vols. Tokyo: Tōjusha, 1968.

Sakaguchi Ango zenshū. Edited by Karatani Kōjin. 17 vols. Tokyo: Chikuma Shobō, 1998–2000.

AUTOBIOGRAPHICAL ESSAYS AND STORIES

"Onna uranaishi no mae nite." *Bungakukai* (January 1938). Reprinted in *SAZ* 1:434–448.

"Koto." *Gendai Bungaku* (January 1942). Reprinted in *SAZ* 2:356–371.

"Ishi no omoi." *Hikari* 2, no. 11 (November 1946). Reprinted in *SAZ* 3:93–106.

"Gūtara senki." *Bunka Tenbō* 2, no. 1 (January 1947). Reprinted in *SAZ* 3:107–117.

"Kaze to hikari to hatachi no watashi." *Bungei* 4, no. 1 (January 1947). Reprinted in *SAZ* 3:220–234.

"Nijūnanasai." *Shinchō* 44, no. 2 (March 1947). Reprinted in *SAZ* 3:316–333.

"Kurai seishun." *Chōryū* 2, no. 5 (June 1947). Reprinted in *SAZ* 3:369–381.

"Sanjussai." *Bungakukai* 2, no. 5 (May 1948) and vol. 2, no. 7 (July 1948). Reprinted in *SAZ* 4:142–158.

"Aoi jūtan." (Originally titled "Ikō.") *Chūō Kōron* 70, no. 4 (April 1955). Reprinted in *SAZ* 6:606–614.

"Yo ni deru made." *Shōsetsu Shinchō* 9, no. 5 (April 1955). Reprinted in *SAZ* 8:516–522.

EARLY EXPERIMENTAL FICTION

"Kogarashi no sakagura kara." *Kotoba*, no. 2 (January 1931). Reprinted in *SAZ* 1:9–19.

"Furusato ni yosuru sanka." *Aoi Uma*, no. 1 (May 1931). Reprinted in *SAZ* 1:20–26.

"Kaze hakase." *Aoi Uma*, no. 2 (June 1931). Reprinted in *SAZ* 1:27–32.

"Kurodani mura." *Aoi Uma*, no. 3 (July 1931). Reprinted in *SAZ* 1:33–55.

WAR-RELATED STORIES AND ESSAYS

"Nihon bunka shikan." *Gendai Bungaku* (March 1942). Reprinted in *SAZ* 7:122–141. Excerpts trans. by James Dorsey as "A Personal View of Japanese Culture." In *Columbia Anthology of Modern Japanese Literature.* Edited by J. Thomas Rimer and Van Gessel. New York: Columbia University Press, forthcoming 2002.

"Shinjū." *Bungei* (June 1942). Reprinted in *SAZ* 2:384–394.

"Dentō no musansha." In *Tsuji shōsetsushū.* Edited by Kume Masao. Tokyo: Hakkōsha Sugiyama Shoten, 1943. P. 105.

"Sensō to hitori no onna." *Shinsei*, special fiction supplement (October 1946). Reprinted in *SAZ* 3:51–63. Trans. by Lane Dunlop as "One Woman and the War." In *Autumn Wind and Other Stories.* Rutland, Vt., and Tokyo: Charles E. Tuttle Company, 1994. Pp. 140–160.

"Darakuron." *Shinchō* (April 1946). Reprinted in *SAZ* 7:197–203. Trans. by Seiji M. Lippit as "Discourse on Decadence." In *Review of Japanese Culture and Society* 1:1–5 (October 1986).

"Hakuchi." *Shinchō* (June 1946). Reprinted in *SAZ* 2:447–467. Trans. by George Saitō as "The Idiot." In *Modern Japanese Stories.* Edited by Ivan Morris. Rutland, Vt., and Tokyo: Charles E. Tuttle Company, 1961. Pp. 383–410.

"Zoku darakuron." *Bungaku Kikan*, no. 2 (December 1946). Reprinted in *SAZ* 7:239–245.

SETSUWA (FOLKTALE)-INSPIRED STORIES

"Murasaki dainagon." *Buntai* (February 1939). Reprinted in *SAZ* 1:456–468.

"Sakura no mori no mankai no shita." *Nikutai* 1, no. 1 (June 1947). Reprinted in *SAZ* 3:352–368. Trans. by Jay Rubin as "In the Forest, under Cherries in Full Bloom." In *The Oxford Book of Japanese Short Stories.* Edited by Theodore W. Goossen. Oxford and New York: Oxford University Press, 1997. Pp. 187–205.

"Yonaga hime to mimio." *Shinchō* 49, no. 6 (June 1952). Reprinted in *SAZ* 5:378–405.

LITERARY CRITICISM

"FARCE ni tsuite." *Aoi Uma*, no. 5 (July 1932). Reprinted in *SAZ* 7:13–22.

"Bungaku no furusato." *Gendai Bungaku* (August 1941). Reprinted in *SAZ* 7:111–115.

"Gesakusha bungakuron." *Kindai Bungaku* (January 1947). Reprinted in *SAZ* 7:246–260.

OTHER WORKS

Fubuki monogatari. Tokyo: Takemura Shobō, 1938. Reprinted in *SAZ* 2:9–261.

"Gaitō to aozora." *Chūō Kōron* (July 1946). Reprinted in *SAZ* 2:468–482.

"Ren'airon." *Fujin Kōron* (April 1947). Reprinted in *SAZ* 7:291–295.

"Furenzoku satsujin jiken." Serialized in *Nihon Shōsetsu* 1, no. 3 (August 1947) to vol. 2, no. 7 (August 1948). Reprinted in *SAZ* 10:9–165.

"Pan pan gāru." *Ōru Yomimono* (October 1947). Reprinted in *SAZ* 7:345–349.

"Ango kōdan." Serialized in *Bungei Shunjū* 28, no. 1 (January 1950) to vol. 21, no. 6 (December 1950). Reprinted in *SAZ* 9:9–162.

"Ango shin nihon chiri." Serialized in *Bungei Shunjū* 29, no. 4 (March 1951) to vol. 29, no. 16 (December 1951). Reprinted in *SAZ* 9:163–358.

SECONDARY WORKS

CRITICAL AND BIOGRAPHICAL STUDIES

Hyōdō Masanosuke. *Sakaguchi Ango ron.* Tokyo: Tōjusha, 1972.

Ikoma, Albert Ryue. "Sakaguchi Ango: His Life and Work." Ph.D. diss., University of Hawaii, 1979. (Includes a translation of "Darakuron" as "On 'Corruption,' " pp. 176–192.)

Isoda Kōichi. "Bunka shugi e no hangyaku." In *Sakaguchi Ango.* Vol. 22. Kanshō Nihon Gendai Bungaku series. Edited by Kamiya Tadakata. Tokyo: Kadokawa Shoten, 1981.

Kamiya Tadakata, ed. *Sakaguchi Ango.* Kanshō Nihon Gendai Bungaku series, vol. 22. Tokyo: Kadokawa Shoten, 1981.

Karatani Kōjin. *Sakaguchi Ango to Nakagami Kenji.* Tokyo: Ōta Shuppan, 1996.

Kubota Yoshitarō and Yajima Michihiro, eds. *Sakaguchi Ango kenkyū kōza.* 3 vols. Tokyo: Miyai Shoten, 1984–1987.

Nishikawa Nagao. "Two Interpretations of Japanese Culture." Trans. by Mikiko Murata and Gavan McCormack. In *Multicultural Japan: Palaeolithic to Postmodern.* Edited by Donald Denoon, Mark Hudson, Gavan McCormack, and Tessa Morris-Suzuki. New York: Cambridge University Press, 1996. Pp. 245–264. (This article compares Ango's conception of culture, as expressed in "Nihon bunka shikan/A personal view of Japanese culture," to that of Bruno Taut.)

Ogino Anna. *Ai rabu Ango.* Tokyo: Asahi Shinbunsha, 1992.

Okuno Takeo. *Sakaguchi Ango.* Tokyo: Bungei Shunjū, 1972. (This is the standard critical biography.)

Pulvers, Roger. "Refilling the Glass: Sakaguchi Ango's Legacy." *Japan Quarterly* 45, no. 4:56–64 (October–December 1998).

Sakaguchi Michiyo. *Kura kura nikki.* Bungei Shunjū, 1967.

Sekii Mitsuo. "Denkiteki nenpu." In *SAZ* 13:369–464. (Contains very detailed biographical and bibliographical information. However, beware of typographical errors in the subsection headings and in information on Ango's early school years, which has since been superceded by Kamiya [see above].)

———. *Sakaguchi Ango no sekai.* Tokyo: Tōjusha, 1976.

———, ed. *Sakaguchi Ango kenkyū.* 2 vols. Tokyo: Tōjusha, 1973.

Steen, Robert Adam. "To Live and To Fall: Sakaguchi Ango and the Question of Literature." Ph.D. diss., Cornell University, 1995. (Includes translations of "Kaze hakase" as "Doctor Wind," pp. 228–238, and "Bungaku no furusato" as "The Birthplace of Literature," pp. 239–249.)

Suzuki Sadami. " 'Nihon bunka shikan' ni tsuite." *Kokubungaku: Kaishaku to Kanshō* 58, no. 2:98–102 (February 1993).

Takahashi Haruo. " 'Nihon bunka shikan' to 'Darakuron' no aida." In *Sakaguchi Ango kenkyū.* Edited by Mori Satofumi and Takano Yoshitomo. Tokyo: Nansōsha, 1973. Pp. 297–312.

Ueno Takashi. "Kōtei no undō." *Kaie* 2, no. 7:184–191 (July 1979).

RESOURCES IN ENGLISH

Dower, John W. *Embracing Defeat: Japan in the Wake of World War II.* New York: W. W. Norton and Co., 1999. (Includes a brief discussion of Ango in the context of postwar popular culture. See particularly Chapter 4, "Cultures of Defeat," pp. 121–167.)

———. *War without Mercy: Race and Power in the Pacific War.* New York: Pantheon Books, 1986. (A sensitive analysis of Japan's wartime ideologies and propaganda.)

Keene, Donald. "Dazai Osamu and the Burai-ha." In *Dawn to the West: Japanese Literature of the Modern Era.* Vol. 1, *Fiction.* New York: Holt, Rinehart and Winston, 1984. (Includes a brief summary of some Ango works.)

LaFleur, William R. *The Karma of Words: Buddhism and the Literary Arts in Medieval Japan.* Berkeley: University of California Press, 1983. (Helpful introduction to the Buddhist concepts that inform Ango's works. See particularly Chapter 1, " 'Floating Phrases and Fictive Utterances': The Rise and Fall of Symbols," pp. 1–25.)

Rubin, Jay. "From Wholesomeness to Decadence: The Censorship of Literature under the Allied Occupation." *Journal of Japanese Studies* 1, no. 1:71–103 (spring 1985). (Includes a discussion of Ango's connection to the postwar obsession with the corporeal body.)

ATOMIC BOMB WRITERS

KAREN L. THORNBER

JAPANESE WRITERS have created thousands of essays, novels, plays, poems, and short stories about the atomic bombing of Hiroshima on 6 August 1945, and that of Nagasaki on 9 August 1945. Their texts often challenge scientific and historical accounts that focus primarily on the physical destruction of these cities as well as traditional Japanese literary modes of expression that privilege an aesthetic sensibility. They discuss in great detail the deep impact of the physical and psychological wounds from which hundreds of thousands suffered and died, and with which countless *hibakusha* (survivors of the atomic bomb) continue to live. Writers of the atomic bomb frequently examine both the memories and the guilt that plague *hibakusha* and often comment on the discrimination that confronts them daily in a society that would prefer to forget. While strongly believing it is their responsibility to translate into words what they saw and heard, they recognize the pitfalls inherent in any writing about an atrocity; the same words that make the trauma at least somewhat intelligible to themselves and to those who did not witness the destruction also tame it beyond recognition. Thus, writers of the atomic bomb rarely adhere to conventional literary forms and generally compose extremely fragmented texts. Moreover, many refuse to

allow Japan to see itself solely as a victim, and they criticize not only the United States for developing and deploying the atomic bomb, but also Japan's wartime government for demanding the complete loyalty of its people and for committing atrocities in other parts of Asia. In addition, writers of the atomic bomb often voice outrage at the continued proliferation of nuclear weapons. Therefore, Japanese literature of the atomic bomb not only discusses what happened to the people of Hiroshima and Nagasaki, the fate of both the victims and the survivors, but it also calls upon individuals all over the world to devote themselves to the creation of a more peaceful future. There follows a brief discussion of Ibuse Masuji's *Black Rain*.

Because literature about the atomic bomb places such demands on the reader, it has been confronted by fervent detractors at most every turn. During the Occupation, censors allowed the publication of scientific accounts of the destruction but prohibited that of literary works. Atomic bomb writers had difficulty publishing their texts in the mainstream press even after the Occupation, because the *bundan*, the Japanese literary establishment, believed that literature should refrain from discussing such matters. The first publicized debate on this topic took place between January and April 1953, in the pages of the *Chū-goku Shinbun*, Hiroshima's daily newspaper; some claimed the atomic bomb to be an improper theme for literature, and one partici-pant urged the *hibakusha* to concentrate on more "important" topics. In 1960, Hiroshima survivor and poet Kurihara Sadako (1913–) set off the next debate, protesting against the con-tinued marginalization of atomic bomb litera-ture; her opponents urged her and other atomic bomb writers to "transcend" the bomb. In the late 1970s and early 1980s, Nakagami Kenji, one of contemporary Japan's most prominent writers, mercilessly censured Hayashi Kyōko (1930–), a Nagasaki survivor, for continuing to depict the atomic landscape in her work.

Although most writers of the atomic bomb are *hibakusha*, a small but significant group did not experience the bomb themselves, and, perhaps because of their ability to distance themselves from the horrors, have met with more critical success than *hibakusha* writers. The most famous non-*hibakusha* writers are Ibuse Masuji (1898–1993), whose *Kuroi ame* (1966; *Black Rain*, 1978) was received very favorably both in Japan and in the United States, and 1994 Nobel Prize winner Ōe Kenz-aburō (1935–), whose *Hiroshima nōto* (1965; *Hiroshima Notes*, 1981) was surprisingly pop-ular. Generally, however, atomic bomb writers and their texts have been dismissed by critics and scholars in both Japan and the West. Because of ingrained attitudes of hostility toward this genre, its first major anthology, the fifteen-volume *Nihon no genbaku bungaku* (Japanese literature of the atomic bomb), did not appear until 1984, and then only after its editors had been rejected by several publishers. American scholars also have been very hesi-tant to work with Japanese literature of the atomic bomb. Few translations of this genre were undertaken before the 1980s, and it was not until Richard Minear's 1990 *Hiroshima: Three Witnesses* and 1994 *Black Eggs* that the biographies and the major works of Kurihara, Hara Tamiki (1905–1951), and Ōta Yōko (1903–1963), three of the greatest atomic bomb

writers, were made accessible to Western read-ers. The first comprehensive study of atomic bomb literature in English, John Treat's *Writ-ing Ground Zero: Japanese Literature and the Atomic Bomb*, did not appear until 1995, half a century after the bombing.

This essay gives a cross-section of the genre, focusing on six of its most prominent writers: Hara Tamiki, Hayashi Kyōko, Kurihara Sadako, Ōta Yōko, Tōge Sankichi (1917–1953), and Ibuse Masuji.

Hara Tamiki (1905–1951)

Hara Tamiki, the first published novelist of the atomic bomb, and a prolific writer since child-hood, is best known for his trilogy *Natsu no hana* (1949; *Summer Flowers*, 1990). Also a greatly admired poet, Hara has been called a founder of Japanese atomic bomb poetry. Because he had been preoccupied with death and catastrophe since childhood, many feel he was destined to be a voice for the *hibakusha*. Hara often has been criticized for his failure to speak out more strongly against both the United States and Japan, as many atomic bomb writers have done. However, despite its often relatively muted tone, his poetry and prose offer a moving picture of the atomic aftermath.

Background

Hara Tamiki was born on 15 November 1905 into a wealthy Hiroshima family, the eighth of twelve children. He read widely as a child and was particularly attracted to the writing of Rainer Maria Rilke, Walt Whitman, and Russ-ian authors including Fyodor Dostoevsky and Anton Chekhov. Having kept a journal since elementary school, by middle school Hara was determined to become a writer. He entered Keiō University in Tokyo in 1924 and gradu-ated in 1932; he wrote his thesis on William Wordsworth. While at Keiō, he became active in radical politics, but after his arrest in 1931 he abandoned politics for other pursuits. In

1933 he married Nagai Sadae, and he became extremely dependent upon her. Shutting himself off from the world, he wrote countless short stories and fairy tales. When Sadae became ill, Hara returned to poetry and began working outside the home, first as an English teacher and then for a film company. In January 1945, several months after Sadae's death, Hara returned to Hiroshima and moved in with his older brother Nobuhide.

The Atomic Bomb

Although Nobuhide's house was located just over a kilometer from ground zero, Hara miraculously escaped with only minor injuries. In 1946, he returned to Keiō, and his writing began to appear regularly in the prestigious literary journal *Mita Bungaku*. Hara strongly believed he had survived to report what had happened to the people of Hiroshima. Between 1945 and his death in 1953, he composed both poetry and prose on the bombing and its aftermath as well as essays discussing his newfound purpose and the fate of society.

Summer Flowers

In June 1947 Hara published "Natsu no hana" ("Summer Flowers"), which he had completed in December 1945; this story would become the first part of *Summer Flowers*. The second part, "Haikyo kara" ("From the Ruins") was published later in 1947, and the third part, "Hametsu no jokyoku" ("Prelude to Annihilation"), was published in 1949. "Summer Flowers" and "From the Ruins" are narrated primarily in the first person by a writer and *hibakusha* whom we know only as *watakushi* ("I"), and whose circumstances closely parallel Hara's own; "Prelude to Annihilation" is narrated in the third person and tells the story of Shōzō, the *watakushi* of the first two parts. *Summer Flowers* is a disturbing and powerful account of the year of the bombing, one that is filled with poignant descriptions of the ruins and that challenges traditional notions of time and genre.

"Summer Flowers" takes the reader from 4 August to September 1945, "From the Ruins" from 8 August to December 1945, and "Prelude to Annihilation" from the early months of the year to 4 August 1945. Retracing in "From the Ruins" much of the ground that he covered in "Summer Flowers" and, more important, bringing *Summer Flowers* to a close on the same day it opens (two days before the bombing of Hiroshima), Hara denies the disaster a beginning and an end. Most striking in this regard is the transition between "From the Ruins" and "Prelude to Annihilation." The narrator concludes "From the Ruins" with descriptions of the survivors' continued search for friends and relatives; he opens "Prelude to Destruction" with the depiction of a nameless traveler on a snowy bridge, whose relished memories of the distant past suddenly are interrupted by a vision of the world coming to a terrible end. The reader first assumes that this man is haunted by memories of Hiroshima, the landscape that was described on the preceding pages. Yet, as we soon discover, he actually is foreseeing the dropping of the atomic bomb, as will many characters and the narrator of "Prelude to Annihilation." The narrator's final comment in *Summer Flowers* is that more than forty hours remain before the dropping of the bomb. Returning the reader, at its conclusion, to the hours before the bombing, this text underlines the fate of many survivors, virtually strangled within their memories.

Like many writers of the atomic bomb, Hara underlined the responsibility of those who had witnessed the destruction to record what had happened. Within the text of "Summer Flowers," the narrator remarks that, immediately after regaining his senses, he knew he had to set everything down in writing, and in "From the Ruins," he states that, although everything had been destroyed, he would write what he could. Hara's concern with finding the proper form in which to record the disaster was evident as early as his "Genbaku hisaiji no nōto" (1945; Notes from the atomic destruction), written only days after the bombing. The notes begin in diary form, with the dates and times

51

of the events to be described set off from the body of the text. This technique quickly is abandoned, however, as the horror around the narrator renders such overt structuring almost obscene. Written in *katakana* (an alphabet used primarily for the transcription of loanwords) and Chinese characters, the notes are terse, concise, and fragmented. They are a much more straightforward account of the immediate atomic aftermath than that found in "Summer Flowers" and "From the Ruins." In fact, parts of these latter texts can be read as attempts to make the notes more authentic. For instance, the first sentence of the notes reads: "Suddenly   air raid   in one instant the entire   city crumbles." In *Summer Flowers*, however, the narrator goes to great lengths to underline the utter confusion that characterized the days following the dropping of the bomb; he describes the attempts of various individuals to determine just what happened to their city, suggesting that the "reality" of Hiroshima was far more complex than what was presented in "Genbaku hisaiji no nōto."

The text of *Summer Flowers* raises questions of its own objectivity. In his essay "Shi to ai to kodoku" (1949; Death, love, and loneliness), Hara wrote that in *Summer Flowers* he had "recorded" his experiences. Yet in this text, certain moments are described so many times and from so many different perspectives that, thanks particularly to the active imaginations of the characters in "Prelude to Annihilation," the reader becomes even less certain as to what really "happened." This, of course, is precisely the point. Denying the existence of a single description, Hara implies that one story, one account cannot hope to capture even the smallest fraction of the disaster. Thus, in addition to providing the reader with graphic portrayals of the destruction, Hara attempts to prevent the structure of the literary text from further taming the horrors. Moreover, alluding to the totality of the disaster by denying his narrative a unified structure, Hara calls attention to the severe limitations of the only medium at his disposal.

Atomic Bomb Landscapes

In his poetry, Hara speaks in more general terms about the condition of his people. Although he was prolific long before the bombing of Hiroshima, his reputation as a poet comes primarily from the nine poems of "Genbaku shōkei" (1950; Atomic bomb landscapes). The first eight poems in this collection are written in a combination of *katakana* and Chinese characters; the presence of *katakana* underlines the "foreign" nature of the events discussed. At the same time, however, the poet continually reminds us that those whose fate he describes remain human beings, regardless of the degree to which their bodies have been deformed. For instance, the first poem, "Kore ga ningen na no desu" (1950; "This Is a Human Being," 1995), translated by John Treat in *Writing Ground Zero*, reads:

> *This is a* human being.
> *Please note what* changes *have been*
> *affected by the* atomic bomb.
> The body *is grotesquely* bloated,
> Male *and* female characteristics *are*
> *indistinguishable.*
> *Oh that* black, seared, smashed *and*
> Festering face, *from whose swollen* lips
> oozes a voice
> *"Help me"*
> In faint quiet words.
> *This is a* human being.
> *The* face *of a* human being.
>
> (p. 474; tr. p. 168)

The opening of the poem echoes its conclusion; the figure on the road is a human being. Also significant is the contrast made between the body and lips swollen beyond recognition, and the thin and quiet words that emanate from these lips. It might be impossible to tell man from woman, but the words of this individual, a powerful reminder of his/her humanity, remain intelligible. "Mizu o kudasai" (1950; "*Give Me* Water," 1995), the eighth poem of the collection, expands the definition of "humanity." In the first thirteen lines, the poet transcribes the pleas and moans of the victims. The following eight lines concern the landscape, the poet writing that the heavens have been split apart and the city has disappeared. However, in the final seven lines, he gives us a physical description of the faces that, though allowed to speak in the opening lines, now have been reduced to groans. Yet although the eyes are burned, the lips festering, and the faces distorted, the groans from these faces are those "of a human being / Of a human being" (p. 478; tr. p. 171), as translated by Treat in *Writing Ground Zero*.

Despite Hara's faith in the humanity of the people of Hiroshima, life as a *hibakusha* became more and more difficult for him. He committed suicide on 13 March 1951, lying down on the tracks between the Kichijōji and Nishi-Ogikubo train stations in Tokyo, as he had suggested he might do in his autobiographical short story "Shingan no kuni" (1951; "The Land of My Heart's Desire," 1985). Many believe the catalyst of his suicide was President Harry Truman's comment that the United States was actively considering the use of the atomic bomb in Korea.

Hayashi Kyōko (1930–)

In an often quoted passage from Hayashi Kyōko's novel *Naki ga gotoki* (1981; As if it weren't there), the narrator expresses her desire to be the "tribal chronicler" of Nagasaki. Her countless novels and short stories have made Hayashi herself a modern chronicler of her city. Hayashi differs from many writers of Nagasaki— including Nagai Takashi, author of the highly acclaimed *Nagasaki no kane* (1949; *The Bells of Nagasaki*, 1984)—who as Christians believe that the bombing of their city was the will of God and that the people of their city were His chosen martyrs. Finding little solace in religion, Hayashi has continued to depict the suffering of the people of Nagasaki, focusing on the permanent physical and psychological scars left by the bombing, questions of survival guilt, the difficulties of second-generation *hibakusha*,

and the particular burden felt by female *hibakusha*. Hayashi also has written about her childhood in Shanghai, at times juxtaposing her experiences before and after 9 August 1945. For instance, in her short story "Futari no bohyō" (1975; "Two Grave Markers," 1989), the protagonist contrasts the dead bodies tied to the stern of the police boats that patrolled Shanghai with the bodies covering the burned fields of Nagasaki. She had perceived the former to be the emblems of a peaceful return to nature, despite the protestations of her Chinese nurse, but the latter nothing but horrific.

Background

Hayashi Kyōko was born in Nagasaki on 28 August 1930; in 1931, her family moved to Shanghai, where her father worked for Mitsui Industries. In 1945, she returned to Nagasaki with her mother and her three sisters and enrolled in Nagasaki Girls' High School. On the morning of 9 August 1945, she was working at the Mitsubishi Munitions Factory, less than a kilometer and a half from ground zero. Seriously ill for several months, Hayashi would suffer the effects of radiation sickness for many years. She eventually enrolled in the nursing program of the Welfare Faculty for Women of Nagasaki Medical School, but she did not graduate. Hayashi began writing in 1962, yet her work was not recognized until the 1970s.

"Ritual of Death" and "Two Grave Markers"

Two of Hayashi's most famous stories are her "Matsuri no ba" (1975; "Ritual of Death," 1984) and "Two Grave Markers." Hayashi was awarded both *Gunzō* magazine's New Writer's Prize and the Akutagawa Prize for the former. Although lengthy descriptions of the immediate atomic aftermath make up the largest part of "Ritual of Death," this text also explores the fate of long-term survivors. Narrated some thirty years after the bombing by a *hibakusha* whom we know only as *watakushi* ("I"), this story opens with the letter that several American scientists had written to a professor at the University of Tokyo, warning of the potential annihilation of Japan. *Watakushi* speaks of the pain that this letter causes her, and, almost as though reciting from a history book, she discusses the moments immediately before and after the explosion. She then describes in some detail what her mother and sister saw, twenty-five kilometers from ground zero, and she follows this with a narration of her own experiences. Having been virtually unharmed, thirty years later she still is hesitant to contact the friends who were with her in Nagasaki that day: although it is difficult to hear that so many continue to suffer, the fact that her pain is not as great as that of her friends is even more troubling. Brief comments on societal attitudes toward the *hibakusha*, no matter how minor their injuries, appear among the discussions of the immediate atomic aftermath. *Watakushi* describes the endless red tape that prevents many *hibakusha* from receiving proper medical treatment; the red tape exists to prevent non-*hibakusha* from receiving benefits, but as *watakushi* remarks, the label "*hibakusha*" is no badge of honor. She also explains how difficult it is to acquire the "death payments" to which each victim is entitled. At the same time, however, *watakushi* is able to overlook a Japanese magazine's portrayal of *hibakusha* as monsters, writing that she will accept anything that conveys the pain of those who were in Nagasaki on 9 August 1945, regardless of whether or not it is "factual." All she asks is that someone feel something about the bombing. In her concluding paragraphs, she describes the October 1945 memorial ceremony for the dead. She brings her story to a close with a citation from what she ironically terms a "beautiful line" from the final scene of an American documentary film on the atomic bomb: "the destruction ended. . . ." The film, the commemoration ceremony, and the narrative of the destruction all come to an end, yet, as *watakushi* had remarked only several lines before, people con-

tinue to die. The deaths, it is implied, easily will overrun the temporary boundaries established by the structures of ceremony and art. Six years later, in her essay "Shanhai to hachi-gatsu kokonoka" (1981; Shanghai and 9 August), Hayashi would write that 9 August marked the beginning, not the end, of the destruction.

"Two Grave Markers" addresses issues of *hibakusha* guilt as they concern not a long-term survivor but a young girl, Wakako, in the days and weeks immediately following the dropping of the atomic bomb. The third-person narrator opens her text inside the dream of Wakako's mother: Wakako is sitting in the trees with a dead baby covered by ants and maggots. In the following paragraphs the reader learns that Wakako's tomb is one of the many that cover a Nagasaki hillside. The story then flashes back to Wakako's return home, without her friend Yōko, four days after the bombing of Nagasaki. Yōko died in the ruins, and neither Wakako nor her neighbors are certain just how to interpret her failure to rescue her friend. "Two Grave Markers" is colored with numerous returns to the hours after the bombing, mirroring the obsession of its characters with discovering what happened between Wakako and Yōko.

We are told that Wakako met Yōko in the ruins, Yōko was too weak to run any farther, and Wakako was not certain what she should do. Wakako remembered that in the instants after the bombing, Yōko had run away from her; should she now do the same? Yōko would not stay to help her, she reasoned, so why should she stay? Failing to resolve the matter, the narrator leaves the two hand in hand and returns to Wakako's first days at home; the sight of a girl catching dragonflies makes her think of Yōko. After Yōko's body is recovered, Wakako falls seriously ill with radiation sickness. The narrator then jumps back in time, returning to Yōko and Wakako on the hillside, and finally describes what happened between them. Wakako sat with Yōko, until the maggots began swarming into her wounds. She believed that, having sucked Yōko's blood, the maggots were becoming reincarnations of her friend and soon would turn on her. Wakako ran away, covering her ears so she would not hear Yōko's cries. The narrator returns to Wakako's deathbed, remarks that she had breathed her last, and then describes her final days; having believed a group of Yōkos to be circling around her bed, she had been haunted by hallucinations not unlike those she experienced on the hillside immediately before leaving her friend. Wakako's feelings of guilt are not entirely self-imposed, of course. Rumors that she abandoned Yōko have been running rampantly through town; in fact, Wakako's mother determines to bury her daughter beside Yōko, rather than in the family's ancestral tomb, in an attempt to prove her innocence. The final paragraphs impose a happy reconciliation, the narrator writing that Wakako's mother, bringing orange branches to Wakako's and Yōko's graves, believes she hears their laughter. Yet this conclusion rings hollow when placed in the context of the work as a whole. Throughout "Two Grave Markers," the narrator juxtaposes the stories created by the villagers in an attempt to hide from the awful truth of Nagasaki, with those created by Wakako, who was forced to live through the incomprehensible. The former give a false sense of calm to those who were not there; the latter only add to the personal tragedy of the one who was.

"The Empty Can"

In "Akikan" (1977; "The Empty Can," 1985), one of the twelve short stories in *Giyaman bīdoro* (1978; Cut glass, blown glass), the first person narrator, a *hibakusha* whom we know only as *watakushi* ("I"), discusses her return with her friends to their old school, several decades after graduation; she includes numerous flashbacks to the months and years following the bombing. Questions of survival guilt loom large in this story, as does an exploration of the long-term effects of being a *hibakusha*. Significantly enough, the opening pages of the tale do not reveal that these women are *hibakusha*; they are simply nostalgic alumnae recalling the idiosyncrasies of their teachers. Painful memories soon come to the surface, however. Looking closely at the windows of the school, the narrator is struck by the polished glass and remarks that from the atomic bombing until her graduation two years later, the windows had not had a single pane of glass. The narrator's musings on the repair of each window are interrupted by her friend Nishida, who suggests that they go inside the school. Entering the auditorium, now stripped of its benches and tables, the narrator writes that she and her friends were flooded with memories, not of the concerts and graduation ceremonies they had attended in this room, but of the memorial service held in October 1945 for the three hundred students who had been killed. Nishida remarks that she feels extremely awkward and guilty whenever talk turns to the bombing: having transferred to the school on the day of the memorial service, she had escaped the bombing. Her friend Oki comments that it naturally is better not to have been exposed, to which Nishida repeats that she wishes she had been with the others on 9 August 1945. There is no assuaging the guilt of those who escaped.

Attention then turns to the difficulties of the survivors. A teacher for Nagasaki prefecture, Oki runs the risk of being transferred to an outlying island where the doctors know little of radiation sickness. The women lament the fact that only one of them is happily married. Yet there are more serious problems that stem from something deeper. Their friend Kinuko could not attend the reunion because she was having an operation to remove glass from her back. Thirty years after the bombing, she felt a stabbing pain while demonstrating a somersault for her second grade students; the doctor determined embedded glass to be the culprit. Oki also has just had glass removed from her back. Most painful, however, are these women's memories of Kinuko. Though physically absent in "The Empty Can," Kinuko nevertheless dominates the thoughts of the story's characters. This text concludes with a discussion of the can of the title; Kinuko had placed the bones of her dead parents in this container and had brought it to school with her every day until a teacher had told her that it would be better to leave it at home. The narrator speaks of this incident with the can as an awl that was driven into her childhood. "The Empty Can" contains no explicit condemnations, yet its relatively muted tone can be deceptive. In the opening paragraphs of her story, the narrator seduces the reader with images of nostalgic alumnae worried over the future of the phoenix palm that sits in the driveway of their school. Then she gradually draws us deeper and deeper into the narrative, leaving us with women scarred for life.

In some works Hayashi has also discussed at great length the particular burden of female *hibakusha*: even if a woman still is able to have children, she is plagued with worry about what diseases her children will suffer as a consequence of having been born to a *hibakusha* mother. For instance, in "Seinen-tachi" (1977; Young men), one of the stories in *Giyaman bīdoro*, Hayashi describes the fears both she and her son have concerning his future. Although he currently enjoys good health, they both worry that he eventually will succumb to an atomic bomb related illness. In "Zanshō" (1985; Afterglow), she speaks candidly about the great fear that arose within her every time her son had so much as a nosebleed. In *Summer Flowers*, Hara had denied the bombing a beginning and an end. Nearly forty years later, Hayashi did the same, refusing to be deterred by a literary world that still did not understand why she had no choice but to write of the horrors of her city.

Kurihara Sadako (1913–)

The first published atomic bomb poet, Kurihara Sadako, is also the most prolific, having completed more than ten books of poetry and five volumes of essays. In both her writing and her political activities, she has been one of the most outspoken critics not only of American and Japanese policies during World War II, but also of Japanese treatment of Koreans (particularly Korean *hibakusha*), of the continued proliferation of nuclear weapons, and of the apathy of individuals all over the world. She also has written extensively on literature of atrocity, including literature of the atomic bomb and literature of the Holocaust, and she has made little secret of her opinions of the postwar Japanese literary establishment, which would like to see the horrors of the atomic bomb erased from literature.

Background

Kurihara Sadako (maiden name Doi Sadako) was born in Hiroshima on 4 March 1913. She began writing at the age of thirteen and published her first poem when she was only seventeen, the year she completed formal schooling. At the age of eighteen, she met Kurihara Tadaichi, who had been involved in anarchist politics. The Kuriharas were quite poor, and their first child, born in 1932, died of malnutrition. They managed a store in Hiroshima between 1937 and 1944. Many of the poems Kurihara wrote during the war years were published in *Kuroi tamago* (1946; *Black Eggs*, 1994). Composing both tanka and free verse, she spoke of everything from the love she felt for all people, to her difficult relationship with her husband, to the absurdity and inhumanity of Japan's wartime policies. In July 1945, Kurihara evacuated to Gion, a town north of Hiroshima where Tadaichi was working in a factory. In a footnote to one of her poems, she mentions that on 5 August 1945 she was mobilized to clear firebreaks at what the following day would become ground zero.

The Atomic Bomb

Kurihara was in her kitchen, four kilometers from ground zero, on the morning of 6 August 1945 and began writing about the atomic bombing almost immediately. She created

"Umashimen ka na" ("Let Us Be Midwives," 1994), which was included in *Black Eggs* and has remained both her most famous poem and one of the most famous poems of the atomic bomb. Here, the speaker takes us into the dark basement of a building in ruins, crowded with victims of the atomic bomb. From the moans, the smells, and the blood comes a voice crying, "The baby's coming." The people forget their own pain, and a midwife, who moments before had been moaning in agony, offers her services. Richard Minear's translation of the poem concludes:

And so new life was born in the dark of
that pit of hell.
And so the midwife died before dawn, still
bathed in blood.
Let us be midwives!
Let us be midwives!
Even if we lay down our lives to do so.

(p. 116; tr. p. 67)

In the foreword to the 1983 edition of *Black Eggs*, Kurihara expresses her embarrassment at the "naïve" vision of the poems in this collection. Clearly, the answer offered in "Let Us Be Midwives" is hardly sufficient, and, many would say, reprehensible: lives cannot be exchanged so easily. At the same time, however, this poem does underline Kurihara's faith in human compassion, a theme that would resurface repeatedly in her work. Although her poems and essays often mercilessly expose the dark underside of human society, the fact that she continues to protest reveals a powerful faith in our ability to replace hatred and violence with friendship and authentic concern.

Other poems in *Black Eggs* also paint the atomic landscape of Hiroshima. The five tanka in the second section of "Yakeato no machi" (1945; "City Ravaged by Flames," 1994) offer more subtle portrayals of life beginning in the ruins than what we find in "Let Us Be Midwives." Each tanka begins with "Yakeato no . . ." ("In the burned-out ruins . . .") and continues with the description of a flower that has bloomed; even the gardens around the shacks are turning green, and this in the months before winter. The first and third sections of "City Ravaged by Flames" present a more disturbing picture of the aftermath, however, as the poet concludes with the image of a pine grove in which only trunks remain, charred black. Even more graphic are the twenty-three tanka of "Akumu" (1946; "Nightmare," 1994), which outline the poet's journey through the city on 9 August to help her neighbors bring home the body of their daughter. After loading the corpse onto a cart, the poet looks out at the encroaching dusk and stares at the fires that continue to burn in the hills around the city. In the final tanka, she brings the bodies and the dusk together, remarking that "cremation" flames have stained the black night red and concludes with a note on the sorrow of the landscape. Yet although no refuge is to be found here, the poems on the atomic aftermath included in *Kuroi tamago* are not nearly as strong as those Kurihara would write decades after the bombing.

The 1960s and Beyond

Kurihara's husband was a member of Hiroshima's prefectural assembly from 1955 to 1967, and she assisted him in his activities, becoming more and more interested in a variety of political movements. Kurihara continued to write in the 1960s, composing poetry that protested against the resumption of nuclear testing by the United States and the Soviet Union. However, it would be almost a quarter century after *Black Eggs* before she would publish her second book of poetry, *Watakushi wa Hiroshima o shōgen suru* (1967; I give testimony for Hiroshima). This work was followed by numerous other collections, including the uncensored version of *Black Eggs*. All written in free verse, the poems of these collections cover a myriad of topics. Never one to mince words, Kurihara spares little in her criticism of Japan, the United States, and all whom she believes to be working against the best interests of humanity.

For instance, her third collection, *Hiroshima to iu toki* (1976; When we say "Hiroshima"), contains a poem of the same title that has become one of her most famous. In "Hiroshima to iu toki" (1972; "When We Say 'Hiroshima,'" 1994) Kurihara speaks of the consequences of the Japanese government's failure to acknowledge its war crimes. The poet begins by telling us that people do not respond to the word "Hiroshima" with a gentle sigh; rather, this single word evokes memories of Pearl Harbor, the rape of Nanking, and the women and children in Manila who were thrown to the ground, doused in gasoline, and burned alive. The opening of the second stanza echoes that of the first; the poet states that the word "Hiroshima" is not met with gentle sighs. Rather, Asians, both dead and alive, spit out the anger of the many who were victimized. Kurihara does provide an answer, however. In the second half of this stanza, she writes that if the Japanese want to receive sympathy, they must lay down their arms and send foreign soldiers home. Until then, she declares, the Japanese will be pariahs, burning with latent radioactivity. In the third and concluding stanza, she states that, to receive sympathy, the Japanese first must wash the blood off of their hands. "When We Say 'Hiroshima'" spares little in its attack against Japan's imperialist policies and the postwar government's continued refusal to take responsibility for the atrocities committed in Asia.

Yet Kurihara does not deny Japan the role of victim. For instance, she writes a scathing critique both of the American decision to use the bomb and of contemporary American attitudes in her "Amerika yo mizukara horobiru na— Genbaku tōka shō ni kōgi shite" (1976; "America: Don't Perish by Your Own Hand!— Protesting the Atomic Bomb Air Show," 1994), included in her fourth collection of poetry, *Mirai wa koko kara hajimaru* (1979; The future begins now). The poet begins by stating that a generation has passed since the bombing, and the words on the cenotaph in Hiroshima Peace Park now are seen as remains from the distant past, as people all over the world have forgotten the horrors of the atomic aftermath. She criticizes the participants of an air show in Texas who reenacted Hiroshima and describes in graphic detail the fate of those who were in Hiroshima on 6 August 1945, both those who died almost instantly and those whose children and grandchildren have been born deformed. Kurihara's severest condemnation comes in the second half of the final stanza, however: the poet writes that when the "million Hiroshimas" explode in the United States, she will send a message of condolence. God may forgive the hell they created, the poet concludes, but human beings will not. The final lines reveal the emotions behind the scarred and burning faces described in the body of the poem.

Kurihara's intense anger and powerful statements are in large part responsible for her continued marginalization, greater than that of other writers of the atomic bomb. Yet she has refused to remain silent. In his 1999 translation of Kurihara's poems, Richard Minear, a friend of Kurihara for many years, reported that Kurihara was still continuing her work as an activist, despite a traffic accident in 1994 that left her unable to walk.

Ōta Yōko (1903–1963)

Ōta Yōko, one of the most prolific Hiroshima writers and an established literary figure well before the dropping of the atomic bomb, is known primarily for her *Shikabane no machi* (1948; *City of Corpses*, 1990). Although much of her writing is concerned with portraying the physical destruction of Hiroshima and the lingering effects of the bombing on the *hibakusha*, in her novels she also questions at length the duty of the writer confronted with tragedy of such magnitude, and she makes no secret of her anger—at the United States for dropping the bomb and at the apathy of the Japanese before, in the immediate aftermath of, and in the years following the bombing of Hiroshima and Nagasaki.

Background

Ōta Yōko (maiden name Fukuda Hatsuko) was born in Kushima, a village outside Hiroshima, on 20 February 1903. Her family life was very unstable: when Ōta was seven, her mother left her father, and Ōta was adopted by a family with whom she lived for two years before eventually moving in with her mother and her new husband. She completed formal schooling in March 1921, and in November 1921 she began teaching in an elementary school, where she remained for less than a year. Between 1924 and 1940 she had a number of different jobs. In 1929 she published her first story in the popular feminist magazine *Nyonin gei-jutsu* (Female writers), and in 1939 her first novel, *Ryūri no kishi* (Drifting shores), a description of her tumultuous relationship with a journalist. She was an ardent supporter of the Second World War and wrote many prize-winning patriotic texts, including *Ama* (1940; Women of the Sea), which encouraged selfless devotion to the nation, and *Sakura no kuni* (1940; Land of cherry blossoms), which extolled Japanese aggression in Asia.

The Atomic Bomb

After having lived in Tokyo since 1930, Ōta returned to Hiroshima in January 1945, where she stayed with her step-sister Kazue. Although Kazue's house was less than two kilometers from ground zero, Ōta, her mother, and her sister all survived with only minor injuries. Ōta's earliest depiction of the bombing appeared in the *Asahi Shinbun* newspaper on 30 September 1945; this would be the last time she proclaimed the beauty and the glory of the war and its victims. Increasingly haunted by the tragedy that had befallen her city, Ōta became more and more committed to speaking for the *hibakusha*. Written in 1945 and published in 1948, *City of Corpses* was the first of several novels discussing the effects of the bombing and its implications.

City of Corpses

Containing thirty chapters divided into seven sections, *City of Corpses* is narrated in the first person by a *hibakusha* whom we know only as *watakushi* ("I"). Written by *watakushi* between early September and late November 1945, the text begins with a discussion of the narrator's current situation, flashes back to the day of the bombing, and then with numerous twists and turns gradually moves toward the present where it concludes. In the preface to the second edition of this text (1950), Ōta, speaking of the rather desperate conditions in which it was written, stresses its documentary nature, and emphasizes that what she strove to create was a direct translation into words of the destruction, before she, too, met what she believed to be a certain death. However, in addition to documenting the ruins of Hiroshima, *City of Corpses* also is a depiction of the evolution of an atomic bomb writer. In chapter 17, the narrator's sister asks her whether she can write about what she has seen. She replies that one day she will have to—this is the responsibility of a writer who has witnessed the tragedy. On this and other occasions, *watakushi* reveals herself to be an individual who believes she has no choice but to tell the story, but she is not quite certain just what it means to "tell the story."

Well aware of the fact that she has witnessed just a small fraction of the ruins of Hiroshima, the narrator includes many statistics, newspaper clippings, and medical theories and reports. Yet she often reminds the reader of the inherent limitations of these sources, writing on one occasion, as translated in Minear's *Hiroshima: Three Witnesses*: "It cannot be denied that the issues are of extraordinary interest. . . . However, no one seemed to be interested in understanding the psychology of the victims. . . . things of the body may have been more important; but what we most wanted was consolation for our souls" (p. 37; tr. p. 177). The narrator also transcribes several stories she has heard. Although none is told without interruption, the style of narration and the method of presentation are different in each. *Watakushi* progresses from a writer frightened of speaking about the horrors directly to one who allows herself to penetrate the thoughts of an individual who found himself at the very center of Hiroshima. Thus, in *City of Corpses*, the "reporter" becomes a "novelist" who learns how to make "fiction" out of "fact."

Another important element of *City of Corpses* is the narrator's anger, not so much at the destruction of Hiroshima as at Japan's imperialist government and at the utter passivity of the Japanese people. The opening of the fifth chapter, as translated by Minear in *Hiroshima*, reads:

> In the last days of the war, Japan's opponent employed atomic bombs. Most people seem to react to that fact with resentment. In doing so, they rely more on emotion than on reason. They refuse to face the facts. . . . We lament the ravages of war. But we must lament as well what led up to the ravages of war.

> (p. 23; tr. p. 165)

In addition, *Watakushi* speaks of the virtual dehumanization of the Japanese, even before the dropping of the atomic bomb. Years of wartime silence and enforced apathy had taken their toll. The narrator states that in the weeks following the bombing, people scarcely stopped to look as they walked among the dead bodies littering the road.

The narrator also is concerned with the future of Japan. In chapter 27, she writes that the Japanese reporters' delusion that after the war they had gained freedom of expression troubled her more than did the *New York Times'* article on Hiroshima. In the novel's final chapter, she states that the Japanese must move toward democracy, but that she is not sure whether such a "foreign" mode of thought can even begin to take root on Japanese soil. She concludes the text with images of starving Japanese, their groans the song of the countryside; she writes that the two millstones of war and natural disaster grind against each other, producing a song of death that creeps along the ground. Thus, for

both *watakushi* and Ōta, describing the ruins—the responsibility of those who have seen—necessitates an exploration both of the circumstances that led to their creation and of the impact they will have on the future.

Later Works

Ōta followed *City of Corpses* with *Ningen ranru* (1951; Human rags), *Han-ningen* (1954; Half-human), and *Yūnagi no machi to hito to* (1955; People and the city of evening calm). *Ningen ranru* covers more ground than *City of Corpses*, opening on 6 August 1945 and depicting the lives of six survivors in the first year and a half of the atomic aftermath. The characters of this text attempt to lead "normal" lives, having their share of romantic liaisons, domestic troubles, and the like. The "normal" provides no refuge from memory, however, and the plight of the *hibakusha* becomes more disturbing with the passing of time. *Ningen ranru* was criticized harshly for its arguably disjointed structure. However, as many have noted, it is precisely such disunity that allowed for a more penetrating portrayal of the disaster.

Han-ningen is the story of Oda Atsuko, a fictional atomic bomb writer whose experiences are very similar to Ōta's own. Oda is attempting to receive treatment for psychological problems brought about by the trauma of the bombing. In the hospital, she meets women suffering from similar problems, but there is no refuge to be found in these interactions. Moreover, the doctors and nurses with whom she comes into contact have no idea how to treat her and only make matters worse. In *Yūnagi no machi to hito to*, Oda returns to Hiroshima, seven years after the dropping of the bomb, only to be confronted with the continued suffering of the survivors.

In the eighteen years that she lived as a *hibakusha*, Ōta also wrote numerous essays and short stories. In many of these she outlined the dilemmas she faced as a survivor and a writer of the atomic bomb. She often deplored the indifference of the world to the plight of the *hibakusha* and the failure of the world to understand the broader implications of the bombing of Hiroshima. At the beginning of "Hotaru" (1953; "Fireflies," 1985), for instance, the narrator speaks of an artist from Tokyo who wanted to engrave one of Hara Tamiki's poems on a stone wall in Hiroshima. She remarks that she understood his intentions, but that he and the others who had not seen could not comprehend the inappropriateness of such a gesture. Often becoming extremely frustrated with those who could not understand and would not listen, Ōta worked tirelessly to make the world appreciate the plight of the *hibakusha*, just as she struggled to reclaim a place within it.

Ōta died of a heart attack 10 December 1963, having outlived Hara and Tōge by more than a decade.

Tōge Sankichi (1917–1953)

Although the creator of thousands of poems, numerous essays, and many short stories, Tōge Sankichi is known primarily for his *Genbaku shishū* (1952; *Poems of the Atomic Bomb*, 1990), which generally is regarded as one of the two principal collections of Japan's atomic bomb poetry. Its opening poem, "Jo" ("Prelude"), is engraved on a stone monument in Hiroshima's Peace Park. A poet from childhood, Tōge devoted the last few years of his life to creating verse that described the destruction of his city, protested the decision to use the atomic bomb, and would help restore to the *hibakusha* their sense of dignity as human beings.

Background

Tōge Sankichi (birth name Tōge Mitsuyoshi) was born in Hiroshima on 19 February 1917, the youngest of five children. His family was politically active; his father participated in a number of socialist movements in the 1920s, and his mother, who died when Tōge was ten, was an ardent feminist. Tōge's oldest sister was a liberal Christian who in 1942 would be responsible for his conversion, and his other

sister participated in various social movements. His oldest brother was repeatedly arrested for his involvement in communist activities; both his brothers were active in the labor movements of the 1920s and 1930s. Because Tōge succumbed easily to illness, his father tried to prevent him from following in the footsteps of his siblings and encouraged him to go into business. In 1935, after graduating from the Hiroshima Prefectural School of Commerce, Tōge began working at the Hiroshima Gas Company. He was, however, no stranger to literature. His parents were both avid readers, so Tōge's attraction to literature blossomed early. Having been strongly impressed by the works of Leo Tolstoy and Kagawa Toyohiko (a Christian social reformer) and by the poetry of Heinrich Heine, Shimazaki Tōson, and Satō Haruo, Tōge began writing at the age of fourteen. Incorrrectly diagnosed with tuberculosis in 1938, he wrote thousands of haiku and tanka, believing that he had only a few years to live.

Already a poet with a heightened political consciousness, in the postwar years Tōge became far more socially active, and his protest poems much more powerful. However, it was not until *Poems of the Atomic Bomb* that the object of his protest became the dropping of the atomic bomb itself.

The Atomic Bomb

Tōge writes in the afterword of *Poems of the Atomic Bomb* that Hiroshima was bombed just as he was preparing to leave his home, located approximately three kilometers from ground zero. His injuries were not severe, and, although he was cut by flying glass, he had enough strength to search the ruins of his hometown for his family and friends. He later experienced a mild case of radiation sickness that required a brief hospitalization.

Tōge composed "Ehon" ("Picture Book," 1995), perhaps the world's first poem of the atomic bomb, on 8 August 1945. This poem describes the death of a mother in a camp for the wounded: she looks at the pictures in the children's book her son holds up for her, gazes vacantly into space, and dies silently in the stench of excrement. "Picture Book" is based on Tōge's experiences at the makeshift aid-station where he had found a friend of his family. When juxtaposed with the poems in *Poems of the Atomic Bomb*, "Picture Book" appears very restrained in its discussion of the horrors. The poet tells us that the mother's face is burned and that she is on the verge of death, but he does not speak explicitly of her pain or disfigurement. The woman still is able to look at the pictures her son is attempting to show her. Moreover, while the man lying next to her had been moaning, unlike in *Poems of the Atomic Bomb*, we never actually are allowed to "hear" this moaning, for the poet speaks only of its cessation. The mother of "Picture Book" dies with her son by her side, enveloped in the stench of excrement, whereas the *hibakusha* of *Poems of the Atomic Bomb* die surrounded by strangers, buried within excrement.

"Kurisumasu no kaerimichi" (1946; "The Road Home from Christmas," 1995) is the first poem in which Tōge refers explicitly to the atomic bomb. The poet speaks of the silent evening walk he and his companion make through their city on the first Christmas after the dropping of the bomb. Over the course of the poem the ruins find a voice; in the first stanza they are simply "burned," in the second stanza they are said to smolder, releasing a terrible smell, and in the third stanza, as translated by Treat in *Writing Ground Zero*, they "whisper discordant sounds about God and war" (p. 88; tr. p. 175). However, the narrator does not attempt to describe the destruction in any detail, focusing instead on the fact that he and his companion continue to walk, despite the great burden the ruins have placed upon them. It would be a number of years before Tōge would be able to face the atomic aftermath in all of its horror.

Although in the immediate postwar years Tōge wrote very little about the devastation wrought by the atomic bomb, it was at this time that he established his mark as a political and protest poet. In February 1947, he joined the Hiroshima Shijin Kyōkai (Hiroshima Poets' Society), an organization committed to using poetry to bring about social change. He became a member of the Shin Nihon Bungaku Kai (New Japan Literature Association), a group of revolutionary writers, in February 1949; later that year, he joined the Japan Communist Party (JCP) and became active in its Bunka Sākuru (Culture Circle) movement. Labor strikes were rife in postwar Japan, and the June 1949 Hiroshima Steel Incident marked a turning point in Tōge's thought and career. After returning home from the confrontation between 10,000 demonstrators and 2,000 police officers that followed the firing of 730 of the 2,000 employees of Japan Steel's Hiroshima factory, Tōge composed "Ikari no uta" ("Song of Rage," 1990). In the first two stanzas the poet describes conditions fairly straightforwardly, stating that the machines have stopped and the workers have been driven away. In the third stanza, he pleads with the workers not to run away, and, in the remaining four stanzas, he speaks of their strength and tenacity. The following day, Tōge read this poem aloud to the strikers. In his diary, he speaks of their extremely enthusiastic response and of his recognition of the great potential of poetry.

In November 1949 Tōge became leader of the Warera no Shi no Kai (The *Our Poetry* Association), established after the disbanding of the Culture Circle. He began to speak more and more of literature as a weapon to be used against those he called the "enemies of humanity."

Poems of the Atomic Bomb

Tōge wrote the poems included in *Poems of the Atomic Bomb* between 1949 and 1951. On 26 May 1949, he composed "Chimata nite" ("In the Streets," 1990), the first poem of this collection to be completed. In this poem no mention is made of the atomic bomb; the poet speaks only of emotions boiling beneath the surface of his people. "Yobikake" ("Appeal," 1990), written in May 1950 on the occasion of the Stockholm Appeal, is a precursor of the poem of the same title included in *Poems of the Atomic Bomb*, and it examines the place of the survivor. Several months later, Tōge created "1950 nen no hachigatsu muika" ("August 6, 1950," 1990). The Occupation authorities had forbidden the Japan Communist Party to proceed with the memorial for the victims of the atomic bomb and with the protest of the Korean conflict that they had planned for 6 August 1950. The Japan Communist Party ignored this prohibition, and their demonstration became violent when the police arrived. Appearing first in the September 1951 issue of *Our Poetry* and later in *Poems of the Atomic Bomb*, "August 6, 1950" discusses the events of that day. Having experienced severe hemorrhaging during the fall of 1950, in June 1951, Tōge entered the hospital, where, over the course of the next four months, he would write and/or revise all the poems eventually included in *Poems of the Atomic Bomb*, with the exception of "Sono hi wa itsu ka?" ("When Will That Day Come?," 1990), which he composed shortly after leaving the hospital. The first edition of *Poems of the Atomic Bomb* was published in 1952.

Poems of the Atomic Bomb is a collection of twenty-four poems (written in free verse ranging in length from eight lines to eight pages), one prose passage, and an afterword, also written in prose. "Prelude," the first poem, is perhaps the best known:

Give me back my father! Give me back
  my mother.
Give back the old people
Give back the children.

Give me back myself. And all those people
Joined to me, give them back.
Give me back mankind.

Give me peace.
A peace that will not shatter!
As long as man, man is in this world.

(p. 161; tr. Treat 1995, p. 172)

The poet cries out, calling for the creation of an everlasting peace. He also demands the return of all who are lost, both those who died and those who are living in death. When, in the second stanza, he calls for his own return, he reminds us that although he and the other survivors might remain physically alive, parts of them have been lost forever. The poet longs for the *hibakusha*'s return to wholeness and to humanity. This is his cry for dignity.

With the exception of "Prelude," the first third of *Poems of the Atomic Bomb* is devoted to a discussion of the immediate aftermath of the atomic bombing. Following the seventh poem, and in many ways summarizing the events of the previous eight days, is the prose piece "Sōko no kiroku" (1951, "Warehouse Chronicle," 1990), which, written in diary form, gives an account of the scene inside the Army Clothing Depot, where many of the injured came to die. Although Tōge includes many graphic descriptions of the horror that befell his city, he will not let the reader forget the humanity of those who gradually begin to emerge from the rubble. Many of his portraits are those of dignified human beings, of individuals who, in spite of everything, refuse to die without a fight. Particularly striking are his descriptions of the white eyes of the wounded. We are first exposed to these eyes in "Hachigatsu muika" (1951; "August 6," 1990), the second poem of *Poems of the Atomic Bomb*, and they gain in strength the deeper we travel into the collection. In "Me" (1951; "Eyes," 1990), the seventh poem, translated by Minear below, the poet describes his experiences in a dark storehouse, surrounded by the bodies of people on the verge of death:

Eyes fastened to my back, fixed on my
  shoulder, my arm.
Why do they look at me like this?
After me, after me, from all sides, thin
white beams coming at me:
eyes, *eyes*, EYES—
from way up ahead, from that dark corner,
  from right here at my feet.
Ah! Ah! Ah! . . .
eyes materialize, *materialize*, do not fade.
Ah, pasted to me, fixed forever on me—
back, then chest; armpit, then shoulder—

I who step into this dark
In search of the one who only this morning
    was my younger sister—
  eyes!

                  (p. 168; tr. p. 317–318)

In the poems following "Warehouse Chronicle," Tōge shifts his concern to a description of conditions in Hiroshima following the immediate atomic aftermath. The poet alternates between describing the *hibakusha* who have been emotionally paralyzed by their experiences, many of whom he knows personally, and discussing what can be done to counteract the apathy that, he suggests, has allowed for the continuation of nuclear testing. He speaks of fighting war with love, urging the children of Hiroshima to disarm with hugs the adults who would start wars, and adults to join hands and work toward stopping the proliferation of nuclear weapons. In many poems, he also describes the rage lying beneath the surface of his people. For instance, "Sono hi wa itsu ka" ("When Will that Day Come?," 1990) concludes with:

the day will come
when the menace of an ugly, grasping will
    seems about to force the people once
    again to war;
when a force that mothers and children and
    sisters can hold back no longer
turns into the wrath of a peace-loving people
and erupts.

On that day
your body will be covered over without
    shame;
the humiliation will be cleansed by the
    tears of the race;
the [curse of] the atomic bomb that [has
    polluted the earth]
will begin to dissipate.
When, oh when
will that day come?

             (p. 202–203; tr. p. 364–365)

In the following and final poem, Tōge speaks of looking through a book of pictures of Hiroshima. He first asks who would be able to resist the need to straighten the mangled legs, to cover the naked loins, and to unravel one by one clenched fingers covered in blood, implying that we all attempt to tame the horrors, to a greater or lesser degree. Yet even though our inclination is to paint a kinder picture of the disaster, the poet alludes to the existence of even deeper emotions. He asks who among us would be able to arrest a deep, awakening anger at the dropping of the atomic bomb and promises to do his best to make certain the events of August 1945 will never be repeated.

Not satisfied with *Poems of the Atomic Bomb*, Tōge dreamed of writing an epic poem entitled *Hiroshima*. Yet weakened both by radiation sickness and the respiratory problems that had plagued him for most of his life, Tōge was betrayed by his health, and he died on the operating table on 10 March 1953. He was soon elevated to hero status.

Ibuse Masuji's *Black Rain*

Distancing itself further from the horrors of the atomic aftermath than most examples of the genre, Ibuse's *Black Rain* has enjoyed unparalleled critical and commercial success. Indeed, it is regarded by many as Japan's foremost work of atomic bomb literature. Yet *hibakusha* have spoken out harshly against this novel, arguing that its aestheticization of Hiroshima trivializes the suffering of the victims and the survivors of the atomic bomb. *Black Rain* describes the protagonist's attempts to retranscribe both his own experiences and those of numerous other *hibakusha*. As such, this text is less a depiction of the atomic bombing of Hiroshima than an exploration of what it means for the survivor to write about atrocity, both in its immediate aftermath and after several years have passed.

Background

Ibuse Masuji was born on 15 February 1898 in a small village in Hiroshima prefecture and died on 10 July 1993. His work having appeared in print since 1923, he was a prominent writer long before the 1966 publication of *Black Rain*, the novel for which he is best remembered. Ibuse first discussed the atomic aftermath in his 1951 short story "Kakitsubata" ("The Crazy Iris," 1984), in which he examined the effect of the bombing on the residents of Fukuyama, a town outside Hiroshima.

Ibuse relied heavily on the oral and written testimony of survivors while working on *Black Rain*. He was especially indebted to Shigematsu Shizuma, a farmer in Kobatake, a village outside Hiroshima, whom he met after the bombing, and after whom he modeled Shizuma Shigematsu, the protagonist of *Black Rain* (in Japanese, the surname and given name were not only reversed but written with different characters). Shigematsu told Ibuse about his niece Yasuko, who had died of radiation sickness; he later provided Ibuse with several hundred pages of testimony, which included both his own story and those of countless other *hibakusha*. Ibuse also made numerous trips to Hiroshima to interview survivors. Arguing that he had gathered as much information as possible on the experiences of the *hibakusha*, he repeatedly stressed the documentary nature of *Black Rain*.

Critics' reactions to the novel were decidedly mixed. Unlike virtually all other works of atomic bomb literature, it was an instant commercial and critical success. Praised by some of Japan's leading critics even before it had been completed, *Black Rain* soon became the world's most widely read and most often translated piece of atomic bomb literature. The Japanese literary establishment applauded Ibuse both for speaking of the horrors in "ordinary" language and for not coloring his text with ideology. American critics were particularly receptive to *Black Rain*'s aestheticization of the atomic aftermath and congratulated Ibuse for transforming Hiroshima into a "work of art."

Yet many *hibakusha* criticized Ibuse harshly for failing to give a more realistic portrayal of the atomic aftermath. In addition, some believed that Ibuse, because he had not personally experienced the bombing of Hiroshima or Nagasaki, had no right to speak of the destruction of these cities. Distressed by the critiques of the *hibakusha*, Ibuse declared *Black Rain* a failure.

The Novel

Deeply disturbed that many in his town seem to have forgotten the horrors of the atomic aftermath, Shigematsu believes it his duty to retranscribe both his own experiences and those of as many other *hibakusha* as possible. Although the task is fraught with difficulty, rewriting and greatly expanding his "Diary of the Bombing"—which makes up more than half the text of the novel—helps him to fulfill some of the tremendous responsibility he feels both toward those who did not survive and to future generations. This enables him to begin to create a new life for himself out of the ruins of the past.

Black Rain opens with Shigematsu worried about the future of his niece Yasuko; the rumor that she was exposed to radiation has made it impossible for him to find her a husband. He believes that if the go-between had a copy of her diary, which supposedly places her far from ground zero, Yasuko's prospects would improve. While recopying her diary, he decides that he must also rewrite his own and attach it to hers as an appendix.

Yet even when Yasuko becomes ill and negotiations with the go-between break off completely, Shigematsu does not abandon his project. He continues to rewrite his diary, now adding to it the stories of numerous other *hibakusha*; he resolves to donate the work, upon its completion, to the reference room of the local primary school, where it will be available to future generations.

Shigematsu's revision and expansion of his "Diary of the Atomic Bomb" soon becomes the focal point of *Black Rain*. Never satisfied with the shape of his journal, he constantly edits and rewrites, so much so, in fact, that when he states that he is inserting a certain passage "today," it is unclear to which day he is actually referring. Shigematsu speaks often of the difficulties inherent in writing about atrocity and makes no secret of his struggle to create a text that will do justice to the plight of his people. He is intent on maintaining objectivity, but he also acknowledges the importance of subjective experience.

Concerned with his inability to transform into writing any more than a small fraction of what he observed, which is itself only a small fraction of the tragedy of Hiroshima, Shigematsu narrates countless stories, both those told to him personally and those that have come to him second, and even third-hand. He makes no attempt to create from this collection of stories a composite image of the atrocity. Shigematsu refuses to transform Hiroshima into a seamless text that can be rapidly perused and easily absorbed.

At the conclusion of *Black Rain*, the narrator states that Shigematsu has finished his transcription. He then adds that all Shigematsu needs to do is reread what he has written and find a cover for his manuscript. However, throughout the novel rereading has led to rewriting; thus, we can assume that Shigematsu will continue with his revisions and additions. Yet in writing about Hiroshima, he begins to fulfill some of the responsibility he believes he has to his people, which makes him more certain of his place within society and gives him more hope for the future. It is suggested that while narration of the bombing might never be completed, since there is no real escape from the past, one need not remain its prisoner forever.

Selected Bibliography

BIBLIOGRAPHIES OF ATOMIC BOMB LITERATURE

Kuroko Kazuo. "Genbaku bungaku shi nenpyō." In *Nihon no genbaku bungaku*. Vol. 14. Tokyo: Horupu Shuppan, 1984. Pp. 543–568.

Lammers, Wayne P., and Osamu Masuoka. *Japanese A-Bomb Literature: An Annotated Bibliography.* Wilmington, Ohio: Translation Collective, Wilmington College Peace Resource Center, 1977.

GENERAL STUDIES OF ATOMIC BOMB LITERATURE

Kuroko Kazuo. *Genbaku to kotoba: Hara Tamiki kara Hayashi Kyōko made.* Tokyo: San'ichi Shobō, 1983.

———. *Genbaku bungaku ron: Kaku-jidai to sōzōryoku.* Tokyo: Sairyūsha, 1993.

Masuoka Toshikazu. *Hiroshima no shijin-tachi.* Tokyo: Shin Nihon Shuppansha, 1980.

———. *Genbaku shijin monogatari.* Osaka: Nihon Kikanshi Shuppan Sentā, 1987.

Nagaoka Hiroshi. *Genbaku bungaku shi.* Nagoya: Fūbaisha, 1973.

———. *Genbaku bunken o yomu.* Tokyo: San'ichi Shobō, 1982.

Rubin, Jay. "From Wholesomeness to Decadence: The Censorship of Literature under the Allied Occupation." *Journal of Japanese Studies* 11, no. 1:71–103 (winter 1985).

Tachibana, Reiko. *Narrative as Counter-memory: A Half-Century of Postwar Writing in Germany and Japan.* Albany, N.Y.: State University Press of New York, 1998.

Treat, John Whittier. *Writing Ground Zero: Japanese Literature and the Atomic Bomb.* Chicago, Ill.: University of Chicago Press, 1995.

ANTHOLOGIES OF ATOMIC BOMB LITERATURE IN JAPANESE

Hiroshima no shi henshū iinkai, eds. *Hiroshima no shi.* Hiroshima: Chūō Kōminkan, 1955. Trans. as *The Songs of Hiroshima.* Hiroshima: YMCA Service Center, 1955.

Hotta Yoshie, Kinoshita Junji, and Ōhara Miyao, eds. *Nihon genbaku shishū.* Tokyo: Taihei Shuppansha, 1972.

Ienaga Saburō, Odagiri Hideo, and Kuroko Kazuo, eds. *Nihon no genbaku kiroku.* 20 vols. Tokyo: Nihon Tosho Sentā, 1992.

Kaku-sensō no kiken o uttaeru bungakusha, ed. *Nihon no genbaku bungaku.* 15 vols. Tokyo: Horupu Shuppan, 1984.

Kashū Hiroshima henshū iinkai, ed. *Kashū Hiroshima.* Tokyo: Daini Shobō, 1954.

ANTHOLOGIES OF ATOMIC BOMB LITERATURE IN TRANSLATION

Goodman, David G., ed. and trans. *After Apocalypse: Four Japanese Plays of Hiroshima and Nagasaki.* New York: Columbia University Press, 1986. (Translations of Betsuyaku Minoru's *Zō* [Elephant], Hotta Kiyomi's *Shima* [The Island], Satō Makoto's *Nezumi Kozō* [The Rat], and Tanaka Chikao's *Maria no kubi* [The Head of Mary].)

Minear, Richard, ed. and trans. *Hiroshima: Three Witnesses.* Princeton, N.J.: Princeton University Press,

1990. (Contains Hara's *Summer Flowers*, Ōta's *City of Corpses*, and Tōge's *Poems of the Atomic Bomb*, and detailed biographical summaries of these writers.)

Ōe Kenzaburō, ed. *The Crazy Iris and Other Stories of the Atomic Aftermath.* New York: Grove Press, 1985. (Contains nine short stories, including Hara's "The Land of My Heart's Desire," Hayashi's "The Empty Can," and Ōta's "Fireflies.")

Selden, Kyoko, and Mark Selden, eds. *The Atomic Bomb: Voices from Hiroshima and Nagasaki.* Armonk, N.Y.: M. E. Sharpe, 1989. (Includes Hayashi's "Two Grave Markers," as well as translations of novellas, poetry, citizens' memoirs, and stories by children.)

Sklar, Marty, ed. *Nuke Rebuke: Writers and Artists Against Nuclear Energy and Weapons.* Iowa City: The Spirit That Moves Us Press, 1984. (Includes Hayashi's "Ritual of Death.")

SELECTED WORKS OF HARA TAMIKI

COLLECTED WORKS

Hara Tamiki zenshū. 2 vols. Tokyo: Haga Shoten, 1965.

Yamamoto Kenkichi and others, eds. *Hara Tamiki zenshū.* 3 vols. Tokyo: Seidōsha, 1978.

Kaku-sensō no kiken o uttaeru bungakusha, ed. *Nihon no genbaku bungaku.* Vol. 1, *Hara Tamiki.* Tokyo: Horupu Shuppan, 1984.

ESSAYS

"Genbaku hisaiji no nōto" (1945). In *Hara Tamiki zenshū.* Vol 1. Tokyo: Haga Shoten, 1965. Pp. 529–530.

"Shi to ai to kodoku" (1949). In *Hara Tamiki zenshū.* Vol. 2. Tokyo: Haga Shoten, 1965. Pp. 301–313.

NOVELS

Natsu no hana. In *Hara Tamiki zenshū.* Vol 2. Tokyo: Haga Shoten, 1965. Pp. 50–113. Trans. by Richard Minear as "Summer Flowers." In *Hiroshima: Three Witnesses.* Princeton, N.J.: Princeton University Press, 1990. Pp. 45–113.

POETRY

"Genbaku shōkei." In *Hara Tamiki zenshū.* Vol. 1. Tokyo: Haga Shoten, 1965. Pp. 474–479.

"Kore ga ningen na no desu." In *Hara Tamiki zenshū.* Vol. 1. Tokyo: Haga Shoten, 1965. P. 474. Trans. by John Treat as "This Is a Human Being." In *Writing Ground Zero.* Chicago, Ill.: University of Chicago Press, 1995. P. 168.

"Mizu o kudasai." In *Hara Tamiki zenshū.* Vol. 1. Tokyo: Haga Shoten, 1965. P. 478. Trans. by John Treat as *Give Me Water.* In *Writing Ground Zero.* Chicago, Ill.: University of Chicago Press, 1995. Pp. 170–171.

SHORT STORIES

"Gyōretsu" (1935). In *Hara Tamiki zenshū.* Vol. 1. Tokyo: Haga Shoten, 1965. Pp. 238–250.

"Honoo" (1935). In *Hara Tamiki zenshū.* Vol. 1. Tokyo: Haga Shoten, 1965. Pp. 106–114.

"Utsukushiki shi no kishi ni" (1950). In *Hara Tamiki zenshū.* Vol. 2. Tokyo: Haga Shoten, 1965. Pp. 287–300.

"Shingan no kuni" (1951). In *Hara Tamiki zenshū.* Vol. 2. Tokyo: Haga Shoten, 1965. Pp. 397–405. Trans. by John Bester as "The Land of Heart's Desire." In *The Crazy Iris and Other Stories of the Atomic Aftermath.* Edited by Ōe Kenzaburō. New York: Grove Press, Inc., 1985. Pp. 55–62.

CRITICAL AND BIOGRAPHICAL STUDIES OF HARA TAMIKI

Kawanishi Masaaki. *Hitotsu no unmei—Hara Tamiki ron.* Tokyo: Kōdansha, 1980.

Kokai Eiji. *Hara Tamiki—Shijin no shi.* Tokyo: Kokubunsha, 1978.

Minear, Richard. "Translator's Introduction." In *Hiroshima: Three Witnesses.* Princeton, N.J.: Princeton University Press, 1990. Pp. 21–40.

Nakahodo Masanori. *Hara Tamiki nōto.* Tokyo: Keisō Shobō, 1983.

SELECTED WORKS OF HAYASHI KYŌKO

ESSAYS

"Mizu" (1975). In *Shizen o kou.* Tokyo: Chūō Kōronsha, 1981. Pp. 33–43.

"Jisho" (1979). In *Shizen o kou.* Tokyo: Chūō Kōronsha, 1981. Pp. 158–161.

NOVELS

Giyaman bīdoro. Tokyo: Kōdansha, 1978.
Naki ga gotoki. Tokyo: Kōdansha, 1981.

SHORT STORIES

"Futari no bohyō" (1975). In *Nihon no genbaku bungaku.* Vol. 3. Edited by Kaku-sensō no kiken o uttaeru bungakusha. Tokyo: Horupu Shuppan, 1984. Pp. 69–93. Trans. by Kyoko Selden as "Two Grave Markers." In *The Atomic Bomb: Voices from Hiroshima and Nagasaki.* Edited by Kyoko Selden and Mark Selden. Armonk, N.Y.: M. E. Sharpe, 1989. Pp. 24–54.

"Matsuri no ba" (1975). In *Nihon no genbaku bungaku.* Vol. 3. Edited by Kaku-sensō no kiken o uttaeru bungakusha. Tokyo: Horupu Shuppan, 1984. Pp. 26–68. Trans. by Kyoko Selden as "Ritual of Death." In *Nuke Rebuke: Writers and Artists against Nuclear Energy and Weapons.* Edited by Marty Sklar. Iowa City: The Spirit that Moves Us Press, 1984. Pp. 21–57.

"Akikan" (1977). In *Giyaman bīdoro*. Tokyo: Kōdan-sha, 1978. Pp. 7–26. Trans. by Margaret Mitsutani as "The Empty Can." In *The Crazy Iris and Other Stories of the Atomic Aftermath*. Edited by Ōe Kenzaburō. New York: Grove Press, 1985. Pp. 127–143.

"Kōsa" (1977). In *Giyaman bīdoro*. Tokyo: Kōdansha, 1978. Pp. 87–105. Trans. by Kyoko Selden as "Yellow Sand." In *Japanese Women Writers: Twentieth Century Short Fiction*. Edited and trans. by Noriko Mizuta Lippit and Kyoko Selden. Armonk: M. E. Sharpe, 1991. Pp. 207–216.

"Seinen-tachi"(1977). In *Giyaman bīdoro*. Tokyo: Kōdansha, 1978. Pp. 67–86.

"Giyaman bīdoro" (1978). In *Giyaman bīdoro*. Tokyo: Kōdansha, 1978. Pp. 47–65.

"Zanshō" (1985). In *Michi*. Tokyo: Bungei Shunjū, 1985. Pp. 233–261.

CRITICAL AND BIBLIOGRAPHICAL STUDIES OF HAYASHI KYŌKO

"About the Authors." In *Japanese Women Writers: Twentieth Century Short Fiction*. Edited by Noriko Mizuta Lippit and Kyoko Iriye Selden. Armonk, N.Y.: M. E. Sharpe, 1991. Pp. 271–272.

"Contributors." In *The Atomic Bomb: Voices from Hiroshima and Nagasaki*. Edited by Kyoko Selden and Mark Selden. Armonk, N.Y.: M. E. Sharpe, 1989. Pp. 248–249.

Kouchi Nobuko. "Hayashi Kyōko ron." *Kokubungaku kaishaku to kanshō* 50, no. 9:47–52 (August 1985).

Treat, John Whittier. "Hayashi Kyōko and the Gender of Ground Zero." In *The Woman's Hand: Gender and Theory in Japanese Women's Writing*. Edited by Paul Schalow and Janet Walker. Stanford: Stanford University Press, 1996. Pp. 262–292.

SELECTED WORKS OF KURIHARA SADAKO

COLLECTED WORKS

Kurihara Sadako shishū. Nihon gendaishi bunko 17. Tokyo: Doyō Bijutsusha, 1984.

BOOKS OF POETRY

Kuroi tamago. Hiroshima: Chūgoku Bunka Hakkōjō, 1946.

Watakushi wa Hiroshima o shōgen suru. Hiroshima: Shishū Kankō no Kai, 1967.

Hiroshima: Mirai fūkei. Hiroshima: Shishū Kankō no Kai, 1974.

Hiroshima to iu toki. Tokyo: San'ichi Shobō, 1976.

Mirai wa koko kara hajimaru. Hiroshima: Shishū Kankō no Kai, 1979.

Kakujidai no dōwa. Hiroshima: Shishū Kankō no Kai, 1982.

Kuroi tamago: Kanzenban. Kyoto: Jinbun Shoin, 1983.

Hiroshima. Hiroshima: Shishū Kankō no Kai, 1985.

Aoi hikari ga hirameku sono mae ni. Hiroshima: Shishū Kankō no Kai, 1986.

Kaku naki asu e no inori o komete. Hiroshima: Shishū Kankō no Kai, 1990.

INDIVIDUAL POEMS

"Umashimen ka na"(1945). In *Nihon no genbaku bungaku*. Vol. 13. Edited by Kaku-sensō no kiken o uttaeru bungakusha. Tokyo: Horupu Shuppan, 1984. P. 116. Trans. by Richard Minear as "Let Us Be Midwives." In *Black Eggs: Poems by Kurihara Sadako*. Ann Arbor: Center for Japanese Studies, University of Michigan, 1994. P. 67.

"Yakeato no machi" (1945). In *Nihon no genbaku kiroku*. Vol. 17. Tokyo: Nihon Tosho Sentā, 1992. Pp. 9–10. Trans. by Richard Minear as "City Ravaged by Flames." In *Black Eggs: Poems by Kurihara Sadako*. Ann Arbor: Center for Japanese Studies, University of Michigan, 1994. Pp. 92–95.

"Akumu" (1946). In *Nihon no genbaku kiroku*. Vol. 17. Tokyo: Nihon Tosho Sentā, 1992. Pp. 7–8. Trans. by Richard Minear as "Nightmare." In *Black Eggs: Poems by Kurihara Sadako*. Ann Arbor: Center for Japanese Studies, University of Michigan, 1994. Pp. 86–90.

"Hiroshima to iu toki" (1972). In *Nihon no genbaku bungaku*. Vol. 13. Edited by Kaku-sensō no kiken o uttaeru bungakusha. Tokyo: Horupu Shuppan, 1984. Pp. 129–130. Trans. by Richard Minear as "When We Say 'Hiroshima.'" In *Black Eggs: Poems by Kurihara Sadako*. Ann Arbor: Center for Japanese Studies, University of Michigan, 1994. Pp. 226–227.

"Amerika yo mizukara horobiru na—Genbaku tōka shō ni kōgi shite" (1976). In *Nihon no genbaku bungaku*. Vol. 13. Edited by Kaku-sensō no kiken o uttaeru bungakusha. Tokyo: Horupu Shuppan, 1984. Pp. 180–182. Trans. by Richard Minear as "America: Don't Perish by Your Own Hand!—Protesting the Atomic Bomb Air Show." In *Black Eggs: Poems by Kurihara Sadako*. Ann Arbor: Center for Japanese Studies, University of Michigan, 1994. Pp. 277–279.

VOLUMES OF ESSAYS

Dokyumento Hiroshima nijūyonen: Gendai no kyūsai. Tokyo: Shinpō Shinsho, 1970.

Hiroshima no genfūkei o idaite. Tokyo: Mirai Sha, 1975.

Kaku-tennō-hibakusha. Tokyo: San'ichi Shobō, 1978.

Kaku-jidai ni ikiru: Hiroshima—shi no naka no sei. Tokyo: San'ichi Shobō, 1982.

Towareru Hiroshima. Tokyo: San'ichi Shobō, 1992.

TRANSLATIONS

Minear, Richard, trans. *Black Eggs: Poems by Kurihara Sadako*. Ann Arbor: Center for Japanese Studies, University of Michigan, 1994. (Contains poems from a number of Kurihara's collections, as well as a detailed introduction to Kurihara and her work.)

———. *When We Say "Hiroshima": Poems of Kurihara Sadako*. Ann Arbor: Center for Japanese Studies, University of Michigan, 1999.

CRITICAL AND BIOGRAPHICAL STUDIES OF KURIHARA SADAKO

Minear, Richard. "Translator's Introduction." In *Black Eggs: Poems by Kurihara Sadako*. Ann Arbor: Center for Japanese Studies, University of Michigan, 1994. Pp. 1–38.
———. "Translator's Introduction." In *When We Say "Hiroshima": Poems of Kurihara Sadako*. Ann Arbor: Center for Japanese Studies, University of Michigan, 1999. Pp. vii–xv.
Nihon gendaishi bunko 17. Kurihara Sadako shishū. Tokyo: Doyō Bijutsusha, 1984.

SELECTED WORKS OF ŌTA YŌKO

COLLECTED WORKS

Ōta Yōko. *Ōta Yōko shū*. 4 vols. Tokyo: San'ichi Shobō, 1982.
Kaku-sensō no kiken o uttaeru bungakusha, ed. *Nihon no genbaku bungaku*. Vol. 2, *Ōta Yōko*. Tokyo: Horupu Shuppan, 1984.

ESSAYS

"Unazoko no yō na hikari: genshibakudan no kūshū ni atte" (1945). In *Ōta Yōko shū*. Vol. 2. Tokyo: San'ichi Shobō, 1982. Pp. 275–280.
"Hara Tamiki no shi ni tsuite" (1951). In *Nihon no genbaku bungaku*. Vol. 1. Edited by Kaku-sensō no kiken o uttaeru bungakusha. Tokyo: Horupu Shuppan, 1984. Pp. 292–293.
"Sakka no taido" (1952). In *Nihon no genbaku bungaku*. Vol. 15. Edited by Kaku-sensō no kiken o uttaeru bungakusha. Tokyo: Horupu Shuppan, 1984. Pp. 242–245.
"Bungaku no osoroshisa" (1956). In *Ōta Yōko shū*. Vol. 2. Tokyo: San'ichi Shobō, 1982. Pp. 321–323.

NOVELS

Ryūri no kishi (1939). In *Ōta Yōko shū*. Vol. 4. Tokyo: San'ichi Shobō, 1982. Pp. 5–255.
Ama (1940). In *Ōta Yōko shū*. Vol. 4. Tokyo: San'ichi Shobō, 1982. Pp. 273–318.
Sakura no kuni. Tokyo: San'ichi Shobō, 1940.
Shikabane no machi (1948). In *Ōta Yōko shū*. Vol. 1. Tokyo: San'ichi Shobō, 1982. Pp. 6–156. Trans. by Richard Minear as *City of Corpses*. In *Hiroshima: Three Witnesses*. Princeton, N.J.: Princeton University Press, 1990. Pp. 147–273.
Ningen ranru (1951). In *Ōta Yōko shū*. Vol. 2. Tokyo: San'ichi Shobō, 1982. Pp. 5–273.
Han-ningen (1954). In *Ōta Yōko shū*. Vol. 1. Tokyo: San'ichi Shobō, 1982. Pp. 261–334.
Yūnagi no machi to hito to (1955). In *Ōta Yōko shū*. Vol. 3. Tokyo: San'ichi Shobō. Pp. 5–294.

SHORT STORIES

"Hotaru" (1953). In *Nihon no genbaku bungaku*. Vol. 2. Edited by Kaku-sensō no kiken o uttaeru bungakusha. Tokyo: Horupu Shuppan, 1984. Trans. by Kōichi Nakagawa as "Fireflies." In *The Crazy Iris and Other Stories of the Atomic Aftermath*. Edited by Ōe Kenzaburō. New York: Grove Press, 1985. Pp. 85–111.
"Han-hōrō" (1956). In *Ōta Yōko shū*. Vol. 3. Tokyo: San'ichi Shobō, 1982. Pp. 295–314.

CRITICAL AND BIOGRAPHICAL STUDIES OF ŌTA YŌKO

Esashi Akiko. *Kusazue: Ōta Yōko hyōden*. Tokyo: Nami Shobō, 1971.
Minear, Richard. "Translator's Introduction." In *Hiroshima: Three Witnesses*. Princeton, N.J.: Princeton University Press, 1990. Pp. 117–142.
Sawada Akiko. "Shikabane no machi." *Kokubungaku kaishaku to kanshō* 50, no. 9:60–65 (August 1985).

SELECTED WORKS OF TŌGE SANKICHI

COLLECTED WORKS

Genbaku shishū. Tokyo: Aoki Shoten, 1952. Trans. by Richard Minear as *Poems of the Atomic Bomb*. In *Hiroshima: Three Witnesses*. Princeton, N.J.: Princeton University Press, 1990.
Tōge Sankichi sakuhinshū. 2 vols. Tokyo: Aoki Shoten, 1975.

INDIVIDUAL POEMS

"Ehon" (1945). In *Tōge Sankichi sakuhinshū*. Vol 1. Tokyo: Aoki Shoten, 1975. P. 123. Trans. by John Treat as "Picture Book." In *Writing Ground Zero*. Chicago, Ill.: University of Chicago Press, 1995. Pp. 174–175.
"Kurisumasu no kaerimichi" (1946). In *Tōge Sankichi sakuhinshū*. Vol. 1. Tokyo: Aoki Shoten, 1975. P. 125. Trans. by John Treat as "The Road Home from Christmas." In *Writing Ground Zero*. Chicago, Ill.: University of Chicago Press, 1995. Pp. 175–176.
"Chimata nite" (1949). In *Tōge Sankichi sakuhinshū*. Vol. 1. Tokyo: Aoki Shoten, 1975. P. 193. Trans. by Richard Minear as "In the Streets." In *Hiroshima: Three Witnesses*. Princeton, N.J.: Princeton University Press, 1990. P. 352.
"Ikari no uta" (1949). In *Tōge Sankichi sakuhinshū*. Vol. 1. Tokyo: Aoki Shoten, 1975. P. 132. Trans. by Richard Minear as "Song of Rage." In *Hiroshima: Three Witnesses*. Princeton, N.J.: Princeton University Press, 1990. P. 285.
"1950 nen no hachigatsu muika" (1950). In *Tōge Sankichi sakuhinshū*. Vol. 1. Tokyo: Aoki Shoten, 1975. Pp. 189–191. Trans. by Richard Minear as "August 6, 1950." In *Hiroshima: Three Witnesses*. Princeton, N.J.: Princeton University Press, 1990. Pp. 347–349.

"Yobikake" (1950). In *Tōge Sankichi sakuhinshū*. Vol. 1. Tokyo: Aoki Shoten, 1975. Pp. 196–197. Trans. by Richard Minear as "Appeal." In *Hiroshima: Three Witnesses*. Princeton, N.J.: Princeton University Press, 1990. P. 357.

"Hachigatsu muika" (1951). In *Tōge Sankichi sakuhinshū*. Vol. 1. Tokyo: Aoki Shoten, 1975. Pp. 161–162. Trans. by Richard Minear as "August 6." In *Hiroshima: Three Witnesses*. Princeton, N.J.: Princeton University Press, 1990. Pp. 306–307.

"Jo" (1951). In *Tōge Sankichi sakuhinshū*. Vol. 1. Tokyo: Aoki Shoten, 1975. P. 161. Trans. by Richard Minear as "Prelude." In *Hiroshima: Three Witnesses*. Princeton, N.J.: Princeton University Press, 1990. P. 305.

"Me" (1951). In *Tōge Sankichi sakuhinshū*. Vol. 1. Tokyo: Aoki Shoten, 1975. Pp. 168–169. Trans. by Richard Minear as "Eyes." In *Hiroshima: Three Witnesses*. Princeton, N.J.: Princeton University Press, 1990. Pp. 317–318.

"Sōko no kiroku" (1951). In *Tōge Sankichi sakuhinshū*. Vol. 1. Tokyo: Aoki Shoten, 1975. Pp. 169–172. Trans. by Richard Minear as "Warehouse Chronicle." In *Hiroshima: Three Witnesses*. Princeton, N.J.: Princeton University Press, 1990. Pp. 319–322.

"Sono hi wa itsu ka?" (1951). In *Tōge Sankichi sakuhinshū*. Vol. 1. Tokyo: Aoki Shoten, 1975. Pp. 197–203. Trans. by Richard Minear as "When Will That Day Come?" In *Hiroshima: Three Witnesses*. Princeton, N.J.: Princeton University Press, 1990. Pp. 358–365.

CRITICAL AND BIOGRAPHICAL STUDIES OF TŌGE SANKICHI

Masuoka Toshikazu. *Hachigatsu no shijin: genbaku shijin Tōge Sankichi no shi to shōgai*. Tokyo: Tōhō Shuppansha, 1978.

———. *Genbaku shijin Tōge Sankichi*. Tokyo: Shin Nihon Shuppan, 1985.

———. *Genbaku shijin monogatari*. Osaka: Nihon Kikanshi Shuppan Sentā, 1987.

Thornber, Karen L. "Toward Human Dignity: The Poetry and Poetics of Tōge Sankichi." Senior thesis, Princeton University, 1996.

SELECTED WORKS OF IBUSE MASUJI

INDIVIDUAL WORKS

"Kakitsubata." In *Ibuse Masuji zenshū*. Vol. 5. Tokyo: Chikuma Shobō, 1975. Pp. 3–22. Trans. by Ivan Morris as "The Crazy Iris." In *The Crazy Iris and Other Stories of the Atomic Aftermath*. New York: Grove Press, 1985. Pp. 17–35.

Kuroi ame. In *Ibuse Masuji zenshū*. Vol. 13. Tokyo: Chikuma Shobō, 1975. Pp. 3–298. Trans. by John Bester as *Black Rain*. Tokyo: Kodansha International, 1978.

CRITICAL AND BIOGRAPHICAL STUDIES OF IBUSE MASUJI

Bester, John. "Translator's Preface." In *Black Rain*. Tokyo: Kodansha International, 1978. Pp. 5–8.

Etō Jun. "Heijōshin de kataru ijōshin: kioi no nai genbaku shōsetsu." In *Asahi Shinbun*, evening edition, 25 August 1966.

Ibuse Masuji. "Oboegaki." In *Ibuse Masuji jisen zenshū*. Vol. 6. Tokyo: Shinchōsha, 1986. Pp. 448–449.

Liman, Anthony V. *A Critical Study of the Literary Style of Ibuse Masuji: As Sensitive as Waters*. New York: The Edwin Mellen Press, 1992.

Matsumoto Tsuruo. *Ibuse Masuji ron*. Tokyo: Tōjusha, 1978.

Treat, John Whittier. *The Literature of Ibuse Masuji: Pools of Water, Pillars of Fire*. Seattle: University of Washington Press, 1988.

OTHER PRINCIPAL WORKS

Nagai Takashi. *Nagasaki no kane*. Tokyo: Hibiya Shuppan, 1949. Trans. by William Johnston as *The Bells of Nagasaki*. Tokyo: Kodansha International, 1984.

Ōe Kenzaburō. *Hiroshima nōto*. In *Hiroshima no hikari: Ōe Kenzaburō dōjidai ronshū*. Vol 2. Tokyo: Nihon Hōsō Shuppan Kyōkai, 1991. Pp. 7–162. Trans. by Toshi Yonezawa and David L. Swain as *Hiroshima Notes*. Tokyo: YMCA Press, 1981.

DAZAI OSAMU
1909–1948

JOEL COHN

PROBABLY NO OTHER modern Japanese writer has been as intensely loved—and loathed—by as many readers as Dazai Osamu. In a culture that frequently turns writers into cult figures, Dazai's cult has consistently been among the largest and most ardent of all. It certainly must be the most enduring, having long ago transcended the specific circumstances of the postwar era that gave birth to it. The date of 19 June, marking both the day of his birth and of the discovery thirty-nine years later of his body, drowned in a double suicide, is still honored by his devotees with a memorial observation at his graveside and dutifully reported by the media to the much larger group of admirers in whose lives Dazai's writing, and his legend, continue to be an important element. His writing compellingly draws the attention of new generations of readers, especially younger ones, who have consistently formed his most devoted audience.

What accounts for this appeal? Much of it, of course, stems from the power of the themes, characters, and language in Dazai's fiction to move his readers; but the charisma of his own largely self-created image and the manifold dramas of his life story have also played a major role. Like the life of Ernest Hemingway (whom Dazai resembled in few other ways as a writer or as a human being), the life and per-

sonality of Dazai can end up overshadowing the writing itself for some admirers. But to a greater degree than in Hemingway's case, it may be hard to understand the attraction that Dazai's personality and life story can exert without having directly experienced the way that he transmuted them into the matter of his own fiction.

This is all the more true because that act of transmutation is the very raison d'être of so much of Dazai's writing. In fact, Dazai can lay claim not only to the the title of ultimate cult writer but to that of ultimate autobiographical fictionist in a land of autobiographical fictionists. Certainly he was unwavering in his commitment to the use of literature as a means of exploring and exposing the self. Although readers cannot take all the assertions made in his writing as expressions of his own beliefs, few would be likely to doubt that the idea, declared in *Tokyo hakkei* (1941; "Eight Scenes from Tokyo," 1991), that "Geijutsu wa watakushi de aru" ("Art is 'I' ") was ever far from his mind (*Dazai Osamu zenshū [DOZ]*, vol. 4, p. 70; tr. McCarthy, 1991, p. 168).

Similar convictions about the relationship between self and art have been embraced by many Japanese writers, and their readers, both before and after Dazai's time. So, for that matter, has the willingness to confess one's darkest secrets and reveal one's deepest fears, no matter how humiliating, in an atmosphere of absolute sincerity—so much so that critics regularly refer to autobiographical or confessional fiction (known in Japanese as *shishōsetsu*, used hereafter in the text) as the mainstream form of modern Japanese literature.

Whether the actions, words, or thoughts of Dazai's fictional characters are or are not identical with those of the author (many of them can be verified, while many others are clearly fabrications), they create an impression of truthfulness and sincerity prized by many Japanese readers. But what sets his writing apart is the way that its confessional impact and sense of honesty are heightened by his distinctive worldview, by the inventiveness and variety of his language, fictive techniques, and moods, and (not least of all) by his engagingly intimate tone. Dazai's devotees admire the finely balanced mix of bitter honesty and gentle sentimentality with which he looked at his own life, and at life in general. Both effects are greatly enhanced by one of Dazai's most outstanding gifts: his ability to make his readers feel like he is talking directly to them. Sometimes this is done through the voices of his fictional characters as they tell their stories; sometimes the author thrusts himself out from behind his curtain to address the reader directly; often there is no curtain at all, and the author addresses the reader directly throughout the piece in an essayistic manner.

Given his propensity to use and reuse a relatively limited set of basic themes and materials, much of Dazai's effectiveness as a writer depends on his ability to vary his treatments, to avoid becoming claustrophobically confined in the repeated details of his own life and personality even while managing to endow his characters and situations with a familiar, indeed unmistakably Dazaiesque, stamp. This stylistic virtuosity, boldness, and versatility enabled him to transcend the realistic strictures that have conventionally been associated with the genre in Japan. Whereas some autobiographical writers strove for a minimalist approach in their language, or regarded atten-

tion to issues of language as a distraction from the pursuit of truth, Dazai reveled in a variety of inventive prose styles and linguistic colorings, moving with seemingly effortless ease between childlike simplicity, keen wordplay, evocative dialect, and archly stilted pseudo-classical diction. His narrative voices can be male or female, young or old, plain or sophisticated, and, while not all of them are equally convincing, they are never less than lively.

Dazai's range of tones and moods also brings a rare variety and richness to the normally earnest *shishōsetsu*. Although he is best known as an exponent of grim despair, Dazai's writing can just as easily be lighthearted or intently serious, witheringly sarcastic, full of poignant longing, stoic resignation, or even uplifting optimism. Irony is rarely far below the surface, even when he proclaims his own utter truthfulness.

Equally notable is the variety of structures and techniques which Dazai employed in presenting his materials. He continually sought new ways to tell his stories, whether by breaking them into collage-like assemblages of brief fragments, by shifting the narrative voice from character to character to provide multiple narrative perspectives, by freely integrating letters and journal entries into the narrative flow, by recasting familiar material in parodic adaptations, or by supplying running commentaries on his stories even in the act of spinning them out.

But the difference between Dazai and other *shishōsetsu* writers is not only a matter of formal inventiveness or stylistic flair and versatility. Dazai stands out also because he had a different conception of the crucial *shishōsetsu* value of "authenticity." Despite his highly developed streak of narcissism, Dazai was in the final analysis concerned not so much with the degree of honesty or sincerity in the author's act of self-revelation as he was with a different kind of relation between self and truth: the ways in which the particular truths of his personality and experiences related to life in general, among all kinds of settings, ages, situations, and people. It is this as much as any other factor that accounts for his enduring appeal.

The principal conclusion that Dazai drew from his own experiences and observations of life and reiterated persistently as the truth in his writings is that an unbridgeable gap separates the few individuals who attempt to live honestly and harmlessly from the society around them. In Dazai's fiction, society is an incomprehensible and often fearsome world of charlatans and predators who are so preoccupied with self-interest that they never even consider their own behavior. The narrator/protagonist of *Ningen shikkaku* (1948; *No Longer Human*, 1958) gives this vision one of its most powerful expressions:

> I am convinced that human life is filled with many pure, happy, serene examples of insincerity, truly splendid of their kind—of people deceiving one another without (strangely enough) any wounds being inflicted, of people who seem unaware even that they are deceiving one another . . . I find it difficult to understand the kind of human being who lives, or is sure he can live, purely, happily, serenely while engaged in deceit. Human beings never did teach me that abstruse secret. If only I had known that one thing I should never have had to dread human beings so, nor should I have opposed myself to human life, nor tasted such torments of hell every night.

> (*DOZ*, vol. 9, p. 377; tr. pp. 37–38)

But inevitably this perspective leads to a moral configuration that the reader recognizes to be double-edged, even if Dazai's outsiders and misfits do not: the very inability to play along with the game that dooms them to the status of loser or victim in society also confers a kind of moral authority on them. Some of them, like Dazai himself, are shrewd enough to realize this and even to exploit it on occasion. In some cases, especially among the male characters in later works such as *No Longer Human* or "Buiyon no tsuma" (1947; "Villon's Wife," 1956), their own shortcomings go beyond matters of weakness or incomprehension: they too can be victimizers whose actions make life miserable for others whom Dazai's outsiders and misfits in general have no reason or desire to hurt. But whether they have been helplessly manipulated into such actions or committed them with malice aforethought, their actions can still be judged in a different light and even justified or at least mitigated, since the characters are at least acutely aware of the suffering they are causing, and feel guilty—unlike the mass of fellow human beings who are so blinded by their self-serving and lies that they remain unaware that they have done anything wrong.

These fundamental truths, as Dazai saw them, form the basis of a worldview that changed little over the course of his writing career. But Japan changed around him—drastically after 1945—and in a time when virtually every aspect of life seemed to have turned upside down, the perpetual outsider and rebel was suddenly and unexpectedly cast as hero and cult object. It was not a role he could play comfortably, and less than three years after the end of the war he self-destructed at age thirty-eight. Death only intensified his legend. Japan has changed again, in ways that would seem to make Dazai irrelevant: comfort and complacency have largely replaced the desperate misery and soul-searching of the early postwar years. Yet the mystique of Dazai, and of his writing, remains a considerable force. The cult lives on.

Shōsetsu and Fiction

Dazai wrote in various prose forms, including drama and essays, but devoted most of his efforts to the category known in Japan as *shōsetsu*, which is often equated in the West with "fiction." While it is his work of this latter type that is most widely read and celebrated, it is worth noting that his writing offers an illuminating example of the discrepancies between the Western notion of "fiction" and its not so exact Japanese counterpart.

Critics sometimes divide Dazai's work between more straightforwardly autobiographical pieces and fictive works with little or no basis in the events of his life, with the latter tending toward a more carefully shaped structure, often adapted from existing narratives, historical incidents, or materials supplied by friends and acquaintances. But this is not really a significant or useful distinction: The contrasts, paradoxes, and contradictions that Dazai saw in himself are reflected throughout his work, no matter what kind of setting or cast of characters he employed. And indeed for all the surface variety, the reader has a sense, comforting or claustrophobic, of rarely being far away from Dazai.

Whether of the autobiographical or "fictive" type, Dazai's *shōsetsu* often do not adhere to the norms of structure and content conventionally associated with fictional writing in the West. In some, such as the early "Ha" (1934; "Leaves," 1968) the structure consists of a collage of fragments ranging from a single word ("Life") to a few pages in length, connected by no narrative story line. Other works such as "Kunō no nenkan" (1946; "An Almanac of Pain," 1985), may be read as *shōsetsu* in Japan but take the form of more or less discursive "memoirs" or essays with little sense of fictional structure at all. Repeatedly Dazai quotes passages, sometimes at length, from his earlier stories in later ones.

In many of the pieces classified as autobiographical, such as the early story "Omoide" (1933; "Recollections," 1985), a series of events is recounted in a form similar to that of a conventional story, but these are largely based on actual experiences. Repeatedly Dazai made a point of assuring his readers that what he had written was the "truth," and at times he explicitly identified himself or a family member or acquaintance by their real-life names in ostensibly fictional works. And yet, scholars have had little trouble identifying passages in ostensibly autobiographical pieces in which Dazai had freely departed from those "facts" of his life that he appeared to be at such pains to convey. Dazai regularly presented conflicting versions in different stories, and sometimes he even used one of his "fictions" to reveal his modifications or fabrications in an earlier piece. In other instances, such as the story "Dasu gemaine" (1935; "Das Gemeine," 1983) and the novel *Shayō* (1947; *The Setting Sun*, 1956), Dazai distributed various traits associated with himself among multiple characters, and it is quite likely that he adopted the same technique when creating characters that were not self-portraits. Moreover, while he returned compulsively to describe and redescribe certain key episodes or situations from his childhood experiences or his double suicide attempt at Kamakura in 1930, there are others, such as an earlier suicide attempt while still a high school student and his activities on the margin of the illegal Communist Party, that he writes about minimally or not at all.

The Dazai pieces conventionally labeled as more "fictive" are often set in ages and locations far removed from Dazai's own, and are drawn from sources ranging from traditional Japanese folk tales and historical records to the Bible and Shakespeare and journals and letters of friends and acquaintances. But in many of these, such as the recountings of familiar traditional tales in *Otogizōshi* (1945; Fairy tales), the narrative framework is repeatedly disrupted by passages in which the author (or a narrative voice that sounds like the author's) directly addresses the reader, offering a running stream of comments or explanations on the events he is recounting, the motivations of the characters, as well as his own, and the circumstances under which he created the story. And here too, despite the remoteness of the setting and events from Dazai's own world, the characters and situations often bear a more than passing resemblance to those in the "autobiographical" works: a cold, remote father; a well-meaning but reserved and vaguely intimidating older brother; a bumbling, defensive husband; the long-suffering but nagging, humorless wife.

Throughout Dazai's writing, the boundary lines between what is "fiction" and what is not, and between what is "autobiographical" and what is not, are often so vague that they are virtually irrelevant. Still, as many commentators have pointed out, and many readers must have sensed on their own, it is possible to read many of Dazai's individual works as components of a single extended more or less autobiographical saga. While some of these, most famously his final novels *The Setting Sun* and *No Longer Human*, stand out as prominent peaks, more enduring in their popularity than others, any reader is likely to pick and choose a set of particularly resonant personal favorites.

Dazai as "Japanese"?

Even outside of the precincts of his fandom, Dazai's name is regularly included in short lists of modern Japan's major writers. Still, he does not enjoy iconic status or compel widespread admiration in the manner of Natsume Sōseki, Mori Ōgai, or Kawabata Yasunari. He is not a writer who is designated (by himself, or by his readers) to speak for his nation, or to represent its traditions or its spiritual essence. Ever the outsider, it is not even clear that he had much interest in glorifying or perpetuating Japanese culture: his occasional comments in praise of tradition not infrequently have a distinctly tongue-in-cheek tone, while his critiques have a genuine sting. Nor was he much inclined to engage in meditations on the fate of Japan, even though the despair and tumult so prominent in his writings of the immediate postwar years have often been taken as emblematic of the nation's condition in the same period.

Thus, for the non-Japanese reader, the experience of reading Dazai is different from that of reading many of the other Japanese writers whose works are well known in translation. Dazai's writing is not an ideal starting place for those in search of a vision of Japanese culture as something exotic or distinctive, except perhaps in the glimpses that he frequently offers into the structure and workings of Japan's traditional family system and his renowned evocations of the spiritual desolation of the late 1940s.

Another possible exception concerns the issue of suicide. The prominence of suicide as a theme in some of Dazai's writing (most strikingly in *The Setting Sun*, where one character or another seems to be proclaiming his or her desire to die every few pages) and the five suicide attempts in Dazai's own life inevitably evoke associations with the prominence of suicide in the morality of Japan's traditional warrior class, or with the large number of modern Japanese writers who have taken their own lives (among them one of Dazai's own early literary heroes, Akutagawa Ryūnosuke, as well as Arishima Takeo, Mishima Yukio, and Kawabata Yasunari, just to name some of the most famous). But in Dazai's works and life suicide does not generally seem to have the functions of redeeming one's honor or remonstrating with one's superiors that it had in traditional warrior society—for whose values, by the way, Dazai rarely expressed much admiration.

Nor is it evident that Dazai's suicide attempts were (like those of some of his fictional characters) motivated by the impulse to forge a way out of a profound spiritual dilemma rather than by such relatively immediate factors as disappointment in love, the strains created by a lack of future academic or professional prospects, or sheer nervous exhaustion. Of course, the same is true for some of the other prominent literary suicides, and to this extent one would be justified in viewing the suicidal compulsion as a distinctively Japanese tendency—but at the same time it is worth remembering that these are causes that might lead to a suicide attempt in many cultures, and not just by writers.

If there is relatively little in Dazai's writing to intrigue seekers after "Japaneseness," at least in its most widely known forms, he offers much to readers who are prepared to accept a Japanese portrayal of themes and characters whose significance transcends national or cultural boundaries. Many such readers will be able to relate what they encounter in Dazai's works to what they have experienced in their own lives with an immediacy that is not likely to be equaled when they read other Japanese authors.

Formative Years

The writer who was later to take the pen name Dazai Osamu was born Tsushima Shūji on 19 June 1909 in the village of Kanagi, Aomori prefecture, northern Honshu, a region commonly viewed by other Japanese as a remote provincial backwater. It has been claimed that one of the reasons for his choice of the pen name was that he was able to pronounce it without revealing his thick country accent, unlike his actual surname, which would have sounded like "Chishima" rather than "Tsushima" in his pronunciation. His family was not only large (Dazai was the tenth of eleven children) but locally prominent, with extensive landholdings that made it one of the wealthiest and most powerful in the region at a time when Japan was still a predominantly agricultural nation and landlords were economically, socially, and politically dominant figures in rural areas. As a consequence of the family's importance, his father, Tsushima Gen'emon, served as a member of the provincial legislature and later in both the lower and upper houses of the national Diet, but he died when Dazai was thirteen. These circumstances may have helped to contribute to Dazai's lifelong sense of being both an outsider who had little in common with the mainstream of Japanese life and a member of a chosen elite—with feelings of guilt due to his family's privileged position—all the more so given the sometimes desperate poverty of much of the rural population.

By Dazai's own account, the family offered little emotional warmth: his mother was sickly and took little direct part in his upbringing. In his early years he was cared for at times by a nursemaid, by an aunt whom he seems for a time to have believed to be his actual mother, and by another of the family's female servants. The death of his father, followed in the next several years by the deaths of two of his brothers, no doubt also contributed to his sense of insecurity.

By the time he was a middle school student Dazai had begun to develop an interest in literature, contributing pieces to school publications and even collaborating with his brothers and friends to produce their own magazines. He continued his literary pursuits as a high school student in his late teens and early twenties (1927–1930), and added to them some new interests which were to have fateful consequences in his later life. One of these new interests was a local geisha named Oyama Hatsuyo, with whom he struck up an acquaintance while taking lessons in traditional Japanese music. Another new interest was an engagement with the leftist political ideas that were then becoming widely known in student circles despite harsh government attempts to suppress them. The awareness that his family's rich landlord status marked it—and thus him—as unconscionably privileged exploiters in the Marxian view of society is generally considered to have been a significant factor in his first attempt at suicide (by an overdose of sleeping medicine) in 1929.

Despite these distractions, Dazai qualified the following year to enter Japan's most elite educational institution, Tokyo Imperial University. However, he was now far more committed to literary and political activities than to his studies and rarely attended classes. He was soon joined in Tokyo by Hatsuyo, and after a difficult round of negotiations with his eldest brother, who had become head of the Tsushima family following Gene'mon's death, they were permitted to marry and receive a comfortable monthly allowance. Because of the unacceptable difference in social status, though, Dazai was officially expelled from the family.

During this period, Dazai also attempted suicide a second time, this time with a partner, not Hatsuyo but a café waitress he barely knew. He again survived, but she died. His family's influence succeeded in forestalling the ensuing police investigation, but Dazai's life was by now firmly embarked on a chaotic course of downward mobility and self-destruction that would continue with little interruption until close to the end of the 1930s. As government pressure on leftist movements intensified, Dazai found his undercover political activities increasingly onerous, and he abandoned them by 1932 following a round of police interrogations, adding yet another dimension to his already well-developed sense of guilt and betrayal.

Early Writings: The *Bannen* Stories

Despite the virtually nonstop disorder of his life in these years, Dazai never abandoned his literary aspirations. He had been composing stories on and off since his school days, and his withdrawal from political activities was followed by a renewed commitment to writing. Having abandoned his comrades, alienated his family, given up hope of graduating from the university, and even suffered the shock of learning that he had not been Hatsuyo's first lover, Dazai sensed that the end was already closing in on him. He resolved to leave behind something that would serve as a legacy and perhaps provide a measure of redemption for all the disasters and failures.

Possessing a new sense of dedication and benefiting from the steadying influence and literary guidance of the writer Ibuse Masuji, whom he viewed as a mentor, Dazai produced a series of stories which began to appear (under, for the first time, the pen name Dazai Osamu) in various magazines in 1933. In 1936 they were published in book form; the volume's title, *Bannen* (Final years), reflected Dazai's belief that he had already experienced a lifetime's worth of suffering by his mid-twenties, and that there was little or nothing to look forward to.

Bannen includes some of the best known of all Dazai's works. It has often been remarked that most of the techniques, themes, and styles that would become hallmarks of Dazai's repertory throughout his career are already represented, or at least foreshadowed, in the fifteen stories of this collection. Among the types of story included here are straightforwardly realistic autobiographical accounts of scenes from the author's childhood and young adulthood, reworkings of material from traditional legend and history, an animal fable, an evocation of the popular fiction of the Edo period (1600–1868), and modernistic experiments in fragmented structure and narrative voice. Even some of the stories not overtly based on the author's life contain elements that with hindsight can be recognized as more or less closely transposed versions of actual events, relationships, and preoccupations. Also frequently apparent are the characteristically Dazaiesque mix of self-absorption and self-irony and the penchant for lightening the prevailing mood of gloom and despair with bright flashes of humor.

Probably the best known of the *Bannen* stories, as much for its contents as its literary qualities, is "Recollections," a summing up of the author's life from infancy to his teenage years. "Recollections" serves as an introduction to Dazai's world, establishing the family background, some of the major characters, and many of the themes and preoccupations that would be revisited repeatedly in his ensuing works. As Donald Keene has pointed out in *Dawn to the West*, two of these preoccupations, the strong interest in language and the impulse to provide "service" to others, particularly by means of clowning, are already present in the primal scene:

> I was standing by the front gate with my aunt at dusk. . . . My aunt told me, His Majesty the Emperor has passed on. "He is a living god," she added. I seem to recall that I too whispered "living god," intrigued. And then I seem to have said something disrespectful. She reproved me: "That isn't what we say; we say he has passed on." "On to where?" I asked deliberately, although I knew what she meant. I remember that made her laugh.

> (*DOZ*, vol. 1, p. 22; tr. Lyons, 1985, p. 189)

One might add that a lack of respect for conventional authority, another characteristic Dazai attitude, is already clearly in evidence here as well.

The story goes on to relate, in loosely chronological order, events that illustrate the steady development of a child's feelings of insecurity and estrangement in a large, sometimes intimidating family as care providers come and go. Ominous signs appear early on: childhood visits to a local temple invariably result in the prognostications of damnation, and later attempts at fortune-telling with playing cards prove equally sinister. Growing tendencies toward narcissism and playacting are unsparingly revealed, and Dazai adeptly captures the volatile mix of youthful curiosity, doubt, and confusion that accompanies the boy's initiation into such bewildering phenomena as social class distinctions and death, as well as his ongoing encounters with the tangled complications of sexuality and romance, culminating in an ardent teenage infatuation with one of the family's maids. The chaotic rush of emotions in first love is depicted with an honesty and sensitivity that make them easy for many readers to identify with, even if the class dimension reminds us of Dazai's highly atypical background.

"Recollections" closes with the disappointment of the protagonist's hopes as the girl disappears, and his growing awareness of the ways that guilt, deception, and betrayal can contaminate the exalted yearnings of love—a theme that would figure prominently in so much of Dazai's later writing. But an earlier passage introduces an equally significant revelation, one that was to provide Dazai's main justification for enduring all the deceptions and misery: "And then I discovered one poor outlet after all: writing. Here, it seemed to me, there were dozens of creatures just like me, all of them subject to the same unfathomable shudders. Oh, that I might become a writer, I secretly prayed" (*DOZ*, vol. 1, p. 45; tr. Lyons, 1985, p. 206).

It is worth stressing that most of the *Bannen* stories, including several of the best, are not of the straightforwardly autobiographical type. Among the most remarkable is the first in the collection, "Leaves." Its epigraph, from a poem by Paul Verlaine, is often taken as one of the definitive expressions of Dazai's own psyche:

The ecstasy and terror
Of having been chosen—
Both are within me.

(*DOZ*, vol. 1, p. 5; tr. Lyons, p. 54)

But what is most striking about this story is its collage-like structure, a sometimes eccentrically juxtaposed succession of fragments in which Dazai was entirely free to experiment with a variety of voices and styles that alternate between lively colloquialism, decorous formality, unctuous politeness, and provincial dialect, and to indulge in his penchant for finely balanced mixes of pathos and cool irony:

I thought of suicide. Last January I was given a present, a piece of fabric for a kimono. The material was linen, woven in narrow gray stripes. It is for a summer kimono. I thought I would live until summer.

(*DOZ*, vol. 1, p. 5; tr. Miyoshi, p. 128)

All he was doing was to drag out his existence from day to day. In his lodgings he drank all alone, got drunk all alone. It was hardest of all at night when he furtively spread out his bedding and lay down. He didn't even dream. He was completely exhausted. He felt listless, no matter what he did. Once he even bought a book called *How Should Privies Be Improved?* and seriously studied it. At the time he was fairly stymied by the traditional methods of disposing of human excrement.

(*DOZ*, vol. 1, pp. 4–5; tr. Keene, 1984, p. 1031)

Among the other sections are passages taken from earlier writings (another practice that he continued in later writings), pithy aphorisms, and bits of poetry, including the following mildly unconventional haiku:

Sleet falls outside—
What is he smiling about,
That bust of Lenin?

(*DOZ*, vol. 1, p. 13)

In several other striking non-autobiographical stories, habitual Dazai concerns are variously tempered and enlivened by a rich strain of fantasy. In "Gyofukuki" (1933; "Undine," 1989), a tragic allegory with strong overtones of traditional legend, a girl seeks escape from a brutish father and a meaningless existence by plunging into a mountain pool and transforming herself into a carp. "Romanesuku" (1934; "Romanesque," 1993), a tale set in the Edo period, shows Dazai in a more light-hearted mood as he tells of three good-for-nothing young men who seek to perfect their talents for magic, brawling, and lying, only to have their pursuits lead to embarrassing disasters. In the final scene, they happen to come together in a tavern, where they tell each other their stories. The concluding statement is left, inevitably, to the liar Saburō: "We three are artists! . . . Our day will come, and soon—I'm certain of it! I'm an artist. I'm going to write the stories of Tarō the Wizard and Jirōbei the fighter and, with your leave, my own story as well, to offer the world three models for living. Who cares what people say?" (*DOZ*, vol. 1, pp. 199–200; tr. McCarthy, 1993, p. 131).

For all of their embracing of self-deprecation, humiliation, and misery, the *Bannen* stories also contain many passages that convey a robust confidence, even a sense of mission. Often, as in two of the passages cited above, these concern the significance of writing and its relation to life. Like many educated young people at the time, Dazai held a conviction that literature was not just a diversion or a game. Rather it was a serious pursuit, one—maybe the only one—that offered its "chosen" devotees a way out and even a redemption from life's confusions and agonies, one that was worth all the sacrifices and suffering that the acts of living and writing demanded. That confidence is expressed eloquently in comments Dazai made on what the *Bannen* stories, and the experience of creating them, meant to him:

I sacrificed ten years of my life for this one volume of stories. . . . Because of this one book I lost my place in the world, was constantly wounded in my self-esteem and buffeted by the cold winds of the world, and I wandered around in a daze. I squandered tens of thousands of yen . . . I burnt my tongue, singed my breast, and deliberately harmed my body beyond any possibility of recovery. I tore up and discarded over a hundred stories. Five thousand sheets of manuscript paper. And all that remained was this one volume. Nothing else. . . . But I believe in it. I believe that [it] will take on deeper colors with the passing years, that it will surely penetrate ever more profoundly into your eyes, your heart. I was born only to write this one volume. From today I am a corpse, through and through. I am merely living out my remaining days.

(*DOZ*, vol. 10, p. 40; tr. Keene, 1984, pp. 1028–1029)

Bannen was not initially a major success, but it helped to establish Dazai as an up-and-coming writer. Two more books were published in 1937, and his stories began to appear in prominent magazines. Meanwhile his personal life was continuing on a downward spiral: his expulsion from the university in 1935 was followed in rapid succession by a third suicide attempt (this time by hanging) and then a life-threatening case of appendicitis that led to his addiction to a pain-killing drug. For over a year his physical condition deteriorated, complicated by a chronic pulmonary ailment, while he alienated devoted friends and supporters and ran up huge debts in an ever more desperate attempt to feed his habit.

A one-month confinement in a mental hospital in the fall of 1936 finally restored him to a modicum of physical and psychological health, but his relationship with Hatsuyo fell apart the next year when he discovered that she had carried on an affair with a friend of his while he was institutionalized. Yet another unsuccessful suicide attempt, this time with Hatsuyo, was soon followed by a final breakup and a year that seems to have been occupied mainly by idleness and drinking. Understandably, Dazai managed to produce relatively little writing in this period, and much of what he did write reflects the calamitous nature of his living conditions and his mental state.

Middle Period

One of the first signs that Dazai was emerging from this prolonged period of turmoil came in the fall of 1938 when he published "Mangan" ("A Promise Fulfilled," 1991), a very short but finely crafted story in which the author's preoccupation with his own tribulations gives way to an affectionate, even romantic, tribute to the optimism with which some more ordinary characters deal with their problems, and "Ubasute" ("Putting Granny Out to Die," 1983), a longer piece in which he manages to evince a measure of mordant humor while coming to terms with the grim final act of his life with Hatsuyo. A definitive turning point was reached soon thereafter when, at the behest of his mentor Ibuse, he began a two-month stay near Mount Fuji in Yamanashi prefecture, west of Tokyo. Ibuse was also instrumental in arranging Dazai's marriage in January of 1939 with Ishihara Michiko, a schoolteacher from the nearby city of Kōfu. These events mark the start of the second, or middle period, of Dazai's career, which was to continue through the end of World War II. It was to be the most stable phase of Dazai's adult life; he wrote steadily and his work enjoyed increasing recognition in the literary world.

The recovery of equilibrium is reflected in both the contents and the tone of his fiction in these years, most notably in the story "Fugaku hyakkei" (1939; "One Hundred Views of Mount Fuji," 1991), which recounts a series of incidents from his sojourn in Yamanashi and engagement to Michiko. This is Dazai at his sunniest, his most endearing. Even as the ghosts of his past periodically come back to haunt him and Japan's most celebrated mountain fails repeatedly to live up to expectations, Dazai's prose sparkles with a refreshingly irreverent quality.

The loosely episodic structure is thematically unified by the appearance of the mountain in each vignette, always impassive yet sometimes contrasting with and sometimes underscoring the mood of the human situation. A hike with Ibuse (mentioned here by name) to a famous Fuji-viewing spot goes badly as the mountain is hidden by clouds: "We couldn't see a thing. Enveloped in that dense fog, Mr. Ibuse sat down on a rock, puffed slowly at a cigarette, and broke wind. He looked decidedly out of sorts." The expedition is redeemed after a fashion when an elderly teahouse proprietress produces a large photograph of the mountain: "That was a fine Fuji indeed. We ended up not even regretting the impenetrable fog" (*DOZ*, vol. 2, p. 156; tr. McCarthy, 1991, p. 74).

The mountain is even given a pivotal role in the delicate proceedings leading up to the engagement:

> The young lady's mother showed us into the parlor, where we exchanged greetings, and after a while the young lady came in. I didn't look at her face. Mr. Ibuse and her mother were carrying on a desultory, grown-up conversation when, suddenly, he fixed his eye on the wall above and behind me and muttered, 'Ah, Fuji.' I twisted around and looked up at the wall. Hanging there was a framed aerial photograph of the great crater atop the mountain. It resembled a pure white waterlily. After studying the photo, I slowly twisted back to my original position and glanced fleetingly at the girl. That did it. I made up my mind then and there that, though it might entail a certain amount of difficulty, I wanted to marry this person. That was a Fuji I was grateful for.
>
> (*DOZ*, vol. 2, pp. 156–157; tr. McCarthy, 1991, p.74)

Several other of Dazai's best-known and most accomplished works were produced in the burst of creative energy in the first years of this marriage. In some of these, Dazai borrowed from European sources but endowed them with his own distinctive stamp in freely imaginative treatments. "Kakekomi uttae" (1940; "Heed My Plea," 1989) reflects his growing interest in the Bible, especially the New Testament. It takes the form of a dramatic monologue in which Judas Iscariot recounts his side of the story of his betrayal of Jesus Christ. Its numerous ironies and paradoxes suggest that Dazai did not possess and was not interested in forming a spiritually coherent view of biblical events or doctrines—a tendency that is also apparent in many other of Dazai's biblical references, which become increasingly frequent in his writing from this point on. If anything, the way that Judas portrays himself as a misunderstood outsider, his abilities under appreciated by Jesus and his insensitive disciples, echoes a pattern already very familiar in many Dazai works with less remote settings.

"Hashire Merosu" (1940; "Melos Run!," 1989) is another Dazai reworking with a Western setting and sources, in this case the ancient Greek legend of Damon and Pythias and a tale by Friedrich Schiller. It is now one of the best known of all Dazai's pieces in Japan, frequently appearing in school textbooks, presumably because its suspenseful plot, idealistic tone, uplifting message of friendship, loyalty, and sacrifice, and the title character's stirring athletic feat (uncommon as these elements may be throughout the rest of Dazai's work) are considered appropriate for young readers. Yet even here there are unmistakably Dazaiesque touches. Both of the heroes confess to moments of weakness and mistrust; Melos at one point muses that "Justice, love, fidelity—they're really worthless when you think about it. We kill others to save our own skin—that's the way of the world, isn't it? Oh, nonsense! I'm just a disgraceful traitor" (*DOZ*, vol. 3, p. 211; tr. O'Brien, 1989, p. 122). Dazai also undercuts the heroics with a fine farcical note at the end when Melos, the virtuous runner, has to be reminded that he has compromised the dignity of his triumphal run by arriving at the finish point stark naked.

A more insouciant tone and more concentrated projection of habitual Dazai qualities and preoccupations—alienation from family, narcissism, lack of fortitude, a sense of victimhood, failure to understand others or to be understood by them, to name a few—onto ostensibly remote materials are evident in a

longer work from this period: the 1941 *Shin Hamuretto* (New Hamlet). Dazai had not, however, abandoned writing in a more directly autobiographical vein. In "Tokyo hakkei" ("Eight Scenes from Tokyo," 1991), written in 1940 and published early in 1941, many of the hallmarks of Dazai-style *shishōsetsu* are on prominent display. After a quick bit of generic scene-setting, the narrator inserts himself into the landscape of a forlorn hot spring village and launches into a brief recapitulation of some of the major events of the ten years since his arrival in Tokyo, followed by the first of several references to "ecstasy and terror" and a declaration that he had long wanted to write a piece entitled "Eight Views of Tokyo" as one of his periodic attempts at a summing-up of one phase of his life. The rest of the story consists of scenes from Dazai's life with Hatsuyo (called "H" in the story) and the suicide attempts, addiction, and hospitalization, largely conforming to actual events in general outline if not always in the details. These are interspersed with the narrator's running commentary, often ironical, on the motives behind his actions and his writings, culminating in the revelation that "Art is 'I'" and concluding with the narrator setting out on the journey, during which he composed the story that the reader has just finished reading.

In the last of these Tokyo scenes, the narrator is seeing off his sister-in-law's fiancé, a soldier whose unit is about to embark for China, which had been invaded by Japanese forces several years earlier. Within a year of the story's appearance, the Japanese attack on Pearl Harbor had placed the nation on a full wartime footing. Like other Japanese writers in these years, Dazai was confronted with a steady decrease in opportunities to publish his work, and with intensifying pressure from the government to have all writing that was published conform with official militarist ideology. Like virtually everyone else in Japan his life was made difficult by wartime shortages and ultimately endangered by air raids.

Despite these problems, Dazai managed to produce and publish several works of distinction during the war years. In 1944 he was commissioned to write a travelogue of his native district. Despite the increasingly grim wartime situation and his still problematic relationship with his family in Kanagi, *Tsugaru* (1944; *Return to Tsugaru: Travels of a Purple Tramp*, 1985), the book-length account of his visit, stands out among all of Dazai's writing for its sympathetic, even affectionate treatment of this often-maligned region and for the intensely human account of a man coming to terms with a home from which he had long been estranged. Many memories are still raw, yet Dazai finds himself realizing how much of his own nature has been indelibly formed by this harsh land and its people, often taciturn and stubborn yet warm and devoted.

Like so many of his writings, *Return to Tsugaru* occupies an indeterminate position between fiction and nonfiction. Frequent quotations from historical records and scholarly studies lend it an air of objectivity, and Dazai's account of his travels is based in a general way on actual experiences and observations, but he has modified them freely for artistic and emotional effect. The reunion with his childhood nursemaid Take, for whom he claims to feel as much affection as he did for his own mother, is unquestionably the most celebrated scene in the book. Near the end of his journey, he finally tracks her down after a tension-filled series of tribulations at a school field day in the village of Kodomari. The almost wordless encounter echoes the earlier description of another emotionally intense meeting in which little is said, his reunion with his brothers in the family home in Kanagi. But where the sense of uneasiness underlying that scene is never completely dispelled, there are no such reservations now: "I was completely happy. I felt utterly secure. . . . Is this the kind of feeling that is meant by 'peace'? If it is, I can say that my heart experienced peace for the first time in my life" (*DOZ*, vol. 7, p. 151; tr. Westerhoven, p. 167).

Perhaps nowhere else in Dazai's entire work is another scene of such absolute contentment presented without any apparent sense of irony.

Yet Take herself later testified that Dazai's version was an imaginative treatment, at variance at key points with the actual course of events.

Like many other writers in the war years, Dazai turned to traditional materials as a way of satisfying governmental demands for patriotic content. He applied his by then well-polished technique of reworking traditional materials with great effect in two sets of stories, *Shinshaku shokokubanashi* (1945; New tales from the provinces) and *Otogizōshi* (Fairy tales).

Based on twelve tales by the great Edo-period writer Ihara Saikaku, *Shinshaku shokokubanashi* presents a gallery of protagonists striving with verve and ingenuity to muddle through various difficult situations, with mixed success: impoverished samurai struggle to keep up appearances; a cheeky laborer tries to outwit a straitlaced official; a would-be playboy attempts to keep playing as his funds run out. The parodic, light-hearted mood is reminiscent of "Romanesuku" ("Romanesque"), but with an even more finely modulated undercurrent of dark irony that sometimes verges on desperation. Although the tone and language are unmistakably Dazaiesque, few of the circumstances in these stories relate to Dazai's own in any readily identifiable way; perhaps because of this distancing, the collection includes some of the most finely crafted of all his writing.

Otogizōshi, a set of four retellings of traditional folk tales, was composed in the spring of 1945 amidst intensifying air raids which led Dazai to evacuate his family to Kōfu and soon thereafter to join them when his Tokyo house was severely damaged. The narrator of *Otogizōshi* introduces himself as a bedraggled father gamely trying to pacify a five-year-old daughter by reading folktales to her from a picture book as his family crouches in a backyard shelter during an air raid. As he reads, he spins out his own versions in his own mind. Unlike the Saikaku stories that formed the basis of Dazai's *Shinshaku shokokubanashi*, these originals are familiar to virtually all Japanese readers, and it is easy to trace the manner in which Dazai combined traditional materials and fanciful inventions, regularly punctuated with narratorial comments that describe in realistic detail the circumstances under which he created them. Here too there are undertones of bitterness, even cruelty, some of them appearing to reflect the stresses of family relationships under increasingly difficult wartime conditions. But as in *Return to Tsugaru*, the emphasis is on acceptance and sympathy rather than despair and alienation, and no knowledge of Dazai's life is necessary to appreciate these stories, which also rank among his most appealing works.

Postwar

Japan's surrender in August 1945 found Dazai with his wife and children in his childhood home in Kanagi, where they had fled a few weeks earlier following the destruction of the Kōfu house in another air raid. They were to stay there for more than a year since postwar turmoil and food shortages prevented a quick return to Tokyo. Despite the dire difficulties created by wartime destruction and the desperate postwar economic situation, the publishing industry burgeoned with the ending of wartime controls and Dazai gradually began to find outlets for his work.

The sweeping political, social, and economic democratization measures instituted by the American Occupation forces were seen by many Japanese as a welcome replacement for the discredited militarism, authoritarianism, and traditionalism of the prewar and wartime order. Dazai, never comfortable with conventional values or authority, might have been expected to welcome these developments as well. But he soon came to see the eager support for the new ideals of peace and democracy by many of his fellow Japanese, including some who had been enthusiastic supporters of the wartime regime, as merely another form of the hypocrisy and opportunism that had been endemic in society all along. In a series of works including "Pandora no hako" (1945–1946; Pandora's box), "Jūgo nenkan" (1946; Fifteen years), "An Almanac of Pain,"

and "Shin'yū kōkan" (1946; "The Courtesy Call," 1962), the onetime Marxist proclaimed his sympathy for the emperor and vented his bitterness at postwar Japan, which he now began to see as a coarse, cheapened world which made prewar Japan look gentle and innocent in retrospect.

This message caught with deadly accuracy the prevailing mood of disillusionment and despair of the immediate postwar years, and for the first time Dazai, the inveterate rebel and outsider, found himself elevated to the first rank among Japanese authors. By the time of his return to Tokyo in late 1946, he was classed with a few other suddenly lionized writers such as Sakaguchi Ango, Oda Sakunosuke, and Ishikawa Jun as a star of the so-called *burai-ha* or "outlaw school," renowned (or notorious) for their frank embracing of decadence and their disdain for all forms of convention.

Dazai's dazzling literary success in the final year and a half of his life following his return to Tokyo seems to have done little to alleviate his personal and professional anxieties, nor did it lead to a more optimistic outlook on Japan's postwar course. To the contrary, his life took on a chaotic tone increasingly reminiscent of the early Tokyo years, now with the added stimuli of intense pressure to meet the insatiable demands of the newly revitalized publishing industry, and the pervasive effects of general social, material, and spiritual collapse. Repeatedly he verged on physical and mental breakdown brought on by a combination of overwork, a renewed flaring up of his chronic pulmonary ailment, and excessive indulgence in alcohol and drugs, as well as the sense of despair that emerges so powerfully in much of his postwar writing.

It was in the midst of this chaos and desperation that Dazai produced the works for which he is now best remembered, especially the novels *The Setting Sun* and *No Longer Human* and a series of shorter fictions such as "Villon's Wife" ("Buiyon no tsuma"). These works present Dazai's bleakest visions of the human condition, but much of their impact is derived from his mastery of expressive technique in dealing with his themes. Joined to the rich variety and eloquence of language which were always Dazai hallmarks is an integration and balance of materials from his own life, sources provided by others such as letters and diaries, and products of his own imagination for maximum artistic effect.

In *The Setting Sun (Shayō)*, the most accomplished and celebrated of these postwar classics, Dazai combined a number of elements familiar since the early part of his career (a female narrative voice; use of letters and journal entries as narrative devices; themes of suicide, alienation, and the sufferings of the small elite of individuals blessed and cursed with superior values and sensibilities) with some features that had become more prominent since the final phase of the war. The most notable of these new features are a structure that focuses on a group of main characters rather than on the usual single protagonist and the theme of Japan's fallen postwar aristocracy as a symbolic representation of the psychological and spiritual dislocation that Dazai now saw as pervasive. The story centers on the tribulations and aspirations of Kazuko, a young woman of noble family, as she struggles to find new values that will sustain life amid the postwar turmoil. Her fate is constantly juxtaposed with those of the other main characters, especially her mother (a figure of impossibly idealized grace and innocence whose death is meant to represent the passing of the gentler and nobler aspects of Japanese life) and her brother Naoji (a would-be writer recently returned from army service in the South Pacific, who finds himself deprived of all grounds for belief and hopelessly cut off from his aristocratic roots yet unable to find a place in the rough-and-tumble world of the common people).

The mother's death and Naoji's suicide are contrasted with Kazuko's growing determination to affirm a new way of life based on a defiance of conventional morality. The key act in her challenge is her resolution to bear a child by Naoji's mentor, the drunken decadent writer Uehara:

I think that in this first engagement, I have been able to push back the old morality, however little . . . And I intend to fight a second and a third engagement together with the child who will be born.

To give birth to the child of the man I love, and to raise him, will be the accomplishment of my moral revolution.

(*DOZ*, vol. 9, p. 240; tr. p. 173)

While each of these characters contains enough elements of self-portraiture to endow them with a strong sense of conviction, they are also sufficiently separate from their creator to take on distinctive identities of their own, and to complement the novel's thematic and structural designs, rather than overshadow them as some other Dazai protagonists have a tendency to do. Moreover, Dazai showed himself capable of treating them with an unaccustomed degree of ironic distance, especially the sodden Uehara, whom Naoji castigates as "a stupid country bumpkin who realized his dreams by coming to the big city and scoring a success in a scale quite unimagined even to himself" (*DOZ*, vol. 9, p. 235; tr. p. 165).

Many of the novel's thematic references to topics such as aristocracy, revolution, and the Bible are idiosyncratic or vague, but their very vagueness gives them a range and richness of potential application that deepens rather than diminishes their power and undoubtedly has helped to give *The Setting Sun* its prominent place not only among Dazai's works but among the landmark works of modern Japanese literature.

In *No Longer Human (Ningen shikkaku)*, Dazai created a narrower but more focused effect by concentrating on a single character, the protagonist-narrator Ōba Yōzō (a name he had already used for one of his earlier fictional alter egos). The narrative structure, which consists of a series of notebooks in which Yōzō records the key events of his life, sandwiched between a brief prologue and epilogue in which other characters provide background information and deliver their own assessments, is more carefully shaped and tauter than usual. This structure also allowed Dazai to exploit his penchant for directly addressing the reader in an intimate, natural-sounding voice even as he created a portrait of a tortured man continually at odds with the world of "normal" human beings. Once again, some of the situations and incidents have recognizable parallels in the author's life, but others do not, and a large part of Dazai's life is left out: significantly, Yōzō's story ends with a collapse analogous to what Dazai experienced around 1937; the recovery, remarriage, and professional success of the following years have no place in the novel.

Again the linguistic touch is deft, and heartfelt pathos is finely leavened with touches of mordant humor. The subsidiary characters are more carefully drawn than usual, some with sympathy, some with devastating irony.

No Longer Human is the most coherent and fully realized expression of the central Dazai theme: the impossibility of living without deceit and victimizing others, and the pain experienced by anyone ingenuous enough to try it. Dazai was clearheaded enough, however, to present Yōzō in the contrasting guises of a sensitive, well-meaning innocent whose appeals for help go unheeded and a spoiled, narcissistic incompetent who creates disasters for himself and those who care for him.

In the epilogue, one of Yōzō's old acquaintances delivers the final and definitive verdict: " 'It's his father's fault,' she said unemotionally. 'The Yōzō we knew was so easy-going and amusing, and if only he hadn't drunk—no, even though he did drink—he was a good boy, divine' " (*DOZ*, vol. 9, p. 470; revised from tr. p. 177). This retroactive vindication of the protagonist's self-proclaimed weaknesses and shame is often cited as an example of Dazai's skillful handling of perspective, but blaming everything on the father (like Dazai's own, a distant and forbidding figure) is not altogether convincing, and Dazai had already filled the novel with opportunities for the sympathetic reader to reach a similar evaluation of Yōzō. The reversal does, however, make for an emphatic ending.

No Longer Human can be read as a kind of summing up of Dazai's literary career, not only because of its scope and thematic clarity but because it was the last major work that he completed. By the time he had finished it, there were signs that Dazai was once again preparing to end his life. Entanglements with women had been another conspicuous feature of his postwar life; one of these provided much of the inspiration for *The Setting Sun*, but another culminated in a double suicide on the night of 13 June 1948. The drowned bodies of Dazai and his companion were discovered a few days later in the Tamagawa Canal, not far from his home on the western outskirts of Tokyo, on 19 June, which would have been his thirty-ninth birthday.

His final work, left uncompleted at his death, bears the ominous title *Guddo bai (Goodbye)*, but the content centers on the maneuvers of a harried man intent on disengaging from relationships with various women in his life, and the tone is remarkably casual and lighthearted, with Dazai's comic talents displayed to the full.

Conclusion

In his last years, references to the Bible, and especially to the life of Jesus Christ, played an increasingly prominent part in Dazai's writing. This should not be taken to indicate that Dazai had become a believer in Christianity, at least in any conventional sense, any more than his earlier engagement with Marxism suggested a sense of deep-seated political commitment. If anything, Dazai seems to have seen the story of Jesus not so much as a religious text but as a kind of novel whose protagonist was both human and divine, blessed with superior moral and spiritual stature, but cursed with the tragic destiny of having to suffer in redemption for the sins of an uncomprehending humanity that rejected and stigmatized him. The attractions of such a reading to a man like Dazai are obvious, but he remained conscious, sometimes to the point of obsession, of his own shortcomings, and there is little evidence that he sought to be viewed or treated as a latter-day Christ.

Following his own death, however, he has repeatedly been described in divine or Christ-like terms, with art as his religion. In *Dazai Osamu ron* (On Dazai Osamu) a ground-breaking critical study of Dazai published six years after his death, the critic Okuno Takeo describes him as "a Christ who was crucified for us." Yamanouchi Shōshi, one of the most prominent among contemporary Dazai scholars, has written of him as a shamanic figure endowed with the gifts of prophecy and compassionate self-sacrifice. The novelist and playwright Inoue Hisashi, who has himself written a play inspired by episodes from Dazai's life, describes him as the actor in a one-man play of his own composition, the main theme of which is the passion of Christ, with all of "the ecstasy and terror / Of having been chosen"—but just as eager to act out the subsidiary role of Judas.

Not all of the reviews have been so glowing. Even ardent admirers such as Okuno and Inoue are keenly aware of the narcissism, the pratfalls, and the pretensions that accompany Dazai's enactment of his passion play. His writing has been deplored by some of the major figures in modern Japanese literature, most notably Shiga Naoya (a revered authority figure in the Japanese literary world in Dazai's day, whom Dazai, probably in large part for that very reason, had mocked repeatedly and mercilessly) and Mishima Yukio, who castigated Dazai for elevating weakness to a virtue in his life and art and for blaming others for wounds that were self-inflicted, and who suggested that many of Dazai's defects of character could have been remedied by a regimen of cold water treatments, gymnastic exercises, and a more regular lifestyle.

Outside of Japan, Dazai has ranked among the most widely translated and studied modern Japanese writers since the 1950s. The same qualities for which he has been both acclaimed and condemned at home have found their champions and detractors abroad as well.

Through it all Dazai's popularity has endured, but while his life and writing must have inspired much emulation among his many admirers, it is hard to detect much obvious influence on major writers of succeeding generations. Rather, Dazai's work at its best represents the culmination of one of the most important and distinctive major forms in modern Japanese literature, extending its boundaries to achieve a height and richness (or bringing the inherent self-indulgence of the form to a nadir) that has yet to be surpassed.

Selected Bibliography

PRIMARY WORKS
COLLECTED WORKS

Dazai Osamu zenshū. 13 vols. Tokyo: Chikuma Shobō, 1971. (Abbreviated as *DOZ* in citations.)

MAJOR COLLECTIONS OF SHORT STORIES IN JAPANESE

Bannen. Tokyo: Sunagoya Shobō, 1936.
Fugaku hyakkei. Tokyo: Jinbun Shobō, 1940.
Hashire Merosu. Tokyo: Kawade Shobō, 1940.
Tokyo hakkei. Tokyo: Jitsugyō no Nihonsha, 1941.
Otogizōshi. Tokyo: Chikuma Shobō, 1945.
Shinshaku shokokubanashi. Tokyo: Seikatsusha, 1945.
Buiyon no tsuma. Tokyo: Chikuma Shobō, 1947.

COLLECTIONS OF SHORT STORIES IN ENGLISH

Dazai Osamu: Selected Stories and Sketches. Trans. and edited by James O'Brien. Ithaca, N.Y.: Cornell University East Asia Papers, no. 33, 1983. (Contains translations of sixteen Dazai stories.)
A Late Chrysanthemum: Twenty-one Stories from the Japanese. Trans. and edited by Lane Dunlop. San Francisco: North Point Press, 1986. (Contains translations of four Dazai stories as well as translations of works by other authors.)
Run, Melos! and Other Stories. Trans. and edited by Ralph F. McCarthy. Tokyo: Kodansha International, 1988. (Contains translations of seven Dazai stories.)
Crackling Mountain and Other Stories by Osamu Dazai. Trans. and edited by James O'Brien. Rutland, Vt., and Tokyo: Charles E. Tuttle Company, 1989. (Contains translations of eleven Dazai stories.)
Self Portraits: Tales from the Life of Japan's Great Decadent Romantic Osamu Dazai. Trans. and edited by Ralph F. McCarthy. Tokyo and New York: Kodansha International, 1991. (Contains translations of eighteen Dazai stories.)
Blue Bamboo: Tales of Fantasy and Romance. Trans. and edited by Ralph F. McCarthy. Tokyo, New York,

and London: Kodansha International, 1993. (Contains translations of seven Dazai stories.)

INDIVIDUAL SHORT STORIES AND NOVELS

"Gyofukuki." 1933. Trans. by Thomas J. Harper as "Metamorphosis." In *Japan Quarterly* 17, no. 3:285–288 (1970). Trans. by James O'Brien as "Transformation." In his *Dazai Osamu: Selected Stories and Sketches*. Ithaca, N.Y.: Cornell University East Asia Papers, no. 33, 1983. Pp. 51–57. Trans. by James O'Brien as "Undine." In his *Crackling Mountain and Other Stories by Osamu Dazai*. Rutland, Vt., and Tokyo: Charles E. Tuttle Company, 1989. Pp. 68–79.

"Omoide." 1933. Trans. by James O'Brien as "Memories." In his *Dazai Osamu: Selected Stories and Sketches*. Ithaca, N.Y.: Cornell University East Asia Papers, no. 33, 1983. Pp. 16–50. Trans. by Phyllis Lyons as "Recollections." In her *The Saga of Dazai Osamu: A Critical Study with Translations*. Stanford, Calif.: Stanford University Press, 1985. Pp. 189–216. Trans. by Lane Dunlop as "Memories." In his *A Late Chrysanthemum: Twenty-one Stories from the Japanese*. San Francisco: North Point Press, 1986. Pp. 115–130. Trans. by James O'Brien as "Memories." In his *Crackling Mountain and Other Stories by Osamu Dazai*. Rutland, Vt., and Tokyo: Charles E. Tuttle Company, 1989. Pp. 17–67.

"Ha." 1934. Trans. by Eric Gangloff as "Leaves." *Chicago Review* 20, no. 1:31–41 (1968).

"Romanesuku." 1934. Trans. by John Nathan as "Romanesque." *Japan Quarterly* 12, no. 3:331–346 (1965). Trans. by Ralph F. McCarthy as "Romanesque." In his *Blue Bamboo: Tales of Fantasy and Romance*. Tokyo, New York, and London: Kodansha International, 1993. Pp. 103–131.

"Dasu gemaine." 1935. Trans. by James O'Brien as "Das Gemeine." In his *Dazai Osamu: Selected Stories and Sketches*. Ithaca, N.Y.: Cornell University East Asia Papers, no. 33, 1983. Pp. 72–96.

"Mangan." 1938. Trans. by Ralph F. McCarthy as "A Promise Fulfilled." In his *Run, Melos! and Other Stories*. Tokyo: Kodansha International, 1988. Pp. 7–10. Trans. by Ralph F. McCarthy as "A Promise Fulfilled." In his *Self Portraits: Tales from the Life of Japan's Great Decadent Romantic Osamu Dazai*. Tokyo and New York: Kodansha International, 1991. Pp. 65–67.

"Ubasute." 1938. Trans. by James O'Brien as "Putting Granny Out to Die." In his *Dazai Osamu: Selected Stories and Sketches*. Ithaca, N.Y.: Cornell University East Asia Papers, no. 33, 1983. Pp. 97–113.

"Fugaku hyakkei." 1939. Trans. by Ralph F. McCarthy as "One Hundred Views of Mount Fuji." In his *Run, Melos! and Other Stories*. Tokyo: Kodansha International, 1988. Pp. 11–42. Translated by Ralph F. McCarthy as "One Hundred Views of Mount Fuji." In his *Self Portraits: Tales from the Life of Japan's Great Decadent Romantic Osamu Dazai*. Tokyo and New York: Kodansha International, 1991. Pp. 69–90.

"Hashire Merosu." 1940. Trans. by Ralph F. McCarthy as "Run, Melos!" In his *Run, Melos! and Other Stories*. Tokyo: Kodansha International, 1988. Pp. 114–134. Trans. by James O'Brien as "Melos, Run!" In his *Crackling Mountain and Other Stories by Osamu Dazai*. Rutland, Vt., and Tokyo: Charles E. Tuttle Company, 1989. Pp. 110–126.

"Kakekomi uttae." 1940. Trans. by James O'Brien as "Heed My Plea." In his *Crackling Mountain and Other Stories by Osamu Dazai*. Rutland, Vt., and Tokyo: Charles E. Tuttle Company, 1989. Pp. 91–109.

Shin Hamuretto. Tokyo: Bungei Shunjūsha, 1941.

"Tokyo hakkei." 1941. Trans. by James O'Brien as "Eight Views of Tokyo." In his *Dazai Osamu: Selected Stories and Sketches*. Ithaca, N.Y.: Cornell University East Asia Papers, no. 33, 1983. Pp. 123–146. Trans. by Phyllis Lyons as "Eight Views of Tokyo." In her *The Saga of Dazai Osamu: A Critical Study with Translations*. Stanford, Calif.: Stanford University Press, 1985. Pp. 217–235. Trans. by Ralph F. McCarthy as "Eight Scenes from Tokyo." In his *Run, Melos! and Other Stories*. Tokyo: Kodansha International, 1988. Pp. 135–177. Trans. by Ralph F. McCarthy as "Eight Scenes from Tokyo." In his *Self Portraits: Tales from the Life of Japan's Great Decadent Romantic Osamu Dazai*. Tokyo and New York: Kodansha International, 1991. Pp. 145–173.

Tsugaru. Tokyo: Oyama Shoten, 1944. Trans. by James Westerhoven as *Return to Tsugaru: Travels of a Purple Tramp*. Tokyo and New York: Kodansha International, 1985. Trans. by Phyllis Lyons as *Tsugaru*. In her *The Saga of Dazai Osamu: A Critical Study with Translations*. Stanford, Calif.: Stanford University Press, 1985. Pp. 271–385.

Otogizōshi. Tokyo: Chikuma Shobō, 1945. (Dazai's collection contains four stories. James O'Brien has translated one of these in his *Dazai Osamu: Selected Stories and Sketches* and two in his *Crackling Mountain*.)

Shinshaku shokokubanashi. Tokyo: Seikatsusha, 1945. (Dazai's collection contains twelve stories. James O'Brien has translated two of these in his *Dazai Osamu: Selected Stories and Sketches* and two in his *Crackling Mountain*. Ralph F. McCarthy has translated one in his *Blue Bamboo*.)

"Pandora no hako." 1945–1946.

"Jūgonenkan." 1946.

"Kunō no nenkan." 1946. Trans. by Phyllis Lyons as "An Almanac of Pain." In her *The Saga of Dazai Osamu: A Critical Study with Translations*. Stanford, Calif.: Stanford University Press, 1985. Pp. 262–270.

"Shin'yū kōkan." 1946. Trans. by Ivan Morris as "The Courtesy Call." In his *Modern Japanese Stories*. Rutland, Vt., and Tokyo: Tuttle, 1962. Pp. 464–480.

"Buiyon no tsuma." 1947. Trans. by Donald Keene as "Villon's Wife." In his *Modern Japanese Literature*. New York: Grove Press, 1956. Pp. 398–414.

Shayō. Tokyo: Shinchōsha, 1947. Trans. by Donald Keene as *The Setting Sun*. New York: New Directions, 1956.

Ningen shikkaku. Tokyo: Chikuma Shobō, 1948. Trans. by Donald Keene as *No Longer Human*. New York: New Directions, 1958.

SECONDARY WORKS

BIOGRAPHICAL AND CRITICAL STUDIES

Brudnoy, David. "The Immutable Despair of Dazai Osamu." *Monumenta Nipponica* 23, no. 3:457–474 (1968).

Dower, John W. *Embracing Defeat: Japan in the Wake of World War II*. New York: W. W. Norton and Company, 1999. Pp. 158–161.

Inoue Hisashi. "'Nānchatte' ojisan no kufū: Aru sanmon shōsetsuka no kōenroku no nukigaki." *Shinchō* 95, no. 7:142–145 (July 1998).

Keene, Donald. "Dazai Osamu." In his *Landscapes and Portraits: Appreciations of Japanese Culture*. Tokyo and Palo Alto, Calif.: Kodansha International, 1971. Pp. 186–203.

———. "Dazai Osamu and the Burai-ha." In his *Dawn to the West: Japanese Literature in the Modern Era*. Vol. 1. New York: Holt, Rinehart, and Winston, 1984. Pp. 1022–1112.

Lyons, Phyllis. " 'Art is Me': Dazai Osamu's Narrative Voice as a Permeable Self." *Harvard Journal of Asiatic Studies* 41, no. 1:93–110 (1981).

———. *The Saga of Dazai Osamu: A Critical Study with Translations*. Stanford, Calif.: Stanford University Press, 1985. (Includes translations of "Omoide," "Tokyo hakkei," "Tsugaru, "Kunō no nenkan," and two other pieces.)

McCarthy, Ralph. "Dazai Osamu: After the Silence." *Japan Quarterly* 39, no. 2:225–237 (April–June 1992). (Includes "Down with Decadence," a translation of "Dekadan kōgi," 1939.)

Miyoshi, Masao. "Till Death Do Us Part." In his *Accomplices of Silence: The Modern Japanese Novel*. Berkeley, Calif.: University of California Press, 1974. Pp. 122–140.

O'Brien, James. *Dazai Osamu*. Boston: G. K. Hall & Company, 1975.

———. "Dazai's *The Setting Sun*." In *Approaches to the Modern Japanese Novel*. Edited by Kinya Tsuruta and Thomas E. Swann. Tokyo: Sophia University Press, 1976. Pp. 19–24.

Okuno Takeo. *Dazai Osamu ron Zōho kaitei-ban*. Tokyo: Shunjūsha, 1968.

Sōma Shōichi. *Hyōden Dazai Osamu Kaitei-ban*. 2 vols. Hirosaki: Tsugaru Shobō, 1995.

Ueda, Makoto. "Dazai Osamu." In his *Modern Japanese Writers and the Nature of Literature*. Stanford, Calif.: Stanford University Press, 1976. Pp. 145–172.

Wolfe, Alan. *Suicidal Narrative in Modern Japan: The Case of Dazai Osamu*. Princeton, N.J.: Princeton University Press, 1990.

Yamanouchi Shōshi. "Dazai Osamu no miryoku." *Kokubungaku Kaishaku to Kanshō* 61, no. 6:10–13 (June 1996).

———, ed. *Dazai Osamu chojutsu sōran*. Tokyo: Tōkyōdō Shuppan, 1997.

ENCHI FUMIKO
1905–1986

LUCY NORTH

ENCHI FUMIKO is one of the few women writers in Japan who has garnered an incontestable place for herself in the history of modern Japanese literature. Even if she rarely figures in mainstream literary histories, which have until recently tended to focus mainly on male writers and their groups and which often mention women writers as an afterthought (usually as a string of names), Enchi Fumiko is nearly always mentioned, however briefly, as one of the most prominent of these. Her writing is known especially for its depiction of the way women suffered, often silently, under the Japanese *ie*, or household system, as well as for its evocation of female eroticism and mystery.

Above all, Enchi's work is known for its frequent incorporation of themes and texts from the classical Japanese canon. In later life, she translated the text *Genji monogatari* (early 11th century; *The Tale of Genji*, 1976) into modern colloquial Japanese. (*Genji monogatari* was written by Murasaki Shikibu, a lady-in-waiting in the entourage of Empress Shōshi.) Rarely, however, do critics do more than point out the fact of her sheer learnedness as a scholar and translator of the Japanese classics (including *Genji monogatari*): the techniques whereby she incorporates classical texts and themes into her works, and the pos-sible significance of their use, have generally been overlooked.

A prolific writer in the years after World War II, Enchi won numerous literary prizes. She played an important part in encouraging other women writers, particularly in her role as chairperson for eighteen years (1958–1976) of the Women's Literature Committee (Joryū bungakusha kai). She also edited two collections of essays written about prominent women figures in Japanese history and literature titled *Gendai joryū bungaku* and *Jinbutsu Nihon no joseishi*. In 1979 she was honored by her country as a Person of Cultural Achievement (Bunka kōrōsha), and in 1985, shortly before her death in March 1986, she was awarded the Order of Culture (Bunka kunshō), a high national honor bestowed by the emperor. She was praised for having produced "works of eroticism and mystery that explore the depths of female psychology and the obsessive attachments and destiny of human beings."

Enchi was the daughter of Ueda Kazutoshi (1867–1937; also known as Ueda Mannen), a distinguished classical scholar and philologist who is considered the founder of Japanese linguistics. A professor at Tokyo Imperial University, Ueda played a major role in the institution of so-called national language studies *(kokugogaku)*, a discipline that linked linguistics with a sense of national identity. As a powerful bureaucrat in language education policy for the Meiji government, Ueda was a member of his nation's cultural and educational elite, and in 1926 he was appointed to the house of Peers. Ueda is now generally remembered for the important dictionaries he produced, but he was also one of the founding fathers of the modern academic canon of classical Japanese literature, teaching courses in the national literature at Tokyo Imperial University. As one of the prime movers behind the government's efforts toward colloquialization of the modern written language *(genbun-itchi)*, he was one of the shapers, on a linguistic level, of the very medium in which modern Japanese literature itself was created.

As the daughter of such an important and influential academic, Enchi could take access to books, scholars, and libraries for granted. She also knew the importance of appealing to male scholars, critics, and academics, who held the key to getting published and getting noticed. By her own admission, she had an Electra complex with regard to her father, and the cachet of her father's name must have served her well (although she later professed to having had a profound ambivalence about this in her early years as a writer). At the same time, Enchi had yearnings to be independent, and she had an interest in feminist thought. During her association with left-wing writers in the 1920s and 1930s she read Friedrich Engels, Karl Marx, and Rosa Luxemburg. She also participated in the women's left-wing journal *Nyonin Geijutsu* (Women's arts).

It is interesting to consider the implications of her need, conscious or unconscious, to appeal to father figures—scholars, academics, and critics, many of whom had connections with her father—and the interaction between this and her developing feminist sensibilities. Enchi's relationship with the canon of Japanese classical literature can be seen in the light of her relationship with her father as a symbolic figure of literary patriarchy. Enchi wrote about her father all her life, in memoirs and in reminiscences—and the impression is of an adoring, grateful daughter who felt nothing but admiration for her scholarly, liberal father. However, it is possible that the uses she made of classical Japanese literature in her fictional prose reflected in part a dutiful daughter's attempt at rebellion.

A Literary Childhood

Enchi Fumiko (née Ueda Fumiko) was born in 1905, in Mukōyanagihara-machi, in what was then Asakusa Ward in Tokyo, the youngest of three children of Ueda Kazutoshi and his wife, Murakami Tsuruko. Both parents were of samurai stock: her father's family had originally been based in Owari domain (present-day Nagoya), and her mother had come from a family in the Hosokawa domain in Kyushu. By the time Fumiko was born, her father was an established professor at Tokyo Imperial University and had held a number of prominent positions on several government boards of education. Though not wealthy, the family was financially comfortable—able to support three maids, a rickshaw man and his wife, a nursemaid, and several live-in students (some of whom later became prominent government officials). From Enchi's later memoirs, it is possible to detect other accoutrements of bourgeois life: her father had a marvelous library filled with books and exotic European furniture. To his book collection was later added the collection of his former teacher at the Imperial University, Basil Hall Chamberlain.

The Ueda family moved several times and in 1911 settled in Kiyomizu-chō (Ikenohata in present Taitō Ward); in 1926 they moved again, to Koishikawa Ward (present Bunkyō Ward). Fumiko moved away from home when she married Enchi Yoshimatsu, settling eventually in Nakano Ward. She also spent summers in a villa in Karuizawa after 1938. However, in 1946, she and her husband moved back to the house in Kiyomizu-chō, where they lived with Enchi's mother until her death in 1956; and it was in this location that Enchi lived for the rest of her days. The location of Enchi's home in

Ikenohata is important for an understanding of her writing: situated near Western-oriented Ueno with its museums and the modern space of the park and, also, in the opposite direction, near Tokyo University, it was also near the *shitamachi*, or "low city," the old neighborhoods associated with the imaginary and actual space of the past ("Edo," or "traditional" Tokyo). Enchi's writing, too, places itself on a border between the premodern and modern, high and low culture, between the university and the *shitamachi*. In some of Enchi's text, protagonists traverse the space between the premodern and modern by means of a slope, or hillside.

As the last daughter of the family, Fumiko was coddled by everyone, including maids and houseboys, but her father and grandmother are the two people who figure most prominently in her reminiscences. Her father seems to have been especially fond of Fumiko—and proud of her precocious intelligence, often telling her he wished she had been a boy. Her memoirs abound with descriptions of the walks they took together in Ueno Park, which was just above their house, and their special closeness. Mentions of her father always include descriptions of his stupendous collection of books, old and new, which overflowed from his study out into the corridor and down into the parlor, making, as Enchi described it, the "very joints of the house creak with their weight." The house was also filled with a variety of the latest journals, and it was among these journals and books that Fumiko played, even before she learned to read.

Notwithstanding her father's tremendous book collection, however, Enchi later wrote in her memoirs that the person who provided "the bridge" between her and literature, and who was the original impetus for her to become a "writer of tales" *(monogatari sakusha)*, was in fact her father's mother, her grandmother, Ine. Ine had lived the first half of her life in the Edo period, and she had a strong interest in products of the Edo imagination, in ghost stories and tales of *bakemono*, or monsters, and in plots of Kabuki and Bunraku plays. She was a consummate storyteller, and she could also recite whole passages straight out of the Edo-period writer Kyokutei Bakin's classic *Nansō satomi hakkenden* (1814–1832; The tale of eight virtuous heroes) from memory. Fumiko was given a thorough priming by her grandmother in ghost stories, fictional romances, and in the plots of Kabuki plays—especially in those of late-Edo playwrights Tsuruya Namboku and Kawatake Mokuami, whose plays feature an eroticized blend of cruelty and beauty, of cruel women torturing weak, beautiful girls. Enchi's reminiscences abound with descriptions of the way, in the mornings, she would go in to lie with her grandmother, who would tell her these stories, adding her own slant to them, utterly entrancing her little granddaughter. The significance of orally told versions of stories, and the difference between these and stories that are apparently fixed in books, and thus authoritative, are important issues to bear in mind when reading Enchi's work.

Fumiko entered a primary school at age seven, but she was sickly and frequently missed classes or had to be collected and taken home by rickshaw. When she learned to read, she immersed herself in the early-eleventh-century text *Genji monogatari (The Tale of Genji)*. At thirteen, she entered a girls' school affiliated with Japan Women's University. A precocious student, Fumiko regarded her fellow students as uncultured and unsophisticated. In one reminiscence she recalls being repulsed by their provincial accents. She later reported that the sanctimonious atmosphere of the school, run by the educational innovator Naruse Jinzō, did not accord with her own aesthetic sensibilities, already thoroughly steeped by then in the amours of Prince Genji, the dashing, romantic adventures of Bakin's eight virtuous heroes, the ghostly tales of the Edo-period writer Ueda Akinari, and the decadent drama of late-Edo Kabuki. By this time, she was extremely widely read: besides the various works in Yūhōdō's 121-volume collection of classical Japanese literature published during the years 1911 through 1917, she was reading modern Japanese writers such as Izumi Kyōka, Nagai Kafū, and Tanizaki Jun'ichirō and, in translation, Western writers such as Oscar Wilde, E. T. A. Hoffman, and Edgar Allan Poe.

Fumiko quit school in 1922, at the age of seventeen: she later claimed it was because she had read Nagai Kafū's *Shōsetsu sahō* (1920; How to write *shōsetsu*), in which he argued that a vital qualification for a writer was a thorough knowledge of a variety of literatures. A sense of amazement, gratitude, guilt, and obligation to her father for allowing her to quit school stayed with her throughout her life. Considering that she only had one more year before graduation, it does seem a remarkable indulgence. From then on, Fumiko pursued a course of reading and tutoring tailored to her every whim. Tutors were chosen by her father to instruct her in English language and literature, Chinese literature, Bible studies, and French and Russian literature. She read whatever she fancied in her father's study, and for foreign literature she went to Ueno Library.

Coming of Age in the 1920s

In 1924, having heard a lecture by Osanai Kaoru, a leader of the New Theater Movement, which presented in translation plays by Western playwrights such as Henrik Ibsen, August Strindberg, and Maurice Maeterlinck, Fumiko tried her hand at writing plays. Beginning in 1926, she attended Osanai's lectures on drama at Keio University, the only woman in an auditorium full of men, and she managed to publish some of her plays in Osanai's literary coterie magazine *Geki to Hyōron* (Drama and criticism). In 1928, Osanai introduced Fumiko to Hasegawa Shigure, the editor of the women's journal *Nyonin geijutsu*. She began submitting her plays to this journal, and some of them were published. Through *Nyonin geijutsu*, Fumiko became acquainted with many left-wing writers, including Hirabayashi Taiko, who became a lifelong friend; and she also embarked on an affair with a leading light of the left-wing movement, Kataoka Teppei. In October 1928, Fumiko's play *Banshun sōya* (A turbulent night in late spring) was produced for the stage at Osanai's Tsukiji Little Theater.

Fumiko reached adulthood in the 1920s, a time when Japan was flooded with various streams of left-wing thought, including socialism, Marxism, and anarchism. Many educated, intelligent young people hoping to be writers were affected by these ideas; Enchi was no exception. However, despite her dramatic aspirations and her interest in left-wing literature, the fact that she was a daughter of an extremely high-ranking government official was in these circles a definite disadvantage. Fumiko sensed this herself and she was made aware of it by colleagues. Fumiko seems to have been anxious to tone down her comfortable financial state. In one reminiscence, she recalls wearing dowdy kimonos and stripping herself of jewelry to go to *Nyonin geijutsu* meetings. She also seems to have been tormented by guilt about the consequences that her literary activities might have for her beloved father. The dilemmas she felt are evident in her early plays and stories, in which pairs of political (or pragmatic) and artistic women are contrasted. The artistic women suffer from intellectual and emotional paralysis: they are held back by their appreciation for the artistic production of the past from joining any political movement, which seems to demand a rejection of art and tradition.

In 1930, Fumiko married Enchi Yoshimatsu, an editor for the daily newspaper *Tokyo nichinichi shinbun*—despite the fact that she professed an immediate repugnance for the provincial manner and opinions of the man, who hailed from the San'in region in western Japan. She later wrote that her strongest motivation for marriage was the desire not to be an embarrassment to her father because of her literary aspirations. By marrying, she could leave her family and change her name. There was also the desire for financial security. In 1931, Enchi gave birth to her only child, a daughter, Motoko. The marriage proved disappointing and dissatisfying.

War and Classics

Beginning in 1935, Enchi turned seriously to writing prose fiction, managing to publish several stories, some of them lengthy, in a coterie magazine. In 1939, she published a miscellany of her previously published works (short stories, essays, critical works, and plays). By this time, however, Japan's government was firmly in the grip of the military, and the more liberal atmosphere that had allowed for left-wing literary activity had given way to repression and to cultural chauvinism. Suddenly Japan's literary heritage was very much in vogue. Responding to this changed atmosphere, Enchi began after 1938 to read and study ancient texts and to contribute to a magazine called *Murasaki* (named after the author of *The Tale of Genji* and run by the *Genji* scholar Ikeda Kikan) that published articles on classical literature.

During the war, Enchi participated in government efforts to requisition writers' support for the war effort. In 1941, she accompanied several other writers on a month-long trip to Taiwan, South China, and Hainan Island as a member of the Navy Ministry Writers War Support Group. In 1943, she visited northern Korea on a two-week trip as a member of the Japan Patriotic Writers Association. The wholeheartedness of Enchi's participation in these trips is a subject that has yet to be explored.

The years just before, during, and just after the war brought loss after loss for Enchi. In 1937, her father died of cancer. In 1938, at the age of thirty-three, Enchi contracted tubercular mastitis and had to undergo a single mastectomy. In the air raids on Tokyo in May 1945, her house in Nakano was burned to the ground. Enchi saw out the war's end in her Karuizawa villa. The following year, she and her husband returned to the family home of her childhood in Tokyo, which thenceforth became her residence. Enchi was diagnosed that year with uterine cancer, and she had to have a hysterectomy, at the age of forty-one. She was in poor health for two years thereafter. (Enchi's ill health later led her to call herself a veritable wholesaler in illness: she had an operation for a detached retina in her right eye in 1969, and another for a detached retina in her left eye in 1973.)

For several years after the war, Enchi's attempts at getting her manuscripts published were met with rejection: she considered this period her time of "bleakness," a time when she was "locked out" of the literary establishment, having to "roam around aimlessly before its tightly shut gates." This was a second time when she had to feel like an outsider. The literary scene at this time was dominated by the left-wing writer Miyamoto Yuriko and her husband Kenji, and other intellectuals and writers surrounding the journal *Shin Nihon Bungaku* (Literature for the new Japan). Hayashi Fumiko, who had participated enthusiastically for the government as a war reporter in Malaysia, also enjoyed popularity. In contrast to Miyamoto and Hayashi, however, Enchi seemed to have been regarded as a writer whose time was over—and at this time, the cachet of her father's name may have been a hindrance rather than a help. The first few years after the war saw a trickle of stories published in minor journals; in 1949, she published what later became the first part of the first chapter of one of her most successful novels, *Onnazaka* (1957; *The Waiting Years*, 1971). In the immediate postwar years of soaring inflation, Enchi's financial situation was precarious and she resorted to writing lightweight romances, which may have further hindered her reputation.

Postwar Recognition

The transition for Enchi from outsider to insider status in the literary world seems to have come with the help of establishment male scholars and literati. Even during her years of being shut out of literary coteries, Enchi managed to cultivate, and make use of, her connections. For some years after the war, she held a study group known as the Yanaka Salon at her own home, in which scholars, writers, and members of the cultural establishment participated. In 1950, a scholar of French literature applied influence on Enchi's behalf that resulted in publication of her short story "Kōmyō kōgyō no e" (A portrait of the empress

Kōgyō) in a major literary journal. In 1953 the publication of her story "Himojii tsukihi" (Bleak months and days) in *Chūō Kōron* brought extravagant praise from male critics in major newspaper reviews and won her the sixth Women's Literature Prize in March 1954. Also in 1954, she published a collection of stories with "Himojii tsukihi" as the title story: the collection garnered praise from the prominent critic and writer Masamune Hakuchō in a 1955 newspaper review (he said the descriptions of men in the title story made his "flesh creep").

After a long period of not knowing how to position herself, and of setbacks, Enchi from this time appears to have found her niche. Her recognition in the literary world was secured, particularly as a writer associated with Japan's classical heritage. There followed a tremendous outpouring of literary work. Enchi's rate of production and publication, which continued unabated over the next few decades, has been compared variously by exuberant biographers to a cascade of shooting stars, or a river that suddenly bursts its banks. It was not unusual for her to publish several collections of short stories a year, and she was often at the same time serializing several long prose narratives simultaneously in different journals. She was also participating in various literary committees, translating, and writing on the Japanese language and Japanese classical literature—as a figure of authority. (For example, in 1958, she participated in a round-table discussion on classical literature with three of the paramount establishment critics of the day, Ikeda Kikan, Nakamura Shin'ichirō, and Yamamoto Kenkichi.) Enchi's newfound authority might simply have been a function of her improvement as a writer, but it seems clear that part of the reason she suddenly became a writer in demand at this time of social upheaval and questioning of national identity was that now the connection she offered with the nation's classics had become a source of solace and nostalgia. At the same time, Enchi had found a way of resolving the dilemma she felt in her youth between her classical heritage and politics: that is to say, her use of classical literature

was made to serve a political, and specifically a feminist, purpose.

From 1955 to 1960, Enchi resumed her early interest in drama. She contributed drama criticism to a magazine, and she wrote numerous scripts based on other writers' fiction (interestingly, these writers were all male). These plays, many of which were directed by Kubota Mantarō, were performed either at the Kabuki-za Theater as *shimpa* plays (a kind of Kabuki-Western hybrid), or at the Shimbashi Enbujō Theater by the Kabuki actor Onoue Kikugorō V and his acting troupe. Among those works of fiction she adapted for the stage were Tanizaki Junichirō's *Bushūkō hiwa* (1932; *The Secret History of the Lord of Musashi*, 1982), Mori Ōgai's *Gan* (1913; *The Wild Goose*, 1959), Izumi Kyōka's *Yushima mōde* (1900; Yushima pilgrimage), Shiga Naoya's "Akanishi Kakita," (1917; "Akanishi Kakita," 1987), and Ueda Akinari's "Asaji ga yado" ("The House amidst the Thickets," 1974). She also made some of her own narratives into plays: for example, *Namamiko monogatari* (1965; *A Tale of False Fortunes*, 2000), performed in 1966. (*The Waiting Years* was also written up as a play by Kikuta Kazuo and performed in 1970.)

Over the late 1950s and 1960s Enchi published a prodigious number of fascinating short stories and longer prose fiction. Several of the short stories she wrote during this time have since taken a paramount position in her oeuvre, including "Yō" (1956; "Enchantress," 1961) and "Nise no en—shūi" (1957; "A Bond for Two Lifetimes—Gleanings," 1982). In March 1957, *The Waiting Years*, which had been serialized sporadically in parts in a variety of journals since 1949, finally came out in a single volume, and in November 1957, this narrative won the prestigious Noma Literary Prize (jointly with Uno Chiyo's narrative *Ohan*). The other novel most widely associated with Enchi's name, *Onnamen* (*Masks*, 1983) was published in 1958. Another important novel, *Komachi hensō* (Visions of Komachi), was published in 1965, and a long narrative that has been seen by some critics as Enchi's pièce de résistance, *Namamiko mono-*

gatari (*A Tale of False Fortunes*, 2000), was published in 1965 (though it had been serialized beginning in 1959), winning for Enchi the Women's Literature Award (Joryū bungaku shō) in 1966 (she had won the Women Writers' Award, or Joryū bungakusha shō, in 1956).

Raiding the Classical Canon

Enchi was well versed in various literatures—English, French, Russian, and Chinese—but without a doubt, she was most versatile in the classical literature of Japan, and she put this versatility to consummate effect in her own writing. Her favorite texts were *The Tale of Genji*, which became a rich source of themes in her own work, the tales of Ueda Akinari, and Kyokutei Bakin's *Nansō satomi hakkenden* (The tale of eight virtuous heroes). Enchi frequently embedded or wove together ancient classical texts in her own narratives, using them in a variety of ways. She used themes and situations from *The Tale of Genji*, the Noh repertory, quotations from *Ise Monogatari* (early tenth century; *Tales of Ise*, 1968), Ono no Komachi's poems, and many other classical texts. In her narrative "A Bond for Two Lifetimes—Gleanings," she included a modern version, or translation, of an entire story by Ueda Akinari. Furthermore, Enchi freely made up her own "classical" texts and embedded them in her narratives. This, for example, is the case in *A Tale of False Fortunes*, in which a narrator, clearly identifiable with Enchi herself, claims to have read an old text in her youth that has since been lost and proceeds to reproduce it from memory in her old age, complete with "actual" quotations. The story she tells fits in with a context provided by actually existing texts (all by women) such as *Izumi Shikibu nikki* (c. 1008; *The Izumi Shikibu Diary*, 1969), *Makura no sōshi* (c. 996; *The Pillow Book of Sei Shōnagon*, 1967), *Murasaki Shikibu nikki* (c. 1010; *The Diary of Lady Murasaki*, 1996), and *Eiga monogatari* (c. 1030; *A Tale of Flowering Fortunes*, 1980). It is also the case in *Saimu* (1976; Colored mist), a narrative that features an ancient scroll consisting of pictures and text, written in "quotations," and swatches of made-up classical Japanese (*gikōbun*, a hybrid of modern and classical language), depicting the erotic relationship between a shrine priestess and her male attendant.

At the same time, in her readings of texts from the classical canon, Enchi picked out female figures that were traditionally regarded simply as horrifying, macabre, or ridiculous and brought out their erotic and creative sides. Such, for example, is the Lady Rokujō, featured in *Masks*, a terrifying presence in *The Tale of Genji* who wreaks havoc when her living spirit (and, later, her ghost) wanders from her body. There is also the "wispy-haired lady" in chapter 63 of *Tales of Ise*, an elderly woman who is beset by sexual desire, featured in "Enchantress." In her oeuvre, Enchi took these figures and overlaid them with the figure of the ancient *miko* (a medium or shrine maiden), as well as the priestess of the Kamo Shrine, or Saiin, to produce a figure who is mature, sexually active, strong, independent, and at the same time creative—and literary. Drawing out literary, creative elements in these figures, Enchi implied an equivalency between erotic and literary powers.

In 1967, Enchi began work on a translation into modern colloquial Japanese of the classic text *The Tale of Genji*, which she had been reading and rereading avidly since childhood. The renowned classical scholars Tamagami Takuya and Inukai Kiyoshi and the scholar and writer Takanishi Hiroko helped advise on the translation, which was published as a ten-volume set in 1972 and 1973. Meanwhile, Enchi also wrote prose fiction. In 1972, she published the story collection *Yūkon* (Playful spirit), a trilogy consisting of three quite separate middle-length narratives, "Kitsunebi" (Foxfires), "Yūkon," and "Hebi no Koe" (Voice of a snake). The collection, which combines narrative categories, situations, and themes characteristic of *The Tale of Genji* with aspects and plot components reminiscent of Kabuki and *shimpa* plays, won the Grand Prize for Japanese Literature the same year.

Enchi's Final Years

Enchi was truly an indefatigable writer, and even at the end of her life, when she was in her seventies and had lost most of the sight in both of her eyes and had to write with the help of an amanuensis, she was still taking on writing assignments. Over the course of 1975 and 1976, she published a long narrative called *Karuizawa* (later changed to *Saimu*, Colored mist). In 1978, she published in serialized form the long prose narrative *Shokutaku no nai ie* (The house with no table), which appeared in two volumes in 1979. In 1982, she published yet another long narrative *Kikujidō* (1984; Chrysanthemum child). She continued to publish essays on a variety of subjects, as well as collections of autobiographical writings. However, in June 1985, Enchi suffered a mild stroke and was hospitalized for nine months; she collected her Order of Culture award in a wheelchair. Having returned home from the hospital in March 1986, she died of heart failure on 14 November 1986.

Enchi insisted before her death that her ashes be deposited with those of her father, Ueda Kazutoshi, in his gravesite, rather than with those of her husband. In the end, they were divided between the two gravesites, both in Yanaka Cemetery. Several more of Enchi's works were published posthumously in 1987, including the incomplete *Yume utsutsu no ki* (Record of reverie), a memoir of her life specifically as the daughter of her father.

Enchi's Feminism

The end of World War II brought the establishment of a new constitution for Japan and new values from abroad. Among these were women's legal equality with men, the right to vote, and the rescinding of the law making married women's adultery a crime. With the postwar occupation, a wave of feminism and a consciousness of the issue of women's rights swept Japan. Simone de Beauvoir's *La deuxième sexe* (1949) was translated and published in Japan in 1953. A comparative liberation of

sexual mores occurred. In the aftermath of wartime censorship, writers started to write about sex in startlingly explicit terms.

Enchi's sudden health crisis in 1946, when she was diagnosed with uterine cancer and underwent a hysterectomy, also had a symbolic significance which, as she put it, is "unique to women" and cannot be underestimated. In Japan, as in other countries, a woman's sexual life, and indeed her gender, is often viewed in terms of her reproductive capacity. Once this is gone, her sexual life can be assumed to be over, and she is considered no longer a woman but still less than a man. Enchi's hysterectomy opened her eyes to the suffering, physical and psychological, that women's bodies can bring them (in her reminiscences, she wrote that it made her feel a bond with other women), to the ideological significance accorded "femininity," and indeed female "reproductivity," and to the grip of that ideology over women's lives.

In the new Japan, Enchi was something of an old, and indeed old-fashioned, woman. But ideas about equality and women's liberation struck a chord with her. Enchi was aware through her unsatisfactory marriage of the constricting power of male authority and the strength given it by the bulwark of patriarchy. Writing about women, and women's plights, provided a release for Enchi's longtime need to write politically engaged literature. Depicting women in marriage and family situations was a much more comfortable thing for Enchi to do than trying to be a left-wing writer: besides being personally significant, it no longer left her vulnerable to the accusation of hypocrisy.

Enchi's early feminism is clear in two narratives that brought her to prominence in the postwar period, "Himojii tsukihi" (Bleak months and days) and *The Waiting Years*, both of which provide stark descriptions of the lives of two downtrodden women in domestic situations. "Himojii tsukihi," set in the immediate postwar period, concerns Saku, a woman who spends her days in drudgery, looking after an oppressive, invalid husband for whom she feels nothing but disgust and resentment. She struggles to make a living for her family (a spiteful daughter and blandly delinquent son), until she collapses and dies. *The Waiting Years*, set in the Meiji period, concerns Tomo, a wife who is entrusted by her husband to select for him a series of live-in concubines to tend to his sexual desires. As she witnesses her egotistical, libertine husband go through these women, and as she is forced to be an accomplice in the process, Tomo, an ordinary woman with no special education, feels sympathy for them, but suffers her own special isolation (and desexualization). The novel shows how the role of upholder of the family system, to which she faithfully adheres, offers nothing to Tomo but emotional pain, crushing responsibility, sacrifice, and exhaustion.

It is possible in these narratives to see a sympathy with a more traditional type of woman, one who is strongly passive and bears up to the unhappy circumstances of her marriage without resorting to active rebellion. The endings are similar in their implications. In "Himojii tsukihi," before her death the downtrodden Saku has a beautiful dream of a white river bird: after a long period of trying unsuccessfully to fly, it rises into the air, transformed into a phoenix. The suggestion is that this is an apotheosis for Saku after her purgatory. In *The Waiting Years*, Tomo relays a bitter deathbed message to her husband after a lifetime of servitude. She tells him not to put her ashes in his family tomb, but simply to "dump" her body into the sea. This message (with an implication that without a proper funeral she intends to haunt him after her death), we are informed, is enough to "break his ego in two." Even if these women spend their lives bound to grossly selfish husbands, the suggestion is that their stoic suffering brings them the moral victory.

The same theme of power within immobility for women is continued in *Masks*. In this narrative, however, the power is made mysterious: it becomes a silent, bewitching force emanating from one woman, Toganō Mieko, which drives and controls others. In this narrative, an abusive marriage like that in *The Waiting Years* has

happened in the past. Having suffered in a traditional family for years, Mieko, the wife (or rather widow, for her husband has died before the narrative begins), is now on a mission to undermine patriarchal lineage—by undermining the line of her husband with her lover's progeny. Though her son Akio's death has disrupted her original plan before the narrative begins, Mieko uses her widowed daughter-in-law Yasuko in the course of the narrative as bait to draw in two unsuspecting men, whom she plays off against each other. One of these men is deceived into impregnating Mieko's mentally disabled daughter Harume, who gives birth to a baby boy to replace Mieko's son. In *Masks*, we see women co-opting male promiscuity, turning it back on itself, and retrieving the power of female reproduction for themselves. Menstrual blood, and thus menstruation, traditionally regarded in Shinto and Buddhist belief and practice as a source of pollution, is revealed for what it is: a source of female power.

In *Masks*, this power within immobility, the ability to control others though taking no action oneself, is referred to as *mikoteki*, or "having the psychic qualities of a medium *(miko)*." Though Enchi never defines what she means by this term, she probably uses it in a loose sense to refer to women's propensity to control or be controlled by each other, in an identification with one another as victims or outsiders, and also in a stance of passive resistance to men. Toganō Mieko's interest in the figure of the Lady Rokujō in *The Tale of Genji*, and her comparison with the figure of the *miko* in her essay at the core of this text, "An Account of the Shrine in the Fields," invites the reader to make a comparison of Mieko herself with a *miko*-like woman. At the same time, it is notable that this fictional essay bears a close resemblance to passages in an essay later published by Enchi herself, *Genji monogatari shiken* (1974; A personal view of *The Tale of Genji*).

In the late 1950s, Enchi started to write stories about older women who are beset by strong sexual desire. Into these categories fall the protagonists of the short stories

"Enchantress," "A Bond For Two Lifetimes—Gleanings," and "Mimi yōraku" (1957; Earrings), as well as the protagonists of longer narratives such as *Hanachiruzato* (1961; Village of falling blossoms), *Masks,* and *Komachi hensō* (Visions of Komachi). Often these women are in their middle or late-middle years; sometimes they are women without wombs. Despite the fact that these women have in every case lost their "first bloom," they are capable of toying with men. These monstrous, unyielding, undomesticated women (whose powers consist of something attractive, mysterious and intimidating—*sei-en,* or "bewitchingly, weirdly beautiful"), women who torment men, represent the other side, the twin sister, of the strong, suffering, stoic, enduring wife. In Enchi's later writing, particularly in *Saimu* (Colored mist), this character of the older desiring woman shifted slightly to become that of the irresistibly attractive elderly—even aged—woman who exercises a compelling force over younger men. In *Saimu,* a new connection is made between the figure of the *miko* (a key figure in Enchi's works) and an ancient mother figure who draws men toward her in a union that is at once sexual and primevally, mythically maternal.

Reading Enchi

Throughout her life, Enchi made a number of translations from classical into modern colloquial Japanese. Her first translations were in 1943 of classical fairy tales, published in a collection titled *Otogi zōshi monogatari* (Tales of fairy tales) which appeared in a series that reflects its nationalist times, *Shōkokumin bungaku* (Literature for little national subjects). She also translated Ueda Akinari's *Ugetsu monogatari* (1768; *Ugetsu monogatari, Tales of Moonlight and Rain,* 1974) and *Harusame monogatari* (1808; *Tales of the Spring Rain Harusame monogatari,* 1975); *Yowa no nezame* (late twelfth century; Awake at night); *Kagerō nikki* (c. 974; *The Gossamer Years,* 1964); *The Izumi Shikibu Diary;* and the Kabuki play *Imoseyama onna teikin* (An example of noble

womanhood). This translating work culminated in her translation of *The Tale of Genji,* carried out between 1967 and 1972.

Enchi emphasized in articles on the process of translating *The Tale of Genji* that her translation was strictly her own reading—an exercise of her own interpretation, judgment, and preferences. She abbreviated, even omitted, poems; she wove explanations into the narrative; she even explained the implied thoughts of various characters, weaving the contexts of their poems into the prose. She also purposely used anachronistic language: her translation of *The Tale of Genji* was affected by her love for Kabuki, as well as by her readings of Nagai Kafū. Referring to the Edo-period writer Ryūtei Tanehiko's version of the original text, *Nise Murasaki inaka Genji* (1829; The false Murasaki and the country Genji), Enchi joked that her translation should perhaps have a title that reflected herself as translator, a modern woman of Tokyo: *Ima Murasaki azuma Genji* (An "eastern" [that is, Tokyo] *Genji* by a modern Murasaki).

The importance of these translation projects in Enchi's intellectual development cannot be underestimated. As her numerous articles on the process of translating *The Tale of Genji* attest, it was through translating that Enchi came to be aware of the importance of the reader's subjectivity in the interpretive process. The meaning of a text is dependent on the reader's interpretation, which necessarily depends on one's readerly understanding, which in turn depends on what one knows, what one has read—other texts. As one's circumstances and understanding change, so may the meaning one makes of a text. For all the numerous times she had read *The Tale of Genji,* Enchi wrote, she was forever discovering new meanings. The meaning of a text is thus never static, or fixed, and to a certain extent it can be changed, given different resonances, with a change of context.

It is in the light of the play between text and context and readerly subjectivity that we can understand one of Enchi's key literary techniques: the setting of classical texts in modern context, or "recontextualization." Just as readerly understanding (informed knowledge, familiarity with literary codes) contributes to an enriched reading of a text, so the setting of an old text within a new context, or "recontextualization," can provide new ideas that unsettle fixed interpretations and provoke new readings.

In many of her narratives, Enchi places the classical texts in specific "reading situations." In "Enchantress," for example, a man and a woman read, ponder, and translate a passage from *Tales of Ise.* In "A Bond for Two Lifetimes—Gleanings," again a man and a woman read and translate a story by Ueda Akinari. In *Masks,* two men read an essay by a woman which itself is a reading of the figure of the Lady Rokujō in *The Tale of Genji.* In *Komachi hensō* (Visions of Komachi), a young man and an old woman read an essay (supposedly by a male academic but probably in fact a composition by his wife that has been altered by him) about the figure of the early Heian poet Ono no Komachi. In *Saimu* (Colored mist), an old woman writer, her secretary, and son-in-law all read and react to an ancient picture scroll consisting of a story written around a series of pictures featuring a love affair between a shrine priestess and her male attendant, and in the course of their reading, it affects them, charging them with its own eroticism.

The way in which classical texts are embedded in Enchi's narratives emphasizes the act of reading and highlights the interpretive and subjective and indeed affective nature of the act of reading. Moreover, the method always involves at least two sets of readers: the readers within the text and readers outside the text. The outside reader, the reader of Enchi's text, is always implicated—provoked, taunted—in a repetitive and imitative act of reading.

This technique is most clearly demonstrated in *Masks.* In this text, an essay, "An Account of the Shrine in the Fields" is read by a male academic. This is a kernel text, an essay concerning the significance of the Lady Rokujō written by the protagonist in the text, Toganō Mieko. The way in which the outside reader encounters this text is by reading it with a male figure—Ibuki, a professor of Heian literature, who gives Mieko's interpretation of Lady Rokujō his own interpretation. The outside reader, however, is given facts that distance him or her from the professor's interpretation—the reader knows it is obtuse. The reader is also given certain details that suggest that Mieko's interpretation of Lady Rokujō is colored by personal experience. Nevertheless, one's understanding of Mieko, and indeed of the events in the narrative of *Masks,* inevitably becomes informed by her reading of Lady Rokujō and by Ibuki's interpretation of her reading. The result is a highly unsettled and unresolved reading by the outside reader. Only the outside reader gains access to all the events and readings—yet precisely because of this, the reader's insight into the truth of the tale remains blurred—everything is seen through a prism comprised of different facets of subjectivity.

Enchi's technique of recontextualization, and her use of reading situations, consistently make the reader conscious not only of the limitations of the viewpoints of the figures within the text, but also of the limitations in his or her own subjectivity, or viewpoint, in the reading process. The reader is never allowed to come away with a fixed idea of the story of the text, and in particular of how to interpret the women figures or their motivations, but is rather made conscious that his or her reading may be only one version of the story. Enchi's narratives demand that the reader accept in the reading process an element of provisionality, a lack of closure, a sense that the particular version of the tale the reader thinks he or she has understood might well not be the last one. In this sense, even though Enchi's texts were written down, in a fashion they also attempted to hark back to *monogatari,* or tales—tales told by a particular subjectivity to a particular subjectivity and destined to be told and retold again. In her writing, she was reaching back to her grandmother's orally told tales.

In *Masks,* the protagonist Toganō Mieko writes an essay titled "An Account of the Shrine in the Fields," in which she identifies two different "types" of women: the "Woman who becomes the object of men's eternal affection," and the "Woman whom men fear." Women who become the object of men's eternal affection are those who blend in and conform with their expectations. Women whom men fear are identified as women of strong desire and strong emotion, whose "egos" *(jiga)* are unable to fuse with those of the men with whom they have relationships and who are thus compelled to live in loneliness, longing, resentment, and frustration.

Many of the women Enchi depicts in her narratives are either suffering or frightening. At the same time, inasmuch as Enchi's women represent real women, her writing suggests that women are like this only because this is what men make them: men have control over what women can do and over how women's actions are interpreted, and so they control the stories of women's lives. What, then, might the "reality" of women be? Time and again in Enchi's narratives, she explores the way that stories about women affect the way women live their own reality and make sense of themselves. By constantly drawing attention to the role, and the limitations, of subjectivity in the reading process, and emphasizing that situations are interpreted by means of the stories we create to describe them, Enchi was able to suggest that there was something outside—beyond the stories—and that situations so read did not in fact capture the "whole" reality of women, which was probably uncapturable. In Enchi's narratives, readings of women become temporary versions of an authoritative one yet to be discovered.

Ake o ubau mono

In 1955, around the time Enchi was making her comeback as a postwar writer, she published a story that became the first chapter of her fictionalized autobiography *Ake o ubao mono* (That which steals redness), which takes its name from the first of the three volumes of the work. This fictionalized autobiography was published serially in journals and then in individual volumes (*Ake o ubau mono*, 1960; *Kizu aru tsubasa*, 1962; and *Niji to shura*, 1968) over the next thirteen years, winning the Tanizaki Jun'ichirō Prize as a trilogy in 1969. Although in the afterword to the first volume, and several times again, Enchi denied that this text was autobiographical, her denial was ambiguous. She admitted at the same time that the fiction was a layer of "unnecessary clothing," a thin disguise over an account of her own life. For all the changes in names, and the highly wrought plotline (especially in the first volume), this account is clearly identifiable with Enchi's life. She may have been prompted to write this text by a wish to justify herself—to re-create herself—as a newly emerging, or reborn, writer after the war. Accounts of Enchi's life rely on this "fictional" text, parts of which overlap with her personal reminiscences (particularly the descriptions of her grandmother's storytelling and her father's book collection and study)—so in this sense, Enchi could be said to have achieved her purpose.

In *Ake o ubao mono*, Enchi presents, albeit in sometimes highly encoded form, her own view of how and why she became a writer. She includes a subtle apology for her naïveté in participating in writers' support of the war. Enchi also weaves into this narrative numerous clues that elucidate several of her other works. For example, in the second volume, Enchi's literary alter ego Munakata Shigeko is shown contemplating attempting to become pregnant with a child fathered by her lover in order to take revenge on her husband and to subvert the demoralizing constraints she experiences in having to play the role of "wife" in a family—something that may strike a chord with the situation in *Masks*. At several points in the narrative Shigeko is shown determining to write in order to assuage the humiliation she experiences as the wife of a philanderer (a man to whom she is tied by bonds of marriage but whom she does not respect) and also to assuage the pain that has come from being "deceived" and "broken" by a lover. She takes it upon herself to write on behalf of all the innumerable other women who must have suffered the same situations.

In the first volume of *Ake o ubao mono*, Enchi seems to explain the effect that having been her father's daughter had on her: she is clearly using the Freudian concept of the Family Romance. Shigeko is born to a literary man, an academic and playwright, a man who has traces of Edo about him and who also has a marvelous study and book collection. Shigeko also has a remarkable grandmother who tells her tales. However, Shigeko's literary father dies (her mother died soon after Shigeko's birth), and thereafter Shigeko is the adopted daughter of her uncle, a well-known high-ranking government official. Her conflicted loyalties to this uncle are suggested over and over again in this first volume.

Particularly thought-provoking is the way Enchi presents the onset of Shigeko's menstruation, in a highly wrought passage set by the sea at Kamakura, where she is staying with her father. Frightened by the sudden appearance of blood, Shigeko is beset by a nameless fear. She goes out to sit by the sea and is joined by her father, who asks her what the matter is. She is unable to tell him—and her father moves off, striding up the beach. She chases him, struggling, unable to catch up and lonely at the thought that "her father, a man" can never understand. In this scene of young girl chasing after her father, set in the context of blood flowing and a sudden awakening to irrevocable sexual differences between men and women (which may echo the chase by Izanami of Izanagi in the Japanese creation myth), there is resentment at having been cut off from him by the fact of being a woman, and perhaps there is the desire for vengeance as well. At the same time, there is a suggestion of a desire to be united with him again.

In the third volume of *Ake o ubao mono*, Shigeko has to undergo a hysterectomy because of uterine cancer, and here she is shown in the aftermath of the operation calling for her father and also dreaming vividly about him. After her hysterectomy, Shigeko writes a proclamation to herself about why she will become a writer. It is from this time on, when Shigeko feels that she has been divested of all that makes her a woman, that she starts to try concertedly to write, to identify her readership, and to identify the kind of story she wants to write. In this project, she is encouraged by a man with whom she has had a long-time intellectual and platonic relationship, and who urges her to put more "fiction" (the Japanese word used is *bakeru*, "to transform") into her writing. In the final pages of this third volume, what could be termed a drama of blood, femaleness, and creativity occurs. Shigeko, painfully conscious of being a woman manquée, finally has sexual relations with this man, who assures her that she is a woman after all; mysteriously, portentously, she experiences blood flowing from her womb again. Her partner, however (presumably having fulfilled his role as "inspiration"), proceeds to contract lung cancer, to cough up blood, and die. It is from this point on that Shigeko comes into her own as a writer.

In the course of *Ake o ubao mono*, the "redness" (*ake*, or *shu*) referred to in the title accumulates various meanings. In the first volume, Shigeko's life is described as being without color, without *ake*, redness (which also suggests the more political use of the word Red, or *aka*), because of the effect by comparison of the too vivid, fictional, escapist world given to her by her grandmother and father. In the third volume, Shigeko is deprived of her womb, from which would issue the red blood that would make her a "real" woman; at the same time, being stripped of her reality as a woman makes her pursue femaleness in fiction. There is the suggestion that it will be in her writing that she will try to *recover* this redness, this blood that was stripped from her. The fact that the redness was taken away from her makes her want to pursue it—in a chase that echoes that original one of desire and resentment for her father. This redness or blood that Shigeko will pursue in her fiction may refer to the bonds between women, born of the common suffering that women had to endure in the traditional *ie* household system that Enchi explores in her writing; it may refer to the specific power—the power to pollute, the power to create—that menstruation and reproductivity give women. At the same time, on a metaphorical level, the redness, the blood, may also refer to the lurid quality of many of Enchi's narratives (many of which would comfortably fall into what Noriko Mizuta Lippit has referred to as "female gothic"). In Enchi's oeuvre, blood becomes a symbol of women's power (which can be stripped from them) and of women's writing (through which women get their power back).

Conclusion

Whereas the lives of other women writers of the day (Miyamoto Yuriko, Hirabayashi Taiko, Hayashi Fumiko, Uno Chiyo) were marked by various combinations of travel and exile, sexual promiscuity and multiple marriages, homelessness and poverty, and sometimes imprisonment, Enchi's life was relatively unremarkable, characterized by inhibition and passivity rather than by impropriety or adventure. The biographer or reader looking for evidence of a forceful, rebellious personality, or a life fully or irrepressibly lived, will be disappointed. If the chronological accounts in collections are to be believed, Enchi's life, especially after she gained success as a writer, consisted almost exclusively of literary activities, literary achievements, and episodes of surgery. Enchi married for the sake of her father, and she also avowedly refrained from divorce at his insistence. Apart from a brief stay in Hawaii when she lectured on Japanese women writers, some trips to Europe and America, and summers spent in Karuizawa, Enchi lived all of her life in Tokyo. She liked to identify herself with the Edokko. The word means literally "child of Edo," an anachronistic term referring to long-term townspeople óf Edo, a group that included lower-ranking samurai as well as merchants, and it implies pride, stoicism, and restraint.

And yet, if Enchi did indeed have an uninteresting life, it was more than compensated for by the richness of her work, much of which has yet to be fully appreciated and commented on even in Japanese as well as translated from Japanese. It could be said that the journey other women writers made, whether through various countries or through series of lovers and husbands, Enchi made through her own extensive travels in Japanese literature.

Enchi made use of the categories of *joryū sakka*, "woman writer," and *joryū bungaku*, "literature of the women's school," categories that tended to be used unreflectively by most critics at the time in which she was writing. And yet she often explored and exploded through her writing the assumptions of such gender compartmentalizations. Though her stance of erudite literary daughter may have made her appear a nonthreatening presence, a good student of her male academic supporters—almost one of "their own"—her narratives often contain stingingly critical portraits of men and male scholars in particular.

Mishima Yukio, a writer who recognized a fellow Edokko in Enchi (they shared a taste for lurid, decadent things, he wrote, but also the same kind of strictness) and who highly admired her writing, identified a mixture of wantonness and restraint in Enchi's narratives. In one of her stories there is a refined elderly writer who appears the epitome of respectability and who always wears a plain, dark-colored kimono with a tastefully combined obi sash. Underneath her sober, appropriate exterior, however, for her own private indulgence, she wears highly "inappropriate," sensuous undergarments in variegated colors and gorgeous designs, more suitable for a young woman at the height of fresh, voluptuous beauty. About the nature of these sensuous undergarments her companions, treated to just an occasional hint of color at the hem of her kimono, can barely guess. The image captures well the mixture of restraint and sensuality, propriety and impropriety in Enchi's writing.

Selected Bibliography

PRIMARY WORKS

SHORT STORIES AVAILABLE IN ENGLISH

"Otoko no hone." *Bungei Shunjū* 34, no. 7:334–342 (July 1956). Trans. by Susan Matisoff as "Bones of

Men." *Japan Quarterly* 35, no. 4:417–426 (October–December 1988).

"Yō." *Chūō Koron* 71, no. 9:338–354 (September 1956). Trans. by John Bester as "Enchantress." *Japan Quarterly* 5, no. 3:339–350 (1958). Rev. ed. Tokyo: Japan Publications, 1970. Pp. 70–93.

"Nise no en—shūi." *Bungakukai* 11, no. 2:55–65 (January 1957). Trans. by Phyllis Birnbaum as "A Bond for Two Lifetimes—Gleanings." In her *Rabbits, Crabs, Etc.: Stories by Japanese Women.* Honolulu: University of Hawaii Press, 1982. Pp. 25–47. Also trans. by Noriko Mizuta Lippit as "Love in Two Lives: The Remnant." In *Japanese Women Writers: Twentieth Century Short Fiction.* Edited by Noriko Mizuta Lippit and Kyoko Iriye Selden. Armonk, N.Y.: M. E. Sharpe, 1991. Pp. 97–111.

"Kikuguruma." *Gunzō* 22, no. 7:59–75 (July 1967). Trans. by Yukiko Tanaka and Elizabeth Hanson as "Boxcar of Chrysanthemums." In their *This Kind of Woman: Ten Stories by Japanese Women Writers, 1960–1976.* Stanford, Calif.: Stanford University Press, 1982. Pp. 69–86.

"Hana kui uba." *Shinchō* 71, no. 1:26–33 (January 1974). Trans. by Lucy North as "Flower Eating Crone." In *The Oxford Book of Japanese Short Stories.* Edited by Theodore W. Goossen. Oxford: Oxford University Press, 1997. Pp. 172–181.

LONG PROSE FICTION

(Dates represent first editions of book publication. For details of serialization in journals, see Shinchōsha's *Enchi Fumiko zenshū*, vol. 16.)

Onnazaka. Tokyo: Kadokawa Shoten, 1957. Trans. by John Bester as *The Waiting Years.* Tokyo: Kodansha International, 1971.

Onnamen. Tokyo: Kōdansha, 1958. Trans. by Juliet Winters Carpenter as *Masks.* New York: Knopf, 1983.

Rijō. Tokyo: Chūō Kōronsha, 1960.

Watashi mo moete iru. Tokyo: Chūō Kōronsha, 1960.

Minami no hada. Tokyo: Shinchōsha, 1961.

Hanachiruzato. Tokyo: Bungei Shunjū, 1961.

Fuyu no sumika. Tokyo: Kōdansha, 1962.

Onna no mayu. Tokyo: Kōdansha, 1962.

Onna-obi. Tokyo: Kadokawa Shoten, 1962.

Otoko no meigara. Tokyo: Bungei Shunjū, 1962.

Yasashiki yoru no monogatari. Tokyo: Shūeisha, 1962.

Gendai kōshoku ichidai onna. Tokyo: Kōdansha, 1963.

Shishijima kitan. Tokyo: Bungei Shunjū, 1963.

Yuki moe. Tokyo: Shinchōsha, 1964.

Azayaka na onna. Tokyo: Shinchōsha, 1965.

Komachi hensō. Tokyo: Kōdansha, 1965.

Namamiko monogatari. Tokyo: Chūō Kōronsha, 1965. Trans. by Roger K. Thomas as *A Tale of False Fortunes.* Honolulu: University of Hawaii Press, 2000.

Ningyō shimai. Tokyo: Shūeisha, 1965.

Senhime shunjūki. Tokyo: Kōdansha, 1966.

Ake o ubau mono. Tokyo: Shinchōsha, 1970. (A trilogy consisting of *Ake o ubau mono*, 1960; *Kizu aru tsubasa*, 1962; and *Niji to shura*, 1968.)

Saimu. Tokyo: Shinchōsha, 1976.

Uzu. Tokyo: Shinchōsha, 1978.

Shokutaku no nai ie. 2 vols. Tokyo: Shinchōsha, 1979.

Kikujidō. Tokyo: Shinchōsha, 1984.

COLLECTED SHORT STORIES

Kaze no gotoki kotoba. Tokyo: Takemura Shobō, 1939.

Onna no fuyu. Tokyo: Shun'yōdō Shoten, 1939.

Himojii tsukihi. Tokyo: Chūō Kōronsha, 1954.

Taiyō ni muite. Tokyo: Tōhōsha, 1957.

Yō. Tokyo: Bungei Shunjū, 1957.

Tokyo no tsuchi. Tokyo: Bungei Shunjū, 1959.

Koi-zuma. Tokyo: Shinchōsha, 1960.

Yuki-ore. Tokyo: Chūō Kōronsha, 1962.

Kamen sekai. Tokyo: Kōdansha, 1964.

Ki no aware. Tokyo: Chūō Kōronsha, 1966.

Kikuguruma. Tokyo: Shinchōsha, 1969.

Yūkon. Tokyo: Shinchōsha, 1972.

Hana-kui uba. Tokyo: Kōdansha, 1974.

Kawanamishū. Tokyo: Kōdansha, 1975.

Kinuta. Tokyo: Bungei Shunjū, 1980.

Karasu gitan. Tokyo: Chūō Kōronsha, 1981.

COLLECTED MEMOIRS, PERSONAL REMINISCENCES, AND ESSAYS

(Many of these collections contain essays on modern and premodern Japanese writers and their writing.)

Onnazaka. Tokyo: Jinbunshoin, 1939.

Nanshi no haru. Tokyo: Manri Kakuhan, 1941.

Onna kotoba. Tokyo: Kadokawa Shoten, 1958.

Ōbei no tabi. Tokyo: Chikuma Shobō, 1959.

Onna no himitsu. Tokyo: Shinchōsha, 1959.

Hon no naka no saigetsu. Tokyo: Shinchōsha, 1960.

Otoko to iu mono. Tokyo: Kōdansha, 1960.

Onna o ikiru. Tokyo: Kōdansha, 1961.

Tabi yosoi. Tokyo: Sangatsu Shobō, 1964.

Matashitemo otoko monogatari. Tokyo: Sankei Shimbunsha, 1967.

Hi o kou. Tokyo: Kōdansha, 1968.

Haru no uta. Tokyo: Kōdansha, 1971.

Usagi no banka. Tokyo: Heibonsha, 1976.

Kashin. Tokyo: Kairyūsha, 1980.

Uso makoto nanajū yo nen. Tokyo: Nihon Keizai Shinbunsha, 1984.

Yume utsutsu no ki. Tokyo: Bungei Shunjū, 1987. (Uncompleted, published posthumously.)

COLLECTED ESSAYS ON JAPANESE LITERATURE

Koten bungaku kyōshitsu. Tokyo: Popura, 1951.

Genji monotagari shō. Tokyo: Gakushū Kenkyūsha, 1972.

Onna fudoki. Tokyo: Heibonsha, 1972.

Genji monogatari no sekai: Kyoto. Tokyo: Heibonsha, 1974.

Genji monogatari shiken. Tokyo: Shinchōsha, 1974.

Genji monogatari uta karuta. Tokyo: Tokuma Shoten, 1974.

Koten yorubanashi; Keriko to Kamoko no taidanshū. Tokyo: Heibonsha, 1975. (A series of discussions on classical Japanese literature with the writer Shirasu Masako.)

Edo bungaku towazugatari. Tokyo: Kōdansha, 1978.

Koten sainyūmon. Kamakura: Shobō, 1981.

Kokubungaku harimaze. Tokyo: Kōdansha, 1983.

Enchi Fumiko ga kataru "Chikamatsu monogatari." Kataribe Zōshi. Vol. 8. Tokyo: Heibonsha, 1984.

Yūen no hitobito to. Tokyo: Bungei shunjū, 1986. (Discussions on Japanese literature with literary luminaries including Yoshida Seiichi, Edward Seidensticker, Donald Keene, Nakagami Kenji, Ōe Kenzaburō, Tanizaki Jun'ichirō, and Setouchi Harumi. Published posthumously.)

Genji monogatari no herointachi. Tokyo: Kōdansha, 1987. (Discussions between Enchi Fumiko and a selection of other Japanese women writers including Tsushima Yūko, Setouchi Harumi, and Tanabe Seiko on women in *The Tale of Genji.* Published posthumously.)

COLLECTIONS EDITED BY ENCHI

Gendai joryū bungaku. With Sata Ineko. 8 vols. Joryū Bungakusha kai/Mainichi Shinbunsha, 1974–1975. (A series on modern Japanese women writers.)

Jinbutsu Nihon no joseishi. With Satō Aiko et al. 12 vols. Tokyo: Shūeisha, 1977–1978. (A series on prominent women in Japanese history from premodern to modern times.)

GENERAL COLLECTED WORKS

Enchi Fumiko bunko. 8 vols. Tokyo: Kōdansha, 1960–1961.

Enchi Fumiko kikōbunshū. 3 vols. Tokyo: Heibonsha, 1974.

Enchi Fumiko zenshū. 16 vols. Tokyo: Shinchōsha, 1976–1977. (Volume 16 contains a year-by-year account compiled by Wada Tomoko of Enchi's activities and publications, as well as an extensive list of Enchi's works in various categories—plays, short story collections, longer prose narratives, translations, and also the editions in which various publications occur. It also contains an extensive list of the collections of Japanese literature that feature Enchi's writing. "Complete" only through 1977. See next entry.)

Enchi Fumiko: Yō, Hanakui uba. Tokyo: Kōdansha Bungei Bunko, 1997. (The bibliography by Ogasawara Yoshiko at the back of this collection contains a list of Enchi's publications up-to-date through 1997 and cites the various collections of modern Japanese literature in which her work is featured. It also has a useful list of her work in Bunko editions.)

TRANSLATIONS BY ENCHI

(References for translations are selective. For details regarding first editions of translations, see Shinchōsha's *Enchi Fumiko zenshū,* volume 16, pp. 435–437.)

Otogi zōshi monogatari. Shōkokumin bungaku. Vol. 3. Tokyo: Shōgakkan, 1943.

Kagerō nikki. The Gossamer Years, 1964.

Genji monogatari. Enchi Fumiko yaku. 5 vols. Tokyo: Shinchō Bunko, 1980.

Yowa no nezame. Enchi Fumiko yaku. Tsutsumi chūnagon monogatari: Nakamura Shin'ichirō yaku. Nihon koten bunko. Vol. 9. Tokyo: Kawade Shobō Shinsha, 1976–1988.

Ugetsu monogatari, Ukiyodoko, Harusame monogatari, Shunshoku umegoyomi. Nihon koten bunko. Vol. 20. Tokyo: Kawade Shobō Shinsha, 1988. (Enchi translated Ueda Akinari's tales; other translations are by other scholars.)

Kagerō nikki Izumi shikibu nikki. Tokyo: Chikuma Bunko, 1993.

SECONDARY WORKS

CRITICAL STUDIES

Bargen, Doris. G. "Twin Blossoms on a Single Branch: The Cycle of Retribution in *Onnamen.*" *Monumenta Nipponica* 46, no. 2:147–171 (summer 1991).

———. "Translation and Reproduction in Enchi's 'A Bond for Two Lifetimes—Gleanings.' " In *The Woman's Hand: Gender and Theory in Japanese Women's Writing.* Edited by Paul Gordon Schalow and Janet A. Walker. Stanford, Calif.: Stanford University Press, 1996. Pp.165–204.

Carpenter, Juliet Winters. "Enchi Fumiko: 'A Writer of Tales.' " *Japan Quarterly* 37, no. 3:343–355 (July–September 1990).

Cornyetz, Nina. "Bound by Blood: Female Pollution, Divinity, and Community in Enchi Fumiko's *Masks.*" *U.S.-Japan's Women's Journal,* English Supplement No. 9:29–58 (1995).

———. *Dangerous Women, Deadly Words: Phallic Fantasy and Modernity in Three Japanese Writers.* Stanford, Calif.: Stanford University Press, 1999. (A strong feminist-materialist analysis of three writers using the psychoanalytical theory of Jacques Lacan and Julia Kristeva. It includes a highly sophisticated and insightful discussion of Enchi.)

Furuya Teruko. *Enchi Fumiko, Yō no bungaku.* Tokyo: Chūsekisha, 1997. (An exuberant account of Enchi's life. It contains a useful chronological account of Enchi's publications, with details of narratives by Enchi published later than the 1976–1977 Shinchōsha collection of Enchi's works.)

Gessel, Van. "The 'Medium' of Fiction: Enchi Fumiko as Narrator." *World Literature Today* 62, no. 3:380–385 (summer 1988).

Hulvey, S. Yumiko. "The Intertextual Fabric of Narratives by Enchi Fumiko." In *Japan in Traditional and Postmodern Perspectives.* Edited by Charles Weihsun Fu and Steven Heine. Albany: State University Press of New York, 1995. Pp. 169–224.

Kamei Hideo and Ogasawara Yoshiko. *Enchi Fumiko no sekai.* Tokyo: Sōrinsha, 1980. (A solid biographical account of Enchi's life—written while Enchi was alive—with analysis of her works. Contains close readings of a selection of Enchi's texts.)

Kobayashi Fukuko. "Onnazaka: hangyaku no kōzō." In *Onna ga yomu Nihon kindai bungaku*. Edited by Egusa Mitsuko and Urushida Kazuyo. Tokyo: Shin'yōsha, 1992. Pp. 121–148.

McClain, Yoko. "Eroticism and the Writings of Enchi Fumiko." *Journal of the Association of Teachers of Japanese* 15, no. 1:32–46 (April 1980).

Mishima Yukio. *Sakkaron*. Tokyo: Chūō Kōronsha, 1970. (Contains analysis and astute comments on various texts by Enchi.)

Mizuta Noriko. *Heroin kara hero e: josei to jiga no hyōgen*. Tokyo: Tabatake Shoten, 1982. (Contains astute and theoretically informed analysis of Enchi Fumiko's writing.)

———. *Monogatari to hanmonogatari no fūkei*. Tokyo: Tabatake Shoten, 1993. (Contains astute analysis of Enchi Fumiko's writing.)

Nakagami Kenji. "Monogatari no keifu/hachinin no sakka; Enchi Fumiko 1–6." *Kokubungaku Kaishaku to Kyōzai no Kenkyū* 29, no. 5:148–50 (April 1984); 29, no. 6:130–134 (May 1984); 29, no. 7:130–131 (June 1984); 29, no. 11:136–139 (September 1984); 29, no. 14:138–140 (November 1984); 29, no. 15:136–138 (December 1984).

North, Lucy. "Double-speak: The Writings of a Linguist's Daughter: Enchi Fumiko, 1905–1986." Ph.D. diss., Harvard University, 2000.

Pounds, Wayne. "Enchi Fumiko and the Hidden Energy of the Supernatural." *Journal of the Association of Teachers of Japanese* 24, no. 2:167–183 (November 1999).

Sunami Toshiko. *Enchi Fumiko ron*. Tokyo: Ōfū, 1998. (An astute analysis of Enchi's writing, with close readings of *Onnazaka*, "Yō," "Nise no en—shūi," *Onnamen*, and *Komachi hensō*. Contains an abbreviated chronological account of Enchi's life and the most extensive list [current through 1998] of articles and chapters on Enchi in Japanese journals, newspapers, and books; a list of expository critical essays in various books by Enchi; and a list of dialogues and round-table discussions in which Enchi participated.)

Uesaka Nobuo. *Enchi Fumiko: sono Genji monogatari hanshō*. Tokyo: Ubun Shoin, 1993.

Vernon, Victoria V. "Between Osan and Koharu: The Representation of Women in the Works of Hayashi Fumiko and Enchi Fumiko." In her *Daughters of the Moon: Wish, Will, and Social Constraint in Fiction by Modern Japanese Women*. Japan Research Monograph 9. Berkeley, Calif.: Institute of East Asian Studies, University of California, 1988. Pp. 137–169.

BIOGRAPHICAL STUDIES

Enchi Fumiko and others. *Joryū sakka ga kataru*. Tokyo: Shūeisha, 1978. (A collection of dialogues between women writers about their lives.)

Fuke Motoko. *Haha, Enchi Fumiko*. Tokyo: Shinchōsha, 1989. (A collection of reminiscences by Enchi's daughter.)

———. *Dōjo no gotoku, haha Enchi Fumiko no ashiato*. Tokyo: Kairyūsha, 1989. (A second collection by Enchi's daughter.)

Kobayashi Fukuko, ed. *Sakka no jiden 72 Enchi Fumiko*. Tokyo: Nihon Tosho Sentā, 1988. (A collection of Enchi's reminiscences about her life, family, other writers, and her own writing, with an expository essay by the editor.)

Mulhern, Chieko I., ed. *Japanese Women Writers: A Bio-Critical Sourcebook*. Greenwood Press: Westport, Conn. 1994.

Sachiko S. Schierbeck. *Japanese Women Novelists in the Twentieth Century: 104 Biographies, 1900–1993*. Copenhagen: Museum Tusalanum Press, 1994. Pp. 112–118.

FUTABATEI SHIMEI
1864–1909

DENNIS WASHBURN

FUTABATEI SHIMEI is generally credited with writing the first modern novel in Japan. *Ukigumo* (Drifting clouds), which was serialized from 1887 to 1889 in *Miyako no hana*, was read by many at the time as a turn toward serious literary practice, and was hailed by some as a major event in the modernization of Japanese culture. The narrative style developed by Futabatei transformed the conventions of late Edo fiction by introducing elements of the realistic mode that dominated European literature in the nineteenth century: the use of unadorned vernaculars and of circumstantial detail to create a vital sense of presence, and the reliance on psychological verisimilitude to give depth to the depiction and development of character.

Apart from his literary accomplishments Futabatei is also an important historical figure because of the significance attached to his life by his peers. Futabatei was seen above all as a pioneer, a necessary transitional figure who emerged at the beginning of Japan's modern moment. Futabatei himself was self-conscious about his status as an innovator, and, like any transitional figure, often felt as if he were torn between two worlds—a feeling that gave rise to personal tensions that he struggled to resolve throughout his life. Even the name Futabatei Shimei, the literary persona of Hasegawa Tatsu-nosuke, suggests an ambivalence about his position in the literary world. The characters for the name may be read as "double-leaf pavilion, four perplexities"—an echo of the pen names of many writers of *gesaku*, the so-called playful fiction that was a major genre of late Edo literature. But the name is also a play on the phrase "kutabatte shimae," meaning (to employ a mild translation) "Drop dead!" This choice for a pen name is at once a comically defiant assertion and an ironic rejection of his own literary and cultural heritage.

Early Career

Futabatei was born 4 April 1864 in Edo (Tokyo) to a low-ranking samurai family attached to the Owari fief. Because of the turbulent political situation that had overtaken Japan in the final years of the Tokugawa regime, his father, Hasegawa Yoshikazu, moved the family out of the Tokyo residence and back to the home domain in present-day Nagoya, where he took up a position in the local administration. Futabatei's education began in Nagoya. He learned to read and write at a relatively young age and was tutored in the Chinese classics by an uncle. He also began to read the works of popular fiction, especially *gesaku*, that would be a major influence on his development as a stylist.

Although Futabatei began his studies in a traditional manner, he came of age in a generation when the Japanese educational system was undergoing radical transformation. The Meiji Restoration of 1868 brought into political power an oligarchy intent on remaking and modernizing the political economy and social institutions of Japan; and at the center of the project of modernization was the effort to learn as much as possible about the West and its systems. In direct response to this enormous undertaking, the Owari fief established a school of Western studies in 1870. Futabatei enrolled there in 1871, and began his formal training under the guidance of French and English teachers. He returned to Tokyo with his mother, Gotō Shizu, in 1872 and then moved to Matsue in Shimane prefecture in 1875 when his father was appointed to a post in the prefectural government there. That same year he enrolled in two private middle schools. One of them, the Matsue Hensoku Chūgakkō, emphasized Western studies, especially English and the natural sciences. The other was an academy called the Sōchōsha (Academy of Chinese Studies).

The Sōchōsha was run by a neo-Confucian scholar who not only emphasized the Chinese classics in the curriculum, but also inculcated in his charges a strong sense of Japanese nationalism. While attending this school Futabatei became a strong supporter of Saigō Takamori, one of the original oligarchs who had left the government in 1873 in protest over the decision to defer a hardline expansionist policy toward Korea. Saigō led a revolt of disgruntled former samurai in 1877, but he was defeated in the Satsuma Rebellion, and he committed suicide. His charismatic leadership was nonetheless a powerful example for an impressionable youth like Futabatei, and the nationalism he embodied had a major impact on the direction of Futabatei's career.

One of the main issues that the Meiji government confronted in the 1870s was fixing the borders of the Japanese empire, which involved negotiations with the Russian Empire over territories to the north of Japan. Many felt considerable passion about this issue and took

it as a major defeat when Japan ceded its claim to Sakhalin in 1875. Among those with strong nationalist feeling, Futabatei came to be convinced at this time that the greatest long-term threat to Japan's security was Russia; and it was in part this conviction that led him to return to Tokyo in 1879 to enroll in the officer's training school of the Imperial Army. Futabatei, who was very near-sighted, failed the physical examination. He tried the entrance exams two more times and finally gave up his dream of a military career in 1880.

Futabatei's nationalism was not a passing phase, and he decided that if he could not join the army, then he could serve his country through a career in diplomacy. With that goal in mind he entered the department of Russian at the Tokyo School of Foreign Languages in 1881. He proved to be a brilliant student of Russian, and he was deeply impressed by the work of Ivan Goncharov, Fyodor Dostoevsky, and Nikolai Gogol. Although he never lost his nationalist beliefs, his experiences at the school eventually led him to attempt a career in literature as a writer, and his new goal became the reform of literary practice in Japan. In particular he wanted to translate the conventions of Western realism into a Japanese idiom, and so found himself in sympathy with other writers who were seeking to reform and legitimize the writing of fiction. Futabatei began to seek out connections in the literary world, and the most important relationship he established was with Tsubouchi Shōyō, whom he first met in 1886.

Tsubouchi was a critic and translator of Sir Walter Scott and Shakespeare who had begun serializing a seminal literary tract, *Shōsetsu shinzui* (The essence of the novel), in September 1885. Though he was never a successful novelist himself, Tsubouchi exerted tremendous influence on a younger generation of writers with his call for reform and his harsh criticism of the state of Japanese literature. Tsubouchi's project meshed almost perfectly with Futabatei's interests, though in many ways Futabatei's grasp of Western critical theory was already more advanced than that of the man who became his mentor and close friend. Tsubouchi encouraged Futabatei to pursue his career by translating Russian literature, and the first major project he undertook was a translation of Ivan Turgenev's *Fathers and Sons.* This project was never completed, in part because the effort to render the Russian text into a colloquial-style language free of Edo literary conventions proved to be too difficult for him at this stage of his career. Even so, this translation was an important exercise for Futabatei, because it forced him to come to grips with the practical problems of developing a literary language that would make the composition of Western-style fiction possible for him.

Language Reform and Critical Theory

The literary languages employed in the early Meiji period are notable for their sometimes eclectic mixing of various styles. These styles included the balancing of the elegant (classical) and vulgar (colloquial) styles that emerged in certain Edo-period works, notably the genre known as the *yomihon* (reading books—that is, texts without illustrations); the Western-influenced, but still heavily ornate, styles that emerged from translation literature; and a new style based primarily on colloquial speech. Some authors continued to compose in the vein of *gesaku* (playful fiction) writers of the late Edo period, and even translators of Western works often chose to emulate the rhythmic qualities of the ballad style of the *jōruri* or the didactic style of the *yomihon* of Kyokutei Bakin (1767–1848). Many early attempts to modernize literary conventions focused on changes in orthographic usage (such as the simplification of Chinese characters, more liberal use of glosses for characters, and the substitution of characters with hiragana), and avoided the use of the spoken forms of the language as the basis for a new literary style. Indeed, it was not until the mid-1880s that experiments with the vernacular began on a genuinely wide scale, and that the idea of

achieving a style based on a standard spoken language (in this case the dialect of Tokyo) became the focus of debate. What is known as the *genbun'itchi* movement, that is, the movement to find a compromise style that fused elements of the older literary language with contemporary vernacular, gained momentum as a cultural force during this decade.

In an essay on language reform, "Yo ga genbun'itchi no yurai," (1906; The origins of my *genbun'itchi*), Futabatei states unequivocally his reasons for pursuing a fusion style: "I first began writing in the *genbun'itchi* style because otherwise I couldn't write at all" (*Futabatei Shimei zenshū [FSZ]*, 1981, vol. 5, p. 170). He explains that on the advice of Tsubouchi Shōyō he tried to imitate the colloquial style of a popular form of oral storytelling known as *rakugo*, that had been a major influence on late *gesaku* fiction. Futabatei was a little uncomfortable basing his literary experiments on what was seen by some readers as a vulgar style, but his youthful love of *gesaku*—especially the works of Shikitei Sanba (1767–1822)—had instilled in him a preference for directness of expression. His ideal of a literary style based upon the language of everyday speech was a key component in the evolution of literary practice in Meiji Japan—an ideal that may be discerned in other important works of the time, including translations from European literature and *sokkibon* (direct transcriptions of oral narrative performances). Throughout the 1880s and 1890s there was general agreement that a recasting of narrative conventions in line with the aims of *genbun'itchi* was a prerequisite for the creation of a modern literature. Nonetheless, Futabatei's initial experiments with style, though unquestionably groundbreaking, were based on elements with which he and much of his readership were familiar.

Even as he attempted to develop a realistic style, Futabatei admitted his affinity for the vulgar language of *gesaku* fiction and the techniques of *rakugo*. He shared the aims of Tsubouchi Shōyō in that he was concerned with making Japanese literature a serious art; but he was interested in reform that did not altogether reject earlier literary practice. In fact, he employed the frivolous language of *gesaku* as part of the conventions of literary realism. From the outset, then, there was a fundamental division in his view of literature that manifested itself as an ambivalent attitude about his place as a transitional figure—an attitude that exemplified the divided sensibility of a generation that had undertaken radical cultural modernization. The Meiji literary establishment saw in Futabatei a true original who nonetheless had about him the aura of Edo literature, and it discovered in his ambivalence the birth of a modern literary self-consciousness.

The conflicting elements of Futabatei's literary project are laid out clearly in a brief essay entitled "Shōsetsu sōron" (An overview of the novel), written in 1886. The essay is simultaneously an explanation and a defense of narrative realism that borrows heavily from the work of the Russian critic Vissarion Belinsky (1811–1848). Futabatei was attracted by the directness and immediacy of the performance language of *rakugo* and *gesaku*, because he saw in that language certain resources that could be employed by a novelist to conjure the illusion that the world was being presented as it really is. Futabatei believed the Western novel was a flexible form that facilitated the creation of the illusion of reality, and he championed this mimetic representation as the foundation for modern literature, asserting that the seriousness and honesty of the novel rested entirely on its ability to copy the world.

The Japanese word for "copy" used here, *mosha*, suggests mimesis, not reproduction, and Futabatei argued that the novel functions by finding direct equivalents in language for objects in the world. In this respect, the importance he placed on the mediating presence of word in the act of representing reality indicates his debt to Edo-period critical values. Yet Futabatei remained aware that realism is just another mode of writing. He did not give mimetic representational forms a privileged place over the earlier presentational forms of narrative he had enjoyed as a child. He gained

from *gesaku* writers an essentially comic, skeptical view of the tricks of fictional narrative, which is never wholly trustworthy because it is always dependent on the playful whims of the author. Thus, even though he argued that mimesis is the true essence of the novel, his theoretical view found room to accommodate his fondness for Edo fiction.

Still, for all his admiration of elements of *gesaku* style and his debt to native critical theory, Futabatei can hardly be described as a late *gesaku* author. In one sense, the modernity of his work may be said to arise as much from the struggle to suppress the *gesaku* author within himself as from his efforts to create a realistic style. His sense of difference from his beloved Edo forebears was something that Futabatei accepted as the cost of creating a new literary culture in Japan. That cost was a heavy one that came in the form of cultural dislocation and an anxiety over the loss of tradition. That anxiety is every bit as much a defining characteristic of Futabatei's modernity as his ambition to create a new literature; and those two qualities, ambition and anxiety, were the motivating forces behind the composition of his first novel, *Ukigumo*.

Ukigumo

The ideas about literature that guided Futabatei's experiment with realism must be understood within the context of the general awareness of discontinuity in Meiji Japan. *Ukigumo* is an account of the struggle of its protagonist, a young man named Bunzō, to find a place for himself in a society undergoing rapid change. Bunzō is a bit of a stick-in-the-mud who has very strong, old-fashioned notions about proper behavior. His inability to adapt to the shallow, materialistic outlook of his age causes him to lose his job and also, as a result, the attention of the woman he loves, Osei. Bunzō is far from a heroic protector of traditional values, however, and his indecisiveness, penchant for introverted behavior, and self-pity prevent him from tackling the problems created for him by a changing society.

The story of Bunzō is in its basic conception less anecdotal than *gesaku* fiction, because it reproduces the more continuous structure of Western novels of the time that present the inner psychological development of a character. This overall shift to a Western mode of narrative, however, does not completely obscure the presence of certain *gesaku* elements of style, which remain an important part of the experiments undertaken by Futabatei. The following passage is an example of how Futabatei fuses Edo and Western techniques. The scene occurs at a crucial point in the novel, following Bunzō's falling out with Osei. Bunzō has just returned home to find Osei entertaining Noboru, a crass and thoroughly up-to-date acquaintance whose very name (which means "to climb") suggests the nature of his ambitions:

> When he peeked into the inner room, Noboru was standing, with round pieces of white paper stuck to his back, loitering in the midst of things scattered around as if there had been a drunken revel. Osei and Onabe [the maid] were nearby holding their sides and convulsed with laughter, though he couldn't see all of Osei. Even though their eyes met his, no one welcomed him home, or answered him when he asked about his aunt. When Bunzō passed by fuming like that, suddenly from behind him he heard a ruckus of loud voices.

> Noboru: All right now, who's the wiseguy?

> Osei: It's not me. It's Onabe. Ho-ho-ho-ho.

> Onabe: What are you saying? It's the young mistress. O-ho-ho-ho-ho.

> Noboru: It's neither one, it's both of you. Let's start with this little piggy.

> Onabe: Hey, it's not me! O-ho-ho-ho-ho. Stop that. . . Hey, Miss Osei!

> Bunzō also heard the *dotapata* of feet scurrying, and another voice laughing, "O-ho-ho-ho." He also heard Osei shouting over and over, "Scratch him, scratch him!"

(*FSZ*, vol. 1, pp. 89–90; revised from tr. p. 293)

This passage shows a visual debt to *gesaku* in the clear marking out of the dialogue and the speakers, and a linguistic debt in the style of speech Futabatei imitated. However, the most important aspect of this *gesaku*-like scene is the use Futabatei makes of it within the context of the narrative. After nearly running into Osei in the hallway and being scolded by her, Bunzō retires to his room upstairs and tries to read a work, written in English, on British political parties. Apart from the tedious subject matter and the incomprehensibility of the foreign language, which is reproduced in the narrative to establish a visual contrast between the alien English and the native Japanese, the noise of the young people downstairs having fun distracts him. Soon Noboru comes up to visit, and the contrast between the serious, boring Bunzō and the shallow, witty Noboru is starkly drawn, especially in the repetition of the latter's ingratiating, scornful laugh, which is always conspicuously spelled out on the page.

They argue, and Bunzō breaks off their friendship; but when Noboru demands an explanation as to why he is being cut off, Bunzō cannot answer. When Noboru presses him further, Bunzō counters that everything Noboru says is an "evasion." But when he is asked to clarify that statement, Bunzō is reduced to asserting, in English, that his comment is a "self-evident truth." Bunzō has no language to express his interior feelings, and so he is always positioned outside the action in the story as either a passive observer or as a passive subject. Futabatei has extended the literary nature of his *gesaku* model in part by showing the psychological basis for the misunderstanding of language among the characters, and, more important, by making the cause of Bunzō's failure and isolation not simply a flaw in his character but a fundamental lack of the kind of social language or discourse that would make it possible for him to fit more easily into his world.

As the novel progresses Bunzō becomes more isolated, inward looking, and silent; and the fact that Bunzō always seems to be at a loss for words indicates that he is a man out of his time. His problems stem from his inability to reconcile his ideals, which are presented as belonging to the past, with the economic realities and practical needs of the new Japan. In this respect the influence of Russian literature on the development of character in the novel is important to note in order to understand how Futabatei achieved the effect of psychological realism. Bunzō's inability to redefine himself leads to both his inner turmoil and the central crisis of the novel, which is the problem he begins to have with Osei after he loses his job. He is by nature inclined to inactivity and thus is more of an antihero, a figure whose inability to control or create his fictional world creates the predicament at the core of the book. This predicament is not his alone, for after his prospects of marrying Osei are dimmed, she too begins to lose her bearings and is in danger of ruining her own chances of happiness through her reckless relationship with Noboru. Yet the sense of dislocation, of being out of place and time, is so strong within Bunzō that he is rendered incapable of redeeming either Osei or himself. Marleigh Ryan's formulation of Bunzō as a superfluous hero modeled after the protagonists in the fiction of Turgenev certainly suggests the central problem of the narrative, which is the protagonist's marginality in his fictional world.

Futabatei discovered in the course of writing his novel that the want of a traditional hero makes narrative difficult to sustain, and this discovery had a major impact on the structure of the novel. Near the end Bunzō ponders ways to save the situation for himself, but he does not act on this thoughts. Luckily for him, Osei breaks off with Noboru on her own, but the story ends with Bunzō still weighing his options and taking a passive wait-and-see attitude. The sense of dislocation at the heart of the characterization of Bunzō is mirrored in the open-ended, inconclusive structure of the story. One of the achievements of the work is the way in which the structure of the narrative meshes so well with the consciousness of the central character. And yet the open-ended

nature of the story presented a challenge to Futabatei, who, as installments of the novel continued to appear, struggled to find an appropriate way to bring the narrative to a close.

Futabatei wanted to write a form of fiction that avoided the easy, seemingly unrealistic endings of typical Edo-style narratives, but his efforts led him right into the dilemma that always confronts the writer of realistic fiction, which is that true, or absolute, mimesis of the open-ended nature of human experience makes closure impossible. The notion of the novel as an artistic means of copying reality expounded by Futabatei in 1886 is vulnerable to this dilemma. Although Edo fiction and performance arts provided Futabatei with certain elements from which he could construct a realistic style, the dominant structural form in Edo literature was anecdotal narrative, which was used to suggest the ephemerality and fragmentation of human experience. For Futabatei and others of his generation the outlook on human experience suggested by that narrative model was no longer valid, and anecdotal fiction was judged to be formally inferior to the large-scale coherence of the European novel. In the effort to adapt a Western narrative model, Futabatei realized that the transitory formlessness of reality, which is suggested by the title of the work, *Ukigumo* (Drifting clouds), forces any so-called realistic depiction to be similarly formless and open-ended with no hope of resolution in an artistic sense. The fact that *Ukigumo* was not finished to Futabatei's satisfaction indicates just how difficult the challenge to create a modern literature was.

Though it still shows traces of Edo literary practice, *Ukigumo* altered the form of the novel in Japan by employing shifting perspectives, which complicated the determination of what is true in the text, and which introduced a greater self-awareness or self-consciousness on the part of the characters. The narrator often intervenes to explain or judge the actions of the characters or to interject humorous digressions, but that voice is not the sole source of information, and the characters, especially Bunzō and Osei, frequently perform the narrative function of commenting on or judging their own actions or those of the other figures. The characters provide perspectives that call into question the absolute reliability of the text, and that raise the crucial issue of how a realistic mode reconciles its attempt to depict the world as it is with the formal demands of fictional narrative. This represents a significant shift from the practices of *gesaku* fiction, and justifies critical judgment that *Ukigumo* is a work of lasting historical importance.

The Silent Years

Looking back on the composition of *Ukigumo* in "Yo ga hansei no zange" (1908; Confessions of my life so far), Futabatei describes the difficulties he encountered in terms similar to those he used to represent his character, Bunzō: namely, that writing the novel opened an irreconcilable split between idealism and practicality. He recalls that he wrote the novel in order to make money, but that at the same time he was driven by a desire to live a lifestyle guided by the ideal of honesty (*shōjiki*). Futabatei tells us that this ideal was the product of several influences, primarily Russian literature, Confucianism, and socialism. He wonders whether ideology really has any bearing on the composition of literature, and then proceeds to outline the troubles caused by his attempts to write within the dictates of his ideal of honesty. Although he was guided by humility, honesty, and a reverence for art, the demands placed on him by family and society led him to desire money. Thus his efforts to write became an affront to his ideals. He tells us that he used Tsubouchi Shōyō's name to get published, putting his own petty interests first and deceiving the readers as well.

It is not hard to believe that Futabatei was sincere in his recollections when we consider that at the center of his career is a nearly twenty-year period in which he did not write another novel. As the composition of *Ukigumo* continued, he grew increasingly skeptical about his own aims for literature, and

he felt that he had no choice but to withdraw from literary activity. His silence was perhaps the only way he could adequately express his skepticism. Shortly after the third part of *Ukigumo* appeared, he became a civil servant. Although he continued with his work as a translator, his long silence contributed to the impression that he was ahead of his time, a pioneer, and an anomaly.

Futabatei acutely felt the need for a narrative form and language that would allow him to break free of his tradition. However, the alternatives to which he turned to address that need were Western, and he understood that, by reforming traditional practices according to the normative values of the West, he was in effect placing himself at the margins of modern culture. To renew his tradition on those terms ran the risk of extreme cultural alienation. The fact that it was possible to identify a correspondence between some traditional narrative techniques and elements of the Western realistic novel helped Futabatei salvage some native practices, but that merely underscored the Western novel as the norm by which such practices were judged. Futabatei's silence, then, was an expression of his skepticism toward realistic narrative, and a response to his marginality as a Japanese writer. He felt that, perhaps like his character Bunzō, he did not possess a voice that would enable him to establish his literary identity against either the West or his native tradition.

Futabatei's ethical and artistic doubts were compounded by personal problems, especially the precarious financial situation of his family. He had left a fairly secure position as an instructor of Russian language in 1886 when his school was merged with what is now Hitotsubashi University. Futabatei had opposed this administrative change and had resigned as a matter of principle. Shortly after he left this job, *Ukigumo* began to appear in print, but he was not able to make an adequate living from the proceeds. Over the three years that the book was being serialized the author's share averaged less than ten yen a month. This was not a living wage, and he had to supplement his income by teaching literature at a school for women. When his father's health began to fail this arrangement also proved inadequate, and in August 1889 he found a position in the Government Printing Office of the Treasury. He held this job for about eight years.

His family circumstances were a major consideration in Futabatei's decision to change careers, and they were also a source of the feelings of personal failure, mediocrity, and frustration he suffered for the rest of his life. His strong idealism, inflexible temperament, and stubborn perfectionism exacerbated the loss of confidence he experienced. Together with Shōyō his goal in the mid-1880s had been nothing less than the reform of literary practice in Japan. Futabatei had been a strong critic of contemporary Japanese society and literature, but his extreme honesty led him to criticize his own work just as severely. Thus, he took his failures to make a living at writing and to complete *Ukigumo* to his satisfaction as indications of his lack of talent.

There is no simple explanation for Futabatei's decision to stop writing. His sense of personal failure, his disillusionment, and his intellectual temperament were all important factors, and taken together they led to the skepticism with which Futabatei came to view literary activity. For almost six years after taking the job at the Government Printing Office, Futabatei produced very little writing of any kind. He married Fukui Tsune in 1893, but the marriage was not happy, and the couple divorced in 1896. He quit his government job the following year and began teaching to support himself. During this period he began to translate more actively, and at the urging of Tsubouchi Shōyō and Uchida Roan he became involved in a modest way with the activities of the literary establishment. He married again in 1902, and then spent much of the next two years working in China and Korea. When he returned in March 1904, he took a job in the Tokyo office of a daily newspaper, the *Asahi Shinbun*.

An Adopted Husband

The Russo-Japanese War provided the stimulus that Futabatei needed to try his hand at another novel. The war held special significance for Futabatei. Twenty-five years earlier he had begun his study of the Russian language under the influence of what he himself termed a kind of imperialism that made him consider language study essential for the security of the nation. He never entirely ceased viewing Russia as a potential threat, but his long association with that country created severe doubts about the course of his own nation's modernization. He shared in the nationwide sense of revulsion and dissatisfaction over the terrible costs of victory, for which no compensation could be adequate, and this feeling was amplified in his case by his personal ambivalence about the war. His moral values had been shaped to a large extent by Russian authors, and so his perspective on events was broader than that of most observers at the time.

Futabatei was approached by the editors at the *Asahi Shinbun* to write a story depicting the domestic troubles created by the war, especially the difficulties faced by women who had been widowed by the fighting. His investigation into the problems of women cut off from family and economic support because of widowhood gave way to a wider examination of the family system and of the rights of the individual within that system. The novel that grew out of this change in conception, *Sono omokage (An Adopted Husband)*, was serialized in the *Asahi Shinbun* between 10 October and 31 December 1906.

The novel traces the disintegration of the marriage between Ono Tetsuya and his wife Tokiko. Tetsuya is an adopted husband who assumed the Ono family name when he married. After coming into the household he finds that Tokiko and her mother Takiko have grown used to luxurious living as a result of the extravagance of his late father-in-law, Reizō, and are completely dissatisfied with Tetsuya's inability to provide for them. Because they measure success in material terms, they force him to take on several teaching jobs, and once his energies are spread so thin, Tetsuya finds it is impossible to advance. His continued failure adds to the unhappiness of his wife and mother-in-law, and a terrible cycle of distrust and recrimination is created. As life becomes unbearable for Tetsuya, both husband and wife feel justified in their complaints and reconciliation becomes impossible. Divorce is no solution because Tetsuya cannot get the money he needs to settle his educational debts, and, even if he could get the money, his departure would leave the Ono family destitute. The driving force of the plot is thus the lack of trust in the relationship between husband and wife.

Their domestic discord is complicated by another problem. When Reizō died, he left behind an illegitimate daughter, Sayoko. Although he had tried to care for this daughter, her presence in the house was a painful affront to his wife Takiko. Sayoko was forced out and spent much of her childhood in Christian boarding schools. After her father's death, she is forced to leave school and get married. Tragically she is widowed shortly after her marriage and has to return to Tetsuya's house. Because of Tetsuya's strained relationship with Tokiko, Sayoko begins to look after her brother-in-law, performing many of Tokiko's wifely duties. Her return is quickly perceived by the other women not just as a burden, but as a threat. Tetsuya feels sorry for Sayoko and wants to help her in some way. When she begins to look after him, he sees her as his only source of comfort and then as his ideal love.

Tokiko looks for ways to get Sayoko out of the house. At this point a family friend, Hamura Kōsaburō, approaches Tetsuya with a job offer for Sayoko. Hamura sees in Sayoko a way to help further his own career by recommending her as a governess to his boss, a man named Shibuya. When he makes his proposal Tetsuya wavers, for there are rumors that Shibuya has raped some of his female servants. In spite of these allegations, Tetsuya is too weak-willed to make a firm decision, and he is unable either to refuse or to accept his friend's

proposal. So Hamura goes over his head to Tokiko and her mother. The two of them jump at the opportunity to be rid of the potential threat to their security, and once again they ignore Tetsuya's desires. Sayoko is sent off to the Shibuya house, only to return soon after when, as Tetsuya feared, her master tries to rape her. This precipitates a violent argument during which Tokiko strikes Sayoko. Sayoko leaves the family for good, intending to join a Christian group in a rural province. Because she decides to leave so abruptly, she has no time to say good-bye to Tetsuya, who is at his school. Feeling a sense of obligation to him, she contacts him just before her departure. He convinces her to stay, and they become lovers, living together in a hideaway.

Their life quickly deteriorates. Tokiko vows that whatever happens between her and Tetsuya, she will do all she can to keep Sayoko away from him. In spite of her attitude, Tetsuya is moved to feel pity for his wife, and he becomes desperate to find a way to leave with Sayoko and still not place Tokiko in a hopeless position. A solution seems to present itself when he is unexpectedly offered a job teaching in China. He accepts the position, but before he can flee his hideaway is discovered. The leaders of the Christian group that Sayoko had originally planned to join take her away, and Tetsuya is unable to find her. Psychologically broken, he becomes an alcoholic, and eventually disappears in China. The Ono house is ruined, and Tokiko and her mother are forced to return to their ancestral home in the countryside. Sayoko reportedly becomes a nurse on a hospital ship. The only figure in the book who ends successfully, at least in material terms, is Hamura.

An Adopted Husband shares many of the elements found in *Ukigumo*. At a basic level it may be said that both works are attempts to portray realistically the consequences of the failure of an individual to cope with the pressures of personal and social obligations. However, it is also apparent that in *An Adopted Husband* the author's ideas have evolved and deepened, and that there is a more mature artistry at work. The protagonist of *Ukigumo*, Bunzō, is a man so hamstrung by his scruples that he is incapable of rising to heroic action to achieve success in the world and thereby win Osei, the woman he loves. Tetsuya is also a stubborn, ineffectual antihero, yet his characterization is more complex, because he rouses himself to have a self-destructive love affair with his sister-in-law, Sayoko. He also constantly questions the nature of his actions, giving the reader a clearer idea of the defeats and disappointments that shape his motivations. Tetsuya is not a self-portrait of the artist, any more than is Bunzō, but certainly an older author was able to draw upon the experience of defeat and disappointment to create a darker fictional world.

The techniques developed in the course of composing *Ukigumo* were brought to bear and perfected in Futabatei's second novel in a number of ways. Following his early belief that ideas shape the structure of a novel, Futabatei began to fashion *An Adopted Husband* out of his concern with the often unacceptable choices forced upon individuals by social institutions. The institution in this case is the family system, which was widely perceived to contain vestiges of the old Japan, where individual rights and desires were subordinated to the interests of socially sanctioned behavior.

Futabatei was not content, however, with just exploring external causes for the mistreatment of individuals or the wrecking of individual lives. Instead he pushed his narrative toward an exploration of the interaction between external, social factors and internal motivations. He developed that interaction by presenting the main characters in this novel as incapable of personal reconciliation because of their stubborn adherence to their own version of the truth of events. Even though Tetsuya tries to understand events from the viewpoint of Tokiko or Hamura on a number of occasions, he finally never doubts his own justification for his attempt to get away from his family burdens and achieve personal happiness. Throughout the novel there is an implied criticism of the inflexibility and narrow abso-

lutism not only of the family system, but also of the actions of the characters; and this criticism is the product of an intellectual position that refused to acknowledge the possibility of a single narrative version of the truth. The unreliability of the voices that relate the story is a key component of *An Adopted Husband.* Because the text never gives a clear-cut reason for believing one character's story over another's, the fundamental contradictions are beyond resolution.

The realistic style Futabatei developed in *Ukigumo* involved more than moving away from the reliance upon stock figures and improbable action. If fiction were to reflect or record the realities of modern society, then the means by which the characters try to overcome their difficulties had to seem commonplace. For example, in Edo-period drama and fiction double suicide was a frequently used device to resolve the otherwise irreconcilable conflict between the desires of the individual and the dictates of social behavior. In choosing to die, the lovers in Edo literature opted for a heroic course of action. The literary convention of double suicide reflected the realities of a society where individual rights were subordinated to social obligations. That convention also gave tacit acknowledgment to the primacy of those obligations. If, in a modernizing society, a critique of older social customs was to have any force, then the actions taken in the past to overcome the conflicts caused by those customs had to be rejected. To the extent that literary conventions reflect the nature of social conflicts, heroic action had to be redefined. After all, his failure to do so in his first novel had left Futabatei profoundly dissatisfied.

An Adopted Husband was one of the earliest works of its era to fully explore the ambivalent nature of tragedy. It was also a sophisticated attempt to elaborate on traditional characters and situations in ways that were antiheroic in order to reconcile the formal necessities of literature with contemporary ideals and principles. It was one thing to try to achieve realism, but quite another to lose the rhetorical qualities that gave value to the novel as an art form in the attempt. The striking characteristic of *An Adopted Husband* is the way in which the conflicts among its main characters parallel the tensions in the narrative form itself. If the form of the modern novel itself seems to preclude any absolute determination of what is true or real, then is it possible to write literature that seriously engages social or ethical questions? For Futabatei the question of the possibility of a new literature was never laid to rest; and that question would in fact be the central subject of his third and final novel, *Heibon (Mediocrity)*.

Mediocrity

Mediocrity was published serially in the Tokyo *Asahi Shinbun* from October to December 1907. It enhanced Futabatei's critical reputation and helped him return to prominence within the literary establishment. But for a number of reasons Futabatei viewed the attention he was receiving as a mixed blessing. He had garnered acclaim early in his career but had not handled it well. More important, he had re-emerged at a time of important developments in Meiji literature. The rise of the naturalist movement in particular, with its emphasis on the tightly controlled realism of confessional or first-person narratives, had created a lively atmosphere in which the purpose and nature of fiction were being reconsidered.

Mediocrity consists of three main stories that deal with a love relationship of importance to the narrator. These stories involve his grandmother, his dog, and his father respectively, and each exemplifies a different kind of love. The novel is cast as a memoir that details the coming of age of the narrator, Furuya Sekkō, who must come to grips with the loss of these three figures and with the true nature of love.

The story of his relationship with his grandmother takes place when the narrator is very young. She is depicted as a tyrant who uses her position in the household to bully the narrator's mother. One way in which she exercises power is to pamper her grandson and protect

him from the discipline of his parents. Furuya tells us that at a very early age he learned how to manipulate the situation to his advantage; and though he caused his mother many problems, he also secretly thought that his grandmother was foolish to be taken in by his childish calculations. When his grandmother died, Furuya says that he made a show of grief, but that he did not really feel any loss until after the public mourning was completed. He only felt the absence of the grandmother when he returned to the normal routine of the household, and he speculates that what was taken to be a love relationship was instead nothing more than the selfish gratification he and his grandmother gained by using one another.

As a child, love has no real meaning for Furuya, except in its most narrow and grasping sense, until he comes to a different understanding of it through caring for a pet dog. Of all his relationships, he tells us, it is his love for this animal that he regards as the highest type of love in his experience: a love valued because it was selfless and natural. And of all the incidents in the narrator's life, it is the death of the dog at the hands of a dogcatcher that prompts his deepest speculations on the ideal of love. After telling us how the dog was killed and how the episode affected him, Furuya abruptly interrupts his narrative with a series of aphorisms, concluding with the following observation: "I could go on scribbling such things, but having just written them I'm bored. They are all lies. I would like to write just one thing that isn't a lie. For a long time after Pochi was killed, the faces of people all looked like dogcatchers. That alone is the truth" (*FSZ*, vol. 4, p. 132).

All of the aphorisms express a deep distrust of the intellect and a reliance upon intuited experience. The inadequacy of rationalism appears to be a crucial argument in the story as a whole, but intuition is not being idealized. The aphorisms carry more rhetorical than intellectual weight, and Futabatei uses them to good effect to make us feel the grief and resentment of the young man. The emptiness of intellect, the faculty that idealizes, is revealed in its contrast with innocent emotion. The effect of the passage, not its content, seems to confirm the importance of emotional attachments while showing that such attachments are never permanent and cannot become an ideal. This recalls what takes place in *An Adopted Husband* when that novel shifts near the end from the question of credibility to the question of emotional consequences. The truth that each of the aphorisms tries to convey gives way before the formal literary effect of the passage, which creates the illusion that the final statement about human brutality is an absolute truth.

We soon learn that this skepticism extends to literature. Almost half of the novel deals with the education of the narrator, and the turning point in his education comes when, as a middle school student, Furuya obtains his parents' consent to go to Tokyo to study. Moving to Tokyo from the provinces was an experience shared by many Meiji intellectuals—an experience that took on symbolic meaning as an expression of the kinds of anxiety and ambition shared by Futabatei's generation. Furuya's story thus takes on a quasi-mythical, literary quality. He arranges to stay and work in the home of his uncle while attending school. There he experiences his first pangs of adolescent love for his cousin, Yukie, but she turns out to be a shallow young woman, and he is disappointed. He also grows indignant at his uncle, who treats him like a servant. As a result he strikes out on his own, moving to a boarding house where he becomes friendly with some young men who are interested in literary pursuits. He affects a literary name, Sekkō, which is the Sinitic reading of the characters for Yukie, and he portrays his early literary endeavors as a youthful, pretentious kind of romanticism. Eventually, Furuya becomes convinced that his involvement with literature is a corrupting influence. Looking back on that time of his life, he feels that he was seduced by the concept that literature provided a way to get at the truth, to describe reality. He asserts that "literature embellishes human corruption with rhetorical flourishes," and he wonders

whether the reality of literature isn't "already more prejudiced in favor of evil than my view of it?" (*FSZ*, vol. 4, p. 171).

Furuya tells us that he enjoyed some early critical successes with his writing, but that he was hard-pressed to continue because he really did not have the imagination to create fiction. To compensate for his weakness, he decided to try writing according to the formula of some artistic doctrine, and the doctrine he eventually settled on resembles naturalism. At this point the narrative turns itself inside out, with the narrator telling in mock-naturalist style about himself as a young author who writes as an insincere naturalist. Once he had adopted this literary creed, he concluded that formal realism depends upon the subjectivity of the author, and that he must therefore broaden his experience as much as possible. This leads him into a meaningless relationship with a woman named Oito, and it is in this section of the novel that Futabatei makes his sharpest attack against the methods of the naturalists, exposing the pretense of honesty underlying the confessional mode and deploring the hypocrisy of authors who absolve themselves of responsibility in real life by using the novel as a confessional.

When Furuya embarks upon a literary career, he is estranged from his parents; and the lifestyle he keeps with Oito causes him to neglect them further. This neglect becomes a serious matter when his father becomes gravely ill. And when his father dies, Furuya is shocked into the realization that he has been chasing after false values and ideals. He feels that this realization is somehow inextricably bound up with his views about literature.

This brutal moment of understanding is a defining one in Meiji literature. It comes right before the abrupt ending of the novel, which is revealed to be an unfinished manuscript, and is a recapitulation of the doubts about literature that Futabatei struggled with for most of his life. He saw a powerful link between idealism and literature in the formal, intellectual, and thus fictional qualities they share. He is skeptical of both because they fail to touch on reality, and it is on this point that he sees moral and literary questions overlapping. Nonetheless, if that were all there was to his position, then surely he would not have bothered to write *Mediocrity* at all. Skepticism was at the core of Futabatei's thought and writing predicated on an irreconcilable conflict between the ideal and the practical, which in turn, he thought, reflected a larger crisis within Meiji culture. He was ambivalent toward the novel: he recognized its emotional power and artistic potential, and yet finally he was unable to find in it the seriousness that he considered the essential characteristic needed to break with the practices of Edo narrative.

The title itself indicates the extent of Futabatei's skepticism toward literature, in particular the confessional novel. *Mediocrity* is a self-parody that calls attention to the inherent artificiality of the first-person narrative. It also recalls the mediocrity of the characters in his earlier works, as if to point out that modern literature can no longer deal in heroic absolutes. The title loudly announces the fictive, formal quality of the narrative, and the self-consciousness contained within it. In chapter 2, even as the narrator begins to tell us about his personal background, he decides right before us the subject and mode of his narrative:

> Well now, a title. . . . "What should I do for a title? These matters have always been damned hard for me to decide." . . . And so, thinking aloud like this for a moment, I suddenly slap my knee. *Mediocrity!* That's the title. When a mediocre person writes about his mediocre life with his mediocre pen, that title's a natural.
>
> Now for the style of writing, although that is not something you can really plan out. I hear that of late it has become the rage to write out all manner of trivial things experienced by the author, just as they are without adding any artifice, like a cow dribbling slobber. . . .
>
> So let's see. My title is *Mediocrity*, and my style of writing will be as natural as the slobber of a cow.
>
> (*FSZ*, vol. 4, pp. 102–103)

The tone of this passage seems like a return to the playfulness of *gesaku*. The satire is directed at the form and pretense of the novel, as Futabatei takes up again the question of the possibility of literature as a vehicle for expressing serious ideas. *Mediocrity* is for that reason not merely a polemical attack on idealism, but an examination of the possibility of maintaining ideals in the face of the disappointments of life. Although Futabatei was uncomfortable with the contrivances of the confessional mode, he uses that form, which became dominant in modern Japanese literature first among the naturalists and then in the guise of the I-novel, as a means of examining idealism while maintaining a skeptical frame of mind.

Futabatei's Legacy

In June 1908 Futabatei left for St. Petersburg to work as a special correspondent for the *Asahi Shinbun*. Shortly after he arrived, he suffered a nervous collapse and spent most of the rest of the year recuperating. The following February he was diagnosed as having either pneumonia or tuberculosis (probably the latter). He entered a hospital in March, but a high fever persisted, and in April 1909 he was sent home. He went to London first where he boarded a Japanese ship. On 10 May 1909, while the ship was en route to Singapore, Futabatei died.

Shortly after Futabatei's death his friends Tsubouchi Shōyō and Uchida Roan organized a memorial volume to which all of the major writers of the time contributed essays. A consistent judgment emerges from the volume, for all the contributors—even some who were critical of Futabatei to the end—acknowledged the impact of his work on them. Futabatei's influence is in part the result of timing, that is, of his historical position, and in part the direct stylistic impact that he had on others. His peers looked upon him as an emblematic figure of an age marked by enormous hopes, change, and anxiety, a figure who gave expression to many of the concerns that came to define modern literature. The literary terrain he first mapped out was of vital interest to his contemporaries, and remains of interest today, because it is the same landscape that almost all twentieth-century writers in Japan have had to traverse.

Selected Bibliography

PRIMARY WORKS

COMPLETE WORKS

Futabatei Shimei zenshū. 9 vols. Tokyo: Iwanami Shoten, 1981. (In-text references are to this edition.)
Futabatei Shimei zenshū. 5 vols. Tokyo: Chikuma Shobō, 1984–1985.

WORKS IN ENGLISH TRANSLATION

An Adopted Husband. Trans. by Buhachiro Mitsui and Gregg M. Sinclair. New York: Knopf, 1919; New York: Greenwood Press, 1969.
Japan's First Modern Novel: Ukigumo of Futabatei Shimei. Trans. and with critical commentary by Marleigh Grayer Ryan. New York: Columbia University Press, 1967.
Mediocrity. Trans. by Glenn W. Shaw. Tokyo: Hokuseido Press, 1927.

SECONDARY WORKS

CRITICAL AND BIOGRAPHICAL STUDIES

Kamei Hideo. *Futabatei Shimei: Sensō to kakumei no hōrōsha.* Tokyo: Shinkōsha, 1986.
Nakamura Mitsuo. *Futabatei Shimei den.* Tokyo: Kōdansha, 1958.
Oketani Hideaki. Futabatei Shimei to Meiji Nippon. Tokyo: Bungei Shunjū, 1986.
Satō Seiro. *Futabatei Shimei kenkyū.* Tokyo: Yūseidō, 1995.
Tanaka Kunio. *Futabatei Shimei "Ukigumo" no seiritsu.* Tokyo: Sōbunsha Shuppan, 1998.
Togawa Shinsuke. *Futabatei Shimei ron.* Tokyo: Chikuma Shobō, 1984.
Tsubouchi Shōyō and Uchida Roan, eds. *Futabatei Shimei.* Tokyo: Ifūsha, 1909.
Washburn, Dennis. *The Dilemma of the Modern in Japanese Fiction.* New Haven, Conn.: Yale University Press, 1995.

ICHIYŌ
(HIGUCHI ICHIYŌ)
1872–1896

ANN SHERIF

HIGUCHI ICHIYŌ wrote about poor and marginalized people in the great capital of Tokyo. She took as her heroines such characters as a young woman from a poor family who aspires to end her marriage to a rich and powerful man, a maid whose life is on the line because of a minor indiscretion, and a teenage girl for whom the future means work as a prostitute. Her stories portray adolescent love, lust, and identity before it was fashionable even to recognize youth as a time of significant social, emotional, and physical change. At a time in Japan when a progressive person might have sought inspiration from Anglo-European ideals about the sanctity of the individual and the rights of people to challenge unjust social structures and conventions, Ichiyō created stories that boldly presented the humanity of her characters and highlighted the social and economic constraints upon the lives of Tokyo's less honored inhabitants—in particular, the lives of women.

Yet Ichiyō has never been regarded as a renegade or an innovator. On the contrary, she is the only woman whose writings have been consistently included in the canon of Meiji period (1868–1912) literature. Ichiyō's stories retain this status because she was an intelligent and incisive observer of Japan in the transitional period that was her age. In addition, she is ranked among the most accomplished stylists—a writer steeped in the classical literary and aesthetic tradition. Ichiyō wrote in a consciously traditional style that was heavily allusive and rich; the sumptuous style of her earlier stories and diary passages draws upon the aristocratic prose and verse from the Heian period (794–1185), the golden days of the aristocracy. While in her early twenties, she helped to uncover for contemporary readers the wonders of the Edo-period (1600–1868) writer Ihara Saikaku, with his witty tales of the merchant class and the amorous goings-on of the pleasure quarters. Through her fascination with and use of Saikaku's brand of realism, she confirmed that realism was indeed the most promising path for modern Japanese literature. In her own works, she offered penetrating and witty observations about social class, gender relations, and the fault line dividing the forward-looking Meiji state from the complex social patterns and practices remaining from the past.

In 1913 the feminist writer and political activist Hiratsuka Raichō (1886–1971) took a critical view of Ichiyō, asserting that although Ichiyō produced unforgettable and beautifully crafted portraits of late-nineteenth-century women and their lot, she ultimately proved to be a "woman of old Japan" in both her life and her art. Ichiyō, Hiratsuka asserted, sacrificed herself by working ceaselessly in order to support her family, rather than devoting herself exclusively to her art; and her writings failed to produce an adequate critique of Confucian ideology. While Hiratsuka Raichō was correct in viewing Ichiyō as working outside the progressive circles of writers and artists who embraced Western notions of social change, in the end the limitations of her critical estimations of Ichiyō both as a person and as a writer have placed her among a distinct minority.

For over a century readers both in and out of Japan have continued to praise Ichiyō's wonderfully detailed and nuanced short stories. In fact her reputation has grown enormously, especially in the postwar period. In response to readers' demands for more accessible versions of Ichiyō's works, respected novelists such as Matsuura Rieko have delighted in rendering Ichiyō's classical prose into modern Japanese. Along with three annotated editions of Ichiyō's complete works, the significant number of scholarly and critical studies devoted to her work attests to Ichiyō's literary status.

Until the 1960s it was mostly male critics and writers who commented on and annotated Ichiyō's works (if only because men comprised most of the active critical community). Subsequently, feminist critics and readers have expressed their high regard for Ichiyō by vigorously debating the meanings of her writings and by studying her life and the age in which she worked. Far from condemning Ichiyō's writing or her life as regressive remnants of a bygone era, as Hiratsuka Raichō did, it is possible to view Ichiyō as both of her time and ahead of her time, like the best writers able to reach an audience living in a world vastly different from her own.

Unlike many of the writers in this volume, Ichiyō did not write literary criticism per se, but her works, the course her writing career took, and her diaries constitute a kind of literary and cultural criticism in themselves. For years, Ichiyō kept to a strict regime of writing in her diary. The multiple volumes offer scholars and readers an invaluable source of information about Ichiyō's daily and professional life as well as her outlook on the world. Judging from the changing writing styles and the high quality of the hundreds of entries, clearly Ichiyō also considered diary writing to be a means of honing her craft. She penned some entries in a stiff, formal style most often used by men in official documents and public diaries, some in the flowing, poetic style associated with the diaries of aristocratic women of old, and some in a mixed or more colloquial manner. Ichiyō's use of a wide range of written Japanese styles suggests her reverence for the rich and varied literary tradition of Japan and her desire to show its vitality in the modern age. Ichiyō's generation was one of the last to be educated so thoroughly in the classics. Understanding her writings demanded a certain level of education in literary genres, even for her contemporaries. Both her fiction and her diary writing were informed by her knowledge of *waka* (classical poetry in the court tradition), which she also composed.

Biography

Born Higuchi Natsuko in Tokyo on 2 May 1872, Ichiyō was the third child of Higuchi Noriyoshi and his wife Taki. Both her mother and father grew up in farm families in Yamanashi Prefecture and moved to the city of Edo (present-day Tokyo) in the 1850s. As was the case with many prosperous peasants, Ichiyō's father Noriyoshi was well educated and knew the Chinese classics. For a time Ichiyō's mother Taki found employment as a wet nurse for the children of one of the shōgun's retainers. Noriyoshi worked as an assistant in a shogunal office and bought the samurai rank for himself. After the advent of the Meiji period and the dissolution of the central military government, he found new employment in Tokyo municipal offices.

Recognizing his daughter's aptitude for learning, Noriyoshi doted on Ichiyō and encouraged her scholarly tendencies. He taught her classical poetry and Edo-period fiction at home and chose to send her to private schools rather than to the newly established public schools. Private schools instructed students in modern subjects such as geography, hygiene, and chemistry but also emphasized the study of the Japanese classics—poetry in particular. In the Japanese literary tradition, the verse of the imperial anthologies of poetry had long formed the core of the canon, and it was these poems that Ichiyō learned from early childhood. Though an excellent student, Ichiyō withdrew from school for several years at her mother's insistence, partly because her older brother Sentarō, a dissolute and sickly boy, had quit school.

Ichiyō was allowed to return to formal schooling in 1886 at age fourteen, but this time at a school that would make her fully aware of the potential of literature and of the literary life. The Haginoya (Bush Clover Hut) was a private school that mainly offered its students training in poetry composition and lessons in the prose and verse of the glorious Japanese literary past. Poet Nakajima Utako (1844–1903), who headed the poetry school, encouraged her students to excel by holding poetry contests, in which Ichiyō vied for attention. She also found herself in the company of the daughters of upper-class families for the first time in her life, an experience that gave her a new perspective on her own family's precarious financial and social status. Haginoya proved stimulating to Ichiyō's career as a writer in a number of ways: in addition to the exposure to the classical literary canon and opportunities to emulate such elegant modes of writing, Haginoya introduced Ichiyō to women who dedicated their lives to writing—Nakajima Utako presented a formidable model for Ichiyō. One of Ichiyō's classmates at Haginoya, Miyake Kaho, proved successful in her determination to become a professional novelist. In 1888 Kaho published her first novel and was paid handsomely for it. Impressed by Miyake Kaho's cash earnings, Ichiyō resolved to put her talents to good financial use by writing and selling stories. Unlike the many privileged young women at the Haginoya, Ichiyō's family had managed to climb into a respectable social class but now found itself sliding back rapidly into poverty. While still in her teens, Ichiyō began to see herself as one of the family bread-winners.

Not long after the father's business attempts failed, the Higuchi family's fortunes shifted from bad to worse. Noriyoshi died in 1889. Ichiyō's older brother had succumbed to tuberculosis the previous year, and her other brother was estranged from the family. Consequently, the Higuchi family now consisted only of women—Ichiyō, her mother, and her younger sister Kuniko. Ichiyō, moreover, was named the legal head of the family. Her desire to earn money by writing, then, came not so much from a spirit of rivalry with her classmate Miyake Kaho as from a pressing need to support herself and her family. Nakajima Utako had given her the opportunity to help out in the poetry school, but Ichiyō did more busy work than writing or teaching, and the financial rewards were extremely limited.

But how was she to earn a place in literary circles outside the small world of the elegant Haginoya? Unlike Miyake Kaho, whose education had afforded her broad exposure to Anglo-European culture and literature, Ichiyō could boast a deep knowledge of Japanese and Chinese classics. From 1892, through the sponsorship of the novelist Nakarai Tōsui, Ichiyō succeeded in publishing some of her earliest stories, such as "Yamizakura" (1892; "Flowers at Dusk," 1981); "Umoregi" (1892; "In Obscurity," 1981), and "Koto no ne," (1893; "The Sound of the Koto," 1981), in *Musashino, Bungakukai,* and other literary journals. Although Ichiyō's great talent and potential were evident in the accomplished style, mixing classical and colloquial elements, the stories were flawed by Ichiyō's rigid adherence to formulaic plots and archetypical characters common in classical fiction. The reader finds in them sentimentality, melodrama, baroque turns of phrase, and heavy dependence on allusion to *The Tale of Genji,* a novel of the Heian period by Murasaki Shikibu, and other classical romances.

The Higuchi women worked hard to maintain the lifestyle that they had managed when

123

Ichiyō's father was alive. But they soon realized that their rapidly reduced earning power meant they would have to change the way they lived. Ichiyō determined that they would sell off most of their belongings—kimonos, painting scrolls, furniture—and use the proceeds for the purpose of setting up a small shop selling stationery and sweets. Ichiyō, planning to manage the shop, resigned from her position as assistant to Nakajima Utako, the head of the Haginoya. The Higuchi women could no longer afford to reside in their comfortable middle-class neighborhood, nor would they be able to rent a shop there. This pressing financial reality led to what proved to be the most significant journey in Ichiyō's life—a journey of less than five miles, but one leading to an encounter with a section of the city, people, and ways of life that would permanently alter Ichiyō's approach to her writing and her understanding of herself as a woman.

In 1893 Ichiyō, Kuniko, and their mother moved to the Ryūsenji neighborhood of Tokyo, which bordered on the Yoshiwara pleasure quarter. They managed to procure a tenement house that was barely clean enough and found themselves living among the pleasure quarter's denizens: courtesans, prostitutes, teahouse owners, street musicians, craftspeople, and many other sorts they had never before had close contact with. The women of the teahouses produced a world of fantasy and entertainment for men of all classes, but none of them, not even the most successful and celebrated *oiran* (high-class courtesan), could make claims to bourgeois respectability.

During her days in the Ryūsenji area, the work of stocking the shop and managing a business exhausted Ichiyō. Even so, she found time to write fiction, to hone her skills by keeping her diary, and to read as much as she could, from Edo-period fiction to the daily newspaper. Her world had narrowed to the business of survival. Yet intellectually and artistically, Ichiyō continued to grow, to become aware of new possibilities for her fiction, to monitor current events, and to learn about the humbling circumstances of life on

the boundaries of the Yoshiwara. With a classmate from the Haginoya, she made plans to found a new school of classical poetry, but this scheme proved impossible for a woman who could barely put food on the table. Even the economic prosperity brought on by Japan's early efforts as an imperial and colonialist power, including the war waged on the Korean peninsula in the Sino-Japanese War of 1894–1895, did not improve the Higuchi family's lot.

However trying, this period spent near the pleasure quarter was highly significant in Ichiyō's career as a writer. It provided her with direct and intimate exposure to the community of people who worked and lived there, especially the women. Ichiyō and her family got to know the prostitutes and other pleasure quarter dwellers who came to the shop and who sought out Kuniko and Taki's tailoring expertise. Some of Ichiyō's most accomplished and lasting works—"Takekurabe" (1894–1896; "Child's Play," 1981), "Nigorie" (1895; "Troubled Waters," 1981) and "Wakaremichi" (1896; "Separate Ways," 1981)—were inspired by her days in this realm.

As fruitful as the Ryūsenji period proved to be artistically, financially it was a disaster. Ichiyō, Kuniko, and their mother, unable even to pay the rent on their house regularly, admitted defeat in their attempts as shopkeepers. In May 1894 the family closed the shop and moved to a more respectable and somewhat more prosperous neighborhood called Maruyama-Fukuyama. To make ends meet, Ichiyō returned to her position assisting Nakajima Utako at the Haginoya. Kuniko and their mother continued to take in piecework from courtesans and prostitutes. With the stress of the shop gone, Ichiyō had more time to write—and write she did. Some call this time from mid-1894 the "miraculous fourteen months" because Ichiyō turned out one brilliant story after another, published in literary magazines: in addition to "Child's Play," "Troubled Waters," and "Separate Ways," she wrote "Yamiyo" (1894; "Encounters on a Dark Night"), "Ōtsugomori" (1894; "On the Last

Day of the Year"), and "Jūsan'ya" (1895; "The Thirteenth Night"). Most of these pieces met with the highest praise from critics and readers alike. Prominent novelists such as Kōda Rohan, Kunikida Doppo, and Mori Ōgai visited Ichiyō to offer congratulations on her brilliant success and to talk about literature with her.

Ichiyō's tremendous burst of energy and creativity was cut short by tuberculosis. After years of a meager diet, hard work, and the undiagnosed illness, Ichiyō weakened quickly. Her last attempts at fiction were half-hearted. Save for sporadic, brief entries, in which she chronicled her physical distress, she stopped keeping her precious diary. Ichiyō died on 13 November 1896.

"Child's Play"

Ichiyō's most famous and revered work, the novella "Child's Play," has long delighted and intrigued readers. The characters—adolescents who live around the pleasure quarters in Tokyo—come so fully to life that the thinness of the story's plot hardly matters. The story begins several days before the annual Otori summer festival. Young people around the Ryūgeji Temple compete to make the best floats and most eye-catching outfits for the festival parade. Rude and obnoxious Chōkichi's group has always lost out to Shōta's, but this year Chōkichi is determined to outdo his rivals. Surely if he enlists the help of Nobu, the respected son of the Ryūgeji's priest, his group will triumph. Shōta is proud to have Midori on his side, the girl who has been dubbed the "queen of the neighborhood kids" because of her generosity and spunk. For several of those involved in what begins as a frivolous yet earnest competition between two cliques of kids, the preparations for the festival result in realizations about the meaning of impending adulthood and a loss of intimacy with childhood companions.

Ichiyō makes a point of explaining each character's class background and schooling, clearly emphasizing these as integral aspects of identity. Chōkichi, the son of a firefighter,

attends the less prestigious private school, the Ikueisha, whereas Shōta, whose family runs a pawnbroking and money-lending operation, thinks highly of himself because he goes to a progressive public school. Fourteen-year-old Midori finds herself entranced by the pleasure quarter where she lives with her parents and her sister, the popular courtesan Ōmaki, who works at the brothel Daikokuya.

Midori and her friends have played together innocently in the shadow of the pleasure quarter. Ichiyō's story traces the precarious days of summer when they take their first steps toward adulthood. For the first time, they realize the brevity of their carefree adolescence. The serious Nobu becomes uncomfortably aware of his feelings for the lovely Midori and, at the same time, of the gossip that surrounds them—rumors of marriage that cast their relationship in terms of adult ties between a man and a woman. Arrogant Chōkichi taunts Midori openly because her sister is a courtesan and because a similar fate awaits her. Gentle and innocent Shōta is always Midori's ally and not one to lord his masculinity over Midori or to feel threatened by her beauty and dubious future. In the end, though, Shōta, who is a few years younger than his friends, reacts like an unknowing child to the change in Midori's life, and she rejects even his friendship.

Over the course of the novella, it is Midori whose transformation strikes the reader as the most painful and complete. Midori the child adores her sister Ōmaki's beautiful robes, her suitors, and her status as the brothel Daikokuya's prize princess and product. The generous allowance she receives from Ōmaki and the neighbors' effusive praise of Ōmaki's beauty fuel Midori's pride. Much of "Child's Play" concerns the gradual process of Midori's coming to understand what her future will bring and the harsh reality of her sister's seemingly gorgeous world.

Ichiyō depicts this tragic shift in Midori's awareness of the world gradually and delicately. In the beginning Midori presents herself as full of pluck and overflowing with confidence. When Chōkichi calls her a whore and flings a muddy sandal at her face, her pride is a bit wounded, but she manages to keep her head up. When Nobu snubs her she is in a quandary, but she comforts herself that "she, after all, was Midori of the Daikokuya, and not beholden to him in the slightest" (*Higuchi Ichiyō zenshū [HIZ]*, vol. 1, p. 421; tr. Danly, p. 269). Beautiful though she is, she refuses to connect her own physical and sexual allure to that of the courtesans and prostitutes who surround her. In other words, for much of the story Midori remains unaware of her own sexual potential and of the traffic in the bodies of young women that drives commerce in the quarter. "A headstrong girl by nature, Midori indulged herself by fluttering around in a world that she had fashioned from the clouds" (*HIZ*, vol. 1, p. 424; tr. Danly, p. 271). She has even forgotten the tears she shed when the owner of the Daikokuya came to the family's country home to "appraise" and purchase her sister Ōmaki. Despite the reader's growing awareness of Midori's self-delusion and the inevitability of her transformation, Ichiyō conjures up a highly sympathetic, multidimensional portrait of this troubled young girl as she becomes a woman.

Although the focus of "Child's Play" is on character, the story's famous opening passage describes the setting:

It's a long way round to the front of the quarter, where the trailing branches of the willow tree bid farewell to the nighttime revellers and the bawdyhouse lights flicker in the moat, dark as the dye that blackens the smiles of the Yoshiwara beauties. From the third-floor rooms of the lofty houses the all but palpable music and laughter spill down into the side street. Who knows how these great establishments prosper? The rickshaws pull up night and day.

(*HIZ*, vol. 1, p. 402; tr. Danly, p. 254)

This famous opening passage suggests the emphasis on a sense of place. Not until the very end of the first chapter does the narrator mention the children who live around the

Yoshiwara, let alone the protagonists of the story. This and other lengthy passages that evoke the sights, sounds, smells, and population of the pleasure quarter serve to ground Midori, Nobu, and the others in a specific time and place. By contrast, in many of her earlier, less mature works, Ichiyō conjured poetic settings that suggested the landscapes of classical poetry, gardens of the imagination. Her first published work, "Flowers at Dusk" ("Yamizakura," 1892), for example, begins with a generalized, lyrical description of setting marked by untranslatable allusions to classical poetry: "Only a bamboo fence separated the two houses. They shared the same well, whose waters ran deep and pure, untroubled as the concord between the neighbors. The flowering plum beneath the eaves of one home brought spring to the other" (*HIZ*, vol. 1, p. 3; tr. Danly, p. 167).

Although the title "Child's Play" refers to a tenth-century poem on the sudden blossoming of childhood fondness into married love, its primary inspiration was not the delicate sensibilities and lovely imagery of aristocratic poetry. In "Child's Play" Ichiyō creates a prose version of Edo-period comic *haikai* linked verse, a genre distinguished from court poetry in its focus on the details of daily life and its celebration of wit. A sequence of *haikai* linked poems always started with a stanza (called a *hokku*) that established setting and tone for the piece. The opening of "Child's Play" has a similar function. Ichiyō's use of this structure also recalls the works of the renowned Ihara Saikaku (1642–1693), whose prose incorporated *haikai* techniques, especially the loosely linked structure and the emphasis on tone and setting. Saikaku found this genre, infused with wit and faithfully realistic, most suitable to describing the people who intrigued him. Rather than write about emperors and court ladies, Saikaku focused on the ordinary people of the growing "middle" classes of Edo-period Japan: the merchants, craftspeople, courtesans, and prostitutes.

In "Child's Play" Ichiyō thus turns away from the aristocratic modes of writing that she learned to love during her days at the Hagi-noya and searches for a more suitable approach to painting vivid portraits of Tokyo's people, their struggles and joys. Ichiyō's choice of Saikaku as a model and her use of a mixed classical and colloquial writing style mark her as unusual among writers of her period. Unlike many of her fellow writers, she chose not to emulate Anglo-European realist and naturalist novelists. Even her older contemporaries, such as Mori Ōgai and Kōda Rohan, favored writing in a manner much closer to the spoken language. Mori Ōgai praised Ichiyō's own brand of realism, her disinclination to copy foreign examples:

> What is extraordinary about "Child's Play" is that the characters are not those beastlike creatures one so often encounters in Ibsen or Zola, whose techniques the so-called naturalists have tried imitating to the utmost. They are real, human individuals that we laugh and cry with. . . . I do not hesitate to confer on Ichiyō the title of a true poet.
>
> (tr. Danly, p. 148)

Ōgai's description of Ichiyō's creation of Midori, Nobu, and others as the work of a poet points not only to the lyricism of the novella but also to the restraint and subtlety with which Ichiyō treats the emotions and changing psychologies of her characters. Ichiyō refuses to portray Midori as an uncomplicated victim of an unjust society but rather evokes the complex mental, physical, and social demands on an individual living in a society that offers her few choices. Ichiyō subtly depicts Midori's reactions to the small outward changes that signal she is no longer a child. In the following passage Midori has her hair done for the first time in the style of an adult—or a courtesan—and goes out into the street, where she meets Shōta:

> When she felt so awkward and unhappy, flattery only sounded like an insult. People turned to admire her and she thought they were jeering. "Shōta, I'm going home."

"Why don't you play? . . ." Midori felt her face color. Shōta was still a child, clearly. Where did one begin to explain?

> (*HIZ*, vol. 1, pp. 441–442; tr. Danly, p. 284)

Generations of critics have debated the cause of Midori's sudden transformation from spitfire to cringing young lady. Is it simply because of the new hairstyle that acts as an external sign of her passage to adulthood, or is her body showing signs of maturation? Ichiyō's subtleties are such as to keep the reader slightly off-balance and unsure of what prompts her characters to behave as they do.

Another poignant transformation is Nobu's sad acquiescence to his future as a priest and his rejection of his beloved Midori—perhaps because she is socially unacceptable. In one of the story's climactic moments, Nobu finds himself standing in the rain in front of the Daikokuya, stranded because the strap of his shoe has broken as he walks through the muddy alleyway. Not knowing that it is Nobu, Midori comes out to lend a scrap of fabric for the unfortunate traveler to use in mending his clog. Rather than scolding him for his clumsiness, as she would have only months before, Midori "cringed in the shadows of the gate. She didn't move, her heart throbbed. This was not the old Midori" (*HIZ*, vol. 1, p. 436; tr. Danly, p. 280). The two do not speak, and Midori flees into the house:

> He heard her walk away; his eyes wandered after her. The scarlet scrap of Yūzen silk lay in the rain, its pattern of red maple leaf near enough to touch. Odd, how her one gesture moved him, and yet he could not bring himself to reach out and take the cloth. He stared at it vacantly, and as he looked at it he felt his heart break.
>
> (*HIZ*, vol. 1, pp. 437–438; tr. Danly, p. 281)

In the end Nobu goes off to train for the priesthood, following the course expected of him. In fact, the narrator refers to him throughout by his formal priestly name, Shinnyo, as if to foretell his fate; "Nobu" is just the children's nickname for him.

But Midori's future looms more threatening than that of the other children because she will be the one bought and sold by men, her body no longer her own. There is no happy ending here. In the context of this tight-knit community, Midori is the one young person whose fate after her childhood has come to an end is to be torn from the fabric of respectable society and be relegated to the marginalized population of the women of the pleasure quarter. Paradoxically, the move of Midori's family from the countryside toward the center of the urban social realm in search of a better life will result in a social death for Midori once she is a prostitute or courtesan. Her future contrasts with that of other adult women in the community who will work as productive members of family units, as wives and mothers. When Chōkichi throws his dirty sandal at Midori's forehead, declaring, "You're nothing but a whore, just like your sister. . . . This is all you're worth" (*HIZ*, vol. 1, p. 414; tr. Danly, p. 264), he signals the community's view of Midori as tainted and as an outsider.

Since the 1980s, literary scholars such as Maeda Ai and Seki Reiko have sought to explain to modern readers what the Tokyo neighborhoods portrayed in the story reveal about that city as a whole and about the nation in the late nineteenth century. The pleasure quarters, some sanctioned by the authorities and some more clandestine, were a holdover from the Edo period, when urban dwellers sought out these spaces as escapes from a system of marriage based on financial and familial benefit rather than on romantic love. Edo-period literature and art glorified the courtesans and even the prostitutes of the quarter as aesthetic beings in a special place untainted by the demands of day-to-day life. But in the Meiji period, the country aimed at becoming a modern nation-state, one that respected the rights of all its citizens; how could such spaces thus persist alongside modern ideals? Or did their very existence serve to demarcate and define what was respectable and modern?

Maeda points out that the quarter where Midori and her friends grow up is on the fringes of the rapidly growing city of Tokyo, a place where the religious festivals and sense of tight-knit, almost rural community still figured prominently. However, scholars suggest that the willingness of the Daikokuya owner, who comes to the country to purchase Ōmaki, to bring the entire family to Tokyo so that it can remain intact stems from wishful thinking on Ichiyō's part rather than being modeled on actual examples of kind and gentle whorehouse owners. During this period the government instituted plans for economic growth and industrial prosperity at home and expansion into an empire abroad. Yet, many citizen farmers were so poor that they resorted to selling their daughters; and many women's prospects for earning a living wage were so limited that they sold their own bodies. Ichiyō's great achievement in "Child's Play" was to represent some of these people in their fullness, with all their ordinary joys and extraordinary sorrows. She also vividly evoked their particular cultural and social space: the miserable tenement houses they lived in, things that made life bearable despite it all, and the entertainment districts where customers believed they were visiting "lofty houses" that even a young woman like Midori could believe were beautiful.

Contemporary Japanese readers may be particularly drawn to Ichiyō's portrait of Midori and the freedom of her adolescent girlhood. In late-twentieth-century popular culture, audiences have been fascinated by evocations of the *shōjo*, or presexual adolescent girl, in literature, art, and film because of the freedom from adult responsibilities suggested by this transitional period in life. The *shōjo* as evoked in art appears free of the constraints of sexuality and oppressive gender roles in a patriarchal system. Although the Yoshiwara pleasure quarter and the highly organized system of sex and pleasure workers that it commanded has long since vanished from Tokyo, the refuge of adolescence that Ichiyō dramatizes in "Child's Play" strikes readers as particularly modern.

"Troubled Waters"

Critics have debated the meanings of "Troubled Waters" perhaps more than any of Ichiyō's other works. The figure of Oriki, a woman of the pleasure quarters and one of the story's main characters, has provoked much controversy. Oriki is a *shakufu*, a "waitress" or "barmaid" in Kikunoi, one of the establishments known euphemistically as a *meishuya*, or "bar with superior sake." Such bars often featured only displays of empty bottles, and the women who worked there poured, not excellent wine, but sweet words and flattery for their customers—all men. The story opens with a description of several of the women of the house as they attempt to lure potential customers. Among them,

> [Oriki] was a true beauty, slender and of average height. Her hair, just washed, was done up in a great chignon knotted with a twist of new straw. Her white complexion seemed in need of no make-up. . . . Her kimono was loosely tied, as if to show off the fairness of her breasts. Rather indecorously, she sat with one knee hoisted up and puffed away on her long pipe. . . . She was fortunate there was no one to scold her.

> One didn't have to ask her line of work. She had the uniform of all the girls in the district. . . . Oriki was surprisingly kind. Even women found themselves attracted to her.

(*HIZ*, vol. 2, pp. 4–5; tr. Danly, pp. 218–219)

Indeed, Oriki's natural beauty and independent spirit have made her the most sought after courtesan: "Not a man visited the quarter who didn't know of Oriki at the Kikunoi House. One hardly knew whether it was Oriki of the Kikunoi or the Kikunoi of Oriki, such was the success of this recent and rare find. Thanks to her, the fledgling quarter had blossomed with bright lights" (*HIZ*, vol. 2, p. 5; tr. Danly p. 220). The spirited and likable Oriki even has a handsome, wealthy gentleman suitor, Yūki Tomonosuke, who acts as though he is more interested in Oriki as a person than as a body. He encourages her to speak frankly about her past and her problems; he even brings up the subject of marriage to her. Oriki, though, finds herself plagued by headaches, and, what is worse, another man she should forget but cannot.

Although Oriki downs large cups of sake she still finds herself thinking of Genshichi. Genshichi has lost his credit at the Kikunoi House because his futon business has failed and his family is destitute—as a result of spending all of his money on Oriki. One fateful day, Oriki and Tomonosuke run into Genshichi's four-year-old son, and they buy him a package of fancy *castella* spongecake. When the boy brings it home and tells his mother, Ohatsu, that the "demon lady" bought it for him, Ohatsu flies into a rage and pitches the cake out. The argument that ensues between Genshichi and Ohatsu ends with the husband demanding a divorce and the wife fleeing the miserable shack where they live, with child in tow. At the end of "Troubled Waters," people on the street are gossiping about what seems to have been the most recent lovers' suicide, as they watch a pair of coffins being carried away. The bodies are those of Oriki and Genshichi. He appears to have slit his belly open with a sword. But Oriki "was slashed across the back, down from the shoulder. There were bruises on her cheek and cuts on her neck. . . . Obviously she tried to flee" (*HIZ*, vol. 2, p. 33; tr. Danly, p. 240).

Ichiyō does not present the interaction between Oriki and Genshichi that leads to their deaths, or the fate of Ohatsu and her son, or why Oriki resists Yūki Tomonosuke's offer to rescue her from her life as a prostitute. The critic Seki Reiko points out the ironic parallels between this story and the well-known play by Chikamatsu, "The Love Suicides at Amijima," from the Edo period. In Chikamatsu's drama, a merchant and a prostitute plan their suicides and are willing to die together in order to escape the unbearable social reality that thwarts their love for one another. Chikamatsu's lovers end their lives believing that they will be reborn together on the same lotus blossom in a Buddhist heaven. In "Troubled Waters," Ichiyō casts a doubtful eye on the romanticized fantasy of love suicide presented in "Amijima" and other plays of the genre. Through her creation of Ohatsu, Ichiyō also calls into question Chikamatsu's evocation of the merchant's self-sacrificing wife, Osan, who puts her own sense of duty and obligation to the other woman over her own needs.

Despite Oriki's low status in society, Ichiyō makes her a woman of considerable complexity. She is much more than a stock character of the Edo period, the women-who-loved-love type. That Genshichi and his destructive behavior are partly responsible for Oriki's headaches is clear, but in her confession to Tomonosuke she also hints at a troubled family history. She tells him, "You, I've liked from the start . . . But if you asked me to be your wife, I don't know . . . I guess you could say I'm fickle. And what do you think made me this way? Three generations of failure, that's what" (*HIZ*, vol. 2, p. 25; tr. Danly, p. 234). The scholar Takada Chiname notes that a confessional speech is not unusual for such geisha or prostitute characters in the literature of the pleasure quarter. But the fact that Oriki speaks not only of a legacy of failure but of a kind of madness suggests that Ichiyō aims to distinguish Oriki from the standard good-hearted whore. Oriki tells Tomonosuke that her proud father "was a craftsman." "His father was a learned man. My grandfather even read Chinese. But he was mad. In other words—like me. He wrote worthless scraps of things; they were banned by the authorities and he starved to death, I've been told" (*HIZ*, vol. 2, p. 25; tr. Danly, p. 235). In an earlier draft of "Troubled Waters," Oriki's speech differs slightly: her grandfather was an ardent admirer of Confucius, and other people called him a failure and crazy. In being a failure, Oriki claims, she most resembles her grandfather. Thus, Ichiyō's final version of the story emphasizes the psycholog-

ical rather than the social—specifically, the connection between the "craziness" of Oriki's passion and whatever (ambiguous) craziness she attributes to the grandfather and father.

Although "Troubled Waters" immerses itself in Edo-period dramatic situations and characters, the critic Isoda Kōichi reads the story as a commentary on the Meiji-period clash between old—pre-existing patterns of thought and social behavior—and new—the profound influence of Anglo-European thought, social constructs, and art. If Oriki—and Genshichi's passion for her—signifies the old "barbarian" (*yaban*) world carrying over from Edo, then Yūki Tomonosuke can be read as the new "civilization and enlightenment" (*bunmei kaika*) world of Meiji. Oriki seems to plead for salvation from the curse of failed generations before her and sees herself as mad, thus emphasizing the personal over the social. Genshichi's ruinous passion for Oriki, the prostitute in the pleasure quarter, resonates with that of many antiheroes from Edo plays. Even Genshichi's choice of *seppuku* ("ritual suicide") represents a regressive, anachronistic mindset. Yūki Tomonosuke, who, though a visitor to the quarter, is definitely not part of it, serves as contrast. This well-heeled gentleman has something of the modern psychologist in him, logical and rational as he almost scientifically observes Oriki. After hearing Oriki's confession about her past, he responds with what seems almost a non sequitur: "You want to be successful, don't you?" His comment represents the Meiji mindset that puts high value on social ambition and success at any price.

"The Thirteenth Night"

Together with the works discussed above, the stories "On the Last Day of the Year," "The Thirteenth Night," and "Separate Ways" form the set of five pieces widely regarded as Ichiyō's best and most significant work. "On the Last Day of the Year," a piece in the style of Saikaku, depicts the struggles of Omine, a young maid, to support her impoverished family at the year's end, as well as her fears that her rich employers might accuse her of theft.

The moving story "The Thirteenth Night" concerns a young married woman named Oseki, who desperately wishes to escape her cruel husband, even if it means giving up her only child. The husband demanded Oseki's hand in marriage from her parents, even though the parents "told him over and over again that [their] social standing was no match for his" (*HIZ*, vol. 2, pp. 103–104; tr. Danly, p. 246). Oseki finds her plans complicated by the dependence of her lower-class family on her powerful husband, for he has secured employment for her brother and paid for small comforts for her aging parents. When she visits her parents to inform them of her plan, they eventually talk her out of leaving her husband and especially her young son, Tarō. After much agonizing, Oseki decides that from "tonight I will consider myself dead—a dead spirit who watches over Tarō. That way I can bear Osamu's cruelty for a hundred years to come" (*HIZ*, vol. 2, p. 107; tr. Danly, p. 249).

In "The Thirteenth Night" Ichiyō examines the hazards of the kind of rapid class mobility that was idealized in the Meiji period. Oseki's parents are so conscious of their social inferiority that they are ashamed even to send their favorite cakes to their daughter and her rich husband for fear that nothing they could offer would be good enough for someone of the upper class. Her father's demands that she keep climbing the social and economic ladder are so great that she can only capitulate. Ichiyō ironically comments, "It was Oseki's misfortune to have been born so beautiful, and to have married above herself" (*HIZ*, vol. 2, p. 106; tr. Danly, p. 248). As Rebecca Copeland points out, "The Thirteenth Night" is one of several Meiji short stories that focus on women trapped in unhappy marriages. Not all these stories, however, end as fatalistically as "The Thirteenth Night." In a twist of fate in this story, the rickshaw driver who takes Oseki home from her visit to her parents turns out to be her childhood sweetheart, who has been widowed. The story ends with an image of the two of them, "one living on the

second floor of Murata's boardinghouse; the other, the wife of the great Harada: each knew his share of sadness in life" (*HIZ*, vol. 2, p. 114; tr. Danly p. 253). What it lacks in subtlety, "The Thirteenth Night" makes up for in drama worthy of the kabuki stage. The characters' extended monologues, indeed, seem like passages from a Chikamatsu play imported into modern fiction.

"Separate Ways"

Critical estimations of "Separate Ways," one of Ichiyō's last stories, have changed drastically in the century after Ichiyō's death. In 1896 the fiction writer Saitō Ryokuu wrote in a letter to Ichiyō that "Separate Ways" was not up to the usual high quality of her work. In 1981 Robert Danly called the story Ichiyō's most accomplished work. Written with utmost control and beautiful delineation of its characters and their milieu, the story features elements of character and plot familiar from her other stories: a lovely woman hidden away in some obscure corner of the city; her friendship with a somewhat younger man; the ending of their friendship as they make difficult decisions about their futures. Okyō, a seamstress in her early twenties, dotes on the sixteen-year-old Kichizō, who because of his small stature has been cruelly nicknamed "Dwarf."

Although Okyō and Kichizō's relationship is tinged slightly with eroticism, the core of their bond is a quest for family and for friends—without the entanglements of sex. At the end of the story, Okyō informs Kichizō that she will leave the neighborhood soon in order to become the mistress of a wealthy man: "It's just as you once said—good luck has come riding in a fancy carriage. So I can't very well stay on in a back tenement, can I?" Kichizō feels betrayed and says to Okyō, " 'I don't know, maybe it's a step up for you, but don't do it. It's not as if you can't make a living with your sewing. The only one you have to feed is yourself. . . .' The boy was unyielding in his notion of integrity" (*HIZ*, vol. 2, pp. 140–141; tr. Danly, p. 293). For

Kichizō, who grew up in the most poverty-stricken slum in all of Tokyo, keeping food on the table through his own hard work is enough of a goal. Kichizō rejects Okyō's friendship, but Ichiyō is able to make the reader sympathize with both characters: Kichizō in his "integrity" and Okyō in the making of her dubious, yet difficult, moral choice.

Conclusion

The year 1868 marked a vast political divide between the Edo period—the age of the Tokugawa shoguns—and the modernizing Meiji period, which would last until 1912. Edo culture had censured fiction as a vulgar form of writing, one vastly inferior to poetry and history, and the political changes of 1868 did nothing to change that. Gradually, however, exposure to Western models demonstrated that fiction could serve serious intellectual and social purposes and even have high artistic aspirations. By the 1890s Japanese writers and critics found themselves engaged in a common project of elevating the status of prose fiction. Higuchi Ichiyō was one of the more noteworthy participants in that project, but while others began turning more toward the West and away from anything redolent of premodern writing, she steadfastly defended the elaborate style, realism, and allusiveness of premodern prose and theater as a valid path for modern Japanese literature.

On one hand, one of Ichiyō's nearest contemporaries, and an admirer of her work, Kunikida Doppo (1871–1908), stopped writing in classical Japanese and rejected attempts by Kōda Rohan, Ichiyō, and Ozaki Kōyō to revive Saikaku. Instead, he embraced Christianity and found inspiration in Wordsworth's poetry and Anglo-European Romantic conceptions of man and nature. He and the proponents of naturalism viewed their writing as an individualistic art and fiction's evocation of a sense of selfhood as an exalted undertaking, one entirely separate from what they regarded as the vulgar conventionality of Edo fiction. They insisted that an economical, colloquial language was the proper style for fiction in a modern nation and eschewed the linguistic exuberance of Heian- and Edo-period writings.

On the other hand, Higuchi Ichiyō loved the very artifice of premodern fiction, especially the self-conscious writing styles that expressed both the virtuosity of the storyteller and a reverence for and an emulation of narrative forms of the past. She found Saikaku's realism, with its emphasis on common people, sharp wit, and detailed descriptions of city people and city life, highly adaptable to evocations of the crowded urban society of modern Tokyo. Although readers of the twenty-first century may struggle with her semiclassical style and may find the pleasure quarters of Tokyo an exotic locale of the distant past, Ichiyō's delight in language, her compassion for myriad types of city dwellers whom she made her characters, and her astute observations about social class and nationhood retain a compelling immediacy.

Selected Bibliography

PRIMARY WORKS

COLLECTED WORKS

Higuchi Ichiyō. In *Nihon kindai bungaku taikei* series. Vol. 8. Tokyo: Kadokawa Shoten, 1970.

Higuchi Ichiyō zenshū. Edited by Shioda Ryōhei, Wada Yoshie, and Higuchi Etsu. Tokyo: Chikuma Shobō, 1974. (Abbreviated as *HIZ* in citations.)

Zenshū Higuchi Ichiyō. Edited by Maeda Ai. Annotated by Noguchi Seki et al. Rev. ed. Tokyo: Shōgakkan, 1996.

TRANSLATIONS OF NOVELLAS AND SHORT STORIES

"Takekurabe." Trans. by Edward Seidensticker as "Growing Up." In *Modern Japanese Literature: An Anthology.* Edited by Donald Keene. New York: Grove Press, 1956.

"Nigorie." Trans. by Hisako Tanaka as "Muddy Bay." *Monumenta Nipponica* 14:173–204 (1958).

"Jūsan'ya." Trans. by Hisako Tanaka as "The Thirteenth Night." *Monumenta Nipponica* 16:157–174 (1960–1961).

Danly, Robert Lyons. *In the Shade of Spring Leaves: The Life and Writings of Higuchi Ichiyō, a Woman of Letters in Meiji Japan.* New Haven: Yale University Press, 1981. (Includes a literary biography and translations of "Yamizakura" ["Flowers at Dusk"], "Yuki no hi" ["A Snowy Day"], "Koto no ne" ["The Sound of the Koto"], "Yamiyo" ["Encounters on a Dark Night"], "Ōtsugomori" ["On the Last Day of the Year"], "Nigorie" ["Troubled Waters"], "Jūsan'ya" ["The Thirteenth Night"], "Takekurabe" ["Child's Play"], "Wakaremichi" ["Separate Ways"], and excerpts from Ichiyō's diary.)

SECONDARY WORKS

CRITICAL AND BIOGRAPHICAL STUDIES

Copeland, Rebecca L. *Lost Leaves: Women Writers of Meiji Japan.* Honolulu: University of Hawaii Press, 2000.

Danly, Robert Lyons. *In the Shade of Spring Leaves: The Life and Writings of Higuchi Ichiyō, a Woman of Letters in Meiji Japan.* New Haven: Yale University Press, 1981. (Includes a literary biography and translations.)

Itagaki Naoko. *Meiji, Taishō, Shōwa no joryū bungaku.* Tokyo: Ōfūsha, 1960.

Iwahashi Kunie et al., eds. *Higuchi Ichiyō.* In *Gunzō Nihon no Sakka* series. Vol. 3. Tokyo: Shōgakkan, 1992. (An extremely useful collection of critical and biographical essays dating from Meiji to the 1990s.)

Maeda Ai. *Higuchi Ichiyō no sekai.* Tokyo: Heibonsha, 1978.

———, ed. *Higuchi Ichiyō.* In *Shinchō Nihon bungaku arubamu* series. Tokyo: Shinchōsha, 1985. (Contains useful photographs.)

Matsuzaka Toshio. *Higuchi Ichiyō kenkyū.* Tokyo: Kyōiku Shuppan Sentā, 1970.

Sata Ineko. " 'Takekurabe' kaishaku e no hitotsu no gimon." *Gunzō* (May 1985).

Seki Reiko. *Kataru onnatachi no jidai: Ichiyō to Meiji josei hyōgen.* Tokyo: Shin'yōsha, 1997.

Seki Ryōichi. *Higuchi Ichiyō: Kōshō to shiron.* Tokyo: Yūseidō, 1980.

Shioda Ryōhei. *Higuchi Ichiyō kenkyū.* Tokyo: Chūō Kōronsha, 1975.

Tsukada Mitsue. *Gokai to henken: Higuchi Ichiyō no bungaku.* Tokyo: Chūō Kōron Jigyō Shuppan, 1976.

Wada Yoshie. *Higuchi Ichiyō.* Tokyo: Kōdansha, 1974. (This is one of many books by Wada on Ichiyō.)

KAFŪ
(NAGAI KAFŪ)
1879–1959

STEPHEN SNYDER

THE CAREER OF Nagai Kafū, while long and productive, is not easily explained in terms of literary movements or periods. His work reflects the changes and modernization Japan experienced during his lifetime, but the image is often distorted or inverted, telling the reader as much about the author's unique personality as it does about the time and place he inhabits. While Kafū is remembered largely for his elegiac depictions of the vanishing culture of the Edo period (1600–1868), these portraits are often filtered through his fascination with French literature, a combination that has interested and confounded critics of his work. Still, Kafū is almost universally regarded as one of the finest prose stylists of modern Japan and as perhaps the most sensitive and loving chronicler of his native Tokyo. Although he does not fit neatly into the narrative of modern Japanese literary history, his ambiguous position nevertheless illuminates several key themes.

Nagai Sōkichi (Kafū is a pen name) was born in Tokyo on 3 December 1879. Though he was proud of his status as a native of Tokyo, his parents had in fact moved to the capital from the province of Owari shortly before the Meiji Restoration of 1868. Kafū's father, Nagai Kagen (also a pen name), the son of a wealthy farmer, married the daughter of his teacher, Washizu Kidō, a renown Confucian scholar. Kagen him-

self became a notable *kanshi* (Chinese-language) poet, and saw that his eldest son, Sōkichi, was educated in the Confucian classics; but Kagen's career was spent as a successful bureaucrat in the Ministry of Education, where he helped draft the Imperial Rescript of 1890 that served as one of the ideological foundations of the Meiji state, and later as a shipping executive of Japan Mail Lines. Kagen was, by Kafū's own account, an example of the Meiji elite who embraced many of the trappings of modernization while maintaining a strong sense of traditional decorum. Kafū's mother and maternal grandmother present similar contradictions: the wife and daughter of the famous Confucian scholar both converted to Christianity after the Restoration, thus providing Kafū with yet another set of potentially conflicting influences.

Kafū's career bears out this background. In his early years he became fascinated with the arts of Edo, studying the *shakuhachi* flute in the geisha quarters and reading the popular novels of Japan's premodern period. But while he maintained a lifelong love for the world of Edo depicted in the woodblock prints of Utamaro and the erotic fiction of Tamenaga Shunsui, he went on to develop an equally active and enduring passion for French literature and culture that affected his work in equally profound ways. In 1900, while working at a Tokyo newspaper, Kafū began reading the work of Émile Zola, the writer who inspired the early Japanese naturalists; and after a number of youthful literary experiments in imitation of Shunsui, under the tutelage of the Ken'yūsha writer Hirotsu Ryūrō, Kafū produced three "Zolaesque" novels and a summary translation of Zola's *Nana* in 1902 and 1903. The best of the novels, *Yume no onna* (1903; Woman of the dream), introduces a theme that Kafū would pursue throughout his career: the figure of the prostitute and her sad yet touchingly beautiful life in the demimonde. The heroine, O-nami, is the daughter of a samurai family that flounders during the transition from the feudal world of the Tokugawa era (1600–1868) to the modern era of the Meiji Restoration (1868–1912), forcing O-nami into increasingly degrading situations until she at last becomes a prostitute in the Suzaki quarter of Tokyo. The effect of the novel, like so much of Kafū's work to follow, is hybrid, as naturalistic, generally dark social observation mingles with more lyrical passages that owe much to Kafū's reading in Edo fiction. But the final impression is one of youthful experimentation. In his *Kafū the Scribbler*, the critic Edward Seidensticker admires *Yume no onna* as a "quiet, straightforward, and touching chronicle of a woman's life," but most critics agree with the critic Nakamura Mitsuo that Kafū's career as a mature writer began with his next major work, a product of his years abroad.

In October 1903, after a series of academic failures and personal indiscretions, Kafū was sent to America by his father, who hoped to salvage a business career for his dissolute son. Kafū arrived in Tacoma, Washington, ostensibly with the goal of studying commerce in the United States, but his interests lay elsewhere. Though he spent most of the next four years in America, he continued to long for France and to lobby his father for permission to cross the Atlantic to the home of his literary idols. He enrolled in the local high school in Tacoma and began studying French, the language of Zola, and of the writer under whose spell he

increasingly found himself: Guy de Maupassant. During his stay in America, Kafū wandered from Tacoma to Kalamazoo, Michigan, to Washington, D.C., where he had a job sweeping floors at the Japanese legation, and finally to New York City, to take up a job his father had secured for him at a Japanese bank. During his travels, Kafū recorded his experiences and musings in a series of short stories and essays that were published as *Amerika monogatari* (1908; *American Stories*, 2000).

American Stories is a departure for Kafū from his earlier, Zolaesque style in many senses. Taken as a whole, the style, as Isoda Kōichi has observed in his *Nagai Kafū*, exhibits a "sense of the ephemeral" (*mujōkan*; p. 63) typical of classical works such as *The Tale of the Heike*; and the descriptive passages in particular exhibit an extraordinary naturalness, as in the following depiction of autumn in the Maryland countryside from "In the Woods":

About half an hour after sunset, the fiery evening glow gradually fades and leaves only a faint rosy hue around the edges of the white clouds floating in the sky. The vast grass-covered surface of the fields turns into a misty blue sea, and at the distant horizon it is difficult to tell where sky ends and earth begins. On the other hand, the whiteness of certain objects—the pure white walls of the farmhouses here and far away, the white skirts of four or five women who are probably driving cattle across the fields, the treetops tinged here and there with yellow leaves, or the flowers of some unknown plants—is truly striking as it reveals itself, perhaps reflecting the rays of light from the sky, against the surroundings that are slowly growing darker.

(*Kafū zenshū [KZ]*, vol. 3,
p. 108–109; tr. pp. 74–75)

Such lyricism aside, however, as Akase Masako has suggested, the collection is heavily indebted to Maupassant for its ironic tone, its lightly decadent subject matter, and for the variety of narrative frames and other devices.

Moreover, the beauty of Kafū's prose, which the critic Donald Keene, in his *Dawn to the West: Japanese of the Modern Era*, has called a "glory of modern Japanese literature," first becomes fully evident in *American Stories*.

Kafū writes about Japanese immigrants in the Pacific Northwest, about Japanese students at a Midwestern college, a visit to the World's Fair in St. Louis, an evening at a New York brothel, or a stroll through Chinatown. Some of the narratives amount to little more than travel sketches by a tireless *flaneur* who would, in later years, record his native Tokyo with equal care and affection. Other stories feature slender, melancholy plots that also presage Kafū's eventual de-emphasis of storytelling in favor of setting and character. But each of the twenty-four pieces provides a fascinating glimpse into American life from a Japanese perspective, and it is no doubt this aspect of the work that explains its enormous popularity with readers and the considerable boost its publication provided to Kafū's career even before his return from abroad.

In the summer of 1907, after years of petitioning his father to be allowed to visit the object of his literary desires, the bank at which Kafū had been working in New York transferred him to its Lyon branch, no doubt at Kagen's request. Kafū worked there until the spring of the following year, when he was fired for his lackadaisical performance and, after a brief stay in Paris, returned to Japan. He found, on his arrival, that *American Stories* had made him perhaps the most famous *shinkichōsha* (recent returnee) of his day, a position only enhanced by a protracted battle with the censors over the publication of *Furansu monogatari* (1909; French stories), a second, somewhat more irreverent collection of travel vignettes. Suddenly a central figure in the *bundan* (literary establishment), Kafū realized that his art and his thinking about the uses of fiction had changed radically during his years abroad. Despite his earlier association with the Japanese version of Zolaism, he allied himself with a loose-knit group of writers, including Natsume Sōseki and Mori Ōgai, that came to

be known as anti-naturalists, not so much for any shared literary aesthetic but for their opposition to the dreary self-absorption that characterized Japanese naturalism *(shizenshugi)* in the first decade of the century. Ōgai, whom Kafū came to consider his mentor, recommended the younger writer for a position involving teaching French at the school that would later become Keiō University; and at the same time, Kafū became editor of Keiō's literary magazine, *Mita Bungaku*, which became the primary mouthpiece of the anti-naturalists.

The period following his return was productive for Kafū and one in which he developed the themes that he pursued for the remainder of his career, among them, a relentless criticism of the changes that modernization had brought to Japan and the search for remnants of the lost culture of Edo. Both are expressed in a work such as *Reishō* (1909–1910; Sneers), where Kafū states his agenda rather bluntly:

> In writing *Sneers*, I have attempted to provide a serious assessment of the vulgar confusion of Tokyo life in 1909; to lament the predicament of those who attempt to live quietly in the current period; and to seek out and examine those places where things authentically Japanese can still be found.
>
> (*KZ*, vol. 13, p. 41)

Essays written around this period and collected in 1920 as *Edo geijutsuron* (Arts of Edo) constitute one aspect of this search. Kafū looks to *ukiyo-e*, Edo prose fiction, and the Kabuki theater for their ability to recapture the vanishing world that becomes his refuge from the tastelessness of modern Tokyo. But in his fiction it is more often the women of the demimonde and the tawdry quarters they inhabit that provide the most promising possibilities for recovering the past. The critic Yoshida Seiichi has pointed out that more than half of Kafū's fiction following *Shinkyō yawa* (1912; Night tales from Shimbashi) is set in the demimonde; and it is certainly true that all Kafū's finest narrative achievements feature prostitutes of one variety or another.

Among the works from this period, *Sumida-gawa* (1909; "The River Sumida," 1965) is the most memorable. As Isoda Kōichi has pointed out, Kafū wrote at least three separate works with this title, including an opera and two short stories. The multiple uses of the river indicate the role it came to play in his fiction as a symbol of the traditional plebeian culture he loved. The Sumida River runs through the heart of the merchant quarters of Edo, and it is this lively, earthy world of the riverbanks that Kafū archived in his role as a self-proclaimed latter-day *bunjin* (literatus). It is, moreover, a culture quite distinct from the aristocratic world of the classical Heian court that attracted such writers as Kafū's friend and protégé, Tanizaki Jun'ichirō—and one better suited to Kafū's temperament.

The plot of Kafū's short story "The River Sumida," which is often compared to Higuchi Ichiyō's *Takekurabe* (1896; *Child's Play*, 1981), concerns a young man, Chōkichi, who falls in love with O-ito, a young woman destined to become a geisha. Chōkichi's ambition is to become an actor, a profession that would allow him to remain near O-ito; but his mother, herself a teacher of traditional music, is anxious that he follow a more legitimate Meiji path to success. Chōkichi is forced to enroll in school, despite his lack of interest and aptitude, and grows increasingly despondent as he watches O-ito prepare for her debut as a geisha. At the end of the story, he runs out into a storm, determined to destroy himself rather than live without O-ito. The plot of "The River Sumida" is as melodramatic as it sounds and quite similar, in fact, to the Edo-period romances the author so admired. But the genius of this short story, as with so many subsequent works, is the evocation of obscure and moldering neighborhoods in the old quarters of the city, and a number of modern narrative touches Kafū added to distinguish his work from that of such Edo precursors as Shunsui or Tanehiko. The most important of these is the character of the haiku master Ragetsu, Chōkichi's uncle, whose point of view informs much of the action, and who functions to situate the whole

of Kafū's narrative as a self-conscious act of literary ventriloquism. In the final lines of the story, the elegiac tone and Edo subject matter are identified and framed as willful acts of recollection filtered through the modern consciousness:

> The flame in the lamp wavered and wavered. Ragetsu thought of the beautiful young couple, Chōkichi with his thin, pale face and his large eyes, and the round-faced O-ito, her mouth winsome and her eyes turning up at the corners. He drew the picture over and over again in his heart, like an artist working out the frontispiece for an old romance. Rest easy, Chōkichi, he said. No matter how ill you may be, you are not to die. I am with you.

> (*KZ*, vol. 5, p. 59; tr. Seidensticker, p. 218)

This conspicuously placed passage signals yet another important development in Kafū's thinking about his craft: the rise of a self-conscious interest in the role of the artist in shaping narrative and the appropriation of the figure of the artist as a thematic element.

Another work from this period that deserves mention is *Sangoshū* (1913; Coral anthology), a collection of Kafū's translations of French poetry by Charles Baudelaire, Henri de Régnier, and Paul Verlaine, among others. The translations, while at least as suggestive of Kafū's own literary preoccupations as those of the original poets, were nevertheless instrumental in introducing modern French poetry to Japanese readers. They also suggest the range of Kafū's literary activity, which included translation, the essays mentioned previously, and a monumental diary, the *Danchōtei Nichijō* (Dyspepsia house days), which he kept from 1917 until his death in 1959. This latter, named after a retreat Kafū built on family property in the Western suburb of Ōkubo while suffering from chronic stomach disorders, has been the subject of extensive study for the biographical and literary light it sheds on Kafū's career and for its abundant information on Tokyo life and literary politics

138

of the times. Edward Seidensticker's seminal English-language study of Kafū's life and works, and of the city in which they are set, is based on a close reading of the *Danchōtei Nichijō*, as are later works such as Kawamoto Saburō's *Kafū to Tōkyō*, which uses the diary as a map of Kafū's city and literary practice. Still, it is the fiction itself that is the principal basis for Kafū's reputation, and among the many works of varying quality and substance that he published up until his death, a handful stand out as masterpieces. In addition to "The River Sumida," these include *Udekurabe* (1916; *Geisha in Rivalry*, 1963), *Okamezasa* (1918; Dwarf bamboo), *Tsuyu no atosaki* (1931; *During the Rains*, 1994) and *Bokutō kidan* (1937; *A Strange Tale from East of the River*, 1965). These works constitute Kafū's central achievement, and they were all written during his middle years, as he increasingly withdrew from literary society and slowly developed a reputation as a misanthropic, if brilliant, eccentric.

Kafū's retreat from the center of literary activity, which has also been characterized as a process of unwilling marginalization brought on by changing literary tastes, began around the time of his father's death in 1914. At that point, as Kagen's eldest son and heir, Kafū became financially independent; indeed, his father's fortune allowed Kafū to live in considerable comfort for his remaining years. Without the necessity of supporting himself, Kafū soon lost interest in his duties as teacher and editor; and by the spring of 1916, he had resigned from both Keiō and *Mita bungaku*. He had cut ties in other ways as well. In the years between his return from France and his departure from the university, he had married twice, once to a respectable merchant's daughter and once to a geisha, but both had ended in divorce. Disputes over the distribution of Kagen's estate and Kafū's unfilial behavior had alienated him from his family; and, finally, he found himself increasingly at odds with the literary establishment, responding with vituperative attacks on such longtime foes as Kikuchi Kan, the highly entrepreneurial founder of the literary journal *Bungei Shunjū*. But in time Kafū seemed to come to the realization that he was simply uninterested in the forms in which Japanese culture was remaking itself, uninterested in Japan's version of modernity. His response was the creation of a public persona as a latter-day *gesakusha*, or "writer of frivolous works," a reclusive, cantankerous, figure who filled his days with antiquarian research on Edo culture and peripatetic wandering in the demimonde, both of which become inspiration for his fiction. Kafū was consciously following in the footsteps, too, of Narushima Ryūhoku, who liked to pose as an individual "useless" in modern society. (See the essay on Ryūhoku in this volume.)

Geisha in Rivalry was serialized in the journal *Bunmei* beginning in the summer of 1916. The heroine Komayo, one of Kafū's greatest creations, is a geisha in the traditional Shimbashi entertainment district of Tokyo. Most critics agree that she must have been modeled in part on Kafū's second wife, Yaeji, who was herself a geisha from the same quarter, though Isoda has speculated that Kafū was able to achieve the richness of characterization by combining aspects of all the women he had known, from the American prostitute, Edyth Girard, to the imperious Yaeji. The somewhat melodramatic plot, which owes much to premodern Japanese fiction in its penchant for contrivance and coincidence, describes Komayo's "rivalry" with the other geisha of the quarter for money, fame, and the affections of desirable *danna* ("patrons"). The action begins at the Imperial Theater when the twenty-five-year-old Komayo, who has returned to the quarter after a brief absence, encounters Yoshioka, an ambitious businessman with whom she had an affair early in her career. Komayo, conscious that she is no longer young by the standards of her profession, is anxious to secure the patronage of men who can establish her as one of the most successful women in the quarter, thereby assuring her future prosperity. To that end, she resumes her relationship with Yoshioka, despite his brutal, calculating nature, while at the same time accepting the advances of a wealthy antique dealer, known only as Umibōzu ("the sea monster").

Komayo's immediate goal is to be known as the finest dancer in Shimbashi. Having secured the financial resources for costumes and lessons from Yoshioka and Umibōzu, she seeks additional help by beginning yet another affair, this time with the Kabuki *onnagata* actor, Segawa Isshi, who will serve as coach and teacher, but who will also attract the envy of the other women of Shimbashi, the ubiquitous rivals. Komayo's rise to stardom in the quarter is traced through several brilliantly rendered theater scenes in which the Machiavellian stratagems of both the geisha and their patrons are carefully dissected. Komayo, in particular, plays the game almost too well, at least until Yoshioka discovers the affair with Segawa and plots an elaborate revenge that leaves her disgraced. The novel ends on an uncharacteristically optimistic note, however, as Komayo is rescued from her predicament by a former employer who asks her to take over as mistress of his house of assignation *(machiai)*.

The plot of *Geisha in Rivalry*, such as it is, unfolds in these relatively naturalistic scenes, which include at least two graphic depictions of the sexual brutality experienced by Komayo in her profession. But, as Takemori Ten'yū, among others, has pointed out, these Zolaesque passages alternate with more pastoral descriptions of the refined traditions of Shimbashi or scenes set in the suburban retreat of Kurayama Nansō, a writer who serves as Kafū's surrogate in the novel. The most famous of these passages comes in the twelfth chapter, "Sayo shigure" ("Rain on an Autumn Night"), when Nansō and his wife wander out into their garden to peek through the fence in hopes of catching a glimpse of a tryst between Segawa and Komayo:

"There's something pleasant about walking in the garden at night with a lantern. For all you know, I might be playing the role of the handsome young lord in the twelfth act of *Genji*," Nansō mused. "But it's a strange kind of jealousy that makes a man take his wife with him when he goes to spy on the house next door." Nansō laughed exuberantly.

"They'll *hear* you! Laughing in a loud voice like that."

"Listen! It's sad, isn't it? So many crickets still alive and singing. Ochiyo, you can't get through that way. There's always a puddle under the pomegranate tree. It's better to go under the crape myrtle over there."

Picking their way from one stepping-stone to another, the two of them shortly entered the thick shrubbery. Ochiyo, concealing the lantern behind one of her kimono sleeves, held her breath. Just then, the Sonohachi music came suddenly to an end, and after that there was nothing but the faint light shining through the paper doors of the veranda. A lonely silence had come over the villa, and there was neither the sound of talk nor of laughter nor of anything else.

(*KZ*, vol. 6, p. 337; tr. pp. 121–122)

The tone of this passage and others like it is, in fact, more melancholy and subdued than the ones that precede and follow it, but Nansō is nevertheless participating in the voyeuristic economy of Shimbashi, as if the disease of competition that infects the quarter has begun to affect the distant suburbs as well. The critic Takemori suggests that the immediate cause for the pattern of inserting calmer, more poetic scenes between the "rawer" *(namagusai)* ones is the practice of serial publication: each subsequent installment would have had a contrasting tone, adding to the reader's enjoyment. At the very least, the pastoral interludes provide relief from the claustrophobic, sexually charged world of Shimbashi, encouraging a certain ironic distance from Komayo's dilemma, a distance reinforced, perhaps, by the unrealistic "happy" ending Kafū gives his novel.

Kafū began keeping his diary, *Danchōtei Nichijō* (Dyspepsia house days), in the autumn of 1917 while living alone at his family home in Ōkubo, to the west of the city. The diary is named for the cottage Kafū built in the garden of the Ōkubo house to serve as a study, but he sold this house in 1918, moving to the plebeian eastern district of Tsukiji. Despite its proximity to Shimbashi and the other areas where traces of Edo remained, however, Tsukiji proved too noisy and dirty for Kafū's tastes. In 1920, he moved to a house he had built in the fashionable western district of Azabu, former home to samurai aristocrats during the Tokugawa period. Kafū dubbed his new dwelling "Henkikan" or "Eccentricity House," in tribute, one imagines, both to its Western-style architecture, still relatively rare for residences at the time, and for its occupant's growing reputation for unconventional behavior. The move from the old quarters of the city to the newer, relatively Westernized Azabu is mirrored in *Okamezasa* (Dwarf bamboo), the novel Kafū published during the same year.

Okamezasa, in contrast to *Geisha in Rivalry*, is set in the bourgeois neighborhood of Fujimichō, and in Azabu itself. Like the Shimbashi novel, it concerns women in the demimonde, though in this case not an artistically accomplished geisha like Komayo and her compatriots but women of more humble achievements who are being established in cheap *machiai* ("house of assignation") outside of the traditional entertainment quarters. In a sense, Kafū's fiction from this period traces the movement of these women, often in a downward trajectory, as they abandon elegant neighborhoods such as Shimbashi and Yanagibashi, and with them all pretense of traditional refinement, and fan out across the modern city into small pockets of degradation. Interestingly, one senses that Kafū's affection and sympathy for women in the demimonde—geisha, cafe waitresses, dancers, common prostitutes—never wavers through these transitions, though his nostalgia for a vanished city grows stronger. In *Okamezasa*, however, the women share center stage with a group of painters and antique dealers whose greedy and duplicitous trade in art is analogous to the more basic form of prostitution being practiced at the *machiai*.

All the characters in *Okamezasa* are corrupt in a manner reminiscent of French naturalism, and the tone is bleak, if ironic. The novel as a whole resembles the naturalistic chapters of *Geisha in Rivalry*, without the relief of the pastoral interludes nor a character like Komayo

with whom the reader is encouraged to sympathize. Isoda has suggested, in fact, that the darker tone is due to this absence, that *Okamezasa* can be seen as "*Udekurabe [Geisha in Rivalry]* without Komayo" (p. 186). The ostensible hero of *Okamezasa* is Uzaki Kyoseki, a mediocre painter who survives by running errands and keeping accounts for the master to whom he had been apprenticed, Uchiyama Kaiseki. Kaiseki, though a famous painter, is apparently selling the work of other artists—including Uzaki—as his own for a handsome profit, and other members of Kaiseki's circle of bourgeois artists and dealers are revealed to be equally unsavory. The proprietor of a prosperous shop known as the Unrindō is trafficking in forgeries; Kaiseki's profligate son, Kan, is in the habit of proposing marriage to every geisha or maid with whom he spends the night; and Kan's eventual father-in-law, a haughty former governor, is apparently selling fake antiques as originals. The women in the story are similarly unreliable. Kimiyū, a geisha with whom Kan had carried on an affair, makes a show of writing a letter to express her heartbreak on the eve of his marriage, only to forget to send it; and Kan's slatternly wife, Chōko, is revealed to be the illegitimate daughter of the governor, passed off as his real daughter in order to ensnare the unsuspecting Kan. The portraits of these less-than-appealing characters are drawn with Kafū's usual precision and wit, though with little of the lyricism that is evident in most of his other fiction. Yoshida Seiichi has called *Okamezasa* the "most prosaic" of Kafū's works (p. 133), claiming that it is perhaps the only example in Japanese literature of true naturalism in the tradition of Zola. He is particularly impressed with the way Kafū treated these disreputable characters, revealing their faults with absolute clarity and hardly a trace of sympathy. For Yoshida, Kafū's "nihilism" reaches its nadir in this work (p. 133).

At the same time, however, *Okamezasa* is also the most skillfully plotted and, in many senses, the funniest of Kafū's novels, a feature to which Kafū himself pointed in the afterword to the book, where he labeled the work a "comic novel" *(kokkei shōsetsu)*. The comic element is to be found in the plot, which concerns a series of chance events—quite un-naturalistic coincidences, in fact—that befall Uzaki, leading eventually to his financial security and erotic gratification. The action is set in motion when Kan visits Uzaki in hopes of borrowing enough money to buy Kimiyū, the geisha with whom he is currently infatuated. Though Uzaki, in keeping with his modest means, rarely visits *machiai*, he agrees to accompany his master's son to one of the establishments that has opened near his house in order to keep him out of trouble. Instead, he meets Kohana, a young geisha to whom he is strongly attracted. The next day, Uzaki wanders into a brush shop in Asakusa and discovers a painting of a chicken that he remembers as his own (due to a some brush strokes made to cover up a mistake) but which now bears the signature of his famous master, Kaiseki. The owner of the shop, fearful that Uzaki will reveal the forgery scheme, seizes on the idea of bribing the hapless artist by sending him to another of his business ventures—the same *machiai* Uzaki has visited with Kan. After this second encounter with Kohana, Uzaki is all but addicted to physical pleasure. As Uzaki becomes accustomed to dissolute ways, however, in an ironic reversal, Kan has grown weary of the role of spoiled *waka-danna* ("young master") and agrees to marry Chōko, the daughter of the retired governor.

Chōko, while little more than a cipher, is a brilliant embodiment of Kafū's theme of duplicity; she is, in effect, a human "forgery." Though Kan is initially charmed by her laziness and slovenly habits, so similar to his own, he is shocked at how different the real woman is from the image she had projected:

In the morning, when he caught sight of Chōko after she had been to wash, Kan had something of a shock: her face was so dark in color that he would have sworn this was a different woman from the one he had seen at their initial meeting. The complexion of the Chōko he had seen on that occasion had seemed exceptionally white indeed; but even allowing that she would have taken added care with her face powder given the importance of the event, Kan was surprised how completely unaware he had been of what lay beneath. She must have used even more makeup than a geisha, he thought, utterly taken aback.

(*KZ*, vol. 7, p. 86)

Still, he is willing to overlook this fault until he learns of the more serious one, that Chōko's lineage has also been "forged," and she is actually the daughter of the governor's mistress rather than his wife. In the end, the painting of a chicken that begins the narrative becomes emblematic of every person and thing in Uzaki's world: unauthentic and deeply flawed. If *Geisha in Rivalry* explored the dark side of the highly refined Shimbashi quarter, revealing it to be a place of brute competition and bald prostitution, *Okamezasa* turns a still harsher light on the respectable neighborhoods of the "high city," suggesting that the economics of prostitution had come to dominate the bourgeois art world—and perhaps, by implication, the literary world it resembled. As a "comic" novel, the action of *Okamezasa* occasionally provokes laughter, but as the critic Moriyasu Masafumi has suggested, it is a "dark laughter" that negates the very possibility of faith in modern society (p. 196).

The novel lacks a proper conclusion, but the reader is informed in summary fashion that Chōko dies of a venereal disease contracted from Kan, who is temporarily banished to America. Uzaki, on the other hand, has prospered from his encounter with the forgery, and from the fact that he has spotted the governor's wife leaving a rendezvous with her lover, and is able to set up Kohana in an establishment of her own where he can visit her daily.

After the publication of *Okamezasa* in 1920, Kafū entered a fallow period lasting for the next decade. The subdued and melancholy *Ame shōshō* ("Quiet Rain," 1964) was published in 1921, but it is more essay than fictional narrative. "Kashima no onna" (1926;

142

The woman in the rented room) includes a convincing description of the city following the Great Kantō Earthquake of 1923, but there is little else of note. Opinion differs on the immediate cause of this silence, but it seems clear that Kafū felt marginalized by the literary establishment, which was controlled largely by the practitioners of politically engaged Proletarian fiction, and increasingly alienated in the modern city. Still, the changing forms of the demimonde continued to fascinate him, and he frequented not only the alleys and temples near the banks of his beloved Sumida River but the Western-style cafes emerging in the Ginza and other new entertainment districts. Whatever the reasons for this period of inactivity, however, Kafū began publishing again in 1931 and produced, over the next six years, a small group of stories that are among his finest work. Of these, two are particularly important, and, indeed, stand as a summation of his career: *During the Rains* and *A Strange Tale from East of the River.*

During the Rains is generally regarded as a "comeback" work by an aging writer losing touch with the times (Kafū was fifty-two in 1931). Tanizaki called it the "oldest" of Kafū's novels, complaining that there were too many coincidences and too little psychological realism. But it is doubtful that Kafū had ever really sought realism in his fiction; it seems he favored storytelling that evokes a strong sense of place while self-consciously calling into question conventional devices for creating literary illusion. As early as *American Stories*, he had experimented with a variety of narrative frames that insist on the "told" quality of his stories by dramatizing the act of the telling of the core tale. Many of his subsequent fictions, as well, employ devices—including authorial interruptions, inserting letters and other "found" texts, and complex narrative structures—to remind readers that they are reading a story and insist on the author's (and reader's) role in constructing the meaning of the work. Kafū's diary contains a detailed account of his reading habits, and from it scholars know that in addition to Chinese classics and Edo

romances, Kafū continued to read modern French fiction throughout his career. As Ōno Shigeo has shown, during the 1920s and early 1930s, Kafū revisited works by Maupassant and Pierre Loti, while beginning to explore modernist writers such as Guillaume Apollinaire, Sidonie-Gabrielle Colette, Marcel Proust, and, most importantly, André Gide. These influences had a powerful effect on *During the Rains* and *A Strange Tale from East of the River*, which successfully wed Kafū's interest in narrative experiment with his project of chronicling his beloved demimonde.

In *During the Rains*, Kafū appears to have returned to his naturalist roots to portray the fashionable if somewhat unsavory world of a Ginza café called the Don Juan, where the waitresses are in reality unlicensed prostitutes. Beginning in 1926, Kafū had been an almost nightly customer at an actual Ginza café known as Tiger, and his extended research is reflected in *During the Rains*, particularly in the lively characterization of the protagonist, Kimie. Unlike Komayo or the women in *Okamezasa*, Kimie has become a "waitress," not out of necessity or ambition but because the work suits her somewhat careless and altogether lascivious nature. She comes from a respectable country family, but has fled to the city to avoid the marriage her parents had arranged; after working briefly in an office, she drifts into work at the cafe. Kimie is content with her life at the Don Juan and her less-than-monogamous relationship with her patron, a popular novelist named Kiyooka, until she is plagued by a series of mysterious misfortunes—a cut sleeve on her kimono, a stolen ornamental comb, a dead kitten in her closet, and, most ominous, an anonymous article in a scandal sheet detailing a change in the moles on her inner thigh, a fact known only to herself and to a few male friends.

The novel begins as Kimie goes to consult a fortune-teller about her troubles; the reading, however, is ambiguous at best, an outcome that presages the mood and structure of the novel as a whole. Descriptions of the Don Juan and Kimie's cluttered room are interspersed with seemingly aimless details about her past and accounts of casual encounters with a variety of men. As the story unfolds, numerous characters are introduced in such a way as to arouse expectations that they will play significant roles, only to have them vanish after a single scene. As Seidensticker has noted, the novel "seems to have too much in it and not enough," suggesting either that Kafū was unable to control his material, as a number of critics have concluded, or that he is consciously manipulating reader expectations, playing with the conventions of naturalism and the realistic novel—a theme that will recur in *A Strange Tale from East of the River.*

Certain characters, however, are given fuller treatment and play more central roles in the rambling plot, though not necessarily in a positive sense. The description of Kimie's patron, Kiyooka, is among Kafū's most scathing portraits, prompting some critics to speculate that it might have been based on Kafū's sworn enemy, Kikuchi Kan, the founder of the journal *Bungei Shunjū.* Kiyooka is a despicable man who is more interested in profits than the quality of his prose. He is imperious with colleagues and controlling with Kimie. He also mistreats his wife, while keeping a second mistress in addition to Kimie. Moreover, it eventually becomes clear that he is not only professionally and personally reprehensible but is the villain in Kimie's little drama as well. In a scene that strains credibility, he secretly follows Kimie across the city to a *machiai* and spies on her engaged in a lurid encounter with another woman and an elderly man. Kiyooka, like Nansō in *Geisha in Rivalry,* is clearly titillated by the act of voyeurism, but he is also infuriated at Kimie's infidelity and decides to exact an elaborate revenge. Readers learn that it is Kiyooka who has orchestrated Kimie's misfortunes and that he is determined to continue his sinister attacks.

Kiyooka is, in short, an unappealing figure but a complex one and the object of some critical disagreement. Yoshida, on the one hand, has regarded him as the "embodiment of Kafū's hatred of contemporary writers" (p. 156) and as

a sign of his complete alienation from the literary establishment. Oddly enough, however, Akiba Tarō, Kafū's foremost biographer, has described a number of similarities between Kiyooka's actions and Kafū's own, arguing that Kiyooka is, in fact, an ironic self-portrait of the author. The sharp division of opinion suggests that the characterization of Kiyooka is intentionally ironic, imitating the autobiographical identifications of the I-novelists (successors of the Japanese naturalists of whom Kafū was sharply critical) while at the same time undercutting them. At the very least, however, the portrait of Kiyooka seems to indicate that Kafū was consciously manipulating reader response, much as he did elsewhere in raising expectations with portentous introductions of characters only to immediately disappoint them.

The novel ends as ambiguously as it begins. Kimie discovers Kiyooka's plot and breaks off the relationship, turning her attention, at least temporarily, to an older man named Kawashima whom she rescues from despondency through her sexual favors—a kindness typical of Kimie if of no one else in the novel. The efficacy of her sacrifice, however, remains unclear, as she wakes the next morning to read the note he has left behind:

Last night, when I happened to meet you, I was walking around looking for a place to kill myself. Thanks to you, I was able once more to experience the pleasure of the past, which I had completely despaired of. Now there is nothing in this world that I will regret leaving. By the time you meet with Kyōko and are talking about this, I will most likely no longer be in this world. I am profoundly grateful to you for your kindness. To tell you the truth, in that moment I wanted to take you with me, all unknowing as you were, to that other world. I was shocked at myself. What a terrible thing a man's will is, I thought. So then, farewell. As thanks for your kindness in this world, I will watch over you from that other world. I pray for your future happiness.

Kawashima Kinnosuke

"Auntie! Auntie!" Leaping up from the bedding, Kimie went on desperately calling out for the old woman.

(*KZ*, vol. 8, pp. 357–358; tr. p. 133)

Kafū's work continued to appear well into the 1950s, including some interesting stories and sections of his diary, but scholars generally agree that his career reached its conclusion with the publication of *A Strange Tale from East of the River* in 1937. For whatever reasons, the repressive censorship and nationalist rhetoric of the years leading up to the war seem to have inspired a final burst of energy in Kafū, encouraging him to create what many consider to be his masterpiece, *A Strange Tale from East of the River*. The work is so well loved by Kafū's readers, and forms such a contrast with the troubled period of its composition and publication, that in the immediate postwar years, the novelist and critic Satō Haruo pointed to it as rare evidence that "art still existed in contemporary Japan" (p. 167). The novel itself, however, seems an odd candidate for such high praise. It is relatively slight, full of digressions and personal observations, and, as many critics have noted, slightly misshapen. Indeed, Seidensticker has concluded that it is "scarcely a novel at all." Yet it is also extraordinarily evocative of its time and place—places that would be destroyed shortly afterward in the fire bombing of Tokyo—and of the moods of its author as he wanders through the urban landscape in search of the final traces of traditional charm.

The novel is set in Tamanoi, a tawdry, newer district of tiny brothels and cheap restaurants built in the marshy lands east of the Sumida River. Kafū had begun exploring the area in 1936 and found there an unexpectedly lively and welcoming destination for his incessant wanderings. The action concerns a brief, desultory affair between an aging novelist, Ōe Tadasu (whose biography overlaps with Kafū's in a variety of ways), and a charming denizen of the quarter, O-yuki. They meet by chance under a shared umbrella in a sudden shower, a coincidence that reminds the author of the Edo-period romances of Tamenaga Shunsui, and part for no particular reason except, perhaps, Ōe's desire to experience the melancholy of parting. Suffering as it does from relatively thin characterizations and the lack of a coherent plot, the work would be unremarkable but for the addition of a narrative device, the "novel within a novel," that activates a series of questions about Kafū's understanding of his craft and the nature of fiction.

Ōe Tadasu's visits to Tamanoi are occasioned by the noise of the radio in the house next door to his home in Azabu. Driven out by the constant blaring of popular music, he is in the habit of disguising himself as a laborer and wandering off to the poorer quarters in search of material for *Whereabouts Unknown*, the novel he is writing. Rather than simply telling his reader about this work, however, Kafū allows the fiction-within-a-fiction to become an integral part of his novel, following Ōe as he researches his subject, describing the plot and characters of his novel in some detail, and even including chapters from the "fictional" work interspersed with the chapters of the "real" fiction. The effect is rather startling, as the boundaries between the various levels of the narrative become blurred; but it is also the sort of experiment that is common in European modernist writing from this period. As a number of critics have pointed out, and Kafū himself admitted shortly after the publication of *A Strange Tale from East of the River*, this particular device, the "novel within a novel," is borrowed from two works by André Gide, the 1920 story "Paludes" and *Les Faux-Monnayeurs* (1925; *The Counterfeiters*, 1927), which Kafū read first in 1931. Each work focuses on the character of a writer who is writing a novel within the novel, a novel which is in turn about a writer writing yet another (or the same?) novel, a cycle threatening infinite regress (Gide dubbed it the *mis en abyme*), and thereby challenging the ontological status implied in more conventional fictions. It is not certain that Kafū intended this sort of radical experiment in *A Strange Tale from East of the River*, but it is clear that his novel takes writing itself as a central theme. Ōe is constantly musing on his profession, cataloguing advice on compositional practice from such Kafū favorites as Lafcadio Hearn and Pierre Loti, and making self-conscious asides such as this famous apology for the clichéd way he first meets O-yuki.

> After the manner of Shunsui, I should like to make a remark or two here. The reader may feel that the woman was just a little too familiar when she met me there by the road. I merely record the facts of our meeting, however, and add no coloring, no shaping or contriving. Inasmuch as the affair had its beginning in a sudden thundershower, moreover, certain readers may be smiling at me for having used a well-worn device. Precisely because I am mindful of the possibility, I have refrained from giving the incident another setting. Put in motion by an evening shower, it seemed to me interesting for the very reason that it was so much in the old tradition. Indeed I began this book because I wanted to tell of it.

(*KZ*, vol. 9, p. 119; tr. p. 292)

A Strange Tale from East of the River fuses Kafū's various literary and personal concerns into a single, and singularly beautiful, story. It is his most successful evocation of the debased, tenuous, yet fascinating world of the demimonde; and O-yuki, herself a great storyteller, is the embodiment of the potential for narrative he sees in the lives of women caught up in prostitution. The fantasies of desire created by these women become, in effect, an analogy for Kafū's own activities as a creator of modern fictions.

Kafū's concerns were not, of course, shared by many of his compatriots in the late 1930s. *A Strange Tale from East of the River* was greeted as an impressive feat for an author long out of the center of literary activity, but its quiet, elegiac tone did not accord with the increasingly nationalistic and militaristic mood of the times, and its complex narrative experiment was largely lost on critics accustomed to the relatively transparent confessional forms of the I-novel.

Kafū lived in the Henkikan until March 1945 when it was destroyed, along with his large personal library, in the Tokyo air raids. He wrote little during these years and published nothing, silenced by censors and his own lack of enthusiasm for the war. There is evidence in his diaries from this period, in fact, that he was among the few writers who were consciously opposed to his nation's policies, and there are expressions of regret, for instance, over the German occupation of France. These attitudes, potentially dangerous during wartime, were partially responsible for a revival in Kafū's popularity in the postwar years. Identified as an anti-militarist (a label he fostered through the publication of sections of the *Danchōtei Nichijō* [Dyspepsia house days]), Kafū was sought out by literary journals and publishers anxious to reform their image in the new political climate. In 1952, he was awarded the Bunka Kunshō Medal (Imperial Cultural Decoration), the highest distinction granted to writers by the Japanese government. The citation commended him as a poet, social critic, and researcher in Edo culture, and for his contribution in introducing foreign literature to Japan—all in all, an accurate assessment. The following year he was elected to the Geijutsuin (Academy of the Arts). His reputation for eccentricity, however, grew along with his literary fortunes. Postwar cultural lore is replete with stories of Kafū wandering his old haunts—or what remained of them—armed with a purse full of cash and his indefatigable curiosity for the underside of Tokyo life. He died during the night of 29 April 1959, alone in his house on the eastern edge of the city.

Selected Bibliography

PRIMARY WORKS

COLLECTED WORKS

Kafū zenshū. 28 vols. Tokyo: Iwanami Shoten, 1962–1965. (Abbreviated as *KZ* in citations.)

NOVELS AND SHORT STORIES

Amerika monogatari. Tokyo: Hakubunkan, 1908. Trans. by Mitsuko Iriye as *American Stories.* New York: Columbia University Press, 2000.

Sumidagawa. 1909. Trans. by Edward Seidensticker as "The River Sumida." In his *Kafū the Scribbler.* Stanford, Calif.: Stanford University Press, 1965. Pp. 181–218.

Udekurabe. Tokyo: privately published, 1916. Reprinted, Tokyo: Shinbashidō, 1918. Trans. by Kurt Meissner and Ralph Friedrich as *Geisha in Rivalry.* Rutland, Vt.: Charles E. Tuttle Co., 1963.

Tsuyu no atosaki. Tokyo: Chūō Kōronsha, 1931. Trans. by Lane Dunlop as *During the Rains.* In *During the Rains & Flowers in the Shade,* by Nagai Kafū. Stanford, Calif.: Stanford University Press, 1994. Pp. 3–133.

Bokutō kidan. Tokyo: Iwanami Shoten, 1937. Trans. by Edward Seidensticker as *A Strange Tale from East of the River.* In his *Kafū the Scribbler.* Stanford, Calif.: Stanford University Press, 1965. Pp. 278–328.

SECONDARY WORKS

CRITICAL AND BIOGRAPHICAL STUDIES

Akase Masako. *Nagai Kafū to furansu bungaku.* Tokyo: Aratake Shuppan, 1976.

Akiba Tarō. *Nagai Kafū den.* Tokyo: Shun'yōdō, 1976.

Isoda Kōichi. *Nagai Kafū.* Tokyo: Kōdansha Bungei Bunko, 1989.

Kawamoto Saburō. *Kafū to Tōkyō.* Tokyo: Toshi Shuppan, 1996.

Keene, Donald. "Nagai Kafū." In his *Dawn to the West: Japanese Literature of the Modern Era.* New York: Columbia University Press, 1998–1999. Pp. 386–440.

Moriyasu Masafumi. *Nagai Kafū: Hikage no bungaku.* Tokyo: Kokusho Kankōkai, 1981.

Nakamura Mitsuo. *Hyōron Nagai Kafū.* Tokyo: Chikuma Shobō, 1979.

Ōno Shigeo. *Kafū nikki kenkyū.* Tokyo: Kasama Shoin, 1976.

Satō Haruo. *Kafū zakkan.* Tokyo: Kokuritsu Shoin, 1947.

Seidensticker, Edward. *Kafū the Scribbler: The Life and Writings of Nagai Kafū, 1879–1959.* Stanford, Calif.: Stanford University Press, 1965.

Snyder, Stephen. *Fictions of Desire: Narrative Form in the Novels of Nagai Kafū.* Honolulu, Hawaii: University of Hawaii Press, 2000.

Takemori Ten'yū. "*Udekurabe* no josetsu." *Kokubungaku Kaishaku to Kanshō* 49, no. 4:59–66 (March 1984). (Special Kafū issue.)

Yoshida Seiichi. *Nagai Kafū.* Tokyo: Shinchōsha, 1971.

KAWABATA YASUNARI
1899–1972

CHARLES CABELL

ON 16 APRIL 1972 Kawabata Yasunari turned on the gas in a small, seaside apartment in Hayama, Japan, and killed himself. Just a few years earlier, in October 1968, he had become the first Japanese and the second Asian ever to receive the Nobel Prize for literature. The award had confirmed his position as unquestionably the most famous Japanese writer alive. In the wake of such unparalleled acclaim, Kawabata's death, unaccompanied by any explanatory note, left admirers nonplussed, mirroring the author's well-known penchant for shunning resolution in his literary works. For one last time, the author had frustrated the element of his readership yearning for tidy explanations. Readers were left on their own to assign meaning to an act designed to end a story without bringing it to conclusion.

On the other hand, the very enigma of Kawabata's suicide coincided with a stereotypically Western perception of Japanese inscrutability, especially coming as it did less than two years after the histrionic *seppuku* (ritual suicide) of Kawabata's longtime friend and fellow writer Mishima Yukio. The back-to-back suicides of Japan's two most famous writers provided more grist for the mills of those convinced of a unifying mentality common to natives of the archipelago but unfathomable to outsiders. Kawabata's death reinforced an understanding of his writing and life in the West as representative of a cultural legacy largely inaccessible to non-Japanese. In his self-consciously traditional works, the writer had struck Japanese and Westerners alike as something of an anachronism, in possession of a Heian sensibility that inspired in admirers a nostalgic longing for an imagined past destroyed during Japan's economic and social transformations. The author spoke to the acute sense of loss experienced by a generation that had lived through the war years only to witness the erosion of local custom in the "miraculous" growth within the American-dominated, postwar global economy.

The Swedish Nobel committee certainly viewed the writer in this role. Anders Österling, the permanent secretary of the Swedish Academy, in his "Presentation Address," commended Kawabata "for his narrative mastery which with great sensibility expresses the essence of the Japanese mind." Although, among scores of literary works, only three of Kawabata's novels and a handful of short stories had been translated into Western languages at the time of the prize, Österling expressed confidence that the sampling provided "a sufficiently representative picture" of Kawabata's personality. The secretary linked Kawabata to Murasaki Shikibu, Japan's most famous classical author, who wrote at the turn of the eleventh century. He identified in Kawabata's literature "a whole network of small, mysterious values," while admitting to feeling excluded by a root system "of ancient Japanese ideas and instincts." Österling nevertheless praised the author for his attempt "to save something of the old Japan's beauty" during the "violent Americanization" of the postwar era. At the conclusion of his remarks, the secretary congratulated Kawabata for his contribution "to the spiritual bridge-building between the East and West."

Österling's concluding statement, which positioned Kawabata as representative of not just Japan but Asia in its entirety, ironically echoed claims made by militarists during Japan's war in Asia and the Pacific. During the 1930s and 1940s, Japanese propaganda conveyed an image of Asia, led by Japan, bound together by a common spirituality at odds with the West. In retrospect, one can find in the praise of the committee an unmistakably orientalist bent. The committee assumed an irreducible divide forever separating Asians and Westerners, and thus the necessity of a spiritual bridge-builder who could link the opposed mentalities. The reference to the author's ability to express "the essence of the Japanese mind" further revealed a belief that, on a fundamental level, Japanese were bound together by a common understanding of the world.

According to E. Wight Bakke and Mary S. Bakke in "Student Activism in Japan," the year that Kawabata received the Nobel Prize witnessed in Japan "a nationwide explosion of student activism directed against university authorities." The protestors demanded, among other things, the right to organize politically, the reform of educational policy, an end to governmental support of the American war in Vietnam, the development of a foreign policy independent of the United States, and the return of Okinawa. One wonders whether the Nobel committee viewed such actions (if they were aware of them) likewise as expressions of the Japanese mind. Most likely not, for the notion of a shared national essence precludes the occurrence of such conflict. When Österling praised Kawabata for his "clear tendency to cherish and preserve a genuinely national tradition of style," he rather audaciously implied that certain writers (and certain activities?) were less genuinely national, less Japanese. In a manner reminiscent of militant nationalists during the war years, the Nobel committee delineated norms of "Japaneseness" based on a construction of tradition that devalued engagement with present-day political realities.

Kawabata's reception of the Nobel Prize for literature represented the Western resurrection of Japan. The delicate beauty of Kawabata's prose helped to erase the image of fanatical savages utilized by the allies during the war in order to dehumanize their Asian foe, as described by historian John Dower. The choice of the Nobel committee signified a new willingness by the West to bestow upon Japan a semblance of cultural equality. Little wonder that interpreters before and after have felt compelled to distance this standard-bearer of traditional beauty from the totalitarianism of Japan in the 1930s and 1940s. The author's incorporation of Buddhist thought in many of his works and his well-known fascination with pre-modern art and literature have assisted critics intent on disassociating him from the violent economic, social, and political changes that shook Japan during his lifetime.

Partly as a result of his own self-projection, Kawabata has become the ghost of Japan Past, a writer who represents the continuation of a classic sensibility into the modern era. Were this the entire story, Kawabata would provoke scant response from students of Japan interested in understanding not the eleventh century but the twentieth. Fortunately, a glimpse behind the curtain of Kawabata's beautiful Heian stage reveals machinery of unmistakably twentieth-century design. This is to deny neither the author's profound knowledge of traditional poetics nor his incorporation of it within certain texts. At different stages in his career, however, Kawabata greedily read European writers, enthusiastically participated in modernist projects, navigated government censorship, traveled in the colonies to proclaim the superiority of imperial culture, supported Japanese aggression in Asia, mourned the nation in its defeat, and tantalized readers with surrealist fantasies. Even the author's concern with tradition belongs to a decidedly modern moment in Japanese history. Depending where one looks, one can find in Kawabata's writing all-embracing cosmopolitanism or xenophobic nationalism, the demand for constant revolution or a deep reverence for the past. The rumors of Kawabata's absence from the twentieth century, one may say, have been greatly exaggerated.

Early Years

Japan had possessed a modern constitution for nine years by the time of Kawabata's birth on 14 June 1899 in the city of Osaka. The promulgation of the constitution had been an important step in allowing the country to begin re-negotiating the unequal treaties it had concluded with the Western powers and to emerge from the subsequent forty-year period of national disgrace. Kawabata thus grew up in a nation struggling to emerge from Western domination and gain recognition as an advanced, modern civilization. One means of joining the ranks of the world powers was to participate in the global land-grab, which in Japan's case meant invading its Asian neighbors. This geopolitical landscape framed Kawabata's understanding of Japanese, Asian, and Western culture.

In his early years, however, concerns of a more personal nature would occupy Kawabata. Though not born an orphan, he quickly became one. His father, Eikichi, died when he was two; then his mother, Gen, died when he was three; both were probably victims of tuberculosis. His grandmother passed away when he was seven. His sister Yoshiko, who had been living with an aunt since the death of their mother, died two years later. Kawabata grew up virtually alone with his almost-blind grandfather. The boy's isolation was exacerbated by

frail health and a sense of estrangement from the children of his school. The critic Van C. Gessel in his *Three Modern Novelists* follows several Japanese commentators in viewing the spiritual damage the orphan Kawabata must have suffered from the deaths of so many close relatives as a means of understanding his literature, which frequently depicts alienated males yearning for acceptance, affirmation, and a sense of belonging.

In one of his earliest stories, "Jūrokusai no nikki" (1925; "Diary of My Sixteenth Year," 1998), Kawabata movingly describes the pain he experienced as a boy nursing his dying grandfather. Kawabata did not publish the short piece until 1925, though he assured his readers in an afterword that the story remained virtually as he had written it eleven years previously at the age of fourteen (sixteen by traditional East Asian reckoning). Critics tend to be rather skeptical of such claims. In any case, Kawabata unforgettably describes in this piece the mixed feelings of agony, disgust, compassion, and love experienced by a young boy called upon to help his slowly deteriorating grandfather with everything, including basic bodily functions. The diary records the frustrations of a helpless boy and a dying old man. Each day the boy must listen to the relentless moaning of his grandfather, who worries himself over the boy's future.

In 1948 Kawabata eventually published a second afterword, as the critic Donald Keene records, in which he asserted that the first afterword should be read as fiction. Together the two afterwords act as overlapping memories reinterpreting and even re-creating the past. Kawabata's confession that he has no recollection of certain scenes in the diary confronts the unreliability of memory over time and the subsequent threat to identity, a problem he took up often in his literature:

I wrote in the afterword, "What seemed strangest to me when I found this diary was that I have no recollection of the day-to-day life it describes. If I do not recall them, where have those days gone? Where had they vanished to? I pondered the things that human beings lose to the past." The mystery of having experienced something in the past but not remembering it is still a mystery to me now at the age of fifty.

(*Kawabata Yasunari zenshū [KYZ]*,
vol. 2, p. 42; tr. pp. 65–66)

Shortly after the death of his grandfather on 24 May 1914, as Gessel relates, Kawabata moved in January 1915 to a middle school dormitory, where he first experienced romantic love. Only more than thirty years after leaving the school, however, did the author finally feel secure enough to publish an account of the relationship. In *Shōnen* (Youth), serialized from 1948 to 1952, the author describes how, in 1916, during his fifth and last year at the school, he entered into a homosexual relationship with a second-year student referred to as Kiyono. The author expresses his sense of being purified and saved by the younger boy. After graduating from middle school, Kawabata moved to Tokyo, where he entered the English Department of the First Higher School. Separated from Kiyono and uncomfortable with the rules governing his new living quarters, Kawabata seems to have been severely depressed in his new surroundings. Unable to meet the younger boy at all during 1919, Kawabata returned to Osaka in the summer of 1920 to see his first love for the last time.

Perhaps the beginning of a new political era following the nation's defeat at the end of World War II, coupled with the knowledge that his close colleague Mishima was at the same time working on *Kamen no kokuhaku* (1949; *Confessions of a Mask*, 1958), which similarly engages homosexual themes, encouraged Kawabata to return to the text he had so long shelved. Although much of Kawabata's literature portrays heterosexual love among characters who act within rigidly fixed gender roles, a few works, such as the short story, "Shizen" (1952; "Nature," 1999) provide a more fluid rendering of gender and sexuality. The narrative depicts an incipient homosexual affair between the protagonist-writer and a strikingly handsome young actor whom the writer hap-

pens to meet at a seaside resort. In this moving portrayal of homoerotic desire, the author relies on the same combination of silent yearning and indirect revelation that would become the hallmark of his more famous works.

In 1918, Kawabata embarked upon a walking tour of the Izu Peninsula, which was to serve as the basis of one of his most popular and enduring stories, "Izu no odoriko" (1926; "The Dancing Girl of Izu," 1998). As Keene relates, the author devoted his first rendering of the experience, the unpublished "Yugashima no omoide" (1922; Memories of Yugashima), primarily to his love for Kiyono, material which he would eventually rework into *Shōnen*. Only a third of the original manuscript concerned the dancer.

"The Dancing Girl of Izu" depicts the simple story of a young student's unspoken yearning for the youngest girl in a troupe of itinerant performers. As he travels with the group and begins to know them, he comes to realize that the girl's age is much younger than he had first imagined. The knowledge that the girl is a mere child, rather than disappointing him, fills him with joy at the discovery of her innocence. In a key passage, the boy overhears the girl remarking to her companion, "He's a nice person." This simple statement of affirmation leads the boy to recall the impetus behind his journey:

Twenty years old, I had embarked on this trip to Izu heavy with resentment that my personality had been permanently warped by my orphan's complex and that I would never be able to overcome a stifling melancholy. So I was inexpressibly grateful to find that I looked like a nice person as the world defines the word.

(*KYZ*, vol. 2, p. 318; tr. p. 27)

The story introduces elements that became familiar to Kawabata's readers. In the years to come, according to the critic Seiji Lippit, the author produced several narratives "associated with nature, lyricism, classical aesthetics and sentimentalism" that would turn on a similarly structured romance. The narrator's habit—in contrast to his treatment of the other characters—of exclusively referring to the object of his affection as "the dancing girl" even after learning her name, ensures that the girl's personality does not intrude upon his fantasy of her, which requires the maintenance of a certain distance. The discovery of a younger, impoverished, virginal girl by an urban, well-educated male creates a gender hierarchy often repeated in Kawabata's literature. Her youth and decidedly lower status, reinforced by the prejudices voiced against her family, render the girl a nonthreatening, sympathetic figure. This accounts partly for the gratitude she and her family feel toward the socially, economically, and intellectually superior student.

Kawabata's employment of a quest motif also became a familiar device. The spiritually dysfunctional urban male is transformed by his journey through the natural world and by his relationship with the purifying female he encounters there.

One aspect of "The Dancing Girl of Izu" that disappeared in otherwise similar narratives written between 1935 and 1945, at the height of Japanese nationalism, is the straightforward description of rural suffering, as in this early passage presenting a man, paralyzed by palsy, buried in a mountain of paper scraps:

> An old man sat cross-legged by the fire, his body pale and swollen like a drowning victim. He turned his languid eyes toward me. They were yellowed to the pupils as if putrefied. . . . An automobile navigating the pass rattled the house. I wondered why the old man did not move down to a lower elevation, with the autumn already this cold and snow soon to cover the pass. . . . "Please take care of yourself," I said to the old man. "It's going to get colder."

> (*KYZ*, vol. 2, pp. 296–298; tr. pp. 5–7)

The critic S. Harrison Watson has found in the omission of this and other references to rural poverty from Edward Seidensticker's original English rendition, which appeared in the *Atlantic* in 1955—at a time when the United States government was committed to fighting communism in Japan and elsewhere in Asia by promoting positive images of liberal democracy—evidence of selective translation in order to alter the ideological content of the text.

Modernism

Kawabata graduated from the First Higher School in 1920, according to Gessel, whereupon he entered the Department of English at Tokyo Imperial University, only to transfer to the Department of Japanese Literature at the end of his first year. Soon after entering the university, he began publishing, with several classmates, the journal *Shinshichō* under the auspices of the luminary writer Kikuchi Kan, who took great interest in the young Kawabata's career. His new mentor introduced the aspiring student to Yokomitsu Riichi, who became one of his closest colleagues, and to such notable figures as Akutagawa Ryūnosuke and Kume Masao. In 1923, Kikuchi launched the journal *Bungei shunjū*, inviting Kawabata to join the editorial staff. Kawabata was involved with the journal throughout his life, publishing in it regularly.

The following year, however, the author joined with Yokomitsu to found *Bungei Jidai*, a modernist journal that heralded the advent of a new literature in Japan. Kawabata played a leading role in the magazine, which soon became the mouthpiece of the movement known as the *Shinkankakuha* (new sensationalism). It was in *Bungei Jidai* that the author first began to publish his so-called palm-of-the-hand stories *(tanagokoro no shōsetsu)*. By the time of his death in 1972, Kawabata had written 146 of these lyrical, evocative pieces, which, though generally running to no more than two or three pages, are indispensable to any attempt to understand his writings. As in the case of his best-known novels, the author's delicate prose and abrupt juxtaposition of lyrical images have led some critics to compare his writing to *haiku* or *renga*, Japanese linked poetry. Others have uncovered an equally strong affinity with stream-of-consciousness techniques and experimental writing, dating from Kawabata's association with new sensationalism.

In sharp contrast to the view of the author as a traditional writer, Lippit argues that, "Kawabata's work reveals the ultimate destination of modernism, as the collapse of forms of literary representation within a cultural field whose borders were perceived to be in the process of dissolution." In opposition to mainstream "pure" literature, represented primarily by realism, modernist fiction represented a move to destroy the borders defining the novel.

Kawabata's employment of mass-media technologies—in the areas of journalism, film and radio—in *Asakusa kurenaidan* (1929–1930; The crimson gang of Asakusa) demonstrated a clear break with naturalist writing. The author, who moved to Asakusa in 1929, took copious notes in order to create the text, which, "as the destruction of literary form and an exploration of the hybrid culture of modernity," notes Lippit, deserves a central position in any attempt to understand Japanese modernism. Among Kawabata's groundbreaking accomplishments in the text are: the use of collage, incorporating quotes from contemporary writers, a cafeteria menu, popular song lyrics, and advertisements from the subway; reliance on techniques of montage borrowed from film; and what Maeda Ai has called the jazz-like narrative. As a result, Lippit suggests, *Asakusa kurenaidan* "represents the most radical formal experimentation of any new sensationalist work, pushing the generic boundaries of the novel toward its disintegration into the various forms of mass culture."

First serialized in daily installments that appeared in the evening edition of the *Tokyo Asahi Shinbun*, the text provided readers with the latest news on contemporary Asakusa. According to Lippit, information-as-commodity replaces plot as the driving force behind the narrative, which is written in a somewhat journalistic style of urban reportage. In its semblance to journalism, the work destroys the border separating fiction from nonfiction. Indeed, narrative time seems to coincide perfectly with actual time, as Kawabata in places speculates on how his publishing of the installments will affect the characters about whom he is writing. At other times, the author insists on the fictionality of the work, even as he incorporates known personages of Asakusa. The authorial voice relates events that it later recants, leaving readers confused about what is real in the story. The journalistic nature of the work was attested to by the increase in popularity of the Casino Follies after Kawabata described them in one of the installments. At the same time, Kawabata employed a variety of narrative voices and disarming interruptions that forced readers to participate in the construction of meaning. In Lippit's words, Kawabata situates readers "in the gap between the text and the urban landscape," so that the act of reading itself leads readers to engage with the actual world of Asakusa.

Although the roles of men and women appear rigidly prescribed in the classical Kawabata canon, the world of *Asakusa kurenaidan* (The crimson gang of Asakusa), like the postwar work "Nature," is a place of shifting gender and sexuality. According to Lippit, Kawabata depicts the collapse of family and state, which destabilizes gender and allows the central character Yumiko to fluctuate between female and male. In contrast to several of his better-known works, this piece, by focusing on the suffering of homeless beggars and prostitutes, offers a critique of the social displacements that result from Japan's ongoing capitalist transformation. Kawabata portrays Asakusa as a hybrid culture greedily consuming novelties from the West, especially America. The revolutionary quality of *Asakusa kurenaidan* makes the break that follows it all the more remarkable. The author's shift in the middle of the 1930s has been described as a retreat from the attempt to grapple with the exterior realities of the eclectic culture of urban modernity to an internalized narrative ensconced within "the enclosed and secure boundaries of a native culture."

The Importance of the Female Savior

During the decade of 1935 to 1945, Kawabata repeatedly portrayed rural female characters whose redemptive qualities allowed them to heal spiritually broken urban males in texts such as *Maihime no koyomi* (1935; The dancer's calendar), *Hana no mizuumi* (1936; Lake of flowers), *Tabi e no sasoi* (1940; Call to travel), *Tōkaidō* (1943; The Tōkaidō), and, most famously, *Yukiguni* (1937, 1948; *Snow Country*, 1956). Readers could only speculate as to what forces had driven such men from the city, or what fates they would have met if, instead of receiving the comforting sense of national, ethnic unity provided by the "traditional" maidens, they had confronted women of a more revolutionary bent.

A possible answer to just such questions lies in "Kinjū" (1933; "Of Birds and Beasts," 1969), one of Kawabata's most disturbing stories. The examination of a male denied the reassuring stability of the Japanese maiden underscores how critical her role is to the nativism of later texts.

The fragmented narrative revolves around the musings and recollections of a misanthropic protagonist who favors animals over people and whose spiritual life has become deformed by the effects of the nation's capitalist transformation. His rejection of society appears tangentially related to his past and present relationship with a dancer named Chikako. Rather than serving as a source of reassuring stability, she reflects the turmoil of the times.

Kawabata details in the narrative the corrosive effects of capitalism on human relations that had once been regulated by Confucian obligation and infused with Buddhist compassion. The protagonist's recognition of the cruelty of capitalist society—demonstrated by its treatment of pets as commodities—has caused him to retreat from it. Chikako's story frames the narrative and helps explain why the protagonist cannot overcome the upheaval brought about by the economic changes at

work in Japan, as do protagonists in other stories by Kawabata. Rather than be a static, eternally pre-modern source through which the man can uncover his Japanese roots, Chikako represents a loss of purity and the absence of continuity.

The protagonist initially wishes to treasure forever an image of Chikako formed ten years previously, when she was a beautiful prostitute willing to be killed in order to satisfy his momentary whim. After a stay in the puppet state of Manchukuo (in Pinyin, Manzhouguo; in Japanese, Manshūkoku), however, Chikako has changed. She seems to have absorbed the erotic appeal of the colonial frontier. The wild, lascivious dancer first shocks and then fascinates the protagonist. Chikako's downfall results not from her metamorphosis abroad but from her attempt to transgress the border that separates the erotic woman from her domesticated counterpart. She audaciously believes that she can simultaneously play the parts of whore and mother.

Regardless of her desires, in the reality of the text, pregnancy immediately brings about the collapse of Chikako's "strange power" (*KYZ*, vol. 25, p. 170; tr. p. 148). Despite the man's exasperated demand that she choose either sexuality (dancing) or motherhood, Chikako insists she will have both. In adopting such a position, she directly challenges the patriarchal division of female gender between the wifely and the erotic, a decision that hastens her demise and transforms her from a goddess of salvation and renewal into a symbol of the threat of modernity. The author wastes little space in relating the predictably disastrous outcome of each of Chikako's endeavors. The mother abandons her child; the wife is divorced by her husband; and, after two years, the art of the dancer has "degenerated so greatly that the man had to look away" (*KYZ*, vol. 25, p. 178; tr. p. 156).

When the male protagonist can no longer sustain the dream of the eternal maiden, faith in the national community disintegrates. The man becomes condemned to the loathsome world described in the text, a society in which human conduct is guided only by the grim, unrelenting logic of modern capitalism. The Buddhist and Confucian references in "Of Birds and Beasts" allude to the protagonist's unexpressed yearning for a spiritual foundation. The text suggests that the journeys of later protagonists such as Shimamura (protagonist of *Snow Country*) may be seen as religious quests upon which alienated, urban males embark in order to find and worship mountain maidens—Shinto goddesses capable of restoring to these men their belief in a timeless, aboriginal Japanese community.

The War Years

In 1948, writing under a new system of censorship enforced by the United States Occupation, Kawabata denied any association with the thoroughly discredited militarism that had resulted in the nation's disastrous defeat:

I am one of the Japanese who was affected least and suffered least because of the war. There has been no conspicuous change in my prewar, wartime, and postwar works and no noticeable break. I did not experience any great inconvenience because of the war either in my artistic or my private life. And it goes without saying that I was never caught up in a surge of what is called divine possession, to become a fanatical believer in or blind worshiper of Japan. I have always grieved for the Japanese with my own grief; that is all.

(Keene, p. 823)

This image of Kawabata and his wartime beliefs has been adopted with little modification by a great many critics writing in Japan and in the United States. The author's writings demonstrate, however, that his detachment from Japan's imperial ambitions did not come about until after Japan's defeat. Because Kawabata has been interpreted as a man who lived and wrote at a far remove from the politics of his day, few people are familiar with his wartime works or the manner in which they create an intimate relationship between gender, nation, and empire.

Any discussion of the political significance of Kawabata's wartime texts to Japanese nationalism must take into account the very real threat presented by Western imperialism. According to the critic Edward Said in *Culture and Imperialism*, in 1914, when Kawabata was fifteen years old, Europe held dominion over approximately eighty-five percent of the inhabited globe. It was a time of unparalleled Western domination of the earth. The colonization of the non-Western world was justified by an unquestioned belief in the superiority of the white race, a belief sustained by military and technological superiority.

After half a century of "modernization," however, many Japanese felt keenly the impossibility of climbing out of the Eastern past and into the Western present. To the extent that the Japanese adhered to a concept of global progress, they would, it seemed, be damned to spend eternity in the temporal and geographical periphery. The movement in Japan to overcome modernity in part represented an attempt to repudiate the teleological claims of Western-dominated history, which located the West in the present, or the modern, and relegated the non-West to the past, or the traditional. The equation of the West with the modern assumed that non-Western world was destined to become more Western as it "developed." Many prominent Japanese thinkers attempted to remove Asia from global (that is, Western) history and locate it in a pure realm of Asian culture led by the Japanese. In order to exempt Japan from Western notions of progress, Japanese attempted to establish their uniqueness. Agrarian nationalists Gondō Seikyō and Tachibana Kosaburō stressed the divine links to the land, and the mythic origins of the Japanese people. The insistence on an eternal community was expressed through the idea of the *kokutai*, the national essence. The nation constituted a single family with mystical links to the land and was headed by the divine emperor.

Kawabata's literature between 1935 and 1945 reflected the dominant intellectual trends of the period. His wartime works may be profitably read alongside the literature of Japanese Romantics who similarly sought to eliminate vulgar Western influences from their writings and return to the authentic literature of Japan. In the idea of the return (kaiki), according to the critics Tetsuo Najita and H. D. Harootunian, writers expressed their nostalgic yearning to recover a sense of unity with their compatriots, the land, and the aesthetic tradition.

Snow Country

Examination of Kawabata's best-known novel, *Snow Country (Yukiguni)*, as a single text obscures the relationship of the disparate segments to the circumstances surrounding their production. Kawabata delivered the work, bit by bit, over a thirteen-year period. The first edition appeared in May 1937, but Kawabata had been working on it since late 1934, relying on several different magazines to publish what initially appeared as independent stories. Even after the first edition came out, Kawabata, who from the beginning had conceived of concluding the work with a fiery calamity, continued to publish additional chapters in various magazines. Two sections, "Yuki no naka no kaji" (December 1940; Fire in the snow) and "Ama no gawa" (August 1941; The milky way), were re-written by Kawabata after the war as "Yukiguni shō" (May 1946; *Snow Country* Extract) and "Yukiguni zoku" (October 1947; *Snow Country* Continued). As a result, the two texts written at the height of the Pacific war were eliminated from what became the standard version of the book in 1948, and disappeared—along with a great deal of Kawabata's wartime writings—from public memory.

Snow Country tells the story of the nihilistic dilettante Shimamura's three journeys to an inn in the northeastern region of Japan, and of the relationship he develops with Komako, a young woman who, while still a novice upon their first meeting, becomes a full-fledged geisha over the course of their relationship. The novel opens with the train that carries

Shimamura emerging from a long tunnel into the snow country. Shimamura is on his second journey, returning to see Komako, who has long awaited his return. On the train, Shimamura is held spellbound by the partial reflection of another young woman, Yōko, in the train window. Yōko occupies herself with caring for Yukio, a young man who is dying. *Snow Country* presents to the reader, through the lens of Shimamura, various impressions of Komako, Yōko, and Yukio, and their relationship to one another, to him, and to the land.

Kawabata's first two installments, "Yūgeshiki no kagami" (1935; Mirror of the evening scenery) and "Shiroi asa no kagami" (1935; Mirror of the white morning), reflect the complexity that characterized issues of censorship in Japan in the mid 1930s. *Fuseji* (marks such as *X*s or *O*s) were applied to "Yūgeshiki no kagami" from the first page. Substituted for words that could potentially incite the wrath of a government ministry and lead to bans, fines, suspensions, or imprisonment, *fuseji* were employed by publishers often with cooperation from writers in acts of preemptive self-censorship. As their experience with such self-censorship increased, writers learned to use *fuseji* in such a way as to invite readers to imagine a sexual content more erotic than what could be explicitly expressed.

Tajima Yōko has commented, for example, on the phallic symbolism in Shimamura's use in *Snow Country* of his "finger" to remember Komako. The implied phallus loomed even larger in "Yūgeshiki no kagami" due to Kawabata's use of *fuseji* to omit the word "finger" from the text, an act that resulted in sentences such as "Only the *x* in his left hand remembered her well. Shimamura gazed at his *x* as if it were a strange, mysterious object. It was a living creature existing totally apart from him" (*KYZ*, vol. 34, p. 75). "White Morning" was also published with *fuseji* to similar effect.

In the months of November and December 1935, Kawabata published, respectively, "Monogatari" (Tale) and "Torō" (Wasted effort). Before the writer could complete the next two sections, "Kaya no hana" (August 1936; Kaya flowers) and "Hi no makura" (October 1936; Pillow of fire), elements within the military had brought about what became known as the February 26 Incident, a failed coup during which 1400 troops seized the center of Tokyo, assassinating prominent members of the government. In March 1937, the Ministry of Education published and distributed *Kokutai no hongi* (*Kokutai no Hongi: Cardinal Principles of the National Entity of Japan*, 1949), which, according to the critic Richard Mitchell, advocated "a new synthesis of Western and Eastern thought, firmly based upon the indigenous tradition." The booklet was the product of a committee appointed in November 1935 by the Okada Cabinet to promote the *kokutai* and weed out foreign ideology.

In May 1937, Kawabata published "Temari uta" (Children's songs), the last work in what appeared to be the completed novel. Sōgensha published *Snow Country* to critical acclaim in June. As if in celebration of the outbreak of full-scale war with China, on 7 July, Kawabata accepted the Third Prize of the Literary Chat Committee, to which he had belonged since 1934. The repressive nature of the committee became clear at least by 1935, when Matsumoto Gaku had removed the leftist writer Shimaki Kensaku from a list of finalists. Though Kawabata complained of Shimaki's removal, as related by Kawabata's biographer Shindō Sumitaka, he remained in the society. With the money from the prize, he bought a villa in Kamakura.

Snow Country portrays a community of rural Japanese who inhabit a magical landscape where giant cedars tower above Shinto shrines. The sacred mountains of the northern country purify the aboriginal folk. The city-dweller, Shimamura, in contrast, appears polluted by Western ideas that have seeped into the urban areas. Kawabata creates a division between beautiful mountain natives whose cultural wellspring is found not in other regions of East Asia but in the native soil, and an urban man whose interest in the West is emblematic of his degeneracy. The text displays an anxiety over Western influence and a concomitant desire to demonstrate the uniqueness and spiritual superiority of indigenous culture. Propaganda tracts such as *Cardinal Principles of the National Entity* written during the same period convey a similar set of concerns, albeit less subtly and less persuasively.

A modern man who has rejected tradition in favor of the frivolous translation of meaningless Western works, Shimamura discovers a people living in harmonious unity with the land, a country whose sacred, magical qualities suffuse those who reside within it. In contrast to the treatment of rural suffering and class prejudice in earlier texts such as "The Dancing Girl of Izu," class strife, economic injustice, competing interests, ideological differences, dirt, and conflict seldom appear in the snow country with the exception of the brief appearance of a filthy, incongruous Russian peasant. The indigenous women of the mountains purify themselves through acts of self-sacrifice, or through unflagging dedication to the traditional arts of Japan. (For an opposing interpretation, see Torrance, p. 257.)

Shimamura's brief encounter with the geisha Kikuyū at the start of his last visit to the snow country and Komako's subsequent recounting of her story reinforce the message that every Japanese has a duty and place that must not be questioned. Instead of meekly taking over the restaurant built by her patron, Kikuyū leaves him to follow the man she loved. Ultimately, she realizes that she has been abandoned and must take her leave of the snow country where, until the time of her impulsive action, she has been "at the center of everything, . . . making more money than any of the rest." Komako attributes Kikuyū's plight to the "gradual rise of individualism" (*KYZ*, vol. 10, p. 78, cf. tr. p. 97). However good-natured and popular Kikuyū may have been, Komako in the end finds her a weakling. A weakling thus is one who yields to individual desires, the fulfillment of which lead to the abandonment of one's determined social role. The unmistakable parallel between the plights of Kikuyū and Komako seemingly forecloses any possibility that either Shimamura or

Komako might, as a result of their feelings for each other, attempt to depart from the fixed orbits of their lives.

The act of writing *Snow Country* itself parallels the quest of Kawabata's main protagonist to uncover a pristine realm of Japanese culture. The author's numerous classical allusions represent an attempt to create a literature that will connect to a pre-modern, purely Japanese tradition. The critic Dennis Washburn has written, in a discussion of Kawabata, that the conscious employment of pre-modern motifs "implies a sentimental longing or nostalgia on the part of social elites whose order is threatened by cultural change." The revival of a literary tradition within the pages of *Snow Country* is, as Washburn recognizes, a sign of a previous radical break with the past. Kawabata's text seems to leap over the modern period into an ahistorical Japanese cultural heritage.

Paradoxically, this attempt to reclaim a lost literary past more than anything else firmly marks the text as modern. Kawabata must attempt to re-establish an authentic Japanese literature precisely because he is writing in an era that follows the wholesale abandonment of pre-Meiji literary forms. The author's nostalgic reliance on canonical literary tropes defines *Snow Country* as uniquely and authentically Japanese. The work creates an illusion of seamless unity with the classical literature of previous centuries. Even as the author incorporates elements of traditional aesthetics, he unhesitatingly borrows, as the critic Richard Torrance notes, "popular literary languages" from the era. Kawabata's intricate, unobtrusive weaving into the text of layer upon layer of modern techniques and classical allusions has caused it to be celebrated as a masterpiece. Despite the evidence of such hybrid origins, the construction of Japanese tradition within the work has given it a reputation of being impenetrable to foreigners, reinforcing myths regarding the uniqueness and homogeneity of the people and the mystical, divine power of the language.

After Japan's defeat in 1945, Kawabata himself recognized the significance that his depiction of the homeland had held for Japanese colonizers and soldiers throughout Asia. In the afterword of the edition published by Kamakura Bunko in December 1945, Kawabata wrote:

> In the year that *Snow Country* was published, the China Incident began. . . . My work was read with more poignant love than would have been the case during peacetime. Contrary to what one would expect, it was I who received numerous consoling letters from soldiers at the front. Even in Manchuria and Northern China, I met housewives who read my work as if it were the evening daily. There were even people who said that, in the trenches dug for protection against air raids, they felt calmed upon coming across my work.

> (*KYZ*, vol. 33, p. 610)

In the afterword of the 1948 edition, Kawabata added, "During the war, I knew that when Japanese living outside of Japan read the work, it stirred up their nostalgic yearnings for their home villages. Knowing this deepened my own awareness of the meaning of my work" (Isogai, p. 32). In a July 1955 letter to Harold Strauss, who oversaw publication of the English translation for Knopf, Kawabata repeated that the work originally had "stirred up nostalgic feelings for home in soldiers in the Outer Territories of the empire" (*KYZ*, vol. 37, p. 371).

Snow Country was drawn from a crucible of rising censorship, resistance to Western narratives of universal progress, fascination with cinematic techniques, naturalism, agrarian romanticism, nativist returns, and quests for racial purity. Both Kawabata and his protagonist flee the corrupt internationalism of the city in search of a subjective realm of culture that is authentically Japanese. More than merely "apolitical," the text denies domestic conflict, and in doing so further stigmatizes politics as an illegitimate activity for the citizenry. In this, and in its portrayal of an organic community existing across the millennia, *Snow Country* supports depictions of the *kokutai*, the national essence.

159

Yet, the text cannot be reduced to a propaganda tract for the state and ultimately presents a more complex, contradictory image of Japan than the comparison implies. Shimamura's unstable, self-deceiving, highly subjective perceptions throw into doubt the reality of the narrative and prevent it from being read as political dogma. *Snow Country* is told from the perspective of an alienated, urban, modern, cosmopolitan man who seems to have no interest in dedicating himself to fulfill the aims of the government authorities. The text invites readers to identify with this wanderer and his search for authenticity. The very motivation of the story, Shimamura's quest, reveals his deep-rooted unease with modern society. Like his contemporaneous Japanese readers, Shimamura lives in a nation irrevocably transformed by the forces of Western-driven modernity. He recognizes that he has been shaped by such forces, but he yearns to identify with characters such as Komako and Yōko, who somehow manage to exist in a pre-modern past. Readers are invited to share in Shimamura's nostalgic yearning for a distilled Japan even as they are reminded by his indulgent fantasies that such a Japan does not exist.

The Master of Go

Kawabata's assertion of Japanese cultural superiority and advocacy of empire—which was repostulated after the war as the defense of (or eulogy for) decaying tradition—can also be witnessed in the wartime version of the author's well-known work *Meijin* (1952, 1954; *The Master of Go*, 1972). Donald Keene interprets the text as "a statement by Kawabata on the nature of men's consecration to art. The master and his successor immerse themselves completely in a game that has no political, economic, or social significance; this was also Kawabata's chosen stance." Van C. Gessel echoes Keene, citing the writing as evidence of "Kawabata's secession from contemporary society." Certainly, *The Master of Go* does poignantly convey the feelings of loss experienced as one watches a traditional way of life

yield to the forces of modernization, but, during the war, the text pointedly conveyed another set of messages as well.

Kawabata began writing the text in 1938, reporting on a match between Go Master Hon'inbō Shūsai and Kitani Minoru of the Seventh Rank. Kawabata's column, "Hon'inbō meijin intai go kansenki" (Eye-witness report of Master Hon'inbō's final match) appeared in forty-one installments from 23 July to 6 September in the evening editions of the *Tokyo Daily News* and the *Osaka Daily News*. On 25 August 1942, two years after the death of the master, Kawabata began serialization of *The Master of Go* in the journal *Yakumo* based largely on the column he had written four years earlier. Kawabata reworked the material several times (August 1944; *Yūhi* [Evening sun]; 1947; *Hana* [Flower]; *Mibōjin* [1948; The widow]) before including a rewritten version in an anthology of his works published in August 1951. He continued to write on the subject, however, adding to the ending material from two additional short works when the work was next anthologized in 1952. Kawabata finally completed the work in 1954, incorporating yet another short piece into the ending (*KYZ*, vol. 25, p. 472; *KYZ*, vol. 11, pp. 597, 598). The preface to Seidensticker's English translation, however, seems to indicates that this translation is based on the edition of 1952.

Rather than as a means to withdraw from society, the author clearly uses the game/art of Go as a metaphor for expressing views on the pressing political issues of the day. Go provides the writer with an apt symbol for all sorts of competitions—tradition versus modernity, East versus West, and Japan versus China. In *Master Hon'inbō Shūsai* (1940), Kawabata introduces his perspective on the game: "That this competition of a depth and mystery unparalleled in the world has developed to such an extent in Japan is most probably due to the extraordinary superiority of Japanese intelligence, but there is no one to contemplate the nature of this superior intelligence" (*KYZ*, vol. 25, p. 355). For Kawabata, Go provides a key to understanding the unique character of the Japanese people.

In addition to exploring the spiritual profundity of Go or lamenting the passing of tradition, Kawabata seems intent on using the game as a pretext for demonstrating Japanese cultural superiority in the world while justifying at the same time Japan's imperial ambitions. The potential of the people of China, readers discover, for example, will never be realized without the loving help of the Japanese. This lesson is driven home in Kawabata's account of the rise of a phenomenal Chinese player, Wu Qingyuan of the Sixth Rank. Wu has come to Japan at the age of fourteen or fifteen as a Go prodigy. The narrator proclaims great admiration for the young "genius" who, able through the power of intellect to overcome the backward traditions and present benighted conditions of his native land, has recognized Japan's wisdom and benefited from it.

One felt the glory of human wisdom when one merely considered how he had escaped from the history of his motherland, to say nothing of how he had removed himself from its present circumstances. . . . While a multitude of people remained unknowing, he alone had seen the light and leaped forward of his own accord. All of it owed to the gift of genius. On more than a few occasions, a single youth has purified the emotions flowing back and forth between Japan and China. I felt at times as if this youth were a bright ray shining with the wisdom of China. Behind him a great pool of light lay submerged deep beneath the mud.

(*KYZ*, vol. 25, p. 411)

By expressing the relationship through the attractively benign analogy of Go, the Japanese invasion of China—and the rape, plunder, and carnage it entails—can be expressed as "purifying the emotions between the two countries." Kawabata's narrative convinces readers of the Chinese potential to become a lesser partner in a Great East Asia Co-Prosperity Sphere naturally headed by Japan.

In sharp contrast with China, the West appears in Kawabata's text as irreducibly alien.

The narrator describes his utter distaste upon being pressed into playing a game of Go with an American while riding on the train:

In this manner, I suffered his play almost all the way from Ueno to Karuizawa Station, becoming thoroughly irritated in the process. . . . Yet, for him, this was apparently quite an absorbing match. Trapped by this simple-minded barbarian opponent, I was at a loss to extricate myself. Perhaps due to the novelty of seeing a foreigner playing Go, four of five passengers gathered and stood over us as if in search of diversion.

(*KYZ*, vol. 25, pp. 413–414)

Go becomes a device for revealing a spiritual hierarchy, and the top position is occupied by the Japanese race. Unfortunately, the wisdom of their neighbors, the Chinese, lies buried deep in the mud, waiting to be uncovered by their charitable Japanese superiors. Yet how enviable the position of the Chinese appears when contrasted with the true enemy of Japan, the simple-minded, disgusting barbarians of the West.

The Puppet State of Manchukuo

On 2 April 1941, Shindō records, Kawabata first traveled to Manchukuo—the puppet state under Japanese control since its creation in 1932—at the invitation of the *Manchurian Daily News*. He visited again in September, this time at the invitation of the occupying Kwantung Army. At the end of his tour, Kawabata decided to remain in Fengtian at his own expense in order to carry out further research. He invited his wife to join him, and, in December, the two set out for Beijing. Rumors of the coming war in the Pacific drove him back to Japan on 30 November, eight days before the attack on Pearl Harbor (For more information about the author's travels in Manchukuo and his writings in support of empire, see "Maiden Dreams: Kawabata Yasunari's Beautiful Japanese Empire, 1930–1945" by Charles Cabell).

In the handful of articles he wrote on Manchurian literature, Kawabata urged his Japanese audience to respond more passionately to the cultural imperative for Japanese involvement in the new nation, which, according to the author, lacked any cultural history. In addition to Manchukuo, Kawabata dreamed of publishing in Japan anthologies of literature composed by each race of what, at the successful conclusion of the war, would be the newly independent nations of Great East Asia. As in the case of Manchukuo, these new nations, which presumably would also lack histories and cultures, undoubtedly would demand a great deal of Japanese guidance. On 30 March 1944, Kawabata wrote:

The fateful significance and mission borne by the literature of Manchukuo have become even more lofty and awesome as a result of the Great East Asian War. Not only has the relationship of Manchurian literature with Japan become even closer, the expansion of the corpus of one literature for all of Great East Asia has gained new urgency. Even as war in the South rages, we Japanese especially must not forget that the only place where already for many years numerous members of the Japanese race have helped create a culture and stimulate literary activity—as citizens and writers of the new nation—is this very land of Manchukuo.

(*KYZ*, vol. 34, pp. 112–115)

Joshua Fogel, in an extensive survey of Japanese travel writing on China, concludes that, after 1938, no account demonstrated any form of "resistance to the dominant ideology of the state." Even suggestions of dissatisfaction with the war or with Japan's policy in China disappeared after that year. Kawabata's writings on Manchukuo, the empire, and the war effort are paradigmatic rather than exceptional. Although Kawabata hoped to become the driving force behind anthologies of Manchurian literature, which were to be published in Japan and Manchukuo for generations to come, Japan's defeat curtailed the writer's plans and insured that his projects never amounted to more than a footnote in the history of the puppet state.

The Postwar Period

Recognizing the degree to which Kawabata supported the war makes more understandable the intense grief he felt in the aftermath of the defeat. Kawabata would write, "When Japan surrendered, I felt as if I were dead" (Shindō, p. 453). Despite such depression, the immediate postwar era would witness some of Kawabata's most productive years.

In 1949, the author began publishing installments of *Senbazuru* (1952; *Thousand Cranes*, 1959). A few months later saw the appearance of the first chapters of *Yama no oto* (1954; *The Sound of the Mountain*, 1970), the work some critics believe to be his finest. Both texts continue a style perfected in *Snow Country*. Rather than being plot-driven, the works are composed around series of emotionally charged images. Consequently, individual sections are quite capable of standing alone just as the ends lack an air of finality.

Thousand Cranes presents the story of Kikuji Mitani, a man who enters into a brief affair with his deceased father's former mistress, Mrs. Ōta, after meeting her at a tea ceremony hosted by a rival mistress of his father, Kurimoto Chikako. Mrs. Ōta commits suicide, leaving behind her daughter Fumiko, to whom Kikuji is also attracted. Chikako strongly opposes their relationship, however, and urges the protagonist to marry Miss Inamura, to whom he has been introduced at a tea ceremony. Perhaps one of Kawabata's great achievements in this story of karmic guilt is his skillful integration of the tea ceremony in the narrative. Tea bowls, the critic Matthew Mizenko suggests, seem to convey the ability of the dead to hold power over the living.

If *Thousand Cranes* reminds readers of the continued presence of the dead, *The Sound of the Mountain* tells the story of approaching death. The failing memory and encroaching senility of the aging protagonist, Shingo, address questions of self and identity that Kawabata first took up in "Diary of My Sixteenth Year." Kawabata made a famous comment in his Nobel speech that *Thousand Cranes* concerned the degradation, not the beauty, of the tea ceremony in postwar Japan. *The Sound of the Mountain*—in addition to unforgettably describing Shingo's private world of intensely felt moments in time, premonitions of death, and the interplay of reality and dream—presents a powerful critique of postwar society, as the critic Neil Donahue has noted. The nation's failed war has robbed the characters of their morality and their identity, leaving instead cynicism, decadence, and pain.

The Sound of the Mountain, as *Snow Country* before it, bears the unmistakable traces of the social moment in which it was created. Shingo, however, does not flee his family in favor of an idyllic wonder world. On the contrary, he witnesses in his former classmates, in his family, and in himself the malaise of Japanese society in the wake of defeat. He and his wife have settled into a thirty-year marriage of lost opportunity and indifferent tolerance, each a poor substitute for the truly desired lover of the other. Addiction eventually destroys Shingo's emotionally crippled son-in-law. His daughter-in-law aborts her child as a consequence of her strained relationship with her husband. The protagonist's daughter, distraught by her own ruined marriage and loveless childhood, bitterly attacks him.

The character who binds the breakdown of the family to the nation's defeat, however, is the son, Shūichi, a deeply scarred veteran whose life is characterized by spiritual paralysis and decay. Shūichi drunkenly beats his mistress and reacts to her pregnancy first by dragging her down the stairs and later by treating her with callous indifference. His own wife's abortion and anguish leave him similarly cold. The narrative suggests that Shūichi's experience as a soldier has stripped him of any sense of moral responsibility. His cruelty and brutality pale next to the acts he was encouraged to commit against the enemy and against women on the mainland. Shingo, the "indirect" murderer unable to alleviate the suffering of his family members, shares his son's paralysis. He can no more heal his family than rid the nation of the neocolonialist American occupation forces, represented in the text by sexually predatory soldiers who occasionally appear in the background. Such external threats, however, appear minor compared to the spiritual collapse of the nation, manifested in the warped, lonely lives of the primary characters.

The Sound of the Mountain helped establish Kawabata as one of the leading writers of the postwar era. In 1948, at the age of forty-nine, as Kawabata's biographer Shindō relates, he had become the fourth president of Japanese P.E.N., following Shimazaki Tōson, Masamune Hakuchō, and Shiga Naoya. One of his most noteworthy achievements as president was undoubtedly the hosting of the Tokyo International P.E.N. convention in September 1957. At the time, Japan was still recovering from the war, and the estimated 30 million yen cost of accommodating 150 participants created a great deal of resistance. Members of Japan P.E.N. had hotly debated whether or not Japan should sponsor the meeting, and it was said that Kawabata's fervent support was decisive.

In order to encourage a sizeable international turnout, in March 1957, Shindō records, Kawabata left for Europe. He visited London, France, West Germany, Italy, and Denmark, meeting with well-known writers and encouraging their participation in the coming gathering in Tokyo. The convention provided a great boost to the standing of Japanese literature in the West, and Kawabata's dominant role increased his stature at home and abroad. The critic Van C. Gessel has gone so far as to credit the present status of Japanese literature in the world to the author's activities.

In February 1958, as noted by Shindō, Kawabata received the Kikuchi Kan prize for his "efforts and achievements regarding Japan's hosting of the International P.E.N." In March, he was unanimously elected to serve as vice-president of International P.E.N. In May 1960, the author visited the United States as the guest of the State Department. In July he continued on to Rio de Janeiro, where he was the guest of honor of the meeting of International P.E.N. In the same year, he received an award from the French government on behalf of his achievements in promoting French-Japanese cultural exchange. The next year, he received Japan's award for cultural achievement. In June 1964, he participated in the meeting of International P.E.N. in Oslo, again as the guest of honor. Once again, he traveled throughout Europe before returning to Japan in August. When Kawabata resigned as president of Japan P.E.N. in 1965, he had dominated Japanese literary circles for almost two decades and was rivaled in global fame only by Tanizaki Jun'ichirō and Mishima Yukio.

Misogynist Fantasy or Social Critique

In the early 1960s, Kawabata completed two surrealist works—"Nemureru bijo" (1961; "The House of the Sleeping Beauties," 1969) and "Kata ude" (1964; "One Arm," 1967)—which objectified female characters to an unprecedented degree. While such treatment of women was not new to the author's literature, seldom had it been so central or conspicuous. On the other hand, the symbolism of the texts created a space that invited readers to look critically at society, the human condition, and male-female relations in a way that the author's more realistic novels precluded. The fantastic aspects of the modern fairy tales de-naturalized the texts, opening up discussion of such themes as the exorcism of desire from the modern, the dehumanizing nature of lust, male manipulation and control of women, the impossibility of communication, and human capacity for self-delusion. The analysis below is limited to "The House of the Sleeping Beauties."

The protagonist of the narrative, Eguchi, describes violent acts and fantasies directed toward women that include molestation, rape, mutilation, pedophilia, and murder. The text is divided into five chapters, each one describing a night spent by the protagonist next to a naked and drugged young woman. Each of the women functions as a kind of Proustian memory jog, calling forth in the protagonist different sensations felt during sexual encounters long ago forgotten.

As the writer and critic Mishima Yukio discusses in the introduction to the English translation of "The House of the Sleeping Beauties," the maidens are mere "fragments of human beings." The narrative creates a structure, common to many of Kawabata's texts, of a dominant man fantasizing about women placed in passive, non-threatening positions. Like Chikako in the story "Of Birds and Beasts" and Komako in *Snow Country*, the sleeping beauties exist within the economy of the sex trade. Unlike Chikako and Komako, however, the drugged nudes present no danger of asserting their identities or lessening the distance separating them from the protagonist. Instead, they resemble other virgin ciphers whom males can interpret as pure and innocent due to a perceived lack of sexual desire or awareness—women such as the dancing girl of Izu and Yōko from *Snow Country*.

Assertiveness, proximity, middle age, and sexual experience often render women unattractive in Kawabata's narratives. Shimamura's attraction to the distant Yōko never wanes, whereas his relationship with Komako grows burdensome as he learns the quotidian details of her life. In *The Sound of the Mountain*, Shingo's wife is but a poor parody of her dead sister. The attempt at self-assertion by the prostitute/dancer Chikako in "Of Birds and Beasts" results in self-destruction. In *Thousand Cranes*, the repulsive birthmark of the tea instructor Chikako mirrors the spiritual defect of her soul, demonstrated by her attempts to manipulate Kikuji. In contrast to conscious women who may threaten men by undergoing changes or asserting their identities, the salvation offered by drugged beauties, likened in the texts to Buddhas, is absolute. In them, spiritually broken men no longer capable of tolerating the despair of old age find brief respite. "The House of the Sleeping Beauties" shares with *Snow Country* a nostalgic male yearning to return to a time of innocence.

Under the surface of what appears the most blatant misogyny, Kawabata's narrative plants seeds of social criticism. Eguchi's manipulation of drugged women calls attention to itself. Their stories may be read as allegories for the ways in which women are abused and degraded to satisfy male desire. According to Mizenko, readers, aware that Eguchi has no possibility of knowing anything of the women, must view his indulgent interpretations of them with some skepticism. Eguchi's descriptions, Mizenko asserts, reveal little more than his penchant for categorizing young females in ways that stimulate his fantasies. The death of a woman at the end of the work and her easy substitution underscore the inhumanity of the house, a microcosm of modern society, and the culpability of the protagonist.

Texts such as *Snow Country* invite realistic readings in which a masculine perspective of gender may be interpreted as natural. Österling, along with the Nobel committee, followed in the footsteps of numerous American and Japanese critics, for example, when he declared that, in the creation of Komako, Kawabata had demonstrated himself to be "a subtle psychologist of women." In contrast, the fairy-tale framing of "The House of the Sleeping Beauties" prevents readers from "naturalizing" either the manipulation of the author or the protagonist. The author demonstrates that Eguchi's interpretations of the women have no basis in reality. Readers also see at once that the drugged virgins represent a vision of women distorted in order to satisfy one kind of purely masculine fantasy. Ironically, the story reveals the manipulation at work throughout Kawabata's oeuvre. After reading "The House of the Sleeping Beauties," one can retrospectively return to the author's earlier texts and see much more readily similarly manipulative processes at work.

Conclusion

The announcement that Kawabata would receive the Nobel Prize for literature was made on 18 October 1968. The ceremony took place on 10 December 1968. One might well argue that no one benefited more from the author's ceaseless efforts to promote Japanese literature than Kawabata himself. As noted, the author won the prize as "the heir to Japanese literary tradition" and promoted himself in an appropriate manner. In the years that followed, he wrote several essays devoted to explaining traditional aesthetics, taking, as Mizenko says, "his new role as spokesman for Japanese culture to an almost absurd extreme." He wrote little fiction, however, in the four years that followed the prize.

Kawabata's death has inspired, as one might imagine, many a parlor guest to try on the hat of the amateur detective, searching through the author's life and letters for clues that will solve the riddle of his suicide. One would-be psychoanalyst holds forth on Kawabata's seeming inability to recover from the shock suffered from the suicide of his protégé and rival for the Nobel Prize, Mishima Yukio. Another dwells instead on the author's incurable insomnia and problems with drug addiction. "The writing block suffered in the years following the Nobel must surely have depressed him," adds a third.

There is, however, another clue, as intriguing and no more improbable than the others. In 1977, Usui Yoshimi published a scandalous account of Kawabata's infatuation, in the last year of his life, with a teenage girl who had worked for the author as a maid and occasional driver. The girl in no way reciprocated the author's feelings and eventually, despite the protestations of Kawabata and his wife, announced her decision to terminate her employment at the end of the month. According to Usui, the same day the girl made her announcement, 16 April 1972, the author walked away from his house, only to be discovered by the girl and another female employee several hours later in the apartment at Hayama, his body collapsed against the sink, his right hand clutching a blue rubber tube connected to a gas heater in the kitchen.

The young maid standing over the old man's body searching his expression for hints of his final thoughts presents an ironic reversal of "The House of the Sleeping Beauties." The girl describes an image of his peaceful and handsome face, flushed as though he were yet alive, as she tries in vain to nudge him from his slumber. As we join in the maiden's gaze, the author's story reminds us of the inevitable violence interpretation wreaks upon its object. Kawabata, like the fatally willful maid, refuses to yield to our demands. His remarkably eclectic literature continues to thwart the attempts of successive generations of critics to categorize it. Just when we think we have grasped the man, we suddenly discover upon arriving home that we hold nothing but a fragment, Kawabata's disembodied arm reminding us of our epistemological limits. In the end, the arm—our incomplete, disjointed understanding of Kawabata—reveals as much about us as about him.

Selected Bibliography

PRIMARY WORKS

COLLECTED WORKS

The House of the Sleeping Beauties and Other Stories. Trans. by Edward Seidensticker. Tokyo: Kodansha International, 1969.

The Izu Dancer and Other Stories. Trans. by Edward Seidensticker. Rutland, Vt.: Tuttle, 1974.

Kawabata yasunari zenshū. Tokyo: Shinchōsha, 1983. (The complete works of Kawabata Yasunari. Abbreviated as *KYZ* in citations.)

Miniature Masterpieces of Kawabata Yasunari. Trans. with notes by James Kirkup and Tsutomu Fukuda. Tokyo: Eichōsha-shinsha, 1983.

Palm-of-the-Hand Stories. Trans. by Lane Dunlop and J. Martin Holman. San Francisco: North Point Press, 1988.

The Dancing Girl of Izu and Other Stories. Trans by J. Martin Holman. Washington, D.C.: Counterpoint, 1998.

First Snow on Fuji. Trans. by Michael Emmerich. Washington, D.C.: Counterpoint, 1999.

INDIVIDUAL WORKS

"Jūrokusai no nikki." 1925. Trans. by J. Martin Holman as "Diary of My Sixteenth Year." In *The Dancing Girl of Izu and Other Stories.* Washington, D.C.: Counterpoint, 1998.

"Izu no odoriko." 1926. Trans. by J. Martin Holman as "The Dancing Girl of Izu." In *The Dancing Girl of Izu and Other Stories.* Washington, D.C.: Counterpoint, 1998.

"Kinjū." 1933. Trans. by Edward Seidensticker as "Of Birds and Beasts." In *The House of the Sleeping Beauties and Other Stories.* Tokyo: Kodansha International, 1969.

Mizuumi. 1936. Trans. by Reiko Tsukimura as *The Lake.* Tokyo: Kodansha International, 1974.

Yukiguni. 1937. Trans. by Edward Seidensticker as *Snow Country.* New York: Knopf, 1956.

"Shizen." 1952. Trans. by Michael Emmerich as "Nature." In *First Snow on Fuji.* Washington, D.C.: Counterpoint, 1999.

Meijin. 1952, 1954. Trans. by Edward Seidensticker as *The Master of Go.* New York: Knopf, 1972.

Yama no oto. 1954. Trans. by Edward Seidensticker as *The Sound of the Mountain.* New York: Perigee Books, 1981.

Utsukushisa to kanashimi to. 1961. Trans. by Howard Hibbett as *Beauty and Sadness.* New York: Knopf, 1975.

Nemureru bijo. 1961. Trans. by Edward Seidensticker as *The House of the Sleeping Beauties.* In *The House of the Sleeping Beauties and Other Stories.* Tokyo: Kodansha International, 1969.

Koto. 1962. Trans. by J. Martin Holman as *The Old Capital.* San Francisco: North Point Press, 1987.

"Kata ude." 1964. Trans. by Edward Seidensticker as "One Arm." In *The House of the Sleeping Beauties and Other Stories.* Tokyo: Kodansha International, 1969.

SECONDARY WORKS

CRITICAL AND BIOGRAPHICAL STUDIES

Bakke, E. Wight, and Mary S. Bakke. "Student Activism in Japan." In their *Campus Challenge: Student Activism in Perspective.* New York: Archon Books, 1971. Pp. 24–76.

Cabell, Charles. "Maiden Dreams: Kawabata Yasunari's Beautiful Japanese Empire, 1930–1945." Ph.D. diss., Harvard University, 1999.

Donahue, Neil. "Age, Beauty, and Apocalypse: Yasunari Kawabata's *The Sound of the Mountain* and Max Frisch's *Der Mensh ersheint im Holozan.*" *Arcadia: Zeitschrift fur Vergleichende Literaturwissenschaft* 28:291–306 (1993).

Dower, John. *War without Mercy: Race and Power in the Pacific War.* New York: Pantheon, 1986.

Fogel, Joshua. *The Literature of Travel in the Japanese Rediscovery of China 1862–1945.* Stanford, Calif.: Stanford University Press, 1996.

Gessel, Van C. *Three Modern Novelists: Sōseki, Tanizaki, Kawabata.* Tokyo: Kodansha International, 1993.

Isogai Hideo. "Yukiguni no shasei." In *Kawabata yasunari: gendai no biishiki.* Edited by Takeda Katsuhide and Takahashi Shintarō. Tokyo: Meiji Shoin, 1978.

Hall, Robert K., ed. *Kokutai no Hongi: Cardinal Principles of the National Entity of Japan.* Trans. by

John O. Gauntlett. Cambridge, Mass.: Harvard University Press, 1949.

Keene, Donald. *Dawn to the West: Japanese Literature in the Modern Era.* New York: Holt, 1984.

Lippit, Seiji. "Japanese Modernism and the Destruction of Literary Form: The Writings of Akutagawa, Yokomitsu, and Kawabata." Ph.D. diss., Columbia University, 1997.

Mishima Yukio. Introduction to *The House of the Sleeping Beauties.* Trans. by Edward Seidensticker. Tokyo: Kodansha International, 1969. Pp. 7–10.

Mitchell, Richard. *Censorship in Imperial Japan.* Princeton, N.J.: Princeton University Press, 1980.

Mizenko, Matthew. "The Modernist Project of Kawabata Yasunari." Ph.D. diss., Princeton University, 1993.

Najita, Tetsuo, and H. D. Harootunian. "Japanese Revolt against the West: Political and Cultural Criticism in the Twentieth Century." In vol. 6 of *The Cambridge History of Japan.* Edited by Peter Duus. Cambridge, Mass.: Cambridge University Press, 1988.

Österling, Anders. "Presentation Address." In *Nobel Prize Library: Yasunari Kawabata, Rudyard Kipling, Sinclair Lewis.* Edited by The Nobel Foundation. New York: Helvetica Press, 1971. Pp. 2–5.

Said, Edward. *Culture and Imperialism.* New York: Knopf, 1994.

Shindō Sumitaka. *Denki Kawabata Yasunari* (A biography of Kawabata Yasunari). Tokyo: Rokkō Shuppan, 1976.

Tajima Yōko. "Komako no shiten kara yomu *Yukiguni*" (*Snow country* from the perspective of Komako). In *Onna ga yomu Nihon kindai bungaku: feminizumu hihyō no kokoromi* (Women's readings of Japanese literature: An attempt at feminist criticism). Edited by Egusa Mitsuko. Tokyo: Shin'yōsha, 1993.

Torrance, Richard. "Popular Languages in *Yukiguni*." In *Studies in Popular Japanese Literature.* Edited by Dennis Washburn and Alan Tansman. Ann Arbor: University of Michigan, 1997. Pp. 247–260.

Usui Yoshimi. *Jiko no tenmatsu* (The entire story of the incident). Tokyo: Chikuma Shobō, 1977.

Vernon, Victoria. "Creating Koharu: The Image of Woman in the Works of Kawabata Yasunari and Tanizaki Jun'ichirō." In her *Daughters of the Moon: Wish, Will, and Social Constraint in Fiction by Modern Japanese Women.* Berkeley, Calif.: University of California Press, 1988. Pp. 171–204.

Washburn, Dennis. *The Dilemma of the Modern in Japanese Fiction.* New Haven, Conn.: Yale University Press, 1995.

Watson, S. Harrison. "Ideological Transformation by Translation: *Izu no Odoriko*." In *Comparative Literature Studies* 28, no. 3:310–321 (1991).

Kōno Taeko
1926–

DAVINDER L. BHOWMIK

AMONG THE MANY authors who emerged in the period of recovery following World War II, Kōno Taeko is surely one of the most sensational. Known primarily as a writer of erotic fiction, she has also gained a reputation as an essayist, playwright, and literary critic. Kōno established herself in Japan in the early 1960s with a series of short stories that depicted with startling frankness the sexual desires of her typically middle-aged, married, but childless heroines. Kōno usually writes about everyday events, focusing on the minutest details with obsessive intensity and incorporating glimpses of an extraordinary level of violence lying hidden beneath the quotidian surface. A Kōno narrative is immediately recognizable as uniquely her own. A major figure in the heyday of postwar "women's literature" *(joryū bungaku)*, she has by example helped to render the very notion of such a category obsolete. Indeed, she is one of the truly original voices of the twentieth century, beyond questions of gender or even nationality.

Kōno's reputation for bluntness is evident in her critical writing as well. In an essay called "Jikai" (1974; Self-discipline) Kōno writes of Japan's utter submission to the United States after World War II in these terms: "The victors might just as well have raped every woman in Japan" (pp. 11–12). Having lost several years of her youth to the war effort, Kōno knows whereof she speaks. Her critics have pointed out that, more than anything else, Kōno's war experience, in which she endured constant deprivations of food and shelter, as well as regular interruptions in her studies, ingrained in her the notions of dominance and submission that pervade her works. The fact that a disproportionate number of sadomasochistic narratives characterize her literary output lends credence to the idea that the war played a critical role in shaping Kōno's mind.

In her literary debut, "Yōjigari" (1961; "Toddler-Hunting," 1996), Kōno graphically depicts a heroine who abhors girls, fetishizes boys, and delights in a sexually brutal relationship with her lover. Kōno thus burst onto the literary scene in the early 1960s, shocking readers unaccustomed to tales of sadomasochism, pedophilia, and spouse-swapping—at least ones told from a female point of view. Since the 1960s, Kōno has written scores of works in which her often sterile protagonists engage in sexually deviant behavior. While the shock value of Kōno's works has naturally abated with time, and certainly, with the proliferation of younger writers who have followed Kōno's lead in writing about sexual freedom, the sexually liberated, childless females who people her stories continue to intrigue readers in a country where females are still expected to devote their lives to child-rearing and homemaking.

Despite having won Japan's top literary prizes for decades, surprisingly, Kōno has taken a battering from the critical community. While impressed with her writing, many critics fail to comprehend Kōno's trademark masochistic trope, calling it "incomprehensible" *(nankai)* and "abstract" *(kannenteki)*. Even feminist critics, whom one would expect to endorse Kōno's many determinedly independent heroines, fault her for the extremely negative portrayals of young girls she repeatedly includes in her works. Some of the most sophisticated criticism of Kōno comes from feminist critics, such as Yonaha Keiko and Hotta Kazuko in Japan and Gretchen Jones and Chizuko Uema in the United States, each of whom has grappled intelligently with Kōno's use of masochism.

Even perennially dismissive senior writers and critics cannot fail to acknowledge Kōno's leading presence in Japan's literary establishment. Ōe Kenzaburō, Japan's Nobel laureate, called her the most "lucidly intelligent" female writer in Japan; Masao Miyoshi found her to be among the most "critically alert and historically intelligent." In recent years, several of her most important works have been translated into English, German, and Italian, attesting to the interest in her work outside Japan. Many of her pieces have found a home in anthologies of Japanese women writers, as well as in collections of international feminist writing.

In addition to her impressive number of fictional works, Kōno has written critical studies on topics ranging from the Brontë sisters to her own countryman and literary idol, Tanizaki Jun'ichirō. Astounding, too, is Kōno's political clout in the literary establishment. Having served on the committee for the coveted Akutagawa Prize and for smaller yet prestigious awards such as those given at the Kyūshū Arts Festival, Kōno is a pioneer among women writers, who are usually left out of the big business of determining who gets what literary prize in Japan. There is no question she occupies a dominant place in the literary establishment today.

More than her steady stream of writing or even her prominence in the literary establishment, what finally sets Kōno apart from many of her contemporaries is the imaginative quality of her work. While there are certain similarities between the author and her protagonists, namely, the fact that her protagonists are generally married and without children, as Kōno is, these resemblances are slight when one considers her fiction in its entirety. Kōno's trademark surrealism, her penchant for sado-masochistic themes, and her remarkable eye for detail make her works truly crafted and not merely vehicles for plotting the events of her own life, interesting though it may be.

Kōno's Early Years

The year 1926 was the founding year of the lengthy and tumultuous Shōwa era (1926–1989). Shōwa, which means "bright-peace," was the reign name adopted when Emperor Hirohito succeeded to the throne. Kōno was born that year into a merchant family in Osaka, the third largest city in Japan following Tokyo and Yokohama, and the business center for western Japan. Known primarily for its textiles, chemicals, steels, machinery, and metal, Osaka is also where *bunraku*, Japan's professional puppet theater, originated in the early seventeenth century and still enjoys a following today.

Kōno was the fourth child of five, and the second daughter in her family. Her father, Tameji, operated a wholesale business selling a variety of mountain produce such as shiitake mushrooms. Her mother, Yone, the daughter of a local druggist, assisted Kōno's father in this venture. Prone to sickness, Kōno repeatedly suffered from autointoxication, which, in turn, led to difficulties adjusting to school. Having to move repeatedly from school to school, Kōno found pleasure in reading, particularly in high school, when she devoured the works of Tanizaki Jun'ichirō and Izumi Kyōka, both giants of modern prose far removed from the autobiographical mainstream. Judging from Kōno's literary output, it was Tanizaki's imaginative skill and his interest in sadomasochism, clearly evident from his debut piece "Shisei" (1910; "The Tattooer," 1963), that drew her to him, while Kyōka's intensely gothic style appealed to her literary sensibility and served as a model for her more mature works.

The War Years

In 1941, at the age of fifteen, Kōno's favorite subject in school was world history, a topic of grave import in this year that marked the outbreak of the Pacific War. Air raids, relief drills, forced marches, and farm work further disturbed her education, already impeded by bouts of illness. As the war escalated, Kōno performed stints of patriotic duty sewing military fatigues and serving as a student worker in a munitions factory. When she was eighteen and bone-tired of wartime drudgery, Kōno aspired to enter the Japanese language department at a professional school for women in Osaka (later Osaka Women's University), but failed the entrance exam. She then joined the English department where she became absorbed in the Brontë sisters until nationalistic policies forced her to abandon her newfound interest in English literature. Undaunted, she settled on economics, the study of which has led some critics to identify Marxist elements in her works, namely, the fusion of extremely concrete details (production) with a highly abstract style (capital). Her fascination with master/slave relations, too, they argue, is related to the economic principles with which she was no doubt familiar.

Kōno's scholarly desire was so fierce, she claimed in an essay called "Toki kitaru" (1977; The time has come), that she wished to go to university even if she might be bombed during the entrance ceremony. Once admitted to the university, however, Kōno spent most of her time performing compulsory work until the war ended the following year, when she turned nineteen. In Kōno's first essay collection, *Bungaku no kiseki* (1974; The miracle of literature), she relates the extent to which her ambitions were constrained by the war and just how

free and hopeful she became when the war finally ended.

Not surprisingly, Kōno's wartime experience during the five precious years from age fifteen to nineteen informs her early fiction. In her best-known war pieces, "Michishio" (1964; "High Tide," 1996), "Hei no naka" (1962; Inside the fence), and "Tōi natsu" (1963; A far-off summer), her female protagonists endure the daily deprivations wartime austerity brought to Japan's civilians. Physical hardships that resulted from dwindling food sources were accepted as a matter of course; more difficult to bear, however, was the lack of material goods used for personal ornamentation. The absence of items as trivial as hair ties, deemed by authorities to be extravagant "luxuries," was intolerable for teenage girls struggling with self-image. Kōno's wartime stories detail the increasingly psychic toll military conflict took on the lives of adolescents robbed of their youth. It was not until she wrote "Tōi natsu" in 1963, eighteen years after the war ended, that the frustration Kōno felt at being stifled by the war at last dissipated. The story's cathartic concluding lines succinctly describe the life of her heroine Keiko in the postwar years: "It was a dark, cold road . . . completely different from the road on which she was returning home that bright summer day after being released from within the factory fence" (*Kōno Taeko zenshū [KTZ]*, vol. 1, p. 294).

In March 1945, during the height of the war, Kōno became one of the many casualties of the air raids that besieged most of Japan's major cities at the time. She moved in June of that year to bombed-out ruins in southern Osaka where she resided temporarily. From 15 August 1945, the day of Japan's surrender, to 15 September 1945, Kōno spent a particularly unforgettable summer holiday observing those around her grappling with Japan's defeat. In a 1992 reflection of these critical wartime years, Kōno wrote that amid the chaos she concentrated on her deepest passion—music. Naturally, American tunes were banned due to the outbreak of hostilities between Japan and the United States, but to Kōno's delight, a steady stream of Italian and German classics accompanied the daily air-raid news report. Kindled during military conflict, Kōno's love of music, especially opera (Giacomo Puccini's *Madame Butterfly* and Giuseppe Verdi's *Rigoletto* are but two operas featured in her writing), remains strong.

Postwar Hopes

As Kōno recounts in her first essay collection *Bungaku no kiseki,* she only began to enjoy life at the age of nineteen. It is not coincidental that her outlook on life changed with the war's end. Millions of Japanese besides Kōno harbored desires for productive and prosperous lives following the shambles of the war. Kōno's own postwar dream was to become a novelist, much to her parents' dismay. When, at the age of twenty-one, she informed her parents of her writerly desires, they objected on the grounds that she was supposed to marry after graduating from university. Her parents' reaction is far from startling given prevailing cultural norms that dictated that a woman should marry when she reached age twenty, the year that marks an individual's passage to adulthood in Japan. Kōno, however, in a rare act of rebellion, disobeyed her family and stuck to her decision.

In order to save money for a move to Tokyo, the center of literary activity, Kōno worked full-time and wrote during whatever free time she had available. Most nights she slept for scarcely three hours. Overwork cost her dearly; after two years she contracted tuberculosis, which robbed her of another two years of her youth. While still recovering from her illness, she participated in a coterie organized by Niwa Fumio, an important male *shishōsetsu* ("personal fiction") writer and critic of the time. Her first story, "Yojin" (1951; Embers), was published in *Bungakusha,* the literary magazine created by the group. Encouraged by the publication of her work and by discussions with other members of the coterie, Kōno resolved to go to Tokyo. In 1952, the very next year, she moved there.

Despite being in Tokyo, a city full of literary activities and literary personae, Kōno endured several more unproductive years, encountering a particularly severe setback in 1957 when at the age of thirty-one she again contracted tuberculosis. After struggling for several years to recover from the illness, Kōno began to publish a stream of short fiction beginning in the early 1960s. These stories differ from the experimental pieces she wrote as a member of *Bungakusha* in that they deal with female protagonists who indulge in masochism and are obsessed with small boys. Japanese critics have speculated, as they often do, that the author's literary predilections might be tied to her own physical state. Though tuberculosis primarily affects the lungs, other organs of Kōno's body were no doubt also affected. In later stories, many of Kōno's protagonists are sterile owing to tuberculosis; thus, perhaps her adherence to sadomasochistic narratives is a manifestation of her own questions about what life as a physically unproductive woman might hold in store. By focusing on masochistic relationships, which tend not to yield children, Kōno offers her readers, many of whom are Japanese mothers, a vision of another life as well as some reflection of her own.

Kōno's Literary Debut

After years of encountering obstacles ranging from deadly air raids, to grave illness, to meager finances, Kōno's ambitions were realized at long last in 1961 with the publication of "Toddler-Hunting." Spurred on by a recommendation from her coterie, Kōno wrote a submission for consideration at *Shinchō,* a major literary magazine. As fate would have it, her literary success in 1961 coincided with a personal loss, the death of her father that same year. *Shinchō* began serializing her stories, and in 1962 she was awarded its Dōjin Zasshi ("coterie magazine") Award for "Toddler-Hunting," the work with which most critics begin their discussions of Kōno.

"Toddler-Hunting," Kōno's first prize-winning story, centers on the life of a single woman, Hayashi Akiko. Trained as a musician, Akiko belonged to a chorus until she contracted tuberculosis, a disease that deprived her of the strength to sing, as well as the ability to conceive a child. Subsequent to her illness she leads a seemingly independent life translating Italian and cohabitating with her lover, Sasaki.

The story begins with a very brash opening statement: "Hayashi Akiko couldn't abide little girls between three and ten years old—she detested them more than any other kind of human being" (*KTZ*, vol. 1, p. 7; tr. *Toddler-Hunting and Other Stories*, 1996, p. 45). What follows is a detailed analysis of Akiko's abhorrence of girls fused together with a parade of concrete images of belittled and idolized children. Akiko's specific dislike of girls is a phobia that produces in her a physical revulsion akin to the discomfort she experienced as a child observing a dark, squirming pupa in science class. The source for her aversion is not made explicit, yet Akiko senses it has something to do with her own femininity. Beneath Akiko's superficially pleasant childhood, Kōno reveals a disturbing element of suffocation: "in the pit of her stomach, she'd been conscious of an inexplicable constriction. Something loathsome and repellent oppressed all her senses—it was as if she were trapped in a long, narrow tunnel; as if a sticky liquid seeped unseen out of her every pore—as if she were under a curse" (*KTZ*, vol. 1, p. 7; tr. p. 46). Akiko's feelings of repulsion for the female sex seem to originate from subconscious memories of this feeling of entrapment.

Small boys are the antithesis of Akiko's phobia. In them she sees the essence of a "wholesome world," one that cleanses and sustains her. The fact that Akiko would tolerate a foreign female child or a female child of mixed heritage indicates the degree to which she is revolted by young girls of her own race, and is certainly connected to her own self-loathing. As an adult Akiko fears she might spawn a female child, whom, if born, she would cruelly punish. Her self-loathing, then, projects itself onto an imagined daughter whose femaleness

arouses in her the desire to harm. Unborn daughters are not the sole objects of Akiko's rage. What offends her senses most is her own body, which she has Sasaki ruthlessly torture with a clothesline rope to the point that neighbors come inquiring after her health. Inured as they are to the brutal relationship she enjoys with Sasaki, they fear Akiko may die in the course of her thrill-seeking.

The only respite from the discomfort Akiko feels most days is the thought of, or—better yet—the sight of, a young boy. The story's title refers to Akiko's quest for these male children. Dissatisfied with the pleasure that comes from merely observing in-store displays of young boys' apparel, Akiko madly purchases unnecessary items that she later bestows on the children of friends surprised by the abruptness of Akiko's gesture. One of the most vivid descriptions, among many, in "Toddler Hunting" is Akiko's state of arousal brought on by a fantasy in which she imagines giving such a gift:

Akiko stroked the garment tenderly—she could just see a little boy, about four years old, pulling on this cozy, lightweight shirt, his sunburned head popping up through the neck. When the time came he would definitely want to take it off himself. Crossing his chubby arms over his chest, concentrating with all his might, he would just manage to grasp the shirttails. But how difficult to pull it up and extricate himself. Screwing up his face, twisting around and wiggling his little bottom, he would try his hardest. Akiko would glimpse his tight little belly, full to bursting with all the food he stuffed in at every meal. The shirt, though, was not going to come off, however hard he tried.

(*KTZ*, vol. 1, p. 9; tr. p. 48)

While many critics note that Kōno's fascination with boys is intimately related to her aversion toward girls and her own self-loathing, in an interview, Kōno remarked that the reason she likes boys is that they encapsulate all that is good in life. When they are angry they show it; when they are happy it is plain to

173

see, she explained. Their utter transparency charms Kōno and accounts for why her fiction is strangely positive, despite being chock-full of dark secrets hidden in the lives of seemingly ordinary people.

Given Kōno's statements about her fondness for boys it is difficult to fathom why in a later episode of "Toddler-Hunting" her lover abuses a young boy, presumably their son. The scene progresses from the boy being gently scolded to being severely beaten while at the same time a woman's voice is heard. In a twist of logic the object of scorn is now a boy and not a girl. Critics have pointed out that if one imagines that Akiko, in the height of her passion, is transformed into the beaten boy *and* is present as the child's mother, then the logic of the story, based on the sadomasochistic principle of desiring to inflict or receive pain for erotic pleasure, is again in operation.

The story ends as Akiko searches once more for a young boy who will revive her body, weary from the sexual torture she endured the previous night. As luck would have it, she chances upon a perfect specimen—a three-year-old boy engrossed in eating a slice of watermelon. Rich in detail, the final scenes describe the boy poking out seeds and chomping on the melon before relinquishing the fruit to Akiko, who likens the warm pulpy fruit to live flesh. As she swallows the melon she relishes the taste of the child's sweat, grime, and saliva. The boy, not wanting to take back the slice of melon that Akiko has eaten from, runs off, leaving her rooted to the spot. Thus, Kōno's debut ends.

At the time of the publication of "Toddler-Hunting" in 1961, critics and readers were shocked by the subject matter. That Kōno wrote about the pursuit of sexual desire from the point of view of an unmarried female engaged in a sadomasochistic relationship was utterly new and had not been seen previously in serious women's writing. Moreover, the coupling of Kōno's heroine's far-out fantasy world with detailed descriptions of completely familiar concrete objects such as watermelon, children's garments, and clothesline rope,

made for fresh writing. The story is all the more impressive since it came a full decade after Kōno's "maiden" work, "Embers," was published in the coterie magazine *Bungakusha*. During the intervening ten years, Kōno suffered a slump in her creative energies, brought on by massive strain from overwork, a recurrence of tuberculosis, and failed love affairs, all of which occurred after her move to Tokyo. When she first saw her "Toddler-Hunting" in as important a literary journal as *Shinchō*, Kōno could scarcely contain her joy: "It's in! It's in!" she reportedly cried. The dark, cold road of which she wrote in "A Far-off Summer" had at last come to an end.

In an attempt to reconstruct how Kōno arrived at the novel masochistic theme of "Toddler-Hunting," critics have traced elements of masochism in her early experimental fiction. For instance, they argue that in stories that touch on the war, Kōno depicts her protagonists' sense of victimhood as would-be students ordered to live in residential dormitories and work in munitions factories. These early hints of victimization are magnified in "Toddler-Hunting," a work in which she ironically affirms the pleasure Akiko receives at the hands (literally) of her sadistic lover Sasaki. Save for a few minor comments, such as one made by a senior critic who lamented that, had Kōno told the story from Sasaki's point of view, it would have been more like fiction (and presumably less autobiographical), praise for "Toddler-Hunting" was overwhelmingly positive. With so few detractors, Kōno swiftly regained the courage she had lost during her slump, and she went on to write a steady stream of critically praised fiction.

Masochistic Heroines

In the months that followed Kōno's publication of "Toddler-Hunting," several more stories appeared in succession. Among the most notable was "Yuki," (1962; "Snow," 1996), a piece that was nominated for the prestigious Akutagawa Prize. A beautifully told story, "Snow" centers on a woman named Hayako who has feared snow since she was a small child. As she matures, her fears become so excessive that she experiences migraines whenever the weather turns snowy. During childhood, Hayako once innocently remarked on the beauty of a sudden snow shower only to be cruelly thrust out into the deep snow and stranded by her mother. Uncomprehending, Hayako does not learn the reasons behind her mother's abrupt and irrational behavior until some years later.

After one of her parents' frequent quarrels, she is told that she is actually the child of her father's mistress and that her name and birth date are incorrect. Her mother had had another small child whom she buried in the snow in a fit of madness brought on by the child's incessant crying. Not wishing to arouse suspicions, her parents secretly entered Hayako into their family register, giving her the name and birthdate of her dead half-sister. This revelation shocks Hayako, but she begins to understand why the topic of snow is forbidden in their household. The brutality that Hayako's mother inflicted on the children in her life is reminiscent of the cruelty shown to children in "Toddler-Hunting," and is a theme that recurs in Kōno's subsequent writing.

As an adult Hayako is courted by a man named Kisaki whom she likes for his "boyishness" but puts off because she is "terribly uncomfortable" at the thought of marriage. Ironically, the strongest bond she has is with her mother, who, like Hayako, suffers from headaches whenever it snows. Again, like Akiko in "Toddler-Hunting," Hayako feels especially alive when she is cruelly treated, an essential paradox of masochism. Kōno writes, "Hayako felt that her mother was the mainstay of her tenuous existence. Her father had been the one to rescue her from the garden that snowy day, but her impulsive violent mother occupied a special place in her heart" (*KTZ*, vol. 1, p. 106; tr. p. 93). The hold Hayako's mother has on her is underscored when Hayako has a dream reminiscent of a Heian period (late eighth–late twelfth century) story of spirit possession. In it, her dying mother's

spirit attacks her for failing to be a filial daughter. The cruelty continues at a funeral home where Hayako is blasted by a stream of blood that spurts out of her dead mother's nose, a phenomenon she is told is caused by her mother's fervent wish to see Hayako.

In a scene that foretells the story's ending, Hayako defiantly trudges through bone-chilling conditions in snowbound Hakone. Kōno describes the transformation that occurs in her heroine as the snow penetrates her body:

> At such times Hayako would feel that the person whom her mother had murdered that night in the snow had been none other than her own self. The self who had survived was only the ghost of the self who'd died. Like a ghost, she was destined to pass through the world, never knowing her own age or birthday. Even when she died, her funeral would be held in somebody else's name.

> (*KTZ*, vol. 1, p. 104; tr. p. 90)

This chilling story concludes as Hayako spies a hollow in the snow where she crouches in hiding. Distraught by thoughts of her own lack of identity, she begs Kisaki to bury her alive, stating in no uncertain terms, "I want to die just this once" (*KTZ*, vol. 1, p. 112; tr. p. 100).

Though less explicit and graphic than "Toddler-Hunting," Kōno's hallmark sadomasochistic narrative is nevertheless discernable in the portrayal of a cruel mother whose daughter is aroused only when she is punished. Reaching beyond death, the mother's powerful hold over Hayako forces her to obliterate herself in the snow, since embracing pain—even pain that leads to death—is, in all its irony, a life-affirming act. Many critics praised "Snow," and it was nominated for an Akutagawa Prize. In particular, the beautiful prose and haunting story caught their attention. Some felt, however, that the work was too obvious a display of technical virtuosity, and that Kōno's day was yet to come, as indeed it was.

Virtually assuring her a successful future, the literary establishment gave Kōno its seal of approval, the Akutagawa Prize, in 1963 for the publication of "Kani" (1963; "Crabs," 1996). In this work, Kōno fully explores the revitalizing effect small boys have on her heroines. This theme, traces of which appear in "Toddler-Hunting," is what makes a simple story of a woman looking for crabs to delight a child left in her care become a complex portrait of the inner workings of a woman who has been stricken by disease.

In "Crabs," Yūko is in frail health owing to a serious case of tuberculosis. Like most of Kōno's protagonists, Yūko is in her thirties. Unlike the protagonists of "Toddler Hunting" and "Snow," Yūko is married, though unhappily so. In keeping with the sexual preferences of Kōno's earlier heroines, Yūko enjoys it when her husband treats her cruelly during sex. Despite the pleasure she receives in this sphere of her life, she is discontent with her choice of a partner. For one thing, her husband, Kajii, does not understand Yūko's wish to go to a coastal town for recuperation. Showing the same sort of defiance Hayako displays in "Snow," Yūko ignores his arguments and proceeds to embark on a "rest cure." Just as Hayako's defiance leads to probable death, Yūko's rebellious act endangers her well-being.

Once at the coast, Yūko feels immeasurably better. When Kajii's younger brother comes for a visit with his seven-year-old son, Takeshi, Yūko is all the more invigorated. In Takeshi, Yūko discovers a sense of completeness that she herself lacks: "[His outfit] was adorable. The hooks under his little chin; the white collar of his shirt, just visible within his jacket's black collar; the two neat rows of gold buttons on his chest; the square cuffs, with a line of three small buttons accentuating the manliness of his chubby little wrists. Everything was there, in miniature" (*KTZ*, vol. 1, p. 178; tr. p. 145). The energy she witnesses in Takeshi during his visit leads her to persuade his parents to allow him to stay on with her. So desperate is Yūko for Takeshi not to go that she promises to find bright red crabs with pincers for him. It is of little consequence to her that a reckless pursuit of crabs is sure to endanger her already precarious health.

Kōno might well have named the work "Crab Hunting" rather than "Crabs" to reiterate the quest theme of her debut "Toddler-Hunting." In an effort to please Takeshi, Yūko goes to great lengths to secure a crab. For his part, Takeshi is undeterred by her lack of success. His unflagging optimism further drives Yūko. Still, her efforts are unrewarded. Eventually, Takeshi senses that Yūko will not deliver the promised goods and tells her that Kajii might be able to catch a crab for him. This betrayal unhinges Yūko, releasing in her the pent-up anger and frustration she feels at her own incompleteness and her dissatisfaction with Kajii. The story concludes with a mortified Yūko begging Takeshi not to displace her by asking Kajii to hunt for crabs.

Drawing an analogy between the shape of a crab and that of a womb, symbolic of life, some critics have conjectured that the obsessive crab hunt that Yūko is engaged in is, in fact, a search for the motherhood that her illness has deprived her of. No matter how much she toils, Yūko cannot unearth a crab. Similarly, as hard as she may try, she will never bear a child. Yūko, another of Kōno's literally dysfunctional heroines, makes obvious the possibilities that are closed to females not equipped with effective reproductive organs. At the same time, she, like the other sterile heroines, is freed from traditionally assigned sex-roles for women.

The early 1960s were especially good years for Kōno. After Kōno had tried various means to come out of the slump she was experiencing during the late 1950s, her desperation knew no bounds, and she reportedly consulted a fortune-teller for the first time in 1960. The fortune-teller chose an auspicious section of the city for her to reside in, and she moved there straightaway. This move, one among several she made in her efforts to survive as a writer in Tokyo, apparently was effective. Within months, Kōno's "Toddler-Hunting" appeared, followed by scores of other short stories that, taken together, made her a leading new writer of the 1960s. Of these successful years, 1963 was doubly rich for Kōno. Not only did she capture the Akutagawa Prize at the relatively late age of thirty-seven, she also married the western-style artist Ichikawa Yasushi, her partner for decades to come.

A year later, Kōno published "Ari Takaru" (1964; "Ants Swarm," 1996), which deals explicitly with maternity. Kōno's protagonist Fumiko has been married for six years to a man named Matsuda, with whom she has decided not to have children. Matsuda is willing to accept this condition of their marriage, but, when Fumiko fears she may have accidentally become pregnant after an act of impromptu sex minus the usual precautions, she is astounded to learn Matsuda is not unhappy about the news. While Fumiko had never wanted to have children because the "very thought of giving birth and having to raise a baby repelled her" (*KTZ*, vol. 2, p. 41; tr. p. 171), Matsuda cannot help but exude masculine pride at the idea of fathering a child, despite their strict agreement.

The story details the changes in Fumiko's thoughts concerning her possible pregnancy. Initially, she thinks only of how to terminate it. Matsuda's surprising reaction leads her to feign interest in the child and eventually, Fumiko, who herself is a willing victim of Matsuda's violent lovemaking, enjoys fantasies in which she severely punishes their expected baby. She especially relishes the idea of being a cruel mother to a daughter whom she would instruct to serve others and not voice opinions. After marrying her off as soon as possible, she plans to encourage her daughter's husband to be abusive as well. If the girl complained, she would show her no sympathy and tell her to endure the tyranny of her husband just as she has suffered at the hands of her spouse. " 'Look!' I'll tell her: 'Look at what your father does to me. I can bear it, and so should you!' " (*KTZ*, vol. 2, p. 46; tr. p. 178). As the violent fantasy continues, Fumiko punishes the daughter by shouting, pinching, jabbing, and even scalding her with butter. Just as in "Toddler-Hunting," the small child who is tortured in the protagonist's fantasy is none other than the protagonist herself. It is she who is punished for neglecting to buy butter for Matsuda's breakfast. More importantly,

critics write, she is punished for speaking her mind and not capitulating to the demands placed on females in her society.

In Kōno's literary world, the choice not to bear children comes with brutal consequences; the unproductive, unyielding body must be repeatedly punished. This logic explains why Fumiko endures Matsuda's sadism. She begs him to torture her as a means of punishing herself for not assuming motherhood, the expected role for a woman. The ants of the story's title appear in the final scene swarming over a slab of meat. Fumiko recalls that she has never seen ants in their home because she and Matsuda do not use sugar, an item she links to domesticity. Musing upon her lack of domestic experience, Fumiko hits upon the idea that the ants "must have forgotten the taste of sugar—or else never sampled it," just as she has never known motherhood (*KTZ*, vol. 2, p. 50; tr. p. 183).

"Toddler-Hunting," "Snow," "Crabs," and "Ants Swarm" are typical examples of the stories upon which Kōno's reputation as a writer of serious fiction rests. The heroines of these early stories, whether single or married, pursue a life that does not revolve around children and home life. However, despite making an active choice in this regard, each is a passive sexual partner. Their deviation from cultural norms leads to self-destruction, usually in the form of a sadomasochistic relationship. Dissatisfied with themselves for their lack of completeness and their failure to maintain a meaningful relationship, Kōno's heroines remain only outwardly free. At this stage in her career, self-annihilation is the only means by which her protagonists can ease their suffering.

A Sadistic Turn

As if Kōno's writing had not been daring enough, in the late 1960s her work took a different, bolder turn. *Fui no koe* (1969; A sudden voice) differs from earlier works both in its form and its content. Unlike the short pieces Kōno customarily writes, this work is a full-length novel. It tells the story of a woman, Ukiko, who sadistically kills three people: her mother, the son of her former lover, and a man she knows only casually. That a typically passive Kōno heroine would commit cold-blooded murder is striking in itself; more bizarre is the fact that among the murder victims is a young boy. The wholesome boy, a figure much adored by Kōno's earlier heroines, is in this instance strangled to death. Moreover, where Kōno's previous stories often alternate between reality and fantasy, *Fui no koe* goes a step further by juxtaposing events from the everyday world Ukiko inhabits with those of the supernatural world. Several appearances by the ghost of Ukiko's father, long since deceased, show Kōno's interest broadening to encompass the spiritual world.

In the novel, Ukiko is unhappily married to a man named Kiichi, who regularly abuses both alcohol and his wife, in that order. Wishing to escape her marriage, Ukiko's dependence on Kiichi prevents her from doing so. After one of their intense quarrels, Kiichi orders Ukiko out of the house. Unlike previous occasions, this time Kiichi means business; he leaves Ukiko with little money and no key to return home. Just before she is forced to leave the house, the ghost of her father—who appears in moments of Ukiko's distress—intimates to Ukiko that she should "Do it!" (*KTZ*, vol. 5, p. 150). Ukiko is not sure what her father means by this, but from what follows, it is clear that whatever "it" is, she can do it to as many as three people.

Since Kiichi is her second lover, she initially construes her father's commandment to mean that she should abandon her present relationship for a third one. When she inquires whether she should then divorce Kiichi, Kōno writes: "Her dead father's intense gaze pierced through her soul, and the meaning of his revelation flashed through her mind. She heard her father's sudden voice. . . . It's all right. Just do it!" (*KTZ*, vol. 5, p. 150) In her distraught state, Ukiko reasons that since her father has never encouraged her to stay with Kiichi, he must be urging her to kill him. Ukiko's transformation from a passive housewife to an aggressor is triggered by her father's words, which produce in her "a force that seemed to inspire her. She

knew this was not the first time she had felt this power. This was, however, the first time she was conscious of it, and it was also the first time the power seemed to be coursing through her" (*KTZ*, vol. 5, p. 151). The energy Kōno writes of here emboldens her heroine, allowing her to strike back.

Critics have puzzled over Ukiko's choice of victims. Why does she kill her mother, with whom she had enjoyed a healthy relationship? And, why does she kill a young boy, an object of fetishism in prior works? Finally, why does she kill a casual acquaintance? The reasons behind the odd selection lie in Ukiko's mental state: ever the filial daughter, she has no choice but to obey her father's bidding. Strange as it may seem, in keeping with this logic, she must first kill her mother to spare her from the suffering that the mother would naturally experience when Ukiko committed the two other murders.

Upon returning to Tokyo from Osaka where she has suffocated her mother in her family home, Ukiko visits a friend who teaches at a nursery school. She observes there her ex-lover's son. A disturbing and lengthy passage describing the child innocently playing music with his classmates follows. In the scene, Ukiko's thoughts turn from noting that the boy is plainly the happiest and most childlike child present, to the notion that her abusive husband Kiichi was once such a child, and finally to the idea that the child could very easily have been her own son. These musings lead her to murder a second time. She lures the boy to a side street and strangles him.

Ukiko's brutal stabbing of a man she barely knows is related in a surreal flashback toward the end of the novel. Since she believes "men are all the same" (*KTZ*, vol. 5, p. 192), her seemingly random act makes an odd kind of sense, for it no longer matters that Ukiko is not killing Kiichi, the real target of her rage. The poignancy of this novel arises from the irony of Ukiko's situation. Bound to kill out of a strong sense of filial duty, her murders represent the destruction of an entire family unit: man, woman, and child.

Critics have pointed out that while the graphic details of the murders are crystal clear in *Fui no koe*, the surreal quality of Kōno's writing prevents one from ever knowing whether the violence ascribed to Ukiko is real or imagined. Given Kōno's predilection for interweaving reality and fantasy, the critics' suspicions are warranted. Certain refrains in the novel, such as Ukiko's pattern of returning after each murder scene to the house where she lived with Kiichi, do point to the likelihood that Ukiko's brutal acts take place in her fantasies. Still, the caliber of the violence perpetrated by Kōno's heroine in this novel marks a shift in the mentality of her protagonist. In a bizarre way, the fact that Ukiko suffocates and stabs her victims to death, rather than merely jabbing and pinching them as Kōno's earlier heroines had done, indicates a certain maturation in the development of her protagonists. No longer content with her submissive, masochistic nature, Ukiko assumes (or longs to assume) a sadistic role.

Without a doubt, the transformation of Kōno's heroines struck a chord with her readers. *Fui no koe* won the Yomiuri Prize for Kōno in 1969. This success, as well as that of a thematically similar short piece she wrote the next year, "Hone no niku" (1969; "Bone Meat," first translation 1977, second translation 1989), attests to her growing popularity. "Bone Meat," which portrays a nameless, deserted heroine who apparently succumbs to a long cherished desire to set her home on fire, triggered a storm of critical debate. Some state the protagonist is another of Kōno's masochistic heroines, only engaged in fantasy; others argue the woman is not merely a victim of her husband's neglect—rather, *she* is the aggressor who has killed him in a conflagration so intense it leaves only his bones, which she delights in eating. This debate notwithstanding, the fact that the protagonist is unnamed and referred to as "the woman," allows the story to be easily read as an allegory of woman consuming man. The powerful simplicity of its message, and its easily digestible length (approximately a dozen pages) has made "Bone Meat" Kōno's most-often translated work. There have been at least six translations: one each in English, French, and Czechoslovakian, and three in German.

Kōno's Critical Activities

While continuing to write critically acclaimed fiction, Kōno began to publish in other genres as well, beginning in the 1970s. She wrote a screenplay for Emily Brontë's *Wuthering Heights*, and this successful adaptation was used in several theater productions. Still more Japanese came to know Kōno when she wrote a radio script called "Fushigi na nichiyōbi" (1973; A bizarre Sunday) for NHK, Japan's quasi-official broadcasting network. This project virtually assured her a huge listening audience. An interest in the fiction and drama of the Edo period (1600–1868), which critics note as another influence on Kōno's fiction, led her to do a translation into modern Japanese of *Tōkaidō yotsuya kaidan* (1825; Ghost tales of Yotsuya), a major work by the playwright Tsuruya Nanboku. Kōno's widespread presence accounts for the fact that she was elected to the boards of several prestigious artistic organizations and was asked to judge among selections for new writers' prizes given by a number of literary journals from this point onward.

By far, the most noteworthy work Kōno undertook in the 1970s was *Tanizaki bungaku to kōtei no yokubō* (1976; The literature of Tanizaki and the desire to affirm), a critical study of Tanizaki Jun'ichirō, her long-time idol. In this work, Kōno offers a penetrating analysis of Tanizaki's life and works, focusing on his use of masochism. She concludes her sophisticated analysis with the claim that Tanizaki's desire to write was driven solely by a desire for spiritual affirmation. Etō Jun, a leading critic, considered the book "essential reading for studies of Tanizaki" (*KTZ*, vol. 9, p. 347). His high praise no doubt inspired Kōno to continue in her critical pursuits, which range from topics as diverse as Kabuki drama to the prose of Okamoto Kanoko, a writer of the Taishō period (1912–1926).

Between Two Worlds: The 1980s and Beyond

In the 1980s and 1990s, Kōno's style of publishing changed radically. Rather than writing regularly for monthly magazines, the means of making a living secured by most writers, Kōno was commissioned to do special book projects that, owing to their length, naturally cut down on the frequency of her publications. *Ichinen no bokka* (1980; A year-long pastoral), the first work of fiction Kōno published in the 1980s, is one such book. This novel centers on the life of a single woman ordered by her doctor not to engage in sex for a period of one year. This unusual restriction in her protagonist's sexual activities allows Kōno to explore issues dealing with sexuality in a new way. For this critically acclaimed novel, Kōno received the Tanizaki Jun'ichirō Prize, an award given to exceptionally imaginative works.

In the remaining years of the decade, Kōno's literary output was relatively small since she was working on a much longer novel that was not published until 1990. Kōno was by no means idle, content with her many honors. Aside from her writing, much of her time was devoted to serving on one literary committee after another, the most important being the Akutagawa Prize committee of which she became a member of in 1987.

Perhaps it was to escape onerous committee work that Kōno began to travel abroad extensively in the 1980s. Her international travels began in 1985, when she and several other Japanese writers were invited to the West Berlin Arts Festival. Accompanied by the writer Tomioka Taeko, a fellow Osakan, Kōno went from Germany to England, where she toured for three weeks to gather material for a travelogue that she intended to write with Tomioka. After this trip, Kōno frequently traveled to international destinations, usually with her artist-husband Ichikawa Yasushi.

The 1990s began with Kōno's participation in the thirteenth annual symposium for Comparative Literature Studies held in Tokyo, where she discussed her views of female writ-

ers in Japan and Germany. In January 1992, she returned to Europe, traveling on this occasion with Yasushi to Italy for the purpose of gathering materials for her writing; a few months later in May, the couple moved to New York, where Kōno became a writer in residence at Columbia University. In the following year, Kōno participated in two important conferences—the 1993 Berlin Festival in Germany and the Rutgers Conference on Japanese Women Writers in New Jersey. Though Kōno and her husband had established a second residence in New York City, they returned to Japan two or three times a year until their application for permanent residency in the United States was approved in 1994.

The Kansai earthquake, which killed more than six thousand people in January 1995, completely destroyed Kōno's family home in Ashiya, an affluent suburb of Osaka. This disaster brought Kōno back to the Kansai region where she and Yasushi attended to the laborious task of rebuilding the home. In April, Kōno was named honorary professor of the English Literature Department at Komazawa University in Tokyo; during the same month she traveled yet again to Italy to speak at the University of Venice. There, Kōno presented a paper on the topic of "presentiment" in Tanizaki Jun'ichirō's literature at an international symposium commemorating the twenty-fifth anniversary of Tanizaki's death.

The most outstanding example of Kōno's literary work in the 1980s and 1990s is *Miiratori ryōkitan* (1990; A bizarre tale of mummy-hunting). This specially commissioned novel, Kōno's longest (approximately four hundred pages), took ten years to complete and became a runaway best-seller when it finally appeared. Kumashiro Tatsumi, director for the Nikkatsu motion picture company and best known for his soft-core pornographic films, is said to have been so moved by this erotic novel that he vowed (while strapped to an oxygen tank and dying of emphysema) he would die a happy man if he could just direct a film based on the novel before he died. Others, too, were struck by the mammoth work: in 1991, exactly thirty years after the debut of "Toddler-Hunting,"

Miira-tori ryōkitan won the Noma Hiroshi Prize, reserved for the best work of fiction of the year. In *Miira-tori ryōkitan* Kōno's two most beloved themes—war, a topic seen in her early experimental fiction, and sexuality, for which she is best known—come together richly.

The term *miira* in the novel's title originates from the Portuguese word *myrrh*, which is a spice used in mummification, but now generally refers to mummies themselves. The work's rather complex title, with its evocation of an earlier age, suggests that its contents are set in the past. Indeed, the novel opens as Kōno's protagonist, Hinako, aged nineteen, marries a doctor named Masataka in 1941, the year the Pacific War begins. This marriage, Kōno provocatively writes, is most peculiar.

The bulk of *Miira-tori ryōkitan* is spent on Masataka's teaching the young, inexperienced Hinako about sex. Masataka introduces games in which he binds Hinako with a kimono sash, immobilizing her. He persuades her that being thus constricted will free her of her inhibitions. Paradoxically, Hinako does obtain sexual freedom over the course of Masataka's sadistic teachings. As the novel progresses, their games intensify to the point that Hinako becomes the dominant partner with Masataka playing an increasingly submissive role.

This reversal in Hinako's orientation from masochist to sadist has sparked much critical debate. Some have said that Hinako's assumption of a sadistic role makes her the ultimate Kōno heroine, one who finally breaks out of her passivity and masochistic proclivities. Others—notably, Hasumi Shigehiko—have suggested that *Miira-tori ryōkitan* is a clear demonstration of masochism, not sadism, for Hinako is simply playacting, following Masataka's lead.

One particularly remarkable scene in the novel suggests the complexity of Kōno's sexual theme and serves to explain critics' differing analyses of the work. After their home is destroyed by the fire bombings that leveled much of Tokyo in March 1945, Hinako and Masataka move to Kainami on Sagami Bay,

where Masataka sets up a medical practice. Hinako assists by making her husband a signboard for the clinic. After struggling to gather wood and charcoal, materials hard to come by in wartime, Hinako painstakingly begins her work. With the tip of a knife, she first carves out the letters "Internist" and "Otaka Clinic." Then, with metal chopsticks, she uses charcoal to blacken the wood background. As she labors over the task, Masataka comes to observe.

In this scene, which strikingly resembles the act of the tattoo artist in Tanizaki's "The Tattooer," who carves a spider onto the back of his victim, Kōno demonstrates the power that Hinako wields over Masataka. Both the content and language of the passage suggest that the scene is figurative as well as literal. Critic Minamoto Gorō has pointed out that the power of the description comes from the idea that the wood sign is actually Masataka's back, which Hinako desires to mutilate. The fact that Masataka, standing by Hinako's side, is viewing his own torture makes the scene more gruesome.

In the novel's dramatic conclusion, Masataka suffers death by strangulation. Since he dies while Hinako "rides him like Pegasus," his death is read by many as a crime of passion for which the dominatrix Hinako is clearly responsible; however, Kōno's complex psychological characterization of Hinako and Masataka, makes the final death scene far more ambiguous. While it is true that Masataka is Hinako's sexual slave by the end of the work, this is a role he has actively sought. In educating Hinako, he fulfills his own fantasies of torture. Hinako is the master to Masataka's slave, yet, as the critical inclusion of Masataka as keen observer indicates in the memorable woodcarving scene, she is still, in a sense, the victim of Masataka's machinations.

Just as it is difficult to ascertain whether Ukiko actually murders the three victims Kōno gruesomely catalogs in *Fui no koe* (A sudden voice), written decades earlier, the murder in *Miira-tori ryōkitan* is fraught with ambiguity. While Masataka's death is not framed as a fantasy, as the murders in *Fui no koe* are, Kōno's many reversals in *Miira-tori ryōkitan* rule out the possibility of naming a single victim or aggressor. Despite the lack of clear-cut murders in *Fui no koe* or a clear-cut murderer in *Miira-tori ryōkitan*, these two works do show a marked change in the nature of Kōno's heroines. Ukiko and Hinako are prime examples of Kōno's turn from depicting stereotypically masochistic protagonists who cannot escape their predicaments to knife-brandishing ones who do.

Characterized by variations on the theme of sadomasochism first seen in her graphic debut, "Toddler-Hunting," Kōno's oeuvre is full of stories of childless protagonists who seek independence through sexual liberation. Kōno's resistance to traditionally assigned roles for women is demonstrated in her writing by the frequency with which she makes her heroines sterile. As the course of Kōno's writing shows, her typically masochistic heroines become increasingly more sadistic, yet Kōno does not grant these later heroines greater power, for the females in her work are already powerful. Kōno has said that, for her, both sadist and masochist are forceful in equal ways. Her masochistic heroines actively seek to torment their lovers just as her sadistic heroines routinely submit to their lovers' desires. By refusing to restrict masochism to the female body and sadism to the male body, a theme she brilliantly explores in *Miira-tori ryōkitan*, Kōno rejects the idea that gender determines power relations. When critics such as Hotta Kazuko lament that Kōno is not a characteristically female writer *(joryū sakka rashikunai sakka)*, they fail to see how the many contradictions in Kōno's writing serve to undermine traditional hierarchies. Kōno commands center stage in Japan's literary establishment precisely because she challenges the boundaries between male and female, whether sadist or masochist.

Selected Bibliography

PRIMARY WORKS

COLLECTED WORKS

Kōno Taeko zenshū. 10 vols. Tokyo: Shinchōsha, 1994–1995. (Abbreviated as *KTZ* in the body of the text.)

NOVELS, SHORT STORIES, AND SHORT STORY COLLECTIONS

Yōjigari. Tokyo: Shinchōsha, 1962. Partial trans. by Lucy North as "Toddler-Hunting," "Snow," and "Theatre." In *Toddler-Hunting and Other Stories.* New York: New Directions, 1996. Pp. 45–134. "Toddler-Hunting" also in *Manoa* 3, no. 2:42–57 (fall 1991).

Bishōjo/Kani. Tokyo: Shinchōsha, 1963. Partial trans. by Lucy North as "Crabs" and "Night Journey." In *Toddler-Hunting and Other Stories.* New York: New Directions, 1996. Pp. 1–26, 135–165. Partial trans. by Phyllis Birnbaum as "Crabs." In *Rabbits, Crabs, Etc.: Stories by Japanese Women.* Honolulu: University of Hawaii Press, 1982. Pp. 99–132.

Yume no shiro. Tokyo: Bungei Shunjūshinsha, 1964.

Dan'yūtachi. Tokyo: Kawade Shobōshinsha, 1965.

Saigo no toki. Tokyo: Kawade Shobōshinsha, 1966. Partial trans. by Yukiko Tanaka and Elizabeth Hanson as "The Last Time." In *This Kind of Woman: Ten Stories by Japanese Women Writers, 1960–1976.* Edited by Yukiko Tanaka and Elizabeth Hanson. Stanford: Stanford University Press, 1982. Pp. 43–68. Partial trans. by Lucy North as "Full Tide," "Ants Swarm," and "Final Moments." In *Toddler-Hunting and Other Stories.* New York: New Directions, 1996. Pp. 27–44, 166–184, 185–213. Partial trans. by Noriko Mizuta Lippit as "Ants Swarm." In *Japanese Women Writers: Twentieth Century Short Fiction.* Edited by Noriko Mizuta Lippit and Kyoko Iriye Selden. Armonk, N.Y.: M. E. Sharpe, 1991. Pp. 112–125.

Fui no koe. Tokyo: Kōdansha, 1969.

Hone no niku. Tokyo: Kōdansha, 1969. Partial trans. by Lucy North as "Conjurer" and "Bone Meat." In *Toddler-Hunting and Other Stories.* New York: New Directions, 1996. Pp. 214–266. Partial trans. by Lucy Lower as "Bone Meat." In *Contemporary Japanese Literature: An Anthology of Fiction, Film, and Other Writing since 1945.* Edited by Howard Hibbett. New York: Knopf, 1977. Pp. 41–52.

Kusaikire. Tokyo: Bungei Shunjūsha, 1969.

Kaitentobira. Tokyo: Shinchōsha, 1970.

Erabarete aru hibi. Tokyo: Kawade Shobōshinsha, 1974.

Mukankei. Tokyo: Chūō Kōronsha, 1974.

Isutorietto. Tokyo: Kadokawa Shoten, 1977.

Suna no ori. Tokyo: 1977. Partial trans. by Yukiko Tanaka as "Iron Fish." In vol. 2 of *The Shōwa Anthology: Modern Japanese Short Stories.* Edited by Van C. Gessel and Tomono Matsumoto. New York: Kodansha International, 1985. Pp. 348–360. Partial trans. by Yukiko Tanaka as "Iron Fish." In *International Feminist Fiction.* Edited by Julia Penelope and Sarah Valentine. Freedom, Calif.: Crossing Press, 1992. Pp. 227–237.

Tōi natsu. Tokyo: Kōsōsha, 1977.

Yojutsuki. Tokyo: Kadokawa Shoten, 1978.

Ichinen no bokka. Tokyo: Shinchōsha, 1980.

Shuken. Chūō Kōron 95, no. 11 (summer 1980). Trans. by Yukiko Tanaka as "Crimson Markings." *Literary Review* 30, no. 2:184–231 (winter 1987).

Tori ni sareta onna: Kōno Taeko jisen tanpenshū. Tokyo: Gakugei Shorin, 1989.

Miira-tori ryōkitan. Tokyo: Shinchōsha, 1990.

En'en no ki. Tokyo: Kōdansha, 1992.

Akai kuchi kuroi kami. Tokyo: Shinchōsha, 1997.

Toddler-Hunting and Other Stories. Trans. by Lucy North, with an additional translation by Lucy Lower. New York: New Directions, 1996.

Gojitsu no hanashi. Tokyo: Bungei Shunjū, 1999.

ESSAY COLLECTIONS AND LITERARY CRITICISM

Bungaku no kiseki. Tokyo: Kawade Shobōshinsha, 1974.

"Jikai." *Bungei* 12, no. 7:10–11 (July 1974).

Watakushi no nakidokoro. Tokyo: Kōdansha, 1974.

Tanizaki bungaku to kōtei no yokubō. Tokyo: Bungei Shunjūsha, 1976.

Mō hitetsu no jikan. Tokyo: Kōdansha, 1978.

Kibun ni tsuite. Tokyo: Fukutake Shoten, 1982.

Ikutsumo no jikan. Tokyo: Kairyūsha, 1983.

Arugaoka futaritabi. With Tomioka Taeko. Tokyo: Bungei Shunjū, 1986.

Kabuki. With Furuido Hideo. Tokyo: Shinchōsha, 1992.

Kaeru to sanjutsu. Tokyo: Shinchōsha, 1993.

Tanizaki bungaku no tanoshimi. Tokyo: Chūō Kōronsha, 1993.

Okamoto Kanoko. With Kumasaka Atsuko. Tokyo: Shinchōsha, 1994.

Jein Ea to Arashigaoka: Buronte shimai no sekai. Tokyo: Kawade Shobōshinsha, 1996.

"Presentiments." In *A Tanizaki Feast: The International Symposium in Venice.* Edited by Adriana Boscaro and Anthony Hood Chambers. Ann Arbor: Center for Japanese Studies, University of Michigan, 1998. Pp. 117–124.

Ikani shite Tanizaki Jun'ichirō o yomu ka. Tokyo: Chūō Kōronshinsha, 1999.

Nyūyōku meguriai. With Ichikawa Yasushi. Tokyo: Chūkō Kōronshinsha, 2000.

WORKS EDITED BY KŌNO

Kojima Nobuo o meguru bungaku no genzai. Tokyo: Fukutake Shoten, 1985.

Nihon no meizuihitsu 98 (Aku). Tokyo: Sakuhinsha, 1990.

Josei sakka shiriizu. Tokyo: Kadokawa Shoten, 1999.

SECONDARY WORKS

COMMENTARY ON KŌNO IN ENGLISH

Ariga, Chieko M. "Text versus Commentary." In *The Woman's Hand: Gender and Theory in Japanese Women's Writing.* Edited by Paul Gordon Schalow and Janet A. Walker. Stanford: Stanford University Press, 1996. Pp. 352–381.

Bargen, Doris. "Translation and Reproduction in Enchi Fumiko's 'A Bond for Two Lifetimes—Gleanings.'" In *The Woman's Hand: Gender and Theory in Japanese Women's Writing.* Edited by Paul Gordon Schalow and Janet A. Walker. Stanford: Stanford University Press, 1996. Pp. 165–204.

Gessel, Van C. "Echoes of Feminine Sensibility in Literature." *Japan Quarterly* 35:409–416 (October–December 1988).

Jones, Gretchen. "Deviant Strategies: The Masochistic Aesthetic in Tanizaki Jun'ichirō and Kōno Taeko." Ph.D. dissertation, University of California, Berkeley, 1997.

Langton, Nina. "On the Edge: Mother and Child in the Works of Kōno Taeko." In *Mothers in Japanese Literature.* Edited by Kin'ya Tsuruta. Vancouver: University of British Columbia Press, 1997. Pp. 291–317.

Minamoto Gorō. "Fresh Insights into Human Nature: Kōno Taeko's *Miira-tori ryōkitan.*" Trans. by Janet Goff. In *Japanese Literature Today* 17:22–25 (March 1992).

Miyoshi, Masao. *Off Center: Power and Culture Relations between Japan and the United States.* Cambridge: Harvard University Press, 1991. Pp. 26, 212, 237.

Molasky, Michael S. *The American Occupation of Japan and Okinawa: Literature and Memory.* London: Routledge, 1999.

Mori, Maryellen Toman. "'Jouissance' in Takahashi Takako's Texts." In *The Woman's Hand: Gender and Theory in Japanese Women's Writing.* Edited by Paul Gordon Schalow and Janet A. Walker. Stanford: Stanford University Press, 1996. Pp. 205–238.

Orie, Muta. "Aspects of Love in Contemporary Japanese Fiction by Women Writers." *Hecate* 16, no. 1:151–163 (1990).

Uema, Chizuko. "Resisting Sadomasochism in Kōno Taeko." Ph.D. dissertation, University of Oregon, 1998.

STUDIES ON KŌNO IN JAPANESE

Hayes, Carol. "Dansei shakai no kanata e: Kōno Taeko, Ōba Minako, Tsushima Yūko no ayumu michi." *Hikaku Bungaku Kenkyū* 62:128–140 (December 1992).

Hotta Kazuko. *Joryū sakka no shinzui.* Tokyo: Fuji Shuppan, 1987. Pp. 13–86.

Kamei Hideo. "Hito to bungaku: Onna ni seibetsu sarete—Kōno Taeko." In *Chikuma gendai bungaku taikei 83.* Tokyo: Chikuma Shobō, 1977. Pp. 465–474.

Kanda Yumiko. "Kōno Taeko: Bosei dōkei no gyakusetsu." *Kokubungaku Kaishaku to Kanshō* 45, no. 4:46–52 (April 1980).

Matsumoto Tsuruo. "Kōno Taeko." In *Joryū bungei kenkyū.* Tokyo: Nansōsha, 1973. Pp. 335–347.

———. "Kōno Taeko." *Kokubungaku Kaishaku to Kanshō* 50, no. 10:77–78 (September 1995).

Yamada Yūsaku, ed. *Joryū bungaku no genzai.* Tokyo: Chikuma Shobō, 1985.

Yonaha Keiko. *Gendai joryū sakkaron.* Tokyo: Shin-bisha, 1986. (This insightful study contains a comprehensive bibliography of Kōno criticism from 1960 to 1985.)

Yoshikawa Atsuko. "Osore to yorokobi—Manchaku to chinmoku o yaburu kotoba: A. Rittchi to tomo ni yomu Kōno Taeko." *Shin Nihon Bungaku* 544:42–50 (autumn 1993).

RESOURCES IN ENGLISH

Ericson, Joan E. *Be a Woman: Hayashi Fumiko and Modern Japanese Women's Literature.* Honolulu: University of Hawaii Press, 1997. (Contains an informative section on the origins of the concept of "women's literature" in Japan.)

Lippet, Noriko Mizuta, and Kyoko Iriye Selden, eds. *Japanese Women Writers: Twentieth Century Short Fiction.* New York: M. E. Sharpe, 1991.

Schalow, Paul Gordon, and Janet A. Walker, eds. *The Woman's Hand: Gender and Theory in Japanese Women's Writing.* Stanford: Stanford University Press, 1996. (Contains a useful bibliography.)

KURAHASHI YUMIKO
1935–

ATSUKO SAKAKI

KURAHASHI YUMIKO is a short-story writer, novelist, and critic who has maintained a proud isolation from most of her contemporaries—and a distance from the modern Japanese literary establishment—in her refusal to write *watakushi shōsetsu*, or prose fiction meant to be taken by its reader as thinly disguised autobiography. Kurahashi thus looms as an inconvenient figure in modern Japanese literature, undoing perceptions of a field conventionally described as sentimental, confessional, transparent, and structureless. Her writing, in contrast, is logical, parodic, rhetorical, and well plotted. Her fiction is notably absurdist, fantastic, or otherwise autonomous of facts and expectations of the real world.

Despite her unorthodox stance and the candor with which she manifests and defends it, Kurahashi has earned several awards (the 1960 Meiji University President's Prize, the 1961 Women's Literature Prize, the 1963 Tamura Toshiko Memorial Prize, the 1987 Izumi Kyōka Memorial Prize) and award nominations (the prestigious semiannual Akutagawa Prize, twice, both in 1960) for her unique and not-to-be-dismissed talent that has attracted a large number of loyal readers. One of the reasons for her enduring popularity is the lucidity of her style, which is arguably unparalleled among contemporary Japanese authors and is particularly noteworthy, given the complexity of the stories she tells.

To write Kurahashi Yumiko's biography is in part to defy the author's intent, which is manifest in her essays and evident in her fiction. She declares that she does not write fiction in order to represent something about her life, but that she does so in order to build a world quite apart from what we ordinarily conceive as the real one. Her self-assigned mission is to perfect the intrinsic logic of fiction that one might call "rhetoric," and to see to it that everything that happens in the "anti-world," as she terms it, should make sense within the hypothetical premise.

Her renunciation of the autobiographical mode, however, is not coupled with a life of reclusion and obscurity. In fact, Kurahashi publicized facts about her life by personally editing an annal for what then constituted her complete works (published by Shinchōsha in 1975–1976). Although this is not an uncommon practice for an established contemporary Japanese author, her intent is not to help her readers draw easy analogies between facts in her life and her work, as it is for other authors. Instead, she mocks a predominant mode of reading her autobiographical details as the primary, if not the exclusive, sources of information for her fiction.

As we shall see shortly, there are many biographical facts that resemble aspects of Kurahashi's fictional texts, which are then confronted by unrealistic or unaccountable turns of events that could not possibly figure in any autobiographical narrative. Her life indeed provides a source for her fiction but does not contribute to the making of an "authentic" portrait out of which we would see her true self emerge; rather, it contributes to the making of a caricature, and a sardonic one at that, into which she disappears. In other words, Kurahashi's life story does not "feed" her fiction; her fiction "cannibalizes" her life. Her insidious scheme of self-projection exclusively for the sake of self-annihilation is obvious in the fact that two of her few published interviews are not actual but imaginative, both the interviewee's and the interviewer's speeches entirely invented by her.

Interestingly enough, the perpetual gesture of self-mocking and self-erasure is shared by many of her fictional characters who are writing or talking about themselves in order to further confuse their identities. Indeed, Kurahashi's fiction is autobiography-obsessed, and to that extent, she uses autobiographical elements generously, not in order to express herself but to test her ideas as to what constitutes selfhood and to explore how self-consciousness operates in attempts at writing self-histories.

Given the strategic displacement of the lived experience of the author in her fiction, any survey of Kurahashi's work along the lines of her life would have to be an attempt to expose a degree of distortion of her biographical facts in her text, rather than confirming a correspondence between the author's life and work. Another axis that should play itself out in the survey is to trace her reading experience, that is, her life in books, as the reader.

Claiming a Territory of Her Own: The Early Years

Born the eldest daughter of a dentist (Kurahashi Toshirō) and his wife (Misae) in the countryside of Kōchi, a prefecture not far from Ōe Kenzaburō's hometown on the island of Shikoku, on 10 October 1935 (the same year that the 1994 Nobel laureate was born), Kurahashi does not exude a sense of nostalgia as he does. Whereas the homeland became and remains for Ōe a ceaseless source of inspiration, Kurahashi's relation to her home is ambiguous. This is not to say that she had a bitter childhood or adolescence. Kurahashi simply denies home as the origin of one's creativity: not necessarily somewhere that one should flee from but a place that one does not culturally belong to. For her, identity is culturally constructed, not naturally given.

Kurahashi's denial of the concept of home as origin and place of perpetual attachment speaks most loudly in "Doko nimo nai basho" (1961; The place that exists nowhere), a dystopian novella that comes across as the most abstractionist in her entire oeuvre. In it the famous fellow countryman and colleague is relentlessly caricatured as a sex-obsessed compulsive speaker and the protagonist's mother is institutionalized in a mental asylum. Importantly, the protagonist expresses little despair or sorrow. It is not that the particular countryman or particular mother she happens to have disappoints her; she has no expectations from elements of her homeland because she does not belong there. She defines herself not in terms of where she is from, but of how she thinks.

Having graduated from an elite private high school in the city of Kōchi in 1953, Kurahashi spent a year in Kyōto, studying Japanese literature at a women's college. She then aspired to become a medical doctor but was unable to pass the entrance examinations to several medical schools. Her father wanted her to become a dental hygienist (an occupation within his field and considered inferior to his own profession), and sent her to a professional school in Tokyo in 1955. "Yōjo no yōni" (1964; Like a witch), *Seishōjo* (1965; partial trans., *Divine Maiden*, 1983), and "Nagai yumeji" (1968; "The Long Passage of Dreams," 1998), to mention but a few, present a dentist father who has a free-spirited daughter. The father's profession is not chosen simply for biographical reasons. It allows the father figure to look into the darkness each human being envelops within his or her body, while giving the patient (or the voyeur, either of which roles the daughter figure can take on) an opportunity to indulge in imagined oral sex and, by extension, to make associations with the journey into another hole (vagina). Kurahashi's fascination with holes in the human body is not incidental, but epistemological: for her the space inside the human body serves as a metaphor of the world of negativity, "the anti-world."

Kurahashi remained in Tokyo after she graduated and obtained a professional certificate in 1956, this time to study French literature at Meiji University. She shared Ōe's interest in Jean-Paul Sartre; the French existentialist was the subject of her senior thesis. The only (yet significant) difference from Ōe's reception of Sartre is that Kurahashi's focus is on his early immersion in the world of books rather than his later engagement in politics. Her first work, "Zatsujin bokumetsu shūkan" (1959; "Week for the Extermination of the Mongrels," 1983), is a satire of fanatic political movements, and for that reason was not published until later. Unlike the female narrator-protagonist in her next story and first published piece, "Parutai" (1960; "Partei," 1973 and 1982), who joins the Communist Party and gets pregnant by another member, Kurahashi journeyed through the season of politics as a bookworm, devouring the works of Franz Kafka and Albert Camus, who, with Sartre, constitute for her the "trinity." Her life as a student seems to have been quiet until the success as a professional writer, brought to her by "Partei."

Kurahashi's mission, stated most clearly in an essay titled "Shōsetsu no meiro to hiteisei" (1966; partial trans., "The Labyrinth and Negativity of Fiction," 1977), is to build and perfect an autonomous world of language that has its own logic (or rhetoric, if you will) and is not subject to the principles, ideological or political, operating outside the text. Since the earliest days of her career, Kurahashi has maintained this policy and has remained textbound. Her adherence to this policy may have resulted in her proud isolation from a majority of the rest of her contemporaries who write confessionally.

In order to accomplish her self-defined mission, Kurahashi often relies on intertextual plays. Unlike Akutagawa Ryūnosuke, who was defeated by his sense of incapacity to deal with the exterior, she has never been shy about creating works of art for the art's sake. Kurahashi even calls herself a "parasite" that, instead of building up something anew on the ground, excavates under the ground, into the world of negativity. She thus defines herself without any hint of self-humiliation but with defiance. Indeed, she "cannibalizes" not only her own life but the texts that she reads as well. She voraciously draws upon preceding works of literature and art, a compositional practice that did not meet with critical approval by the Japanese literary establishment.

Kurahashi's talent was first exhibited in her absurdist and abstract short stories à la Kafka. "Hebi" (1960; Snake) showcases this tendency, beginning with a man who wakes up to find that he is about to swallow a long snake, tail first, for no conceivable reason, and ending with the snake having completely swallowed the man feet first. It is difficult to find any (auto)biographical resonance in the plot, so it seems more rewarding to interpret the story as a fable of postmodern self-reflexivity or of baroque mutual erosion of the subject-object position. "Kon'yaku" (1960; Betrothal) features Kafka himself as a commitment-phobic man who is perpetually engaged but never gets married.

The intellectuality evident in this work as well as others was highly esteemed by some influential critics (for example, Hirano Ken, Okuno Takeo, Haniya Yutaka), who all but chaperoned her as a headstrong young woman who could use their support—in other words, a literary daughter. Many others (such as Niwa Fumio, Etō Jun, Nakamura Mitsuo), however, were troubled by what they saw as a combination of pedantry, cosmopolitanism, and almost airy lightness in the transgression of taboos of incest, masturbation, matricide, bisexuality,

187

hermaphroditism, and bestiality. There are several disputes among literary critics involving, if not centering on, Kurahashi's fiction in regard to missions to be accomplished by fiction writers and propriety of the content and style of literature.

With such sensations that her debut caused to literary journalism on the one hand, and her father's untimely death from heart failure on the other, Kurahashi, who dropped out of graduate school at Meiji University, tried to come to terms with her life as a professional writer. Although she was doubtful of the future of her career, she continued to produce stories that are both disturbingly powerful and profoundly philosophical. "Sasori tachi" (1963; Scorpions) relates a siblings' conspiracy to murder their mother—another conceptual attempt at denial of the origin. "Koibito dōshi" (1963; "We Are Lovers," 1998) presents a human couple and a feline pair, while suggesting that the real bond is established between the man and his female cat, and the woman and her male cat. "Uchūjin" (1964; "An Extraterrestrial," 1998) tells a story of potentially incestuous young siblings who wake up one morning to find an extraterrestrial egg. It hatches and turns out to be a hermaphrodite, a revelation that leads to the siblings' shared possession of the extraterrestrial as their sexual object, or a substitute for one another. Eventually, the two decide to consummate their relationship, not in the real world, but within the body of the extraterrestrial, entering the "anti-world" inside through the hermaphrodite's vaginal opening.

Common criticisms of Kurahashi are that her logical and intellectual style are inappropriate for literature, that her use of alphabetic letters as names is incongruous with Japanese cultural practice, and that she writes with an absence of the anguish that, to the conventional understanding of the "universal" human nature, should accompany any sexual misconduct or inadequacy. Kurahashi occasionally inserts mathematical formulas into her texts, explicitly questioning disciplinary boundaries between science and "humanities." Her characters are named with alphabetical letters that

bear consistent characteristics: L (intelligent and unconventional woman who does not have a womanly reproductive body), K (L's male counterpart), S (convention-bound man of poorly developed physique and intelligence), M (convention-bound woman of well-developed body and scanty intelligence), P (patronizer and womanizer), and Q (masochist). Kurahashi thus denies any root in the native culture of Japan and excludes room for lyricist aestheticism. Central characters—K and L—do not express sorrow, remorse, or guilty consciences, as expected in conventional novels, even when they are engaged in "inhuman" acts such as incest and matricide. The author's intent is not to report sensational incidents or to portray merciless deviants. Rather, she intends to suggest the contingency of human values.

The practice of reading fiction in search of truth about the author, which was predominant in Japan and had lent itself to the establishment of the *shishōsetsu* genre, was baffled by this intellectual woman who did not conform to the indigenous ethnic cultural standard, who was none other than a contrived product of fancy—or, if real, an unacceptable deviant who did not deserve to be represented. Women writing of their bodies in intellectual and often foreign terms were constructs. Kurahashi thus became prey to the anti-intellectualism, essentialism, empiricism, and ethnocentrism that plagued a majority of the Japanese literary critics. By their standards, any writer who would not write out of his or her own experience, in his or her own indigenous voice, was unnatural, a labeling that could be a death verdict for a new author. Fortunately for Kurahashi, there were readers versatile enough to understand her mission and appreciate her deft execution of her vision.

Autobiography's Many Faces: Quartet of Anti-novels and Metanovels (1961–1966)

Kurai tabi (1961; Blue journey) marks a shift in Kurahashi's career in two senses: it is the first book-length work; and it is full of references to persons, things, and places that we find in reality. However, some qualifications regarding the work's length and referentiality are necessary in order to avoid misunderstanding. The length does not help the work earn the title "novel"; the author herself classifies it as an "anti-novel," because it challenges the very notion of the genre as a coherent narrative that works to resolve a mystery about or surrounding the protagonist. Instead, *Kurai tabi* consists of fragmentary thoughts and retellings of events presented out of any visible temporal order, and it does not offer any conclusion as to what had happened in the past, what the events in the narrative present mean, or what may happen in the future. The referentiality to the "real" world does not amount to realism; rather, the flood of mentions of names accentuates the work's concern with exteriority. It proposes the material and sensual understanding of the surface of the surrounding world, rather than ideological and psychological inquiry into the interior, which more often than not accompanies versions of realism in Japan and elsewhere.

The story centers on a woman's search for an existentialist presence of her fiancé, who has disappeared without a trace. For years she has been engaged to him, her high school sweetheart and a fellow graduate student in French literature, on the contract that they no longer make love with one another, that they have one-night-stands with others, that they confess "faithfully" to one another about their affairs with strangers, and that they do not plan marriage. They are engaged not to be married and are faithful to one another in keeping their promise to be unfaithful. Their uniquely defined engagement, which is said to evoke the image of incestuous intellectual twins, falls apart when he departs not only physically but also discursively—without a word. To the heroine this means a loss of her own identity, as it is defined in terms of the role she plays vis-à-vis her fiancé, and also in discursive rather than essential terms. Her travel from Tokyo, where the two have lived and studied,

to Kyōto, the ancient capital of Japan that the two used to visit, inevitably entails incessant slippages into the past, shaping the narrative in a distinct mode of stream of consciousness. Although her journey in the spatial and physical sense does not come to an end—no destination is specified, no possibility of a new relationship confirmed—she comes to a definite conclusion about the discursive search for lost identity: to look for his unfinished manuscripts and to build her own image of him by writing of him. Thus, the ending of the novel is a declaration of the birth of a female writer, a resurrection of faith in language/text, and a rebuilding of the identity in textual terms.

Another not-to-be-dismissed narrative feature of *Kurai tabi* is the absence of the "I" and the impersonal narrator. Narrated neither in the first person nor in the third person, this novel refers to the protagonist as "you," producing the illusion that the reader is the subject of action, thought, and speech. This choice of the narrative mode gave antagonistic critics the opportunity to accuse Kurahashi of plagiarizing Michel Butor's *La modification*, an experimentalist novel in the second person that was translated into Japanese a few years prior to the publication of *Kurai tabi*. The author defended herself by claiming that she wrote the novel partly as a parody of Butor's work, assuming a high level of the reader's reading knowledge, and that no literary work is entirely original but is indebted to the pre-existing body of literature.

The irony in this much publicized dispute is that no critic seems to have grasped the depth and breadth of autobiographicality of the novel. Set aside experimentalist features, and you will see a most rare portrayal of Kurahashi as a young woman, surviving serious conflicts with her mother, visiting Kyōto, living in Tokyo, studying French literature, aspiring to become a professional novelist, and breaking up with a boyfriend with whom she was also intellectually intimate. The overlooking of the autobiographicality accounts for the critics' lack of insight into the differentiation of the narrator from the protagonist.

"Kekkon" (1965; Marriage), a sequel to *Kurai tabi*, is another parody of autobiography. Its refusal to get serious about the most serious matters of one's life (such as marriage and infidelity) sets it outside the norm of the *watakushi shōsetsu*. The text is largely epistolary, consisting of several letters that the heroine, now called L, writes to her former boyfriend, K, about her betrothal to and marriage to a man named S, framed within the narrative present in which K reads the letters and finally sees L again. Seemingly silly disputes over S's former girlfriend M's accusation that he had impregnated her, S's layoff, L's consideration of divorce, and her decision to continue to work as a professional writer, despite her husband's wish to be the sole breadwinner, work to suggest that marriage is an institution and that as such it is based not on romantic love but instead on a social contract involving family register and finance. Those who base their judgments and decisions on sentiments are relentlessly mocked, because they are unaware of the contingency of the institution called marriage.

The heroine of *Kurai tabi* and "Kekkon" reincarnates in *Divine Maiden*; she makes a cameo appearance as a professional writer called Y. K., none other than Kurahashi's own initials, who has written a second-person narrative about herself and her lost boyfriend (referred to as K) called *Blue Journey* (the title is given in English in the original). The author-within-the-text's information that she has written a piece about her own marriage matches the content of "Kekkon." There are many other biographical and bibliographical facts that pertain to Kurahashi. The author's presence within her own text, and as a most marginal character, presents a metafictional paradox. A conventional idea of the author as the creator of the text is reversed, and the text is now seen as the source of images of the author. This device showcases Kurahashi's unique handling of autobiography mentioned earlier.

Both the warped autobiographicality that the character exhibits and her pivotal role in showing as well as telling how to read autobiography largely escaped the critics' attention; such "technical" points were eclipsed by the eye-catching theme of incest. The female central character and secondary narrator, Miki, proves to have been engaged in father-daughter incest, and the male primary narrator-protagonist, "I," also referred to as "K," slept with his elder sister, L. Miki writes first-person fictitious "confessions" of incest, loses her memory, regains it but fakes continuation of amnesia, and asks "I" to read her past "memoir" and help her rebuild her self-history. During the process of reading and trying to decode her mystifying text, "I" ends up retelling Miki his own past, including his relationship with L. These and other perpetual changes of positions between writer and reader, and speaker and listener, call into question the stability of the relationship between the subject and object of any action. The fleeting and interchangeable pairing of the two may not be entirely irrelevant to the theme of incest; both involve loss of identity and narcissism. Miki's father and L having been existentially erased, due to his death and her self-silencing, respectively. Miki and "I" agree to marry, in order to complete the closure of the self-reflexive system maintained in the practice of incest.

Whereas the three works in the sequence mock convention-bound characters for their blind faith in contingent social and behavioral norms and expectations, "Kyōsei" (1966; Cohabitation) suggests that challenges to the social norms can be as petty as blind conformity to them. The story belittles the reincarnation of K, the idealized accomplice of the female protagonist in intellectual and sexual experimentations. K in this story sneaks into the life of the married couple, L and S, as a spy and crawls beneath their bed for close observation of L's married life. A voyeur and nothing else, K appears dimensionless and purely conceptual, his presence merely filling an empty space allocated to him. L, on the other hand, is judged by her doctor to be "genderless," and thus more like a plant than a human being. The lack of substance, an asset positively viewed in *Kurai tabi*, *Divine Maiden* and

"Kekkon," has come to be mocked in this story, which concludes Kurahashi's journey through the world of negativity.

Satire without a Devil: *The Adventures of Sumiyakist Q*

Whereas Kurahashi in her real life went through events such as marriage (to Kumagai Tomihiro, a photographer), a one-year stay in the United States, return to Japan and the birth of a daughter (and later a second daughter), she produced a novel that is most abstract and autonomous of reality: *Sumiyakisuto Kyū no bōken* (1969; *The Adventures of Sumiyakist Q*, 1979). The eponymous protagonist, who is soon to be revealed as an anti-hero, lacking intelligence, dignity, and physical beauty, is sent to the dystopian community of an isolated reformatory, in the guise of a newly appointed teacher, to convert every member to the imaginary ideology called Sumiyakism. His blind devotion to the dogma is challenged by the head of the institution (Rector), who "violates," intellectually or sexually, any other human being with his insatiable interest in knowing the Other; a theologian who cannot communicate with anyone else due to stammering; the overseer who cannot see anything but his own eyes; the man of letters called Bukka—presumably a multiple pun involving Kafka, Book, and Sakka ("professional writer" in Japanese)—who cannot deal with anything except textually; and the doctor who rapes both men and women, and cannibalizes. They are all caricatures of Q himself and thus exhibit many kinds of self-reflexivity or colonization of others. In total, the mechanisms of self-assertion and self-annihilation are multifariously ubiquitous in the novel.

We can detect the enduring presence of themes from earlier periods: incest and autobiography. K and L, the twins born to the rector's wife by immaculate birth, commit double suicide. Bukka tries to educate Q, albeit in vain, because he cannot understand that the first-person narrative is not necessarily the narra-

tor's autobiography; Bukka shows Q a work of his, "Memoir of the Doctor," in which the narrator-protagonist retells his practice of cannibalism, and which Q can read only as a transparent confession made by the author-narrator. Committed to a revolutionary ideology and its promotion, Q reads fiction only as representation of reality. Bukka then develops a thesis of autonomy of literature, much the same as Kurahashi's own in "The Labyrinth and Negativity of Fiction" (mentioned earlier). Bukka is thus the most obvious caricature of Kurahashi herself, and his accidental death in the middle of the story marks the exit of the author incognito, materializing another metafictional paradox similar to one in *Divine Maiden*.

The novel has resemblances to some modern classics: Thomas Mann's *The Magic Mountain* in terms of the setting (a reformatory remote from the rest of the world, arrived at and left behind by the protagonist, who is an outsider); Dostoyevsky's *The Brothers Karamazov* in terms of the philosophical discussions (especially the ones presented by the doctor whose cynicism reminds us of Ivan Karamazov); Cervantes' *Don Quixote* in terms of the naming of the character as well as his absurdly idealistic views; and Laurence Sterne's *Tristram Shandy* in terms of the intrusive and occasionally digressive narrator who changes the pace and focus of the narration, depending on the focus and distance from the object of observation at a given moment.

Kurahashi took pains to stress that the novel is not meant to mock any existing ideology or political party, as had been suspected. Her cynicism toward political engagement being well known, many thought that the novel was a satire, intended to criticize communism, to which Sumiyakism seems to have similarities: the oppressed population (in this case, the students in the reformatory) should revolt and take charge of the governing board. However, the author, as usual, did not intend a political satire of a particular political belief; instead, she intended satirical effects, negating the stability of any hierarchy presupposed by political beliefs. With the subject-object position in any type of negotiation constantly being reversed, it is theoretically impossible to determine who is threatening, conquering, enslaving, or oppressing whom.

A Traveler Returns?: Transitional Period (1968–1971)

Kurahashi spent a year in the United States as a Fulbright artist, affiliated with the Creative Writers' Workshop at the University of Iowa, in 1966–1967. Her husband followed her to study in the film department of the same university. This absence from and subsequent return to Japan were generally taken by critics to mark a radical change in Kurahashi's career. Many argued that she transformed herself from a Europhile to a nativist. That they were simply misguided by an increased number of references to classical Japanese literature, most notably to Nō theater, medieval *waka* poetry, and *The Tale of Genji*, should become evident in a survey of her later development as a writer.

What is obvious and noted, but nonetheless has not been incorporated into the discussion of Kurahashi's "transformation," is that she also began to refer extensively to European classics. In addition to the contemporary experimentalist fiction, she came to draw liberally on Greek myths, tragedies, and high-modern European novels. If Kurahashi had entered a new stage in her career, that stage should be defined as classicist rather than nativist. This is just another example which reveals that her desire to draw a contrast between East and West as entities of intrinsic essences was so strongly felt by critics that any other contrast was outshadowed by it. The "return to the native" scenario—any young Japanese writer would be attracted to the West, only to be drawn back to his or her native culture—is applied to interpretations of Kurahashi as well.

Kurahashi herself may have been entrapped in the fallacy when she wrote "Vāzinia" (1968; Virginia), a novella that does not appear to create the "anti-world." In this piece, the first-person narrator (Yumiko), a professional writer visiting Iowa with her husband, relates her friendship with the eponymous Swedish-American woman, a divorcee with two sons who is studying filmmaking. The content relies upon the author's experience in the real world, and the style remains descriptive. The relationship between the two friends culminates in a lack of understanding: the narrator concludes that Virginia cannot appreciate the values specific to the Japanese and decides to leave her, with no intention to keep in touch, when the narrator finds herself to be pregnant. Thus, from behind the facade of the unassuming narrative emerges the formula that "East is east, West is west," as well as the conventional belief that women mature when they become mothers.

Although the unabashed and unframed conventionality of "Vāzinia" is disappointing, one of the works most representative of Kurahashi's arts of storytelling and pastiche was written in the same year: "The Long Passage of Dreams," which paints a more nuanced portrait of home than her earlier works. In this novella of finely woven texture of numerous references to Nō plays and Greek myths, a grown-up daughter (of a dentist) comes home from the United States to see her father die, feeling bound to her adolescent struggles with the hallucinatory father and the chastising mother. Although the story conveys a degree of poignancy as well as intimacy with the author's experience (facts from different stages of her life are anachronistically juxtaposed), supernatural themes and self-reflexivity, for which Kurahashi had become famous, are not sacrificed. The viewpoint in the narrative alternates between the dying father's and the daughter's several times, and the sections narrated from the father's viewpoint reveal several personae of the father: from his past, present, and moments of hallucinatory identification with characters in theater playing roles from Nō plays and Greek tragedies. The transformation being done very quickly, the effect is that of the postmodern art of bricolage. The instability and inconsistency in the subjecthood that Kurahashi revealed in earlier fiction are reconfirmed in this novella.

The juxtaposition of Nō and Greek plays in "The Long Passage of Dreams" is sustained in the next series of works, a five-part omnibus titled *Han higeki* (1968–1971; Anti-Tragedies). The storylines of Euripedes' plays—centering on Electra and Orestes (conspiratory siblings), who murder Clytemnestra (their mother, who had conspired with her lover to murder their father)—and those of Nō plays about homicides *(Adachigahara)* are transplanted into an unspecified place or into contemporary Japan. None of the stories—"Himawari no ie" (1968; The house of sunflowers), "Suikyō nite" (1969; Being inebriated), "Shiroi kami no dōjo" (1969; "The Little Girl with the Silver Hair," 1987), "Kakō ni shisu" (1970; "To Die at the Estuary," 1977), or "Kamigami ga ita koro no hanashi" (1971; When there were gods)—displays a complex narrative structure, though there is absurdity in parts of the plot, and the tone of speech, whether in the third person or first, is calm, distant, and rational.

The Narrator in Control: Novels and Tales since 1971

Kurahashi, who became the mother of two daughters (Madoka and Sayaka), continued with the seemingly neutral narration for the subsequent decades. *Yume no ukihashi* (1971; The floating bridge of dreams) introduces Keiko, the figure central to the still-ongoing multivolume saga, as a female college student (majoring in English literature, rather than in French, which is significant in characterization) whose senior year coincides with the apogee of the student movement. Choosing to stand alone, if not aloof, from the majority of her fellow students, Keiko writes a thesis on Jane Austen, revealing her inclination toward sense and stability, breaks up with her boyfriend Kōichi, who perhaps is her half brother (as a result of partner-swappings that his and her parents were engaged in), and marries her thesis adviser, with whom she is not in love. The story closes with the beginning of a new cycle of partner-swapping, involving Keiko, her husband, her ex-boyfriend, and his wife. Although the title, taken from the last chapter of *The Tale of Genji*, and seasonal references in the narrative may give the impression that this is a very "Japanese" piece, *Yume no ukihashi* could not be further from it.

Shiro no naka no shiro (1980; The castle within the castle) functions as a sequel, portraying Keiko in her thirties. Two problems threaten her marriage: her husband's secret conversion to Christianity, which she considers a variation on infidelity, and his potential relationship with one of his female students. Kōichi's marriage is also on the rocks. The two former lovers consummate their relationship sexually (which, we are told, they could not do at the end of the previous work) and continue to be intimate both in physical and intellectual terms.

In these two works, Kurahashi tried a narrative mode new to her: the third-person narrative unfolded by the impersonal, omniscient narrator. All the characters, including the protagonist Keiko, are referred to as "he" or "she." Much closer to, if not identical with, the conventional novel of nineteenth-century Europe, both works convey the impression that they are the only possible account of truth, presented by the objective narrator who has no trace of his/her positionality within the text. The reader is to stay outside the text, rather than invited into it as the hypothetical protagonist, as in *Kurai tabi*. Neither is the author thrown into the text, as in *Divine Maiden*, to question the subject-object positions in textual production. The stability of the narration matches conservatism in the story.

The next two volumes of the saga represent yet another mode of telling. Although the narrator of each is anonymous and unidentified, he or she is not impersonal, as is obvious from the way each character is addressed. The narrator employs "san," "kun," and "shi" to denote the gender and relative rank of a given person, suggesting that the narrator is in a specific relation to the person in question. Thus, the narrator is personified within the text, if outside the storyline.

193

In *Kōkan* (1989; Pleasure exchange), which covers the next stage of Keiko's life (in her forties), she appears as a widow with three children and is surrounded by many sophisticated male friends who admire her. The reader sees her enter a new stage of her life, in three senses: she recognizes and respects Kōichi's second marriage, which places him in a confinement that even Keiko cannot tread; she develops a lesbian relationship with the student of her late husband who used to adore him; and she meets Irie, a political and business entrepreneur, a lover to spend the rest of her life with. *Shunposhion* (1985; Symposium) places Keiko, now in her sixties, in the background, focusing on the romance between her granddaughter Satoko, a precocious young woman, and Akira, Kōichi's son by his second marriage, a widowed professor of classics in his thirties. The narrative reminds us of two banners flown high in Kurahashi's earlier days: defense of pastiche and conscious use of autobiography. The entire story exhibits theories and practices of pastiche, letting characters validate the art of reproduction and displaying its own indebtedness to preexisting works of literature, art, music, and culinary art by innumerable quotations and allusions. Satoko writes an autobiography that takes on the appearance of fiction, featuring Akira's former object of affection as the protagonist. This text within the text echoes the theme of potential incest between a woman and her mother's ex-boyfriend in *Divine Maiden*, and also the act of writing autobiography as self-annihilation.

Kurahashi turns to the first-person narrative in *Popoi* (1987), which centers on and is recounted by Mai, the granddaughter of Keiko's long-term partner (Irie, introduced in *Kōkan*). As is often the case with Kurahashi's female protagonists, Mai is a precocious young woman of discriminating taste. The story is confined to her observations, with no challenge made to her subjecthood from the exterior. This does not mean, however, that the novel suggests the stability of subjecthood in general. The questions pertaining to identity and subject-object positions, raised throughout Kurahashi's earlier

works, are evoked by the eponymous character, who is in fact a severed head of a terrorist kept alive owing to modern medical technology. Deprived of a body, Popoi the head lives on its (his?) own memory. Thus, Popoi makes a chiasmatic contrast with Miki, the amnesiac, in *Divine Maiden*: memory without the body, and the body without memory—which, if either, would be better able to claim to have a coherent identity?

Kurahashi continued the story of Keiko in two anthologies of short stories: *Yume no kayoiji* (1989; Passage of dreams) and *Gensō kaigakan* (1991; Fantastic gallery). The reader is thus allowed a few glimpses into Keiko's life in her seventies and thirties, respectively, in the two. *Yume no kayoiji* collects episodes of Keiko having rendezvous with spirits of deceased historical figures, taken by them into the fictional or historically remote worlds that they created or lived in. This leads the reader to ask the medical question that is not irrelevant to the one asked in *Popoi*: How is the state of death to be determined? Written during the author's serious illness, the stories in the volume still do not convey the pain and suffering that should concern *watakushi shōsetsu*. Instead, Kurahashi clothes the question of how to define death in the heroine's supernatural affairs with literary immortals, which presents a junkyard of ahistoricized fragments from the past—a symptom of postmodernism.

Gensō kaigakan centers on Keiko's grandson, Kei, an exceptionally gifted young man who develops a communication network with an indefinite number of people, and multiple relationships with women either in cyberspace or in the real world. Scientific knowledge and literature again are found compatible. In fact, the loss or maintenance of identity may not be more relevant than in computer communication, where the sender and recipient of messages are physically absent in the site of communication, and they can remain anonymous or not have to reveal their identities in the real world. Cyberspace may have been an appropriate model for Kurahashi in envisioning the "anti-world."

194

The works in the saga, especially those after the first two, share a strong interest in European literature and arts, citing numerous works as characters' favorites and providing materials for pastiche. This defies the theory of "returning to the native," persistent in modern Japanese literary studies. Kurahashi, who began her career by writing stories set in no specific nation, sojourned in the Japanese cultural heritage and has come to terms with heterogeneous culture, which indeed is Japan.

Miscellaneous Fiction since 1985

Kurahashi's first abstractionist work after *The Adventures of Sumiyakist Q*, *Amanon koku ōkanki* (1986; An account of a round trip to the Amanon), was awarded the Izumi Kyōka Prize of 1987—the first literary prize for the author in a quarter-century. This reveals both the literary establishment's neglect of her many accomplishments and the tenacity of her popularity, which enabled her to stay professionally active. Indeed, Kurahashi remained productive and marketable, as is evident in her publication list during the 1970s and 1980s, which consists of new works and older works reprinted in paperback editions. This is rather unusual for authors whose writings are not primarily for entertainment—mysteries, science fiction, or historical narratives.

Amanon koku ōkanki recounts the adventures of the protagonist, P, a missionary of an imaginary religion called Monokamism (pun intended for monotheism and the Japanese term for fetishism), sent to the land of the Amanons, lesbians and eunuchs, the former of which P is to initiate sexually. Despite its resemblance to Kurahashi's previous satire, however, this superficial parody of feminist society does not match the previous satire in stylistic rigor and vigor; although the content may be imaginative, the language of the text remains referential and does not engage threatening changes in subject-object positions. The narrative also does not display any self-reflexivity to lead us to epistemological questions.

Kurahashi may have succeeded in nailing down worldly honor, but she failed here to construct an autonomous "anti-world" founded upon a perfect rhetoric of its own.

Kurahashi does not lose her sharp edge when it comes to short stories. Some of the stories collected in *Kurahashi Yumiko no kaiki shōhen* (1985; Horror short stories by Kurahashi Yumiko) reconfirm her concern with the contrast between exterior and interior while demonstrating the mastery of storytelling that makes her text accessible to a wider audience. "Kubi no tobu onna" (1985; "The Woman with the Flying Head," 1998), the story of a woman whose body is violated by her adopted father while her head flies to her sweetheart, provides a parable on the binary opposition between the body and the mind, in the guise of a ghost story (based on ancient Chinese sources) and a classical quasi-incest tale (in *The Tale of Genji*). Thus, Kurahashi manages to create and maintain a balance between philosophical questions to be asked and familiar plots and settings recycled from literary conventions.

Although Kurahashi has not been as productive in recent years, due to her chronic illness, younger writers have been publishing works reminiscent of many of the experimentations she first attempted. For example, Kanai Mieko, a longtime lover of Kurahashi's fiction, challenges the reader with questions about identity, subjectivity, and the body in similarly complex narratives that consciously display language games. Although official recognition may be long overdue, Kurahashi's accomplishments are visible in Japanese literature of the postmodern age.

Selected Bibliography

PRIMARY WORKS

NOVELS AND SHORT STORIES

"Zatsujin bokumetsu shūkan." 1959. Trans. by Samuel Grolmes and Yumiko Tsumura as "Week for the Extermination of the Mongrels." *Mundus Artium: A Journal of International Literature and the Arts* 14, no. 1:103–113 (1983).

"Natsu no owari." 1960. Trans. by Victoria V. Vernon as "The End of Summer." In her *Daughters of the Moon: Wish, Will, and Social Constraint in Fiction by Modern Japanese Women.* Berkeley: Institute of East Asian Studies, University of California, 1988. Pp. 229–240.

"Parutai." 1960. Trans. by Samuel Grolmes and Yumiko Tsumura as "Partei." In *New Directions in Prose and Poetry* 26:8–22 (1973). Also trans. by Yukiko Tanaka and Elizabeth Hanson as "Partei." In *This Kind of Woman: Ten Stories by Japanese Women Writers, 1960–1976.* Edited by Tanaka and Hanson. New York: Putnam, 1982. Pp. 3–16.

Kurai tabi. Tokyo: Tōto Shobō, 1961.

"Kyosatsu." 1961. Trans. by Carolyn Haynes as "The Monastery." In *The Shōwa Anthology: Modern Japanese Short Stories.* Vol. 2, *1961–1984.* Edited by Van C. Gessel and Tomone Matsumoto. Tokyo: Kodansha International, 1985. Pp. 218–231.

"Koibito dōshi." 1963. Trans. by Atsuko Sakaki as "We Are Lovers." In her *The Woman with the Flying Head and Other Stories of Kurahashi Yumiko.* Armonk, N.Y.: M. E. Sharpe, 1998. Pp. 29–38.

"Uchūjin." 1964. Trans. by Atsuko Sakaki as "An Extraterrestrial." In her *The Woman with the Flying Head and Other Stories of Kurahashi Yumiko.* Armonk, N.Y.: M. E. Sharpe, 1998. Pp. 3–28.

Seishōjo. Tokyo: Shinchōsha, 1965. Partial trans. by Bertha Lynn Burson as "Divine Maiden." In her *"Divine Maiden:* Kurahashi Yumiko's *Seishōjo."* Ph.D. diss., University of Texas at Austin, 1983. Pp. 1–66.

"Shūma tachi." 1965. Trans. by Lane Dunlop as "Ugly Demons." In his *Autumn Wind and Other Stories.* Rutland, Vt.: Tuttle, 1994. Pp. 201–221. Also trans. by Samuel Grolmes and Yumiko Tsumura as "The Ugly Devils." In *New Directions in Prose and Poetry* 24:55–67 (1972).

"Nagai yumeji." 1968. Trans. by Atsuko Sakaki as "The Long Passage of Dreams." In her *The Woman with the Flying Head and Other Stories of Kurahashi Yumiko.* Armonk, N.Y.: M. E. Sharpe, 1998. Pp. 105–155.

"Shiroi kami no dōjo." 1969. Trans. by Kumiko Nakanishi as "The Little Girl with the Silver Hair." In her *"The Life and Works of Yumiko Kurahashi."* Master's thesis, San Diego State University, 1987.

Sumiyakisuto Kyū no bōken. Tokyo: Kōdansha, 1969. Trans. by Dennis Keene as *The Adventures of Sumiyakist Q.* St. Lucia: University of Queensland Press, 1979.

"Kakō ni shisu." 1970. Trans. by Dennis Keene as "To Die at the Estuary." In *Contemporary Japanese Literature: An Anthology of Fiction, Film, and Other Writing since 1945.* Edited by Howard Hibbett. New York: Knopf, 1977. Pp. 248–281.

Yume no ukihashi. Tokyo: Chūō Kōronsha, 1971.

Shiro no naka no shiro. Tokyo: Shinchōsha, 1980.

Shunposhion. Tokyo: Fukutake Shoten, 1985.

Amanon koku ōkanki. Tokyo: Shinchōsha, 1986.

Popoi. Tokyo: Fukutake Shoten, 1987.

Kōkan. Tokyo: Shinchōsha, 1989.

COLLECTED WORKS

Parutai. Tokyo: Bungei Shunjū Shinsha, 1960.

Kon'yaku. Tokyo: Shinchōsha, 1961.

Ningen no nai kami. Tokyo: Kadokawa Shoten, 1961.

Yōjo no yōni. Tokyo: Tōjusha, 1966.

Sasori tachi. Tokyo: Tokuma Shoten, 1968.

Vāzinia. Tokyo: Shinchōsha, 1970.

Han higeki. Tokyo: Kawade Shobō Shinsha, 1971.

Kurahashi Yumiko shū. Tokyo: Kōdansha, 1971.

Kurahashi Yumiko zen sakuhin. 8 vols. Tokyo: Shinchōsha, 1975–1976. (Each volume includes the author's notes on the works in it. Volume 8 includes the chronological record of the author's life and work mentioned in the text.)

Otona no tame no zankoku dōwa. Tokyo: Shinchōsha, 1984.

Kurahashi Yumiko no kaiki shōhen. Tokyo: Ushio Shuppansha, 1985.

Yume no kayoiji. Tokyo: Kōdansha, 1989.

Gensō kaigakan. Tokyo: Bungei Shunjū, 1991.

COLLECTED ESSAYS

Watashi no naka no kare e. Tokyo: Kōdansha, 1970.

Meiro no tabibito. Tokyo: Kōdansha, 1972.

Jishaku no nai tabi. Tokyo: Kōdansha, 1979.

Saigo kara nibanme no dokuyaku. Tokyo: Kōdansha, 1986.

Mugen no utage. Tokyo: Kōdansha, 1996.

SECONDARY WORKS

CRITICAL AND BIOGRAPHICAL STUDIES

Aoyama Tomoko. "The Love That Poisons: Japanese Parody and the New Literacy." *Japan Forum* 6: 35–46 (April 1994.)

Burson, Bertha Lynn. "*Divine Maiden:* Kurahashi Yumiko's *Seishōjo.*" Ph.D. diss., University of Texas at Austin, 1983.

Etō Jun. "Kaigai bungaku to sono mozōhin." *Tokyo Shinbun,* 9–11 December 1961, evening ed., p. 8.

———. "Kaigai bungaku to sono mozōhin saisetsu." *Tokyo Shinbun,* 28 December 1961, evening ed., p. 8.

Hirano Ken. "Shōwa 35-nen 2-gatsu." In his *Bungei jihyō.* Vol. 1. Tokyo: Kawade Shobō Shinsha, 1969.

Itō Sei, Haniya Yutaka, and Hirano Ken. "Zadankai bundan 1961-nen." *Tokyo Shinbun,* 26 December 1961, evening ed., p. 8.

Kanai Mieko. "Bungakuteki fūdo to sakuhin: Kurahashi Yumiko ganzō no bigaku." *Nihon Dokusho Shinbun,* 24 November 1975, p. 1.

Kleeman, Faye Yuan. "Sexual Politics and Sexual Poetics in Kurahashi Yumiko's *Cruel Fairy Tales for Adults.*" In *Constructions and Confrontations: Changing Representations of Women and Feminisms East and West.* Edited by Cristina Bacchilega and Cornelia N. Moore. Vol. 12 of *Literary Studies: East and West*. Honolulu: College of Languages, Linguistics, and Literature, University of Hawaii, 1996. Pp.150–158.

Kurahashi Yumiko Tokushū. Special Issue of *Yuriika (Eureka)*, March 1981.

Nakamura Shin'ichirō. "'Bungei Ōrai': Roman wa kanō ka." *Bungei* (April 1962): 183.

Napier, Susan J. "The Woman Lost: The Dead, Damaged, or Absent Female in Postwar Fantasy." In her *The Fantastic in Modern Japanese Literature: The Subversion of Modernity*. London and New York: Routledge, 1996. Pp. 53–92.

Ōe Kenzaburō. "Hihyōka wa muyō no chōbutsu ka: Etō-shi ni kamitsuita Kurahashi-shi no iken ni omou." *Sankei Shinbun*, 28 July 1961, evening ed., p. 2.

Okuno Takeo. "Etō Jun shi no Kurahashi Yumiko ron e." *Tokyo Shinbun*, 25 December 1961, evening ed., p. 8.

———. "Riarizumu e no gimon: Nakamura Mitsuo hihan." In his *Bungakuteki seiha*. Tokyo: Shun-jūsha, 1964. Pp. 16–33.

Orbaugh, Sharalyn. "The Body in Contemporary Japanese Women's Fiction." In *The Woman's Hand: Gender and Theory in Japanese Women's Writing*. Edited by Paul Gordon Schalow and Janet A. Walker. Stanford, Calif.: Stanford University Press, 1996. Pp. 119–164.

Sakaki, Atsuko. "The Intertextual Novel and the Inter-relational Self: Kurahashi Yumiko, a Japanese Postmodernist." Ph.D. diss., University of British Columbia, 1992.

———. "Denaturalizing Nature, Dissolving the Self: An Analysis of Kurahashi Yumiko's *Popoi*." In *Nature and Selfhood in Japanese Literature*. Edited by Kinya Tsuruta. Vancouver: Jōsai International University and the University of British Columbia, 1993. Pp. 241–256.

———. "'Watashi' to 'kare' no aida: Kurahashi Yumiko ni miru 'tasha' gainen tono tawamure." In *Nihon bungaku ni okeru "tasha."* Edited by Kinya Tsuruta. Tokyo: Shin'yōsha, 1994. Pp. 342–363.

———. "A Gallery of 'Severed Heads': A Comparative Study of Kurahashi Yumiko's *Popoi*." In *Dramas of Desire/Visions of Beauty*. Edited by Ziva Ben-Porat, Hana Wirth-Nesher, Roseann Runte, and Hans R. Runte. Vol. 1 of *Forces of Vision*. Tokyo: International Comparative Literature Association, 1995. Pp. 386–393.

———. "Autobiographizing Fiction? Fictionalizing Autobiography?: A Contemporary Japanese Woman's Experimentations with Meta-Autobiography." In *Constructions and Confrontations: Changing Representations of Women and Feminisms East and West*. Edited by Cristina Bacchilega and Cornelia N. Moore. Vol. 12 of *Literary Studies: East and West*. Honolulu: College of Languages, Linguistics, and Literature, University of Hawaii, 1996. Pp. 194–206.

———. "Re-configuring the Dyad: Mother-Daughter Relationships in Kurahashi Yumiko's Fiction." In *The Mother in Japanese Literature*. Edited by Kinya Tsuruta. Vancouver: University of British Columbia, 1997. Pp. 397–443.

———. Introduction to *The Woman with the Flying Head and Other Stories* by Kurahashi Yumiko. Armonk, N.Y.: M. E. Sharpe, 1998. Pp. xiii–xxii.

———. "(Re)Canonizing Kurahashi Yumiko: Toward Alternative Perspectives for 'Modern' 'Japanese' 'Literature.'" In *Ōe and Beyond: Fiction in Contemporary Japan*. Edited by Stephen Snyder and Philip Gabriel. Honolulu: University of Hawaii Press, 1999. Pp. 153–176.

Shirai Kenzaburō. "Kaigai bungaku shōkai no mondaiten." *Tokyo Shinbun*, 19 December 1961, evening ed., p. 8.

Shirai Kōji. "Mohō to dokusō." *Tokyo Shinbun*, 2 March 1962, evening ed., p. 8.

Takano Toshimi. *Kurahashi Yumiko ron*. Tokyo: Sanrio Shuppan, 1976.

Tokushū Kokubungaku kaishaku to kanshō. Takahashi Kazumi to Kurahashi Yumiko. August 1971.

Vernon, Victoria V. "The Sibyl of Negation: Kurahashi Yumiko and 'Natsu no owari.'" In her *Daughters of the Moon: Wish, Will, and Social Constraint in Fiction by Modern Japanese Women*. Berkeley: Institute of East Asian Studies, University of California, 1988. Pp. 107–134.

KYŌKA
(IZUMI KYŌKA)
1873–1939

CHARLES SHIRŌ INOUYE

IZUMI KYŌKA wrote over 300 novels, stories, and plays. At a time when Japanese writers were looking to the European novel for inspiration, he declared his indifference to those Western narrative practices that were rapidly redefining Japanese literary culture during the Meiji (1868–1912) and Taishō (1912–1925) periods. While realism came to dominate, he chose to write in a more lyrical, imagistic vein that echoed the much-decried conventions of the late Tokugawa period (1600–1868). For this, he was relegated to a place outside the literary mainstream. Of course, no one writing at this time could easily avoid the larger cultural trends that were transforming Japanese society. Along with the naturalists, Kyōka also shared an obsessive interest in exploring issues of personal identity, especially as made manifest in sexual behavior. But he did not share their assumptions about how to express the modern self. In particular, he could not accept the possibility of a transparent linguistic medium that would supposedly make possible the undistorted representation of reality as perceived by the observant mind. Preferring to cultivate a highly visual, poetic style, he spent his career creating a wildly imaginative, mythopoeic universe situated far beyond the realistic confines of the plausible and the quotidian.

This is not to say that Kyōka's rejection of positivism flowed from a well-articulated philosophical position. His famous depictions of the uncanny resulted from his own emotional need for literary ritual and a language that could address the sense of loss and profound fear—of death, of disease, of dogs, of thunder—that plagued him throughout his life. Referring to his unflagging interest in emotion and monstrosity, he declared that "there are two supernatural powers in this world . . . the power of [the benevolent Buddhist deity] Kannon, and the power of evil spirits. In the face of either of these forces, human beings are powerless" (*Kyōka zenshū [KZ]*, 1940–1989, vol. 28, pp. 677–678). Kyōka was an author who needed to believe that literature could make possible the trespass of the living into the realm of the dead. Only there could they experience the possibilities of unconditional love and salvation, however implausible the circumstances of engagement might be.

Early Life and Education

Izumi Kyōka (given name, Kyōtarō) was born on 4 November 1873. The oldest of four children, he spent the first 16 years of his life in Kanazawa, a provincial castle town on the Japan Sea coast. His father, Izumi Seiji, was a craftsman of precious metals and a member of the city's artisan class, descendants of generations of craftsmen whom the wealthy Maeda clan had nurtured throughout their long reign in the Kaga domain. With the political and economic changes brought about by the Meiji Restoration of 1868, demand for the luxury items of Seiji's craft—intricately fashioned sake cups, elaborate hair pins, and the like—declined sharply, leaving the Izumi family in poverty. Even in these straitened conditions, however, Kyōka's father refused to take on projects he deemed unworthy of his abilities. Perhaps his uncompromising attitude provided a precedent for his son, who would later become a consummate craftsman of words, and equally stubborn about what he would and would not create.

Kyōka also owed much to his mother, Nakata Suzu. She was a native of Edo and the daughter of a musician for the Noh theater. Patronage of the theater also fell off dramatically following the Meiji Restoration, and her family, too, suffered financially. Upon her family's retreat to Kanazawa, she brought with her a library of illustrated fiction (or *kusazōshi*), which became Kyōka's entry into the world of imaginative letters. Long, serialized works such as Mantei Ōga's *Shaka hassō Yamato bunko* (The eight lives of Siddhartha, a Japanese library) left a lasting impression, even to the point of supplying much of the iconography that Kyōka would later draw upon as a writer. As an adult, he made a point of acquiring copies of the books that his mother once possessed; and he associated the often violent and monstrous images in these graphic books with his mother, who died on 24 December 1882, when he was only nine. Crushed by this loss, he came to spend the rest of his life trying to recapture his memories of her. Not only would he seek out and marry a woman like his mother, a geisha by the name of Itō Suzu, but he would also populate his writings with female characters who were reflections of her.

As a schoolboy, Kyōka enjoyed the companionship of women who became proxies for his mother: his maternal grandmother Meboso

Kite, a cousin Meboso Teru, a childhood girlfriend Yuasa Shige, and, interestingly, a woman from Tennessee named Francina Porter, who taught at the local Hokuriku Eiwa Gakkō. The school was established by Presbyterian missionaries from the United States who came at a time when there were few foreigners in Kanazawa. Kyōka studied there for three and a half years, concentrating on English. As one of his teachers, Miss Porter made a powerful impression, for he later wrote about a woman like her—fair and angelic, powerful yet fated to suffer—who transforms into a mother-figure as she lies dying upon her sickbed. Like the other women already named, she informed Kyōka's image of the typical heroine—usually in her mid-twenties, sexually attractive yet maternal and nurturing, slightly older or more experienced than the male characters who depend on her for their safety and salvation.

Kyōka left the Eiwa Gakkō in 1887. He tried to enter the Senmon Gakkō (soon to become the prestigious Fourth School and, eventually, Kanazawa University) but failed the mathematics portion of the examination. Kyōka went on to complete his education at a private boarding school owned and managed by a family friend. He read voraciously during this time, borrowing books from lending libraries and dreaming of someday becoming a writer. To aspire to a career as a novelist at this point in time was highly questionable, due to a continuing Confucian bias against fiction. Moreover, the *bundan* (that social complex of writers, publishers, and critics who created Meiji literary society) had yet to coalesce, and so the financial possibilities were also a question. These difficulties notwithstanding, he successfully lobbied his father and other family members, and on 28 November 1890 was allowed to set off for Tokyo.

Kyōka's specific reason for going up to the capital was to align himself with Ozaki Kōyō (1868–1903), who was one of the two leading writers of the day and a figure of considerable influence. When he arrived at the Shinbashi Station, however, the clamor of the crowds and the size of the city stole his courage away so completely that Kyōka did not actually arrange to meet Kōyō until 19 October 1891, almost a year later. In the meantime, rather than return home to Kanazawa, he wandered between Tokyo and Kamakura, relying on the kindness of others. The details of this year of wandering are hard to recover, but we do know that Kyōka was practically penniless. The personal knowledge of poverty and hunger that he gained at this time most certainly sharpened his sympathy toward the poor. Later, he consistently sided with the lower classes in his stories and plays, and his attitude toward the powerful and wealthy was almost always caustic.

Development of Kyōka's Archetype and Style

The noble poverty of a young man and the nurturing sacrifice of a slightly older woman is the subject of "Giketsu kyōketsu" (1894; Noble blood, heroic blood), Kyōka's first major work. The manuscript bleeds red with corrections, showing just how much Kōyō influenced Kyōka's early style. Because the novella was published jointly, many assumed that this story about a carriage driver, Murakoshi Kin'ya, and a street performer, Taki no Shiraito, was Kōyō's. But the figure of Shiraito, a woman who sacrifices all so that Kin'ya can pursue a law degree, is clearly Kyōka's creation. With Shiraito's help, Kin'ya rises from obscurity to prominence, eventually becoming a judge. In the tragic denouement, Kin'ya finds himself trapped in a situation where he must sentence Shiraito to death for a crime she has committed. Having fulfilled his social responsibility by passing harsh judgment against her, Kin'ya confirms his personal debt by taking his own life. By setting social obligation against personal emotion, Kyōka built upon a long-established theme of Tokugawa-period letters.

The dramatic possibilities of this tale were quickly exploited by others who adapted the story for the *shinpa* stage and also for cine-matic production. From the beginning, the linguistic richness of Kyōka's prose was often appreciated by the masses in a rather debased form, as script and screenwriters quickly churned out their simplified adaptations of his work. One result of this early effort to popularize "Giketsu kyōketsu" was the emergence of the resourceful and self-sacrificing Taki no Shiraito as an icon of Meiji popular culture.

Real fame did not come to Kyōka, though, until the critical reception of two short stories, "Yakō junsa" (1895; The night patrol) and "Gekashitsu" (1895; "The Surgery Room," 1996). These works were labeled *kannen shōsetsu* ("conceptual novels") by the writer and critic Shimamura Hōgetsu. "The Surgery Room" tells of yet another double suicide, but it does so critically and conceptually, hence the generic tag. It poses the question of whether or not the behavior depicted is morally acceptable. Is it right that Countess Kifune and Doctor Takamine should burn with passion for each other even though she is married to another man? "Religious thinkers of the world, I pose this question to you. Should these two lovers be found guilty and denied entrance into heaven?" (*KZ*, 1940–1989, vol. 2, p. 38; tr. p. 20). Kyōka's own answer is suggested in the way he highlights the intensity of their passion: after exchanging glances one day while walking in a park, neither the Countess nor Takamine can think of anyone else. Nine years later, near death, she finds herself on the operating table of this man for whom she has been so fervently pining. In a shocking display of emotion, she plunges Takamine's scalpel deep into her chest and dies knowing that he has not forgotten her. To the bitter end, she remains true to love, an absolute value within Kyōka's system of morality. The doctor similarly follows the dictates of true love by killing himself later that day.

In a famous article printed in the *Tokyo Nichinichi Shinbun* (Tokyo daily news), Aku-tagawa Ryūnosuke described Kyōka's sense of right and wrong as an "ethics based on poetic justice." The author's aestheticized sense of morality is indeed borne out by the way he ignored the critics and their calls for more social criticism. Rather than repeat the established pattern, he went on to write a series of imaginative and even fanciful stories in which the principal male figures are young boys. Some have suggested that Kyōka was following the lead of Higuchi Ichiyō, whose recently published "Takekurabe" (1894–1896; "Child's Play," 1981), a story about children coming to an awareness of their sexuality, had won the praise of Mori Ōgai and numerous others. In writing about a child's world, however, Kyōka was only developing what he had begun with "The Surgery Room." Needless to say, Hōgetsu and others did not appreciate how that story was not so much a burning critique of Meiji society as an early step toward Kyōka's creation of a narrative paradigm that would allow him to ritualize the practice of literature.

The best in this string of boy stories is "Kechō" (1887; A bird of many colors). It makes Kyōka's continued apotheosis of the mother figure much clearer. Gazing at a river on a rainy day, the young protagonist recounts an incident in which he was plucked from the water by a giant bird with brilliantly colored wings. He suspects that this mysterious bird was his mother, but its true identity remains an enigma. To discover the truth will require a flirtation with death. Enticed by the river that nearly killed him once before—water being a traditional image of violence, death, and metamorphosis—the boy risks its danger, knowing that his mother will save him once again. "Mother says to stay away, but I'm going to . . . fall into the river again. I know she'll pull me out. But, then again, maybe—No, I'll be fine. My mother is here. My mother was here" (*KZ*, vol. 3, p. 149).

The critics did not appreciate this strangely fractured and highly imagistic story. Many thought that Kyōka had reverted back to an earlier, thoroughly discounted age of implausible and irrelevant fiction. His interest in metamorphosis and monstrosity, so reminiscent of earlier Edo-period popular fiction, was strangely out of place in an age of realism and reason, even though Kyōka's richly figural

style was emerging just at that moment when he himself switched to the new, more colloquial idiom that had developed as a part of the *genbun'itchi* ("melding of literary and colloquial") movement. The dissonance caused by this simultaneous move in opposite directions—both toward and away from literariness as it had been established by the previous era—did not reach a satisfactory resolution until 1900 with Kyōka's writing of *Kōya hijiri* (1900; *The Holy Man of Mt. Kōya*, 1996). In this account of the trials of a young monk in training, Kyōka set down the archetype that had been slowly developing in his work. In this personal myth, a young (or otherwise sexually hesitant) male passes through a watery barrier in order to encounter an alluring yet maternal female figure. His movement toward her is also a trespass into the realm of death, violence, and mystery. Aided by the woman, who sacrifices herself for his sake, he is allowed to survive and to return from the journey, undeniably shaken but having learned something important about his own nature and about the deeper meaning of love.

The Holy Man of Mt. Kōya is one of the author's most well known and readable stories, largely because of the way the narrative takes the time to develop each element of the archetype. Here the important images of the myth—water, man, woman, forest, mountain—are introduced in ways that explain their relationships to each other with unusual clarity. The young priest crosses over a flooded road; he journeys deep into the heavily wooded mountains; he discovers an alluring yet maternal woman; he resists her temptations because of his priestly celibacy. At the story's climactic moment, when the young priest gazes at a waterfall and sees the woman's body being torn to pieces by the current, the clarifying mode of narration that has so carefully brought the reader along breaks down and is replaced briefly by a more lyrical, fractured style.

When I remembered how I had bathed with the woman in the headwaters of this stream, my imagination pictured her inside the falling water, now being swept under, now rising again, her skin disintegrating and scattering like flower petals amid a thousand unruly streams of water. I gasped at the sight, and immediately she was whole again—the same face, body, breasts, arms, and legs, rising and sinking, suddenly dismembered, appearing again.

(*KZ*, vol. 5, p. 539)

It was in this mode that Kyōka preferred to write during the years ahead. Having established the archetype, he continued to deploy its principle images as a shorthand to connect future stories with this larger metanarrative, thus allowing the imagery to develop the story rather than using the story to develop the images. Partly for this reason, his work is often hard to follow.

Another way to describe the change is to say that Kyōka became largely freed from thematic considerations from this point on. Knowing exactly what he wanted to write about, he was able to concentrate on the process of writing at the level of the word itself, exploring the metaphoric and metamorphic possibilities of language. To quote from Mishima Yukio's *Sakkaron* (Study of authors), Kyōka remembered the "*renga*-like leaps of association and the imagistic splendor of the Japanese language that modern Japanese literature had forgotten" and worked to "raise the Japanese idiom to an extravagant level, to its highest potential" (p. 560). In his fetishistic belief in the power of language, he collided with the naturalists who were coming to dominate the literary world with their call for a transparent linguistic medium that would allow for the precise and truthful description of an objectively observed reality. Although he did not see himself as espousing any particular ideology, and although he did not actively participate in the many literary debates or *ronsō* that marked the development of literary taste over the first half of the twentieth century, he did strike out against the naturalists. In their assertion that language ought to function as a tool, accurately representing the reality of the modern mind in its perception of the world "as it is" (*ari no mama*), the naturalists were compared to an archer who, rather than stand afar and let an arrow fly toward the target, prefers to walk up to the bull's-eye and stick the point in by hand. For Kyōka, the notion of linguistic transparency was not only an impossibility, but it denied the wonder (*myō*) of language that is the very essence of literature itself: "Words themselves are already an artificiality" (*KZ*, vol. 28, p. 694). Unfortunately for Kyōka, it was too easy for others to dismiss his anti-utilitarian regard for language as a fallback to an earlier, outdated time. For one thing, the improved social status of the Meiji writer came to depend on a seriousness of purpose that could only discount the seemingly frivolous and superficial literary pursuits of an earlier age. Slowly but surely, with the rise of this new pseudo-scientific vision of the world, Kyōka's chances for gaining widespread recognition changed. As naturalism rose in prominence, Kyōka was increasingly relegated to the periphery.

Kyōka's Mature Style

Kyōka's mature style emerged by the time of "Chūmonchō" (1901; The order book), a story that is as much a collection of images—snow, mirror, and knife—as it is a telling of the actions and thoughts that link the main characters—the geisha Owaka, who becomes possessed by the vengeful spirit of a woman named Onui, and the handsome Wakiya Kinnosuke, who is Onui's former lover. The influential naturalist critic and writer Masamune Hakuchō disliked the story's plot because to him it seemed little more than coincidental. Truly, the gap between Kyōka's standards of plausibility and that of the realists had already widened considerably by this time. While the fragmented structure of the story can be explained by the way its images refer to the already established archetype, the images themselves are not well developed within the story and do seem to occur randomly. More and more, Kyōka's best works after this date were oblique and fragmented tales that, like Noh librettos, pulled the past into the present through numerous flashbacks, through the use of multiple and non-omniscient narrators, and by way of the highly polysemic, visual texture of his poetic prose.

Assailed by the naturalists and deprived of the backing of Ozaki Kōyō, who died of stomach cancer in 1903, Kyōka began to experience difficulty in getting his work published. The death of his grandmother Meboso Kite also contributed to the mental and physical decline that eventually drove him from Tokyo to the more restful setting of Zushi, near Kamakura on the Shōnan Coast. There he and his wife Itō Suzu lived for the next four years in relative isolation. Kyōka described himself at this time as "able to eat nothing but gruel and potatoes" and "practically in a trance" (*KZ*, vol. 1, p. viii). In this state of mental confusion, he wrote some of his most masterful stories, including "Shunchū"/"Shunchū gokoku" (1906; "One Day in Spring," 1996) and "Kusa meikyū" (1908; The grass labyrinth). The mysteriously verdant Zushi provides a setting for both.

"One Day in Spring" revisits Chuang-tzu's famous butterfly anecdote (which posed the question "Was Chuang-tzu a man dreaming he was a butterfly or a butterfly dreaming it was a man?"), in which the boundaries between dream and reality are declared unknowable. A certain gentleman visits a temple tucked high in the hills overlooking the sea. From the lonely priest who presides over the dilapidated temple grounds, he hears an engrossing story of passion and madness. A little later, he encounters Tamawaki Mio, the beautiful temptress about whom he has just heard. Perhaps reflecting Kyōka's own mental confusion, the protagonist, referred to simply as "the wanderer," represents one of three versions of the same man.

The gentleman stood transfixed. Then someone quickly stepped forward, brushing his back as he passed. It was a dark shadow.

"Is someone else here?" he thought. But how could that be? And yet the shadow staggered onto the stage and sat down back to back with the woman. When it looked his way, the wanderer saw his own face. It was he.

"It was who?" The wanderer asked the priest, who was telling him the story.

"It was the gentleman himself. Later he told me, 'If that were really I on stage, I should have died there.' I remember how he sighed and turned pale."

(*KZ*, vol. 10, p. 284; tr. p. 113)

Here and elsewhere, Kyōka utilizes the possibilities of doppelganger to emphasize the ability of love and passion to both heighten and fracture one's sense of identity. In this case, the self-awareness expressed is not so much split and set against itself—which so often occurs in the numerous *kattō* ("conflict and confrontation") texts that were being produced by Shimazaki Tōson and others—as it is a construction of multiple selves—a wearing of numerous identities that looks back to early-modern paradigms and ahead to post-Freudian notions of identity.

No less concerned with self is "Kusa meikyū" (The grass labyrinth), another effective tale of yearning and wandering. (In terms of structure, the story closely follows the *jo, ha, kyū* (introduction, development, climax) pattern of a classical Noh play.) The protagonist, Hagoshi Akira, has been searching for five years to hear the song that his dead mother once sang. His travels bring him to a deserted mansion, long abandoned as a place of misery and death. Despite the obvious threat to his life, Hagoshi is compelled to trespass. He is assailed by spirits from the other side of the veil. But the purity of his motives spares him the destruction that would normally come to any "real" man. In the remarkable concluding scene, a number of spirits stand around Hagoshi as he sleeps, and they sing the sought-after song while batting a ball *(temari)* back and forth between them.

Their voices joined together in song
In the swamp a rising snake
Is thinking of the plans she'll make,
Young Princess of King Hachiman,
The daughter of cruel Hachiman.
In her hands two jewels she holds,

And on her feet are shoes of gold,
Cruel daughter of King Hachiman.

The walls and sliding doors become maple leaves, the sitting room a brocade spun from the ball. The thickly falling foliage surrounds the lantern and turns its glowing light into crimson. Cross-stitched into the color is the falling snow of countless hands, white here and white there. As their fingertips brush against the priest, his hands dance of their own accord.

(KZ, vol. 11, p. 330)

Again, at issue in this show of language is Kyōka's profound sense of loss and his compulsion to find answers to the enduring question of what can and cannot be gained through belief in myth, beauty, and narrative ritual. Perhaps Kyōka's use of such traditional material is one reason why, despite its experimental nature, his writings seem so grounded in past traditions.

We can clearly see the heroic influence of Noh in what many critics consider to be Kyōka's most perfectly structured story, *Uta andon* (1910; *The Song of the Troubadour*, 1990). This carefully crafted narrative builds toward the heroine's performance of a dance from the play *Ama* (The diver), which is appropriately about a woman who sacrifices herself so her son can survive and prosper. What makes the novella particularly satisfying is how it arrives at a denouement by way of two separate stories that finally come together as the hero of one substory unites with the heroine of the other. This shifting narrative focus between two different stories and two different sites has caused numerous critics to note a cinematic influence here. There had always been something dramatic and visual about Kyōka's style. Moreover, other writers, such as Tanizaki Jun'ichirō, had been adapting Kyōka's work for the cinema. In truth, Kyōka was fond of both the Noh theater (to which he gained exposure through his mother's relatives in Tokyo) and films, especially foreign ones. His writing both looks back to the Tokugawa-period and ahead to the present age of increasingly visual modes of narrative expression, and in doing so it provides a counterpoint to prevailing notions of premodern, modern, and postmodern.

Until now, I have stressed the strongly imaginative and even fantastic qualities of Kyōka's writing, but it would be misleading to characterize all of Kyōka's work in this way. Indeed, during his lifetime his most well known stories were those that were more easily accessible, or were made to be so, due to their conformity with stock melodramatic patterns. *Onna keizu* (1907; A woman's pedigree) is a rather straightforward and biographical narrative based on Kyōka's romance with Itō Suzu. The work dares to divulge Kōyō's contempt for her, as well as Kyōka's subtle but, it seems, unmistakable resentment of his mentor's interference. The novel is long and poorly structured, and, in this form, it was not widely read. But it contained a dramatic seed that was quickly planted by others as they adapted parts of the story for the stage, and in this form it has survived in the popular imagination. Kyōka himself was asked to write the crucial scene, "Yushima no keidai" (1914; The Yushima temple grounds), in which Hayase Chikara (modeled after Kyōka) and Otsuta (modeled after Suzu) bid each other a bitter farewell.

Hayase: I apologize. I bow my head to you.
Otsuta: So you're breaking it off? Is that it? That's what you say to a geisha, not to me. You might as well ask me to die. You might as well tell your Ivy [the "tsuta" of "Otsuta"] to shrivel up and blow away.

(KZ, vol. 26, p. 226)

As an indication of how well Kyōka could write in this more domestic vein when he wished to do so, this scene has since become a signature piece for the *shinpa* theater. As the representative part of the whole, it is still performed independently with regularity.

Kyōka's Plays

This sort of involvement with the stage allowed Kyōka to develop relationships with actors and playwrights, and his interactions with them eventually led to his extraordinary flurry of activity as a writer for the theater himself. Throughout the Taishō era, Kyōka found in the space of the stage many of the same things that W. B. Yeats sought in his flirtations with the Noh theater, including a realm for the supernatural and a territory for the ritual presence of lyrically conjured meaning. Kyōka had always been concerned with establishing such a space in his works of fiction. Indeed, one can probably say that his best works succeed precisely because they so effectively create just that sacred, magical sphere. In the case of the plays, Kyōka so readily accepted the stage as an already established otherworld that much of the tension that contributes to the mystery of the stories is lost. In some cases, the author's reliance on this shortcut is so wholehearted that the trespassive aspect of his aesthetic vision becomes severely diminished. Thus, a play such as *Kaijin bessō* (1913; *The Sea God's Palace*, 2000) comes across as rather ridiculous and even farcical. On the other hand, the stark two-act play *Yamabuki* (1923; Wild roses), which has never been performed to the author's knowledge, manages well in its absurdity to deliver a very Kyōkaesque message: in the end, even if one cannot distinguish reality from illusion, one can still derive some amount of comfort in doing one's work.

One play that does not stray very far from the trespassive techniques of the stories is *Yashagaike* (1913; *Demon Pond*, 2000). Unlike *The Sea God's Palace*, it meanders across the border between the familiar and the strange, the believable and the incredible, and gains dramatic tension because of this. The play is grounded in a nearly forgotten legend: if the village bell is not rung faithfully—once in the morning and once at night—a demon that has been contained in a lake situated above a mountain village will flee captivity, thus inundating the inhabitants below. Tension builds between the few who still believe and the many who do not. In the end, the believers—including two anthropologists, Hagiwara Akira and Yamazawa Gakuen (modeled after Kyōka's friend, the famous anthropologist Yanagita Kunio)—lose to the skeptics. The bell is not rung, and a flood occurs as the demon of the lake takes advantage of this lapse and flees to her lover's pond. Only Gakuen survives the deluge. He lives to provide a familiar point of condemnation for the crass, unfeeling patriarchal order that has so thoroughly rejected him and the things he holds dear.

The most famous of Kyōka's plays is *Tenshu monogatari* (1917; *The Castle Tower*, 2000). Like *Demon Pond*, it is also a negotiation between the supernatural and the mundane. But from the opening curtain, the eponymous castle tower is directly presented to the audience as a no-man's-land in a very literal sense. In this land, Princess Tomi dwells with her all-female retinue, far above the heartless world of men who are to be both pitied and condemned for their petty displays of power and violence. Princess Tomi's world is a space for the dispossessed. It is thoroughly uncanny and provides a decidedly Kyōkaesque perspective from which to look down upon the barbarous. Although men are not allowed to enter, the tower is breached by one young warrior, Zushonosuke, who, searching for his lord's wayward falcon, discovers Tomi's terrible yet comforting powers of love and beauty. Once he has come to know her, he becomes unfit for the world of men. Unable to understand what Zushonosuke has come to know, his fellow warriors try to kill him when he attempts to return to them. Ultimately, the only place of safety left for him is her castle tower.

Kyōka's abiding interest in the pursuit of a feminine ideal, as expressed in the figure of Princess Tomi and the many heroines who both preceded and followed her, has given to some an essentialized image of the suffering-yet-heroic Japanese woman. Predictably, Kyōka has been both praised and criticized for this idealization. During his lifetime, for instance, most of his loyal readers were women; and of this number, many appreciated his writings especially for their depictions of female suffering. To give just one example, the lesbian novelist Yoshiya Nobuko, writing in "Izumi-sensei no kakareru josei" (The women in Master Izumi's writings) in May 1926, described Kyōka as being exceptionally sympathetic to women:

> I believe that of all the writers working today the strongest feminist [feminisuto] among them is Izumi Kyōka. No other author writes about women so frequently. The warm sympathy he extends to them, his gentle praise, his sense of appreciation, and the strength of his passionate love for them are infinitely greater than the concern of politicians who champion women's participation in government. Many of his works praise beautiful, noble women who shine in body and spirit, and his understanding and observation of them is utterly complete.... I know of no other writer who is as inspired in his depiction of women.

(pp. 11–14)

Judged by the standards of Kyōka's own day, one might say that Kyōka's favoring of romance over marriage put him in the progressive camp. In his opinion, matrimony enslaved young women. It stole away their happiness and reduced them to property. On the other hand, it is also true that his obsessive apotheosis of female saviors required their unhappiness. In order to qualify for the privilege of saving men, they must endure more, suffer more. This seems to go beyond a simple expression of sympathy toward women. How is one to understand Kyōka's compulsion to witness the trauma and even torture of so many heroines in his fiction? In fact, even Kyōka was able to see that the carnage required by his own emotional survival was a lot to ask. But until this admission came, the sacrifice of beautiful women was a necessary and eagerly paid price.

Return to Prose Fiction

The intensity of Kyōka's quest for salutary powers in women gained near perfect expression in two works written toward the end of the Taishō period, when Kyōka's main interest turned once again to writing fiction. *Yukari no onna* (1919; Women of acquaintance) stands as his most comprehensive expression of the archetype. Reflecting a growing biographical interest, this lengthy novel is a sustained contemplation of a man's return to his childhood home. Almost all the women who had ever been important to the author—his wife Suzu; his mother; his cousin Meboso Teru; and his childhood sweetheart Yuasa Shige—are models for the work's unusually large number of heroines. What all these women have in common is their shared concern for the protagonist, Asagawa Reikichi, who is a thinly veiled proxy for Kyōka himself. He stands at the center of these relationships, loved by all. Together, they struggle on the side of the weak and against the powerful in one of the more politically nuanced novels of Kyōka's oeuvre.

The same ethos of poverty and struggle prevails in "Baishoku kamonanban" (1920; "Osen and Sōkichi," 1996). A remembrance of Kyōka's penniless year of wandering aimlessly in Tokyo, the story resembles "Giketsu kyōketsu" (Noble blood, heroic blood) in its treatment of a woman's dedication to and sacrifice for an otherwise helpless young man. The heroine, Osen, prostitutes herself in order to provide clothing and shelter for Sōkichi. She literally gives him her soul by blowing her breath into a folded paper crane that, so inspired, flies through the air and leads the young hero to the home of the wealthy family that takes him in and cares for him. Many years later, on a day of unseasonably heavy spring rain, they meet again. She is insane, en route to an asylum; he has become a famous physician, recently returned from abroad. Exercising his authority, he takes her to his private hospital, assuming responsibility for her care. In sympathy for her suffering, he enters her room with the blade that will end her life.

After the example of "The Surgery Room" (and alluding to the much earlier precedent of Tsuruga Wakasanojō's "Akegarasu yume no awa yuki" [c. 1772; The crow at dawn, a dream of thinly falling snow]), they end their lives in a double suicide.

Stubbornly pursuing such a pattern, Kyōka came to be dismissed as a man who had squandered his considerable linguistic talents on strangely outdated matters—vengeful spirits, monstrosities, and the like. In this unsympathetic environment, his literary survival was very much helped by a generation of younger writers who rallied to his support because he had had the courage to stand up to the naturalists and to pursue his own personal artistic vision regardless of the costs. Of course, they themselves had much to gain by surpassing their seniors in influence, and their support of Kyōka might be seen as a self-serving maneuver within a larger generational conflict. Still, it is undeniable that writers such as Akutagawa Ryūnosuke, Kawabata Yasunari, and Tanizaki Jun'ichirō—all vocal supporters of Kyōka—shared with him a respect for the free reign of the imagination and an appreciation for the well-chosen word. The *Akutagawa zenshū* (Complete works of Akutagawa) reprints Akutagawa's forward to the first edition of *Kyōka zenshū* (Complete works of Izumi Kyōka), published by Shun'yōdō in 1925, in which Akutagawa describes the hard-fought battle between the "master" (Sensei), Kyōka, and the naturalists.

With the rise of naturalism, the masses blindly followed the crowd. Delighting in the dust of this world, they saddened the crane that preferred to soar among the heights. Enamored of mud and sand, the naturalists frequently troubled the ancient dragon. Yet Sensei resisted. He fought against the decline of romanticism, faithfully taking upon himself the mantle of his mentor, Ozaki Kōyō. . . . We who make a living by crafting words cannot know the full value of a swift horse by simply hearing it neigh in the marketplace, yet countless are the times when we were encouraged by the sight of the white crane circling above the moors as we watched from afar. Now the divine wind has dispelled the fog, and what was once pushed off to the margins has become the center.

(*Akutagawa zenshū*, vol. 12, pp. 198–200)

If anyone could, the brilliant yet emotionally fragile Akutagawa was able to understand the depth of Kyōka's fear and his motivations for writing. While admiring Kyōka for the way he never lost his faith in language and literature, Akutagawa himself finally succumbed to his own anxiety and lack of faith. Shortly after the publication of the final volume of Kyōka's completed works, Akutagawa took his own life. When Kyōka visited the Akutagawa home upon hearing of his friend's death, he found the final volume of the completed works, just opened, there in his friend's study.

Kyōka's single-mindedness won him passionate supporters and equally determined detractors. Perhaps for this reason, defenders of Kyōka's work often overlook the way his sensibilities coarsened during the final decade or so of his career. His last masterpiece was "Mayu kakushi no rei" (1924; The ghost of matrimony), an engaging short story about a traveler's encounter with the uncanny. Perhaps no other work so clearly expresses the author's desire "not to describe reality as reality, but to pass through reality to reach a greater level of power" (*KZ*, vol. 28, p. 696). The story's gradual and steady accumulation of imagery leads to a flood of poetic language. Yet the destabilizing effect of this narrative—powered as it is by the protagonist Sakai Sankichi's masochistic fear of becoming prey to the woman/bird figure that looms throughout—signals both the fullness of the archetype and the end of its effectiveness. To the extent that the seduction described here is both horrible and unbearably attractive, Kyōka's male characters have, like Kyōka himself, matured considerably. Now more at home with sexual desire, they are no longer so hesitant. As such, they face a crisis. For if the women in Kyōka's world are no longer untouchable, how can the structure of the archetype continue to preserve the men who encounter them?

Abandonment of and Return to Archetype

Toward the end of his career, Kyōka's mythical framing of sexual passion did gain a certain degree of realism, and this shift, noticeable in the ways that relationships between men and women lose their earlier sense of idealism, helps to explain the loss of narrative coherence that one notices in later works. No longer guided by the archetype, novels such as *Sankai hyōbanki* (1929; Of the mountains and the sea) and *Yuki yanagi* (1937; The snow willow) largely fail as narratives because they lack the structuring principles that once gave coherence to Kyōka's tendency to ramble. However fragmented and elliptical the earlier stories might have been, they were still held together by their constant reference to the larger myth of salvation. In contrast, *Sankai hyōbanki* and *Yuki yanagi* are not held together in this way, and they do not succeed in establishing a new and satisfying method of giving coherence.

One might ask why Kyōka finally turned away from a formula that had sustained him for so long. Did he finally tire of the repetition? Or did his reasons for writing change in some fundamental way, so that he no longer needed the comfort that the archetype had provided? Perhaps one can locate a hint of a possible explanation in a comment made by Minakami Takitarō, Kyōka's lifelong friend and patron. Minakami held that Kyōka, in his old age, tried to retain his sexual vigor at all costs, to the extent that he did not seem to mature appropriately as an older man. Perhaps Kyōka's fineness of sensibility suffered as he came to feel the need to prove what had not been an issue earlier. Whatever the reason, Kyōka's late attempts to write about sexually aggressive men are hard to defend from a literary point of view.

Kyōka must have sensed the futility of this detour from a pattern that had served him so well for so long. In the final months of his life,

and against the protestations of his wife, Suzu, who knew the physical toll that writing exacted of him, Kyōka managed to grind out one last story that squarely returned him to the archetype. Entitled "Rukōshinsō" (1939; The heartvine), this work stands as a final memory of Kanazawa and of that horrible moment in 1894 when Kyōka himself nearly committed suicide by jumping into the black waters of the city's castle moat. At that moment, so many years earlier, his father had just died, and Kyōka suddenly had to shoulder responsibility for his penniless family. Called home from Tokyo, he feared that his dream of becoming a writer had just been ruined, and he considered ending his life. Sensing the danger, Kōyō wrote an impassioned letter from Tokyo, berating him for entertaining thoughts of death and encouraging him to endure the trials that would someday make him a great writer:

> To be born amid crumbling walls in a ramshackle house, to chew bread and drink water, is this not heaven? Enjoy that heaven! A great poet is one whose soul is like a diamond. Fire cannot burn it, water cannot drown it, no sword can pierce it, no cudgel can smash it. How much less, then, can it be damaged by hunger for a bowl of rice!"

(Muramatsu Sadataka, 1966, pp. 85–86)

Despite Kōyō's encouragement, Kyōka probably would have killed himself had it not been for the intervention of a young woman. The details are not clear. In one account, his cousin Meboso Teru discovered him missing from his bed and ran to the moat to rescue him. In another, an unnamed young woman emerged from the darkness to jump into the moat just as Kyōka was about to cast himself in. Kyōka had written of such an event earlier in a minor story called "Shōsei yahanroku" (1885; The night bell tolls). Now, in the last months before his death, he returned to the scene again. But this time he did so with remorse for having survived at the expense of so many young women who, in his many literary creations, had paid such a dear price for the privilege of saving the men who required their love. In this sense, "Rukōshinsō" culminates a lifetime of artistic pursuit. A depth of sorrow and a mature understanding of sacrifice finally complete Kyōka's endless fight against fear and dread. For Mishima Yukio, this somber yet strikingly imaginative story of an old man's visit to a temple graveyard would become the very embodiment of the medieval dramatist Zeami's aesthetic ideal of the flower or *hana*. Within months after its completion, Kyōka, the redeemed artist, died of lung cancer on 7 September 1939.

Standing

From the vantage point of the twenty-first century, one can see that Kyōka's artistic vision has survived remarkably well. Perhaps his eccentricity has worked to his advantage: the space captured by his fictive imagination is so rarified that it has not aged as have, for instance, the confessional I-novels of his naturalist detractors. As Donald Keene asserts in *Dawn to the West*, "no other author of modern Japan is less likely to be affected by the changing tastes of the times." And yet the evolution of technology and culture has surely played a role in making Kyōka's gothic imagination both more appealing and more accessible to contemporary readers and viewers. Having passed through the horrors of total war, the wrenching changes of the Occupation, and the technological and social developments brought about by decades of high-growth economics, Japan has finally caught up with Kyōka's sensibilities. Mishima correctly predicted that a resurgence of interest in Kyōka's work would occur in the postwar period, and that it would be led by performances of his more experimental plays—bizarre pieces such as *The Castle Tower* and *The Sea God's Palace*. Plays that were simply too strange to find an audience during the author's lifetime finally appeared with some regularity in the 1970s. Throughout the 1980s and 1990s, interest in Kyōka's work was kept alive by the famous *onnagata* ("female impersonator") Bandō Tamasaburō,

who played the leading female roles in a number of the plays and, more recently, turned to directing and producing cinematic adaptations of pieces such as "The Surgery Room" (1991) and *The Castle Tower* (1995). His understanding of Kyōka's work is excellent, more deeply informed than that of either Shinoda Masahiro or Suzuki Seijun, whose films *Demon Pond* (1979) and *Kagerō-za* (1981) are less successful in capturing the essence of the works they draw upon. Indeed, the latter two films leave one wondering if this renewed interest in Kyōka's world is anything more than a growing appetite for heightened visual effects.

Finally, even if film and video technology have made it easier for people living now to see representations of Kyōka's rich imagery, the linguistic difficulties posed by his texts have certainly not lessened with time. For today's reader, the difficulties of reading his words are real. Annotation is helpful for those wishing to understand the full nuances of this or that kimono fabric or to be privy to what has been left out at the numerous points of ellipses that one encounters at all levels. Such difficulties notwithstanding, his work continues to be bought, read, and seriously studied, continuing as a significant influence upon contemporary writers as diverse as Kōno Taeko, Tsushima Yūko, and even Murakami Haruki. Now that translations of his work are starting to appear in various languages (including contemporary Japanese!), one can anticipate a widening of the circle of readers who will finally be able to gain access to this singularly fearful and brilliant artist whom Mishima Yukio crowned as the only true genius among modern Japanese writers.

Selected Bibliography

PRIMARY WORKS

COLLECTED WORKS

Kyōka zenshū (Complete works of Izumi Kyōka). 15 vols. Shun'yōdō, 1925. Reprinted, Emutei Shuppan, 1994.
Kyōka zenshū. Iwanami Shoten, 28 vols., 1940–1942. 29 vols., 1973–1976. 30 vols., 1989. (Abbreviated in citations as *KZ*.)

NOVELS AND SHORT STORIES

"Giketsu kyōketsu." *Yomiuri Shinbun,* 1–30 November 1894. Reprinted in *KZ.* Vol. 1. Tokyo: Iwanami Shoten, 1940. Reprinted, 1973.

"Gekashitsu." *Bungei Kurabu* 6 (June 1895). Reprinted in *KZ.* Vol. 2. Tokyo: Iwanami Shoten, 1942. Reprinted, 1973. Trans. by Charles S. Inouye as "The Surgery Room." In *Japanese Gothic Tales.* Honolulu: University of Hawaii Press, 1996. Pp. 11–20.

Teriha kyōgen. Yomiuri Shinbun, 14 November–23 December 1896. Reprinted in *KZ.* Vol. 2. Tokyo: Iwanami Shoten, 1942. Reprinted, 1973.

"Kechō." *Shinchō Gekkan* 1 (April 1897). Reprinted in *KZ.* Vol. 3. Tokyo: Iwanami Shoten, 1941. Reprinted, 1974.

Kōya hijiri. Shin Shōsetsu 5 (February 1900). Reprinted in *KZ.* Vol. 5. Tokyo: Iwanami Shoten, 1940. Reprinted, 1974. Trans. by Charles S. Inouye as *The Tale of the Wandering Monk.* New York: The Limited Editions Club, 1995. Reprinted as *The Holy Man of Mt. Kōya.* In *Japanese Gothic Tales.* Honolulu: University of Hawaii Press, 1996. Pp. 21–72.

"Chūmonchō." *Shin Shōsetsu* 6 (April 1901). Reprinted in *KZ.* Vol. 6. Tokyo: Iwanami Shoten, 1941. Reprinted, 1974.

"Shunchū" and "Shunchū gokoku." *Shin Shōsetsu* 11 (November 1906). Reprinted in *KZ.* Vol. 10. Tokyo: Iwanami Shoten, 1940. Reprinted, 1974. Trans. by Charles S. Inouye as "One Day in Spring." In *Japanese Gothic Tales.* Honolulu: University of Hawaii Press, 1996. Pp. 73–140.

Onna keizu. Yamato Shinbun, 1 January–28 April 1907. Reprinted in *KZ.* Vol. 10. Tokyo: Iwanami Shoten, 1940. Reprinted, 1974.

"Kusa meikyū." Tokyo: Shun'yōdō, 1908. Reprinted in *KZ.* Vol. 11. Tokyo: Iwanami Shoten, 1941. Reprinted, 1974.

Uta andon. Shin Shōsetsu 15 (January 1910). Reprinted in *KZ.* Vol. 12. Tokyo: Iwanami Shoten, 1942. Reprinted, 1974. Trans. by Stephen W. Kohl as *The Song of the Troubadour.* Kanazawa: Committee Office, Committee of the Translation of the Works of Izumi Kyōka, 1990.

Yukari no onna. Fujin Gahō, 1 January 1919–1 February 1921. Reprinted in *KZ.* Vol. 19. Tokyo: Iwanami Shoten, 1942. Reprinted, 1975.

"Baishoku kamonanban." *Ningen* 2 (May 1920). Reprinted in *KZ.* Vol. 20. Tokyo: Iwanami Shoten, 1941. Reprinted, 1975. Trans. by Charles S. Inouye as "Osen and Sōkichi." In *Japanese Gothic Tales.* Honolulu: University of Hawaii Press, 1996. Pp. 141–158.

"Mayu kakushi no rei." *Kuraku* 1 (May 1924). Reprinted in *KZ.* Vol. 22. Tokyo: Iwanami Shoten, 1940. Reprinted, 1975.

"Rukōshinsō." *Chūō Kōron* 54 (July 1939). Reprinted in *KZ.* Vol. 24. Tokyo: Iwanami Shoten, 1940. Reprinted, 1975.

PLAYS

Yashagaike. First produced in Tokyo at Hongōza, July 1916.

Tenshu monogatari. First produced in Tokyo at Shinbashi Enbujō, November 1951.

Kaijin bessō. First produced in Tokyo at Kabukiza, August 1955.

ENGLISH TRANSLATIONS

Inouye, Charles S. *Three Tales of Mystery and Imagination: Japanese Gothic by Izumi Kyōka.* Kanazawa: Takakuwa Bijutsu Insatsu, 1992.

———. *The Tale of the Wandering Monk.* New York: The Limited Editions Club, 1995.

———. *Japanese Gothic Tales by Izumi Kyōka.* Honolulu: University of Hawaii Press, Vol. 1, 1996; Vol. 2, in progress.

Kohl, Stephen W. *The Saint of Mt. Kōya; The Song of the Troubadour.* Kanazawa: Committee Office, Committee of the Translation of the Works of Izumi Kyōka, 1990.

Poulton, M. Cody. *Of a Dragon in the Deep.* Kanazawa: Takakuwa Bijutsu Insatsu, 1987.

———. *Spirits of Another Sort: The Plays of Izumi Kyōka.* Ann Arbor: Center for Japanese Studies, University of Michigan, 2000.

Seidensticker, Edward. "A Tale of Three Who Were Blind." In *Modern Japanese Literature.* Edited by Donald Keene. New York: Grove Press, 1956. Pp. 242–253.

FILMS BASED ON THE WORKS OF IZUMI KYŌKA

Yashagaike. Directed by Shinoda Masahiro. 1979.

Kagerō za. Directed by Suzuki Seijun. 1981.

Gekashitsu. Directed by Bandō Tamasaburō. 1991.

Tenshu monogatari. Directed by Bandō Tamasaburō. 1995.

PAPERS

Most of Kyōka's manuscripts are held in the Rare Book Room of the Keiō University Library in Tokyo on the Mita campus. A smaller number of manuscripts, along with certain personal effects and letters, can be seen at Ishikawa Prefecture's Museum of Modern Literature in Kanazawa. A replica of Kyōka's study, which includes portions of his library, has been built in the old Keiō library, also on the Mita campus. A collection of first printings of Kyōka's monographs is also held there in the Mita Bungaku Collection. Izumi Natsuki, Kyōka's adopted daughter, keeps the bulk of the author's notebooks, photographs, and personal effects at her residence in Zushi. The most accessible collection of magazines and newspapers in which Kyōka's work first appeared is the Kindai Bunko at the Shōwa Joshi Daigaku in Tokyo. Other collections can be found at the Kindai Bungakukan, the Chūō Toritsu Toshokan, and the Kokkai Toshokan, all in Tokyo.

SECONDARY WORKS

CRITICAL AND BIOGRAPHICAL STUDIES

Akutagawa Ryūnosuke. "Kyōka zenshū ni tsuite." In *Akutagawa zenshū* (Complete works of Akutagawa). Vol. 12. Tokyo: Iwanami Shoten, 1978. Pp. 198–200.

Carpenter, Juliet. "Izumi Kyōka: Meiji-Era Gothic." *Japan Quarterly* 32:154–158 (April–June 1984).

Inouye, Charles S. "Kyōka and Language." *Harvard Journal of Asiatic Studies* 56, no. 1:5–34 (1996).

Kasahara Nobuo. *Izumi Kyōka: bi to erosu no kōzō.* Tokyo: Shibundō, 1976.

———. *Izumi Kyōka: erosu no mayu.* Tokyo: Kokubunsha, 1988.

———. *Hyōden Izumi Kyōka.* Tokyo: Hakuchisha, 1995.

Kawabata Yasunari. "Izumi Kyōka no Kushigeshū nado." In *Kyōka ron shūsei.* Tokyo: Rippū Shobō, 1983. Pp. 204–207.

Keene, Donald. "Izumi Kyōka." In *Dawn to the West.* New York: Holt, Rinehart and Winston, 1984. Pp. 202–219.

Kindai bungaku kenkyū sōsho. Vol 45. Tokyo: Shōwa Joshi Daigaku Kindai Bunka Kenkyūsho, 1977. (An index to reviews and articles written on Kyōka's work during his lifetime.)

Kobayashi Hideo. "Kyōka no shi sono ta." *Bungaku* 2 (November 1930). Reprinted in *Bungei tokuhon: Izumi Kyōka.* Tokyo: Kawade Shobō Shinsha, 1981. Pp. 15–19.

Mishima Yukio. "Ozaki Kōyō, Izumi Kyōka." In *Sakkaron.* Tokyo: Chūō Kōronsha, 1970. Reprinted in *Mishima Yukio zenshū.* Vol. 33. Tokyo: Shinchōsha, 1976. Pp. 553–567.

Mita Hideaki. *Izumi Kyōka no bungaku.* Tokyo: Ōfūsha, 1976.

Muramatsu Sadataka. *Izumi Kyōka.* Tokyo: Bunsendō, 1966.

———. *Izumi Kyōka kenkyū.* Tokyo: Tōjūsha, 1974.

———. *Izumi Kyōka jiten.* Tokyo: Yūseidō, 1982.

———. *Ajisai kuyōshō—waga Izumi Kyōka.* Tokyo: Shinchōsha, 1988.

Noguchi Takehiko, ed. *Izumi Kyōka.* Kanshō Nihon gendai bungaku. Vol. 3. Tokyo: Kadokawa, 1982.

———. *Izumi Kyōka.* Shinchō Nihon bungaku arubamu. Tokyo: Shinchōsha, 1985.

Poulton, M. Cody. *Spirits of Another Sort: The Plays of Izumi Kyōka.* Ann Arbor: Center for Japanese Studies, University of Michigan, 2000.

Tanaka Reigi. "Izumi Kyōka sankō bunken mokuroku (zasshi no bu)." *Dōshisha Kokubungaku* 13: 102–136 (March 1978). (Journal articles and reviews, 1925–1980.)

———. "Izumi Kyōka sankō bunken mokuroku (zasshi no bu) hoi." *Izumi Kyōka Kenkyū* 5:72–83 (1980). (Journal articles and reviews, 1928–1980.)

———. "Izumi Kyōka sankō bunken mokuroku (zasshi no bu) hoi 2." In *Ronshū Izumi Kyōka.* Tokyo: Yūseidō, 1987. Pp. 223–261. (Journal articles and reviews, 1980–1987.)

———. "Izumi Kyōka sankō bunken mokuroku (zasshi no bu) hoi 3." In *Ronshū Izumi Kyōka.* Tokyo: Yūseidō, 1991. Pp. 224–247. (Journal articles and reviews, 1987–1990.)

Tanizaki Jun'ichirō. "Junsui ni 'Nihonteki' na 'Kyōka sekai.' " In *Tanizaki Jun'ichirō zenshū.* Vol. 22. Tokyo: Chūō Kōronsha, 1968. Pp. 336–338.

Tanizawa Eiichi, Watanabe Ikk, eds. *Kyōkaron shūsei.* Tokyo: Rippū Shobō, 1983.

Teraki Teihō. *Hito, Izumi Kyōka.* Tokyo: Nihon Tosho Sentā, 1983.

Tōgō Katsumi, ed. *Izumi Kyōka.* Nihon bungaku kenkyū shiryō sōsho. Tokyo: Yūseidō, 1980.

———. *Izumi Kyōka: bi to gensō.* Nihon bungaku kenkyū shiryō shinshū. Vol. 12. Tokyo: Yūseidō, 1991.

———. *Izumi Kyōka.* Gunzō Nihon no sakka. Vol. 5. Tokyo: Shōgakkan, 1992.

Waki Akiko. *Gensō no ronri: Izumi Kyōka no sekai.* Tokyo: Kōdansha, 1974.

Yoshimura Hirotō. *Izumi Kyōka geijutsu to byōri.* Tokyo: Kongō Shuppan Shinsha, 1970.

———. *Izumi Kyōka no sekai: gensō no byōri.* Tokyo: Makino Shuppan, 1983.

———. *Makai e no enkinhō: Izumi Kyōka ron.* Tokyo: Kindai Bungei Sha, 1991.

Yoshiya Nobuko. "Izumi-sensei no kakareru josei." In *Shin Shōsetsu,* May 1926, pp. 11–14.

MISHIMA YUKIO
1925–1970

DENNIS WASHBURN

MISHIMA YUKIO is one of the most important writers of the postwar era in Japan, yet his reputation remains a subject of controversy. He was brilliantly prolific, in just over two decades churning out an enormous body of work in a wide range of forms: novels, plays, short stories, poetry, and criticism. Mishima's career, however, was not confined to his work as a literary artist. He was among the first Japanese writers to gain an international audience, and his commercial and critical success gave him the status of a celebrity. Mishima exploited the freedom that came with his status to assume a variety of other public roles. Starting out as a literary aesthete, he transformed himself into a boxer, a bodybuilder, and a martial arts devotee. He acted in films and plays and assumed the guise of a cultural critic lamenting the state of postwar Japanese society. He eventually became a political ideologue who created his own private military group devoted to a return to rule by the emperor.

Given his idiosyncratic right-wing views and his penchant for publicity stunts, it is hardly surprising that judgments of his work should be so conflicted. In a way, Mishima brings out the worst in some of his readers. All too often those outside Japan have looked uncritically upon Mishima's works and his antics as the embodiment of Japanese culture. Conversely, some Japanese critics have taken the worst aspects of the international reception of Mishima as confirmation of their belief that his literature is an anomaly, and that interest in him is proof that Western readers will never truly understand Japanese culture.

Looking back over his career, it appears that reactions to his literature have always been colored in one way or another by the suspicion that as a writer Mishima is playing a role—a suspicion that forces the reader to pause when considering the seriousness of the work. There is something of the poseur about Mishima, creating the impression of an emptiness at the core of his art and of his being. It is regrettable that the propensity for role-playing, which Mishima exhibited throughout his life, has led some to devalue his achievements. For it is not at all unreasonable to make the claim that Mishima was the most accomplished Japanese writer of the second half of the twentieth century, and that a number of his works may legitimately be listed among the most important of modern world literature. This is not to make a claim for the bulk of his writing, however, which suffered from the demands imposed by the role of literary savant. Nonetheless, it is possible to reconcile the serious and superficial aspects of his career by recognizing that

Mishima embraced the notion that all of his narratives, his literary works as well as the roles he assumed in life, were created, and thus empty at the core. The almost desperate willingness of Mishima to exploit his celebrity was also the wellspring of his literary genius.

Early Life and First Writings

Mishima Yukio was born Hiraoka Kimitake in Tokyo on 14 January 1925, the oldest of three children in a middle-class family. His father, Azusa, was a midlevel bureaucrat who served in the Bureau of Fisheries of the Agriculture Ministry. His mother, Shizue Hashi, was the daughter of a family of neo-Confucian educators.

The bare facts of his family background sound rather pedestrian laid out in this manner, but his upbringing was far from normal. The Hiraoka family was beset by financial problems caused by Mishima's paternal grandfather, Jotarō. Moreover, the relationship between his grandparents was strained and difficult. Mishima's paternal grandmother, Natsuko, prided herself on her samurai ancestry—a lineage that Mishima himself would later point to with pride—and she had never been happy with her arranged marriage to a man who, in her eyes, came from lower stock. Her husband's financial ineptitude and serial infidelity were further blows, and she was often difficult to deal with. Worsening her situation were a number of physical and psychological problems, some of which were brought on by venereal disease that she had contracted from her husband.

The situation in the household in 1925 was thus volatile. On the fiftieth day following his birth, right after the customary forty-nine days of ritual abstinence, Natsuko took possession of the infant Kimitake. The supposed reason for this act was that the parents lived on the second floor of the house, and the stairs might be a danger to the child. Thus, Mishima was separated from his parents and spent the first twelve years of his life under the strict control and obsessive scrutiny of his ill and unstable grandmother.

The environment of Mishima's upbringing seems obviously unwholesome, and in fact, he grew up a frail, weak child given to bouts of illness that Mishima himself later described as psychosomatic in nature. He was also a bookish, effeminate boy who early developed a taste for fantasy and imaginative escape through role-playing. Mishima seems to have been aware from a young age that his circumstances were strange, and there is no doubt that his early upbringing had a profound effect on his entire career, in that he developed a marked, near-obsessive tendency for self-reflection and introspection.

At the age of six Mishima entered the Gakushūin, the Peers' School that had been established in 1877 for the education of the children of the imperial family and the peerage that was newly created after the Meiji Restoration in 1868. Mishima came from a commoner family, but Natsuko had insisted that her grandson attend the school, claiming that her lineage entitled him to admission. In fact, by 1931 almost a third of the students at Gakushūin were commoners, so there was nothing extraordinary about Mishima's enrollment.

Despite the constraints imposed on him at home, Mishima did well academically and showed a precocious talent for composition. This talent began to flourish when his grandmother relinquished control on his twelfth birthday and he entered the middle school at Gakushūin. That same year he went to live with his parents, who had earlier moved to a separate residence, and his mother gave strong encouragement to his literary endeavors. At school he was given formal guidance by his Japanese literature teacher, Shimizu Fumio, a minor figure who had connections in the literary world through his work on the journal *Bungei bunka* (Literary culture).

The main influences on Mishima during his school years were two poets, Tachihara Michizō, a classicist, and Itō Shizuo; the writers of the Nihon Rōman-ha (the Japanese romanticists); and two Western authors, Rainer Maria Rilke and Oscar Wilde. Mishima had an affinity for romantic, decadent lyricism, a reflection of Natsuko's tastes, that he expressed in a range of juvenilia he published in the school journal. In 1941 he wrote a short prose piece, "Hanazakari no mori" ("A Forest in Full Bloom," 1997), that gave a clear indication of his potential. This work, which was published in *Bungei bunka*, is a meditation on ancestors and memories. Mishima later dismissed the piece as a youthful and pompous imitation of a Rilkean novel. Nevertheless, there are many passages that give tantalizing evidence of Mishima's talent. For example, it is hard not to detect the first inklings of the style and imagery that would become the hallmarks of his mature work when we read a line such as the following: "Just as the glow of sunset foreshadows the invasion of night, the end of something occurs in a moment of eternal time, a beautiful instant of tension, like extremely still water, which at the height of tension and fear flickeringly maintains itself just as it is, resisting the slightest flaw—straining to maintain 'perfection,' if for only one second" (*Mishima Yukio zenshū [MYZ]*, vol. 1, p. 137; tr. p. 344).

It was the publication of "A Forest in Full Bloom" that led to the creation of his pen name. Mishima admired the poet Itō Sachio, and because the name Itō is also the name of a famous resort in Shizuoka prefecture, it was decided by his mentors that Kimitake would use the name of another famous resort, Mishima, which was known for its views of Mount Fuji. The name Yukio was chosen apparently because of its metrical similarity to Sachio. The use of a pen name was to protect the young man's privacy, but it also marked the special regard in which the teenage writer was held.

Over the next few years, as World War II intensified, Mishima began to expand his circle of literary and intellectual acquaintances. He met Yasuda Yojūrō, a leading figure in the Rōman-ha and a well-known polemicist, and Itō Shizuo; as a result of his contacts he became more deeply interested in classical literary forms, including the Nō drama. Mishima graduated from Gakushūin in 1944 at the top of his class and received a silver watch from the emperor, who presented it in person. Mishima would always look on this occasion as a highlight of his life. Another important event took place the following month with the publication of a collection of his stories, including "A Forest in Full Bloom." It is often noted that the publication of this work in wartime, when paper shortages were severe, was an unusual distinction. The print run of 4,000 soon sold out, suggesting the hunger of the public for a work not about the war and the approval of the censors for a work that was considered safe subject matter.

Early in 1944 Mishima passed the physical examination for conscription at his father's ancestral home of Shikata in Hyōgo prefecture, and he took part in military training. After graduation he was subject to the draft under the general mobilization that now included students. When he went back to Shikata to be inducted, he was ill, and the doctor misdiagnosed him as having tuberculosis. Mishima was thereafter exempted from service, but as part of the labor mobilization he was sent to live and work at a naval arsenal. He ended up working in the base library, and with time off for illness he was able to concentrate on writing and study until the war ended in August 1945.

The Creation of a Literary Persona

In the immediate postwar years Mishima confronted a number of difficulties in his effort to establish himself as a writer. His first mentors were relatively minor figures, and many of the more famous associates of the Rōman-ha were either purged or ostracized following Japan's defeat. In addition, the collapse of the military government brought with it a brief resurgence of the Left, and the tastes prevailing in the late 1940s tended toward writing that was politically aware and socially engaged—qualities that were not in harmony with Mishima's dreamy, decadent sensibility and apolitical leaning.

For all that, even though Mishima struck the pose of an aesthete, he was a young man on the make, and he was not shy about seeking out established writers to find a new mentor or sponsor to promote him. He courted Itō Shizuo for a while, but Itō apparently could not stand him personally or professionally. Nakamura Mitsuo, who would later become a close associate, at first thought he had no talent at all. Mishima called on the distinguished writer Satō Haruo as well, but he abruptly dropped his pursuit of Satō when he met the future Nobel laureate Kawabata Yasunari in January 1946. Mishima brought two stories, "Chūsei" (The Middle Ages) and "Tabako" (Cigarettes), to that meeting, and at Kawabata's recommendation both were published in the journal *Ningen* (Humanity) later that year.

The years 1946 and 1947 were harsh ones in Japan, and Mishima's self-absorbed work struck some as out of place in a world where the need to address pressing social and economic problems appeared to be far more appropriate aims for literary activity. The prestige and authority of the Left at this time worked in favor of certain styles and subjects, and that was a constraint on Mishima. However, there were other important trends, represented by the work of Shiina Rinzō, Ōoka Shōhei, Noma Hiroshi, and Dazai Osamu, which shared elements of deep introspection and a concern with finding personal meaning, identity, and reintegration into society in the face of postwar despair. Thus, even though Mishima's early lyrical evocations of despair and death were criticized as forced and attenuated, the situation in the literary world was rather fluid and not entirely hostile to a writer with great ambitions.

In late 1944 Mishima had been accepted as a student at the prestigious school of jurisprudence at Tokyo Imperial University (now Tokyo University). He graduated in 1947 and accepted an appointment in the Ministry of Finance. He left the prestige and security of this position after less than a year to concentrate on his literary career. That same year he joined a coterie of writers associated with the journal *Kindai Bungaku* (Modern literature), an unusual move, given the magazine's leftist political orientation. However, the motivation for joining was certainly a pragmatic one dictated by his desire to become a writer. In 1948 he published his first novel, *Tōzoku* (Thieves). Set in the mid-1930s, the story presents the lives of a fashionable group of upper-class youth. The protagonist is Akihide, an idealized version of Mishima himself as a student. Akihide has an affair with a beautiful socialite, Yoshiko, but their relationship is discovered and broken off by Yoshiko's parents, and Yoshiko finally rejects Akihide's pleas that she marry him. He then resolves that death is his destiny, and he enters into a pact with another young woman, Kiyoko, who also has been jilted by her true love. Because the two see in one another phantom reflections of their ideal lost loves, they decide to marry and then commit suicide on their wedding night.

This first novel did not receive favorable notices and did not sell well. Like much of Mishima's youthful work, the story not only is over the top, but also shows the explicit influence of other writers—in this case Raymond Radiguet, a writer whose work fascinated Mishima. As he did with other works that did not live up to his expectations, Mishima dismissed the novel as a mere exercise. But here again, as with "A Forest in Full Bloom," it is not hard to find in *Tōzuku* a continuity in his development that would reach its first, and perhaps fullest, expression in his next novel, *Kamen no kohuhaku* (1949; *Confessions of a Mask*, 1958).

Confessions of a Mask is the fulfillment of Mishima's precocious promise and the work that established him as a major figure in Japan's postwar literary scene. The complexity of the narrative arises from the nature of the confessional form. As the title suggests, it is not clear if this confession is true or false, and the ambiguity is important to the conception of the work. The story is based closely on the details of Mishima's childhood and youth, but at the heart of the narrative is a protagonist whose identity is defined by the ambiguities that are inherent to a confession. The novel is the account of a young man who, tormented by his growing awareness of his homosexuality, strives to mask the real self that makes him different and thus isolated. However, the narrator is so self-aware and so critical of his stratagems to hide his real identity that he cannot tolerate those self-delusions. The endlessly regressive self-exposure of the narrative, which reduces self-identity to nothing more than a mask, is the insoluble problem that the narrator must confront; but rather than try to overcome this dilemma, the narrator identifies what he takes to be his true nature not only in his homosexual longings, but also in the unstable act of self-exposure, in which the real presence of identity always slips away. The narrator describes his method of self-analysis: "my powers of introspection had a structure that defied one's imagination, just like those circles made by twisting a long narrow piece of paper once, and then pasting the ends together. What you think is the outer surface turns out to be the inner. And what you take to be the inner surface is really the outer" (MYZ, vol. 3, pp. 291–292; revised from tr. p. 177).

The paradox that confronts the narrator when he tries to define his identity is given wider significance by his questioning of the way in which all people create their identities. The narrator gains honesty and credibility by his self-questioning, but at the same time he forces himself and the reader to see that self-questioning as just another pose or mask. The mere utterance of the paradox of an individual who cannot speak of his true identity does nothing to resolve that dilemma. For example, at the beginning of chapter 3 the narrator tells us that the idea that life is a stage, a kind of dramatic performance, became an obsession with him, and that he came to believe that life was nothing more than assuming roles. Accordingly, when he begins to be troubled by what he sees as his different sexuality, he looks for models to define himself as a "normal" boy. At this point in his life his early tendency to define himself in terms of the literature he

has read becomes pronounced. The narrator's dissociation and inability to connect with others is explicitly connected to the literary quality of his life, and he relies on fiction to learn about normal behavior. He pretends to be the same as the other boys, but the desires that drive them, especially their sexual desire for women, are beyond the vocabulary of his self-created identity, because he suffers from what he calls a deficiency in the power of his mental associations. If his confession can be reduced to the act of donning a mask, then that implies that all efforts to define the self are empty and illusory. When self-awareness becomes an end unto itself, then meaning spirals forever inward, like the narrative structure of *Confessions of a Mask*, making genuine knowledge of the self impossible.

At one point the narrator claims to desire death as a way to conceal his difference from others. The appeal of death is its promise of nothingness, its erasure of the divide between the narrator's perception of his "abnormal" self and the "normal" reality of the world. Yet when he has the chance to seek out death at the time he is drafted into the army, he receives a medical discharge on the basis of a misdiagnosis of a lung inflammation as tuberculosis. By accepting what he knows to be false, he rules out the possibility of death in war. This failure to embrace death complicates the narrator's already severely conflicted identity, and he is forced to try to justify his lie by confessing his fear of death, which he takes to be a universal emotion. His normal reaction to death ironically reinscribes his sense of difference from others, for he then twists his justification to stress the uniqueness of his situation by making the outrageous claim that he alone has been refused by death. He readily admits the falsehood of his romanticized sense of uniqueness—his sense of immortality—but even the honesty with which he confesses his self-serving actions does not give them a sense of authenticity, and so does not allow him to connect with the world.

Mishima pushes the autobiographical confession, with its narrow perspective, to a radically new use. The maddening circularity of the narrator's self-analysis is not a sign of indecision, but signifies an irreparable breach between reality and the means to express it. Once the narrator is conscious of the fact that the narrative of his life (the expression of his selfhood) is a pose, then he can never express his true identity, nor can he connect with his ideal of beauty. Instead, his story is reduced to a series of paradoxes. There is the paradox of his identity. He wants to confess his difference and assert his uniqueness, and yet he fears the isolation that would result. To overcome his isolation, he confesses his tendency to masquerade, but in the end the mask becomes the image of himself, suggesting once again that he cannot connect with the reality of his life. The confession of a mask is by nature an empty narrative, and the narrator's obsession with surfaces and false appearances, which dominates *Confessions of a Mask*, would become one of the most important recurring elements in Mishima's writing.

Toward an International Reputation

The explicit nature of *Confessions of a Mask*, especially the depiction of the narrator's violently sadistic sexual fantasies, raised some critical eyebrows, but on the whole the novel was lavishly praised and established Mishima as a rising star. Because *Confessions of a Mask* is a tour de force, it was a hard act to follow, and the works Mishima wrote immediately afterward in 1950 do not seem as innovative. Instead they emphasized some of the more sensationalist tendencies of his art. Perhaps that sensationalism explains their commercial success. *Junpaku no yoru* (1950; A pure white night), for instance, was a serialized novel written intentionally as an entertainment (it was also the first of Mishima's stories to be adapted to the screen). Mishima wrote sixteen more of these serialized pieces over the next two decades, usually composing them simultaneously with works that he considered serious.

The self-styled serious work of 1950 was *Ai no kawaki* (*Thirst for Love*, 1969). This novel tells of a young widow, Etsuko, who in order to survive in the postwar years has stayed on in her deceased husband's house as the mistress of her father-in-law. Desperately unfulfilled, Etsuko conceives a passion for a young farmhand named Saburō. Jealous of Saburō's affair with a peasant girl, Etsuko reaches a breaking point during a local festival when she watches the frenzied, half-naked dance of the young men of the village. She longs to lose herself in what she imagines is the depthless sea of Saburō's back; drawn into the dance and pressed up against him, she digs her nails into his skin until she draws blood.

In her turmoil Etsuko finally gets Saburō to meet her late one night and attempts to extract a statement from him in which he reciprocates her fantasies. But when he then tries to make love to her, she panics and screams. Her father-in-law appears, armed with a sickle, but is too irresolute to take any action. Etsuko grabs the implement and murders Saburō.

Etsuko's acts parallel the sadistic, homoerotic fantasies depicted in *Confessions of a Mask*, but the turn from autobiographical material to a fictional story creates a distance from the fantasy that makes the sadism less explicit. This distance may partly explain the popular success of *Thirst for Love*. However, if Mishima was consciously suppressing his personal life as a subject for writing, he was beginning to explore other outlets to give expression to his homosexual identity. During the Occupation a thriving gay subculture, stimulated in part by the presence of a large foreign contingent, had sprung up in Tokyo. Mishima began to visit a number of cafés and bars, often accompanied by someone from his publishing house, as if he were gathering material for his writing. At times it seems that Mishima was rather uptight about the scene, or at any rate was keeping himself at a safe distance, even though he made no effort to disguise his homosexuality. Whatever his true feelings, his activities formed the basis for the novel *Kinjiki* (1951; *Forbidden Colors*, 1968). *Forbidden*

Colors is a depiction of Tokyo's gay world in which the protagonist expresses a deep ambivalence about his identity. Although the novel at points appears to exult in its exposé of that world, there is also an underlying unease, a palpable desire of the narrator to escape from himself. Again, the novel sparked some controversy, but it was another in what would become a long line of successes for the author in the 1950s.

Mishima's reputation was further enhanced by the publication of the short story "Manatsu no shi" (Death in midsummer) also in 1951. He was in the midst of an extremely productive period when he made his first overseas trip, which took him around the world from December 1951 to May 1952. His visit to New York fired his ambition to capture an international readership and started his process of reaching out to make Western contacts. Mishima traveled on to Brazil, Paris, and London, but the place that had the greatest impact on him was Greece. Upon his return home he immersed himself for a time in the study of the Greek classics, and in 1954 published the novel *Shiosai* (*The Sound of Waves*, 1956), a reworking of the Daphnis and Chloe myth transposed to a fishing island.

This work was a departure in style and content. The story of the lovers Shinji, a fisherman, and Hatsue, a diving girl, is told in a style that is pared down and generally devoid of the irony typical of Mishima's other works. Indeed, given the sorts of material that had occupied Mishima up to that point, the innocent, wholesome nature of the romance is unexpected. Mishima later claimed that this style was a joke, in part because he felt the enormous popularity of the book meant that readers were not taking it as the serious, high-art novel he intended. To add insult to injury, in his eyes, the book was awarded the Shinchōsha Literary Prize and was his first major work to be translated into English. Mishima's reservations aside, even though the work seems to lack the weightiness of some of his other novels, it is noteworthy insofar as it suggests Mishima's willingness to stretch himself as an artist, even to the point of trying to remake himself as a classicist with appeal in both Japan and the West.

Another important outcome of the visit to Greece was Mishima's determination to remake his body as well as his image. He began boxing lessons in 1953, and in 1955 he extended his physical routine by taking up bodybuilding. He started weight training in earnest, sculpting the upper body that would later become famous in a number of publicity stills. Of course, it was this type of activity that made some of his critics doubt the seriousness of his intentions in all endeavors; after all, going from the stereotypical 98-pound weakling to a 120-pound muscle man is a relatively minor result in the larger scheme of things. In retrospect, it may have been that as Mishima realized the fullness of his creative powers, his exhibitionist tendencies were emphasized in the difficult process of remaking himself.

For all the peculiarity of his hobbies, Mishima was reaching maturity as a writer, and in 1956 he published one of his most important works, *Kinkakuji* (*The Temple of the Golden Pavilion*, 1959). Mishima finds a metaphor in the burning of the famous Zen temple in 1950 for the creative-destructive duality that marks nihilist aesthetics. The young acolyte, Mizoguchi, the narrating I who commits the infamous act of arson, is a stutterer who is incapable of connecting with the world around him. The weariness and impotence that come over him as he contemplates the beauty of the Kinkakuji, which has been an object of veneration for him since his childhood, are the result of his unceasing struggle to reconcile reality with his perceptions of it. He had hoped that the war would provide a way out of his predicament, either through his death or through the destruction of the Kinkakuji by American bombs. Because neither happened, he resolves to overcome his weariness by the nihilistic acts of arson and suicide. Destroying the barrier between his vision of beauty and the reality of the temple will, Mizoguchi hopes, resolve his struggle.

In the buildup to the climax of the novel, Mizoguchi ponders the beauty of the temple one last time. That beauty has so enthralled him that it is now as much a product of his memory as it is the product of his direct experience of it. Therein lies the discovery of the true nature of the temple's beauty. Unable to make out the details of the building in the darkness of the night on which he sets the fire, he closes his eyes and relies on his own vision to determine what it is that has such a hold on him: "Through the power of memory, the details of beauty came sparkling one by one out of the darkness, and, as the sparkling diffused, at last the Kinkakuji gradually became visible beneath the light of a mysterious time that was neither day nor night. Never before had the Kinkakuji appeared to me in such a completely detailed form, glittering in every corner. It was as though I had gained the powers of vision of a blind man" (*MYZ*, vol. 10, p. 265; revised from tr. p. 253).

The beauty of the temple is the creation of the young acolyte's memory of it. Beauty is no longer connected to the real presence of the temple, but arises out of the individual mind contemplating it. The world of art and the world of experience are completely sundered for Mizoguchi, who is forced to create an architecture of the mind. And in that architecture he finds the beauty of each detail "filled with an uneasiness in itself. While dreaming of perfection, it was drawn toward the next beauty, the unknown beauty, never knowing completion. Foreshadowing was linked to foreshadowing, and each foreshadowing of beauty, *which did not exist here*, became, as it were, the theme of the Kinkakuji. Those foreshadowings were the signs of emptiness. Emptiness was the structure of this beauty. Thus, naturally the foreshadowings of emptiness were contained in the incompleteness of the details; and this delicate construction of fine timber, like a devotional necklace swaying in the breeze, was trembling in the foreshadowing of emptiness" (*MYZ*, vol. 10, p. 267; revised from tr. p. 255). The nature of beauty is likened to the Buddhist notion of the emptiness of experience. The existence of beauty is not an absolute but depends on the relationship of individual details, images, or memories. And the subjective ordering of those relationships in turn requires an acceptance of the relative, empty nature of aesthetic values.

Mizoguchi's aesthetic discovery, then, is double-edged. The recognition of the beauty of the Kinkakuji, which is nothing more than the recognition of his own concept of the temple, gives him the freedom to control the reading of the temple's beauty; but in his understanding of that beauty he also feels an uneasiness that foretells the emptiness of his own aesthetic concepts. Mizoguchi, of course, cannot resolve the nihilist-relativist problematic. He is limited to making a gesture toward nihilism by destroying himself along with the temple: an act that would at least conjure up the sense of authenticity that comes with death. Mizoguchi's failure to kill himself in the end is an explicit critique of the inauthentic; Mizoguchi is a false artist. He is capable of destroying the object he blames for reflecting back at him his own ugliness, which makes him different and isolated. But his self-awareness causes him to lose nerve, and he is incapable of completing his vision of immolation. Having committed arson, he retreats to a nearby hill and watches the blaze, casually smoking a cigarette. By failing to extinguish the self, Mizoguchi fails to destroy the subjective, inner vision of the Kinkakuji that is the cause of his turmoil.

The Temple of the Golden Pavilion is a disturbing portrait of how values may be perverted. The concern with the inauthentic, which was first fully explored in *Confessions of a Mask*, is a powerful theme, but also a problematic one, for it is highly self-reflective, raising questions about how seriously any work of art should be taken. Is it possible to distinguish between inauthentic art and art that is about (that critiques) the inauthentic? In 1956 the answer would appear to be yes, because Mishima plays upon the question to brilliant formal and psychological effect in both *Confessions of a Mask* and *The Temple of the*

Golden Pavilion. Events that were to follow, however, would muddle the issue for Mishima and bring the question back into play.

Mishima continued to enjoy popular successes with his novels and plays, and with the favorable reception of *The Temple of the Golden Pavilion* his financial situation was secure. Despite that success he seems to have not been entirely satisfied with his situation and evidently felt his ambitions had not been fulfilled. In 1958 he began work on *Kyōko no ie* (Kyōko's house), a novel that would take him fifteen months to finish, longer by far than any other single volume he wrote. In one sense this novel, which was published in 1959, is a highly personal work. Although not autobiographical to the same degree as *Confessions of a Mask*, it was nonetheless intended to summarize his experience of the previous decade. There are four protagonists in the story: a boxer, a businessman, a painter, and an actor, all of whom represent aspects of Mishima's life. The narrative is fragmented, however, and the separate stories do not come together successfully to create a coherent work of art. The book is at points self-indulgent and meandering, as if there is an underlying ironic recognition that the wearing of masks is not enough to hide the fractured self of which each character represents a facet. The design of the narrative is meant to convey that sense of being broken up, of lacking a true center, but that design is not sufficient to sustain the work, and the result was the first major critical failure for Mishima—a failure in which he had invested so much of himself.

The Search for Authenticity

Mishima was married to Sugiyama Yōko in 1958, soon after he had begun *Kyōko no ie.* Yōko was the daughter of a well-known painter, and she and Mishima had two children. The marriage brought a kind of anchor into his life, but at the same time the failure of *Kyōko no ie* seemed to accelerate his restlessness. Over the next few years he starred in films and plays, posed as a model for photo-

graphs, and continued his interest in body-building. He also began to be more outspoken in his conservative political views—ideas that had been inculcated in him since childhood. As with some of his other activities, there emerged a good deal of skepticism surrounding the sincerity with which he held his rightist views, in particular his gradually evolving support for a return to imperial rule. It may well be that his peculiar ideological bent was nothing more than a way to provide a different anchor in his life—a way, however artificial it may have looked from the outside, of providing some core to his being that could serve as the ground for the poses he struck.

The effect of this ideological shift is apparent in the short story "Yūkoku" (Patriotism), which he wrote in 1960 and published in 1961. The style tries to strip away all sense of irony and achieve a sincere invocation that glorifies a young, beautiful, heroic couple, Lieutenant Takeyama and his bride, Reiko. The backdrop to the story is the 2-26 Incident, the coup d'état attempted by radical officers of the Imperial Army on 26 February 1936. The officers and their men managed to take over parts of central Tokyo and demanded a complete end to civilian government. They claimed their actions were undertaken in the name of the emperor, but Hirohito denied his support and insisted that the army put down the revolt. Takeyama is a fervent loyalist in sympathy with the conspirators, but he was left out of the plot because he is married. When he is ordered to lead the attack against the revolt, he is caught in a moral bind between his duty as an officer, his loyalty to his friends, and his devotion to his ideal of the emperor.

In some ways the historical background is a pretext to set up what follows. Unable to resolve his dilemma, the lieutenant chooses suicide, and his wife decides that she must follow him in death. The major portion of the narrative is comprised of two scenes: one of the couple having heroic sex (which is also remarkably chaste), and the other of the lieutenant's *seppuku* (ritual disembowelment) and his bride's death, both of which are related in disturbing detail. In 1965 Mishima starred in a film version of this story, and many commentators have wondered if the work is not a rehearsal for Mishima's own suicide. Such an interpretation is a stretch, but at the very least it is clear that the aim of the work is to turn political ideology into subject matter that could be linked to Mishima's obsession with violent death, and thereby exploited for art. Because the story is drained of irony, what is left is an aestheticized version of politics, a celebration of an idealized attitude by which Mishima evidently wanted to express something emotionally and culturally authentic.

Because Mishima was always able to work on several projects simultaneously throughout his career, the gradual shift toward his uniquely aestheticized politics should be read within a larger context. The same year he wrote "Yūkoku," for example, he published a very different style of work, *Utage no ato* (*After the Banquet*, 1963). This novel is based on the life of the politician Arita Hachirō, a conservative who turned Socialist and ran for governor of Tokyo in 1959. The primary focus of the story is a middle-aged woman, Kazu, who owns a stylish traditional restaurant famous for its gardens. The restaurant is favored by politicians, and it is through that connection that Kazu meets and marries Noguchi (the Arita character). She backs his losing campaign with her money and her zeal, but after the electoral defeat the marriage dissolves. The depiction of Kazu, especially the growth of her self-awareness, is one of Mishima's most sharply drawn and sympathetic character studies, and the novel was well received—a welcome success after the disappointment over *Kyōko no ie.* The joy was short-lived, however, for the portrayal of the characters was so credible that Arita sued Mishima and won in a landmark privacy case.

Much of Mishima's writing in the early 1960s deals with figures who embody or betray an authentic ideal. *Gogo no eikō* (1963; *The Sailor Who Fell from Grace with the Sea*, 1965) tells of a sailor who at first is utterly devoted to his life at sea, but turns his back on that life in order to live with a young widow in the port city of Yokohama. In the eyes of the widow's teenage son, this act of betrayal of the romantic glory of the seafarer's life is unforgivable, and so the boy and his gang of friends punish the sailor by murdering him.

The linking of aestheticized ideals and sadism is a feature that Mishima explored in his drama as well, in particular two plays from the 1960s: *Sado kōshaku fujin* (1965; *Madame de Sade,* 1967) and *Waga tomo Hitor* (1968; *My friend, Hitler*). Although I have concentrated in this essay primarily on Mishima's prose works, he was, as mentioned at the outset, a prolific playwright. Beginning in the 1950s, Mishima wrote both experimental pieces, such as his modern Nō plays, and mainstream drama for the popular stage. He had a number of successes, including *Sangenshoku* (1955; *Primary Colors*), *Rokumeikan* (1956), and *Asa no tsutsuji* (1957; *Morning Azaleas*). Although Mishima was not a notably innovative dramatist, his talent for incisive characterization and for building to powerful climaxes in his prose served him well in his plays, which show a command of dramatic structure and a talent for creating striking, memorable tableaux. Still, in the late plays in particular—*Madame de Sade* and *Waga tomo Hitor*—Mishima achieves a powerful expression of the major elements of his fiction in the 1960s: his obsession with violent death, his longing for an ideal beyond practical existence, and his search for the authentic in a degraded culture.

The Final Years

Visions of death haunt Mishima's work from the beginning, but those visions took a decidedly militaristic turn by the mid-1960s. In 1968 he formed his own private brigade, the Tatenokai, or Shield Society, which was dedicated to a strange blend of aesthetics and emperor worship. Some critics derided the group as Mishima's toy army, but the game apparently was deadly serious for Mishima. He wrote a commentary on *Hagakure* (Hidden among the leaves), an eighteenth-century tract on the way of the warrior, and his interest in Japan's martial past may be thought of as a kind of repayment of his debt to the Rōman-ha, whose thinkers had so deeply impressed him in the 1930s. Mishima was a radical modernist insofar as his nostalgia and his contempt for the sterility of postwar Japanese society was turned inward, and yet the expression of his critique of modern Japan was a fascist swerve toward a martial code that, because self-consciously revived, was anachronistic and inauthentic. In the end, what distinguishes Mishima from the writers of the Rōman-ha is his degree of self-consciousness toward the inauthentic, which he recognized but accepted as a way to make the present moment timeless through a return to Japan's martial past. In a late autobiographical piece, *Taiyō to tetsu* (1968; *Sun and Steel*, 1970), Mishima states his idealized vision of the moment of death as the point when the literary and the martial are fused—a moment that leads inevitably to the realization that outside such an idealized vision both the pen and the sword are inauthentic and void:

> To devote death to one's heart each day, and to converge moment by moment on death, which must come to us, is to place the power to imagine the worst possible outcome in the same location as the power to imagine glory. . . . In that case, that devotion is sufficient to be able to transfer things carried out in the world of the spirit to the world of the flesh.
>
> As I have stated before, in order to receive this kind of violent transformation, even in the world of the flesh, I thoroughly prepared myself and readied an attitude to be able to receive it any time. Thus the theory that everything had the potential to be reclaimed was born within me. Because it had been proven to me that even the flesh, which ought to be a prisoner by virtue of growing and decaying moment by moment with time, had the potential to be reclaimed. It is therefore not strange at all that the thought that even time itself could be reclaimed should have come to life within me.

> (*MYZ*, vol. 32, pp. 101–102;
> revised from tr. p. 58)

Mishima is convinced that he can break through his self-consciousness and reconcile the momentary with the eternal by returning to those traditions epitomized by the selfless life of the warrior, who accepted the inevitability of death.

Because *Sun and Steel* is a late autobiographical piece, Mishima's statement of his aesthetic purpose is based on a retrospective look at his life experiences. Mishima's aesthetics are inseparable from the context of his critical self-interpretation, and thus it would be a mistake to indiscriminately project this statement back onto his earlier works of fiction as a guide for reading. However, if we separate the self-destructive purpose for which he put his principles to work late in his career, we find a remarkably consistent presentation of his ideas about art and beauty. The sad irony of Mishima's career is that the very nature of his aesthetic breakthrough imprisoned him within his early achievement. By 1968 Mishima apparently came to believe that his identity as an artist held no absolute meaning. This could not have been a happy situation for such a self-absorbed man; and by the time he wrote *Sun and Steel*, his critique of the inauthentic had played itself out. Mishima surely recognized what was happening, and no matter how much he may have enjoyed the masquerade, his knowledge about himself was obviously a burden heavy enough to make him long for the authenticity of death.

In 1963 Mishima decided to undertake a very long novel that would stand as his masterwork. By the spring of 1964 he had developed the main idea for a tetralogy, *Hōjō no umi* (*The Sea of Fertility*). Mishima's ambitions were always large-scale, and his failure to come up with a grand work continued to fuel that ambition. Rather than try to sum up through four characters the experience of a single writer over a decade, as he had in *Kyōko no ie*, Mishima tried in *The Sea of Fertility* to encapsulate the whole of twentieth-century Japan.

The four books are united through the perspective of a single character, Honda. Honda is in turn the witness of the story of four people who are different incarnations of the same being. In the first novel, *Haru no yuki* (1966; *Spring Snow*, 1972), the protagonist is a young aristocrat, Kiyoaki, who has an illicit affair with Satoko, a young woman who is betrothed to an imperial prince. To avoid a scandal Satoko retreats to a Buddhist convent and takes the vows of a nun. Kiyoaki, in the course of trying unsuccessfully to see her again, falls ill; and shortly before he dies, he tells Honda that he will see him again beneath a waterfall.

The first reincarnation of Kiyoaki is Isao, the subject of the second volume, *Honba* (1969; *Runaway Horses*, 1973), which is set nineteen years later, in the 1930s. Honda is now a prominent jurist who recognizes Isao by the distinctive birthmark he shares with Kiyoaki when Isao is undergoing ascetic discipline beneath a waterfall. Isao is a young right-wing radical who becomes involved in a plot to assassinate several prominent political and business figures. He is arrested but is released when the police think he will not act on the plot; but he carries out his mission anyway, and in the end commits *seppuku* alone as dawn is breaking. The style and tone of Isao's story are different from those of *Spring Snow*, which is a lyrical, tragic romance. In contrast, *Runaway Horses* returns to the depiction of the warrior ideal in the modern age, and Mishima even goes so far as to insert a long political tract in the middle of his story to establish the motivations of the young fanatics.

The third volume, *Akatsuki no tera* (1970; *The Temple of Dawn*, 1973), is set initially in Thailand a few years after Isao's death. Honda learns of a young Thai princess who claims to be Japanese; and when he meets her she is able to tell him all about Kiyoaki and Isao. The story then jumps about ten years later, when Honda again meets the princess, this time in Japan. At this moment in the story Honda's role as witness undergoes a transformation. The princess and her female Japanese companion are staying at Honda's estate, which he has set up so that he can spy on his guests. Honda is now a voyeur, and he is eager to confirm the princess's claim of reincarnation by spying the

birthmark. What he also discovers is that the princess and her companion are lesbian lovers, and this discovery makes him conscious of his own sordid role in the story. The princess returns to Thailand, and several years later Honda learns that she died of a cobra bite at age twenty (like the first two incarnations).

The dual settings of *Temple of Dawn* allowed Mishima the scope to use the opening parts of the novel as an extended commentary on Buddhist practice and doctrine, particularly the concept of the transmigration of souls. The novel is thus rather slow-paced, creating a voluptuous sense of ripeness and impending decay. The degradation of Honda is a key turn in the emerging tone of decadence and malaise, which is brought to completion in the final novel, *Tennin gosui* (1970; *The Decay of the Angel*, 1974). The last incarnation is a young man named Tōru, whom Honda discovers, through the telltale birthmark, who works at a harbor signal station. Honda decides to adopt Tōru without verifying the date of his birth. A doubt thus lingers with Honda, and the story centers on the question of whether Tōru is an authentic incarnation. Honda's doubts seem to be strengthened by Tōru's background and his character. The young man is cunning, ungrateful, and fond of humiliating his patron. He is finally confronted by the former lover of the Thai princess, who challenges his claim to special birth and calls him a fake who will not die at the age of twenty. Tōru attempts suicide by poison, but he fails to kill himself and is blinded. The process of dissolution of the divine being sets in, and he is doomed to live out a meaningless existence.

The tetralogy ends with Honda going to visit Satoko at her temple. When they meet again, after nearly six decades, Satoko stuns Honda by denying any knowledge of Kiyoaki. She suggests instead that Honda may have dreamed up the whole story. Mishima turns his final work in on itself, pointing up one last time the fundamental emptiness of narrative, identity, and memory. The novel ends with Honda listening to cicadas as he looks out onto the temple garden: "He had come, thought

Honda, to a place that had no memories, nothing. The noontime sun flowed over the still garden" (*MYZ*, vol. 19, p. 647; tr. p. 236).

With this ending we are back to where Mishima started in "A Forest in Full Bloom." This contrived sense of a complete return, of a perfect ending, to Mishima's art as well as his life, is heightened by the fact that he left the final installment of *The Decay of the Angel* for his publisher on a table at the front entrance of his home as he went out on the morning of 25 November 1970. A few hours later, at 12:15 P.M., after a hopeless and blundering attempt to foment an uprising among the Self-Defense Forces that would restore the emperor to power, Mishima ended his life by committing *seppuku*.

The attempt by Mishima to impose a final, authoritative reading on his life grew out of a lifelong project of narrating and renarrating his literary self. His suicide was a response to the irreconcilable loss of values and meaning. And unlike such fictional characters as the narrator of *Confessions of a Mask* and Mizoguchi in *Temple of the Golden Pavilion*, who were objects of his critique of the inauthentic, Mishima sought to resolve the problem of the inauthentic, to make whole again the breach between himself and the world, and to reclaim time itself by consciously opting to overcome his self-consciousness in the only way he thought possible.

In the end, the irony of his death is that it was widely interpreted as just another expression of the inauthentic. There is a disturbingly literary quality about his suicide, with its contrived political motives, that shapes the expectations we bring to his fiction. A parallel may be drawn with the suicide in 1927 of Akutagawa Ryūnosuke, whose death was also interpreted as evidence of the crisis of modern culture. In that interpretation Akutagawa's death became a literary act, a way to take control over life and identity by imposing a form onto it, by constructing an ending that turns life into a work of art. Such a reading of course may seem to trivialize his death, but it also reveals the severity of the shock felt by many of Akutagawa's contemporaries at his suicide.

In the case of Mishima his death in effect rewrote all of his works by making his career seem developmental. He imposed his own interpretation of his life and art as inseparable, as leading inexorably toward that final moment when his desire to achieve mastery over the forms and meanings of his own being found fulfillment in an absurd act of self-immolation. Even if we resist his efforts at control, Mishima's suicide makes a claim on us by highlighting the contradiction at the heart of his lifework. The horror of the event is grounded in Mishima's drive to give his life a formal closure, but the overt staging of his death seems out of proportion to the finality of the event. Perhaps Mishima intended his *seppuku* to be read as if it were also another work of art.

Selected Works

PRIMARY WORKS

COMPLETE WORKS

Mishima Yukio zenshū. 36 vols. Tokyo: Shinchōsha, 1973–1976. (Abbreviated as *MYZ* in citations.)

WORKS IN ENGLISH TRANSLATION

The Sound of Waves. Trans. by Meredith Weatherby. New York: Knopf, 1956.

Confessions of a Mask. Trans. by Meredith Weatherby. Norfolk, Conn.: New Directions, 1958.

The Temple of the Golden Pavilion. Trans. by Ivan Morris. New York: Knopf, 1959.

After The Banquet. Trans. by Donald Keene. New York: Knopf, 1963.

The Sailor Who Fell from Grace with the Sea. Trans. by John Nathan. New York: Knopf, 1965.

Death in Midsummer, and Other Stories. New York: New Directions, 1966.

Five Modern Nō Plays. Trans. by Donald Keene. New York: Knopf, 1967.

Madame de Sade. Trans. by Donald Keene. New York: Grove Press, 1967.

Forbidden Colors. Trans. by Alfred H. Marks. New York: Knopf, 1968.

Thirst for Love. Trans. by Alfred H. Marks. Introduction by Donald Keene. New York: Knopf, 1969.

Sun and Steel. Trans. by John Bester. New York: Grove Press, 1970.

The Sea of Fertility. 4 vols. New York: Knopf, 1972–1974.

Spring Snow. Trans. by Michael Gallagher. New York: Knopf, 1972. (Vol. 1 of *The Sea of Fertility*.)

Runaway Horses. Trans. by Michael Gallagher. New

York: Knopf, 1973. (Vol. 2 of *The Sea of Fertility.*)

The Temple of Dawn. Trans. by E. Dale Saunders and Cecilia Segawa Seigle. New York: Knopf, 1973. (Vol. 3 of *The Sea of Fertility.*)

The Decay of the Angel. Trans. by Edward G. Seidensticker. New York: Knopf, 1974. (Vol. 4 of *The Sea of Fertility.*)

The Way of the Samurai: Yukio Mishima on Hagakure in Modern Life. Trans. by Kathryn N. Sparling. New York: Basic Books, 1977.

Acts of Worship: Seven Stories. Trans. by John Bester. Tokyo and New York: Kodansha International, 1989.

"A Forest in Full Bloom." Trans. by Michael Rich. In *Studies in Modern Japanese Literature.* Edited by Dennis Washburn and Alan Tansman. Ann Arbor: Center for Japanese Studies, University of Michigan, 1997.

SECONDARY WORKS

CRITICAL AND BIOGRAPHICAL STUDIES

Hasegawa Izumi. *Mishima Yukio no chiteki unmei.* Tokyo: Shibundō, 1990.

Horie Tamaki. *Bara no sadizumu: Wairudo to Mishima Yukio.* Tokyo: Eichōsha, 1992.

Isoda Kōichi. *Mishima Yukio zenronkō: Hikaku tenkōron josetsu.* Tokyo: Ozawa Shoten, 1990.

Kosaka Shūhei. *Hizai no umi: Mishima Yukio to sengo shakai no nihirizumu.* Tokyo: Kawade Shobō Shinsha, 1988.

Matsumoto Ken'ichi. *Mishima Yukio kakeochi densetsu.* Tokyo: Kawade Shobō Shinsha, 1987.

Miller, Henry. *Reflections on the Death of Mishima.* Santa Barbara, Calif.: Capra Press, 1972.

Napier, Susan. *Escape from the Wasteland: Romanticism and Realism in the Fiction of Mishima Yukio and Ōe Kenzaburō.* Cambridge, Mass.: Harvard University Press, 1991.

Nathan, John. *Mishima: A Biography.* Boston: Little, Brown, 1974.

Ogawa Kazusuke. *Mishima Yukio: Han "Nihon romanha" ron.* Ageo: Rindōsha, 1985.

Petersen, Gwenn Boardman. *The Moon in the Water: Understanding Tanizaki, Kawabata, and Mishima.* Honolulu : University of Hawaii Press, 1979.

Scott-Stokes, Henry. *The Life and Death of Yukio Mishima.* New York: Farrar, Straus & Giroux, 1974.

Starrs, Roy. *Deadly Dialectics: Sex, Violence and Nihilism in the World of Yukio Mishima.* Honolulu: University of Hawaii Press, 1994.

Tomioka Kōichirō. *Kamen no shingaku: Mishima Yukio ron.* Tokyo: Kōsōsha, 1995.

Tsushima Katsuyoshi. *Mishima Yukio "Hōjō no umi" ron.* Osaka: Kaifūsha, 1989.

Yourcenar, Marguerite. *Mishima: A Vision of the Void.* Trans. by Alberto Manguel in collaboration with the author. New York: Farrar, Straus & Giroux, 1986.

MURAKAMI HARUKI
1949–

JAY RUBIN

IT IS SOMETHING OF a miracle that anyone outside of Japan has ever heard of Murakami Haruki. Instead of being the one Japanese novelist of the 1990s most widely read abroad, with full-page reviews of his fiction in the *New York Times Book Review* and his works translated into no fewer than sixteen languages in nineteen countries, he could easily have grown up to be a high school teacher like his parents with a specialty in medieval war tales and a pile of papers to grade every night. Or, even more likely, because he rebelled against his parents and became the owner of a successful jazz club in downtown Tokyo, he might have destroyed his hearing in the continual blast of music from a huge stereo system and chopped a pile of onions every night for the rest of his life. In fact, he was still working hard in his club at the age of thirty-two when the success of his first two novels convinced him to try writing fiction full-time.

As long as one is speculating about roads not taken, one might point out here that, if he had become a teacher and stayed in the area near his birth city of Kyoto, Murakami could have died at forty-six in the Great Kansai Earthquake of January 1995, which killed over six thousand people and destroyed his parents' home. On the other hand, because he never did show signs of becoming an ordinary salaried worker, he would almost certainly not have been among the twelve people killed or the 3,800 injured on the Tokyo subway system when members of a fanatical religious cult attacked it with poison gas during the morning rush hour of 20 March 1995. Instead of becoming a victim of either of these two back-to-back violent subterranean incidents that cast a further pall of gloom over a Japan that had recently been shocked by the bursting of its economic bubble, Murakami found in them inspiration to write about the ills of his society and to expand on the dark themes of memory and mystery and violence that had always lain beneath the surface of his musical, mind-teasing stories and novels.

To hear him tell it, though (and he had friends who agreed with him), Murakami was nobody special. Born in 1949, he had an unremarkable education in the Japanese public school system, earning moderately good grades with moderate amounts of study, entering a fairly good private university after a fairly typical year of boning up for the college entrance exams, and graduating without either difficulty or distinction somewhat later than usual, owing to the disruption of the university system caused by the student uprisings of 1969 and his work at the jazz club. An only child, he read a lot and had definite tendencies toward introversion, but he was no hermit, and he had no notable hobbies or vices, no obsessions or special areas of expertise, no dysfunctional family background to deal with, no personal crises or traumas, no experience of vast historical or social dislocations to interrupt a normal life course, no problems of extreme wealth or deprivation, no handicaps or exceptional talents. In other words, he had none of the life-warping experiences that seem to propel certain sensitive individuals toward literary creation as a form of therapy for themselves or their generation. Like other Japanese boys, Murakami grew up liking baseball and jazz and mah-jongg, learned to drink in high school, got interested in girls along the way, and ended up marrying a college classmate. People who knew him only as a nice guy who ran a cool jazz joint were shocked and amazed when, in 1979, he won an award for new writers and started shooting off novels and stories and translations and essays like a newly-awakened volcano.

There would seem, then, to be nothing in his early life that prepared Murakami to be a writer. Indeed, Murakami himself likes to tell the story of the mystical moment that came out of nowhere and turned him in the direction of literature at the age of twenty-nine. He was at a baseball game in April 1978, drinking beer in the outfield stands. His favorite team, the Yakult Swallows, was playing the Hiroshima Carp. An American player named Dave Hilton hit the first ball pitched to him for a double. "And that's when the idea struck me: I could write a novel. It was like a revelation, something out of the blue. There was no reason for it, no way to explain it. It was just an idea that came to me, just a thought. I could do it. The time had come for me to do it. When the game was over—and by the way, the Swallows won the game—I went to a stationery store and bought a fountain pen and paper" (from Murakami's Una Lecture, "The Sheepman and the End of the World," delivered in English at the University of California, Berkeley, 17 November 1992).

Well, it makes a good story, and who knows, the inexplicable suddenness of Murakami's writing of his first novel with his new pen and paper may literally be true. But maybe it would be helpful to go back and look more closely at the details of the early experiences that nurtured Murakami the writer.

Murakami's Early Years

The city of Kyoto was Japan's capital for over a thousand years (794–1868), the downtown streets are still laid out according to the original eighth-century plan, and the city remains today the site of the ancient palace and of thousands of shrines and temples that comprise the heart of the country's religious life. Kyoto draws millions of tourists in search of the kind of ancient roots that seem to have been obliterated from Japan's contemporary capital, Tokyo. Murakami was born in this venerable city on 12 January 1949 and spent his early years in the Kyoto-Osaka-Kobe area with its cultural, political, and mercantile traditions. There he grew up speaking the region's dialect and was taught to distrust anyone whose speech did not have its distinctive locutions and soft accents. Both his father, Chiaki (son of a Kyoto Buddhist priest), and his mother, Miyuki (daughter of an Osaka merchant family), were tradition-minded high school teachers of Japanese language and literature, and he often heard them discussing eighth-century poetry or medieval war tales at the dinner table. They were rather strict, and Murakami sees this, along with his being an only child, as one source of his early tendency toward introversion.

In one area, though, his parents allowed him great freedom. He was permitted to buy books on credit at the local bookstore. Murakami became a voracious reader, as his parents no doubt wished him to be, but their liberal policy on book purchases may have backfired. After the family moved to the nearby city of Ashiya when Murakami was twelve, they subscribed to two separate libraries of world literature, the volumes of which arrived at the bookstore each month, and Murakami spent his early teens devouring them. His father forced him to spend two hours every Sunday morning reading the Japanese classics, but Murakami loved Stendahl (Marie-Henri Beyle) and went on to develop a taste for Leo Tolstoy and Fyodor Dostoyevsky. The Japanese classics never interested him.

At Kobe High School, where he wrote for the school newspaper and avoided studying for the most part, Murakami's reading branched out to the likes of hard-boiled detective novelists Ross MacDonald, Ed McBain, and Raymond Chandler, then Truman Capote, F. Scott Fitzgerald, and Kurt Vonnegut. Significantly, Kobe, an international trading capital, had many bookstores that sold foreign residents' used paperbacks, so that literature in English was available at less than half the price of its Japanese translations. The reading and translating of foreign—primarily American—literature became one of the central activities of his life as Murakami turned himself into one of the pre-eminent translators of American literature in Japan, his own style heavily influenced by the rhythms of his favorite authors.

The foreign language that most enthralled the young Murakami could hardly have been anything but English. Despite his early attraction to Russian literature, Murakami had begun life during the Allied (largely American) occupation of his country following Japan's defeat in World War II, and he had grown up in an increasingly affluent Japan that still admired America for its wealth and the energy of its culture.

America's indigenous music also attracted Murakami. After hearing Art Blakey and the Jazz Messengers at a live concert in 1964, the fifteen-year-old Murakami often skipped lunch to save money for records. Murakami's encyclopedic knowledge of jazz and many facets of American popular culture are immediately apparent to even the most casual reader. He has not invested such references with weighty symbolic significance, however. Whereas America has been an obsessive nightmare for some older writers, Murakami has been called the first writer completely at home with the elements of American popular culture that per-

meated Japan in the 1990s and the beginning of the new millenium.

Fiction was not the only thing that Murakami read with interest in high school. He has claimed to have read and re-read up to twenty times a multivolume, unabridged world history. Although many critics have dismissed his works as apolitical and ahistorical, the majority are set in carefully defined time periods and, taken in aggregate, can be read as a psychological history of post-postwar Japan, from the heat of the student movement to the "Big Chill" of the 1970s, then to the emphasis on moneymaking of the 1980s, and perhaps to a re-emergence of idealism in the 1990s.

One particular area of historical interest for Murakami seems to have been inspired, almost unintentionally, by his father, who served in the Japanese military that invaded China during World War II and who told the boy war stories that left a terrible impression on him. Perhaps as a result, Murakami has long had ambivalent feelings about China and the Chinese. These emerged in the very first short story he published, "Chūgoku-yuki no surō bōto" (1980; "A Slow Boat to China," 1993), a delicate, strangely touching account of how the narrator came innocently to harbor feelings of guilt toward the few Chinese people he had met in his young life. The theme later emerged more concretely in the passages of *Hitsuji o meguru bōken* (1982; *A Wild Sheep Chase*, 1989) that touched upon Japan's violent encounters with the other peoples of Asia and reached their most harrowing development in the gruesome descriptions of war in the massive *Nejimakdori kuronikuru* (1994–1995; *The Wind-Up Bird Chronicle*, 1997).

Murakami hated studying for exams in school, and the feeling was only compounded when it came time for him to confront Japan's notorious "exam hell." He spent most of 1967 studying (or, as he tells it, dozing) at the local library in preparation for his second round of exams after failing the first. English was usually considered one of the most challenging of the entrance exams, but Murakami had no patience for the study of grammar and instead translated passages from the American thrillers he loved. One exam preparation book, though, contained something that moved him in a new way. It was, he said, his first piece of real literature after all those hard-boiled novels: the opening passage from Truman Capote's story "The Headless Hawk." He sought out a collection of Capote stories and read and reread them. The relaxed year of reading and reflection convinced him that he was far more interested in literature than in law, and so he took and passed the exam for the department of literature at Waseda University in Tokyo.

Murakami claims that, like most Japanese college students, he attended few classes. Instead, he spent his time in jazz clubs in the Shinjuku entertainment district. In *Yagate kanashiki gaikokugo*, Murakami says "I didn't study in high school, but I *really* didn't study in college" (p. 242). As usual, though, he read voraciously on his own.

Waseda, a private institution with its strong tradition in drama studies, had always been a good school for literary types. Murakami entered the drama program at Waseda, though he never went to the live theater while enrolled there, and he found the professors' lectures disappointing. Instead, he loved the movies and planned to be a scenario writer. When the scenario study group proved boring, however, he began to spend a lot of time in Waseda's famous drama museum, reading scenarios. In retrospect, he saw this as the single most valuable experience he had gained at Waseda. He always seemed to opt for solo activity and was never at home in groups.

One thing that Murakami thoroughly enjoyed was living alone for the first time in his life. And then there were girls—or rather, one special girl. He didn't have many friends—just two in college, one of whom is now his wife. Yōko Takahashi had grown up in a Tokyo neighborhood of merchants as the daughter of a self-employed futon maker. Many of the quirky young women in Murakami's novels—most notably the energetic, somewhat eccentric character Midori of *Noruwei no mori* (1987; *Norwegian Wood*, 1989 and 2000)—are fictionalized portraits of Yōko.

The year after Murakami met Yōko, Waseda's student strike put an end to any classroom meetings for five months. Even when the barricades went up at school, Murakami fought with the police as an individual but chose not to participate in organized student activities. In October 1969, the police were called onto campus to end the deadlocked confrontation and did so without violence. The students' mood of excitement and idealism collapsed all at once, leaving in its wake a terrible sense of boredom and pointlessness. The Establishment had gained total victory, and the students had given in with barely a whimper. Murakami and Yōko shared this startling shift in mood as a defining experience of their lives. Later, when Murakami began to write his fictional history of the era, there would be the time before and the time after; there would be the promise of 1969 and the boredom of 1970 and beyond.

Murakami's parents were opposed to his plans to marry Yōko, who, though well educated herself, did not come from an educated background. He went ahead with his plans in spite of their wishes. The marriage was registered without ceremony in October 1971, and the young couple moved in with Yōko's father, a widower.

Murakami's studies were on hold—and in the end it took him seven years to finish his undergraduate degree. He decided to take a year off, but he knew he couldn't keep receiving financial support from his father-in-law forever. He thought about getting a job with a television station and actually went for a few interviews, but he decided instead to open his own jazz club.

To prepare for this new phase of their life, Murakami and Yōko began working part-time to amass a down payment. With a matching bank loan, they were able to open a cozy little establishment in a western suburb of Tokyo in 1974, naming it "Peter Cat" after the pet that Murakami had been keeping for the past five years. The place had Spanish-style white walls and wooden tables and chairs and generally resembled J's bar in *A Wild Sheep Chase* and

230

the earlier novels. Yōko and Murakami worked there as truly equal partners. They were so successful that they were able to move the club to a location in downtown Tokyo in 1977.

They were still working hard in the jazz club in April 1978 when Murakami attended the afternoon baseball game that mysteriously aroused in him the desire to write a novel.

The Birth of Boku

Not only did the impetus to write *Kaze no uta o kike* (1979; *Hear the Wind Sing*, 1987) seem to come out of thin air, but the book itself has an unpredictable, fragmented, almost random quality. According to Kawamoto Saburō's record of Murakami's reminiscences, Murakami didn't write the novel in chronological order but "shot" each "scene" separately, "almost like automatic writing," and later strung them together (pp. 38–39). This may sound like an invitation to chaos, but the book is recognizable as something approaching a novel. It traces the experiences of an unnamed narrator who calls himself Boku (I) and his friend "the Rat" during a few weeks in the boring summer of 1970 following the collapse of the student movement. The two spend long hours in a bar run by a Chinese proprietor, J, listening to his "wisdom" and drinking. They try to joke away their disgust at the victory of the establishment, but their almost surreal thirst for beer suggests an unsatisfied inner need. Of the two, "Boku/I" is the more detached, whereas "the Rat" is beginning to turn his inner musings into literature. A postscript tells us that in the years following the action of the novel, "I" has turned twenty-nine, has married, and lives in Tokyo; and the Rat, now thirty, is writing unpublished novels (containing neither sex nor death) that he sends to "I" as combined Christmas/birthday presents.

As the writer of the novel we are reading, Boku imparts his coolness to the language of the book. The most attractive feature of this slight first novel is the style, Murakami's entertaining use of words, many of them for-

eign words—names of American rock and jazz musicians, for the most part. Even the sentences and paragraphs have a certain foreignness to them, with influences from writers like Richard Brautigan and Kurt Vonnegut more in evidence than those of Murakami's Japanese predecessors. This was an effect that Murakami had to work hard to achieve. When he saw his first attempts at writing beginning to resemble typical mainstream Japanese prose, he threw them out and tried writing in the language of the writers he most admired. In English, his vocabulary was limited, and he was unable to compose long sentences. These limitations themselves imposed a kind of rhythm on his language, with which he began to feel comfortable. His final step was to make a literal translation of his own English "back" into Japanese. This is reminiscent of Samuel Beckett's experience writing in French. The effect in both cases was a certain coolness and distancing, not only in the language but also in the humorously detached view of life—and death—that in Murakami's case itself became a central theme of his first novel and the subsequent works.

The narrator that Murakami created for this first novel (and used almost exclusively for the next twenty years) was another feature that attracted a young and enthusiastic audience. Although the "I-novel" was a long-established fixture of serious Japanese fiction, the word most commonly used for the "I" narrator had a formal tone: *watakushi*, or *watashi*. Murakami chose instead the casual *boku*, another pronoun-like word for "I," but an unpretentious one used primarily by younger men in informal circumstances.

Murakami was by no means the first Japanese novelist to adopt "Boku" as the "I" of a nameless narrator, but the personality with which Murakami invested his Boku was unique. First of all, it resembled his own personality, with its generous fund of curiosity and its cool, distanced, bemused acceptance of the inherent strangeness of life. Murakami chose to call this fictional persona "Boku" because he felt the word was the closest thing

Japanese had to the neutral English "I": less a part of the Japanese social hierarchy, more democratic, and certainly not the designation of an authority figure. Murakami said early in his career that he was uncomfortable assuming the stance of a godlike creator, deigning to impose names on his characters and narrating their actions in the third person. The choice of the first-person "Boku," then, was part of Murakami's instinctive decision to eschew all hint of authority in his narrative.

Having reached the age of twenty-nine himself, Murakami made his narrator a twenty-nine-year-old man writing about events in his life from nearly a decade before. In effect, this made the narrator his own and the reader's kindly elder brother, someone who could offer some sense of what it was like to survive one's turbulent twenties and achieve a degree of self-knowledge (but with nothing approaching adult smugness). Boku has seen death and disillusionment, but he is above all an ordinary, beer-drinking kind of guy, not a hypersensitive artist or outstanding intellect. He is polite and well-behaved; he likes baseball and rock and jazz; he's interested in girls and sex but is not consumed by them; and he is gentle and considerate toward his bed partners. He is actually a kind of role model, and the book is a more or less didactic novel giving gentle advice on how to get on with one's life despite the setbacks after one's teens.

Without any extreme traits of his own, Boku is often the least interesting individual in his crowd but a comfortable guy to be around—a kind of Charlie Brown who provides us access to the Lucys and Linuses and Schroeders of the world with their various personality quirks. He is the kind of person whom people trust with their innermost thoughts—a great listener (he keeps his ears clean so as not to miss a beat), and as with an analyst, people seem to feel better once they've told him their stories. As he puts it, "All sorts of people have come my way telling their tales, clumped over me as if I were a bridge, then never come back. All the while I kept my mouth shut tight and refused to tell my own tales. That's how I came to the final year of my twenties. Now, I'm ready to tell" (*Murakami Haruki zensakuhin [MHZ]*, vol. 1, p. 11; tr. in *Hear the Wind Sing*, p. 11).

Most of what Boku has to tell about himself at this stage involves talk: the conversations he shares with the Rat at J's bar, the story of his own late verbal blossoming as a child, and musings on the telling of stories. The Rat at first professes a disinterest in literature, but soon he becomes almost obsessed with ponderous Western classics, and before long he is writing novels himself. Murakami gives a comic portrait of the birth of a novelist, someone who, like a rat, burrows into dark, half-forgotten places to come up with the material for his fiction. *Hear the Wind Sing*, in its jumpy unpredictability, reads nothing like an autobiography, but in Boku and the Rat Murakami is giving us two sides of himself.

Boku Matures

Having satisfied his phantom desire to write a novel, Murakami might never have written another one, but he was encouraged to try again when he won *Gunzō* magazine's New Novelist Prize for 1979. The Japanese literary establishment, however, seemed at a loss as to what to do with this jazzy new writer called Murakami. Standing apart from the cliques that control a large part of "serious" literary production in Japan, Murakami tended to be dismissed as a pop novelist and was never granted the Akutagawa Prize, which conferred a seal of approval from the critical community and served as the traditional entrée to a successful literary career. Murakami's career forged ahead nevertheless, unhindered by the lack of the coveted benchmark.

The changing portrait of Murakami's Boku through the next seven novels is the story of the growth of a writer from youthful cult figure to novelist of world stature. The novels and some sixty stories came out in rapid succession, along with a prodigious number of translations, essays, and travel books. Including the first novel and the story anthologies (marked *; see the bibliography for translations of individual stories from these collections), the list of Boku-narrated works looks like this:

Hear the Wind Sing, 1979

1973–nen no Pinbōru (1980; *Pinball, 1973*, 1985)

A Wild Sheep Chase, 1982

*Chūgoku-yuki no surō bōto (1983; A slow boat to China)

*Kangarū-biyori (1983; A loverly day for kangaroos)

*Hotaru, Naya o yaku, sono-ta no tanpen (1984; "Fireflies," "Barn burning," and other short stories)

Sekai no owari to hādoboirudo wandārando (1985; *Hard-Boiled Wonderland and the End of the World*, 1991)

*Kaiten mokuba no deddo hiito (1985; Dead heat on a merry-go-round)

*Pan'ya saishūgeki (1986; The second bakery attack)

Norwegian Wood, 1987

Dansu dansu dansu (1988; *Dance Dance Dance*, 1994)

*TV Piipuru (1990; TV people)

Kokkyō no minami, taiyō no nishi (1992; *South of the Border, West of the Sun*, 1999)

The Wind-Up Bird Chronicle, 1994–1995

Murakami's second and third novels feature the same cast of lead characters as the first, including the Rat and J, the Chinese bartender, and of course Boku, who narrates. *Hear the Wind Sing*, *Pinball 1973* and *A Wild Sheep Chase* comprise a trilogy, in which the characters grow older and the novelist's ability to convey his view of the world improves dramatically.

Whereas Boku was twenty-one and the Rat twenty-two in *Hear the Wind Sing*, and the action confined to a few weeks in August 1970, *Pinball, 1973* takes place from September through November in the year of its title, with Boku now twenty-four and the Rat twenty-five. Their student days are over, and the boredom ushered in by the 1970 collapse of the student movement has grown deeper. Boku is living in Tokyo, unerotically sharing his bed with twin girls who materialized one day out of nowhere, and listlessly pursuing his career as a commercial translator, working with a friend and an attractive office assistant. The Rat is still hanging out in J's Bar, 700 kilometers away in Kobe, trying to tear himself away from a woman with whom he has become involved and planning to leave the town once and for all.

Boku and the Rat never meet in the course of the book; rather, chapters alternate (somewhat unpredictably) between first-person descriptions of Boku's life and third-person descriptions of the Rat's, inevitably suggesting that the Rat is more a "made-up" fictional character, whereas Boku is closer to the author. The didactic element surfaces in this novel again, not from Boku, who does not speak in this book as his older self, but most directly from the mouth of J, who had very little to do in the first novel.

The overall tone of the book is far more somber than that of *Hear the Wind Sing*, but rather than having Boku return to the most agonized chapter of his past, when his beloved Naoko died, Murakami has him embark on a quest for, of all things, a pinball machine that, until it disappeared with the closing of a Tokyo arcade three years earlier, he had spent many mindlessly happy hours on—as he had on a similar machine in J's bar. Suddenly one day, while on a corridor-like golf fairway, the memory of the machine comes to him, and he feels the need to find it. It is part of the "parade of trivia" that can unpredictably surface from long-lost memory (usually via corridors in Murakami's symbolism) and become nearly an obsession. These images from memory may not be much, but they are all we have: they are what we—and all of life—are made of. They are not necessarily meaningless, however, depending on our attitude. Herein lies the "lesson" of the book, as articulated by J:

> Me, I've seen forty-five years, and I've only figured out one thing. That's this: if a person would just make the effort, there's something to be learned from everything. From even the most ordinary, commonplace things, there's always something you can learn. I read somewhere that they say there's even different philosophies in razors. Fact is, if it weren't for that, nobody'd survive
>
> (*MHZ*, vol. 1, p. 190; tr. in *Pinball, 1973*, p. 96.)

In 1981 Murakami and Yōko sold their jazz club so that he could become a full-time writer. The business was doing well and Murakami still enjoyed the work, but the success of the first two novels had convinced him that he wanted to be able to write without distractions. The time had come to switch from the kitchen table to an actual desk.

When one encounters Boku, the Rat, and the Chinese barkeep J in *A Wild Sheep Chase*, the time is July 1978, although there is a prelude labeled (in the original, not in the translation) "November 25, 1970"—the date of the ritual disembowelment and beheading of novelist Mishima Yukio. The older novelist's dramatic gesture is seen here as nothing more than a series of pictures flashing on TV, part of the ennui following the 1969 student uprisings. Boku, now twenty-nine, has since married and divorced the attractive office assistant of *Pinball, 1973* (owing to boredom), has expanded his translation service into a moderately successful ad agency, and has lost track of the Rat,

who has simply disappeared (as suggested at the end of *Pinball*) without sending novels each December (as suggested in the postscript to *Hear the Wind Sing*).

A Wild Sheep Chase is the book in which Boku catches up with himself. In the novel's "present," he has reached the age he had attained as the retrospective narrator of *Hear the Wind Sing*. He is no longer looking back, but acting. This was a new kind of book for Murakami. For the first time, he was consciously trying to tell a story. For his model, he chose the American detective writer Raymond Chandler, and he had Boku embark on "an adventure surrounding a sheep"—the literal meaning of the title in Japanese—that takes him from Tokyo to the wilds of Hokkaido, Japan's northernmost island.

Boku is still bored in this novel. As he puts it, "I don't know how to put it, but I just can't get it through my head that here and now is really here and now. Or that I am really me. It doesn't quite hit home. It's always this way. Only much later on does it ever come together. For the last ten years it's been like this" (*MHZ*, vol. 2, p. 182; tr. in *A Wild Sheep Chase*, p. 142).

"Ten years ago" marked the end of youthful student idealism, opening the way for the deadening twenties of the routine, workaday world, in which a gap seems to open between "me" and "myself." Boku feels nostalgia for the time before the gulf opened. But the action does not give him time to dwell on the past. Just as a threatening man dressed in black is about to reveal to Boku (and to the reader) what his interest is in a certain sheep that has appeared in an ad produced by Boku's agency, the narrative leaps into a flashback. Last December 1977, the reader learns, a package arrived from the far north, containing a letter from the Rat and a novel. In May, another letter from "some place totally different" arrived, containing a photograph of a bucolic scene with sheep and a request that the narrator put the photo on public display. The Rat also asked Boku to visit the woman he abandoned in *Pinball, 1973* and to say good-bye for the Rat to her and to J. (Conveniently for the plot, the postmark on this second package was obliterated when Boku tore off the forwarding slip.) Boku put the photo into an advertisement produced by his firm, and he made the trip as requested, a sentimental journey to his hometown.

When Boku returns the narrative to the present, the reader learns that the sinister man in black has searched out Boku because of some undefined interest he has in the sheep photo. The man, lieutenant of a right-wing "Boss" who is dying from a huge blood cyst in his brain, compels the hero to embark on a search for one sheep in the photo that has a faintly-discernible star-shaped mark on its back. This means that Boku must find the Rat, who originally sent the photo to him. Boku takes along his new girlfriend, a part-time call girl with an ordinary face but "perfectly formed ears," which she—like several other Murakami characters—is endlessly cleaning.

The search takes Boku to Hokkaido and its sheep ranches. There, Boku reads about a (fictional) town called Jūnitaki and learns that the raising of sheep there and elsewhere in Hokkaido had originally been encouraged by the Japanese government as a means to keep troops dressed in wool for winter military operations in the Asian continent.

Murakami may take a fanciful slant on history, but it is significant that this first novel of his to step beyond the narrow confines of the student movement and its aftermath finds him probing Japan's tragic encounter with the Asian mainland—that area of concern to which he was sensitized by his father—and to which he would return in full force in *The Wind-Up Bird Chronicle* of 1994–1995. *A Wild Sheep Chase* won for Murakami the 1983 Noma Literary Prize for new writers.

After bringing *A Wild Sheep Chase* to a close, Murakami gave up smoking (cold turkey, from three packs a day to nothing) and took up running (as Boku did in *Sheep*). As he began burrowing more deeply inside himself for material, he felt the need of physical discipline to keep on an even keel. The image of the typical member of the Japanese literary establish-ment has always been that of a hard-drinking, heavy-smoking "decadent" whose pursuit of a physically wasting life is the major source of his material, but Murakami decided that physical health would be the foundation of his professional life. Never a heavy drinker, he enjoys an occasional beer or glass of wine. As he says in *Brutus*, "I've heard it said a million times that fiction comes out of something unhealthy, but I believe the exact opposite. The healthier you make yourself, the easier it is to bring out the unhealthy stuff inside you" (p. 28).

By 1999 Murakami had run in sixteen marathons and so strongly identified himself with physical training that the magazine *Brutus* did a twenty-five-page spread on the connection between his running and his writing. "You've got to have physical strength and endurance," he said, "to be able to spend a year writing a novel and then another year rewriting it ten or fifteen times." He decided that he would live as if each day were twenty-three hours long, so that no matter how busy he might be, nothing would prevent him from devoting an hour to exercise. "Stamina and concentration are two sides of the same coin. . . . I sit at my desk and write every day, no matter what, whether I get into it or not, whether it's painful or enjoyable. I wake up at 4:00 a.m. and usually keep writing until after noon. I do this day after day, and eventually—it's the same as running—I get to that spot where I know it's what I've been looking for all along. You need physical strength for something like that. . . . It's like passing through a wall. You just slip through" (pp. 25, 27, 28). The physical discipline is thus inseparable from the enormous professional discipline that has kept Murakami so incredibly productive year after year. In time he came to feel that, whereas jazz might have supplied the energy for the clipped beat of his earlier works, the sustained power of his later style owed much to his long-distance running.

In 1983, the year after he wrote *Sheep Chase*, Murakami took his first trip out of the country, running the course of the Athens Marathon and later that year completing his first competitive marathon, in Honolulu. He has since run in marathons both in Japan (including the 1996 100-kilometer "ultramarathon" in Hokkaido, which he completed in eleven hours) and abroad (five Boston marathons as of 1997; best time, in 1991: 3:31:04).

If *A Wild Sheep Chase* was a major advance over Murakami's first two books, it was still the third novel to treat characters that Murakami had created at the outset of his career. *Hard-Boiled Wonderland* moves into a wholly different world. It represents a still more enormous leap forward in scope and imaginative bravura. Where *Pinball, 1973* had treated Boku and the Rat in two parallel narratives that never intersected, Murakami split the hero of *Hard-Boiled Wonderland and the End of the World* into Boku and Watashi, assigning the formal Watashi-"I" to the more nearly realistic world of a vaguely futuristic Tokyo and the familiar Boku-"I" to an inner, fantastic world with a largely medieval European atmosphere. Discerning the relationship between the two alternating narratives is the great adventure of reading the novel.

Both of the "I" narrators share qualities with earlier Bokus. Most notably they accept events in their respective worlds with an almost surreal equanimity and live lives punctuated by music and devoid of deep involvement with other people. However, neither of Murakami's protagonists is a veteran of the student movement or a reflection of any particular stage of postwar Japanese society. Murakami probes here into the deepest workings of the mind and into the role played by memory and storytelling in the formation of individual identity. The plot elements are distinctly those of science fiction. The narrative of Watashi-"I," entitled "Hard-Boiled Wonderland," features an information war between two ruthless organizations, the "System" and the "Factory," peopled respectively by "Calcutecs" and "Semiotecs"; the latter want access to the secret work of the Professor, an apostate Calcutec from the same System for which Watashi works. The Professor keeps his laboratory in the middle of Tokyo in an underground cavern surrounded by man-eating creatures known as INKlings.

The setting of the Boku part of the story, called "The End of the World," seems to be a medieval walled town, but later references to abandoned factories, electric lights, and obsolete military men suggest something more like a post-nuclear world with ruined reminders of a past that cannot quite be remembered. A herd of unicorns spends its days inside the town walls and is let outside at night by the gatekeeper, who seems to have tyrannical powers over the residents. "Boku" is not a native of the town, but he is not sure how he got to be there. Shortly after he arrives, the gatekeeper insists upon cutting Boku's shadow off at the ankles, though he promises to take care of the shadow and let Boku visit him. Separated from Boku, the shadow begins to die, and he urges Boku to find an escape route for them before it is too late. Boku must decide whether to join his shadow in the escape attempt or to stay forever in the town's forest.

Hard-Boiled Wonderland and the End of the World won Murakami the prestigious Tanizaki Jun'ichirō Prize, named after Japan's grand champion of unabashedly fictional fiction.

The year 1986 marked the beginning of nearly a decade of wandering for Murakami and Yōko. They moved several times in Japan that year, and in October they left for Europe, stopping ten days in Rome before continuing on to the Greek island of Spetsai and from there to Mykonos in November. In January, they moved to Palermo, Sicily, then returned to Rome in February, and took trips to Bologna, Mykonos again, and Crete. All the while, Murakami kept writing, the main product being a novel called *Norwegian Wood* after the Beatles' tune.

The Boku narrator of *Norwegian Wood* has a name. And although that name, Tōru Watanabe, is not "Murakami Haruki," the very fact that he has a name at all invites the reader to feel that he is only a slightly fictionalized version of the author. More important, he is presented as writing directly to the reader, a narrative strategy that intensifies the impression of sincerity. Watanabe is thirty-eight as he begins writing "his" book, which covers his life from the age of eighteen until a few weeks before his twenty-first birthday. Of Watanabe's later life we know little, but what we do know suggests that he is an unhappy person. In the opening paragraph, he is flying into Hamburg at the age of thirty-seven, without enthusiasm, probably for business purposes, as he has before. He is some kind of world-traveling journalist, a lonely wanderer.

The bulk of Watanabe's retrospective narrative concentrates on the years 1968–1970, when, like Murakami, he first came to Tokyo to enter college, only to have his education interrupted by the student movement, which is depicted with far more realistic detail here than in any of the novels of the trilogy. In fact, the novel was Murakami's first attempt to write a piece of realistic fiction ("I had never written that kind of straight, simple story, and I wanted to test myself" [from Murakami's Una Lecture, "The Sheepman and the End of the World," delivered in English at the University of California, Berkeley, 17 November 1992]), and so he borrowed much from his own experience, modeling one of Watanabe's loves on his own love, Yōko, whom he first met under circumstances not too different from the college setting in the book. Although the experiment was a great success, attracting millions of readers to what turned out to be one of the all-time best-selling novels in Japan, many of Murakami's regular readers saw the book as a commercial sellout. The uproar over the book kept Murakami living abroad, where he could concentrate on his work and avoid the sensationalism of the media. He and Yōko have had to go to great lengths to preserve their privacy ever since. The Japanese literary establishment took years to forgive Murakami for having written an authentic blockbuster.

The Murakamis were still living in Rome when Murakami's next novel appeared. *Dance Dance Dance* is a sequel to *A Wild Sheep Chase*; its appearance transformed the early trilogy into a tetralogy. Four and a half years have gone by, and Boku is now thirty-four

years old and writing articles for PR magazines, a job that he describes as "cultural snow shoveling." He returns to the Dolphin Hotel, his Hokkaido base of operations in the earlier novel, where he hopes to find clues to the whereabouts of his old girlfriend with the magical ears. The tattered, old hotel, he finds, has been transformed into a modern, hi-tech wonder, but in an undefined dimension it also "contains" the chilling world of the Sheep Man, who speaks to Boku on the importance of his ties with other people: life has never had any "meaning," he says, but you can maintain your connectedness if you keep dancing as long as the music plays. Again, boredom is seen as central to commodified modern urban life, and Boku (along with the reader) spends an inordinate number of pages in this 600-page novel experiencing just that. Whereas *Sheep Chase* was a wild swing at right-wing politics and continental adventurism, *Dance* is a more systematic pursuit of what it means to find a profession and make a living in a culture in which meaning has been replaced by media. Still fascinated by existential questions of life and death and memory, Murakami has his gaze more obviously trained on the ills of modern society. There is a new level of seriousness here, a growing sense that, as Murakami later verbalized it, the writer has a certain responsibility toward the society in which he lives.

On 12 January 1989, Murakami turned forty. Especially for a writer who had focused so steadily on the decade between twenty and thirty, and whose readership was always young, that milestone fell with a thud. He saw death approaching and began to feel how little time he had left in which he could write with real concentration. The last thing he wanted was, some time in the future, to feel regret that he had wasted part of his life when he was still mentally and physically capable of doing concentrated work. He wanted to know that he had given it everything he could. That feeling has perhaps been the single greatest driving force behind his subsequent amazing productivity. He writes of the turning point in his life with passion—and with surprising frequency.

Still living in Europe, Murakami visited New York briefly near the end of 1989 in connection with the publication of *A Wild Sheep Chase*, the book that brought him to the attention of a broad Western readership for the first time. He and Yōko tried settling in Japan again the following January, but the strains of celebrity status were greater than they had imagined, and Murakami was finding it difficult to write. He decided to accept an invitation from Princeton University to live there for a year as a sort of artist-in-residence, with no teaching duties, convinced that the pastoral campus he had visited on an earlier trip (as Fitzgerald's alma mater) would give him the peace he needed. They arrived in Princeton in January 1991 and were dismayed by the jingoistic atmosphere surrounding Operation Desert Storm, America's war against Iraq. The growing anti-Japanese attitude accompanying the approach of the fiftieth anniversary of Pearl Harbor, on 7 December 1991, ironically helped Murakami to write by keeping him indoors more than normal, often in the library.

Murakami found materials in the Princeton library on events leading up to World War II, most notably the four-month-long Nomonhan Incident (or "War") of 1939, a military fiasco that had fascinated him in his youth. He began doing research for a big novel he had in mind— perhaps one that was too big, for, as he states in *Yagate kanashiki gaikokugo*, "through a mysterious process of cell division," his next novel became his next two novels, *South of the Border, West of the Sun* and *The Wind-Up Bird Chronicle*, the first of which would tie up loose threads from his earlier work, while the second, growing out of his historical research, would open up whole new worlds (p. 14).

South of the Border, West of the Sun seems initially to be something of a return to the world of *Norwegian Wood*, the sexual experiences of a teen-age protagonist occupying several chapters of the book. Whereas the earlier novel began with a retrospective frame that never returned to its thirty-eight-year-old narrator, this one concentrates on the later Boku, now in mid-life. Hajime (another Boku with a

name) is the owner of a successful jazz club and bar. We see him at the age of thirty-six (soon thirty-seven), happily married, and the father of two daughters. As perfect as Boku's life may seem—not only on the surface to others but to Hajime himself—he is not completely fulfilled; there is something missing, some ideal, indefinable quality that lies in a half-imagined world "south of the border" or, even more impossibly, "west of the sun." Not surprisingly for a Murakami protagonist, this realm lies in the past and is associated with those early sexual experiences. The first object of his childhood affections reappears in his life as a gorgeous but mysterious woman, with whom he has a passionate affair, only to have her disappear as mysteriously as she had appeared. Hajime begins to realize that she is not the only mystery in his life. His own wife is as much of a mystery to him as anyone else, and, because of that, the missing percentage points that stand in the way of perfection will always be missing. The book ends in middle-aged defeat.

Extending his stay for a year and taking on some teaching duties, Murakami stayed at Princeton from January 1991 to July 1993, after which he moved to Cambridge, Massachusetts, and became affiliated with nearby Tufts University and, less formally, with Harvard. He stayed in Cambridge for two years. He was still there in 1994 when the first two volumes of *The Wind-Up Bird Chronicle* were published, and it was in Cambridge that he completed the final volume of the novel.

In many ways, *The Wind-Up Bird Chronicle* can be read as a re-telling of *A Wild Sheep Chase*. It is as if the author had asked himself, "What if the Boku of that novel had *not* been so cool about the breakup of his marriage?" And whereas the tragic history of Japan's continental depredations had only been hinted at in the fanciful story of Jūnitaki Village and the government's exploitation of its farmers by turning them into sheepherders to aid in the waging of war against the Russians in China, here the scene shifts for many pages at a time to wartime action on the Manchurian-Mongolian border to explore the violent heritage of modern-day Japan. Most of the time, the thirty-year-old Tōru, an out-of-work paralegal who has been married for six years, is a typical Murakami "Boku," a first-person narrator of interest to us less for himself than for the stories he hears from the more colorful, even bizarre characters who surround him: a death-obsessed nymphet; a pair of sisters with supernormal powers; a deaf old fortuneteller who had been wounded at Nomonhan; an old veteran of continental military operations preceding Nomonhan; an evil media figure/politician (Tōru's own brother-in-law!) with ties to Japan's imperialist past; and a shaman-like storyteller nicknamed Nutmeg and her voiceless son, Cinnamon, who puts her stories through infinite permutations on his computer.

Ostensibly, Tōru is searching for his wife Kumiko, who leaves him partway through the book, but his search for her is more a search inside himself for the meaning of his marriage to her and the meaning of his life as a product of Japan's modern history. Her mysterious departure is no doubt the point at which the "process of cell division" split *South of the Border, West of the Sun* off from *The Wind-Up Bird Chronicle*, with their shared concern for meaning in human relations.

In his search, Tōru/Boku listens to one "long story" after another, and one of the major attractions of the novel is in the sheer fascination of the stories themselves. Murakami's continued use of Boku, however, forces him to go to considerable lengths to find rationales for telling stories not within the experience of the narrator. The frequent quotation of such external sources as newspaper articles, letters (some supposedly never even received by Tōru), and long third-person narratives of military action (arguably the best chapters of the book), suggests that Murakami has taken Boku as far as he could. *The Wind-Up Bird Chronicle* marks the culmination of Murakami's seventeen-year-long "Boku period," after which his fictional narratives began to open to a broader world.

For *The Wind-Up Bird Chronicle*, an obvious product of his growing commitment to

what he felt to be his responsibility as a writer toward society, Murakami received the coveted Yomiuri Literary Award. In a ceremony held on 23 February 1996, the award was presented to Murakami by one of his harshest longtime critics, winner of the 1994 Nobel Prize for literature, the novelist Ōe Kenzaburō. In this "beautiful" and "important" novel, said Ōe, Murakami had been able to respond to the expectations of a huge audience while remaining utterly faithful to the exploration of themes that were purely and deeply his own.

After Boku

In 1995 two catastrophes seized the attention of the Japanese people. In January, a few months before Murakami completed the third volume of *The Wind-Up Bird Chronicle*, a massive earthquake devastated much of his home region around Kobe. On the morning of 20 March, members of the Aum Shinrikyō cult, using the poison gas sarin, made a coordinated attack against several different Tokyo subway lines. The two events came with impeccable timing, as Murakami wrote in *Andāguraundo* (1997; *Underground*, 2000), just as the bubble economy burst so spectacularly, as the age of confidence in Japan's unstoppable development began to wane, as the cold war structure came to an end, as values were faltering on a worldwide scale, and as the Japanese began to examine closely the foundations of their nation:

> The events marked an important and meaningful turning point in Japan's postwar history—events of such magnitude that it is no exaggeration to say that the consciousness of the Japanese underwent a major change by having passed through them. They will remain as a single great catastrophe, a milestone that cannot be ignored in any account of our psychological history.
>
> (pp. 714–715)

The gas attack came to occupy the major portion of Murakami's attention over the next two years, resulting in *Andāguraundo*, a seven-hundred-page book consisting primarily of Murakami's interviews with victims of the event as well as his comments and vivid character sketches of the interviewees. He followed this with a second volume on the gas attack, *Yakusoku-sareta basho de: Andāguraundo 2* (1998; *The Place That Was Promised: Underground 2*, 2000), a book of interviews with members and former members of the Aum Shinrikyō cult that was responsible for the incident. In both volumes (abridged and combined in English translation), Murakami has attempted to convey how little separates the sick world of Aum from the everyday world in which ordinary Japanese have grown accustomed to living. According to Murakami in *Underground 2*, the individuality-crushing pressures of late twentieth-century Japanese society can lead highly educated, ambitious, idealistic young people to abandon the places that have been promised them in that society and search for worlds of unknown potential under misguided religious leaders, just as similar young members of the elite abandoned the positions that could have been theirs in Japanese society before World War II in order to join the government's misguided ventures in Manchuria in the name of utopian slogans that masked a bloody reality. The greatest distinction between victims and perpetrators is that the latter are desperate enough to try to do something about the emptiness that both feel (pp. 262–268).

Before he undertook the work on Aum, however, Murakami faced one more trial of sorts: returning home to Japan. The writing of *The Wind-Up Bird Chronicle* had turned his gaze increasingly on his home country. *Underground* was a continuation of the process for him. He wrote in a postscript to that volume:

One of the major reasons I decided to write this book was because I wanted to learn more about Japan. I had been living abroad for a very long time—close to eight years. . . . During my final two years . . . I was amazed to find myself wanting desperately to know about this country, Japan. I felt increasingly

that the time for me to be wandering far from Japan and groping in search of myself was coming to an end . . . and that I was reaching a time in life when I should be fulfilling the social obligations that had been presented to me.

(pp. 709–711)

He took it slow on his return to Japan, leaving Cambridge in June 1995, driving across the U.S. with an old friend, and meeting Yōko in Hawaii for a month's rest before resuming life in his home country. Shortly after his arrival in Japan, he gave two public readings in the Kobe area to benefit libraries severely damaged in the earthquake.

Although it, too, is narrated by a Boku, the first novel to follow *The Wind-Up Bird Chronicle* is clearly a new departure for Murakami, concentrating as it does on a female character swept away by a lesbian passion. The opening passage, on the tornado of first love that sweeps Sumire away and crosses the sea to destroy the temples of Angkor Wat, is one of Murakami's most energetic and hyperbolic pieces of writing. Murakami has often been paired with Yoshimoto Banana as representative of a new generation of Japanese writers, but only in this novel, *Supūtoniku no koibito* (1999; *The Sputnik sweetheart*), do the resemblances appear as anything more than superficial. The central character, Sumire, is a kind of Yoshimoto Banana figure: cute, lively, a driven (but, unlike Banana, unsuccessful) writer, so her presence naturally colors much of the atmosphere of the book. "I'm not sure if this counts as praise," wrote Banana in a rave review of *Supūtoniku no koibito* for *Yomiuri shinbun kokusaiban*, "but I *loved* this novel; it was as if I had written it myself" (p. 8). Overall, the book reads more like a compendium of rather too familiar Murakami motifs than a fresh creation, but the focus here has clearly moved away from Boku.

Boku disappears entirely in the series of six linked stories that began to appear in August 1999 under the series title "Jishin no ato" (After the earthquake) and were anthologized the following February as *Kami no kodomo-tachi wa mina odoru* (2000; All God's children can dance). As we have seen, the devastating Kobe earthquake of January 1995 and the subway gas attack of March made a great impression on Murakami as paired epoch-making events in the psychic history of the Japanese. The gas attack he has chosen to pursue in nonfiction, but the earthquake stirred his fictive imagination in a new way. This was the first time that Murakami adopted a fully third-person narrative perspective, and the result is a glumly humorous panorama of the mid-1990s Japanese shocked awake to the emptiness of life in a society in which people had more money in their wallets than they knew how to use. That emptiness may be what he found in the hearts of the ordinary people he interviewed as victims of the gas attack: a vague sense (like Hajime's in *South of the Border, West of the Sun*) that there is some indefinable thing missing from their lives. By moving outside the limited focus of Boku, Murakami implies that the malaise goes beyond the somewhat privileged few who live on the periphery of society and observe it from a place apart: he has broadened his scope to examine the very fabric of everyday life.

In his postscript to *Underground*, Murakami uncharacteristically calls upon the Japanese government to correct some of the systemic problems that prevented it from responding to the subway gas attack effectively. Thus we see a creator of haunting, dream-filled images calling for broad social action in a way that is perfectly consistent with the developing vision of his fiction. Neither he nor anyone else could have predicted the growth he was to undergo as a writer and as a person. Which is not to say that Murakami is suddenly stepping forth as the leader of a social movement or that this more overt political stance should be seen as either a rejection or a validation of the earlier work. Murakami continues to see himself as a writer, one who may, in the course of telling his stories, contribute to a process of healing both for himself and for his readers, but who will do so, if at all, through the power of his words.

Selected Bibliography

PRIMARY WORKS

NOVELS AND SHORT STORY COLLECTIONS

Kaze no uta o kike. Tokyo: Kōdansha, 1979. Trans. by Alfred Birnbaum as *Hear the Wind Sing.* Tokyo: Kōdansha English Library [distribution limited to Japan], 1987.

1973-nen no pinbōru. Tokyo: Kōdansha, 1980. Trans. by Alfred Birnbaum as *Pinball, 1973.* Tokyo: Kōdansha English Library [distribution limited to Japan], 1985.

Hitsuji o meguru bōken. Tokyo: Kōdansha, 1982. Trans. by Alfred Birnbaum as *A Wild Sheep Chase.* Tokyo: Kodansha International, 1989.

Chūgoku-yuki no surō bōto. Tokyo: Chūō Kōronsha, 1983. Partial contents trans. by Alfred Birnbaum as "A Slow Boat to China," "The Kangaroo Communiqué," and "The Last Lawn of the Afternoon." In *The Elephant Vanishes: Stories by Haruki Murakami.* Translated by Alfred Birnbaum and Jay Rubin. New York: Knopf, 1993.

Kangarū-biyori. Tokyo: Heibonsha, 1983. Partial contents trans. by Jay Rubin as "On Seeing the 100% Perfect Girl One Beautiful April Morning," and "A Window." In *The Elephant Vanishes.*

Hotaru, Naya o yaku, sono-ta no tanpen. Tokyo: Shinchōsha, 1984. Partial contents trans. by Alfred Birnbaum and Jay Rubin as "Barn Burning" and "The Dancing Dwarf." In *The Elephant Vanishes.*

Kaiten mokuba no deddo hiito. Tokyo: Kōdansha, 1985. Partial contents trans. by Alfred Birnbaum as "Lederhosen." In *The Elephant Vanishes.*

Sekai no owari to hādoboirudo wandārando. Tokyo: Shinchōsha, 1985. Trans. by Alfred Birnbaum as *Hard-Boiled Wonderland and the End of the World.* Tokyo: Kodansha International, 1991.

Pan'ya saishūgeki. Tokyo: Bungei Shunjūsha, 1986. Partial contents trans. by Alfred Birnbaum and Jay Rubin as "The Second Bakery Attack," "The Elephant Vanishes," "Family Affair," "The Fall of the Roman Empire, The 1881 Indian Uprising, Hitler's Invasion of Poland, and the Realm of the Raging Winds," and "The Wind-Up Bird and Tuesday's Women." In *The Elephant Vanishes.*

Noruwei no mori. Tokyo: Kōdansha, 1987. Trans. by Alfred Birnbaum as *Norwegian Wood.* Tokyo: Kōdansha English Library [distribution limited to Japan], 1989. Trans. by Jay Rubin as *Norwegian Wood.* London: Harvill Press, 2000, and New York: Vintage, 2000.

Dansu dansu dansu. Tokyo: Kōdansha, 1988. Trans. by Alfred Birnbaum as *Dance Dance Dance.* Tokyo: Kodansha International, 1994.

TV Piipuru. Tokyo: Bungei Shunjūsha, 1990. Partial contents translated by Alfred Birnbaum and Jay Rubin as "Sleep" and "TV People." In *The Elephant Vanishes.*

Murakami Haruki zensakuhin 1979–1989. 8 vols. Tokyo: Kōdansha, 1990–1991. (Contains all above texts except "TV People," some significantly revised by the author. Abbreviated as *MHZ* in citations.)

Kokkyō no minami, taiyō no nishi. Tokyo: Kōdansha, 1992. Trans. by Philip Gabriel as *South of the Border, West of the Sun.* New York: Knopf, 1999.

Nejimakidori kuronikuru. 3 vols. Tokyo: Shinchōsha, 1994–1995. Trans. by Jay Rubin as *The Wind-Up Bird Chronicle.* New York: Knopf, 1997.

Yoru no kumozaru. Tokyo: Heibonsha, 1995.

Rekishinton no yūrei. Tokyo: Bungei Shunjūsha, 1996. Partial contents trans. by Alfred Birnbaum and Jay Rubin as "The Little Green Monster" and "The Silence." In *The Elephant Vanishes.* Also trans. by Jay Rubin as "The Seventh Man." *Granta* 61 (spring 1998).

Supūtoniku no koibito. Tokyo: Kōdansha, 1999.

Kami no kodomotachi wa mina odoru. Tokyo: Shinchōsha, 2000.

ESSAYS, INTERVIEWS, TRAVEL WRITING, PICTURE BOOKS, REPORTAGE

Uōku, donto ran. With Murakami Ryū. Tokyo: Kōdansha, 1981.

Yume de aimashō. With Itoi Shigesato. Tokyo: Tōjusha, 1981.

Zō-kōjō no happiiendo. With Anzai Mizumaru. Tokyo: CBS-Sony, 1983.

Murakami Asahidō. With Anzai Mizumaru. Tokyo: Wakabayashi Shuppan Kikaku, 1984.

Nami no e, nami no hanashi. With Inakoshi Kōichi. Tokyo: Bungei Shunjū, 1984.

Eiga o meguru bōken. With Kawamoto Saburō. Tokyo: Kōdansha, 1985.

Hitsuji-otoko no kurisumasu. With Sasaki Maki. Tokyo: Kōdansha, 1985.

Murakami Asahidō no gyakushū. With Anzai Mizumaru. Tokyo: Asahi Shinbunsha, 1986.

Rangeruhansu-tō no gogo. With Anzai Mizumaru. Tokyo: Kōbunsha, 1986.

Hi-izuru kuni no kōjō. With Anzai Mizumaru. Tokyo: Heibonsha, 1987.

'THE SCRAP' Natsukashi no 1980 nendai. Tokyo: Bungei Shunjū, 1987.

Za Sukotto Fittsujerarudo bukku. Tokyo: TBS Britannica, 1988.

Murakami Asahidō Hai hō! Tokyo: Bunka Shuppan Kyoku, 1989.

Tōi taiko. With Murakami Yōko. Tokyo: Kōdansha, 1990.

Uten enten. With Matsumura Eizō. Tokyo: Shinchōsha, 1990.

Yagate kanashiki gaikokugo. Tokyo: Kōdansha, 1994.

Murakami Asahidō jānaru: Uzumakineko no mitsukekata. Tokyo: Shinchōsha, 1996.

Murakami Haruki, Kawai Hayao ni ai ni iku. With Kawai Hayao. Tokyo: Iwanami Shoten, 1996.

Andāguraundo. Tokyo: Kōdansha, 1997. Partial contents trans. by Alfred Birnbaum as *Underground.* New York: Knopf, 2000.

Murakami Asahidō wa ikanishite kitaerareta ka. With Anzai Mizumaru. Tokyo: Asahi Shinbunsha, 1997.

CD-ROM-ban Murakami Asahidō: Yume no sāfushitii. Tokyo: Asahi Shinbunsha, 1998.

Henkyō/Kinkyō. Tokyo: Shinchōsha, 1998.

Henkyō/Kinkyō shashin-hen. With Matsumura Eizō. Tokyo: Shinchōsha, 1998.

Yakusoku-sareta basho de: Underground 2. Tokyo: Bungei Shunjūsha, 1998. Partial contents trans. by Philip Gabriel as *Underground.*

TRANSLATIONS BY MURAKAMI HARUKI

Mai rosuto shitii (My lost city, and other stories, by F. Scott Fitzgerald). Tokyo: Chūō Kōronsha, 1981.

Boku ga denwa o kakete iru basho (Where I'm calling from, and other stories, by Raymond Carver). Tokyo: Chūō Kōronsha, 1983.

Seifū-gō no sōnan (The wreck of the Zephyr, by Chris Van Allsburg). Tokyo: Kawade Shobō Shinsha, 1985.

Yoru ni naru to sake wa . . . (At night the salmon move, by Raymond Carver). Tokyo: Chūō Kōronsha, 1985.

Kuma o hanatsu (Setting free the bears, by John Irving). Tokyo: Chūō Kōronsha, 1986.

Idai-naru Desurifu (The great Dethriffe, by C. D. B. Bryan). Tokyo: Shinchōsha, 1987.

Kyūkō Hokkyoku-gō (The polar express, by Chris Van Allsburg). Tokyo: Kawade Shobō Shinsha, 1987.

Wāruzu endo (World's end and other stories, by Paul Theroux). Tokyo: Bungei Shunjūsha, 1987.

and other stories: Totte oki no Amerika shōsetsu 12 hen (12 miscellaneous American stories). Tokyo: Bungei Shunjū-sha, 1988.

Ojiisan no omoide (I remember grandpa, by Truman Capote). Tokyo: Bungei Shunjūsha, 1988.

Za Sukotto Fittsujerarudo bukku (F. Scott Fitzgerald miscellany). Tokyo: TBS Britannica, 1988.

Aru kurisumasu (One Christmas, by Truman Capote). Tokyo: Bungei Shunjū, 1989.

Namae no nai hito (The stranger, by Chris Van Allsburg). Tokyo: Kawade Shobō Shinsha, 1989.

Nyūkuria eiji (The nuclear age, by Tim O'Brien). Tokyo: Bungei Shunjū, 1989.

Sasayaka da keredo, yaku ni tatsu koto (A small, good thing, and other stories, by Raymond Carver). Tokyo: Chūō Kōronsha, 1989.

Hontō no sensō no hanashi o shiyō (The things they carried, by Tim O'Brien). Tokyo: Bungei Shunjū, 1990.

Kurisumasu no omoide (A Christmas memory, by Truman Capote). Tokyo: Bungei Shunjū, 1990.

Reimondo Kāvā zenshū (Complete works of Raymond Carver). 8 vols. Tokyo: Chūō Kōronsha, 1990–1997.

Sora-tobi neko (Catwings, by Ursula K. LeGuin). Tokyo: Kōdansha, 1992.

Kaette kita sora-tobi neko (Catwings return, by Ursula K. Le Guin). Tokyo: Kōdansha, 1993.

Sudden Fiction: chō-tanpen shōsetsu 70 (Sudden fiction, edited by Robert Shepherd and James Thomas). Tokyo: Bunshun Bunko, 1994.

Sayōnara, Bādorando (From Birdland to Broadway, by Bill Crow). Tokyo: Shinchōsha, 1995.

Babiron ni kaeru: za Sukotto Fittsujerarudo bukku 2 (F. Scott Fitzgerald's "Babylon revisited" and three other stories). Tokyo: Chūō Kōronsha, 1996.

Shinzō o tsuranukarete (Shot in the heart, by Mikal Gilmore). Tokyo: Bungei Shunjūsha, 1996.

SECONDARY WORKS

COMMENTARY ON MURAKAMI IN ENGLISH

Aoki Tamotsu. "Murakami Haruki and Contemporary Japan." Trans. by Matthew Strecher. In *Contemporary Japan and Popular Culture.* Edited by John W. Treat. Honolulu: University of Hawaii Press, 1996.

Beale, Lewis. "The Cool, Cynical Voice of Young Japan." *Los Angeles Times Magazine,* 8 December 1991, pp. 36–83.

Buruma, Ian. "Becoming Japanese." *The New Yorker,* 23 and 30 December 1996, pp. 60–71.

Masao Miyoshi. *Off Center: Power and Culture Relations between Japan and the United States.* Cambridge, Mass.: Harvard University Press, 1991.

Napier, Susan. *The Fantastic in Modern Japanese Literature: The Subversion of Modernity.* London and New York: Routledge, 1996.

Rubin, Jay. "The Other World of Murakami Haruki." *Japan Quarterly* 39, no. 4:490–500 (October–December 1992).

———. "Murakami Haruki's Two Poor Aunts Tell Everything They Know About Sheep, Wells, Unicorns, Proust, and Elephants." In *Ōe and Beyond: Fiction in Contemporary Japan.* Edited by Stephen Snyder and Philip Gabriel. Honolulu: University of Hawaii Press, 1999. Pp. 177–198.

Strecher, Matthew. "Hidden Texts and Nostalgic Images: The Serious Social Critique of Murakami Haruki." Ph.D. dissertation, University of Washington, 1995.

———. "Murakami Haruki: Japan's Coolest Writer Heats Up." *Japan Quarterly* 45, no. 1:61–69 (January–March 1998).

———. "Beyond 'Pure' Literature: Mimesis, Formula, and the Postmodern in the Fiction of Murakami Haruki," *The Journal of Asian Studies* 57, no. 2:354–378 (May 1998).

———. "Magical Realism and the Search for Identity in the Fiction of Murakami Haruki." *The Journal of Japanese Studies* 25, no. 2:263–298 (summer 1999).

STUDIES OF MURAKAMI IN JAPANESE

Hisai Tsubaki and Kuwa Masato. *Zō ga heigen ni kaetta hi.* Tokyo: Shinchōsha, 1991.

Imai Kiyoto. *Murakami Haruki—Off no kankaku.* Tokyo: Kokken Shuppan, 1990.

Katō Norihiro et. al. *Gunzō Nihon no sakka 26: Murakami Haruki.* Tokyo: Shōgakkan, 1997.

Kawamoto Saburō. "'Monogatari' no tame no bōken." *Bungakukai* 39, no. 8:34–86 (August 1985).

Konishi Keita. *Murakami Haruki no ongaku zukan.* Tokyo: Japan Mix KK, 1998.

Kuroko Kazuo. *Murakami Haruki: Za rosuto wārudo.* Tokyo: Rokkō Shuppan, 1989; Tokyo: Daisan Shokan, 1993.

———. *Murakami Haruki to dōjidai no bungaku.* Tokyo: Kawai Shuppan, 1990.

Murakami Ryū et. al. *Murakami Haruki: Shiiku & fuaindo.* Tokyo: Seidōsha, 1986.

Tsuge Teruhiko et. al., eds. *Murakami Haruki Sutadiizu.* 5 vols. Tokyo: Wakakusa Shobō, 1999.

Yoshimoto Banana. Review of "The Sputnik sweetheart." *Yomiuri Shinbun Kokusaiban,* 31 May 1999, p. 8.

SPECIAL MURAKAMI ISSUES OF MAGAZINES IN JAPANESE

Brutus 433 (1 June 1999). "Marakami Haruki to kangaeru 'Nikutai no rinri' Nikutai ga kawareba, buntai mo kawaru!?."

Bungakukai. (April 1991). "Murakami Haruki bukku."

Kokubungaku: Kaishaku to Kyōzai no Kenkyū 30, no. 3 (March 1985). "Nakagami Kenji to Murakami Haruki–toshi to han-toshi."

Kokubungaku: Kaishaku to Kyōzai no Kenkyū 40, no. 4 (March 1995). "Murakami Haruki: Yochi-suru bungaku."

Yuriika 21, no. 8 (June 1989). "Murakami Haruki no sekai."

Yuriika 32, no. 3 (March 2000). "Murakami Haruki o yomu."

Nakagami Kenji
1946–1992

EVE ZIMMERMAN

NAKAGAMI KENJI rose to fame in the mid-1970s for vivid and powerful stories of a clan scarred by violence and poverty on the underside of Japan's economic miracle. Wrung from his own experience among the *burakumin* (a group of outcastes viewed as less than human for their "unclean" occupations), Nakagami's fiction burst apart stereotypes of a serene and homogeneous Japan, presenting a clear view of oppression and discrimination. His depiction of the outcaste alleyways of Shingū, winding out from the back of the railroad station, literally drew his middle-class Japanese readers into spaces that they had not seen before.

Nakagami's early fiction struck a chord with critics, who praised his energy and raw style, seeing their own interest in social justice come to life in his pages. At the same time, Nakagami's gritty realism and graphic sex tapped into and enlarged upon the vision of his times, asserting the primacy and the power of human desire. The woman in the story "Akagami" (1978; "Red Hair," 1999), turns to her lover and says, "It's raining again. We can stay in bed all day. But it's not always going to rain like this" (*Nakagami Kenji zenshū [NKZ]*, vol. 2, p. 502; tr. *The Cape*, p. 176). True to Nakagami's vision, the woman knows that pleasure cannot last, but for one more day at least, she will turn back to the warmth of her lover's body, embracing a life lived in the present. Nakagami's fiction begins and ends in the warmth of this present moment.

Rooted in the world, Nakagami's fiction nevertheless transcends realism. Through bursts of lyricism and dazzling rhythms, Nakagami transforms unbearable pain into poetry and forges a fictional voice that astounds with its range and its complexity. Nakagami experimented extensively with literary form, moving from symbolist poetry in the 1960s, to large naturalist canvases in the early fiction, to an examination of myth in his short stories, and finally, in his last year, to romance as he pushed relentlessly at the parameters of modern Japanese literature. Writing until a few months before his death in 1992, at the age of forty-six, Nakagami left the world a body of work that fills fifteen volumes.

Finding a Name

Born on 2 August 1946 into a large and complex family, Nakagami suffered from a surfeit of last names. At birth, he was named Kinoshita Kenji, after his mother's first husband, who had died long before he was born. In high school he became Nakaue Kenji when his mother married a well-to-do contractor who rescued the family from poverty. Interestingly, Kenji never took the name of his biological father, Suzuki Tomezō, a man described by a friend as "strong with men and strong with women, a great fighter" (interview with Matsune Hisao, July 1993). Like the heroes of his own fiction, Nakagami was confronted with the problem of his origins from a young age.

Kenji was not the only boy in an outcaste neighborhood in Shingū (a provincial town in southwestern Japan), who was without a father. Indeed, later in his life, Nakagami would describe his family and the community in general as "matriarchal" (interview with Nakagami Kenji, January 1989). Nakagami's family situation was underscored by the situation of the *burakumin* in general. Denied access to education or advancement, the outcastes of Shingū lived outside the basic social unit of Japanese society, the *ie* ("family system"), in which property and authority were passed down from father to son.

Since the beginning of the Tokugawa period (1600–1868), outcaste status had not only been fixed by birth but also had been formally linked to "unclean," menial jobs, often symbolically aligned with the animal realm or with dirt. Given little choice of employment, the *burakumin* of Shingū worked as day laborers, lumber haulers, shoemakers, or slaughterers. Often dangerous and offering little chance of advancement or security, these jobs did not promote stable family life. As Nakagami explained in *Sabetsu: Sono kongen o tou* (1977; Investigating the roots of discrimination), a debate with other writers, marriage without property to pass along was a more fluid arrangement.

Turning the pages of Nakagami's family history, one can see that men and particularly fathers were scarce. Nakagami's mother, Nakaue Chisato, was born in Koza, a town with an outcaste population. Although her father, a fairly successful cattle dealer, had managed to build his family a house, his early death soon plunged Chisato and her siblings into poverty. Later, after the marriage of her older sister, Chisato moved to Shingū by the

sea where she helped out in her in-law's fish shop (interview with Nakue Chisato, 1993). Eventually she married a Shingū local from the *buraku* ("outcaste neighborhood") and had five children (three girls and two boys; the younger boy died in childhood). Her first husband died at the age of thirty-five, leaving her to raise the children on her own. She conceived her last child, Kenji, during a brief union with Suzuki Tomezō.

The family of Suzuki Tomezō, Nakagami's natural father, was similarly matriarchal. Tomezō's father went to prison when Tomezō was a child, and Tomezo's mother formed a relationship with a one-legged man from Taketō. This affair broke up the marriage, and Tomezō was subsequently raised by his mother. According to Matsune Hisao, an old shoe-seller in the neighborhood, after World War II Tomezō drifted to Shingū looking for work. There he associated with gangster types, working in the black market. After his liaison with Kenji's mother ended, Tomezō had little to do with the family. Although he knew he had a son, Tomezō did not formally meet Kenji until the latter was an adult.

As if being abandoned by his biological father were not enough, at the age of thirteen, Kenji suffered a different kind of family tragedy when Ikuhei, his older half brother by his mother's first husband, hanged himself. According to newspaper accounts of the death, Ikuhei had been suffering from mental illness; moreover, he was an alcoholic. This death would follow Nakagami through the years, stirring ripples of despair, incomprehension, and mournful love.

At the age of eighteen, Kenji graduated from Shingū high school and boarded a train for Tokyo. There he took a third and final name, Nakagami, by giving the characters for "Nakaue" a different reading. Nakagami claimed that he made this change because people in Tokyo misread his name, but the new name also reveals his desire to forge a new identity free from the complications of home. Little by little, the local boy from Shingū made himself over into a Tokyo writer and an intellectual.

Through the invention of a new name, Nakagami attempted to throw off the burden of previous names that had never belonged to him.

Getting Letters

Born in 1946, the year after America occupied Japan, Nakagami's life was dramatically changed by the aftermath of World War II. Under such Occupation reforms as the Fundamental Law of Education (1947), Kenji was sent to school. For the first time his mother, aided by the government in kind (not cash), sent a child past primary school. As Nakagami said in an interview in January 1989, "If Japan hadn't been defeated in World War II, I wouldn't have become what I am today."

In middle school, the young Kenji showed a talent for writing. A sympathetic teacher named Yamamoto Ai recognized his ability, gave him daily "diary" assignments, and encouraged him to publish in the school literary magazine. In high school, however, for the first time Nakagami had to confront the outrage of his readers. A story that had been published in the school magazine was censored when a teacher discovered in its final lines: "I'm going to kill you!" Deeming the story unfit for a teenage audience, the teacher insisted that the offending words be excised. Tamura Satoko, a classmate of Kenji's, writes that she never discussed the incident with him but always wondered about his reaction. As she reports: "At that moment I realized for the first time (as well as I could at that age) that Kenji was fashioning his own unassailable space" (p. 61). For Nakagami, she suggests, writing was not a luxury or a pleasure but a way to shield himself from a harsh environment—a means of survival.

Bodies of Water

Nakagami's early poetry represents his first sustained attempt to sketch out the parameters of an "unassailable space." He began to jot down poems in high school, publishing them in small magazines through the 1960s. In the end, pure poetry did not work for Nakagami; without the mediation of character, poetry proved too raw, and the exploration of the self in its more abstract forms too damaging. Nakagami then took refuge in the writing of fiction. As his biographer Takazawa Shūji states, "Nakagami's poetic flame burned out by 1969" (*Hyōden Nakagami Kenji*, 1998, p. 47). Nevertheless, the poems provide a glimpse of a young writer wrestling with the particulars of his own experience and struggling to find a voice. In particular, Nakagami showed a fascination for Arthur Rimbaud. In high school, he began to write "imitations" of Rimbaud's poems: of the twenty-four poems included in the *zenshū* (Collected works), nine make direct reference to *A Season in Hell*, Rimbaud's 1873 "poetic record" of travel, catharsis, and descent into the lower depths.

To the young Nakagami, the poetry of Rimbaud offered a road out of the provincial backwaters of Shingū and a means to universalize his own experience. In particular, Nakagami's poems contain images of early male death and the dissolution of the male body in landscape. Taking the form of Icarus, the young man flies too close to the sun in pursuit of his desire, or he drifts, dead, down the Kumano River toward the mouth of the sea. In a short verse which is based on Rimbaud's famous poem "Vowels," the speaker gives the following explication:

It's me—desire melting into the sea, Icarus
   falling, anger spilling
over like powdery lime, cola overflowing
   with sadness in
the white coffin of your glass, it's me. Your,
   your, your, your—me.

(*NKZ*, vol. 14, p. 34)

Nakagami plays with the letter "I," making it into a pun which refers both to Icarus and to the speaker himself—*boku* ("I"). The images of the poem point to the dissolution of "me," to a sea of desire into which he melts, to Icarus whose wings melt because he comes too close to the sun, to liquid overflowing the edges of its container. Finally, the "me" dissolves irrevocably into "you," an action which is emphasized by the repetition of the word *omae* in the phrase "your, your, your—me." In another excerpt from a longer poem entitled "Kisetsu no tame no shigaku" (A poetics for the season), Nakagami elaborates on images of a fragile and dissolving male subject: "Kumano River floods every spring / floating the body of a dead boy" (*NKZ*, vol. 14, p. 41). The river performs a mythic pattern of yearly sacrifice, releasing the body of a boy each spring into the flowing space of the sea. In these poems, the male speaker seems inexorably drawn toward death.

Before Nakagami gave up poetry entirely, he explored his fascination with male bodies and water further in a forty-page prose poem entitled "Umi e" (1967; To the sea). With its alternating passages of prose and poetry, "Umi e" marks a transition in Nakagami's oeuvre. It was his last homage to Rimbaud. Exploring the interstices between prose and poetry, "Umi e" begins to sketch in the story behind the image of the dead, drifting boy, who represents both the suicide brother and the possibility of death for Nakagami himself.

"Umi e" falls into a simple pattern: the speaker gets off a bus and walks through his hometown toward the sea, remembering incidents from his youth in the town. As he reaches the water, he internalizes the wild and angry sea—as a sea of anger inside himself. The reader discovers that the internalized sea is actually the space of the brother's suicide—which occurred in the month of March:

I am walking. Walking toward the sea inside me. The sea that ate me, knocked me down, crushed my throat, and killed me. I'm walking toward that sea. Sea, you showed your beautiful form to me brimming over with the brilliant confidence and pride of March and you took me in. Then you tore my skin, ate me alive. I'm beginning to walk. Walking toward that sea inside of me.

(*NKZ*, vol.1, p. 60)

Through a change of format in the text, the reader moves into the head of the dead brother who hanged himself in March 1959. At the moment that the reader imagines that the speaker will join the dead brother in the waves and embrace death, the speaker transforms himself and the ocean:

I am made pure
I'm not a fallen angel anymore
Look at the golden downy hair shining on
my body
Sea,
you're my brother, my sister, myself
Sea, tide of my blood,
I'm purity itself
The waves send an echo of love wildly

(*NKZ*, vol. 1, p. 76)

Rather than allow the sea to destroy him, the speaker claims the water as a familial space, the purifying tide of his own bloodline, overflowing with the essences of his brother and sister. This renewed vision of the sea allows the speaker to break with Icarus and choose survival. But then the speaker goes further. As he steps into the waves, he ejaculates, crying, "Oh, oh, oh, sea, I'm coming, words won't kill me, it's a real ejaculation, o, o, o" (*NKZ*, vol. 1, p. 78). Through this literal ejaculation, the speaker plays on the meaning of "words won't kill me," suggesting that words alone won't bring him to orgasm. At the end of "Umi e" the speaker expresses his determination to transcend the abstractions of poetry. Nakagami further reveals the tension that will propel the work to follow. The speaker is torn by the promise of blissful dissolution into the sea (and death), on the one hand, and, on the other, by the urge to survive: to bring the world into the text and make things "real."

Secrets and Lies

Nakagami's struggle to resist the pull of the sea and move away from his brother began anew in the pages of his early fiction. In 1969, Nakagami set a story directly in Shingū, the town hemmed in by mountains, rivers, and the sea. The title, "Ichiban hajime no dekigoto" (1969; The first thing that happened), seems to foreshadow the series of stories and novels set in the Kumano region that followed. In a straightforward and prosaic first-person narration, Nakagami moves away from poetic images of male bodies drifting in water; the first-person narrator methodically puts distance between his brother and himself.

The elder brother of the narrator in "Ichiban hajime no dekigoto" nurses the mad delusion that a god in the sea whispers words of wisdom into his ear. Nearly a creature of the water himself, he soon commits suicide in his garden. In contrast, the narrator, the young brother, belongs to a gang of boys who heap scorn on the inhabitants of a poor Korean hamlet nearby, and who build themselves a fort in the mountains which they call "Secret." The reader soon learns that the boys themselves are adept at keeping secrets: one of the boys, the narrator reveals, comes from the Korean hamlet; and the narrator, too, is a "liar," who pretends that his stepfather is his real father. In fact, telling lies is the key to survival. In simple terms, the character who practices fiction-making survives, whereas the brother, a creature of poetry who cannot dissemble and who heeds the call of the sea, dies.

Through the boys' construction of a secret fort, Nakagami also makes reference to the desire to "pass" in the outside world beyond the outcaste alleyways of Shingū. The Korean hamlet, for example, not only stands for the outcaste neighborhood, but also suggests the ways in which the characters internalize self-hatred and discrimination by hiding their origins. At the end of the story, the narrator is confronted with his own immutable status and his link to his brother when he pricks his hand and blood drips from his body. Refusing to submit to the lines of his own family identity, the narrator vows to tear everything apart—his friends, the sky, the sea, the mountain, the dead brother, even the tower where he and his friends had hoped to take refuge. The rage that he feels at the sight of his own blood brings an epiphany: one must reveal secrets and literally "externalize" one's identity in writing in order to confront and measure its power.

The Birth of Akiyuki

Six years passed between the publication of "Ichiban hajime no dekigoto" and the appearance of the Akiyuki trilogy about a laborer named Akiyuki: *Misaki* (1976; *The Cape*, 1999), *Karekinada* (1977; The Kareki straits), and *Chi no hate shijō no toki* (1984; The sublime time at the end of the blood). *The Cape* brought Nakagami the Akutagawa Prize (1976), a rite of passage for any serious Japanese writer, and significant critical acclaim. In addition, *Karekinada* was hailed by critics as a masterpiece of modern Japanese literature, and was said to have fulfilled the promise of Japanese naturalism.

With the emergence of Akiyuki, Nakagami's work attains striking lyrical intensity as it explores the lower depths of the outcaste alleyways and the tortured patterns of Akiyuki's family history. The language of "Ichiban hajime no dekigoto," with its polished tone and deliberate imagery, reads like a studious attempt to write literature. In contrast, *The Cape* flows effortlessly forward, its short, imagistic sentences gradually building into passages that are riveting for their gritty realism and moving for their flights of lyricism. The difference is Akiyuki. Through a third-person narration, Nakagami achieves enough distance from his materials to explore them on firm ground. Along the way, Akiyuki thinks like a poet. Surprisingly, Nakagami's poetic flame has not burned out; it has simply been incorporated into prose. Through Akiyuki, Nakagami also practices repetition, examining the problem of male death and expendability from all angles, as if he were painting different views of the same room. Among all the fragile males, Akiyuki is the sole survivor.

The Cape and *Karekinada* tell the story of Akiyuki, a laborer who struggles with a complex family drama that threatens to swallow him. The bastard son of a shady contractor, Akiyuki has four half-siblings from his mother's first marriage. *The Cape* focuses on the story of an elder sister, Mie, while *Karekinada* develops the figure of the father and Akiyuki's conflict with and murder of Hideo, a half brother with whom he shares his natural father. Both works, however, are haunted by an original trauma: the suicide of a half brother, Ikuo (given a name only in the second work), who suffered from alcoholism and madness.

Set twelve years after Ikuo's death, *The Cape* describes Mie's breakdown, which is triggered by another incident of male violence—this time a murder in her clan of in-laws. Mie's mental collapse, however, functions as a delayed reaction to Ikuo's death and signals her desire to join her beloved elder brother: she attempts suicide twice. In her regression to a childlike state, her mourning for her dead brother, and her illness, Mie represents the realm of poetry and dissolution; when Akiyuki visits her sickbed, he notices that "the rise and fall of her faintly pink ear made her look like another sort of creature altogether" (*NKZ*, vol. 3, p. 235; tr. p. 96). Near the end of the story, the family makes an excursion to the cape to tend to the graves of the clan in a final attempt to save Mie. By showing Mie the graves, the other family members hope to put the dead and the living back in their proper places and restore Mie to sanity.

Watching events unfold around him, Akiyuki finds that the murder has upset the rhythms of life, turning "everything upside down" (*NKZ*, vol. 3, p. 223; tr. p. 80). The source of this inversion, Mie, who lives in the past, attempts to make Akiyuki into a substitute for the dead brother. She reads Ikuo's features into Akiyuki's face, and from her sickbed, she calls to him as if he were her lover (*NKZ*, vol. 3, p. 226; tr. p. 83). Mesmerized and disturbed by her desire, Akiyuki strikes out for his father's territory, pursuing the rumor of another half sister (by his biological father), who works in the town's red-light district. He visits the brothel but notes that his supposed half sister "doesn't resemble anyone" (*NKZ*, vol. 3, p. 224; tr. p. 81). This lack of resemblance is particularly telling in a story in which everyone resembles someone else. In this search, Akiyuki flees from the morass of resemblances and from his stifling and hopeless love for his elder sister, Mie—a love which, if fulfilled, would mean his death—his transformation into Ikuo.

Ironically, however, Akiyuki replaces a potential act of incest with an actual one when he sleeps with his prostitute sister. On the one hand, Akiyuki's reluctance to have sex with outsiders evinces his longing for a racialized, pure communal space in which sex with the sister becomes a metaphor for outcaste identity. On the other hand, however, although Akiyuki operates within the coordinates of his complex bloodline, he also chooses the unknown territory of the father, a realm in which he finds himself a stranger. Sex with the prostitute allows Akiyuki to speak for the first time to his father:

> We two are the pure children of that man, the one I can now call "Father" for the first time. If only we had hearts for sex organs. Akiyuki wanted to rip open his chest, and show his sister, her eyes closing as she strained and moaned, the blood of that man running through his veins.

> (*NKZ*, vol. 3, p. 242; tr. p. 104)

The act of naming the father will save Akiyuki and deliver him from the arms of Ikuo and Mie, who remain caught in the embrace of an impossible love. By claiming the father and recognizing the father's face in his own features, Akiyuki finally achieves a means to act in circumstances that have been beyond his control. Just before he sleeps with the prostitute, Akiyuki once again tests his choices—death or life:

> "Do you ever think of dying?" he asked.
> "Damn, you're really hopeless," the woman said. She wrapped her feet around

his. "At my age why would I think about such things? . . . "

He nodded. She reached for his penis again. A vision came to him of the cape protruding into the sea. Swell up, rise up, he thought. Tear the sea to pieces.

(*NKZ*, vol. 3, p. 241; tr. p. 103)

Akiyuki considers death first, but the sister turns him back into the world. To combat his fear of dissolving into a sea of body fluids (of dying), Akiyuki imagines the cape not simply as a phallic projection but as a sign of differentiation, of fiction itself juxtaposed with the timeless story of the sea. Fraught with danger though sex may be, Akiyuki uses it to rescue himself from resemblances, to break free of the faces of Ikuo and Mie, and to create a semblance of selfhood where none exists.

Claiming a Legacy

Karekinada (The Kareki straits), the second work in the Akiyuki trilogy, picks up events three years later. Now twenty-seven years old, Akiyuki continues to struggle with the same ghosts that haunted him in *The Cape*. Nakagami retells and refines the earlier work, shaping his materials over and over again. According to the critic Karatani Kōjin, it is this repetition that makes *Karekinada* a masterpiece (*Sakaguchi Ango to Nakagami Kenji*, 1996, p. 213). The repetition of *Karekinada* reveals Nakagami's stance as a writer; rather than purporting to tell unique tales, fiction is simply the shaping of endless and varied versions of the same material. Fiction can offer only "revision," not resolution. Perhaps the best example in *Karekinada* is Nakagami's use of names. Unlike *The Cape*, which dispenses with proper names altogether, calling the characters Sister, Brother, Mother, and Father, *Karekinada* does assign the characters proper names, thereby giving this version of the tale a specificity that *The Cape* does not possess.

Karekinada continues to probe the problem of substitution. Early in the novel, Akiyuki wrestles with the aftermath of having slept with his prostitute half sister, now given the name of Satoko. First, he reveals his own act of substituting one sister for another; as the reader learns, his true desire was for Mie: "The secret wasn't that he had slept with his half-sister, Satoko. . . . She was so like Mie. That was the real secret, thought Akiyuki" (*NKZ*, vol. 3, p. 364). Akiyuki's love for Mie, however, cannot be acted upon even if it serves as the secret that propels the story forward. Mie, linked with Ikuo, with madness, and with the sea, would lead Akiyuki to repeat the past and follow his brother into death. In order to survive, Akiyuki must leave Mie, the mother's house, and the matriarchal order these women represent.

Through the figure of Satoko, on the other hand, Akiyuki journeys away from the matriarchy, and toward the realm of his father, Hamamura Ryūzō. His act of incest with Satoko is used to draw the attention of his father. Strangely, however, Hamamura does not remonstrate with Akiyuki and Satoko for having slept together; rather, he offers them land upon which they can raise the fruits of their incestuous union if they ever produce children. Hamamura's offer of land signals a transformation in Akiyuki's status: he has finally come into property and his paternal legacy.

The equation of incest with property is revealed at the yearly festival to honor the dead. The old women of the neighborhood dance and sing a song about brother-sister incest. The song, which is quoted in full in the text, tells of a brother who falls in love with his younger sister and begs for her love. When she acquiesces, they flee and commit a love suicide. In a 1978 lecture in Shingū, Nakagami pondered the meaning of this old song preserved so faithfully by the *buraku* community. He rejects the notion that the song reinforces the taboo against incest, and instead suggests that it encodes the mythic tale of the birth of a country. Specifically, this "country" is a mythic space of resistance and empowerment, a topsy-turvy land. He expands on this by reference to Japan's ancient chronicle of creation, the *Kojiki*:

It seems to me that this song is an inside-out, upside-down song about the birth of a country. An inverted *Kojiki* if you will. Many kinds of myths take this shape. In other words, from a brother and sister you can make a country. And here, in the middle of the *buraku*, doesn't this birth of a country take the form of a brother-sister love suicide? In order to give birth to a country, doesn't something have to die? Or, to put it the opposite way, the country that emerges from the brother-sister suicide is an inside-out country of darkness, an upside-down country, that's my sense of it.

(*Nakagami Kenji to Kumano*, 2000, p. 90)

As the brother-sister incest myth suggests, sex with a sister brings a new space into being, one that is necessarily apart and special. In order to reach the new country, however, Akiyuki must turn away from the sister he truly desires, Mie, who dwells in the matriarchy, and he must embrace the sister who leads him to his father.

But one final obstacle remains—his half brother, Hideo (the legitimate son of Hamamura), who has always shadowed Akiyuki with his gaze, reminding him who is the bastard son. Toward the end of *Karekinada*, Akiyuki murders Hideo during a fight by the river. In one of the most chilling scenes in modern Japanese fiction, Akiyuki kills in order to claim his father. The murder is necessary because it will firmly establish the difference between brothers and, moreover, will finally allow Akiyuki to banish the ghost of Ikuo, the brother who longed to kill him. In its emphasis on blood and bodily fluids, the murder scene returns us to the death and dissolution of the early poetry, in which a young man floats dead down the river.

Hideo struggled to knock him over, but Akiyuki held him down, picked up a wet rock from the riverbank and bashed in his head. He was going to kill the son of a bitch.

Blood streamed from Hideo's nostrils. His shirt was stained black with it. Letting out a scream, Hideo covered his face with his hands, trying to ward off the blows. . . . There was blood everywhere. But in the darkness Akiyuki couldn't distinguish between the black water of the river and Hideo's blood. A flower floating in the swollen waters of the river appeared in Akiyuki's field of vision. . . . Something that could have either been Hideo's blood or the water of the river made little waves as it lapped between the rocks. It flowed black all the way to the sea. To the sea that covered Arima, this region and even the straits of Kareki. "Run!" yelled Tōru.

"Where to?" said Akiyuki.

Akiyuki looked at Hideo. Lying there with blood streaming down and his body convulsing, he didn't look like Hideo. He was somebody without a name.

(*NKZ*, vol. 3, pp. 453–454)

Whereas Hideo proved an insurmountable threat to Akiyuki in life, his death makes the difference between the two visible for all to see, in particular the father, who views the murder from the nearby riverbank. Lying on the ground, bleeding and convulsing, Hideo has lost his name and taken on the role of scapegoat. Like all those other boys before him, his body begins its journey to the sea. Subsumed by landscape, Hideo attains a state of mythic, undifferentiated being. Akiyuki, on the other hand, left behind in the world, continues to struggle with those who would claim his features and control his destiny.

Behind the pairs of siblings stands Akiyuki's father, Hamamura Ryūzō. Unlike other patriarchs in modern Japanese fiction, however, Hamamura does nothing to stem the tide of Akiyuki's anger. In fact, the father does not oppose the son nor stand to defend his territory, but rather shifts position according to Akiyuki's movements. In the final work of the trilogy, *Chi no hate shijō no toki* (The sublime time at the end of the blood), Akiyuki's father commits suicide in front of his son rather than turn and fight. His lack of resistance underscores Karatani Kōjin's point in his afterword to *Chi no hate shijō no toki* that the oedipal vein was an empty one for Nakagami. In a tantalizingly autobiographical essay, "Sakuragawa," Nakagami himself wrote, "It's the same as if I'd never written a word about my real father" (*NKZ*, vol. 5, p. 214). But the father does achieve one important thing for the son: he leads him out of a maze of sameness and death, into the world to struggle.

The "Discovery" of Kumano

In the late 1970s, Nakagami returned frequently to Shingū, becoming more active in his old neighborhood. (By this time he had married Yamaguchi Kasumi, a fellow writer who used the pen name Kiwa Kyō; they had two daughters and a son together.) In 1977, on assignment for the *Asahi Journal*, he traveled around the Kishū Peninsula, recording the stories of people in the hamlets dotted along the coast and through the mountains. Published in serial form in 1977, *Kishū: ki no kuni ne no kuni monogatari* (1978; Kishū: land of trees and roots) stands as a remarkable ethnographic record of voices from an illiterate but thriving oral culture. Using the term *ryōi* ("strange marvels") to describe what he discovered in the mountains, Nakagami reiterated his vision of Kumano as an upside-down country of darkness. In 1978, Nakagami founded the Buraku Youth Association *(buraku seinen bunka kai)* in Shingū and produced a series of events to which he invited prominent intellectuals and spoke on *buraku* culture .

Another "discovery" of these years was the old woman named Oryū no Oba. In March 1978, Matsune Hisao took Nakagami, fresh from his documentary writing about Kishū, to meet Oryū no Oba, a relation by marriage. Eighty-eight years old at the time and lying ill in bed, Oryū, like others in her community, had never learned to read and write. Yet, according to Matsune, she had a mind like a "computer" and held the complex genealogy—the birth and death dates—of everyone in the neighborhood in her head. Intrigued by this discovery, Nakagami took notes on the stories Oryū no Oba told from her bed.

Ironically, Nakagami's "discovery" of Kumano reveals the extent to which he had embraced the role of the Tokyo intellectual. It was only from a distance that Nakagami would recognize the fictional possibilities of the dark region of Kumano, turning it into a site of resistance to the center. Moreover, by this time he was working closely with a group of critics, writers, and thinkers who were in the vanguard of the postmodern movement in Japan, and he saw Kumano through a critical lens. During these years, his friendship with the critic and writer Karatani Kōjin in particular blossomed. Typical of Karatani's assessment of Nakagami is a 1985 essay entitled, "Ima koko e" (To here and now), in which Karatani presents his opinion that Nakagami's value lies not in his being a "good" writer but rather in being a writer who was continually "moving into darkness" (*Sakaguchi Ango to Nakagami Kenji*, 1996, p. 124). In the next phase of his writing, Nakagami fulfilled Karatani's expectations even further as he turned inward to create a fiction of the shadows.

"Twice-Told" Tales

For Nakagami, Karatani, and others in their circle, the concept of the *monogatari* in the late 1970s provided a means to rethink modern Japanese literature. In its classical sense, the word *monogatari* simply means "tale" (as in *The Tale of Genji* [Genji Monogatari]), but the critics were not urging a return to a premodern tradition. Rather, in Noriko Mizuta Lippet's terms, they viewed the *monogatari* as "twice-told tales," or "transmitted recollections," with the emphasis on texts that are overtly conscious of their linguistic and rhetorical underpinnings. Through the term *monogatari*, the critics attempted to liberate modern Japanese literature from its dependence on personal experience, its assumption of a genuine authorial presence, its humanist ideology. Like other postmodernists, they debunked the image of the author as the possessor of unique or original truths and proposed instead that writing is simply self-conscious and repetitive performance.

Nakagami contributed to the discussion of the *monogatari* genre. In 1979, he published a critical essay entitled, "Monogatari no Keifu: Danshō" (The genealogy of the tale: fragments). The essay expresses complex and at times contradictory ideas about Japanese literature. First, Nakagami praises writers who have been identified with the *monogatari* in the early modern and modern periods—Ueda Akinari and Tanizaki Jun'ichirō, for example. According to Nakagami, they at least avoided the worst pitfalls of modern literature: a tendency to water down irreconcilable problems of class and economic disparity in sentimental solutions and to practice an elite form of belles lettres which banished certain topics from literary discourse. Immediately after this, however, Nakagami attacks the very idea of the *monogatari*. Instead of terming it simply a literary form, he describes *monogatari* as an oppressive and deterministic law or system *(hō/seido)*, which manifests itself in every form of Japanese cultural and literary expression, even taking the place of religion. In the final analysis, Nakagami's hostility and ambivalence toward the *monogatari* reads like a thinly disguised critique of Japan itself.

Nakagami's bombastic tone in "Monogatari no Keifu: Danshō" reveals anxiety about his own position, even as he functions as an insider in Tokyo literary circles. His preoccupation with the *hō/seido* (not a term he invented) hints at the obstacles that Nakagami continued to encounter after he had arrived in Tokyo. It is known, for example, that he was not awarded the prestigious Tanizaki prize. Nowhere is Nakagami's tone more tortured than in his discussion of the writer Tanizaki Jun'ichiro, who left Tokyo for the Kansai region of Japan, who parodied the *hō/seido* of Japanese culture through his experiments in sadomasochism, but who, in Nakagami's eyes, remained the consummate insider. But in spite

of Nakagami's stated ambivalence to the *monogatari*, he grappled repeatedly with the form of the "twice-told" tale over the course of the next few years.

If one were to label one Nakagami work as a *monogatari*, it would be *Sennen no yuraku* (1982; Pleasures of a thousand years). Told in the rough voice of Oryū no Oba, the old midwife of the outcaste alleyway named after her model in life, *Sennen* is a classic "twice-told" tale filled with magical and mythic elements. Oryū's "tale" concerns the stories of six young men of the Nakamoto family who were born with extraordinary beauty, who transgress, and who die young. In Oryū's portrayal of the Nakamotos, outcastes of the alleyway with "blood that is defiled because it is pure" (*NKZ*, vol. 5, p. 72), Nakagami upsets symbolic hierarchies, inverting the figures of outcaste and god, revealing that the lotus pond of paradise lies beneath the despised confines of the alleyway, and using the name Nakamoto ("origin of the middle") to show how opposites flow together in special bodies.

The title of the work, *Sennen no yuraku*, with its echoes of Gabriel García Márquez, marks a new phase in Nakagami's writing. Far from the realism of the early works, *Sennen* lacks a stable male protagonist, an Akiyuki or a younger brother who contemplates but then resists the call of death. The Nakamotos have no choice but to die, and *Sennen* intensifies the pattern of early male death. This time six faces, not one, are reflected in the mirror. In six stories, each with the same predetermined ending, Nakagami explores the realm of dissolution and death once again. This time, however, rather than a body floating down to the sea, the blood that flows through young men's bodies dissolves unique names and histories in a pool of sameness and death. One might translate this mechanism into formal terms, too. To Nakagami, the *monogatari* represents a rejection of realism for the parameters of the previously told or repeating tale—to what Karatani Kōjin calls "pure pattern" (*Origins of Modern Japanese Literature*, 1993, p. 164). Again, in his interest in previously set patterns (in the blood itself) one senses Nakagami's consciousness of his own *buraku* origins—the coordinates of an identity that cannot change.

In a further departure from the realism of the early fiction, Nakagami shows an increasing interest in extreme forms of violence and sadomasochism in his *monogatari*. One example of violence is the story of Hanzō, the first Nakamoto, who seeks to escape his own predetermined story. Hanzō becomes fascinated with a bird named Tenko (the name is borrowed from a famous story by Tanizaki entitled "Portrait of Shunkin"), which he brings to Oryū to give her pleasure:

The voices of the little golden birds echoed in Oryū's ears like the voice of Tenko, the bush warbler kept by Hanzō. Hanzō would let Tenko out in the bracken behind the house so that old Oryū, confined to her bed though nothing was particularly wrong with her, could hear the voice of the bird that Hanzō tended so carefully.

(*NKZ*, vol. 5, p. 11)

Hanzō's fascination with the bird signals his desire to invent his own story and transcend his outcaste origins. The reader learns that the bird, with its classical name, was a gift from a lover in the outside world, the widow of Ukijima, who in turn had received it from another lover, a bird trainer of low social status (but not of the outcaste class). Now, filled with confidence in his own virility, Hanzō trains the widow of Ukijima to "sing like Tenko" during sex.

Hanzō's luck in the world beyond the alleyway changes, however, when he meets the bird trainer. Hanzō comes to the widow's house to borrow money for a friend injured in the mountains. There he meets the bird trainer, who feels humiliated to learn that Hanzō now possesses Tenko. The man's reaction makes Hanzō want to punish him. The three go to bed, whereupon Hanzō binds the man's hands behind his back and penetrates him from behind, reveling in the subjugation and domination of his rival.

When Hanzō awakes the next morning, however, his feelings of triumph are shattered. The bird trainer suggests that they walk back to town together, but Hanzō informs him that he will take the opposite route, which leads to the outcaste quarters. Suddenly, the man's attitude changes:

Hanzō explained that he was going round the pleasure quarters of Ukijima, up the mountain and down into the alleyway. At this the man looked shocked and mumbled, "So you're from Nagayama," calling the outcaste area by its other name, which he kept repeating to himself as if he couldn't believe that Hanzō came from that crowd of cattle skinners, geta fixers, and basket weavers, and then suddenly, as if he himself had shot up in status, he remarked, "You're pretty good-looking." Hanzō shrugged off the comment with a "Thanks a lot," adding sarcastically that he would service him again sometime, but now he regretted having taken the man from behind. It didn't matter if he played with women and they played with him, but it was an entirely different thing for a man, a stranger, to treat him like a good-looking gigolo. Hanzō spat. He felt humiliated to be seen as a pretty-boy who had sold his body for a close friend from the alleyway, and spitting again, he started up the mountain path. It was about this time that a deep scar appeared on Hanzō's right cheek. He told everyone that he had gotten it when he fell on a knife in the mountains, but Oryū thought that Hanzō had cut himself in anger at his own masculine beauty.

(*NKZ*, vol. 5, p. 28)

When Hanzō reveals his outcaste identity, the balance of power shifts. Outweighing any event in the narrative, the mark of outcaste status allows even the lowly bird trainer to condescend to him. Hanzō suddenly recognizes himself as another exotic object of desire, a bird in a cage, a commodity to be traded. He cuts his beautiful face in a futile attempt to resist a world that continually objectifies him. In the end, Hanzō dies violently in a knife fight with a jealous husband. The violence of his end—the blood spurting from his wounds as he collapses at the entrance to the alleyway—echoes the narrator's rage in the early story "Ichiban hajime no dekigoto" (The first thing that happened). In an unstoppable torrent of outcaste blood flowing into the world, Nakagami expresses his disgust for a system that randomly ranks one person in relation to another.

In contrast to Hanzō, who rages against the inevitable, Oryū no Oba, the old midwife of the alleyway, quietly spins her tale. Oryū mourns the early deaths of the Nakamotos, searching for the cause of their undoing. At the same time she rehearses these deaths, even taking pleasure in them as she muses about Hanzō: "What if he became the plaything of some violent beast that would chew him limb from limb, ripping open his stomach and taking out his guts, so that no one could recognize his wind-tousled hair, his lips that women had kissed and his arms?" (*NKZ*, vol. 5, p. 23). In her vivid imagination of male death, Oryū uses the Nakamotos as the stuff of narrative, the material she must transform into words. Her tale of pleasure originates in the spectacle of male sacrifice. Through the figure of this cruel mother, who both gives life and takes it away, Nakagami suggests that the tale itself is the instrument of fate.

A heavy sense of doom overshadows *Sennen no yuraku*, gathering force through dense and complex sentences, the most difficult of Nakagami's career to date. In his attempt to give Oryū's tale a rough, oral patina, Nakagami dispenses with sentence breaks for paragraphs at a time. Iguchi Tokio notes the "chaotic sentence construction" as Nakagami switches subjects abruptly and makes intuitive leaps (p. 40). The dense, rhythmic language of *Sennen* takes us back to the texture of the early poetry while Oryū's fatalism bubbles up from every page:

> Oryū was the alleyway itself, and no matter how old she got, as long as she had breath in her body she would preserve this place where the babies tumbled into her hands before reaching the hands of their parents, where she bathed them for the first time. Like the virgin of a shrine, she would continue to take the alleyway's pulse. But when she grew cold and couldn't move or think anymore, the children would lose their place and those yet to be born would wander the world forever. Thinking of her own death, she cried, holding her hands out to the flames.

(*NKZ*, vol. 5, p. 117–118)

Throughout the 1980s Nakagami continued to experiment with the *monogatari* form, dispensing with a realistic, stable narrator and indulging in greater feasts of sadomasochism and violence. "Futakami" (1987; Twin gods), for example, tells the story of an incestuous family in which an elder sister blinds her younger brother with a needle in order to keep him with her in darkness, listening to her stories. The narrative switches back and forth between the communal voice of the old women of the alleyway, who watch the house in horror, and the sister, who lives blithely in her own world of visions.

"Nokori no Hana" (1988; Late blossoms) also experiments with narrative voice in a story that shifts back and forth between Jūkichi, a libidinous worker, and the old women of the alleyway, who tend flowers as they gossip. The story opens with the discovery of bones hidden in a jar behind a wall, and is told in the communal voice of the old women. Soon we enter an embedded narrative: the story of Jūkicihi, who meets a mysterious blind woman on his travels and brings her back to live with him in the alleyway, in isolation from the community. Unfortunately, Jūkichi cannot see what the old women spy during the day: the woman entertaining lovers in the house at his expense. Jūkichi's ignorance (his lack of access to the story itself) proves fatal. He is murdered (by whom it is unclear) and hidden in a jar inside a wall. As in *Sennen no yuraku*, the matriarchal voice of the alleyway spins the web of the protagonist's demise.

Ironically, in his *monogatari* writing, with its pattern of early male death and ever-tightening circles of fate, Nakagami's writing attains an intensity of sensation and purpose that one finds nowhere else. His *monogatari* further highlight his love of experimentation with genre, plot, and, most important, with style itself. Over the course of twenty years, Nakagami moved from allegorical poetry, to the pared-down style of the early works, and finally to increasingly complex and dense prose. Nakagami's willingness to take chances—his daring with language itself—stands as his greatest contribution to modern Japanese literature.

Hard at Work

Ironically, while Nakagami engaged in a struggle with Japanese literary forms into the 1980s and early 1990s, he spent less and less time in Japan. In fact, the short biography in the *zenshū* (Collected works) reveals a dizzying pattern of travel from the mid-1980s until his death. To a certain extent, Nakagami was conforming to the pattern of the successful Japanese writer. In 1990 alone, he attended a symposium in San Francisco (with Ōe Kenzaburō, Tsushima Yūko, and others), went to an international literary meeting in Paris, gave a lecture in Frankfurt on national identity, and moved on to New York. His restlessness also indicated his urge to expand into more international circles. Though English translations of his work did not appear until 1999, Nakagami was known in France in the late 1980s. Translations of *Sennen no yuraku* and *Karekinada* appeared there in 1988 and 1989 respectively.

When Nakagami was in Japan, he was often in Katsuura, a town near Shingū, where he had bought an apartment by the sea. In 1989, he returned to formally establish Kumano Daigaku, a locally funded organization that continues to produce cultural events to this day. In fact, Nakagami was simply formalizing the role that he had played in Kumano for years. Returning to Shingū, however, was not easy for him as his fame and celebrity grew. According to one resident, he had upset certain

people for revealing so much about the town. His restlessness might also be attributed to a growing sense of exile. He stated in a 1989 interview, "I don't feel that I belong anywhere *(ibasho ga nai)*."

Romance and Resignation

Restless or not, Nakagami continued to write. *Kiseki* (1989; Miracles), his last book-length portrayal of the characters in the alleyway, was published in serialized form in 1987 and 1988, and at the same time he began to produce chapters of his next novel, *Sanka* (1990; Hymn), for the journal *Bungakukai*. In 1991, he began to publish *Keibetsu* (1992; Scorn), his last complete novel, in serial form. Described on the cover as a "love story" *(ren'ai shōsetsu)*, the work raises interesting questions about the direction Nakagami's writing might have taken had he lived.

Keibetsu turns its back on many of Nakagami's earlier fictional practices and settings, moving from the alleyways and mountains of Kumano to the harsh lights of Tokyo. It is smoothly written, with language that does not draw attention to itself. The characters include Kazu, the pampered son of a wealthy family, a loyal and gentle strip dancer named Machiko, and a cast of assorted underworld characters. In spite of its strip bar setting and low-level gangsters, however, *Keibetsu* describes the love of the two main characters in innocent terms. Rather than tie each other up, Kazu and Machiko kiss each other's hands, saying, "I love you." Gone are the graphic descriptions of ecstatic and at times violent sex. Instead, we are in a world where strip dancers inspire dreams of love.

At the beginning of the novel, Kazu stages a mock raid on the bar, takes Machiko up to the roof, and professes his love for her; then they run away together. Kazu is fleeing from a loan shark; and Machiko, who originally became a stripper to get away from a difficult family situation, is also eager to leave. They return to Kazu's hometown, where his parents run a liquor business, and Kazu, once a playboy, settles down. But trouble soon divides the lovers: Kazu's parents do not approve of Machiko. The couple eventually separate; Machiko goes back to working in a strip bar; and Kazu dies. After Michiko receives word of Kazu's death, she returns to his hometown and visits the beach where he died under mysterious circumstances—either by murder or by suicide.

The story of lovers on the run has deep roots in Japanese literature—Mariko Ihara, for example, finds many references in *Keibetsu* to the love suicide plays of the Tokugawa period. One might also note that *Keibetsu* once again concerns violent, early male death—by the sea—but this time with a difference. Told from Machiko's point of view, *Keibetsu* is elegaic and peaceful. Instead of railing at death, Machiko mourns quietly and visits the site of Kazu's death in order to comfort his spirit:

> Rather than bunches of white orchids costing thousands of yen, one flower chosen with care, even a wildflower, would do for Kazu, who would always press his flesh to hers as if he felt so lonely to have been born a man. One simple flower, one more likely to be trampled and crushed than admired, would comfort his spirit.

(p. 402)

In this final scene of mourning, Nakagami returns to the ocean—the body of water that called young men to their deaths in his early work. Yet this time, Nakagami softens death through the voice of a sympathetic young female character. Instead of tracing the struggle of the male protagonist who tries to resist his own dissolution, *Keibetsu* explores how the young man will be remembered. In Machiko's tender act of placing flowers of remembrance at the site of Kazu's death, one sees how Nakagami's fiction has changed. Death brings resignation, acceptance, and even a touch of sentiment.

In January 1992, during a trip to Hawaii, Nakagami was diagnosed with kidney cancer. That May he gave his last interview, to Watanabe Naomi, and expressed his desire for life. He began to talk about Akiyuki, the one survivor: "Akiyuki is stirring again. He's the one who was closest to me and then moved so far away. Now it's just a matter of what form he's going to take" ("Shijifosu no yō ni yamai to tawamurete" [Sporting with illness like Sisyphus], *Bungakukai*, May 1992, pp. 213–214). Unfortunately, we will never know what form Akiyuki might have taken, or how Nakagami might have reformulated his approach to writing if he had lived. By July 1992, cancer had spread through his body, and he returned home to his mother's house. There, attended by his wife and family, he died quietly on 12 August. He was forty-six years old.

Selected Bibliography

PRIMARY WORKS

COLLECTED WORKS AND POSTHUMOUS PUBLICATIONS

Kotodama no ametsuchi. With Kamata Tōji. Tokyo: Shufu no Tomosha, 1993.

Nakagami Kenji hatsugen shūsei. 6 vols. Edited by Karatani Kōjin and Suga Hidemi. Tokyo: Daisanbunmeisha, 1995.

Nakagami Kenji zenshū. 15 vols. Edited by Karatani Kōjin, Yomota Inuhiko, and Watanabe Naomi. Tokyo: Shūeisha, 1996.

Nakagami Kenji to Kumano. Edited by Watanabe Naomi and Karatani Kōjin. Tokyo: Ōta Shuppan, 2000.

FICTION

Jūkyūsai no chizu. Tokyo: Kawade Shobōshinsha, 1974.

Jain. Tokyo: Kadokawa Shoten, 1976. Trans. by Andew Rankin as *Snake Lust.* Tokyo: Kodanasha International, 1999.

Misaki. Tokyo: Bungei Shunjū, 1976. Trans. by Eve Zimmerman as *The Cape and Other Stories from the Japanese Ghetto.* Berkeley: Stone Bridge Press, 1999.

Jūhassai, Umi e. Tokyo: Shūeisha, 1977.

Karekinada. Tokyo: Kawade Shobōshinsha, 1977.

Keshō. Tokyo: Kōdansha, 1978.

Mizu no onna. Tokyo: Sakuhinsha, 1979.

Hōsenka. Tokyo: Sakuhinsha, 1980.

Sennen no yuraku. Tokyo: Kawade Shobōshinsha, 1982.

Chi no hate shijō no toki. Tokyo: Shinchōsha, 1983.

Kumanoshū. Tokyo: Kōdansha, 1984. Partial trans. by Mark Harbison as "The Immortal." In vol. 2 of *The Showa Anthology.* Edited by Van C. Gessel and Tomone Matsumoto. Tokyo: Kodanasha International, 1985. Pp. 412–428.

Nichirin no tsubasa. Tokyo: Shinchōsha, 1984.

Himatsuri. Tokyo: Bungei Shunjūsha, 1987.

Jūryōku no miyako. Tokyo: Shinchōsha, 1988.

Kiseki. Tokyo: Asahi Shinbunsha, 1989.

Sanka. Tokyo: Bungei Shunjū, 1990.

Keibetsu. Tokyo: Asahi Shinbunsha, 1992.

Izoku. Tokyo: Kōdansha, 1993. (Uncompleted.)

ESSAY AND DISCUSSION COLLECTIONS

Tori no yōni, kemono no yōni. Tokyo: Hokuyōsha, 1976.

Kishū: Ki no kuni ne no kuni. Tokyo: Asahi Shinbunsha, 1978.

Kobayashi Hideo o koete. With Karatani Kōjin. Tokyo: Kawade Shobōshinsha, 1979.

Yume no chikara. Tokyo: Hokuyōsha, 1979.

Tōyō ni ichi suru. Tokyo: Sakuhinsha, 1981.

Fūkei no mukō e. Tokyo: Tōjusha, 1983.

Sabetsu: sono kongen o tou. Edited by Noma Hiroshi and Yasuoka Shōtarō. Tokyo: Asahi Shinbunsha, 1984.

Amerika, Amerika. Tokyo: Kadokawa Shoten, 1985.

Supanishu kyaraban o sagashite. Tokyo: Shinchōsha, 1986.

Jidai ga owari, jidai ga hajimaru. Tokyo: Fukutake Shoten, 1988.

SECONDARY WORKS

CRITICAL AND BIOGRAPHICAL STUDIES

Cornyetz, Nina. *Dangerous Woman, Deadly Words.* Stanford: Stanford University Press, 1999.

Dodd, Stephen. "Japan's Private Parts: Place as a Metaphor in Nakagami Kenji's Works." *Japan Forum* 8, no. 1:3–11 (1996).

Iguchi Tokio. *Monogatari ron hakyoku ron.* Tokyo: Ronsōsha, 1987.

Ihara Mariko. "Isaku keibetsu no shuhō," *Yurīka,* March 1993, pp. 188–195.

Karatani Kōjin. *Origins of Modern Japanese Literature.* Trans. and edited by Brett de Bary. Durham: Duke University Press, 1993.

———. *Sakaguchi Ango to Nakagami Kenji.* Tokyo: Ōta Shuppan, 1996.

Monnet, Livia. "Ghostly Women, Displaced Femininities, and Male Family Romances: Violence, Gender, and Sexuality in Two Texts by Nakagami Kenji." *Japan Forum* 8, no. 1:13–34 (1996).

Morris, Mark. "Gossip and History: Nakagami, Faulkner, García Márquez." *Japan Forum* 8, no. 1:35–50 (1996).

Takazawa Shūji. *Hyōden Nakagami Kenji.* Tokyo: Shūeisha, 1998.

Tamura Satoko. "Omoide no naka no Nakagami Kenji." *Kumano-shi* 39:60–62 (1995).

Watanabe, Naomi. "Shijifosu no yō ni yamai to tawamurete" (Sporting with illness like Sisyphus). *Bungakukai,* March 1992.

———. *Nakagami Kenji ron: Itoshisha ni tsuite.* Tokyo: Kawade Shobōshinsha, 1996.

Yomota Inuhiko, *Kishu to tensei.* Tokyo: Shinchōsha, 1987.

Zimmerman, Eve. "In the Trap of Words: Nakagami Kenji and the Making of Degenerate Fictions." In *Ōe and Beyond.* Edited by Stephen Snyder and Philip Gabriel. Honolulu: University of Hawaii Press, 1999. Pp.130–152.

FILMS BASED ON THE WORKS OF NAKAGAMI

Akai kami no onna. Directed by Kumashiro Tatsumi, 1979.

Jūhassai, Umi e. Directed by Fujita Toshiya, 1979.

Jūkyūsai no chizu. Directed by Yanagimachi Mitsuo, 1979.

Himatsuri. Directed by Yanagimachi Mitsuo, 1985. (Released with English subtitles.)

NISHIWAKI JUNZABURŌ
1894–1982

HOSEA HIRATA

OFTEN COMPARED to T. S. Eliot, Nishiwaki Junzaburō is considered one of the finest Japanese modernist poets. In addition, Nishiwaki was a well-respected scholar of Old and Middle English literature and linguistics, who taught at the prestigious Keiō University in Tokyo from 1920 to 1967. He was also an accomplished painter.

Modernity in Japanese poetry was influenced by an influx of Western culture beginning in the mid-nineteenth century as the isolationist policy of the Tokugawa government dissolved under pressure from the West. Wanting to dissociate themselves from the traditional Japanese poetic forms of *waka* and haiku, Japanese poets began by making awkward translations of some European poems. By the end of the nineteenth century, however, signs of maturity in modern Japanese poetry were perceptible. During the first few decades of the twentieth century, Japanese poets were rapidly absorbing various Western modernist schools—romanticism, symbolism, dadaism, surrealism, tuturism—and they radically transformed the very concept of Japanese poetry. Nishiwaki played a central role in this revolution in the Japanese poetic language.

While many avant-garde artists and writers of the early twentieth century are remembered today merely for their spirit of experimenta-

tion, Nishiwaki's work transcends such limitations. Several factors clearly distinguished him from his peers. He possessed unparalleled erudition in the history of world literature, and he was exceptionally proficient in several European languages. In addition, he pursued the seemingly paradoxical interest in both ancient and contemporary arts. He is known for his studies of Beowulf as well as for his own surrealist writings. In his final years, Nishiwaki was engaged in a comparative linguistic study of ancient Greek and Chinese.

Recommended by Ezra Pound, who happened to read a poem Nishiwaki had written in English, Nishiwaki was considered for the Nobel Prize in literature by the Swedish Academy starting in the late 1950s. In 1962 a member of the Nobel Prize Selection Committee visited Japan and revealed that three Japanese writers—Kawabata Yasunari (1899–1972), Tanizaki Jun'ichirō (1886–1965), and Nishiwaki—were in contention for the literature prize. In 1968, Kawabata received the first Nobel Prize in literature awarded to a Japanese writer. By that time Kawabata's works had been translated into several European languages, but there were hardly any translations of Nishiwaki's work available. However, no one in Japan dared to translate Nishiwaki's poems into English because of his remarkable ability to write in English. In fact, Nishiwaki had been writing poetry in English and French quite freely long before he began writing poetry in Japanese. Herein lies the enigmatic core of his work: the new poetic language Nishiwaki invented was not an authentically Japanese one but rather a language of translation.

Early Years

Nishiwaki Junzaburō was born on 20 January 1894, the second son of a well-established merchant family in the small provincial town, Ojiya, in Niigata Prefecture. At the time of Nishiwaki's birth, his father Kanzō was thirty-four and his mother Saki was thirty-two years old. Eventually the family grew to include four sons and three daughters, though the youngest son died soon after birth. The family had a long history of dealing in silk crepe, a well-known local product. In 1880 Kanzō's father founded a financial company, which became Ojiya Bank in 1893. When Junzaburō was born, Kanzō was the head of this bank. Kanzō became the mayor of Ojiya in 1901, though, due to his failing health, he resigned the position after only a year or so. Throughout his life, Nishiwaki had an ambivalent attitude toward his home, often expressing a preference for the metropolitan life of Tokyo. There is hardly any trace of Nishiwaki's family members in his work. Although financially the young Nishiwaki relied on his provincial family, spiritually he seemed to want to keep a distance from his family roots.

In elementary school, Nishiwaki was a quiet, introverted boy who was too scared to play with his classmates. He loved art classes, but he was interested in neither mathematics nor Japanese classes. As a child, the future writer did not like reading but loved looking at illustrated children's books. Nishiwaki's unfettered, unique writing style might have resulted from this childhood lack of interest in reading, which freed him from the language and style of established Japanese literature. In junior high school, he began to show an unusual passion for English, which was undoubtedly piqued by

the many foreign books in his family's library. The *Illustrated London News* and the *National Reader* nurtured his early longings for Europe. The foreign books in his house were probably brought back by his uncles who had studied abroad. His fellow students nicknamed this boy, who hardly read any Japanese books but was obsessively engrossed in studying English, *Eigo-ya* ("English-shop"). Nishiwaki also kept his passion for painting, but apparently he paid little attention to other subjects. When literary-minded friends talked about the leading Japanese writers of that time, he never showed any interest. Nishiwaki, however, says that he was enamoured by some classical Chinese poems he read in class.

After graduation from junior high school in March 1911, the eighteen-year-old Nishiwaki decided to become a painter. In Tokyo, he met one of the leading modern Japanese painters, Fujishima Takeji (1867–1943), and became his student. Just as he was preparing to go to France to study painting, however, his father died. Forced to abandon the idea of becoming a painter, he was persuaded by family members to pursue higher education in Japan. In 1912, to please the family, he took the entrance examinations at the most prestigious high school in Japan, the First Higher School. Reportedly, he completed only the English test, ignored the other subjects, went to the courtyard, and read Shakespeare's *A Midsummer Night's Dream*. In September, however, helped by his family connections, he enrolled in the preparatory course for the Department of Economics at Keiō University.

Having abandoned his dream of becoming a painter, Nishiwaki turned his attention to poetry. Outside of class he read works by contemporary Japanese poets—such as Shimazaki Tōson (1872–1943), Kanbara Ariake (1876–1952), Ueda Bin (1874–1916), and Kitahara Hakushū (1885–1942)—but was put off by their old-fashioned rhetorical styles. He began studying Greek, Latin, and German, and he also started to compose metrical poems in English.

As he was finishing the preparatory program for the university, Nishiwaki wanted to enter the Department of Literature at Keiō, but his family pressured him to take a more practical course. Eventually Nishiwaki was compelled to enter the Department of Economics at Keiō University in 1914. He recollects that he had absolutely no interest in economics and secretly read Turgenev or Tolstoy in class as his professors lectured on Adam Smith. He also read the works of Charles Baudelaire, Arthur Rimbaud, Paul Verlaine, Gustave Flaubert, Guy de Maupassant, Arthur Symons, Walter Pater, W. B. Yeats, Oscar Wilde, Fyodor Dostoevsky, Friedrich Nietzsche, émile Vehaeren, and Maurice Maeterlinck.

In 1917 Nishiwaki submitted a thirty-page graduation thesis entitled *Pure Economics* to his supervisor. Amazingly it was written entirely in Latin. Since no one in the department could read that language, he had to submit an abstract in Japanese. After graduation he was employed briefly at the only English-language newspaper in Japan, *The Japan Times,* where he wrote various reviews in English. After a managerial change took place, Nishiwaki quit the newspaper company and was planning to work for the Bank of Japan. However, before he could properly embark on a banker's career, Nishiwaki fell ill with a mild case of amyloid infiltration of the lungs and was forced to move first to the countryside and then eventually back home to Ojiya. There he spent most of his time reading Walter Pater's ten-volume complete works. After recovering from his illness, Nishiwaki returned to Tokyo in 1919 and took a part-time position at the Ministry of Foreign Affairs. The next year he began his academic career by working as a lecturer in the preparatory course for the English Department at Keiō University.

Encounter with Modernism

Nishiwaki began publishing essays and poems in English in the English-language journal, *Eigo Bungaku* (English literature). Nishiwaki paid little attention to his contemporary Japanese poets, for he believed that they all wrote in an overwrought, literary, elegant, but unpoetic, style. By this time, however, a revolution in the Japanese poetic language was already under way. The talented young poet Hagiwara Sakutarō (1886–1942) was beginning to utilize the contemporary colloquial language effectively in free verse for the first time in Japanese poetry. Hagiwara's first collection of poems, *Tsuki ni hoeru* (1917; *Howling at the Moon,* 1978), with its stark images etched in nonliterary, everyday language made Nishiwaki consider the possibility of writing poetry in Japanese for the first time. Yet, still enamored by the poetry of John Keats, Nishiwaki continued writing sonnets in English and did not attempt to compose poems in Japanese until much later.

In 1922 Nishiwaki was sent by Keiō University to England to study English literature, criticism, and linguistics. His ship left Japan on 7 July, stopping at Singapore, Egypt, and Italy on the way and arriving in London on the last day of August. On board Nishiwaki carried his favorite books: *Les fleurs du mal* by Baudelaire, *Thus Spoke Zarathustra* by Nietzsche, and *Howling at the Moon* by Hagiwara. Upon arriving in England, he found that it was too late to register for the academic year at Oxford University. His entrance was thus delayed for a year. This mishap provided an opportunity for Nishiwaki to explore London's artistic circles and to learn about the various avant-garde movements flowing in from the continent. Lodging in South Kensington, he became a friend of the young novelist John Collier (1901–1979), who dismissed Nishiwaki's old-fashioned Keatsian sonnets and introduced him to the dissonance of modernist poetry. The first modernist text Nishiwaki read was *The Waste Land* by T. S. Eliot, which had been published that year. (Exactly thirty years later, in 1952, Nishiwaki published a definitive Japanese translation of this monumental work.) Nishiwaki's initial astonishment soon turned into a passion for the avant-garde. James Joyce's *Ulysses,* banned in Joyce's home country and elsewhere, was published in Paris in the same year, and Nishiwaki was able to purchase a copy at a used bookstore on Fleet

Street in London. Encouraged by Collier, Nishiwaki began to read works by Pound, Eliot, Joyce, and Wyndham Lewis. A circle of artistic friends gathered nightly with Nishiwaki at the Café Royal in Soho and discussed the paintings of Van Gogh, Picasso, and Matisse as well as the Russian ballet by Diaghilev and the music of Stravinsky. Among the regulars at the café was a young painter named Marjorie Biddle, six years younger than Nishiwaki, who instantly fell in love with the Japanese poet. They were married on 25 July 1924 despite the astonished disapproval of Nishiwaki's provincial family. Away from the rigorous academic life that awaited him, Nishiwaki was able to enjoy the freedom and excitement of a bohemian lifestyle for a year. The baptism of modernism he experienced in this atmosphere in 1922 greatly influenced not only his poetic career but also the course of modern Japanese poetry.

In 1923 Nishiwaki enrolled at New College, Oxford University, where he studied mainly Old and Middle English literature. During the Christmas break, he traveled to France and Switzerland. In 1924 his English poem "Kensington Idyll" was accepted for publication by *The Chapbook*, which was edited by Harold Monro. The same issue included a poem by Eliot, "Doris's Dream Songs," an early version of "The Hollow Men." The fact that he was published together with Eliot gave Nishiwaki much confidence in his ability to write poems in English. In 1925 Nishiwaki published his first collection of English poems entitled *Spectrum* at his own expense through Cayme Press in London. The book was favorably reviewed by *The Times Literary Supplement* and the *Daily News*. The same year, without taking a degree, Nishiwaki embarked on the voyage home with Marjorie. On the way, he tried to publish a collection of French poems *Une montre sentimentale* in Paris but was turned down by the publisher. In 1926, after he had returned to Japan, he was appointed Professor of Literature at Keiō University. Through Keiō's own literary journal *Mita*

Bungaku, he began to publish important theoretical essays on surrealism, which were later collected in his first major Japanese publication, *Chōgenjitsushugi shiron* (1929; *Surrealist Poetics*, 1993). As he began lecturing at the university, his brilliance and his peculiar foreign deportment immediately attracted young literary intellectuals, who formed a study circle around him. Several notable avant-garde journals were launched. In 1927 the first surrealist anthology in Japan, *Fukuikutaru kafu yo* (Oh, fragrant stoker), was published under Nishiwaki's leadership. Marjorie designed the cover, and Nishiwaki's contribution, excerpted below from *The Poetry and Poetics of Nishiwaki Junzaburō: Modernism in Translation*, was an exemplary piece of surrealist writing:

A Fragrant Stoker

David's duty and his jewels pass through between Adonis and legumina and rush toward their infinite extinction. Thus, behold! How the smooth quercus infectoria frolics, leaning against the magi who generally came from the east.

In a collective sense approximately very purple and extremely justifiable postponement! Velázquez and game birds and all other things.

In an effective era when kingfishers gabble, viewing the Acropolis in the far distance, what refreshes the nails and stretches the infantile legs is not in a single walnut but is above a single ragman's head.

Continuously bless the water-buffalo that attempts to climb up a maple tree!

(*ZS*, p. 28; tr. Hirata, 1993, p. 53)

Surrealist Poetics

Like T. S. Eliot and Wallace Stevens, Nishiwaki was obsessed with the question of what poetry is, asking this essential question both in his poems and in his critical essays. It is understandable that an innovator of an artistic genre would need to ask such a question. For example, when free verse appeared, one could legitimately ask whether it still fit the definition of a poem. When the dadaist Marcel Duchamp exhibited a urinal in an art gallery, the established concept of art itself became questionable. The modernization of Japanese culture presented a similar problem to Japanese writers, who had to abandon the traditional forms and ideas of literature and find a new definition of literature. In the cultural climate in which everything Western was uncritically adored and everything Japanese was disdained as frivolous and shallow, many simply took the Western definition of modern literature as the most authoritative. But some, notably the writer Natsume Sōseki (1867–1916), who attempted to redefine literature in his own terms before he became a prolific novelist, questioned the "authoritative" definition of literature that the West provided. In 1900 Sōseki was sent to England to study English literature, but unlike Nishiwaki, he was unable to adapt himself to British society, which appeared intolerably snobbish to him. Sōseki isolated himself and worked on his own theory of literature until he had a nervous breakdown. Approximately two decades separated Nishiwaki and Sōseki's sojourns in England, but the contrast between their experiences abroad is stunning. Sōseki carried with him feelings of both pride and inferiority for being Japanese. However, one cannot detect either feeling in Nishiwaki. In a sense, even before he went to England, Nishiwaki was already a self-made foreigner, and a certain sense of transcendence associated with foreignness issues forth from his works. For Nishiwaki, the very notion of poetry was not associated with the Japanese language. Poetry had to be foreign. Sōseki was able to question the authoritative, universalistic notion of Western literature because he was well versed in a different notion of literature informed by his studies of classical Chinese literature. On the other hand, Nishiwaki seems to have been

overwhelmed by the West from the beginning. However, in *Surrealist Poetics*, Nishiwaki was not merely introducing a well-established Western theory of poetry. With bold originality, Nishiwaki scanned the long history of poetry in the West, attempting to discern essential characteristics inherent in the historical conceptions of poetry. The significance of Nishiwaki's vision of poetry lies in his insight that the essence of poetry is always foreign to us. The function of poetry is not to find the most beautiful, authentic song or form of the mother tongue, but to provide a distancing mechanism that makes what is familiar (say, the mother tongue) unfamiliar (a foreign language).

Surrealist Poetics consists of five essays: "Profanus," "Shi no shōmetsu," ("The Extinction of Poetry," 1993), "Esthétique foraine," "Chōshizenshugi" (Supernaturalism), and "Chōshizenshi no kachi" (The value of supernatural poetry). The language and style of these essays are idiosyncratic. It is fortunate that they were published in Japan during a period when academic publishing was not as regulated as in the United States at the beginning of the twenty-first century. Nishiwaki's erudition shines through, yet the central attraction of these writings lies in his peculiar poetic utterances whose insightful power no standardized academic discourse could imitate. For example, after discussing the poetics of Francis Bacon in "Profanus," Nishiwaki inserts the following paragraph, which conveys his peculiar textual flavor:

Poetry must be founded in reality. But it is also necessary to feel the banality of reality. Why does the human spirit feel the banality of reality? Human existence itself is desolate. I wonder if those dogs running around over there are feeling this banality. As one dissects the human spirit and reaches its very bottom, one finds the essential existence of this desolate feeling. We suffer, for we think.

(*NJZ*, vol. 4, p. 15; tr. Hirata, 1993, p. 11)

The Latin title "Profanus" ("not sacred") indicates Nishiwaki's desire to be iconoclastic as well as his insight that poetics is essentially a profane theology. The essay begins with this memorable sentence: "To discourse upon poetry is as dangerous as to discourse upon God" (*NJZ*, vol. 4, p. 8; tr. Hirata, 1993, p. 5). The conclusion echoes this theological opening but with a dry witticism: "It is dangerous to discuss poetry. I have already fallen off the cliff" (*NJZ*, vol. 4, p. 26; tr. Hirata, 1993, p. 19). In between, Nishiwaki haphazardly surveys the history of Western poetics, leaping from Baudelaire to Heine, Shakespeare to Catullus, Humboldt to Homer, Aristotle to Samuel Johnson, Francis Bacon to Max Jacob, Coleridge to Reverdy. Nishiwaki finds it curious that the essential feature of the contemporary poetics put forth by the French surrealists could already be seen in Francis Bacon's idea of poetry, which was inherited by Romantic poets, such as Coleridge and Shelley, in their theory of imagination. French surrealists were asserting that one needed to juxtapose unrelated elements to create a poetic image. Nishiwaki points out that at the beginning of the seventeenth century, Bacon was already aware of this mechanism of modern poetry when he wrote in "The tvvo Bookes of the Proficience and Advancement of Learning Divine and Hvmane":

> Poesie is a part of Learning in measure of words for the most part restrained, but in all other points extreamely licensed, and doth truly referre to the Imagination, which, beeing not tyed to the Lawes of Matter, may at pleasure ioyned that which Nature hath seuered, & seuer that which Nature hath ioyned, and so make vnlawfull Matches & divorses of things.

Thus, Nishiwaki sees surrealism as a logical development of Western poetics centered on the role of imagination.

Although Nishiwaki embraces the surrealist idea that poetry is born out of a forceful or tactful destruction of our familiar idea of reality, he accuses French surrealists of abandoning the all-important sense of reality itself. This is the central paradox in Nishiwaki's thought: He endorses the poetic deconstruction of reality while insisting that poetry be founded in reality. How should one understand Nishiwaki's sense of reality then? He states, "The reality of human existence itself is banal *(tsumaranai).* To sense this fundamental yet supreme banality *(tsumaranasa)* constitutes the motivation for poetry" (*NJZ*, vol. 4, p. 8; tr. Hirata, 1993, p. 5). So, in order to make this banal reality meaningful, one needs to transform it poetically, to make this banality disappear. Nishiwaki is not simply reiterating the Romantic poetics of Coleridge and Shelley, who saw the aim of poetry as making familiar things look unfamiliar, and thus poetically exciting. For Nishiwaki, poetry is not such an escape from reality. It is rather an effort to heighten one's sense of a reality that is fundamentally boring. In other words, poetry does not erase the boredom of reality: it deepens the boredom and insignificance *(tsumaranasa)* of reality. In order to understand this paradox regarding poetry and reality, one needs to pay attention to what Nishiwaki calls *tsumaranasa* ("banality," "boredom," "ennui," "insignificance," or "triviality").

Certainly there is a trace of Eastern aesthetics informed by Zen in Nishiwaki's insistence on *tsumaranasa.* For instance, one may recall the haiku poet Bashō's (1644–1694) cultivation of *karumi* ("the style of lightness") in his late years. Ueda Makoto records a masterful example of Bashō's *karumi* in *Bashō and His Interpreters:*

> Autumn deepening—
> I wonder what my neighbor
> Does for a living.
>
> (aki / fukaki / tonari / wa / nani / o / suru / hito / zo)
>
> (tr. p. 411)

The conventional lyricism of the opening "Autumn deepening" *("aki fukaki")* is broken by the sudden, comical, yet very banal thought

"I wonder what my neighbor does for a living *(tonari wa nani o suru hito zo).*" This aesthetics of banality is clearly visible in Nishiwaki's poetry as well. For example, in a section of the long poem *Tabibito kaerazu* (1947; *No Traveller Returns*, 1993) Nishiwaki focuses on an insignificant, banal object, effecting a deep sense of loneliness:

In an old garden
where tiger lilies bloom
a forgotten
broken watering can
lying . . .

(*ZS*, p. 207; tr. Hirata, 1993, p. 90)

In another long poem, *Eterunitasu* (1962; *Eterunitasu*, 1993), Nishiwaki elucidates this notion of *tsumaranasa* ("banality") as the non-symbolic element that poetry ultimately seeks:

A teacup abandoned in a puddle,
a trace of children's play,
a crest imprinted upon the back of a loach,
a madman crossing a bridge,
the nervous flurry of a stone thrown into a
    bamboo thicket,
the scream of a meteorite struck by a plow,
a louse left on a traveler's hat,
the movement of Pound's Adam's apple,
a man
on the run
chewing
a soil-crusted bitter root
of nipplewort—
these things do not symbolize.
Things that do not symbolize
attract us more. . . .

(*ZS*, p. 621; tr. Hirata, 1993, p. 120)

Nishiwaki's aesthetics of banality is thus not a form of realism in which banal objects are celebrated; it is a philosophical conception of poetry as a movement toward the nonsymbolic, toward something that does not signify anything. Romantic poetics believed that real-ity is made dull by custom and conventions, and that poetry must renew this timeworn, trite reality by creating new associations through imagination. Nishiwaki goes further, stating that reality is made significant by established meanings and codes. Poetry is a process through which true reality is revealed by stripping away all the significance, all the meanings that have been establishing "reality" for us. The ultimate reality is meaningless. It is absolutely banal, boring, and insignificant *(tsumaranai).* And poetry leads us there, if it can. However, one must remember the title and conclusion of Nishiwaki's essay. He announces his failure vis-à-vis his theological poetics: He has fallen off the cliff. Theory will never capture the ultimate poem.

In the second essay of *Surrealist Poetics,* "The Extinction of Poetry," Nishiwaki considers the consequences of this movement of poetry toward meaninglessness. He begins with this bold hypothesis: "The realm of poetry expands infinitely and finally disappears. As a corollary (ipso facto) of this hypothesis the following rule is set forth: 'The most expanded, the most advanced mode of poetry is that which is closest to its own extinction' " (*NJZ*, vol. 4, p. 27; tr. Hirata, 1993, p. 20). Audaciously Nishiwaki embraces the modernist's antimimetic mode of art as the only legitimate one and labels as merely "natural" any artistic endeavor that attempts to represent or express something else. Following Baudelaire's conception of art, Nishiwaki considers that the essential feature of art lies not in its close mimetic relation to nature (including human interiority) but in its artificiality radically divorced from nature. This drastic rejection of mimesis in art and poetry is bracketed as a hypothesis and does not imply that Nishiwaki's poetry lacks any trace of mimesis. Nishiwaki is interested in what happens when the modernist's antimimetic mode is stretched to the limit. He outlines three stages in the development of postmimetic poetry. The first stage, called "the era of expression," embraces most of modern poetry because, despite vari-ous modernist schools' antimimetic manifestoes, the poets still try to express something "natural" (such as truth, a subjective attitude, or inner feelings) through their dissonant antimimetic poems. The second stage, "the era of anti-expression," is far more radically ironic. In this hypothetical period, the poet's effort is focused on not expressing anything at all. Although Nishiwaki refers to the Dadaist Tristan Tzara's work as a possible harbinger of this extreme poetic mode, he believes that Tzara's Dadaism belongs to the first "expressive" period. However, Nishiwaki is convinced that the most extreme development of poetry will appear soon. The third stage is, of course, the extinction of poetry. One's desire to express and not to express disappears. The following quotation constitutes the section entitled "The Extinction of Poetry": "Poetry dies as mankind dies. The lamp is turned off. But things like kangaroos or cactuses may be still trying to survive, fidgeting here and there. How pitiful" (*NJZ*, vol. 4, p. 37; tr. Hirata, 1993, p. 27). This section is followed by "Chapter Three: A Critique of Poetics," which states: "The adage *Ars longa* is merely a children's song. It only appears on the surface that art creates. In fact, art is an effort at self-extinction" (*NJZ*, vol. 4, pp. 37–38; tr. Hirata, 1993, p. 27).

The Birth of a New Poetic Language

In 1933 a small publisher of poetry in Tokyo printed three hundred copies of a little book, whose wine-red cover held the unfamiliar foreign title, *Ambarvalia*. The book included Nishiwaki's first Japanese poems, which revolutionized the language of poetry in Japan. Nishiwaki was forty years old then, divorced from Marjorie and remarried to a Japanese woman, Kuwayama Saeko. Japan's invasion of Korea and China was under way. The exact circumstances of Nishiwaki's divorce and remarriage are not known, but the increasingly xenophobic situation in Japan must have made Marjorie's marriage to Nishiwaki difficult in many ways. Marjorie left Japan for India,

remarried there, and eventually returned to England. Meanwhile Nishiwaki was establishing himself as the foremost theorist of modernist poetry as well as a scholar of European literature. In the same year *Ambarvalia* appeared, Nishiwaki published three important scholarly works: a large collection of essays on European literature, covering antiquity to modernism; translations of Joyce's poetry, including a portion of *Finnegans Wake*; and a monograph on William Langland.

The Latin title, *Ambarvalia*, refers to an ancient Roman agricultural festival in honor of Ceres, the goddess of corn. The book is divided into two sections, each with a French title: "Le Monde ancien" and "Le Monde moderne." An epigraph at the beginning of the section on the ancient world announces the determination of the poet to slough off the mantle of a pedantic scholar:

The Song of Choricos

O Muse, arise.
Of late thou hast been submerged too
    deeply in Poesy.
The music thou blowest forth reaches not
    the Abydos.
May the curve of thy throat be the heart of
    the Abydos.

(*ZS*, p. 6; tr. Hirata, 1993, p. 47)

This poem shows many of the unique characteristics that define Nishiwaki's new language of poetry. The first thing that the ordinary Japanese reader would notice is that the poem contains many foreign words. In Japanese orthography, foreign words (except Chinese) are usually written in a special script called *katakana*. In this poem the following words are written in *katakana*: "Choricos," "Muse," "Poesy," "Abydos," and "curve." The next outstanding thing is that some of the foreign words are very unfamiliar. If they were written in the original Roman alphabet, one might be able to check them in a dictionary, but they are transliterated into *katakana*. What is "korikosu"? What is "abidosu"? A devoted scholar of Nishiwaki's works, Niikura Toshikazu, published a book in 1982, explaining many of the difficult words and allusions in Nishiwaki's poetry. According to this book, "Choricos" is the title of a poem published by Richard Aldington in 1919. The Latin word *choricus* is an adjective pertaining to a chorus. Abydos was an ancient city of Egypt, and Lord Byron wrote a poem entitled "The Bridge of Abydos."

It seems, however, that the poem does not require such information to be appreciated. Without knowing who the Abydos are, the reader seems to understand their distance in time and space, in short, their foreignness. The unfamiliar sound and rhythm of the words in Japanese are also pleasantly surprising. The first half of the last line shows a certain sensuality that is at once foreign and mythological. But its romanticism is abruptly disrupted by the word "heart." In English, this word can be utilized in a sentimental sense, but the original Japanese *shinzō* denotes only the internal organ. If Nishiwaki had wanted to soften the image here, he would have used *kokoro* instead of *shinzō*. By rejecting the potential sentimentality, the last line presents a surreal conjoining of two distant images—the curve of the Muse's throat becoming the heart (organ) of an unknown people. The first two lines awaken the Muse from her slumber in abstract "Poesy." The last line presents her physicality, that is, poetry's palpable corporeality, which is heightened by its surrealism. The poem fuses the atmosphere of a distant mythology with the concreteness of images effected by their surreal juxtaposition. *Ambarvalia*'s strange beauty derives from this fusion.

"Le Monde ancien" opens with a section entitled "Greek Lyrics," which contains some of Nishiwaki's loveliest short poems. It begins with a haiku-like three-line poem, "Weather":

On a morning (like an upturn'd gem)
Someone whispers to somebody in the
    doorway.
This is the day a god is born.

(tr. Hirata, 1993, p. 47)

Tenki

*(kutsugae sareta hōseki) no yōna asa
nanpito ka toguchi nite dareka to
    sasayaku
sore wa kami no seitan no hi*

(*Teihon, Nishiwaki Junzaburō zenshishū*
[ZS], p. 7)

Although disjointed, the images in this poem sparkle marvelously. A logical reading of the poem raises many questions. What is the relation between the title, "Weather *(tenki)*" and the poem? What is the reason for those parentheses? Who is whispering? Who is this god? The poem does not supply any answers, but for that very reason retains its radiance and mystery. Niikura provides one answer regarding the parentheses. They contain Nishiwaki's translation *(kutsugaesareta hōseki)* of a phrase from Keats's *Endymion*. Of course *Ambarvalia* does not have notes that identify the sources of the allusions, and the uninformed reader does not know that the phrase is a quotation. In a sense, then, it does not matter that it is a quotation. More important, the parentheses create a visual effect that isolates the space and time of the image, "an upturn'd gem." In Japanese the poem begins with this parenthetical image. The reader stops there momentarily. It is a breathtaking image that is softly superimposed on another image, "a morning." The effect of this "soft" transposition of images comes from the Japanese word for *like* ("no yauna," pronounced "no yōna" written in *hiragana*). It is right beside the "softest" word in the poem, *sasayaku* ("whispers"), in the next line. The reader senses that something radically new is being born. Perhaps the parentheses form a womb in which the brightness of a fetus (a new poetry) is contained.

The following poem is also considered a masterpiece by many critics:

The Sun

The countryside of Karumojiin produces
    marble.
Once I spent a summer there.

There are no skylarks and no snakes come
    out.
Only the sun comes up from bushes of
    damson
And goes down into bushes of damson.
The boy laughed as he seized a dolphin in a
    brook.

            (tr. Hirata, 1993, p. 48)

Taiyō

*karumojiin no inaka wa dairiseki no
    sanchi de
soko de watashi wa natsu o sugoshita koto
    ga atta.
hibari mo inaishi, hebi mo denai.
tada aoi sumomo no yabu kara taiyō
    ga dete
mata sumomo no yabu e shizumu.
shōnen wa ogawa de dorufin o toraete
    waratta.*

              (ZS, p. 9)

The poem begins prosaically as if it were a
journal entry. But where is this place called
"Karumojiin"? Is it a marble-producing Greek
island? Nishiwaki later admitted that he had
made up the name by thinking about the sleeping pill called Calmotin. Whether this poem
expresses a dream world induced by Calmotin
is irrelevant; what is significant is the fact that
the use of the autobiographical mode ("Once I
spent a summer there") is countered by the fic-
tiveness of the place. That is, the poem stealth-
ily rejects its own seemingly autobiographical
truth. It is not a Romantic expression of the
self; it presents, rather, an ironical commentary on autobiographical truth-value by at once
affirming and negating it. In this strangely fictive place, two common allegorical images are
introduced—skylarks and snakes—but with a
twist. They are introduced negatively—as
absences, echoing the play of presence and
absence enacted in the first two lines through
the strong presence of "I" and the fictive place
"Karumojiin." The countryside is bare,
deprived of allegorical images. Only the eter-

nal repetition of the sun rising from the useless
bush and sinking into another bush is seen.
The scene is thus saturated with *tsumaranasa*,
ennui, and insignificance.

Suddenly, this meaningless repetition is
interrupted by a surreal event, another
instance of meaninglessness but of a different,
poetically elevated kind. The most obvious
illogicality is that dolphins do not inhabit a
small stream. But the image of a boy grabbing
a large dolphin in a brook with a big grin on his
face is striking. But why "the" boy? Who is he?
The narrative voice has changed from the subjective "I" to the omnipresent third person. If
the autobiographical "I" were to continue to
the last line, the poem would have the following sense: "I saw a boy grasping a dolphin in a
brook, and laughing." But there is no place for
"I" in the last line. The abrupt appearance of
the boy is emphasized by the particle "wa" in
the Japanese, which indicates that the reader
has known this boy all along, that he has been
already introduced. Could the autobiographical narrator "I" be this boy? If that were so, the
line would have read: "As a boy, I laughed. . . ."
Thus the poem seems to present a clashing of
two different narrative spheres. This narrative
break produces a tension that negates the bare-
ness of the landscape, the ennui of cyclic time.
The poem effects a synthesized image that is
distant, foreign, youthful, and mythical, with
the brightness of an eternal summer.

Poetry As Translation

Nishiwaki included in *Ambarvalia* translations of poems written by others without noting these poems as such. The title poem
"Ambarvalia" that appears in the "Latin Elegies" section is Nishiwaki's Japanese translation of an elegy written by Tibullus, a Roman
poet of the Augustan Age, a contemporary of
Ovid. In fact, the "Latin Elegies" section consists entirely of Nishiwaki's translations of
Latin poems by Catullus, Tibullus, and several
anonymous poets. Nishiwaki also included a
translation of one of his own poems originally
written in Latin. A scholarly reader might iden-

tify Nishiwaki's translation of Yvan Goll's "Poèm d'amour" nestled anonymously in the "Le Monde moderne" section. The ordinary reader, however, would have no idea that these are translations and not completely original writings. In fact, these translations are so beautifully rendered into Nishiwaki's peculiar poetic language that they easily blend into the main body of the book. In an age obsessed with ownership, copyright, and plagiarism, Nishiwaki's failure to inform the reader that some of the poems are translations may seem irresponsible or criminal. But this type of criticism distracts from a far more crucial question concerning the status of translation in Nishiwaki's texts: Why do the translations blend in so well with other "original" poems in *Ambarvalia*? In fact, just as Pound's translations are highly regarded on their own, Nishiwaki's translations are greatly esteemed by Japanese readers. One might surmise that in *Ambarvalia* the issue of authorship was not important; instead, a new Japanese language reshaped through translation was the crucial issue. In short, *Ambarvalia* presents poetry as being essentially linked to the workings of translation.

In order to avoid the concept of poetry as the cultivation of the most beautifully authentic Japanese language, Nishiwaki first wrote poetry in foreign languages only. When he finally decided to write poetry in Japanese, his strategy was to translate foreign poems into a strangely unnatural Japanese that was affected by the syntax and grammar of the foreign languages. For example, a line in the poem, "Shitsurakuen" (Paradise lost), reads: "Ikko no taripotto no ki ga onkyō o hassuru koto naku seichō shite iru" (*ZS*, p. 46). The original is found in Nishiwaki's French poem, "Paradis Perdu," where the corresponding line reads: "Un palmier se grandit sans bruit" ("A palm tree grows without a sound") (*Nishiwaki Junzaburō zenshū [NJZ]*, vol. 9, p. 688). The original French seems natural, whereas the translated version sounds bizarre to a Japanese native speaker. To begin with, "ikko" is the wrong counter for trees—it should be "ippon no." If, in English, instead of saying "three head of cat-

tle," one said "three foot of cattle," the result would be similarly jarring. "Onkyō o hassuru koto naku" ("without emitting an acoustical phenomenon") is a wildly overblown way of translating *sans bruit* ("without a sound"), for which a simple "oto mo naku" would have done. In the same poem, foreign grammar is applied literally to the Japanese to create a comical effect: "Ore no yūjin no hitori ga kekkon shitsutsu aru" (*ZS*, p. 50). Literally translated into English, it becomes "One of my friends is getting married," not in the common sense of the near future, but in the sense of the present progressive. The original French reads: "Un de mes amis va se marier" (*NJZ*, vol. 9, p. 690), which clearly expresses the immediate future. It is possible that Nishiwaki translated the original French into English, and then into Japanese utilizing the temporal ambiguity of the English construction "be plus a present participle." Although this is grammatically possible, one never hears such an expression as "kekkon shitutsu aru" ("in the process of getting married at this moment").

Can one regard this grotesque deformation of the mother tongue as poetic? Hagiwara Sakutarō, Nishiwaki's major rival and friend at that time, raised such a question. In his essay "Nishiwaki Junzaburō-shi no shiron" (1937; The poetics of Mr. Nishiwaki Junzaburō), Hagiwara interpreted Nishiwaki's poetics as follows: "Nishiwaki says that those admirers of nature who love lilies and violets are not real poets; the poet is the one who can sense the images of beauty in such words. In other words, Baudelaire did not love the animal called cat, but loved the image of the word 'cat'" (p. 200). Hagiwara goes on to criticize this attitude as "the poetics of the dilettante," which entirely lacks the essence of lyricism and poetry, that is, human feelings. Although the two poets became close friends, the gap between their respective notions of poetry points toward the essential feature of modernist poetry that was to influence greatly future generations of Japanese poets. Nishiwaki's attitude is strictly rigorous, facing directly the epistemological fact that a poem is never a faithful representation of reality. The joy of poetry lies within the realm of words and images. In contrast, the lyricist Hagiwara never wanted to abandon the desire to express his innermost feelings and anxieties through poetry. Hagiwara's poetics was intended to be close to the source of what has to be expressed. Nishiwaki's poetics was intended to be as far away as possible from that source, hence the need for poetry as translation. However, Nishiwaki's poetry cannot be understood in such a simplistic manner. In fact, his later poetry blends his peculiar lyricism with surreal irony, wit, and Nietzschean laughter.

No Traveller Returns

As Japan's imperialist government increased its effort toward militarization of the nation, Nishiwaki stopped writing poetry around 1935. Although Nishiwaki was never arrested, some of his fellow surrealist writers were harassed and imprisoned by the police. Many poets abandoned their once-cherished avant-gardism and began writing blatantly xenophobic propaganda poems. Nishiwaki did not participate in the hastily established associations for writers promoting imperial Japan's glorious destiny. Instead, he quietly devoted himself to writing his doctoral dissertation, *Kodai bungaku josetsu* (An introduction to ancient literature). In 1942 Hagiwara Sakutarō died of pneumonia. Hagiwara had just selected a few poems from *Ambarvalia* to be included in an anthology of contemporary poetry that he had edited in 1940 entitled *Shōwa shi shō* (Selections of poems from the Shōwa period). Toward the end of the war, Nishiwaki moved his family from Tokyo to his hometown Ojiya to avoid the U.S. bombardment of the capital. His library of over three thousand books was moved to a rural area near Tokyo. His house in Tokyo was burned down in 1945. In Ojiya he immersed himself in classical Japanese literature and began to think about composing a long elegiac poem. The year after the defeat of Japan, in 1946, Nishiwaki composed a long poem consisting of one hundred sixty-eight sections. The title, *Tabibito kaerazu* (*No Traveller Returns*), was taken from Shakespeare's *Hamlet:* "The undiscover'd country, from whose bourn / No traveller returns." The book was published in 1947 along with the entirely revised version of *Ambarvalia*, with its title now written in the Japanese script *hiragana* as *Amubaruwaria*.

For those familiar with the works of the modernist Nishiwaki, the writings in these books show a shocking waning of Nishiwaki's avant-garde spirit. The revised poems in *Amubaruwaria* seem to have lost the brilliant sharpness and youthful violence of language of the originals. Instead, they look tamed and weathered, although somehow more mature. *No Traveller Returns* also appears to represent a retreat from modernism, showing clear evidence of what is called the "return to Japan" or the "return to the East." This nostalgic tendency was an intellectual and spiritual reorientation on the part of the majority of Japanese intellectuals during the war years, who abandoned their youthful infatuation with the West and its modernism and embraced the mythical image of an authentic Japan through the medium of the Japanese classics. *No Traveller Returns* seems to be saturated with the weariness of an old poet wandering aimlessly in the ruins of his country. The emphasis on the theme of loneliness in an ephemeral world is the most salient feature of classical Japanese literature influenced by Buddhism. Was Nishiwaki a spent poet? Did his poetry no longer sparkle? On the contrary, *No Traveller Returns* opened a new vista Japanese poetry. By combining the new and old, lyricism and wit, theory and practice, Nishiwaki seems to have discovered his mature poetic form. He was fifty-three years old; his country lay in ruins; yet, his poetic career was just beginning.

No Traveller Returns begins as follows:

1

O Traveler, wait
Before thou wettest thy tongue
in this faint spring water,
O think, traveler, of life.
Thou art also merely a water-spirit
that oozed out from the chinks in a rock.

Neither does this thinking-water
flow into eternity.
At a certain moment in eternity
it will dry out.
Ah! jays are too noisy!
Sometimes out of this water
comes the phantasmal man
with flowers in his hand.
'Tis only a dream
to seek life eternal.
To abandon thy longings
into the stream of life ever-flowing
and finally to wish
to fall off the precipice of eternity
and disappear. . . .
O 'tis merely an illusion.
Thus says this phantom water-sprite
who comes out of the water to towns
    and villages
when water plants reach for
the shadows of floating clouds.

2

On the window,
a dim-light—
how desolate,
the human world.

3

Desolate, the world of nature
Desolate, our sleep.

4

A hardened garden.

5

Sorrel.

(*ZS*, pp. 173–175; tr. Hirata,
1993, pp. 72–73)

The length of each section is not uniform. Section 5 contains only one word, *yabugarashi*,

whereas the longest section has over forty lines. It seems that there is no narrative or rational linkage between the sections. Each section seems to form an independent poem. However, in reading through the sections, the reader experiences a sense of music, akin to reading through *renga*, Japanese linked verses.

The word *sabishiki* ("lonely," "desolate") appears over forty times throughout the poem. Why is such a trite word repeated so many times? One needs to remember Nishiwaki's insistence on the notion of *tsumaranasa* ("insignificance," "boredom") in "Profanus." If *sabishiki* is an overtly sentimental, trite, amateurishly "poetic" word, why does Nishiwaki repeat a word that has been over-used in the history of poetry? In order to answer this question adequately, it is helpful to look at another section, which contains Nishiwaki's paradoxical inquiry into "what poetry is" through the repetition of the word *sabishiki*:

39

Early September
from a rock by the avenue
a green acorn hanging. . . .

Desolate is the window.
A person's voice sounds from within.
How desolate, the sound of human speech.
"Hey, mistah, dis time I hear you goin'
    a pilgrimage
to Konpira, eh? Please take dis wid ya.
No, no, it's nothin', mistah, just a
    partin' token.
Take-iit, take-iiiiit."

"I can no longer write poetry.
Poetry exists where there is no poetry.
Only a shred of reality becomes poetry.
Reality is loneliness.
I feel loneliness, therefore I am.
Loneliness is the root of existence.
Loneliness is the ultimate desire
    for Beauty.
Beauty is the symbol of eternity."

(*ZS*, pp. 189–190; tr. Hirata, 1993, p. 80)

This section begins with a haiku-like stanza that depicts in the simplest terms a desolate autumn landscape. The last line of this stanza does not form a complete sentence: "aoi donguri no sagaru." It seems to be modifying the nearest noun, which is *mado* ("window") of the next stanza. This possibility suggests the image of a window perhaps reflecting the landscape with an acorn. But there is a clear stanza break. Perhaps the last line of the stanza modifies the first word of the stanza, *kugatsu* ("September"). This possibility suggests that an endless cyclical movement is established, with the last word always going back to the first. This cyclical movement becomes important because the next stanza breaks the perpetually self-sustaining autumnal sphere. The first line of the second stanza "mado no sabishiki" ("Desolate is the window"), sounds odd, for people do not commonly associate loneliness with the image of a window. A green acorn hanging from a rock, on the other hand, can be thought of as *sabishiki* ("desolate"). Thus, there is an abrupt transition from an object in the first stanza accepted as *sabishiki* ("lonely") according to the classical poetic sense of loneliness to the forceful classification of an object as *sabishiki* ("lonely") that has not yet been coded as such in the tradition of Japanese poetry.

The remainder of the second stanza continues the theme of loneliness and meaninglessness. The third line exhibits a bizarre usage of Japanese: "ningen no hanasu oto no sabishiki" ("How desolate, the sound of human speech"). In normal usage, one would never use *oto* ("sound") to refer to human speech, but rather *koe* ("voice"), which Nishiwaki used in the second line: "naka kara hito no koe ga suru" ("A person's voice sounds from within"). This transition from "human voice" to "the sound of human speech" indicates that the humanness associated with "voice" is replaced by a purely objective "sound." Now the human voice is a mere sound, stripped of humanity and warmth—lonely and meaningless, like the image of the green acorn in the first stanza. Then, suddenly, this dehumanized voice

begins to speak forcefully, in a rural dialect, which emphasizes in turn the humanness of the speech. The comical tension that this speech creates is breathtaking, reminding the reader of Bashō's *karumi*.

The final stanza presents an abrupt transition from the primitive voice of the previous stanza. The new stanza presents the soliloquy of a lonely poet-philosopher pondering on the impossibility of poetry: only when poetry disappears can poetry appear. That is, only when traditionally nurtured poetic meanings and codes are thrown away does true poetry emerge. But this true poetry is deprived of meanings. That is why when poetry disappears reality appears. This fragment of reality is desolate, meaningless, poetry-less. But it is also the ultimate poetry, the symbol of eternity.

The earlier question was why is such a trite word as *sabishiki* repeated so many times? The answer seems to be related to the aesthetics displayed in the final stanza. *Sabishisa* ("desolateness") is a state of meaninglessness, a reality where no human intervention (that is, giving meanings to things) is possible. By repeating the word *sabishiki*, which is already worn-out in Japanese poetry, Nishiwaki seems to be making the word more meaningless and trite, to the point that it becomes something like a nameless pebble. For Nishiwaki, poetry is not a signifying process, but it a mechanism to strip away significance, meanings, and codes, including what has been called "poetry."

Such a paradoxical endeavor is bound to fail, and this failure of poetry to be pure poetry (utterly boring reality) is the source of the comical in Nishiwaki's writing. Moreover, this failure does not end in silence. On the contrary, Nishiwaki kept writing voluminously, almost single-mindedly reworking the theme of the impossibility of writing poetry. After *No Traveller Returns*, Nishiwaki published ten more books of poetry before his death on 5 June 1982 in Ojiya at the age of eighty-eight. *Kindai no gūwa* (Modern fables), which many critics regard as his most satisfying collection of poems, appeared in 1953. Then, inspired by Joyce's *Finnegans Wake*, Nishiwaki began to write increasingly longer poems: *Dai san no shinwa* (1956; The third myth); *Ushinawareta toki* (1960; Lost time); *Hōjō no megami* (1962; The goddess of fertility); *Eterunitasu* (1962); *Hōseki no nemuri* (1963; A gemstone's sleep); *Raiki* (1967; Book of rites); *Jōka* (1969, Earth song), which was Nishiwaki's longest poem with 2000 lines; *Rokumon* (1970; Lu-men); and his final collection, *Jinrui* (1979; Mankind). A year before his death, a large volume of Nishiwaki's collected poems *(Nishiwaki Junzaburō zenshishū)* was published, containing 1,238 pages of his poetry in Japanese.

Selected Bibliography

PRIMARY WORKS

COLLECTED WORKS IN JAPANESE

Nishiwaki Junzaburō. *Nishiwaki Junzaburō zenshū.* Edited by Kagiya Yukinobu et al. 12 vols. Tokyo: Chikuma Shobō, 1982–1983. (Abbreviated as *NJZ.*)
———. *Teihon, Nishiwaki Junzaburō zenshishū.* Tokyo: Chikuma Shobō, 1981. (Abbreviated as *ZS.*)

ENGLISH TRANSLATIONS

Hirata, Hosea. *The Poetry and Poetics of Nishiwaki Junzaburō: Modernism in Translation.* Princeton, N.J.: Princeton University Press, 1993. (Includes "Profanus," "The Extinction of Poetry," and "Esthé-tique Foraine" from *Surrealist Poetics, Ambarvalia* [except Nishiwaki's translations], *No Traveller Returns,* and the long poem *Eterunitasu.*)
Nishiwaki Junzaburō. *Gen'ei: Selected Poems of Nishiwaki Junzaburō 1894–1982.* Trans. by Y. Claremont. University of Sydney East Asian Series, no. 4. Australia: Wild Peony PTY LTD, 1991. (Includes selections from Nishiwaki's entire poetic oeuvre.)

SECONDARY WORKS

CRITICAL WORKS ON NISHIWAKI IN ENGLISH

Hirata, Hosea. *The Poetry and Poetics of Nishiwaki Junzaburō: Modernism in Translation.* Princeton, N.J.: Princeton University Press, 1993.

WORKS CITED

Bacon, Francis. "The tvvo Bookes of the Proficience and Advancement of Learning Divine and Hvmane." In *Critical Essays of the Seventeenth Century.* Edited by J. E. Spingarn. London: Oxford University Press, 1908.
Hagiwara Sakutarō. "Nishiwaki Junzaburō-shi no shiron: junsei shiron to sofisuto teki shiron." In *Gendaishi tokuhon: Nishiwaki Junzaburō.* 1937. Reprint, Tokyo: Shichōsha, 1979.
———. *Howling at the Moon.* Trans. by H. Sato. New York: Columbia University Press, 1978.
Niikura Toshikazu. *Nishiwaki Junzaburō zenshi in'yu shūsei.* Tokyo: Chikuma Shobō, 1982.
Ueda Makoto. *Bashō and His Interpreters: Selected Hokku with Commentary.* Stanford, Calif.: Stanford University Press, 1991.

ŌE KENZABURŌ
1935–

DENNIS WASHBURN

Ōe Kenzaburō is a writer driven by an urgent sense of moral and spiritual crisis. In his 1994 Nobel Prize acceptance speech, "Japan, the Ambiguous, and Myself," Ōe wrote:

> In the history of modern Japanese literature, the writers most sincere in their awareness of a mission were the "postwar school" of writers who came onto the literary scene deeply wounded by the catastrophe of war yet full of hope for a rebirth. They tried with great pain to make up for the atrocities committed by Japanese military forces in Asia, as well as to bridge the profound gaps that existed not only between the developed nations of the West and Japan but also between African and Latin American countries and Japan. Only by doing so did they think that they could seek with some humility reconciliation with the rest of the world. It has always been my aspiration to cling to the very end of the line of that literary tradition inherited from those writers."
>
> (*Japan, the Ambiguous, and Myself*,
> pp. 117–18)

Ōe's sweeping summary of the history of modern Japanese literature and his place in it reveals a number of characteristic attitudes. He is gripped by a powerful historical awareness of belonging to a generation disfigured by the twin forces of modernization and war guilt. The pressures of modernization, of trying to emulate the West while remaining true to an essential conception of Japan, has created a deep anxiety about the authenticity of Japanese identity. The shattering experience of defeat and guilt destroyed the unifying myth of the imperial institution and gave greater urgency to the search for values by Japanese intellectuals across the political spectrum. For Ōe and his generation the ambivalence of identity, the apparently unsettled meaning of values, and the difficulties faced by individuals forced to create their own moral universe were not mere abstractions, but defining experiences.

Ōe's historical awareness has given him a profound sense of living on the periphery. Because he is a highly honored public figure, it seems odd that he insists on representing himself as a marginal writer at "the very end of the line" of his own generation. Taken at face value, his attitude may come across as hypocritical false modesty. His insistence that he is marginalized, however, takes on a different significance when we think of it not as an attitude but as a method that makes Ōe's art possible. Throughout his career Ōe has consistently assumed a self-consciously oppositionist pose that enables him to question not only the values and policies of the Japanese state, but also his personal beliefs and the place of those beliefs in society at large. His absolute rejection of intellectual complacency is a difficult position to maintain, but it has fueled his intellectual curiosity, inspired his passion for the political causes he espouses, and provided an emotional ground for his ethical beliefs. It has also determined to a large extent the continuing freshness and experimental quality of his fiction.

Ōe's challenge to himself and to society to confront the ambiguities of Japanese modernity has found expression in several recurring narrative elements. First, there is his affinity for myth-making. Through the repetition of certain images and themes and the layering of different, sometimes competing, narrative voices, Ōe has constructed a complex literary universe situated around an out-of-the-way village in the forest which lies at an intersection between the historical world of postwar Japan and the timeless realm of myth. Ōe's affinity for myth-making marks him as a "high modernist," a member of a lineage that includes Kawabata Yasunari, Shiga Naoya, Mishima Yukio, and Nakagami Kenji. Ōe might reject his inclusion in this line on the grounds that his constant probing of the truth of myth and his use of multiple perspectives undercuts the cultural essentialism that characterizes his fellow Japanese modernists. Yet even if we recognize the distinctive characteristics of Ōe's myth-making, the fact remains that he has been compelled to construct his village in the woods to give voice to his critique of the sterility and debasement of contemporary culture.

A second element of his fiction is its self-centeredness. In this context self-centeredness does not imply selfishness only, though that is an important trait of many of Ōe's protagonists. Myth-making carries with it the danger of abstraction that blocks a full, honest examination of history, cultural myths, and value systems. When an author chooses to keep a distance from ethical problems (out of a desire, for example, to achieve the illusion of objec-

tivity), the loss of direct engagement can lead to simple didacticism. As part of the creative process of self-probing, then, Ōe places himself and his family at the center of much of his work in an effort to efface the narrative boundaries that serve as a buffer between author and subject matter.

Just as myth-making connects Ōe to the lineage of literary modernism in Japan, so the element of self-centeredness is rooted in the convention of the confessional mode known as the I-novel, the dominant form of Japanese literature throughout the twentieth century. So much of Ōe's fiction is drawn directly from his personal experiences that this connection cannot be ignored, though the particular contours of Ōe's art require some qualification of the point. In the later stages of his career Ōe began to insert into his texts a character/narrator who is unmistakably himself, Ōe Kenzaburō, as identified by autobiographical details and direct reference to Ōe's entire earlier corpus. In these later works, however, the technique of explicit identification of an authorial self creates multi-vocal narratives that fly in the face of the normal expectations of a reader of autobiographical fiction. Far from presuming to offer the reader "sincerity," the self-centeredness of Ōe's fiction undercuts the certainty with which we can interpret the meaning of his stories and thus works against the revelation, or emergence, of self (or subject) that is typical of the I-novel, and toward a dispersal of meaning.

A third major recurring element in Ōe's work is its moralism, a natural outcome of his constant probing of beliefs and questioning of the truthfulness of narrative. The structures of Ōe's stories are so inventive and challenging, his style so playful and self-renewing, and the apparent honesty of his voice (often a product of his willingness to shock) so compelling that it may appear inappropriate to apply the term moralism. Nonetheless, didacticism figures prominently in his work. The typical Ōe protagonist is faced with a profound moral crisis that threatens to tear his world apart. A primal action repeated over and over in Ōe's fiction is the descent of the troubled protagonist into a womb-like enclosure to seek some form of escape or resolution. That enclosure may be a physical space such as a cellar, a darkened room, or a mine, or a psychological space such as the retreat to a past relationship or a memory world, but in every instance it represents a space of deep introspection. Occasionally, Ōe's handling of moral issues may strike the reader as too obvious or heavy-handed—a criticism leveled at even some of his most famous works. At its best, however, Ōe's moralism creates a vision of the possibility of a spiritual rebirth in an absurd universe—a vision simultaneously liberating and terrifying, poignantly sad and brutally funny.

The Creation of a Public Persona

Ōe was born on 31 January 1935 in the small village of Ose in Ehime prefecture on the island of Shikoku. His family was large (there were seven children) and had deep roots in a region steeped in rural traditions that survived the social changes of modernization. He entered the local public school in 1941 and his early education was shaped by the moral training standard to the curriculum at that time, which emphasized loyalty to the emperor. The war with China and the United States increased the urgency of such training, which was a central fact of life during Ōe's childhood.

His father died in 1944, and Ōe was raised by the women in the family, who instilled in him a love of narratives, especially local stories. His mother in particular encouraged the study of literature, including Western works such as *Huckleberry Finn*, which Ōe has cited many times as having had a major impact on him. Near the end of his elementary schooling, when Japan had lost the war and had come under the control of the Supreme Commander for the Allied Powers, the education system underwent radical reforms dictated by the Occupation government. The experience was as unsettling as the announcement of surren-

der or the emperor's declaration of his humanity. Japanese children were suddenly required to unlearn history and values that had been inculcated by the prewar system; and though the reforms were liberating, they were also disorienting, since they swept away old certainties and nurtured a more skeptical outlook.

The reforms of the systems of education and of land ownership transformed the social landscape of rural Japan, and these changes directly touched Ōe's life. For example, when he entered middle school in 1947, he became actively involved in setting up a youth cooperative, a program that arose out of the myriad initiatives decreed by the central government during the early Occupation years. For Ōe this kind of exposure to political ideas in his childhood was undoubtedly an important element in the formation of his intellectual interests, especially his support of democratic movements.

Ōe started at the local high school in 1950 and transferred to Matsuyama East High the following year. He edited a student literary magazine and was active in drama productions. When he graduated in 1953 he traveled to Tokyo to enroll in a private school to prepare for the entrance examinations, which he took the following year. Ōe entered the department of French Literature at the elite Tokyo University in 1954. He began to read widely, especially the works of Albert Camus, Jean-Paul Sartre, and Blaise Pascal, and participated in the remarkable cultural scene of the mid-1950s. With the Occupation over and the Cold War in full force, the currents of Japanese intellectual and political life were turbulent. The conservative coalition that eventually ruled Japan for forty years had not yet been realized, and, as Japan began to re-emerge on the international scene, there was a desire to look beyond the heavy presence of American culture to reinvigorate Japanese intellectual life. These historical circumstances explain the wide appeal of both the existentialists and the French Left as well as the particular turn that Ōe's career took.

In his Nobel speech Ōe pays tribute to his mentor at Tokyo University, Watanabe Kazuo, a specialist on François Rabelais. Ōe credits Watanabe with instilling in him a sense of humanism and decency, but in literary terms the impact of his teaching was just as great. According to Ōe, he learned from Watanabe's translation of Rabelais an image system that Mikhail Bakhtin has termed "grotesque realism." This image system yokes together disparate elements—violence and death/sexuality and rebirth—and utilizes humor to undercut authority. Ōe claims this system "made it possible to seek literary methods of attaining the universal for someone like me, born and brought up in a peripheral, marginal, off-center country" (*Japan, the Ambiguous, and Myself*, p.125). Watanabe helped to direct Ōe's graduation thesis—a study of imagery and style in the novels and criticism of Sartre and Camus that was also an investigation of notions of the good. He was also a father figure. When Ōe was struggling with the sudden fame and success he achieved with his first stories, Watanabe was a stabilizing force who gave him what now seems like prescient advice: to live a normal life, but think about the abnormal.

Some of Ōe's first pieces were plays and sketches he wrote for a student drama group at the university. In 1957 he turned a play, "Kedamonotachi no koe" (1956; The voices of beasts), into the short story, "Kimyō na shigoto" (A weird job), which tells of a college student who takes up a part-time job involving the extermination of dogs used for experiments. This story caught the attention of the critic Hirano Ken, who, along with others, encouraged Ōe to submit more work. Soon after, Ōe brought out the short story "Shisha no ogori" (1957; Lavish are the dead)—about another college student with a peculiar job (in this case transferring corpses from hospitals); and in January 1958 the story "Shiiku" (translated as "Prize Stock," 1977, and as "The Catch," 1981) appeared in *Bungakkai*. In June that year *Memushiri kouchi* (*Nip the Buds, Shoot the Kids*, 1995) was published in the journal *Gunzō*. Thus, from the very beginning Ōe found an outlet in mainstream journals, and the Akutagawa prize in 1958 conferred on

him both canonical status and a reputation as a prodigy.

The site of "The Catch" is Ōe's native village. It tells of a group of village children who secretly befriend an African American airman, who is hiding out near the children's village after his plane was shot down. To the children—most especially the boy who is the narrator—the airman is a god-like pet, an animal of genius whose presence among them lifts this one summer in their lives to the timeless realm of perfect childhood innocence. That state is eventually betrayed when the adults in the village discover the American's presence. When they come to capture him, the airman panics and takes the boy-narrator hostage. In the end the boy's father kills the airman, but he also crushes and mutilates his son's hand. Sacrificial violence is marked by disfigurement, a visible sign of the boy's knowledge of evil as he falls into the world of adulthood.

Nip the Buds, Shoot the Kids is also set in an isolated village, and the title calls to mind the agricultural practice of thinning out to ensure survival. This practice gradually takes on a sinister meaning. The story, narrated by a young man, is set during the war and depicts a group of boys who have been abandoned by adults and left to their own devices. The atmosphere is initially one of apparent innocence. However, we learn that these boys are delinquents who have been abandoned first by their families and then by the government institution that had housed them. Forced to seek a place where they can serve as laborers, the boys find a village in the mountains. Soon after, an epidemic breaks out, and the villagers flee, leaving the boys to fend for themselves. For a time the boys create an idyllic, pastoral community, and there is even a play snow festival that evokes the timeless sense of innocence experienced by the narrator in "The Catch." This moment cannot last, however, and the villagers return and use the threat of violence to take back their homes. The boys are put on trial for breaking into the village houses, and the hypocrisy and brutality of the adult world corrupts the boys, who begin accusing one another. The villagers coerce the boys into accepting an agreement based on a lie: the villagers will not try them if the boys agree not to inform the authorities about these events. The narrator refuses to go along and must flee for his life. Completely abandoned, the narrator's story ends with him rushing for safety into the darkest part of the forest.

Both of these stories were praised for their startling freshness, but they were also read within the context of depictions of youth culture best exemplified by Ishihara Shintarō's 1956 Akutagawa prize-winning story "Taiyō no kisetsu" (Season of Violence, 1966). Ishihara's work gave rise to a wave of stories and films depicting the amoral or even nihilistic sexuality of the so-called taiyōzoku (sun tribe) generation of postwar youth. Critics tended to praise Ōe's work, too, for its powerful realism rather than its mythic elements (which became more evident later in retrospect), but Ōe's treatment of sexuality in his first stories is more positively grounded in social values than representations of the "sun tribe."

This positive treatment of sexuality changed in 1959 with the publication of the controversial Warera no jidai (Our age), a novel in which sex is treated explicitly throughout. The narrator, a college student named Yasuo, recounts his relationships with his younger brother Shigeru, and with his girlfriend Yoriko, a prostitute who services Americans. The brothers present a stark contrast: the ineffectual Yasuo and the active, romantic Shigeru, who is a pianist. Yasuo is an intellectual whose emotional life is bottled up by his fantasies. He considers himself a representative of his age, born too late to have joined the heroic battles of the war, but old enough to have suffered the ignominy and humiliation of the Occupation. He longs to escape to Algeria and join the fight for independence against the French, and he shows his solidarity for the cause by turning down a scholarship to study in France. The scholarship would have freed him from his sterile world and from the clinging sexuality of Yoriko, who is pregnant with his child. After declining the scholarship, however, he is incapable of the commitment required to go to war. Even his obsession with sex is no release. His relationship with Yoriko is entwined with feelings of inadequacy and shame, and in the end he becomes impotent.

Shigeru does not share his brother's introspective nature. He longs to buy a large truck and travel around Japan with his jazz trio. Shigeru is frustrated, but he has a blind faith and hope that he will find a way out. His group is constantly on the lookout for excitement, and one day they turn up at a right-wing rally, where they fantasize about becoming fascists fanatically devoted to the emperor. When they finally see the emperor, they are disappointed by his boring ordinariness and hatch a plot to throw a grenade under his car. The plot is foiled in a bizarre farce when the young men hide the grenade in a public bathroom near the route of the emperor's car. They place the grenade in a sanitary napkin disposal, but when a woman uses the disposal they are so disgusted that they cannot retrieve the grenade in time. A short time afterward, Shigeru's fellow musicians get into an argument and kill themselves with the grenade. Shigeru is then killed in a shootout with police.

Yasuo observes all of this but is powerless to help his brother. He contemplates suicide at the end but defers any action. Far from providing at least the solace of self-understanding, Yasuo's paralysis heightens the absurd futility of Shigeru's death. Yasuo believes that the dilemma of his age is that the times are out of joint. Warera no jidai (Our age) was controversial because it of its explicit treatment of sex, but the power of the novel derives from its darkly satirical critique of a culture that lacks the political or aesthetic vision to find a way out of its malaise.

The political undertones of Ōe's early works may strike the reader as unintentionally subordinated to the pyrotechnics of his language and subject matter. His political aims were nonetheless clear, and his emergence as a writer coincided with his increasingly public participation in political causes. He was sympathetic to the Left and joined the opposition to the

Japan–United States Mutual Security Treaty and to nuclear proliferation. In May 1960 he traveled to China as part of a group representing Japanese writers, and in 1961 he was a member of the committee that organized a conference of Asian and African writers in Tokyo that was intended to build solidarity among postcolonial states. Ōe made a very public move to establish his credentials with the Left, and his fiction began to reflect his involvement.

Ōe's 1962 work *Okurete kita seinen* (The youth who came too late) tells of a young man who feels he has missed out on the war and is caught between the old militarist ideology and the new age of democracy. He is conflicted by his awareness of the evils of the emperor system but attracted to it by its emotional appeal. Ōe's story thus tackles one of the central problems of postwar culture in Japan. The first part of the work is set in a village in Shikoku. The young man suffers a series of humiliations and disillusionments that eventually estrange him from his home and land him in reform school. The second part of the novel deals with his life as a student at Tokyo University. He becomes a tutor of French for a young woman, Ikuko, who is the daughter of an important right-wing politician. When Ikuko is impregnated by her young boyfriend, she asks her tutor to approach her father and somehow obtain enough money from him so that she may have an abortion. He fails to get anything from the old man, and so asks a leftist friend to help him find a cheap abortionist. In return for this favor, the young man agrees to join the friend's radical organization. After joining the group he is accused of being a spy, tortured, and humiliated again. The young man, who is now impotent, decides to work for the politician, becoming not only his follower, but also his plaything. This decision is calculated to put him on the road to success, and the young man closes his story with a sardonic evaluation of his circumstances—he is neither a hero, nor a witness to his age, but is just like the reader.

Satire built on the abject humiliation of the protagonist is a recurring technique in Ōe's fiction. This technique, coupled with the sharp

political turn in Ōe's writing, is even more pronounced in an earlier work entitled "Sebuntīn" (1961; "Seventeen," 1996). The political atmosphere in Japan at the time was exceptionally volatile. In addition to the riots and demonstrations that took place over the renewal of the Security Treaty, the Socialist party head, Asanuma Inejirō, was assassinated by Yamaguchi Otoya, a seventeen-year-old extremist. Yamaguchi committed suicide in jail and was hailed as an exemplar of pure virtue and piety by fringe elements on the Right.

Ōe's story makes reference to these events by presenting a disaffected young man who feels his life is meaningless as he prepares for his college examinations. His only release is masturbation. The evening before the exams he gets into an argument over politics with his older sister. He tries to pose as a leftist, but his sister, who holds mainstream conservative views, overwhelms him and leaves him inarticulate. Flustered and enraged, he kicks his sister in the face, shattering her glasses and injuring one of her eyes. As if to announce his sense of utter isolation, he goes off to sleep in a storage shed.

The following day his exams do not go well, and he is also forced to undergo the humiliating ordeal of a physical-fitness test that involves an 800-meter run. A brilliantly written passage brings to life the painful self-consciousness of an adolescent who is not in control, who feels himself to be the object of the gazes of the teachers and the other students. The fiasco becomes more ludicrous when the young man wets himself during the run. Just as he hits bottom, another student persuades him to become a *sakura*—a paid vocal supporter—for a right-wing politician. At first the young man is self-conscious, but those feelings give way, and in a few weeks he becomes a fascist thug. His Imperial Way uniform becomes a metaphorical armor that provides him with an external identity and covers the shame he feels toward his body. His new-found confidence is expressed in the form of violent attacks against leftist demonstrators, and he is arrested several times. No longer paralyzed by shame, he begins to pay a bathhouse girl, his imagined slave, to masturbate him; and all the while no one—neither his family, nor his teachers—does anything to halt his transformation. The young man believes that the emperor is the one who decides all matters, which relieves him of his anxieties and of the burden of thinking.

The publication of "Sebuntīn" made Ōe a target of stonings and death threats by right-wing extremists. The wife of his publisher was attacked, and her servant was murdered. These terrible events forced the withdrawal from publication of the second half of the story, "Seiji shōnen shi-su" (1961; literally "A political youth dies"). The situation cooled somewhat when Ōe took a trip to Europe. He traveled widely, was able to meet Sartre in Paris, and returned to Japan in December 1961. The following year was less eventful, but he was still forced to keep a low profile and concentrate on his work. In November 1962 he published a collection of essays about his travel in Europe and wrote the novel *Seiteki ningen* (A sexual human; translated as *J*, 1996), which was published the following year.

In spite of the threats he faced, *Seiteki ningen* is very much a continuation of the themes and styles Ōe had been experimenting with for several years. The protagonist, a man referred to as J, is a thirty-year-old who is still at loose ends in his life. His father is extremely wealthy, and that allows him to pursue his grotesque desires as he pleases. There is no real danger in all this excess, however, and J is eventually numbed by his lifestyle. In order to get something real into his life, J decides that he will become a *chikan*, a groper on the subway. Along the way he befriends two fellow *chikan*, a young poet and an older, well-groomed man who apparently has powerful political connections. J associates with these men and engages in anti-social behavior as a way to regain his humanity. A considerable amount of collusion by a hypocritical society enables J to get away with his behavior, and that collusion undermines the thrill he seeks. Still, his year of living dangerously at least holds out the possibility of rebirth, until the hope is dashed by the death of the younger

chikan and by the revelation that J's wife has had an affair and is pregnant. J decides to leave his wife and move back with his father. He completes his rehabilitation by taking a respectable job. His rehabilitation is of course double-edged, in a rather heavy-handed way, in that it requires the loss of his humanity. Though it is not one of his most important works, *Seiteki ningen* is representative of Ōe's early period, and it sets the stage for the more highly charged personal fiction that redefined his place in postwar literature.

Personal Matters: A Family Saga

Ōe married Itami Yukari, the sister of actor/director Itami Jūzō, in 1960. Their first child, Hikari, was born in 1963 with a birth defect that left him brain damaged, and this personal crisis perhaps had the greatest impact on Ōe's career. The shock of confronting his son's condition, following so closely on the controversy and violence that surrounded the publication of "Sebuntīn," forced Ōe to reconsider the connections between his public role and his personal affairs. From the beginning he had drawn on his own background to write fiction, but the birth of Hikari changed the very nature of his literary pursuits.

Ōe's relationship with his son gave rise to a series of works written over three decades that constitute what might be called a family saga. The saga began with "Sora no kaibutsu aguwī" (1964; "Aghwee the Sky Monster," 1977). As in many of Ōe's stories the narrator is disfigured, a young man who has lost one of his eyes. But his impaired sight also suggests the potential for a different power of vision, a power acquired as a result of his acquaintance with the character D. D is a famous composer who had a mentally impaired son. Unable to accept the responsibility for the infant, D agreed with the doctors to let the baby die. The resulting guilt unbalanced D, and he claims now to be able to see an apparition of a monster baby who comes down from heaven, uttering a single inarticulate phrase, "Aghwee." D's family is fearful that the composer will hurt himself, and they hire the young narrator to look after him. The task of protecting D is doomed from the start, and despite the young man's vigilance the composer commits suicide. The story ends with the narrator explaining how he lost his eye. One day as he was walking along he startled some children, who, in reaction to their fear, threw stones at him. The narrator's realization of the randomness of this act, and of his own sacrifice, enables him to finally see the dead child: that is, to become the narrator of D's story.

The issues of guilt and ethical responsibility that haunted the postwar generation in Japan and that provided the ground for Ōe's earliest writings are brought down to an intensely personal level and given immediacy in "Aghwee the Sky Monster." This story, however, is only one possible variation on the relationship between father and handicapped son. D tells the narrator of his theory of multiple lives and pluralistic universes, and the hope for the possibility of regeneration, of a different outcome, is a driving force that injects a deeper strain of humanism into Ōe's fiction.

Humanism informs his next major work, the novel *Kojinteki na taiken* (1964; *A Personal Matter*, 1968). Considered by many one of Ōe's best works, it presents the story of Bird, who has just fathered a handicapped son. The plot turns not on the consequences of a decision to let the baby live or die, but on the process of coming to that decision. We follow Bird's dark, at times comic descent into his soul—a descent set in motion by his desire to escape the heavy responsibility of caring for his deformed baby. Bird seeks escape in drink, in violent and degrading sex with an old flame, Himiko, and in his own sense of self-debasement. Bird tries to prove to himself that he is depraved enough to let the baby die, and it is his self-centeredness, his powerful egotism that forces him into his private hell. With the help of Himiko, he steps to the brink of moral degradation by taking the baby from the hospital and delivering it to an unethical doctor to

be done away with. Yet at this pivotal moment, his self-centeredness offers a means of salvation. Bird is caught in a vicious dilemma in which his fear of responsibility may lead him to do something he fears even more. By accepting that he is alone, he understands that he must assume the responsibility of challenging his own fears. This moment of recognition is like looking into a void, and it rouses a different kind of fear in him that he cannot fully articulate. But the act of acknowledging that there is no way out of his existential crisis permits him to hope that forbearance will provide salvation. He chooses to give up his dreams of escape and rescues the baby.

The novel is brilliantly conceived, and the grotesque realism Ōe employs to depict the squalor of Bird's life makes the ethical dilemma he faces all the more vivid. The narrative is perhaps marred at the end by the sudden unexplained nature of Bird's revelation, as if the good outcome is presented as both inevitable and a random event. Bird's search for escape, however, is not just an empty exercise in self-pity. The loathing and degradation he experiences are the correlatives to his self-doubt and moral uncertainty. Yet his state of extreme doubt also suggests a possible route to redemption, for even though Bird fails to find any moral absolutes, the very struggle transforms him.

A Personal Matter was a major success, and the English-language translation brought Ōe an international readership. The personal turn deepened, even authenticated, the passion he brought to his fiction and gave it much wider appeal. Ōe's personal turn, however, did not eclipse his role as a writer deeply committed to public causes. The personal and the social are not separate concerns in his works, and this is demonstrated in the set of essays entitled *Hiroshima nōto* (1965; *Hiroshima Notes*, 1995) that was written over the same period as the composition of *A Personal Matter* and considered the companion piece to the novel.

During the summer of 1963, amid the turmoil surrounding Hikari's birth, Ōe attended a conference in Hiroshima as part of his work in the anti-nuclear movement. He was turned off by what he perceived as the lack of sincerity exhibited by the participants, and depressed by his family troubles. He hit upon the idea of working through his problems by undertaking an examination of a new kind of humanity— what Ōe called Hiroshima Man, meaning the *hibakusha*, the survivors of the atomic bombing. Ōe had been impressed with the nonfiction work of Norman Mailer, in which the author's presence is manifested in the simultaneous acts of reporting and interpreting. Ōe of course cannot speak for the *hibakusha*, and he has been severely criticized for interloping on the cause of genuine survivors of the atombic bombing. In interviewing the survivors and presenting their stories, however, Ōe insisted that he was creating a different form of literature. To be sure, *Hiroshima Notes* is not merely an examination of *hibakusha* culture. It is also a manifesto that extends the humanism Ōe was starting to articulate in his fiction. As a result, the collection is as much about the author as about Hiroshima survivors. Writing these essays allowed Ōe to get a better sense of himself as an artist. However, the self-centeredness that Ōe brought to these essays is, for all his good intentions, not a comfortable fit with either *hibakusha* experience or with the public issue of nuclear arms. The interweaving of the public and private aspects of his lives seems better realized in his fiction than in *Hiroshima Notes*, which is a fascinating but troubling document that chronicles his transformation from the precocious writer of 1963 to the accomplished novelist of 1965.

The introspective self-probing that allowed Ōe, in the guise of his public persona, to confront the enormity of the Hiroshima bombing is reflected in the existentialist resolution Bird finds at the end of *A Personal Matter*. This resolution is not so much a statement of ideology or a working out of moral values as the method of self-probing that, as noted above, makes art possible for Ōe. The constant returning to the subject of the guilt and responsibility felt by a father who brings a handicapped son into the world is the fictional enactment of that method, an exploration of the possible permutations of the relationship that provides no final answer, only the hope of regeneration in the act of returning to the subject.

The figure of a handicapped son appears frequently in Ōe's fiction, and a brief survey of these stories may help to further suggest the method by which Ōe brought the public and private spheres of his art together. In 1969 he published "Warera no kyōki o ikinobiru michi o oshieyo" ("Teach Us To Outgrow Our Madness," 1977), which for the first time names the son Mori. Mori, which means death in Latin and forest in Japanese, suggests the destructive/regenerative nature of the father's relationship with his son. The son is also given the nickname Eeyore (Hikari was nicknamed Pooh), which in the Japanese pronunciation is a play on the phrase *ii yo*—"it's all right"—an echo of the virtue of patience or forbearance that provides a form of refuge.

As with many of Ōe's characters, the father in this story is physically disfigured, in this case because he is fat. He identifies closely with his son and tries to fully comprehend the pain, terror, and incomprehension of his son's existence. The father becomes convinced that he is the only person who can connect with Mori/Eeyore, though over time he realizes that his son can get along without him. The desire to establish some sort of intimacy sends the narrator back into his own past relationship with his troubled father, who ignored the narrator and eventually confined himself to a storehouse, remaining in silence and darkness until his death. The mystery of his father haunts the fat narrator, and it is conflated with his obsessive desire to connect with his idiot son. That desire is broken by his chance brush with death at the hands of a gang of gamblers. His subsequent realization that the gulf that separates him from his son cannot be closed occurs simultaneously with his discovery of the truth about his father, and the story ends with the fat man feeling trapped by the foreboding that his life is a doomed cycle of repetitions.

"Teach Us to Outgrow Our Madness" refers back at points to an earlier novel *Man'en gan-*

nen no futtobōru (1967; *The Silent Cry*, 1974, discussed below), and the technique of exploring the artistic possibilities of the father/idiot son story by recontextualizing it within other narratives becomes an increasingly important one. For example, the 1973 novel *Kōzui wa waga tamashii ni oyobi* (The waters have come unto my soul) retells the family saga as a parody of the biblical Jonah story. Jin is the idiot son who lives with his father, Isana Ooki (whose name means Brave fish/Big tree), in a nuclear fallout shelter. They have retreated to this shelter because of Jin's self-destructive urges, which creates a strong sympathetic bond with his father. In time the two forge a friendship with radical outcasts called the Freedom Voyagers, a survivalist group that is building a schooner to escape what they believe is the coming apocalypse. Their plans, however, are wrecked before the ship is completed. The Freedom Voyagers and Jin die in a shootout with the Self-Defense Forces, and Isana dies by drowning in the hold of the ship. This ending subverts the story of Jonah, but it also leaves open the possibility that the power of the flood is both destructive and regenerative.

The fantastic quality of *Kōzui wa waga tamashii ni oyobi* raises the father/son saga to the realm of myth. Ōe pushes the fusion of the fantastic and the personal even further in the 1976 novel *Pinchirannā chōsho* (*The Pinch Runner Memorandum*, 1994), and the structural complexity of the narrative is the product of a strange blend of magic realism and the grotesque. The story of a thirty-eight-year-old father and his eight-year-old idiot son is set against the historical backdrop of the violence of the anti-Security Treaty demonstrations of 1960; but the narrative gleefully cuts its ties to historical time by detailing the struggle of competing student factions over which group should have the right to construct a nuclear weapon. As it turns out, these struggles are being manipulated by a shadowy figure, Mr. A, who plays the student groups against one another for his own interests.

Mr. A has another role in the story: the former boss of the father. The father did research at a nuclear plant for Mr. A that involved reading through foreign journals specializing in nuclear energy. Accidentally exposed to radiation, the father retires with a pension; but when his son Mori is born with mental defects the father blames Mori's condition on his own exposure. The key plot twist occurs when the identities of the father and son are switched by a power identified only as the Cosmic Will. The father is now eighteen and the son is twenty-eight, and the confusion created by the switch is compounded by the mode of storytelling. The father is the narrator, but his narration is reported to another character, who sets the work down and comments on it. This is an important move, because the confusion of roles and the shifting of narrators allows the idiot son finally to have a voice and even to become the hero of this fantasy world. Mori foils the plans of Mr. A, killing the boss and then committing suicide.

A reversal of roles that gives voice to the idiot son is accomplished as well in *Atarashii hito yo, mezameyo* (Rouse up, O young men of a new age), which was published in 1983. The title is taken from a line by William Blake, whose poetry is worked into the narrative as a device to allow the idiot son to speak. The father's role in the story is subordinated throughout by the simple utterances of his son, and in this particular work there is a sense that the healing power of art may bring the father's elusive search for acceptance and understanding of his son closer to realization.

In the early 1980s, Ōe began to adopt a narrator even more explicitly identified as himself. The encroachment of the autobiographical narrator is a technique that acts in a manner similar to the radical recontextualizing of stories noted above. One effect of this blatant insertion of himself into his fiction is that it permits Ōe to extend his father/son saga into matters not directly related to his family. An example of this method is the 1989 novel *Jinsei no shinseki* (*An Echo of Heaven*, 1996), in which Ōe interjects himself, his wife, and Hikari into the tale of a woman named Kuraki Marie, a professor specializing in the works of

Flannery O'Conner. The narrator K (Ōe) meets Kuraki at a hunger strike they both participate in to memorialize Hiroshima and to protest nuclear proliferation. The novel then focuses on a series of misfortunes that befall Kuraki. She divorces her alcoholic husband, who dies just before they can achieve a reconciliation. Her older son is born brain damaged and her younger son is crippled in an accident. When her sons commit double-suicide, Kuraki seeks solace in a religious commune that moves to America, and she ends up living in a Japanese-Mexican farm community. Kuraki dies from breast cancer, but her determination to persevere and her patience earn her the reputation of a saint in the community.

The example of Kuraki's life poses a challenge to the narrator to reconsider his views on religious faith, the limits of responsibility, and the healing power of art. These questions are taken up again as the subject of the 1990 work *Shizukana seikatsu* (*A Quiet Life*, 1996), which returns to an exploration of the family tensions created when the boundary between a writer's public and private lives is blurred. The narrator is Māchan, a college student who is the daughter of K, who happens to be the author of all of Ōe's works. K's wife is the sister of a famous director, his mentally handicapped son Eeyore is a composer, and his younger son is preparing to study at Tokyo University. The title is a reference to Māchan's desire to escape the notoriety of the family, and the minimalist plot is set in motion by K's decision to go to America with his wife for eight months to take up a post as a visiting professor. In their absence Māchan has to take over the household, which means that she has to learn to deal with Eeyore. The naturally introspective nature of this domestic situation is reinforced by Māchan's musings, and by the inclusion in the narrative of discussions of film, modernist music, and the novels of Louis-Ferdinand Celine. The interiority of the action and the struggle to create a quiet life are set off by two scenes of threatened sexual violence that frame the novel. The first is an incident from the past in which a child molester hangs around the novelist's house hoping to present the atheist author with some holy water. The second incident is perpetrated by a character who was the model for a murderer in an earlier Ōe story, "A Swimming Man," which is discussed below.

The shift from fictionalized to purportedly defictionalized characters is disturbing because it points to the violence that K's career—the choices that he has made as author of his works and his life—has visited upon his family. The book goes beyond a simple roman à clef; it is a form of confessional literature that through its narrative structure lays bare and examines the charge often leveled at Ōe, namely, that he has exploited personal matters for the sake of his art. This is an accusation that has been thrown at other confessional writers, most notably the naturalist writer Shimazaki Tōson; but the charge is especially loaded in Ōe's case given the underlying method that informs his fiction and his political ideology.

The autobiographical strain of Ōe's writing constitutes a work in progress, and in 1995 he brought out a collection of essays, *Kaifuku suru kazoku* (*A Healing Family*, 1996), that takes a contemplative view of the personal matters that have served as the imaginative source of his fiction. In this straightforward account of his family, Ōe returns to a meditation on humanism. The collection is an autumnal testament, a self-examination of the sensibility and propensities of a writer whose work has grown out of, and been disfigured by, the guilt and responsibility of an author and a father who has struggled to negotiate the divide between his public causes and his private lives.

The Simultaneity of Myth

The personal inflections of the primal relationship between father and idiot son act to break down the divide between fiction and reality. The riffing on this story permits Ōe to conflate and confuse the order and reality of events and to compress narrative time. His radical experiments with narrative form and chronology is a distinctive feature of his fiction best described as a type of myth-making.

The concept of multiple existences or parallel lives introduced early on in works like "Aghwee the Sky Monster" and *A Personal Matter* was translated into narrative form in the 1967 novel *The Silent Cry*. In this work Ōe first fully explores the narrative effects of simultaneity: that is, the effect created when two stories told diachronically begin to seem synchronous when they appear side by side. The effect of simultaneity disrupts the illusion of linear time that realistic fiction (or historical narrative) aims to create, and gestures toward the timeless realm of myth. *The Silent Cry* recounts two incidents about a century apart that take place in a village in Shikoku. The first begins with the return of the narrator, Nedokoro Mitsusaburō, and his wife to the village. Mitsusaburō is emotionally impaired and estranged from his wife because of the guilt he feels over having institutionalized his retarded son.

The couple have brought with them the narrator's disturbed and violent younger brother Takashi. After their arrival Takashi organizes what he calls a soccer team, but the group is really a radical organization dedicated to destroying the encroaching power of a supermarket chain run by a shadowy Korean figure know as "the Emperor of supermarkets." The relationship between the brothers is torn by an atavistic sibling rivalry straight from Japanese mythology. Mitsusaburō is an embodiment of order and rationality, but he is frustrated with his shallow and inauthentic life. Takashi is wild and emotional, but he too is frustrated because he is unable to give full vent to his passions. He recklessly has an affair with his brother's wife and an incestuous relationship with his younger sister. The sister commits suicide, and when Takashi's uprising against the supermarket is aborted, he too takes his own life.

This story runs parallel to the story of the brothers' great-grandfather and his younger brother. A few years before the Meiji Restoration (1868–1912) this younger brother tried to foment a peasant uprising against outside feudal authorities. The legendary account of this uprising had the younger brother escaping into the woods surrounding the village. Mitsusaburō, however, learns the truth of the man's fate, which is that he was forced to live out his life in confinement in the cellar of the Nedokoro estate. Mitsusaburō, who used this knowledge to push Takashi over the precipice of suicide, retreats to the cellar after his brother's death, confining himself to atone not just for his guilt but for the very conditions of his existence. He puts himself on trial for his past life, and the self-knowledge he obtains permits an ambivalent resolution. He reconciles with his wife, but on the condition that he take a job that will require him to travel to Africa. His wife, meanwhile, will raise both their handicapped son and her child by Takashi.

The retreat into the cellar is the moment when the two incidents become simultaneous to the narrator. This doubling up of the story allows Mitsusaburō to break through his self-consciousness and acknowledge the possibility that his brother's life might have been meaningful in its own way. The basic elements of *The Silent Cry* are familiar from earlier works, but the formal manipulation of narrative time strives for universality through a repetition that situates events in the cyclical pattern of myth.

Ōe's experiments with the possibilities of simultaneity are as frequent as his retelling of his family saga. In 1971, in response to the death of Mishima Yukio, Ōe published the novella *Mizukara waga namida o nuguitamau hi* ("The Day He Himself Shall Wipe Away My Tears," 1977). The narrator of this story is in the hospital, reportedly waiting to die from liver cancer. The man is in a state of withdrawal from the world; he wears diving goggles covered in dark cellophane and constantly relives a traumatic moment from his childhood. On 15 August 1945, when the narrator was still a boy, his father led a band of men from his village in the woods to a larger town, where they staged an insurrection as part of an effort to save Japan from defeat. The plan is a hopeless, meaningless suicide mission—a detail intended as a critique of Mishima's actions—and when the father dies in the name of the emperor, his son beholds a golden chrysanthemum in the sky. The circling back on a single moment in the narrator's life generates, among a number of possible interpretations, a political critique of the dangerously affective power of the emperor myth—a power that derives from the sense that the myth is ever-present and thus simultaneous with all human experience.

Ōe's concept of simultaneity reaches it most fully realized formal expression in the 1979 novel *Dōjidai gēmu* (A game of contemporaneity). The incestuous relationship between brother and sister that occurs in *The Silent Cry* is universalized in this story, which is told in a series of letters from the narrator, Tsuyuki, to his sister, Tsuyumi. Their names recall Izanagi and Izanami, the divine brother and sister of the *Kojiki* (Record of ancient matters, compiled 712), who created Japan and the gods by incestuous procreation. Tsuyuki's letters also mimic the jumble of history and myth that makes up the *Kojiki*.

Tsuyuki's father has ordered him to make a record of the history and myths of a village that is explicitly identified as a microcosm of the nation. Through a fragmented multiplicity of stories and perspectives, a master narrative slowly emerges. The village has been founded by a group of samurai who have been exiled from their fief. The samurai look for a new homeland, traveling on a river deep into the woods until they come upon a great rock that blocks their way. The leader of the group, who is identified as the One who Destroys, blasts the rock apart with gunpowder. Rain begins to fall, continuing for forty-nine days, and when the rain clears on the fiftieth day the foul air and stone debris have been washed away to reveal a fertile valley. The village-nation-microcosm is constructed and the founders become giants who live for centuries.

This tiny nation remains isolated and independent until the end of the Tokugawa period (1600–1868), when it is finally discovered. The villagers negotiate with the outside powers to avoid a conflict, but they invent a system of registering only one of every two babies born in the village, thus keeping half the population out of the Japanese Empire. Peace is maintained until just before the outbreak of Japan's war with China, when the village becomes embroiled in what is called the fifty-day War. Defying the authority of the emperor, the village is declared in revolt, and from this point on the narrative becomes a kind of allegorical history of all warfare. When the Imperial Army threatens to burn down the forest with its artillery, the village surrenders. The novel then continues to chronicle the history of postwar Japan and the decline of the village, which now waits for the return of the One who Destroys and the spiritual rebirth that his coming will bring.

In *Dōjidai gēmu* (A game of contemporaneity) Ōe's affinity for myth-making entered its most mature phase, which took him through the 1980s and up to the period of his Nobel Prize. The isolated village in the forest remained the primary setting, but the village itself is slowly supplanted in importance by the image of the tree, which dominates many of Ōe's later works, beginning with the collection of stories *"Rein tsurī" o kiku onnatachi* (Women who hear the rain tree) from 1982. The separate narratives are interconnected by an elaborate play upon different symbolic meanings of the rain tree. The opening section, "Atama no ii 'rein tsurī'" (The clever rain tree) is narrated by a Japanese author who has come to Hawaii. The story centers on a party at a home for psychiatric patients, and the atmosphere is unsettling. A female resident of the home tells him about the clever rain tree that curls its leaves to trap the dew and save the moisture. She takes him out in the dark evening to show him the tree, but he cannot see it. The narrator wonders if his inability to discern the embodiment of the renewal of life is a sign of sanity or of madness. During the party an argument breaks out over love, and when a female patient is found covered in menstrual blood, the party collapses into chaos.

The narrator is still in Hawaii in the second section, *"Rein tsurī" o kiku onnatachi.* He meets a former classmate, Katchan, who is now an alcoholic failed writer. Katchan lives with his Chinese mistress, Penny, who nurtures him and indulges his sexual whims, which the narrator participates in as a voyeur. Penny possesses spiritual healing powers, and even though Katchan kills himself, the association of Penny with the life-affirming symbol of the rain tree implies that death for Katchan may have been a form of salvation. The dual meaning of the rain tree sets up the third section, " 'Rein tsurī' no kubitsuri otoko" (A man who hangs himself on the rain tree). This part of the collection is a meditation on death that was inspired by Malcolm Lowry's *Under the Volcano.* The narrator receives a copy of Lowry's work while he is in Mexico City as an exchange fellow working with a local scholar of Japanese literature, Carlos Nervo. Carlos has cancer, and he has expressed a desire to hang himself if the pain of his disease becomes too great. The narrator, lonely and cut off, is drawn to Carlos because of his plight and winds up getting involved in his personal life to the point that he is dragged into the middle of a fight between Carlos's former and current wives. This farcical moment is undercut when the narrator learns that his brain-damaged son has lost his eyesight. He retreats to his bed, surrounded by images of death, and through his meditation the rain tree becomes entwined with Lowry's tree of life and with the concept of spiritual rebirth through death.

The expansion of the meaning of the rain tree to encompass the cabalistic tree of life is made explicit in the fourth section, "Sakasama ni tatsu 'rein tsurī' " (The rain tree that stands upside down). Katchan is figuratively reborn in his son, Zachary K (whose name means "God remembers K"). Zachary is a musician with his own band whose music is inspired by the incomplete novels written by his father. An upside-down rain tree is pictured on the cover of their album, and this inversion of the image confirms its ambivalence as a symbol of both life and death. Katchan's story comes full cir-

cle when the narrator, who has come back to Hawaii for an anti-nuclear rally, meets Penny again. She tells him about Katchan's funeral and how she scattered his ashes in the Pacific. Penny eventually sets off to start a new life in the South Pacific, and their implied spiritual reunion brings together once more images of death and rebirth.

The final section, "Oyogu otoko, mizu no naka no 'rein tsurī' " (A swimming man, the rain tree in water), plays one final time on the ambivalent meanings of the work's dominant symbol. The narrator goes to a swimming club one day where he observes the sado-masochistic relationship between a young man, Tamari, and a woman named Iguchi. It seems clear to the narrator that the woman is playing out their relationship in front of him as a way to heighten her pleasure and enrage Tamari. When the narrator hears later that Iguchi was raped and murdered in a park, he assumes that Tamari is guilty, until he learns that a middle-aged school teacher, who had hanged himself that day, was charged with the crime. The narrator suspects Tamari and pieces together his own theory of the crime. Tamari, who could no longer bear Iguchi's teasing, tried to rape her but failed because he was impotent. In his rage he strangled her. Tamari was saved from the consequences of the crime by the teacher, who raped the corpse and then killed himself out of guilt and despair. His sacrificial death saved Tamari, but the narrator believes that the young man will kill again. Tamari now suspects him, so the narrator worries that he may be the next victim and wonders who will come to save him.

The use of mystical images, the self-identification of author with narrator, and the dense allusive quality of his prose are techniques that Ōe brought to maturity in *Dōjidai gēmu* (A game of contemporaneity) and *"Rein tsurī" o kiku onnatachi* (Women who hear the rain tree). These works set up the large-scale project that has crowned Ōe's career. Ōe returns again to the village in the woods where he begins completing the construction of his mythic universe in two novels, *M/T to mori no fushigi no monogatari* (A tale of the Matriarch/Trickster and the wonder of the forest) and *Natsukashii toshi e no tegami* (Letter to a nostalgic year), that serve in turn as a prelude to a larger work, *Moeagaru midori no ki* (The burning green tree).

The image of a burning green tree, taken from Yeats conveys the destructive/regenerative power of the tree of life at the heart of Ōe's effort to explore the possibility of spiritual renewal. The basic plot, which is related over the course of three novels, *Sukuinushi ga nagurareru made* (Until the savior is beaten up), *Yureugoku: "vashirēshon"* (Vacillation—a title that is also taken from Yeats), and *Oinaru hi ni* (On the day of grandeur), centers on a man named Gii and is narrated by a hermaphrodite named Satchan. Gii, who has grown up overseas as the son of a diplomat, moves to a village in Shikoku at the urging of his uncle K (Ōe). An old woman, Oba, who possesses miraculous healing powers lives in the village, and when she dies Gii and some other villagers oppose cremation and secretly bury her body in the woods. They burn an empty coffin so as not to disrupt the customs of the village, but during this fake cremation a hawk flies through the smoke and alights on Gii for an instant. The villagers soon believe that Oba or, more precisely, Oba's healing powers have been reborn in Gii.

Gii is skeptical at first, since he knows that the cremation was false, but he has no choice but to accept the role of reluctant healer, since so many come to him for help. When the truth about Oba comes out, Gii is beaten up by the villagers. This act of violence transforms Gii, and he decides to accept his spiritual calling, which has marked him as radically different from the others, by building a church in the village and attempting to write sacred scripture for his new religion. There remains a fundamental ambivalence in this calling, and Gii is challenged by Satchan, who fears that Gii's healing powers may, by resolving all pain, prove to be a false religion that erases all contradictions and oppositions. The fundamental ambivalence that is at the core of Gii's spiritual quest is replicated in the emblem of his church, a burning green tree. Through this image, with its contradictory promise of eternal life and prophesy of conflagration, Ōe gestures toward a completion of his myth-making, toward a discovery of a timeless realm of perfect oppositions and unfolding self-knowledge, where spiritual rebirth is never fulfilled but remains forever a vibrant possibility.

Conclusion

In his Nobel speech Ōe expressed the wish that the trilogy *Moeagaru midori no ki* (The burning green tree) be the culmination of his literary activities and announced that with the completion of the trilogy he would embark, in the late stages of his career, on an attempt to create a new form of literature. The statement is characteristic, for it suggests that the questioning and questing that mark Ōe's distinguished career have not ended but continue to evolve and grow. It is thus impossible to summarize his life and work, both of which are still open books. The short catalogue of narrative elements presented above cannot do justice to the complexity of Ōe's fiction, nor can it give us anything more than a partial view of the imposing world he has constructed. Certainly we can read the separate works as autonomous pieces, and yet Ōe challenges us to read each work not only as the product of a particular time, but also as part of an ongoing literary and cultural project. In effect Ōe demands that we read each work as he himself reads it—on its own and simultaneously with all the other works he has written and read. Both the erudition that he displays and the self-referentiality of his works that appears more and more frequently from the 1970s on impose unusually daunting conditions and expectations on the reader. For that reason it is important to think about the survey above as a summary of a single work. The reader of Ōe must make an imaginative leap to encompass the full body of his work and take the full measure of his prodigious literary achievement.

Selected Bibliography

PRIMARY WORKS

COLLECTED WORKS

Ōe Kenzaburō zensakuhin. 12 vols. Tokyo: Shinchōsha, 1966–1978.

Ōe Kenzaburō shōsetsu. 10 vols. Tokyo: Shinchōsha, 1996–1997.

INDIVIDUAL WORKS

Memushiri kouchi. 1958. Trans. by Paul St. John Mackintosh and Maki Sugiyama as *Nip the Buds, Shoot the Kids.* London and New York: Marion Boyars, 1995.

"Shiiku." 1958. Trans. by John Nathan as "Prize Stock." In *Teach Us To Outgrow Our Madness: Four Short Novels.* New York: Grove Press, 1977. Trans. by John Bester as "The Catch." In *The Catch and Other War Stories.* Selected and with an introduction by Shoichi Saeki. New York: Kodansha International, 1981.

"Sebuntīn." 1961. Trans. by Luk Van Haute as *Seventeen.* In *Two Novels: Seventeen, J.* With an introduction by Masao Miyoshi. New York: Blue Moon Books, 1996.

"Seiji shōnen shi-su." 1961.

Okurete kita seinen. 1962.

Warera no jidai. Tokyo: Shinchōsha, 1963.

Kojinteki na taiken. 1964. Trans. by John Nathan as *A Personal Matter.* New York: Grove Press, 1968.

Seiteki ningen. Tokyo: Shinchōsha, 1964. Trans. by Luk Van Haute as *J.* In *Two Novels: Seventeen, J.* With an introduction by Masao Miyoshi. New York: Blue Moon Books, 1996.

Hiroshima nōto. 1965. Trans. by David L. Swain and Toshi Yonezawa as *Hiroshima Notes.* New York: Marion Boyars, 1995.

Man'en gannen no futtobōru. Tokyo: Kōdansha, 1967. Trans. by John Bester as *The Silent Cry.* Tokyo: Kodansha International, 1974.

Warera no kyōki o ikinobiru michi o oshieyo. Tokyo: Shinchōsha, 1969. Trans. by John Nathan as "Teach Us To Outgrow Our Madness." In *Teach Us To Outgrow Our Madness: Four Short Novels.* New York: Grove Press, 1977.

Sakebigoe. Tokyo: Kōdansha, 1970.

Mizukara waga namida o nuguitamau hi. Tokyo: Kōdansha, 1972. Trans. by John Nathan as "The Day He Himself Shall Wipe Away My Tears." In *Teach Us to Outgrow Our Madness: Four Short Novels.* New York: Grove Press, 1977.

Sora no kaibutsu Aguwī. Tokyo: Shinchōsha, 1972. Trans. by John Nathan as "Aghwee the Sky Monster." In *Teach Us to Outgrow Our Madness: Four Short Novels.* New York: Grove Press, 1977.

Kōzui wa waga tamashii ni oyobi. Tokyo: Shinchōsha, 1973.

Pinchirannā chōsho. 1976. Trans. by Michiko N. Wilson and Michael K. Wilson as *The Pinch Runner Memorandum.* Armonk, N.Y.: M. E. Sharpe, 1994.

Dōjidai gēmu. Tokyo: Shinchōsha, 1979.

"Rein tsurī" o kiku onnatachi.* Tokyo: Shinchōsha, 1982.

Atarashii hito yo mezameyo. Tokyo: Kōdansha, 1983.

Jinsei no shinseki. 1989. Trans. by Margaret Mitsutani as *An Echo of Heaven.* New York: Kodansha International, 1996.

M/T to mori no fushigi no monogatari. Tokyo: Iwanami Shoten, 1990.

Shizukana seikatsu. Tokyo: Kōdansha, 1990. Trans. by Kunioki Yanagishita and William Wetherall as *A Quiet Life.* New York: Grove Press, 1996.

Natsukashii toshi e no tegami. Tokyo: Kōdansha, 1992.

Sukuinushi ga nagurareru made. Tokyo: Shinchōsha, 1993. (The first publication of the trilogy, *Moeagaru midori no ki.*)

Yureugoku: "vashirēshon." Tokyo: Shinchōsha, 1994. (The second publication of the trilogy, *Moeagaru midori no ki.*)

Aimaina Nihon no watakushi. Tokyo: Iwanami Shoten, 1995.

Kaifuku-suru kazoku. Tokyo: Kōdansha, 1995. Trans. by Stephen Snyder as *A Healing Family.* Illustrated by Yukari Ōe. New York: Kodansha International, 1996.

Oinaru hi ni. Tokyo: Shinchōsha, 1995. (The third publication of the trilogy, *Moeagaru midori no ki.*)

WORKS IN ENGLISH TRANSLATION

A Personal Matter. Trans. by John Nathan. New York: Grove Press, 1968.

The Silent Cry. Trans. by John Bester. Tokyo: Kodansha International, 1974.

Teach Us to Outgrow Our Madness: Four Short Novels. Trans. and with an introduction by John Nathan. New York: Grove Press, 1977.

The Catch and Other War Stories. Selected and with an introduction by Shoichi Saeki. New York: Kodansha International, 1981.

The Pinch Runner Memorandum. Trans. by Michiko N. Wilson and Michael K. Wilson. Armonk, N.Y.: M. E. Sharpe, 1994.

Hiroshima Notes. Trans. by David L. Swain and Toshi Yonezawa. New York: Marion Boyars, 1995.

Japan, the Ambiguous, and Myself: The Nobel Prize Speech and Other Lectures. New York: Kodansha International, 1995.

Nip the Buds, Shoot the Kids. Trans. and with an introduction by Paul St. John Mackintosh and Maki Sugiyama. London and New York: Marion Boyars, 1995.

An Echo of Heaven. Trans. by Margaret Mitsutani. New York: Kodansha International, 1996.

A Healing Family. Trans. by Stephen Snyder. Illustrated by Yukari Ōe. New York: Kodansha International, 1996.

A Quiet Life. Trans. by Kunioki Yanagishita and William Wetherall. New York: Grove Press, 1996.

Two Novels: Seventeen, J. Trans. by Luk Van Haute. With an introduction by Masao Miyoshi. New York: Blue Moon Books, c. 1996.

SECONDARY WORKS

CRITICAL AND BIOGRAPHICAL STUDIES

Napier, Susan. *Escape from the Wasteland: Romanticism and Realism in the Fiction of Mishima Yukio and Ōe Kenzaburō.* Cambridge, Mass.: Harvard University Press, 1991.

Snyder, Stephen, and Philip Gabriel, eds. *Ōe and Beyond: Fiction in Contemporary Japan.* Honolulu, Hawaii: University of Hawaii Press, 1999.

Treat, John Whittier. *Writing Ground Zero: Japanese Literature and the Atomic Bomb.* Chicago, Ill.: University of Chicago Press, 1995.

Wilson, Michiko N. *The Marginal World of Ōe Kenzaburō: A Study in Themes and Techniques.* Armonk, N.Y.: M. E. Sharpe, 1986.

Yoshida, Sanroku. "Kenzaburō Ōe: A New World of Imagination." *Comparative Literature Studies* 22:80–96 (spring 1985).

———. "Kenzaburō Ōe's Recent Modernist Experiments." *Critique* 26:155–164 (spring 1985).

———. "The Burning Tree: The Spatialized World of Kenzaburō Ōe." *World Literature Today* 69:10–16 (winter 1995).

ŌGAI
(MORI ŌGAI)
1862–1922

MARVIN MARCUS

MORI ŌGAI IS a figure who commands superlatives. He occupies a unique position in Japanese history as catalyst for the nation's cultural modernization in the late nineteenth and early twentieth centuries. Ōgai's lifetime, which spanned the declining years of Tokugawa-era feudalism (1600–1868) and Japan's emergence as a world power in the Meiji period (1868–1912), came to symbolize the many cultural currents, both native and foreign, that combined to form a modern Japan. Deeply concerned about the moral and philosophical ramifications of the modern condition, Ōgai contributed to the formation of that very condition as a public intellectual and literary craftsman of the highest calibre. Together with his great contemporary, Natsume Sōseki (1867–1916), Ōgai may be credited with laying the foundation not only for a modern literature in Japan but for a modern Japan itself.

The extent of Ōgai's achievement all but defies comprehension. He achieved distinction in virtually every field of literary endeavor—fiction, poetry, essay, criticism, translation, drama, history, and biography—while managing to rise above the factionalism that came to dominate the Tokyo-based literary establishment, the so-called *bundan*, at the beginning of the twentieth century. Unlike writers such as Shimazaki Tōson (1872–1943), who became identified with a specific "school" and a fixed literary persona, Ōgai refused to be bound by convention or the dictates of the marketplace. Intent upon restoring a high sense of purpose to the literary calling, he forged new standards of excellence across the literary spectrum. It is remarkable that even his earliest ventures are marked by a degree of sophistication and self-assurance normally associated with a writer's mature works.

Even more remarkably, the writer and intellectual was also a physician who achieved distinction as a medical researcher, academician, administrator, and ultimately surgeon general of Japan. In fact, the body of writings on medical science comprise a substantial portion of his massive collected works. How, then, is one to make sense of this kaleidoscopic career?

The Ōgai biography is a fixture of modern Japanese history, and his place in the canon of *kindai bungaku*—Japan's prewar literary world—is unshakeable. (See the article on Shimazaki Tōson for the broad implications of the term *kindai bungaku*, which literally means "literature of the modern age.") Yet this is an author who presents uncommon challenges for the present-day reader and who himself cultivated a persona of aloofness and detachment. It is helpful to begin with a look at Ōgai's own

295

beginnings, for they reveal much about the shape of his literary horizons and his traits of character.

Formative Years

Mori Rintarō (Ōgai is a pen name) was born on 19 January 1862 in the remote castle town of Tsuwano, the son of a physician in the service of the local *daimyō*, or samurai overlord. Raised in a family that espoused traditional samurai values—devotion to duty, dedication to learning—and enjoyed its many perquisites, young Rintarō was among the last generation in Japan to be trained in the great Confucian tradition. He was studying Chinese classical texts by the age of five and early on showed signs of genius, eventually achieving a level of mastery that enabled him to write sophisticated poetry in classical Chinese. Expected to follow in his father's footsteps, Rintarō was also educated in Dutch, the language of Western medical texts in pre-modern Japan. He was devoted to his mother, Mine, a woman of strong will who remained at the center of his private life until her death in 1916. The patrician upbringing as pampered son and scion of a family of rank and privilege would have profound consequences for the young Rintarō's subsequent literary career.

In 1872, just prior to the formal abolition of the old shogunal system, the lad received a stipend from the Tsuwano *daimyō* to pursue his education. Like so many provincial youth at the dawn of the Meiji era, Rintarō was sent to Tokyo, the new national capital. There he was taken into the home of Nishi Amane (1829–1897), a relative who had achieved considerable renown as scholar and government official. He excelled in his studies, which entailed a curriculum based on the new Western model, and managed to enter the Tokyo University medical school at the tender age of fifteen. Since Dutch had been supplanted by German, the *lingua franca* of modern medicine, Rintarō added yet another foreign language to his repertoire. Equally significant was his extensive training in science and empirical analysis, which cultivated traits of objectivity and rational inquiry.

Mori Rintarō received his medical degree in 1881 and obtained a post with the army medical service as a commissioned officer. He belonged to an early-Meiji elite, of whom much was expected. Eager to expand his horizons by exploiting his facility with language, the young physician was sent to Germany at government expense. His official mission was to pursue research on medical hygiene. What ensued was a four-year stay in Germany that set the stage for the remarkable dual career that would follow. The research he conducted overseas would indeed position Mori Rintarō at the vanguard of a new field of modern medical study. At the same time, he set himself the task of absorbing the main currents of European literature, philosophy, and arts through comprehensive readings in German. By the time of his return to Japan in September of 1888, he had attained an unprecedented understanding of Western culture at its most sophisticated level. Yet Mori Rintarō remained a sufficiently dutiful son to agree to a traditional arranged marriage in 1889. The match, however, was irredeemably bad, and the couple was divorced within a year.

Bundan Debut

Ōgai's stay in Germany has been likened to a crucible for the emergence of a modern literary sensibility in Japan. Confident in his abilities and eager to disseminate the fruits of his learning, the young medical officer—recently promoted to army captain—took up his pen name and emerged on the Tokyo literary scene with a brilliant debut, a trilogy of stories based upon his experiences in Germany.

The first story, entitled "Maihime" (1890; "The Dancing Girl," 1975), is not only one of Ōgai's "signature" pieces; it has earned a secure niche in the canon of modern Japanese literature. Owing much to the German romanticism of admired writers such as E. T. A. Hoffmann and Heinrich von Kleist, the story tells of a young Japanese living in Berlin who falls in love with a poor dancing girl named Elis. The young man, Ōta Toyotarō, moves in with Elis and turns his back on the duties that have brought him overseas. Elis in turn becomes hopelessly attached to her Japanese lover. A pregnancy results, and Ōta senses circumstances closing in on him when he is offered an opportunity to return to Japan:

> If I did not take this chance, I might lose not only my homeland but also the very means by which I might retrieve my good name. I was suddenly struck by the thought that I might die in this sea of humanity, in this vast European capital.

> (Ōgai zenshū [OZ], vol. 1, p. 444; tr. p. 23)

Caught in the paralyzing grip of guilt and indecision, Ōta falls ill, but he is rescued from his romantic stupor by Aizawa, a concerned colleague who sees to it that his friend will heed the call of duty and return to his homeland. It bears noting that the theme of duty versus passion, a conflict that looms large in pre-modern Japanese literature and drama, would be revisited by Ōgai often in the course of a career that by its very nature embodied this conflict.

"The Dancing Girl" concludes as Ōta, narrating his sad tale aboard the Japan-bound steamship, reflects upon the course of events that led him to abandon Elis, pregnant and mentally deranged:

> I recovered from my illness completely. How often did I hold her living corpse in my arms and shed bitter tears? When I left with the count for the journey back to Japan, I . . . gave her mother enough to eke out a bare existence; I also left some money to pay for the birth of the child that I had left in the womb of the poor mad girl. Friends like Aizawa Kenkichi are rare indeed, and yet to this very day there remains a part of me that curses him.

> (OZ, vol. 1, p. 447; tr. p. 24)

"The Dancing Girl" was greeted by a measure of notoriety far in excess of the story's rather modest scale. This reflects the exoticism of the foreign setting and the heady aroma of oriental conquest—much heightened by the unmistakable autobiographical subtext. Indeed, accounts of Ōgai's affair with a German woman became widespread, as did the fact of her having actually traveled to Japan to be reunited with her Japanese lover. It was only the intervention of family members—a "real-life" re-enactment, in effect, of Aizawa's role in the story—that prevented a potentially scandalous incident. In short, the saga of Ōgai's German adventure has become enshrined in the mythology of modern Japan.

The remainder of the trilogy consists of two equally exotic stories based loosely upon the German experience. "Utakata no ki" (1890; "A Sad Tale," 1974) is an improbable tale of romantic frenzy, madness, and death. Set in Munich and told from the point of view of a Japanese artist named Kose (modeled upon Ōgai's friend Harada Naojirō), the plot centers upon a wildly impetuous model named Marie. She tells Kose of her sad upbringing and of how her mother had been the object of King Ludwig's mad infatuation. Kose is strongly attracted to the free-spirited beauty. They take an excursion to a lake near Munich, where the king happens to be vacationing. He sees Marie, whom he mistakes for the mother, and drowns in an attempt to reach her. Marie falls overboard and drowns as well. Kose, the bemused bystander, remains to lament the bizarre tragedy.

"Fumizukai" (1891; "The Courier," 1971) is a tale told by yet another onlooker—a young Japanese military officer named Kobayashi who gains the confidence of the aristocratic and talented Ida. Shrinking from the prospect of a loveless marriage, Ida enlists Kobayashi as a courier to convey a letter requesting that she be taken into the court as a serving lady. Again, the conflicting demands of social propriety, duty, and personal freedom come to the fore. Aside from their thematic integrity, these early stories foreshadow a tendency toward passive, introspective men and strong, resilient women among Ōgai's literary protagonists.

With the German trilogy of romantic novellas, Ōgai may be said to have created a prototype for the modern Japanese short story, redefining and improving what had long languished as a lowly craft of hack writers. What is more, the strikingly autobiographical narrative helped pave the way for the emergence of a personal voice that would become a defining feature of Japan's modern literature.

Literary Criticism

Despite having been so exceptionally innovative in his literary debut, Ōgai essentially abandoned the writing of fiction in favor of more congenial literary pursuits. His ambivalence toward fiction reflects a deep-rooted dislike of literary fabrication—a Confucianist sentiment shared by modern writers of the first grouping of major literary figures in Japan such as Futabatei Shimei (1864–1909) and Kōda Rohan (1867–1947). For these writers, creative fiction had yet to establish itself as a legitimate literary undertaking.

Instead, Ōgai turned to more purely intellectual pursuits. Among the first Japanese to comprehend the major currents of nineteenth-century European literature and philosophy—romanticism, idealism, aesthetics, naturalism—Ōgai sought a forum for disseminating the fruits of his intellectual apprenticeship in Germany. This he accomplished during a three-year period of intense activity.

The nature of the Meiji *bundan* was such that writers had to rely on periodicals to publish their work. Ōgai took the initiative by founding his own literary journal, *Shigarami Zōshi* (The Weir) in 1889. This was but the first of a series of journals that he would establish as outlets for his own work and that of his circle. Modern intellectual discourse was still in its infancy in Japan, and only the educated elite could grasp the meaning, much less the import, of Ōgai's sophisticated argumentation. Yet his early writings, which relied upon complex formulations of German aesthetics and idealism, had the salutary effect of elevating the level of learned discourse and debate. These continentally inspired, abstract writings brought Ōgai into confrontation with Tsubouchi Shōyō (1859–1935), a leading early-Meiji literary authority whose ideas had their roots in British positivism. The well-known debate that ensued, waged in a give-and-take of journalistic essays, essentially marks the birth of modern literary criticism in Japan, and it established the young Ōgai as a formidable thinker and intellectual arbiter. The philosophical issues that he raised in the 1890s would inform his writing for decades to come.

Translation

In the area of translation, too, Ōgai was to demonstrate unusual capacities. Although the value of such activity may be hard for us to appreciate, it is a truism that Meiji culture—and its literature—owed a great deal to the work of translators, who became a crucial conduit for new ideas and styles. Ōgai was by no means alone among *kindai* writers who devoted unusual energies to translation and whose own creative work benefited from the unique apprenticeship that it afforded. His achievement as a translator was equaled perhaps only by Futabatei Shimei. For both, translation would be a lifelong pursuit, the fruits of which helped mold Japan's modern literature.

For nearly three decades, Ōgai published hundreds of translations in virtually every literary genre and across many national borders. He also wrote numerous essays on the art and craft of translation. In the area of prose fiction, Ōgai translated nearly one hundred works—short stories, for the most part, by authors as diverse as Kleist, Leo Tolstoy, Alphonse Daudet, Gustave Flaubert, Edgar Allan Poe, and Fyodor Dostoyevsky. German works were translated from original texts; others, from German translations. Between 1889 and 1892, few months went by without a new translation appearing in print. And then Ōgai opted for a single project—the translation of a long novel by Danish author Hans Christian Andersen entitled *Impro-*

visatoren (1835; The Improvisatore). It took nearly nine years of intermittent labor to render this obscure romantic tale of an amorous Italian musician who ultimately achieves success both in his art and in his love life.

Setting aside the matter of Ōgai's fascination with a work of questionable value, the publication in 1901 of his exquisitely crafted translation of *Improvisatoren*—entitled *Sokkyō shijin*—was greeted with great acclaim. The novel enjoyed a larger audience in its Japanese incarnation than when originally published in Europe, and Ōgai's stylistic innovations, albeit impossible to convey to the nonspecialist, were hailed as a stunning achievement. Indeed, *Sokkyō shijin* has been praised as *the* finest Japanese literary translation.

In the case of poetry, too, Ōgai made his initial mark as a translator. In 1889 he oversaw the publication of an important anthology of translated verse. Entitled *Omokage* (Vestiges), the collection is an eclectic mix of romantic poetry by Lord Byron, Johann Wolfgang von Goethe, Heinrich Heine, and other lesser lights; a hint of Shakespeare (Ophelia's song, from *Hamlet*); and even some early Chinese poetry. This landmark collection, the bulk of which is Ōgai's work, was instrumental in paving the way for Japan's romanticist movement of the 1890s.

As with fiction, Ōgai continued to translate poetry over the years. However, he composed relatively little original verse, much of which was written during service in the Russo-Japanese War and subsequently published in *Uta nikki* (1907; Poetic diary). His contribution in the sphere of drama is rather more significant. Indeed, Ōgai ranks as the foremost *kindai* translator and interpreter of Western drama, which in turn became a crucial venue for modern themes and ideas. Through the staging of his translations of works by Henrik Ibsen, Gerhart Hauptmann, Arthur Schnitzler, Maurice-Polydore-Marie-Bernard Maeterlinck, and August Strindberg—some fifty plays in all—Ōgai was instrumental in establishing a modern theater in Japan. The Ibsen translations would be particularly significant, given the playwright's stature as a quintessential modernist. In particular, Ōgai's rendering of *John Gabriel Borkman*, staged in November 1909 to rave reviews, is noteworthy as the first production of a modern play in Japan. Finally, as a lifelong admirer of Goethe, Ōgai set himself to the dual task of producing a definitive biography and of translating *Faust*. His *Faust* translation, completed in 1912, remains the standard against which others are judged.

In the same sense that modern literature developed in large measure as a function of translation, individual writers drew inspiration from their own work as translators. The career of Ōgai clearly bears this out. His literary translations served as a technical and stylistic proving ground that benefited his original work while at the same time contributing to the larger project of literary modernization in Japan.

Hiatus

Having emerged as a leading intellectual in the 1890s, Ōgai did not remain at the center of the Tokyo *bundan*. The press of official duties was great, and he was forced to curtail his literary activities. With the outbreak of the Sino-Japanese War (1894–1895), Ōgai was sent to Manchuria where he served as a medical officer. Upon his return, he became preoccupied with his medical research. In the meantime, a new group of younger writers rose to prominence in the *bundan*, and Ōgai, although only in his thirties, was treated as a member of the old guard.

As Japan's leading authority on hygiene and sanitation, Ōgai founded several medical journals that published the newest scientific work in the field. His forcefully held views, evidently perceived as unduly arrogant, aroused the disfavor of his superiors. In June 1899 the rising star of Japan's army medical corps was dispatched to the remote southern city of Kokura, where he would spend three years in virtual exile as a regional medical officer. Relegated to the margins, Ōgai had ample time to reflect on himself as a writer and as a man. The Kokura years (1899–1902) would be a crucial turning point.

New Beginning

Although essentially banished from his two chief spheres of activity, Ōgai turned the Kokura experience to his advantage. In his distant outpost on the island of Kyushu, he took stock of himself. Finding time once again to engage in literary pursuit, he immersed himself in reading and study and indulged a long-held passion for history and folklore. As he would later recount in several essays, the sharper edges of his personality gave way to an attitude of acceptance and forbearance. The turn to a more reflective and meditative frame of mind would mark his mature writings.

Having remained a bachelor for over a decade, Ōgai remarried in 1902. His wife, Araki Shige (1880–1936), was a beautiful and strong-willed woman with literary aspirations of her own. The couple returned to Tokyo and moved in with Ōgai's mother, Mine, a domestic situation that precipitated a period of conflict and marital discord.

No sooner did Ōgai begin to reestablish himself in the *bundan* than he was sent back to the front in 1904, where he saw extensive service in the Russo-Japanese War. Returning in 1906, he gradually resumed his literary activities, and in the following year he earned a promotion to the post of surgeon general, the apex of Japan's medical bureaucracy. Ōgai now enjoyed the prestige accorded members of the Japanese administrative elite, a status all but unheard of for a "mere" literary person. It is important to recognize the extent to which social class factors, all too easily overlooked by the casual reader, would figure in the unfolding of Ōgai's career.

Having written only sporadically over the intervening fifteen years, Ōgai found himself drawn back into the *bundan* in the wake of important developments. On one hand, new avenues for modern fiction had been pioneered by writers such as Tōson and Sōseki. On the other hand, a new literary credo was being promoted by the so-called naturalist *(shizenshugi)* school, which called for a Zola-inspired realism rooted in the objective and unaffected expression of a writer's inner being. The movement engendered great controversy, and Ōgai was among those who dismissed much of the resulting naturalist fiction as little more than tedious accounts of pained introspection, self-pity, and tawdry confession. Nevertheless, he was lured by the possibilities of fictionalization as a vehicle for autobiographical narrative. In 1909, nearly twenty years since he had introduced autobiographical fiction to Japan, Ōgai embarked upon what would be a decade of sustained literary activity, as though making up for lost time.

Novel Writing and the Problem of Fiction

Establishing yet another literary journal—*Subaru* (Pleiades)—to serve as his outlet, Ōgai moved ahead on a number of literary fronts. The bulk of his writing over the next three years (1909–1912) was in the area of fiction. There would be four novels and numerous short stories and "essay-stories." How, then, did the author reinvent himself as a fiction writer following the long hiatus? His second *bundan* debut came in the form of a short story called "Hannichi" (1909; "Half a Day," 1973). A fictionalized account of the marital discord that marked his remarriage, the story is colored by the naturalist concern for domestic realism and frank disclosure. But it is written largely from the wife's point of view, centering on one particularly trying day in her life as an anxiety-ridden housewife and daughter-in-law: "His wife . . . was lost in thought. Her head was spinning. Thinking in an orderly fashion was beyond her, for he would assault her with logic; as she half-hysterically argued back and forth with him, she always felt like a checker piece about to be captured" (*OZ*, vol. 4, p. 475; tr. p. 82).

Ōgai's first attempt at original fiction in colloquial Japanese, "Half a Day" presents an unflattering portrayal of a modern marriage and the clash of egos that thwarts mutual trust and open communication. Interestingly, Shige would later publish her own version of the marital situation in the form of a story that her husband helped get published!

Later in 1909 Ōgai wrote "Konpira" ("Kompira," 1994), another fictionalized account of a Mori family crisis. This moving story, based on the death of an infant son in 1908, painstakingly recounts the boy's progressive illness and the insufficiency of both medical science and religion, as represented by the deity Konpira, in the face of an incurable disease—in this case, whooping cough.

Clearly, Ōgai was not averse to autobiographical narrative per se. What concerned him about the naturalist approach was its excessive indulgence in sordid details of sexual fantasy and personal inadequacy. It was such concern that informed his first full-length novel, *Ita sekusuarisu* (1909; *Vita Sexualis*, 1972). A brilliant parody of naturalist fiction and its propensity for lurid self-exposure, the novel presents a thoroughly detached, dispassionate account of sexual awakening—far more cerebral than physical—narrated in the first person by a philosophy professor named Kanai. An obvious authorial surrogate, Kanai expresses concern over the extent of writers' preoccupation with sex. Wishing to teach his son the facts of life in a clinically objective, hence morally upright, manner, he embarks upon his sexual autobiography.

Kanai methodically traces his emerging sexual awareness from age six to twenty-one. This exercise in pure introspection yields virtually no sex—promiscuous or otherwise. A matter-of-fact encounter with a geisha late in the novel is distinctly anticlimactic. Having completed his extended soliloquy, Kanai tosses the manuscript into a drawer, concluding that his son would be better off not reading it after all.

Vita Sexualis brilliantly challenges both the artistic and moral basis of the prevailing *bundan* trend. It is the height of irony, therefore, that this remarkably inexplicit work was actually banned by the authorities, who evidently found the title itself sufficiently scurrilous!

While naturalist fiction was a ripe target for parody and polemic, the period also witnessed important novelistic breakthroughs. Particularly significant was the work of Sōseki, who had raised the art of fiction—especially in the area of psychological portrayal—to an unprecedented level of sophistication. And so it was that Ōgai went on to write several novels "in the Sōseki style," as though seeking to contest his literary rival. Despite their flaws, these are works of considerable interest.

Seinen (1911; *Youth*, 1994) is a quintessentially *kindai* tale of a young man who comes to Tokyo in search of a literary career and, more broadly, an education in life. Evidently modeled upon Sōseki's *Sanshirō* (1908; tr. 1977), which tells a similar story, Ōgai's longest novel strongly evokes the many moods of the late-Meiji youth subculture in Tokyo. This roman à clef, whose cast of *bundan* characters includes both Sōseki and Ōgai, tells of Koizumi Jun'ichi as he makes his way onto the college-based literary scene and comes into contact with a new world of ideas, egos, and—most importantly—women.

A true *bungaku seinen* (literary youth), Jun'ichi engages in much earnest soul-searching on society, culture, and the meaning of life. He is especially anxious about confronting the opposite sex, a perennial concern of callow Meiji youth. Jun'ichi's rambling diary entries, essentially a novel within a novel, serve to voice the author's position on philosophical, literary, and social concerns. The plot, however, centers on Jun'ichi's evolving relationship with women. He makes the acquaintance of Mrs. Sakai, the sophisticated and obviously liberated widow of a professor. As their relationship deepens, Mrs. Sakai invites Jun'ichi to visit her in a resort hotel in Hakone. In a turmoil of anxiety and expectation, he goes to Hakone, only to discover Mrs. Sakai with another man. Chastened by bitter experience, Jun'ichi realizes that he must rise above temptation and seek loftier goals. And so he leaves Hakone, resolving to devote himself to his writing:

The moment he had perceived he would at long last start to write, all the things around him at present together with all he had experienced in the past lost their value. He no longer cared about that beautiful lump of flesh lying in a cottage . . . only a short distance away. His face was flushed, his eyes large and shining.

(*OZ*, vol. 6, pp. 465–466; tr. p. 513)

Youth is a novel of development, insofar as its protagonist achieves a measure of maturity and self-knowledge in the course of events. On one hand, Jun'ichi's opting for duty and self-control harkens back to "The Dancing Girl." On the other hand, Ōgai betrays his debt to Sōseki in seeking to portray the process of intellectual, moral, and artistic growth—in short, the emergence of character.

This concern would also mark his next novel, *Gan* (1911; *The Wild Goose*, 1995), a tale of romantic longing and unrequited love that ranks among Ōgai's most appealing and accessible works. *The Wild Goose* is set in early-Meiji Tokyo, before the city would be transformed by the juggernaut of modernization and "progress." This is a favorite setting for *kindai* fiction, and the author deftly exploits its nostalgic potential. The novel tells of a young woman, Otama, a dutiful daughter who becomes the mistress of a sleazy moneylender in order to support her impoverished father. Scenes involving Suezō, the petty, conniving moneylender, and his hopelessly dense wife make for an effective comic foil to the novel's unfolding romance. Whiling away the days in her gilded cage, Otama takes notice of a handsome university student, Okada, who regularly passes by beneath her balcony: From her lonely perch, she becomes infatuated with the dashing young man, imagining that he might one day rescue her from an empty existence. The two eventually meet when Okada comes to the rescue and saves one of her songbirds from being devoured by a snake—a scene rife with symbolism. Otama resolves to take the initiative and approach Okada, but that very evening, playing out the theme of chance that governs the novel, Okada accidentally kills the goose referred to in the title and subsequent events thwart the incipient romance.

The novel ends, as did *Vita Sexualis*, with the protagonist leaving Japan to pursue his medical studies. And, as with *Youth*, romantic possibilities die on the vine: Otama must resign herself to an unfortunate lot, yet in the process she has absorbed the hard lessons of life and emerges, despite disappointment and frustration, the better for it. The theme of resignation would become a hallmark of Ōgai's mature literature and the subject of numerous scholarly studies. In this novel as elsewhere, its meaning goes beyond mere fatalistic surrender to circumstance and embraces life-affirming, spiritual possibilities as well.

The Wild Goose has long been a favorite among readers. Together with novels such as Sōseki's *Kokoro*, it is seen as having captured the spirit of an age that holds special significance for the Japanese. Buoyed by his success, Ōgai would make one final attempt at novel writing with *Kaijin* (1912; *The Ashes of Destruction*, 1994). This dark, rather depressing work presents a sardonic view of Japanese society through the figure of Yamaguchi Setsuzō, a brooding, lonely young writer. Having written himself into a corner in the course of serializing the novel, Ōgai chose to abandon the project before completing it. There would be no more novels, but the fictive impulse found ample expression in the form of numerous essay-stories composed during the same period.

A Literature of Ideas

For Ōgai, fiction was most appealing as a vehicle for exploring ideas. But the novel, which bound him to the conventions of plot and characterization, proved unduly burdensome. On the other hand, discursive writing—the open-ended essay form—essentially freed him from such formal constraints. It bears noting that Ōgai's classical education had instilled in him a taste for *zuihitsu*, the traditional essay genre that had remained a canonical form for over a thousand years. Fictional touches could be applied where appropriate, but sustained imaginative writing would ultimately be made in the service of larger social, ethical, and philosophical concerns. Hence, Ōgai's second *bundan* debut featured, in addition to the longer fiction, a veritable miscellany of short narratives that convey his sophisticated intellectual agenda.

The essays do not occupy neat categories. They range from slight pieces of several pages to novellas of considerable length. In terms of subject matter, works such as "Mōsō" (1911; "Daydreams," 1970) are marked by a mood of contemplation and reflection; the problematic state of contemporary society is the subject of works such as "Chinmoku no tō" (1910; "The Tower of Silence," 1994) and "Shokudō" (1910; "The Dining Room," 1994). In these stories, Ōgai employs fictional means to target repressive government policy and bureaucratic venality—precisely the sort of politically sensitive issues that *bundan* writers had tended to avoid.

The bulk of Ōgai's essayistic writing consists of autobiographical vignettes that foreground certain ideas and issues while providing assorted personal glimpses. The typical narrator is a world-weary intellectual trying to make sense of modern society and mankind itself. A series of stories featuring an Ōgai-surrogate named Hidemaro is particularly noteworthy in this regard. The best-known of the Hidemaro series, "Ka no yō ni" (1912; "As If," 1994), is a tour de force of philosophical exposition concerning culture, art, and history. However, the density of learned reference makes it daunting reading for the uninitiated.

In his illuminating study, Richard Bowring aptly refers to Ōgai's discursive writing as a "literature of ideas." The broad humanistic concerns explored in this writing include: 1) the moral and ethical consequences of Japan's modernization, 2) the interplay of "East" and "West" in the forging of modern Japan, 3) the alienation endemic to modern society, and the isolation and inversion that present formidable barriers to communication (a key theme in the novels of Sōseki—for instance, *Kokoro* [1914] and *Michikusa* [1915; *Grass on the Wayside*]), 4) the tension between art and science, artistic truth and scientific truth, 5) the role of the intellectual and the efficacy of scholarly activ-

ity, and 6) the tension between the world of action and the world of contemplation.

In his essay-stories, Ōgai employs a self-referential narrator who is cast as a bystander (*bōkansha*) reflecting upon his world, musing upon events and trends that remain beyond one's control. The following passage from "Daydreams" is revealing:

> Although I study medicine, the most "natural-scientific" of the natural sciences, and make rigorous scholarship my life's work, somehow I've come to feel spiritually starved. I find myself thinking about life. I wonder if what I do can in any way be said to constitute the substance of life. From the time of my birth until this day, what is it that I have been doing? Throughout, as though whipped and goaded by who knows what, I have slaved away at my studies, thinking that this will make me useful, that this will perfect me. . . . It seems to me that what I do is no more than what an actor does who comes onstage and performs his role.

> (*OZ*, vol. 8, p. 200; tr. in Marcus, *Paragons*, pp. 105–106)

Borrowing Friedrich Nietzsche's famous paradigm, the author speaks of his "Apollonian" temperament, his stoic, dispassionate nature. But as he reflects upon his roots, Ōgai also acknowledges the transcendent possibilities of ordinary virtue and the liberating quality of "resignation" to the human condition. Consider the following passage from a personal reminiscence entitled "Casuistica" (1911, Medical records):

> At first he thought that his father was leading an empty, meaningless existence. He was old, after all, and wasn't it only natural that an old man should have nothing to do? It was then that he happened to read something by [the Confucian scholar] Kumazawa Banzan. Devoted service to the state, according to Banzan, is no more a manifestation of the Way than washing one's face or combing one's hair every day.

When he read this, then thought about his father's routine, it struck him. Rather than gazing off into the far distances and casually dispensing with what was close at hand, his father was devoting all of his energies to the performance of small daily tasks. And he came to understand, if only vaguely, that his father's attitude of resignation, of contentment with being a doctor in a small post-town, was in its own way a kind of enlightenment. Thereafter he began treating his father with newfound respect.

(*OZ*, vol. 8, p. 7; tr. in Marcus, *Paragons*, pp. 106–107)

The palpable sense here of Buddhistic and Confucianist value, which in a sense held the spiritual key to ending the cycle of self-doubt and skepticism, was epitomized for Ōgai in a favorite epigram of Goethe. He makes reference to it in "Daydreams":

"How can we attain knowledge of self? Surely not by reflection or meditation, but perhaps by our deeds. See, then, to the fulfillment of your duties and you may come to know your worth. And what are these duties? They are the demands of each day." These are the words of Goethe.

(*OZ*, vol. 8, p. 210; tr. in Marcus, *Paragons*, p. 106)

The final years of the Meiji and the subsequent Taishō era (1912–1926) witnessed an ever-accelerating pace of change. Japanese society underwent a striking transformation, and it was therefore inevitable that Ōgai's literary efforts would engage him with the great issues of his day. Like Sōseki, he would also explore these issues in novelistic form. In other words, Ōgai's entire body of writing from 1909 to 1912 shares a common concern for the quality of contemporary life. Although achieving no resolution, this work points to the possibility of a spiritual wholeness that would transcend the dichotomies and dilemmas endemic to modern society.

The dramatic events of 1912 inspired Ōgai to move in a radically new direction, one that would bring him into contact with his cultural roots and with a renewed passion for understanding the inner workings of the human spirit.

Historical Fiction

Ōgai's critique of Japanese society through fictionalized narratives set in the contemporary period came to a close with *The Ashes of Destruction* (1912). In the meantime, events that marked the end of the Meiji period served as the catalyst for a new literary venture focusing on accounts of the Japanese past.

The death of the Meiji emperor on 30 August 1912 rang down the curtain on a truly epochal chapter in Japan's history. Then, on the very day of the Emperor's funeral (13 September), General Nogi Maresuke committed ritual suicide together with his wife. A figure of heroic stature who symbolized Japan's military prowess, Nogi had chosen a shockingly anachronistic expression of unconditional obligation to one's superior—in this case, the Meiji emperor himself. In the context of a modern Japan, this practice, known as *junshi* in the traditional code of *bushidō*, raised the ugly specter of the nation's feudal past and the samurai obsession with duty, blind obedience, and death.

These unprecedented events sent shock waves through the Japanese literary and intellectual community, which had in a sense collectively sought to fathom the deeper meaning of the great Meiji epoch. They bore special significance for Ōgai, who had been a personal friend of Nogi's. Moved to question the larger import of *junshi* in the context of a modern Japan, the author would devote his final productive years (1912–1919) to an exploration of the Japanese past as a means of coming to grips with the present. What resulted was a body of historical and biographical writings that broadly explore the human condition and, specifically, what it means to be Japanese.

Ōgai's interest in Japan's past and in historical study was nothing new, having figured prominently in his early schooling. This interest was reinvigorated during the years spent in Kokura, where he read widely in Japanese history and folklore. Ōgai would continue to produce essays and translations after 1912, but the historical writings predominated. Pioneering a new genre of historical fiction (rekishi shōsetsu), he embarked first on a literary investigation of certain historical events, with an eye upon assessing human conduct and character in the course of these events. He then moved on to a series of works that focus on historical personages who came to embody key traits of character. Likely episodes were gleaned from a vast body of accounts and records of late-Tokugawa samurai. Given Ōgai's own samurai background, the choice bears particular significance.

The resulting stories would be dramatizations of, and expansions upon, the source episodes. Throughout, the author took pains to maintain the accuracy and integrity of the written record, a concern that would ultimately become an article of faith. Above all, however, this was to be literature with deep ethical and philosophical import.

Events

Ōgai's immediate response to the Nogi junshi was to find a parallel account in the historical record, one that would enable him to explore the notions of obedience and duty underlying the bushidō code. Set in the early Tokugawa period, "Okitsu Yagoemon no isho" (1912–1913; "The Last Testament of Okitsu Yagoemon," 1971) presents a first-person account of Okitsu, a samurai who in the course of preparing to take his own life details the circumstances that brought him to this point. Years earlier he had taken the life of a comrade while carrying out a mission for his master. Despite having requested permission to commit seppuku—ritual disembowelment—for this deed, he was exonerated. Nonetheless, Okitsu bore a debt that could only be repaid through suicide, in the form of junshi. And so, following the master's death, he is at long last able to demon-strate his loyalty and restore his honor as a samurai.

Ōgai's attitude toward the bushidō code would be more clearly revealed in "Abe ichizoku" (1913; "The Abe Family," 1977), a chilling re-enactment of the mass suicide in 1641 of an entire samurai clan. The drama is set in motion by the death of Lord Tadatoshi, which precipitates the junshi of his chief retainers. Such ritual suicide, however, required official sanction, and one retainer, Abe Yaichiemon, was refused permission. All but required by the bushidō code to take his life, Abe found himself in an intolerable bind: "For a man of his status to continue living without committing junshi and have to face the members of his lord's household was something not one man in a hundred would believe to be possible" (OZ, vol. 11, p. 328; tr. p. 81).

Abe defies the authorities and takes his own life, leaving his sons to face the consequences of their father's disobedience. Reduced to the status of common outlaws, the sons band together in defiance. The authorities lay siege to the Abe mansion, where the renegades have chosen to make their stand, and finally move in for the inevitable assault: "Now both front and rear attacking parties broke in, yelling and thrusting their weapons as they came. . . . Just as street fighting is far uglier than fighting in the field, the situation here was even more ghastly: a swarm of bugs in a dish devouring one another" (OZ, vol. 11, p. 347; tr. p. 96).

Propelled along with relentless force and exquisite detail, "The Abe Family" casts harsh light on the manner in which mindless obedience, masking itself as high virtue, becomes a form of enslavement, threatening to reduce its victims to a state of moral depravity and inhumanity.

Yet another historical event that would enable Ōgai to question the authoritarian underpinnings of Japanese society occurred in the port city of Sakai, near Osaka, at the very end of the Tokugawa era. Set on the cusp of the nation's transition to modernity, "Sakai jiken" (1914, "The Incident at Sakai," 1977) recounts the attack on a detachment of French sailors by a group of local samurai enraged by the callous disrespect shown by the foreigners. Several Frenchmen were killed in the ensuing encounter, and the French consul demanded stern reprisal. Ōgai's story centers on the harrowing account of the mass *seppuku* of the guilty samurai, who insist upon the right to disembowel themselves in full view of the French consul and his party. One of the samurai leaders, Shinoura Inokichi, takes the opportunity to address the foreigners:

> "Frenchmen! I am not dying for your sake. I am dying for my Imperial nation. Observe the *seppuku* of a Japanese soldier."

> Shinoura relaxed his garment, pointed the sword downward, made a deep thrust into the right side of his stomach, lowered the blade three inches, and pulled it across the front of his stomach and upwards three inches on the left. Because of the depth of the initial thrust, the wound gaped widely. Releasing his swords, Shinoura then placed both hands within the cut and, pulling out his own guts, glared at the French consul.

> (*OZ*, vol. 15, pp. 191–192; tr. p. 146)

Aghast at the unfolding scene, the consul immediately calls an end to the suicidal orgy, whereupon nine of the samurai are pardoned. It was the dubious fate of these nine, whose moment of glory was denied them, eventually to receive a pardon by order of the new Meiji emperor—a gesture symbolizing the dawn of Japan's modern era, the ambiguous fate of the samurai ethos, and the looming challenge of confronting the foreign Other.

With his brilliant "factual fictions," Ōgai deployed the power and authority of the documentary record to enhance his treatment of events that appear to take on a life of their own, threatening to engulf those caught in the grip of circumstance and unyielding codes of conduct. The densely factual narrative is no mere exercise in pedantry or antiquarian taste. It is rather a means of achieving ideological and artistic ends, whereby the art of selection,

focus, and dramatization creates a stage for the unfolding human drama while raising questions regarding the cultural roots of modern Japanese nationhood. Admirers have spoken of the grandeur of Ōgai's historical narrative—specifically, the solemn, almost liturgical quality of its attention to names and genealogical data. "The Incident at Sakai," for instance, incorporates a detailed enumeration of each samurai implicated in the affair, including mention of rank and family pedigree. In this manner, the simple act of naming is raised to the level of sacrament.

In Ōgai's view, character cannot emerge from the mere probing of psychological states—the virtual standard for literary modernity within the *bundan*—but rather from the unfolding of incident. There is a distinctly Confucianist resonance to the manner in which the author suggests that people are to be judged by their deeds and not their words.

Character

Ōgai's historical investigations brought to light the record of many hundreds of lives. Oriented by a powerful moral compass, the author's interest was increasingly drawn to documentary accounts of individuals who bespoke cherished values. These were accounts worth preserving. What resulted was a series of short works focusing on the ordinary virtues of all-but-forgotten individuals from the past. For instance, "Jiisan baasan" (1915; "The Old Man and the Old Woman," 1977) recounts the reunion of an elderly couple separated for nearly forty years. The husband, having killed a man in a heated argument, had been sent into exile. His dutiful wife, Run, remained faithful and stalwart throughout the decades of separation. This gem of a story, with its spare, elegant narrative, underscores the wife's quiet, enduring strength of character:

> Run's nature was not that of a beautiful woman. If a beautiful woman can be compared to some object for display in a tokonoma, then Run was something made

306

for more practical purposes. She was healthy and had a splendid bearing. She possessed a penetrating intelligence, and there was never any question of her idling herself away, hands empty of something to do. Although it is true that her protruding cheekbones were a flaw in her face, the space around her eyes and eyebrows seemed to indicate a great flow of talent and spirit.

(*OZ*, vol. 16, pp. 136–137; tr. pp. 203–204)

"Yasui fujin" (1914; "The Wife of Yasui," 1977) is a similar account of an idealized marriage. Focusing on Sayo, the wife of Tokugawa-era scholar Yasui Chūhei (1799–1876), the story underscores the simple merits that form the very backbone of the social order: "What kind of woman was Sayo? Wearing rough clothing over her own beautiful skin, she passed her life serving Chūhei with his simple tastes" (*OZ*, vol. 15, p. 563; tr. p. 268).

Ōgai's historical fiction (*rekishi shōsetsu*) includes several works of surpassing lyrical beauty and pathos. "Sanshō Dayū" (1915; "Sanshō the Steward," 1977) is unusual insofar as it derives from an age-old folk legend set in the Heian period (ca. 800–1200). Freely embroidering upon the terse account in the archival record, Ōgai tells the story of two children of noble birth who are separated from their mother when they are kidnaped and sold into slavery. The brother, Zushiō, and his sister, Anju, must endure terrible hardships under the tyrannical eye of the slavemaster, Sanshō the Steward, in hopes of escaping and being reunited with their parents. Clinging to one another in the face of adversity, they manage to survive. But it is the strong-willed sister who perseveres, ultimately sacrificing her own life so that her brother can escape. Thanks to Anju's selflessness, Zushiō makes his way to freedom and is eventually restored to his rightful position. In the famous final scene, immortalized on film by the great director Mizoguchi Kenji, Zushiō is finally reunited with his aged mother, who had never ceased longing for her beloved children.

"Takasebune" (1916; "The Boat on the River Takase," 1971), a story of almost magical beauty and serenity, tells of a court deputy named Shōbē and his conversation with Kisuke, a prisoner under his charge whom he is escorting to a place of exile. Perplexed at the paradoxical display of composure and dignity on the part of this common criminal, Shōbē questions the man about his crime. He learns that Kisuke had assisted his brother in completing a failed suicide attempt, the brother having long suffered from an agonizing disease. Upon further questioning, he learns that Kisuke has come to sense a spiritual liberation owing, paradoxically, to the sentence of exile on a remote island. Having been lifted out of poverty and straitened circumstance and given a generous sum of money to live on, Kisuke anticipates his new life and its limitless possibilities.

Although unsure how to interpret the justification for homicide in this case, Shōbē finds himself deeply moved by Kisuke's enlightened demeanor: "As if seeing him now in a completely new light, Shōbē looked at Kisuke with wide-eyed admiration. It appeared to him as if a halo encircled Kisuke's head as he gazed up at the sky" (*OZ*, vol. 16, p. 230; tr. p. 229). This masterful tale of a chance encounter on a small boat, which raises large questions regarding the meaning of life, ranks as an acknowledged masterpiece of *kindai bungaku* (Japan's prewar literary world) and has perennially figured in the Japanese literary curriculum.

Ōgai's achievement as a writer of historical fiction helped establish this type of writing as a major literary genre in Japan. Recasting and molding his source accounts, the author forged a unique literary style that mixed fact, fiction, and moments of stunning lyricism. Ōgai's historical literature transcended the limits imposed by his earlier writing (with its cynical, sardonic tone) and enabled him to apply a vision of moral integrity and wholeness to his literary labors.

Far from serving as an escape from the sordid realities of contemporary society, Ōgai's profound reading and interpretation of Japanese history amounted to a comprehensive cultural critique. The exemplary qualities of self-sacrifice, self-reliance, loyalty, and duty displayed by his recreated characters—significantly, many of them women—stand as an indictment of egocentrism and anomie that bears comparison with Sōseki's achievement in his celebrated novels. These two figures, so different in temperament and talent, shared a deep understanding of, and concern for, the world in which they lived.

Paragons

Following a long and distinguished career in public service, Ōgai retired from his administrative post in April 1916. His mother had died just a month earlier, and it may be that, like Kisuke in "The Boat on the River Takase," he felt a certain sense of unburdening. Having reinvented himself as a cultural historian who delighted in foraging the vast documentary record, Ōgai was now free to indulge his passion for research and writing.

It was in the course of this research that he happened upon certain names that appeared in the margins of his archival sources. There was tantalizing evidence here of a circle of kindred spirits—obscure physician-scholars and literati of the late-Tokugawa period. Intent upon fleshing out the meager record, Ōgai embarked upon what would become an extraordinary intellectual quest that resulted in a trilogy of biographies spanning centuries in the lives of its three central subjects and their overlapping circles of colleagues and kin.

The individuals in question—Shibue Chūsai (1805–1858), Izawa Ranken (1777–1829), and Hōjō Katei (1780–1823)—hardly appear to be ideal subjects for biography. They were distinctly unspectacular men of learning and cultural attainment, bearing none of the fame and notoriety one would normally expect to attract the attention of a biographer. But in Ōgai's hands their assorted documentary traces would be refashioned into a monumental—and daunting—work of humanistic scholarship.

The first volume of the trilogy, *Shibue Chūsai* (1916), is a many-sided work. At once an exquisitely detailed biography of Chūsai and his circle, it is also a cultural history of nineteenth century Japan, incorporating detailed accounts of traditional medical practice, shogunal politics, arts, and culture. But the true greatness of this work lies in the spiritual bond that came to unite the renowned author and his obscure subject (whom he knew only through the painstaking accumulation of evidence) and in the extraordinary effort he would expend in resurrecting a man of substance and integrity.

In short, the great author Ōgai had at long last discovered an alter ego, an individual who fully commanded his respect and admiration. Yet his interest would be especially drawn to Chūsai's wife, Io, a strong-willed and surprisingly modern woman who figures in many of the work's most memorable episodes. Indeed, what makes *Shibue Chūsai* such compelling reading, notwithstanding its dense erudition, is the rich store of anecdotal detail regarding the everyday lives of its many collateral subjects. Having gleaned much of this material from Chūsai's surviving son, who had in turn heard the stories from his mother, Ōgai reworked hundreds of episodes and accounts into what would become in effect a composite profile of exemplary character. The virtues that he endorses—self-sacrifice, magnanimity, inner strength, dedication, and attention to the demands of each day—echo the moral agenda elaborated in the earlier essays and historical fiction. Among the many meritorious individuals who inhabit this work, Chūsai and Io stand out as true paragons.

Perhaps the most intriguing aspect of *Shibue Chūsai*, though, is the personal voice of the questing biographer as he pursues his research—querying his readers, soliciting information. This work-in-progress quality was made possible by the fact of original publication in a daily newspaper. The serialization attracted a core of dedicated readers who were essentially mobilized as research associates, while the general public, accustomed to rather more entertaining fare, found precious little to their liking. Throughout, Ōgai remained indifferent to the rising tide of popular culture and what he regarded as its debased standards, pursuing his biographical researches with unflagging energy.

Two massive volumes would follow, together with shorter biographies of certain collateral figures. *Izawa Ranken* (1917) is a meticulously researched study of one of Chūsai's colleagues, who himself was part of a large circle. This volume was followed by *Hōjō Katei* (1919), a similar study of a colleague of Ranken's. Lacking the rich anecdotal material that enlivened the Chūsai work, Ōgai immersed himself in philological study and textual analysis. Here he would at long last realize his ideal of *rekishi sono mama*—the unadulterated historical account, free of imaginative reconstruction and empty conjecture. As such, these two works will attract only the most dedicated and historically minded readers.

In a brief essay written in 1917, at the conclusion of his Ranken serialization, the author stepped back to assess the state of his literary career:

> I never set out with the intention of being a writer or an artist, neither did I see myself as a philosopher or a historian. When I happened to be in the countryside I simply cultivated the land, and when I found myself by the bank of a river I went fishing. . . . I am idle. . . . The habits of a lifetime as a writer remain only in the sphere of lyric poetry and history—a *vita minima.*

> (*OZ*, vol. 26, p. 544; tr. in Bowring,
> *Mori Ōgai*, pp. 245–246)

Ōgai's *vita minima,* the life reduced to its bare essentials, bespeaks a Taoist sense of free-spiritedness that marked his transition from public service to genteel retirement as an independent scholar. But the author's ironic self-deprecation belies what many have come to regard as his greatest achievement. The biographical trilogy marks the apex of Ōgai's exquisitely crafted literature of fact. Yet it also stands as a unique form of spiritual autobiography, as the author-researcher ushers an inner circle of readers into his study, inviting them to take part in this deeply personal quest. In other words, through his own example of sheer determination in the face of daunting obstacles

and widespread popular disapproval, Ōgai may be said to have ultimately erected *himself* as paragon. Be that as it may, in lending his name to the resurrection of worthy lives, Ōgai has embraced the time-honored values of the *bunjin*, the traditional literatus dedicated to the highest standard of literary cultivation and humanistic endeavor.

In declining health as of 1918, Ōgai realized that his disease—a kidney disorder that had also afflicted his father—was incurable. Displaying the same spirit of resignation that had figured so prominently in his literature, the author put his affairs in order and quietly prepared to die. He composed a final testament that in effect answers the question he had raised in an essay written twenty years earlier: Who, in the final analysis, is Mori Ōgai?

> I wish to die Mori Rintarō of Iwami province. I have had connections with both the Department of the Imperial Household and the army, but at the very moment of death I repudiate all outward signs of this connection. . . . All I want written on my grave are the words: "The Grave of Mori Rintarō"—not a single word more. . . . No one must be allowed to interfere in what remains.

> (*OZ*, vol. 38, p. 112; tr. in Bowring,
> *Mori Ōgai*, p. 253)

Approaching death, Japan's foremost writer and intellectual chose to abjure his worldly accomplishments, identifying himself instead with his native home, a place he had not seen since leaving it behind in his youth. Mori Rintarō passed away on 6 July 1922. The tombstone was prepared precisely according to his instructions.

Ōgai's Legacy

The legacy of Mori Ōgai is at once obvious and imponderable. His extraordinary literary and intellectual gift, the depth of his grounding in East-Asian and Western arts and culture, the uncommon self-discipline and determination—these factors combined to produce an unparalleled record of accomplishment that transcends the narrowly "literary." It is widely recognized that Ōgai stands at the forefront of Japanese cultural modernization, and his unprecedented achievements in literature, science, and cultural affairs are the stuff of legend. Here, paradoxically, is Japan's first great modernist and its last traditional *bunjin*. Indeed, the shape of his career may be said to recapitulate Japan's own coming of age. Yet the figure atop the pedestal inspires mixed reactions.

A core of admirers—which includes literary luminaries such as Nagai Kafū, Ishikawa Jun, and Mishima Yukio—have hailed Ōgai as nothing short of a sage, pointing to the grandeur and profundity of his inimitable prose style and the enlightened example of his unimpeachable integrity and seriousness of purpose. His detractors, on the other hand, have been critical of his aloofness and patrician indifference, decrying what they regard as a headlong retreat into a world of intellectual snobbery and antiquarian self-indulgence. Indeed, while some of his novels, essay-stories, and historical fiction have retained their appeal, much of his writing—especially the biographical and scholarly work—has become essentially unreadable.

In light of current tastes and trends, a writer such as Ōgai can perhaps best be understood as "classical"—a consummate artist and intellectual who towered above his age and set lofty standards for those who would follow. Ōgai has long inhabited the inner circle of the modern Japanese literary canon. Even in his own day, he was seen as a writer of unusual gravity and authority. This came at the expense of his public image. A man known to have had few close friends, literary or otherwise, and even fewer intimate disclosures in print, Ōgai kept his distance from the *bundan* and the sordid personalism that, in his view, had come to infect it like some malevolent virus. Going directly against the grain of popular culture, he remained steadfast in his commitment to the intrinsic value of serious literary and intellectual endeavor.

The assorted statuary erected in Ōgai's honor belies the fact of a complex, flawed individual and a notoriously difficult and demanding body of writing. Whether venerated as a sage, admired as a "classic," or dismissed as a man hopelessly out of touch with the world of ordinary experience, Ōgai will inevitably be identified with the great watershed in Japan's modern history that bears the mark of his own noteworthy contribution. Without a doubt, his example raises the vexing question of the fate of "literary giants" and "masterpieces" in our own day.

Selected Bibliography

PRIMARY WORKS

NOVELS AND SHORT STORIES

"Maihime." 1890. Trans. by Richard Bowring as "The Dancing Girl." In *Mori Ōgai: "Youth" and Other Stories.* Edited by J. Thomas Rimer. Honolulu: University of Hawaii Press, 1994. Pp. 6–24.

"Utakata no ki." 1890. Trans. by Richard Bowring as "A Sad Tale." In *Mori Ōgai: "Youth" and Other Stories.* Pp. 25–42.

"Fumizukai." 1891. Trans. by Karen Brazell as "The Courier." In *Mori Ōgai: "Youth" and Other Stories.* Pp. 43–57.

"Hannichi." 1909. Trans. by Darcy Murray as "Half a Day." In *Mori Ōgai: "Youth" and Other Stories.* Pp. 71–87.

Ita sekusuarisu. 1909. Trans. by Kazuji Ninomiya and Sanford Goldstein as *Vita Sexualis.* Rutland, Vt.: Tuttle Press, 1972.

Seinen. 1911. Trans. by Shoichi Ono and Sanford Goldstein as *Youth.* In *Mori Ōgai: "Youth" and Other Stories.* Pp. 371–517.

Gan. 1911. Trans. by Burton Watson as *The Wild Goose.* Ann Arbor: Center for Japanese Studies, University of Michigan, 1995.

Kaijin. 1912. Trans. by James Vardaman Jr. as *The Ashes of Destruction.* In *Mori Ōgai: "Youth" and Other Stories.* Pp. 312–370.

COLLECTED WORKS

Ōgai zenshū. Tokyo: Iwanami, 1971–1975. (The standard edition of Mori Ōgai's collected works, comprising 38 volumes. Abbreviated as *OZ* following translated passages, with an indication of volume and page numbers.)

The Historical Fiction of Mori Ōgai. Edited by David Dilworth and J. Thomas Rimer; additional contributions by Richard Bowring and others. Honolulu: University of Hawaii Press, 1991. (A single-volume reissue of the original two-volume edition of 1977. Includes fine interpretive essays by the editors.)

Mori Ōgai: "Youth" and Other Stories. Edited by J. Thomas Rimer. Honolulu: University of Hawaii Press, 1994. (Excellent cross-section of Ōgai's work that incorporates considerable background information and commentary.)

ESSAYS AND ESSAY-STORIES

"Konpira." 1909. Trans. by James Vardaman Jr. as "Kompira." In *Mori Ōgai: "Youth" and Other Stories.* Pp. 102–135.

"Chinmoku no tō." 1910. Trans. by Helen Hopper as "The Tower of Silence." In *Mori Ōgai: "Youth" and Other Stories.* Pp. 215–222.

"Shokudō." 1910. Trans. by Helen Hopper as "The Dining Room." In *Mori Ōgai: "Youth" and Other Stories.* Pp. 223–230.

"Mōsō." 1911. Trans. by Richard Bowring as "Daydreams." In *Mori Ōgai: "Youth" and Other Stories.* Pp. 167–181.

"Ka no yō ni." 1912. Trans. by Gregg Sinclair and Kazo Suita as "As If." In *Mori Ōgai: "Youth" and Other Stories.* Pp. 231–254.

HISTORICAL AND BIOGRAPHICAL WORKS

"Okitsu Yagoemon no isho." 1912, 1913 (two versions). Trans. by Richard Bowring (first version) and William Wilson (second version) as "The Last Testament of Okitsu Yagoemon." In *The Historical Fiction of Mori Ōgai.* Edited by J. Thomas Rimer. Honolulu: University of Hawaii Press, 1991. Pp. 45–64.

"Abe ichizoku." 1913. Trans. by David Dilworth as "The Abe Family." In *The Historical Fiction of Mori Ōgai.* Pp. 65–100.

"Sakai jiken." 1914. Trans. by David Dilworth as "The Incident at Sakai." In *The Historical Fiction of Mori Ōgai.* Pp. 129–152.

"Yasui fujin." 1914. Trans. by David Dilworth and J. Thomas Rimer as "The Wife of Yasui." In *The Historical Fiction of Mori Ōgai.* Pp. 225–270.

"Sanshō Dayū." 1915. Trans. by J. Thomas Rimer as "Sanshō the Steward." In *The Historical Fiction of Mori Ōgai.* Pp. 153–178.

"Jiisan baasan." 1915. Trans. by David Dilworth and J. Thomas Rimer as "The Old Man and the Old Woman." In *The Historical Fiction of Mori Ōgai.* Pp. 199–208.

"Takasebune." 1916. Trans. by Edmund Skrzypczak as "The Boat on the River Takase." In *The Historical Fiction of Mori Ōgai.* Pp. 223–234.

Shibue Chūsai. 1916. Partially translated by Edwin McClellan. In his *The Woman in the Crested Kimono: The Life of Shibue Io and Her Family, Drawn from Mori Ōgai's Shibue Chūsai.* New Haven, Conn.: Yale University Press, 1985.

Izawa Ranken. 1917.

Hōjō Katei. 1919.

OTHER WORKS

Omokage. 1889. (Anthology of translated verse.)

Sokkyō shijin. 1901. (Translation of H. C. Andersen's *Improvisatoren.*)

Uta nikki. 1907. (Collection of original verse.)

SECONDARY WORKS

CRITICAL AND BIOGRAPHICAL STUDIES

Bowring, Richard. *Mori Ōgai and the Modernization of Japanese Culture.* Cambridge and New York: Cambridge University Press, 1979.

Inagaki Tatsurō, ed. *Mori Ōgai hikkei.* Tokyo: Gakutōsha, 1968.

Karaki Junzō. *Ōgai no seishin.* Tokyo: Chikuma Shobō, 1974.

Keene, Donald. *Dawn to the West: Japanese Literature of the Modern Era.* Vol. 1, *Fiction.* New York: Holt, Rinehart and Winston, 1984. Pp. 355–385. (The most comprehensive and authoritative English-language survey of modern Japanese fiction.)

Kobori Keiichirō. *Mori Ōgai no sekai.* Tokyo: Kōdansha, 1971.

Lewell, John. *Modern Japanese Novelists: A Biographical Dictionary.* Tokyo: Kodansha International, 1993. Pp. 250–262. (Part of the entry for "Mori Ōgai".)

Marcus, Marvin. *Paragons of the Ordinary: The Biographical Literature of Mori Ōgai.* Honolulu: University of Hawaii Press, 1993.

McClellan, Edwin. *The Woman in the Crested Kimono: The Life of Shibue Io and Her Family, Drawn from Mori Ōgai's Shibue Chūsai.* New Haven, Conn.: Yale University Press, 1985.

Rimer, J. Thomas. *Mori Ōgai.* Boston: Twayne, 1975.

Shibukawa Gyō. *Mori Ōgai.* Tokyo: Chikuma Shobō, 1964.

Snyder, Stephen. "Ōgai and the Problem of Fiction." *Monumenta Nipponica* 49, no. 3:353–373 (autumn 1994).

Washburn, Dennis C. "The Individual in History: The Narrative Voice of Mori Ōgai." In his *The Dilemma of the Modern in Japanese Fiction.* New Haven, Conn.: Yale University Press, 1995. Pp. 180–194.

Yamazaki Masakazu. *Ōgai: tatakau kachō.* Tokyo: Kawade Shobō, 1972.

Ryūhoku

(Narushima Ryūhoku)

1837–1884

Matthew Fraleigh

Narushima Ryūhoku occupies a complex position in Japanese literary history, a contested status that is suggested most succinctly by the fact that he is the only major writer whose work is regularly anthologized in both classical and modern compendia of the Japanese canon. An enthusiastic celebrant of urban culture in the final years of the Tokugawa era, he might be seen as one of the last exemplars of the Edo literatus. Yet even after the Meiji Restoration, Ryūhoku remained an active participant in public life, and his literary work continued to evolve, exerting significant influence on a new generation of writers, such as Mori Ōgai and Nagai Kafū. Ryūhoku was not only thoroughly steeped in the Chinese literary tradition, but also uncommonly conversant with Western culture. Though he wrote almost exclusively in a Chinese style, he freely experimented with a wide variety of poetry and prose genres. More importantly, he succeeded in using these traditional forms creatively to portray and comment on the cultural changes sweeping Japan during the transition to Meiji.

Though he lived to be only forty-seven years old, Ryūhoku had a truly remarkable range of life experiences. Born into a distinguished family of Confucian tutors, Ryūhoku was known for his erudition even as a young man. Yet as a prolific connoisseur of life in the Edo pleasure quarters, Ryūhoku also savored less scholarly subjects. Even as an official in the innermost circles of shogunal bureaucracy, Ryūhoku never hesitated to voice dissenting opinions. After the Meiji Restoration as well, Ryūhoku remained an outspoken critic and satirist as the editor of the *Chōya Shinbun*, an extremely popular newspaper with a decidedly anti-establishment bent. His mockery of those in power often landed him in serious trouble, both before and after the Restoration, but Ryūhoku never lost his sense of humor. In a life full of change, it is perhaps this sense of whimsy that remains Ryūhoku's most consistent characteristic. A look at Ryūhoku's life and works provides us with the opportunity to reconsider the traditional view that sees the early Meiji period only in terms of the serious business of state-building and the mission of catching up with the West. His irrepressible irreverence and playful spirit offer a refreshing counterpoint to the dominant trend of the times, one that is all the more revealing because it comes from a man so broadly and actively engaged as a contributor to the cultural life of the day.

Family and Education

Narushima Ryūhoku was born in Edo on the sixteenth day of the second month of 1837, or

313

22 March by the Western calendar. As an infant, Ryūhoku was known as Kashimaro, but like many literary men of the time, he adopted a variety of names in the course of his life. In his official duties, Ryūhoku would be identified by such names as Kashitarō, Korehiro, or Kakudō, and he made use of a still wider array of names in his literary activities. He is most widely known, however, by the sobriquet Ryūhoku (literally, "north of the willows"), which he probably chose not only on the basis of the location of his home in Edo, but also because of the association of the willow tree with the world of the pleasure quarters, a setting that provided Ryūhoku with the material for his best known work, *Ryūkyō shinshi* (1859–1874; New chronicles of Yanagibashi).

Although there is some evidence that Ryūhoku was adopted, he is listed in the family's records as the third son of Narushima Yoshimatsu (1803–1853). Ryūhoku's two elder brothers died in infancy, leaving him to assume both the family headship and its hereditary position in the Tokugawa shogunate. As the eighth head of the Narushima family, Ryūhoku was the successor to a tradition of scholarship and official service that spanned the entire Tokugawa period. The earliest of the Narushima patriarchs, Nobutsugu (1590–1659), had served the new Tokugawa government as a priest, but beginning with the third patriarch, Nobuyuki (1689–1760), subsequent generations of Narushima would all serve as Confucian tutors of the shogun. At the time, familiarity with the Chinese canon was identified not only with literacy itself, but was regarded furthermore as forming the core of essential knowledge for men of the samurai class. Inasmuch as the Confucian tradition supplied the vocabulary and principles used to justify the social structure of the period and the stewardship of the state by the Tokugawa house, the office of Confucian tutor to the shogun was a fairly prestigious one.

Holders of the office were responsible not only for explicating the Confucian classics, but also for supervising the shogun's education in general. Moreover, the office included other duties, such as the compilation and editing of official histories. In accordance with the traditional prestige of Chinese learning in Tokugawa Japan, Ryūhoku's father and grandfather oversaw his training in the Chinese classics and his studies of Chinese poetics. As a supplement to this education in the Chinese canon, however, Ryūhoku also received extensive training in Japanese literary history and poetic practice. Although Ryūhoku's poetry in Chinese is undoubtedly his best known, his earliest extant compositions are in fact Japanese poems. Ryūhoku was clearly most comfortable expressing himself in classical Chinese, but he was also a lifelong participant in social groups that gathered to compose *waka, kyōka, haikai,* and other Japanese poetic forms.

Writing in Chinese

Ryūhoku's training in Chinese is readily apparent in the Sinified style and classical intertextuality that characterize nearly all of his literary output. This highly rhetorical style and the literary tradition it represents are no longer core subjects in the Japanese educational system. Consequently, many Japanese people today would not only be unfamiliar with Ryūhoku and his work, but would find his texts quite challenging to read without the benefit of extensive editorial annotations. Still, it must be remembered that Ryūhoku was writing at a time when the educated reader would have readily understood his references to the Chinese classics. As Nagai Kafū recalled in 1926, "There probably wasn't a student around in the Meiji period who was unfamiliar with Ryūhoku's *Ryūkyō shinshi.*" ("Ryūkyō," p. 283). In fact, due to the expansion of education, spread of literacy, and growth of national media in the early years of Meiji, the late 1870s actually saw a resurgence of the Sinified literary style in Japan. At that point, traditional education still emphasized proficiency in Chinese, and thus the number of people who read and wrote *kanshi* (Chinese poetry) increased rapidly. As the editor of the literary journal *Kagetsu Shinshi* (1877–1884), Ryūhoku was one of the leading figures in this revival. With the adoption of a more Western educational system and curriculum in the 1880s, however, the momentary popularity of literary composition in Chinese quickly subsided, and by the twentieth century, only a handful of enthusiasts could be considered active kanshi poets.

Ryūhoku wrote kanshi throughout his life, both for publication and for his personal journals. These poems often provide the best opportunity to glimpse his feelings and reactions to contemporary events, for to Ryūhoku and other men of his background, the form was neither as foreign nor as circumscribed in scope as it might appear to us today. Literary Chinese was still the predominant form of scholarly discourse among educated men in the mid-nineteenth century, but it was by no means limited to serious academic inquiry. Far more than a tool to interpret the limited body of Chinese classics, it was a living means of personal expression. Even as a child, Ryūhoku used the medium to express his own thoughts, freely incorporating Japanese figures and events into his compositions.

Ryūhoku's ease with Chinese literary expression is evident not only in his use of it to treat Japanese subjects, but also in his lifelong experiments in style. Many readers today would find the Sinified style a bit remote and perhaps slightly stodgy, but Nakamura Mitsuo has made the interesting observation that literature in this style was as common a form of diversion and entertainment to the students of the 1880s as literary magazines are to the students of today. Furthermore, one of the main reasons that Meiji students delighted in reading Ryūhoku was that they were able to appreciate the humorous disjunction between his works' erudite form and their vulgar—sometimes even obscene—content. The Chinese of *Ryūkyō shinshi*, for example, was not a pure form of Chinese but rather one that had been whimsically and mischievously adapted to discuss more crass matters.

Ryūhoku was not the first to write in such a hybridized style. In the previous generation, for example, Terakado Seiken (1796–1868) had

written his best-selling *Edo hanjōki* (1832; An account of the prosperity of Edo) in a highly modified version of classical Chinese that strongly influenced *Ryūkyō shinshi*. *Edo hanjōki* is in fact often grouped with *Ryūkyō shinshi* and *Tōkyō shin hanjōki* (1874; New account of the prosperity of Tokyo) by Hattori Bushō (1841–1908) as exemplars of *hanjōki-mono*, a sub-category of the broader genre known as *gibun* or *kambun gesaku* (playful writings in Chinese). Yet the roots of kambun gesaku went back at least another generation to the late eighteenth century, when well-educated samurai, such as Ōta Nampo (1749–1823) and Hatakenaka Kansai (better known as Dōmyaku Sensei, 1752–1801), had begun to compose *kyōshi* (literally "crazy poems") inspired by contemporary Japanese scenes or topics but written in a form of classical Chinese. Their poems treated contemporary urban life and social customs with a startling vividness and a sharp sense of satire. Beyond their humorous tone and content, kyōshi often made liberal use of Japanese terms and place names. To a Chinese reader, these would of course be unintelligible, but to an educated Japanese reader, the surprising interjection of mundane indigenous words into the flow of graceful Chinese created an amusing juxtaposition between the elegant and the base.

Ryūhoku's own creations share many stylistic similarities with the pioneering work of these earlier Tokugawa literati. Though all of their works had a generous dose of earthiness, they nevertheless assumed a certain basic level of familiarity with the refined Chinese style, and thus their readership was restricted to fairly well-educated men. In other words, the reader's knowledge of the traditional style greatly enriched his enjoyment of the author's calculated departures from it. For an excellent discussion of these genres' shared stylistic features, the interested reader should consult the first and second chapters of Chieko Ariga's dissertation on *Ryūkyō shinshi*.

While humor was one effect of writing kanshi about nontraditional subjects, it is important to note that this was only one possible use of the form. Indeed, kanshi permitted an expressive range that native poetic forms simply could not offer. Unlike traditional waka and haiku, for example, which were not only severely limited by their brevity, but also confined to a restricted vocabulary, kanshi could be quite long and could also freely fashion terms for the new ideas and objects then being introduced from the West. Ryūhoku's travel diary *Kōsei nichijō* (1872–1873, Journal of a voyage to the West), for example, contains over eighty kanshi inspired by the landscapes and culture of Europe and America. The kanshi form's greater capacity to accommodate such new topics and scenes is surely one of the major reasons that writers of the next generation, such as Mori Ōgai and Natsume Sōseki, also wrote kanshi during their travels abroad.

Ryūhoku's Diary

Ryūhoku chose classical Chinese not only for his literary work, but also for the personal diary he kept throughout his life. This diary is the best source of information on Ryūhoku's early life, but unfortunately only seven volumes of the original diary are extant. The tangled story of how even these few volumes survived to the present is worth sketching in brief. In 1926 Ryūhoku's grandson Ōshima Ryūichi brought nearly thirty volumes of Ryūhoku's diary to Nagai Kafū, the modern literary figure who was not only the earliest and most enthusiastic devotee of Ryūhoku's literature, but also the one whose aesthetic sensibility and choice of subject matter most closely resembled Ryūhoku's own. In fact, according to Kafū's account of their meeting, Ōshima asked Kafū to write a biography of Ryūhoku because he regarded Kafū as "the only one who could really understand his grandfather's life and times" (pp. 267–268). Although Kafū never did write the biography, he did borrow the diaries, which covered Ryūhoku's life from the age of sixteen until his death.

Kafū began reading the diaries immediately and spent the next ten days completely engrossed in them. No sooner had he finished reading the diaries than he began to make a copy of them, a project that took him over seven months. After Kafū returned the original diaries, Ōshima left them with his aunt Nobu for safekeeping. Unfortunately, neither version of the diaries was to survive the next two decades intact. When American bombs burnt Kafū's home to the ground in 1945, he was barely able to escape with his own personal diaries, and for the rest of his life, Kafū felt a mixture of guilt and grief over the loss of Ryūhoku's diaries. As for the originals that Ōshima left with his aunt Nobu, they too were destroyed in a May 1945 air raid.

In 1974, however, seven volumes of these original diaries mysteriously surfaced at a used book sale in Tokyo, where the scholar Maeda Ai had the good fortune to acquire them (see his account in *Narushima Ryūhoku*, pp. 21–26). As Ōshima later suggested to Maeda, the most likely explanation for their reappearance is that Ryūhoku's son Toshirō, a somewhat lackluster playboy who was down on his luck and taking up residence in the homes of various relatives in the late 1920s, came across the diaries while staying at his sister Nobu's house. Figuring no one would notice their absence, Toshirō sold a few of them for drinking money. Though his readiness to part with his father's diaries might seem especially unfilial in the son of a former Confucian scholar, we must be thankful that Toshirō had inherited Ryūhoku's fondness for Tokyo nightlife, or else the diaries would surely have been completely destroyed in the air raid fifteen years later. These seven volumes, covering Ryūhoku's life from 1854 to 1863 are now all that remains of Ryūhoku's diary. Cornell University recently acquired the originals, but a facsimile edition has also been published under the title *Kenhoku nichiroku* (Kenhoku's diary).

Ryūhoku's Early Career in the Shogunate

Ryūhoku began his training as the shogun's tutor in the first month of 1854, only a few months after the death of his father. The young

Ryūhoku's proficiency in Chinese was soon recognized, and he was rewarded with the responsibility of revising the *Tokugawa jikki* (True record of the Tokugawa), an official history that Ryūhoku's grandfather Motonao (1778–1862) had spent forty years of his life compiling. Around the same time, Ryūhoku also assumed the task of editing the *Nochikagami* (A later mirror), a similarly extensive history of the earlier Ashikaga shogunate that his father, Yoshimatsu, had begun but had not lived to complete. Nevertheless, observing his senior colleagues' lectures and proofreading historical records could not have commanded Ryūhoku's undivided attention at this truly critical juncture in the history of Japan. After having maintained peace in the land for over two centuries, the shogunate now found its very future thrown into doubt by the twin threats of domestic instability and foreign incursion. Only half a year earlier, Commodore Matthew Perry had come to demand that Japan accept a trade agreement with the United States, and just as Ryūhoku was beginning his training, Edo was abuzz with news of Perry's return.

Ryūhoku's diary reflects this mounting anxiety; in a February 1854 entry, for example, he writes of being shocked to hear the "thunderous sound" of cannon fire coming over the water. Apparently the American ships were merely commemorating Washington's birthday, but the gesture seemed more menacing than celebratory to those ashore. Just three days later, Ryūhoku noted, "Throughout the castle, there is nothing but talk about the barbarian ships" (Maeda, 1976, pp. 29–30). One of the shogunate's greatest symbolic responsibilities was the military protection of Japan, but after more than two centuries of peace, the samurai class was no longer proficient in its duties and completely unable to muster a successful defense. Like many samurai, Ryūhoku's first reaction to the unsettling presence of foreign ships was to hone his military skills by studying swordsmanship and archery. Yet during the course of 1854, he gradually came to realize the futility of such last-minute measures in the face of the Western powers' overwhelming technological advantage. At year's

end, he expressed his thoughts in a kanshi that reveals this new awareness, and also suggests how deeply the revelation disturbed him. The poem ends:

> I can only laugh as I realize now that my taste for reading makes me a mere bookworm.
> In an earlier age, my strength with sword in hand would have sundered even the greatest whale.
> What then have I become in these eighteen years?
> I laugh at my uselessness, a mere student of Confucianism.

> (*Narushima Ryūhoku,
> Ōnuma Chinzan*, pp. 3–5)

As this poem suggests, Ryūhoku had begun to question not only his role in the government, but his own identity as well. After he assumed full teaching duties in 1856, Ryūhoku's first official task was to supervise the shogun Iesada's reading of the *Daxue* (Great learning), a text particularly esteemed by the reigning school of Confucianism. While these lectures brought Ryūhoku closer to the shogun, he was likewise brought face to face with his own nagging doubts about the ultimate relevance of such studies in this time of national crisis. The future must have looked fairly bleak to Ryūhoku as the 1850s drew to a close. Just as the United States was forcing Japan to accept a commercial treaty, the sickly Iesada died, and in the midst of a contentious factional struggle over the issue of shogunal succession, a key official was assassinated. Over the next several years, Ryūhoku grew increasingly disenchanted with the direction in which the shogunate was leading the country. This escalating estrangement culminated in 1863, when he was removed from office and ordered confined to his home. Ryūhoku's disaffection stemmed from his distress over the unprecedented unrest that was destabilizing Japan, his growing doubts about the relevance of his official role as a Confucian scholar, and his frustration over his inability to help resolve the crisis. Yet the more immediate factors that led to Ryūhoku's dismissal were his simultaneous discovery of the culture of the pleasure quarters and the world of Western learning.

Ryūhoku's Dismissal from the Shogunate

Shortly after his marriage in the summer of 1857, Ryūhoku began to frequent Yanagibashi, a district in Edo then at the peak of its prosperity. Yanagibashi was a separate world within the boundaries of Edo that offered a momentary escape from the pressures and demands of contemporary life. One could drift leisurely along the river with one's friends and geisha companions by day and patronize the district's many drinking and dining establishments by night. Ryūhoku's diary records his increasingly frequent visits to the pleasure quarters during the late 1850s, and his growing enthusiasm for its unique culture soon started to take concrete form in the literary work *Ryūkyō shinshi*, which he began in 1859.

Beyond providing him with the text's raw material, Ryūhoku's initiation into the playful culture of Yanagibashi transformed him from an unremarkable career bureaucrat into the daring writer who could in fact produce a whimsical work like *Ryūkyō shinshi*. Moreover, in the process of immersing himself in the world of Yanagibashi, Ryūhoku came to associate with a circle of friends who introduced him to yet another new world. The group was centered around Katsuragawa Hoshū (also known as Katsuragawa Kunisaki, 1826–1881), a physician whose family had been famous scholars of Dutch studies since the mid-eighteenth century. Due to Holland's longstanding trade relationship with Japan, Dutch was then the major language through which the Japanese learned about the West, and the Katsuragawa were at the forefront of the field. In the 1850s Katsuragawa had assembled a group of young Western scholars, including Yanagawa Shunsan (1832–1870), Mitsukuri Shūhei (1825–1886), and Kanda Takahira

(1830–1898), to help compile the *Oranda jii*, a new authoritative dictionary of Dutch. These men became Ryūhoku's lifelong friends; after the Restoration, for example, Ryūhoku briefly went into business with Katsuragawa, and near the end of his life, Ryūhoku published a condensed version of Kanda's translation of a Dutch mystery novel. These encounters expanded Ryūhoku's world tremendously and changed the course of his life irrevocably.

Though Ryūhoku remained evasive about the reasons for his dismissal from the shogunate, his new interest in the West was surely a crucial factor. In "Bokujō inshi den" (1868; The story of the recluse of the Sumida River), an autobiographical essay that he wrote just after the fall of the Tokugawa, Ryūhoku admitted only: "One morning I was fired and left without a position. Perhaps it was due to a fault in my conduct, perhaps it was because I offended people by being too blunt, or perhaps it was because I advocated study of the West. It doesn't really matter what the reason was; I spent three years of isolation with Western scholars, devoting myself solely to reading English books" (*Ryūhoku zenshū [RZ]*, p. 1).

The reference to a fault in his conduct suggests that Ryūhoku was dismissed because his dissipated behavior in Yanagibashi did not befit a shogunal official. The second possibility that Ryūhoku offers, that he was too direct in his criticism of official policy, has traditionally been interpreted as a reference to a satirical poem that Ryūhoku wrote to criticize the shogunate for its misplaced priorities in a time of national crisis. There are two conflicting theories about the kanshi's precise wording, but what is clear about the episode is that Ryūhoku had chosen an unacceptably crude and provocative manner with which to vent his frustration that his policy suggestions were being ignored. Ryūhoku did not explain what these policy suggestions were, but when one considers his growing familiarity with the members of the Katsuragawa salon, as well as the fact that he enthusiastically commenced studying Western languages after losing his position, it seems fairly likely that he had angered the shogunal authorities by advocating a more active importation of Western learning.

Whatever the reasons for his dismissal may have been, we do know that Ryūhoku took it in stride. A kanshi Ryūhoku composed immediately after the incident ends with a curiously optimistic and somewhat insolent couplet: "My lord has presented me with such tranquil respite / Now I can read the books I have always wanted to" (*Narushima Ryūhoku, Ōnuma Chinzan*, pp. 56–57). Though Ryūhoku refers to "three years" of isolation, the shogunate's actual order of confinement was only for fifty days. Nevertheless, Ryūhoku ended up spending just over two years in seclusion, during which time his home became a frequent gathering place for members of Katsuragawa's salon.

One product of this ongoing exchange with the Western scholars is *Itsumadegusa* (1865–1866; Ivy), a collaborative work composed in fragments over the course of the group's numerous social gatherings. The work is a miscellaneous collection of frivolous occasional writings in a vast range of styles and languages. Moreover, *Itsumadegusa* makes heavy use of pseudonyms and other forms of coded reference invented on the spur of the moment, as when a geisha's expression of sympathy over Ryūhoku's confinement prompts him to start signing his poems "Kawaisō" ("poor old man"). Foreign readers frustrated with the difficulty of deciphering this daunting text can take comfort in the fact that no less an authority than Kishigami Shikken, the late nineteenth-century editor of Ryūhoku's collected works in *Ryūhoku zenshū*, frankly conceded that there were many names and expressions in *Itsumadegusa* that remained baffling to him. Though the precise meaning of some sections was probably clear only to the participants, the reader can still readily envision the whimsical atmosphere that enlivened their gatherings.

Although these men who gathered at Ryūhoku's home all shared an interest in the potential applications of Western learning, *Itsumadegusa* suggests that the pleasure of language itself was one of the major factors stimu-

lating their enthusiastic study. Ryūhoku's recommendation that the shogunate foster Western learning shows that he must have been convinced of its practical benefits. Yet as *Itsumadegusa* demonstrates, to Ryūhoku there was more to the study of the West than utility. Diversion and entertainment were just as important to Ryūhoku as the functional uses of language. In one of the earliest studies of *Itsumadegusa*, Maeda Ai devotes special attention to a visit by Fukuzawa Yukichi (1834–1901), the famous enlightenment thinker and advocate of "practical studies," to Ryūhoku's home. Fukuzawa insisted on returning home early, refusing to compose any kyōshi or otherwise engage in the group's silly antics. Maeda focuses on the contrast apparent here between Ryūhoku's playfulness and Fukuzawa's unrelieved seriousness. It is one of the clearest manifestations not only of Ryūhoku's whimsy, but also of his self-proclaimed credo of "uselessness," a pose that Maeda identifies as a dominant theme in the latter half of Ryūhoku's life. Like many of the early enlightenment thinkers who translated Western books into Japanese and wrote popular introductions to Western learning, Fukuzawa advocated the use of straightforward and unadorned language as the most efficient means of disseminating knowledge. Yet as the numerous lexical puzzles of *Itsumadegusa* show, Ryūhoku's interest in Western learning had obviously not made him a devotee of such utilitarian simplicity and rational clarity.

As a result of Ryūhoku's association with the Western scholars of the Katsuragawa salon, he became fairly proficient in Dutch, English, and later French. His linguistic ability was undoubtedly the main reason that he was unexpectedly called back into service by the shogunate in late 1865 to lead its new military academy in Yokohama. Ryūhoku took up his new position as a leader of the cavalry unit in the first month of 1866. His job was to organize the troops and make the necessary arrangements before French advisors arrived the following year to instruct the soldiers in Western military techniques. Ryūhoku spent nearly two full years working at the military academy, during which time he befriended the French commander Charles Chanoine. Ryūhoku enjoyed learning French and interacting with Chanoine, but he was not cut out for military office. When the opportunity arose, Ryūhoku resigned his post and shortly thereafter accepted a new assignment as foreign affairs secretary and a joint appointment as treasurer.

Ryūhoku had only held these high offices for a few months when the Meiji Restoration brought the Tokugawa era to an end. Moments before the curtain fell on the shogunate in the fourth month of 1868, Ryūhoku resigned his recently acquired posts and moved to live in seclusion in a new home, which he called the Pine and Chrysanthemum Cottage. The name derives from an image in the "Guiqulaici," a well-known work by Tao Qian (365–427) that celebrates the poet's resignation of his government post and his return to the simple comforts of a quiet mountainside home. Ryūhoku felt a profound affinity for this legendary Chinese recluse and his attitude of contented indifference to public affairs. Around the same time, Ryūhoku closed the autobiographical essay "Bokujō inshi den" with the bold declaration: "Having become a truly useless person, it is only natural that I do not wish to pursue anything useful" (*RZ*, p. 2).

The classically inspired ideal of the "useless" literatus would be the role that Ryūhoku cultivated for the rest of his life. In practical terms, the credo meant that Ryūhoku would refuse to become an official in the new Meiji government in spite of the many offers he received. Yet as Ryūhoku's activities in the early years of Meiji demonstrate, this ideal was ultimately no more than a pose. While he claimed sublime indifference, Ryūhoku in fact remained a perceptive and trenchant observer of Meiji society. His withering criticisms of what he saw as the shallowness of the new era's guiding values, such as the uncritical adoption of Western ways in the name of *bunmei kaika* (civilization and enlightenment) and the sacrifice of playfulness to practicality, found expression in literary works such as

Ryūkyō shinshi. Similarly, Ryūhoku's journalistic activities gave him the opportunity to make equally strident attacks on the new government's policies. Ryūhoku's identification with a classical Chinese recluse and his opposition to aspects of the bunmei kaika agenda might seem to suggest that he had become a traditionalist who rejected Western culture and opposed change. Yet Ryūhoku's travel diaries reveal on the contrary that his enthusiasm for Western culture was undiminished, and his literary works likewise show that his criticism was neither rigid nor reactionary.

Ryūkyō shinshi

Ryūkyō shinshi, Ryūhoku's multi-part chronicle of the pleasure quarters, is by far his longest and best-known work. He had essentially finished the first part of *Ryūkyō shinshi* in the autumn of 1859, but the text was not actually published until well into the Meiji period. The first part, which Ryūhoku supplemented slightly in 1869, circulated privately and was published without the author's permission around 1870. He added a second part in 1871, noting in its preface that the dramatic changes of the last ten years had made the word "New" in the work's title "New chronicles of Yanagibashi" no longer appropriate. Just after this second part was published in 1874, Ryūhoku made some minor revisions to the first part and published it for the first time in an authorized edition. *Ryūkyō shinshi* proved immensely popular among Meiji readers, but in February of 1876 the Meiji government prohibited its sale. The authorities might have been reacting to its critical content, but it was surely no coincidence that Ryūhoku, then the editor of the *Chōya Shinbun*, had just been jailed for violating the new Press Laws. Ryūhoku also completed a third section of *Ryūkyō shinshi*, but the Meiji government prohibited its publication too, and today only the preface of this final part is extant.

In the opening lines of *Ryūkyō shinshi*, Ryūhoku acknowledges his debt to Terakado Seiken's *Edo hanjōki*, a work that was banned for its lewdness in 1835. Both texts are written in the same deviant form of classical Chinese, which gives their treatment of such unorthodox subjects as drinking and consorting with geisha an ironic and amusing twist. Unlike Seiken, however, Ryūhoku still held an elite position in the shogunal government when he started writing *Ryūkyō shinshi*, making his descent into the world of Yanagibashi all the more a potential site of transformative role-playing. In the preface to *Ryūkyō shinshi*, edited by Hino Tatsuo, he adopts the narrative pose of a young and inexperienced student:

> I am just a foolish student. With a worn-down inkstone and brush, I earn barely enough to keep myself from going hungry. I have none of Seiken's talent and learning. On top of that, I haven't a penny to my name, so I have not yet spent even a single day playing in the quarters, and I have no experience of how it really is. How then can I claim the authority to write about it? I have, however, heard the tales told by the playboys, and I have been able to get a glimpse of the quarters' workings by looking at maps of the city. And now, I have taken advantage of a tranquil evening to write it all down. If an upright Confucian gentleman were to read this book, with its vulgar language and obscene contents, he would spit upon it and discard it at once.

(p. 338)

The preface echoes Seiken's *Edo hanjōki*, but whereas Seiken really did write in order to keep himself from going hungry, such concerns were unknown to Ryūhoku. Likewise, though the narrator claims never to have ventured inside the quarter, Ryūhoku had already become a frequent visitor at the time he wrote the passage. This narrative pose, in which the narrator feigns innocent ignorance and contrasts himself to a Confucian gentleman, is an example of what Maeda Ai has called the "aesthetics of dressing down" (Maeda, 1976, pp. 77–78). It shows how entering the world of Yanagibashi allowed one a kind of escape: the privilege of

ceasing to be oneself and the pleasure of enjoying the masquerade. As the narrator's detached speculation about how an "upright Confucian gentleman" might react to *Ryūkyō shinshi* suggests, part of the fun of cavorting in Yanagibashi was the freedom it gave Ryūhoku to step outside his official position. The pleasure was all the more keen, however, since just as the text's detailed descriptions belied the student narrator's pose of innocence, so too did its learned diction and studious allusions make it clear that the author was in fact a Confucian gentleman, if not necessarily an upright one. The disguise was, in other words, transparent; it served no practical function but the amusement of author and audience.

In addition to Terakado Seiken's *Edo hanjōki*, a second major inspiration for *Ryūkyō shinshi* was a Chinese text called *Banqiao zaji* written in the 1640s by Yu Huai (1616–1698). A chronicle of the pleasure quarters in Nanjing, *Banqiao zaji* was written during the collapse of the Ming Dynasty. It reveals how even as the Qing army approached and Nanjing lay imperiled, the culture of the literati continued, with consecutive nights of drinking and poetry carried on in the company of courtesans. As Iwaki Hideo notes in his translation of the text into modern Japanese, *Banqiao zaji* not only documents the disappearing world of the literati and the pleasure quarters, but it also has a significant political undertone since it is "interwoven with a profound sense of longing for the Ming" (pp. 225–226). It is hardly surprising that this text was particularly meaningful to Ryūhoku, who was living through similarly sweeping political changes. Moreover, Ryūhoku could not help but share Yu Huai's sense of nostalgia as he witnessed the waning of the unique culture he had grown to love.

The first part of *Ryūkyō shinshi* is essentially a descriptive guide to Yanagibashi that is organizationally patterned after *Banqiao zaji* and contains numerous direct references to Yu Huai's text. Despite these parallels, Ryūhoku clearly distinguishes between the imaginary world inspired by his reading of *Banqiao zaji* and the real world of Yanagibashi. Near the end of the first part of *Ryūkyō shinshi*, for example, Ryūhoku quotes Yu Huai's lengthy praise of Li Shiniang, a courtesan renowned for her beauty and accomplishments, only to muse disappointedly: "Alas! There are countless geisha in Yanagibashi; if I search deeply among them, won't I find one who reminds me of Shiniang?" (p. 371). As this passage suggests, in spite of its celebratory tone, *Ryūkyō shinshi* also shows a rather sober realism.

This objectivity is further apparent in the text's exploitation of the liminal narrative pose of the student observer to describe the quarters from a detached perspective. While the narrator obviously enjoys venturing into this world and sharing knowledge of its ways with his audience, he cherishes no illusions about it. Beneath his praise of the quarters' popularity, there lingers an unsettling hint of excess:

There are grand drinking establishments with shining roof-tiles and sophisticated tea shops with fluttering banners. The powerful aroma of the roast eel shops strikes your nose and the bright blood from the butcher's shop stains your shoes. The *mochi* rice from the sweet shop would be enough to dam the flow of the Yellow River, and the produce sold in the fruit stands would be sufficient to strike down all the birds in the King of Qi's park. Sushi, soba, whatever you say, whatever your desire may be, there is none that cannot be sated.

(pp. 339–340)

As the narrator's gaze takes in the sights and smells of the quarter, his excitement and enthusiasm are obvious, but no sooner does he describe some superlative feature of Yanagibashi than he deflates it with a jarring turn of phrase. While the narrator marvels at the spectacle of Yanagibashi, a sinister undercurrent relativizes the splendor; although the brightness of the butcher shop's blood attests to the richness of the area, it nevertheless stains one's shoes. The references to the wide Yellow River and the vast garden of the King of Qi are classical Chinese allusions indicating immen-

sity, but when the narrator deploys them in reference to mushy mochi and fruit-struck birds, the effect is an absurd disjunction between form and content. This mock pedantry is typical of the irreverent humor that is found throughout *Ryūkyō shinshi*.

It is often noted that the two halves of *Ryūkyō shinshi* show a marked contrast in tone. The first part is sometimes described as a celebration of the culture of Yanagibashi, while the second part is seen as being much more critical of the changes that occurred in the quarter in the wake of the Meiji Restoration. While this is basically an accurate characterization of the two parts, it is important not to overlook the wry realism of the text's first half. As the examples above demonstrate, Ryūhoku was not an idealist, nor was he merely an uncritical apologist for the quarter. Still, it is undeniable that the second part of *Ryūkyō shinshi* carries this sense of disillusionment to an entirely new level.

Ryūhoku wrote the second half of *Ryūkyō shinshi* after the Meiji Restoration, when a coalition of rural domains wrested political power from the shogunate. As a lifelong servant of the Tokugawa, Ryūhoku naturally saw himself in opposition to the officials of the new Meiji government. *Ryūkyō shinshi* thus targets the boorish behavior of these newly arrived rural samurai, whose ignorance of proper conduct threatened to destroy Yanagibashi's refined atmosphere. Yet these rural samurai were not the only targets of *Ryūkyō shinshi*'s criticism. The text also criticizes the program of "civilization and enlightenment" that had become the credo of the new era. In one amusing episode, Ryūhoku spoofs the excessive seriousness of that definitive Meiji species, the ambitious student of the West:

There was a student who went to school and became extremely fluent in English. One evening, he went drinking at Ryūkōtei, but when he spoke to the geisha, half of what he said was in English. The geisha said, "Only you, my dear, understand English. We don't have any idea what you're saying, and that's no fun at all. Won't you teach us some English?" The student said with delight "You're a genius, I tell you, a genius! If you study for a few months, I guarantee you'll become someone big. I know everything there is to know about English, so . . . I don't know, where should we begin?" The geisha replied "When we women address each other, it's so boring to use the usual terms. Why don't you first teach us how to say our names?" The student responded "A novel idea!" The geisha asked how to say "Otake," and the student answered "Bamboo." She asked, "Oume?" "Plum." She asked, "Otori?" "Bird." She asked, "Ochō?" "Kapel" [Dutch for "butterfly"]. The answers came back like an echo. Then she asked, "Misakichi?" The student tilted his head and thought intently, but couldn't think of what to say. Then, "Ochara?" The student grew more and more perplexed. Wiping sweat from his forehead, he said, "Today I haven't brought my dictionary. Next time I'll come with a copy of *Eigosen* in my breast pocket, and I'll be able to answer all of your questions."

(pp. 392–393)

The student fails to understand that the proper names "Misakichi" and "Ochara" will be impossible to translate no matter what dictionary he brings. Unlike some of his literary contemporaries, Ryūhoku did not parody this aspiring English student out of xenophobia or ignorance. Rather, Ryūhoku's target was the humorless program of advancement and superficial Westernization that was sweeping Japan in the 1870s. It is particularly suggestive that Ryūhoku drew the specific foreign words that appear in this episode from a brief piece in *Itsumadegusa*, for the Meiji student's intensity is the very opposite of the relaxed fun memorialized in the earlier work. The situational inappropriateness of the student's overwhelming seriousness satirizes how the incursion of unrefined utilitarian rhetoric had destroyed the elegant atmosphere of the pleasure quarters.

In articles that focus particular attention on this episode, Okada Kesao and Mizumoto Seiichirō illuminate additional dimensions of

Ryūhoku's satire. Okada notes that *Eigosen* (1861; English handbook) was never more than a rudimentary introduction to English vocabulary and simple phrase structure. Ryūhoku's choice of this text thus amplifies the outrageousness of the student's misplaced assurance that such a basic text would be a panacea for any lexical problem. Moreover, inasmuch as the *Eigosen* was produced by Japanese scholars of Dutch, the text still bore the traces of Dutch terminology and pronunciation. Taking the developmental history of *Eigosen* into consideration, Mizumoto argues that Ryūhoku deliberately used the term "Kapel" as the student's attempt to translate "butterfly" in order to expose the tenuousness of the student's grasp on English and his ignorance of the long tradition of Dutch studies in Japan. In other words, the student was an arriviste, unaware of the history of the movement of which he considered himself an exponent, and moreover, oblivious to the outdatedness of his tools.

A similar episode in the text of *Ryūkyō shinshi* concerns a debate between two young men over which political structure the new government should adopt. Completely insensitive to their surroundings, the two men carry on their endless discussion even though it bores the two geisha in the room to the point of desperation. Finally, one of the geisha interrupts to offer her own explanation of the term *kyōwa* (republic):

How mistaken you are! This debate about the merits and demerits of the feudal and federal systems has been argued by all of the great philosophers since the Qin and Han dynasties. What need is there for you two to prattle on about it now? I hear that in America, they have a republican system, and that means "collective harmony." Fair and enlightened, just and grand, even the governance of those sage kings of antiquity could not surpass it. You two would do well to quit ruminating on these worn-out dregs of the ancients, cease your debate on feudalism versus federalism, and celebrate the beauty of collective harmony. After all, when you have fun, more than anything you need to collectively harmonize in order to enjoy yourself. Here you are in a drinking house, and yet you leave your food and drink untouched, you leave the musical instruments lying silent, and you leave us in the corner while you pursue this empty debate that only puts us to sleep! Is this what you call collective harmony? You two really don't know the first thing about having fun. Now I'll become your President, and do my best to sweep away this somber mood. So please, first have a sip from this chalice as your punishment!

(pp. 401–402)

The geisha's clever word play hinges on the literal meaning of the characters used in *kyōwa*, and its effect is to effortlessly shift the direction of conversation to something more suitable to the occasion. Just as he mocked the earnest English student for his shallow knowledge and humorless attitude, so too does Ryūhoku's satire here point out the men's lack of sophistication not only in political theory but also in how to conduct themselves in the pleasure quarters. The text does not simply reject change out of an inflexible loyalty to tradition, but instead makes light of those who take themselves too seriously.

Ryūhoku and the West

In early 1871 Ryūhoku became head instructor of a private academy in Tokyo run by the priest Gennyo (also known as Ōtani Kōei, 1852–1923). It was through his acquaintance with Gennyo that Ryūhoku was given the extraordinary opportunity to travel to Europe and America the following year. Gennyo's mission was to learn more about Western religious institutions, and he knew that Ryūhoku's linguistic skills as well as his experience as the shogun's treasurer made him well-suited for the job of monitoring travel expenses and facilitating interaction with Westerners. Ryūhoku kept a detailed diary during his travels that he later published as *Kōsei nichijō* (1881–1884). Unfortunately, Ryūhoku's month-long tour of the United States is missing from the surviving text, which ends abruptly just as Ryūhoku arrives in New York. Though incomplete, *Kōsei nichijō* is nevertheless a fascinating work of literature that was not only popular in its time, but was later imitated by such writers as Mori Ōgai and Nagai Kafū. Most interestingly, the diary shows the way in which Ryūhoku enjoyed himself in Europe, not as a studious onlooker, but as an active participant. Though many Japanese had traveled to Paris before him, Ryūhoku was, as Shimamura Teru has pointedly observed, the first Japanese "tourist" to visit Paris.

Ryūhoku left Yokohama aboard a French ship on 15 October 1872. After six weeks of travel through Southeast Asia and the Mediterranean, Ryūhoku's group docked in Marseilles. The following morning, they boarded a train for Paris, where they arrived on 1 December. After several very active months in France, including a brief jaunt to Italy, Ryūhoku sailed for England in May 1873, where he stayed for one month before going on to New York. Though the itinerary was a common one for Japanese who traveled abroad at the time, Ryūhoku's diary is unique for the remarkably personal and individualistic way in which he recorded his experiences. Part of this difference, of course, can be attributed to the fact that Ryūhoku was traveling as a private individual and not as a representative of an official mission. Yet the differences are more profound than such a simple distinction might suggest.

In a fascinating study of the diaries of early modern Japanese who traveled abroad, Masao Miyoshi argues that unlike a Western diarist, who "tends to particularize and individualize any experience," the typical nineteenth-century Japanese diarist writes from the perspective of the entire group (pp. 103–114). In Ryūhoku's diary, however, the author's personal experience is almost never submerged within a group identity. On the rare occasions Ryūhoku even mentions the other four men in his traveling group, he contrasts his own intrepid boldness with their withdrawn cautiousness. On the day the ship leaves Yokohama, for example, Ryūhoku mentions that his traveling companions have shut themselves up in their rooms because of the choppy waves while he alone surveys the view from deck, and when they travel to Hong Kong, Ryūhoku regrets that their timidity kept the group from staying in a hotel on shore.

In spite of the differences in subject matter that separate *Kōsei nichijō* from Ryūhoku's earlier writings about Yanagibashi, the works nevertheless share the same sort of jocular tone and individualistic voice. In the opening section of *Ryūkyō shinshi*, for example, Ryūhoku expresses doubt about the accepted etymology of "Yanagibashi." Similarly, as he passed through the heart of the Mediterranean Sea, Ryūhoku questioned the suitability of the sea's Latin name in a kanshi that ends: "Thousands of years ago, who named this place the Sea Amid the Land? / On all four sides, as far as the eye can see, I can't make out any mountains!" As in many of the other kanshi he composed while abroad, Ryūhoku is showing off a bit of esoteric knowledge in this poem, but he is also drolly displaying his own mischievous suspicion of the standard view. Rather than accepting the role of passive stenographer, Ryūhoku revels in the chance to express his personal feelings and interpretive speculations.

Beyond the diary's distinctively individualistic perspective, *Kōsei nichijō* is unlike other early Japanese travel accounts in its literary intent. Far from a detached documentary record or analysis of Western society, Ryūhoku's diary never attempts to conceal his delighted engagement with the new world around him. *Kōsei nichijō* is also unique because it chronicles the unusual range of activities Ryūhoku engaged in while abroad. Ryūhoku spent the majority of his sojourn in Paris, where he had the opportunity to sample the local culture extensively. He writes of his visits to a brothel on the Rue d'Amboise, his trips to various art galleries and museums, his enjoyment of cabaret shows, and his attendance of several plays. Ryūhoku's linguistic abilities undoubtedly opened up a wider range of cultural activities to him than was available to his companions. Without consider-

able facility with French, for example, Ryūhoku could not have given such an accurate summary of Dumas' *La Dame aux camélias*, based on the theatrical adaptation he saw at the Gymnase in early 1873.

More than linguistic ability, however, it was Ryūhoku's aesthetics and interests that made his diary so unlike those of his contemporaries. Though Ryūhoku was in Paris at the same time as the famous Iwakura mission, a comparison of his diary with this official delegation's *Beiō kairan jikki* shows an astonishing difference in focus. Maeda Ai succinctly summarizes this contrast: "On the Iwakura mission's side was the Paris of fortresses and factories; on Ryūhoku's side was the Paris of theaters and art galleries" (Maeda, 1976, p. 191). Even on those few occasions that Ryūhoku accompanied the Iwakura mission on its tour of various state institutions, he invariably recorded a set of impressions quite unlike those in the mission's official record. The contrast that Maeda constructs here is another manifestation of his characterization of Ryūhoku as an exemplar of "uselessness." Other scholars' studies of these two documents have expanded and refined Maeda's formulation. In an article that focuses on the treatment of music, Nakamura Kōsuke concludes that whereas the Iwakura mission wrote of how music could serve the state, Ryūhoku completely rejected the patriotic or didactic uses of art. It is interesting to note that in his rejection of didacticism, Ryūhoku anticipated one of the central arguments of Tsubouchi Shōyō's *Shōsetsu shinzui*, the influential treatise on the novel that appeared over a decade later.

A few Japanese scholars have come to question the absoluteness of this opposition between uselessness and usefulness. Kobayashi Shigeru, for example, has approached the issue not by comparing *Kōsei nichijō* with *Beiō kairan jikki*, but by comparing sections of *Kōsei nichijō* with each other. He argues that it is misleading to see the Paris of *Kōsei nichijō* exclusively in terms of leisurely "cultural enjoyment," since Ryūhoku actually wrote in greater detail about such "useful" places as prisons, courts, and observatories than he did about such "useless" places as brothels and galleries. Inui Teruo has also problematized the distinction by noting that although museums might seem to be "useless" private places to spend one's leisure time, they also have a very "useful" public role to play in preserving national heritage. Impressed by the Louvre and the British Museum, Ryūhoku became a staunch advocate of nationally sponsored cultural preservation in the late 1870s. He wrote numerous editorials that emphasized the government's obligation to protect Japan's cultural artifacts, and furthermore acted on these ideas by becoming a key figure in the movement to restore the shrine at Nikkō. As these studies of his travels abroad suggest, the tendency to identify Ryūhoku with the posture of "uselessness" has come under increasing scrutiny in recent years. The most provocative challenges to this view, however, have come from scholars focusing on Ryūhoku's journalistic activities.

Ryūhoku the Journalist

Shortly after he returned to Japan, Ryūhoku was offered the position of Minister of Culture by Kido Takayoshi, one of the members of the Iwakura mission whom Ryūhoku had met while abroad. Ryūhoku repeatedly refused to accept an office with the Meiji government and chose instead to continue working for Gennyo. In late 1873 he became the head of a new office for translation in Kyoto, a change of residence that provided him with the opportunity to conduct research for *Keibyō ippan* (A pack of Kyoto cats), a chronicle of the old capital's pleasure quarters. It was as a journalist, however, that Ryūhoku was to make his final great contribution to early Meiji culture. In a certain sense, Ryūhoku's first foray into newspaper production had taken place in 1869, when he had produced a few issues of the *Tōkyō Chinbun* (Strange news from Tokyo), a homemade newspaper that Ryūhoku sent to his brother-in-law in Shizuoka. It can hardly be considered a true newspaper, but as Inui Teruo has dis-

cussed, the issues of *Tōkyō Chinbun* show Ryūhoku's intense concern over the new government's policies as well as his early interest in exploring the medium of the newspaper.

Ryūhoku's opportunity to enter the world of journalism professionally came in 1874, when he became editor of the *Kōbun tsūshi*, a minor newspaper that he relaunched as the *Chōya Shinbun*. His first actions as editor were to expand the paper's political analysis section and to add what became the paper's most popular feature: the *zatsuroku* section of miscellaneous reports and essays, mostly written by Ryūhoku. In addition, the newly designed paper included a special section for kanshi, which not only offered readers advice on style, but also gave Ryūhoku a forum in which to publish his poems. Under Ryūhoku's leadership in the mid-1870s, the *Chōya Shinbun* became the most widely read paper in the country.

Editing the paper also led Ryūhoku into his final confrontation with officialdom. The fledgling Meiji government had been growing increasingly wary of the power of independent newspapers in the 1870s. After a series of measures that progressively restricted the freedom of publishers, the government passed sweeping legislation in June 1875, making criticism of the government "nearly impossible" (Rubin, p. 21). Ryūhoku responded almost immediately with a facetious editorial praising the laws and promising his staff's allegiance to them. When the government punished Suehiro Tetchō (1849–1896), the editor of another newspaper, for presenting a sincere argument against the laws, Ryūhoku borrowed a favorite technique of the kyōshi tradition and cast his criticism as a parody of a classic Chinese poem. Ryūhoku's poem was entitled "Hekiekifu" (Poem of shrinking from fear), a name that resembles the Japanese pronunciation "Sekiekifu" of Su Shi's classic "Chibifu" (Poem of Red Cliff). Ryūhoku meticulously preserved the grammatical structure and many of the words of the original poem but altered the rest to humorously express his frustrations over the new law. Unimpressed with Ryūhoku's erudition, the authorities ordered him confined to his home for five days.

Not long after this episode, Tetchō joined the *Chōya Shinbun* and he and Ryūhoku became a team, setting the stage for the paper's final showdown over the press laws. In late 1875 they wrote a thinly veiled attack of the two government officials who had been instrumental in enacting the press laws: Inoue Kowashi and Ozaki Saburō. The humorous twist, however, was that Ryūhoku and Tetchō's article referred to the two officials as Inoue Saburō and Ozaki Kowashi. In part, it was a strategy to defend the paper from legal action, but it was also another instance of Ryūhoku's infamous word play. Inoue and Ozaki did not see the humor, however, and immediately pressed libel charges against Ryūhoku and Tetchō. The two journalists were sentenced in January of 1876 to serve prison terms of four months and eight months, respectively, and also to pay fines of 100 yen and 150 yen.

The sentence did not destroy Ryūhoku's sense of humor. During his incarceration, Ryūhoku drew on his experience with the *Tōkyō Chinbun* to produce a handwritten newspaper that he circulated among the inmates, most of whom were fellow journalists. Moreover, after he was released, Ryūhoku published an essay entitled "Gokunaibanashi" (Tales from prison) that detailed the hardships of life as an inmate. Though Ryūhoku gradually became less involved in the *Chōya Shinbun* after he was released, he did not become ambivalent about freedom of the press. On the first anniversary of the promulgation of the press codes, Ryūhoku organized a mock memorial service for the "spirit of the newspaper" that had been killed one year earlier. Amid sutra recitations, incense offerings, and extemporaneous prayers, Ryūhoku sarcastically lauded the laws and the "benevolence of our wise government." In a few years, he decided to cede control of the paper to Tetchō, freeing himself to launch a new publishing endeavor.

In 1877 Ryūhoku founded *Kagetsu shinshi,* which might be considered Japan's first literary magazine. The journal published poetry and prose works in both Japanese and Chinese and soon became immensely popular, especially among students. The new journal gave Ryūhoku the opportunity to continue the kind of leisurely writing he had always enjoyed most. Though the life of literary withdrawal that the job allowed would seem to accord well with his self-proclaimed ideal of "uselessness," it soon proved unable to hold Ryūhoku's attention. In 1881 Ryūhoku returned to the world of newspapers and began publishing a column in the *Yomiuri Shinbun.* In the following year, he became more involved in politics as well, joining a newly formed party that sought the immediate drafting of a constitution and the formation of a National Diet. Through a detailed examination of these columns and Ryūhoku's work on behalf of the political party, Inui Teruo has convincingly challenged the idea that Ryūhoku spent his final years in quiet withdrawal. Ryūhoku died of tuberculosis in November 1884. Just months before his death, he was writing spirited editorials that reveal a profound concern for Japan's future.

Conclusion

Ryūhoku's position in Japanese literary history has undergone substantial evolution in recent years. Traditionally regarded as the last of a dying breed of "playful writers," his writings were rejected by many early twentieth-century critics as anachronisms. In one such dismissal from 1935, Ōno Mitsuji called Ryūhoku a prototypical "leftover son of Edo" (p. 46). Part of the reason that Ryūhoku's works were so long neglected is that they were written in a linguistic form that came to be identified as "premodern." In one of the earliest attempts to reevaluate *Ryūkyō shinshi,* for example, Wada Shigejirō had first to make the concession that "insofar as it is written in literary Chinese, a non-modern form of expression, the text cannot be said to have transcended pre-modernity" (p. 13). Moreover, Ryūhoku never attempted to write a novel, the genre that is most conventionally identified with the genesis of modern Japanese literature. Traditional narratives of Japanese literary history that make narrow use of these linguistic and generic markers as indices of modernity have thus delineated boundaries that diminish Ryūhoku's relevance.

Beginning in the 1950s, however, Ryūhoku's life and literature attracted new attention as several Japanese scholars—such as Wada Shigejirō, Ochi Haruo, Nakamura Mitsuo, and Miyoshi Yukio—began to question the established equation of Ryūhoku with the last vestiges of the pre-modern literary tradition. While there were significant differences among their interpretations of Ryūhoku, these scholars agreed insofar as they discovered a unique critical spirit in Ryūhoku. They found that unlike his contemporaries, Ryūhoku was not only able to depict the cultural changes that Japan was undergoing, but he was also able to critique and comment upon this tumult with sophisticated and insightful satire. It is Maeda Ai's pioneering work in the late 1960s and early 1970s, however, that has been most influential in shaping our present understanding of Ryūhoku. Building on the earlier scholars' collective discovery of Ryūhoku's critical spirit, Maeda's most important contribution was his more nuanced and elaborate characterization of Ryūhoku as a critic of the *bunmei kaika* agenda. In Maeda's formulation, whereas humorless practicality was the guiding principle for many intellectuals of the early Meiji period, Ryūhoku might instead be seen as an exemplar of the "spirit of play." Though this playfulness had its roots in the culture of the Edo period, Ryūhoku's oppositional stance earned him admirers among Meiji writers who still had the Chinese training to enjoy his works and carry on their spirit. The wryly alienated protagonist of Mori Ōgai's story "Asobi" (1911; "Play," 1994) is surely an heir to Ryūhoku, as are the "useless" "scribblers" who populate the works of Nagai Kafū.

New research is steadily bringing Ryūhoku's lesser-known writings to light and providing more insights into his life. In recent years, for example, the work of Inui Teruo has greatly advanced our understanding of Ryūhoku's later career, especially his involvement in the publishing industry and his participation in the popular rights movements of the early 1880s. Inui's work has already pointed out some of the limits to Maeda's characterization of Ryūhoku as a critic of practicality and an advocate of uselessness. Among scholars in the West, Chieko Ariga's application of reception theory to *Ryūkyō shinshi* stands out as the most thorough treatment of this work in English to date. Likewise, Jay Rubin has considered Ryūhoku's career from the perspective of censorship laws and the publishing industry, and Donald Keene includes a chapter on *Kōsei nichijō* in his volume on modern travel diaries. With these notable exceptions, however, work on Ryūhoku in English remains fairly limited. With the renewed attention that Ryūhoku has received in Japan, however, this condition cannot be expected to continue for long. Ryūhoku is a fascinating figure whose life and works have much to tell us about such issues as Sino-Japanese literary interaction, the Tokugawa-Meiji transition, the development of literary and journalistic media, and the meaning of modernity in the Japanese literary context.

Selected Bibliography

PRIMARY WORKS

COLLECTED WORKS

Ryūhoku ikō. Edited by Narushima Matasaburō. Tokyo: Hakubunkan, 1892.

Ryūhoku zenshū. Edited by Kishigami Shikken. Tokyo: Hakubunkan, 1897. (Abbreviated as *RZ* in the body of the text.)

DIARY

Kenhoku nichiroku. Edited by Maeda Ai. Tokyo: Taihei Shoya, 1997.

KANSHI COLLECTIONS

Bakumatsu Meiji kaigai taiken shishū: Kaishū, Keiu yori Ōgai, Sōseki ni itaru. Edited by Kawaguchi Hisao. Tokyo: Toriatsukaijo Gannandō Shoten, 1984. (This edition includes good annotations, modern Japanese translations, and supplementary reference material for the *kanshi* in *Kōsei nichijō* on pp. 474–526.)

Narushima Ryūhoku, Ōnuma Chinzan. Edited by Hino Tatsuo. Vol. 10 of *Edo shijin senshū.* Tokyo: Iwanami Shoten, 1990. (This edition includes extremely thorough annotations and modern Japanese translations of *kanshi* from every stage in Ryūhoku's life.)

MAJOR LITERARY WORKS

Ryūkyō shinshi (Part 1, 1859–1874; Part 2, 1871–1874; Part 3 (not extant), 1877–1878). Reprinted in *Edo hanjōki, Ryūkyō shinshi.* Edited by Hino Tatsuo. Vol. 100 of *Shin Nihon koten bungaku taikei.* Tokyo: Iwanami Shoten, 1989. (Hino's edition of *Ryūkyō shinshi* is the one referred to in the body of the text. In addition to *Ryūkyō shinshi*, this volume includes Terakado Seiken's *Edo hanjōki*; it also provides both a facsimile of the original *hakubun* and an annotated *yomikudashi* version.)

Meiji kaikaki bungakushū. Edited by Maeda Ai. Vol. 1 of *Nihon kindai bungaku taikei.* Tokyo: Kadokawa Shoten, 1970. (Contains another edition of *Ryūkyō shinshi.* Maeda's notes are very extensive and detailed, providing substantial background information.)

Itsumadegusa (1865–1866). Reprinted in *Ryūkyō shinshi, Itsumadegusa. Benseisha bunko* series. Tokyo: Bensei Shuppan, 1985. (This edition is a reprint from the 1897 Hakubunkan *Ryūhoku zenshū.*)

Kōsei nichijō (1872–1873; originally published 1881–1884). Reprinted in *Narushima Ryūhoku, Hattori Bushō, Kurimoto Joun shū.* Edited by Shioda Ryōhei. Vol. 4 of *Meiji bungaku zenshū.* Tokyo: Chikuma Shobō, 1969. Pp. 117–144.

SECONDARY WORKS

CRITICAL AND BIOGRAPHICAL STUDIES

Ariga, Chieko M. *Reading "Ryūkyō shinshi": An Investigation in Literary Hermeneutics.* Ph.D. diss., University of Chicago, 1986.

———. "The Playful Gloss: Rubi in Japanese Literature." *Monumenta Nipponica* 44, no. 3:309–335 (autumn 1989).

———. "Dephallicizing Women in *Ryūkyō shinshi*: A Critique of Gender Ideology in Japanese Literature." *Journal of Asian Studies* 51, no. 3:565–586 (August 1992).

Imamura Eitarō. "Shitsuiki no Narushima Ryūhoku." *Bungaku* 46, no. 10:19–26 (October 1978).

Inui Teruo. "Narushima Ryūhoku to Jiyū minken: Meiji 14 nen ikō no 'Yomiuri shimbun' o chūshin ni." *Keiei Jōhō Kagaku* 2, no. 4:349–360 (March 1990).

———. "Meiji jūnendai ni okeru Narushima Ryūhoku no genron katsudō nitsuite." *Keiei Jōhō Kagaku* 6, no. 2:117–161 (August 1993).

———. "Narushima Ryūhoku to 'Tōkyō Chinbun.'" *Keiei Jōhō Kagaku* 7, no. 4:239–255 (March 1995).

Kato Shuichi. *The Modern Years.* Vol. 3 of *A History of Japanese Literature.* Trans. by Don Sanderson. Tokyo: Kodansha International, 1990. (Originally published in 1979; Kato's is one of the few general surveys of Japanese literature to include extensive consideration of Ryūhoku.)

Keene, Donald. *Modern Japanese Diaries: The Japanese at Home and Abroad as Revealed through Their Diaries.* New York: Henry Holt and Company, 1995. (Keene's chapter "Journal of a Voyage to the West" [pp. 119–132] provides an informative introduction to *Kōsei nichijō.*)

Maeda Ai. "Narushima Ryūhoku no nikki." In two parts: *Bungaku* 43, no. 2:109–120 (February 1975); and 43, no. 3:53–63 (March 1975).

———. *Narushima Ryūhoku.* Tokyo: Asahi Shimbunsha, 1976.

Miyoshi Yukio. "Hankindai no keifu." *Kokubungaku: Kaishaku to Kanshō* 25, no. 1:95–102 (January 1960).

Mizumoto Seiichiro. "Shēpuru to iu Eigo: Narushima Ryūhoku 'Ryūkyō shinshi' o yomu." *Bungaku Hihyō Josetsu* 7:84–86 (January 1993).

Nagai Kafū. "Narushima Ryūhoku no nisshi." In *Kafū zenshū.* Vol. 16. Tokyo: Iwanami Shoten, 1964. Pp. 267–281.

———. "Ryūkyō shinshi ni tsukite." In *Kafu zenshū.* Vol. 16. Tokyo: Iwanami Shoten, 1964. Pp. 283–292.

Nakamura Kōsuke. "Ishinki Nihonjin no yōgaku taiken: Kume Kunitake hen 'Tokumei Zenken Taishi Beiō kairan jikki' to Narushima Ryūhoku 'Kōsei nichijō' o chūshin ni." *Hikaku Bunka* 4:69–110 (summer 1987).

Nakamura Mitsuo. *Meiji bungakushi.* Tokyo: Chikuma Shobō, 1963.

Ochi Haruo. "Narushima Ryūhoku ni okeru hankindai." *Kokubungaku: Kaishaku to Kyōzai no Kenkyū* 10, no. 5:32–39 (April 1965).

Okada Kesao. "Jūkyūseiki hyōgen isō no ichi jiten." *Nihon Bungaku* 33, no. 7:37–46 (July 1984).

Ono Hideo. "Narushima Ryūhoku." In *Sandai genronjin shū.* Vol. 2. Tokyo: Jiji Tsūshinsha, 1963. Pp. 171–291.

Ōno Mitsuji. "Gaiyūgo no Narushima Ryūhoku." *Kokugo to Kokubungaku* 12, no. 5:33–50 (May 1935).

Ōshima Ryūichi. *Ryūhoku dansō.* Tokyo: Shōwa Kankōkai, 1943.

Rubin, Jay. *Injurious to Public Morals: Writers and the Meiji State.* Seattle: University of Washington Press, 1984. (The third chapter of Rubin's monograph focuses on Ryūhoku's various conflicts with the authorities over censorship and press laws.)

Shimamura Teru. "Pari o mita Nihonjin, Nihonjin no mita Pari: Narushima Ryūhoku to Kurimoto Joun." *Joshi Bijutsu Daigaku Kiyo* 27:107–117 (March 1997).

Wada Shigejiro. "Ryūkyō shinshi ni okeru hihan seishin." *Bungaku* 18, no. 8:11–21 (August 1950).

OTHER WORKS CITED

Iwaki Hideo. *Hankyō zakki Soshū gabōroku.* Vol. 29 of *Tōyō bunko.* Tokyo: Heibonsha, 1965. (This work

includes an annotated modern Japanese translation
of Yu Huai's *Banqiao zaji*.)
Miyoshi, Masao. *As We Saw Them: The First Japanese
Embassy to the United States (1860)*. Berkeley: University of California Press, 1979.

Shiga Naoya

1883–1971

TED GOOSSEN

SHIGA NAOYA was Japan's foremost practitioner of autobiographical fiction *(shishō-setsu)*, the form that dominated Japanese literature for much of the twentieth century. Although he lived a long life, the works he left are relatively few—one long novel, three novellas, and several volumes of short stories and personal essays—and most of these were published before he turned forty. Nevertheless, as his nickname the "god of prose fiction" *(shōsetsu no kamisama)* suggests, no Japanese writer was more revered, and even his critics praised Shiga's direct and powerful style, which set the standard for modern Japanese literary composition. Shiga's work characteristically focuses on the mental state of a single character and neglects the social realm. Viewed as a whole, it chronicles Shiga's tortuous but apparently successful struggle to achieve a harmony within himself, with his family, and with nature.

Life

Shiga Naoya was born on 20 February 1883 in the town of Ishinomaki in Miyagi Prefecture in northern Japan, where his father Naoharu had been posted by the bank for which he worked. Since Naoharu and his wife Gin had lost their firstborn son shortly before Shiga's birth, he was treasured all the more as the heir—not merely of the nuclear family but of the Shiga line. When the three of them returned to the family's Tokyo home in 1885, his care was taken over by his paternal grandparents, a not infrequent occurrence during that era. When he was twelve Shiga's mother died in childbirth, and his father married a much younger woman who became a warm and supportive stepmother to the adolescent boy. Nonetheless, Shiga's grandparents—Rume, his strong-willed and fiercely protective grandmother, and Naomichi, a paragon of samurai virtue who had been a high-ranking retainer to the Sōma clan—were closest to him during his formative years.

The samurai class had been legislated out of existence more than a decade before Shiga was born, in the reforms that followed the restoration of the emperor, Meiji, in 1868. Nevertheless, some former samurai families were able to hold on to their privileged status by providing an elitist education for their male offspring. Shiga's father, for example, was a graduate of Keiō Gijuku (present-day Keiō University), where he garnered the training and connections that helped him amass a considerable fortune in business, while Shiga was sent to the Peers' School, a prestigious private academy for the youth of Japan's new aristocracy.

331

Shiga was a good-looking, athletic boy but an indifferent student who was held back twice for poor grades. Spoiled by his grandmother, he whiled away his time reading novels, going to the theater, and, beginning around the age of eighteen, attending a Christian study group led by the noted preacher Uchimura Kanzō. He graduated from the Peers' School in 1906 and then attended Tokyo Imperial University for two years before leaving without a degree. In his mid twenties, Shiga broke with Uchimura and turned his energies toward becoming a writer. Although he continued to live in the family compound, his father disapproved of his lifestyle and choice of career. The rift between Shiga and his father deepened in 1907, a year after the death of his grandfather, when Shiga's father thwarted his misguided attempt to marry one of the family maids. Shiga later described this event in the novella *Ōtsu Junkichi* (1912), the first work for which he was actually paid. In fact it was to launch a counterattack against his father's disapproval and Uchimura's puritanical teachings—which forbade all sex outside marriage, including masturbation and the casual homosexual liaisons so common to young men of that era—that Shiga began to write.

In October 1912, three months after the death of the Meiji emperor, Shiga finally left home at the age of twenty-nine. His literary career was already well under way. For several years he had been publishing stories in an arts journal called *Shirakaba* (White birch) that he and some of his schoolmates from the Peers' School had founded in 1910. The group included Shiga's lifelong friend Mushakōji Saneatsu (1885–1976), Arishima Takeo (1878–1923), and Satomi Ton (1888–1983), young writers whose literary approaches varied greatly. All, however, shared a dislike of the prevailing Naturalist school, which was producing gloomy, pessimistic confessional literature. Led by Mushakōji, the *Shirakaba* group instead emphasized the importance of the individual and the value of ideals such as "love" and the "brotherhood of man." This sort of universal humanism may strike modern West-ern sensibilities as trite and overly optimistic, but in Shiga's time it was a novel perspective for educated young Japanese struggling to liberate themselves from the conservative, family-centered legacy of the feudal era. As a result, *Shirakaba* gained a great deal of attention and respect in intellectual and artistic circles.

The popularity of *Shirakaba* brought Shiga's literature into the limelight, but even after achieving literary success he remained a tense and moody man, quick to flare up at those around him and addicted to sex with prostitutes. Thinking that writing about his malaise might prove therapeutic, in 1912 he moved to the town of Onomichi on the Inland Sea, but the isolation proved too much for him and he returned the next spring a psychological wreck. Then, in August 1913, he was struck and almost killed by a train on Tokyo's Yamanote Line, an experience that changed his life. By the end of the following year, Shiga had married the widowed cousin of Mushakōji, had clashed once again with his father (who violently disapproved of the match), and had been formally stricken from the family register. But even after he was officially expelled from the family he continued to receive whatever funds he needed from his stepmother and grandmother. He published little in the four years between the accident and his reconciliation with his father in 1917, yet his experiences during that time—especially his visit to Mount Daisen and the death of his first child—provided the basis for his most lasting work, *An'ya kōro* (1937; *A Dark Night's Passing*, 1976).

Once the reconciliation had been achieved and memorialized in the novella *Wakai* (1917; *Reconciliation*, 1998), Shiga's life went smoothly, too smoothly perhaps for an author who relied on personal conflicts for his material. It seemed that once he had wrested the events of his tumultuous youth into literary form, a project that was more or less complete by the time he turned forty-five, there was little more for him to write about. By that juncture, however, Shiga's reputation had soared to remarkable heights, not only with the reading public but among his fellow writers as well.

Indeed, the reaction he inspired had a religious quality, as if his personal struggles had been undertaken on behalf of his countrymen as a whole. This perception was further strengthened in 1937 when his only full-length novel, *A Dark Night's Passing*—whose climactic scene unites two of Japan's most sacred symbols, the holy mountain and the rising sun—was published in its final form after a quarter-century-long gestation. By then Shiga was as much a revered icon as he was a respected writer.

Prewar icons of any sort were attacked during the postwar era, and Shiga was no exception. Some resented the privilege his wealth had afforded him and questioned whether less fortunate people could follow the path he had taken. It was easy enough to talk about enlightenment, they scoffed, when you never had to worry about finding a job or paying the bills. Others regarded the introspective autobiographical tradition he represented as an obstacle to social and literary progress. What was the good of personal fulfillment, they asked, if it did not translate into political action when the times demanded it? Had not the emphasis on personal material stunted the social vision of a whole generation of writers?

Shiga had no answers to these questions. The opposite side of his finely honed intuitive sense of life and art was a massive indifference to history and politics. Yet he was by no means a conservative man. When the literary world had split into two after the 1923 Great Kantō Earthquake, with the proletarian writers on one side and virtually everyone else on the other, Shiga had stood apart, respected by both camps but belonging to neither. He had even been a kind of literary mentor to several of the proletarian writers, especially the communist Kobayashi Takiji (1903–1933), probably the most gifted of the group. Shiga's advice to Kobayashi was not always very helpful—he rejected outright the idea that ideology had any positive role to play in art. Nevertheless he was a supportive friend, who, despite the risk to his own safety, wrote a public letter to Kobayashi's wife after he was tortured to death by the police. Characteristically, Shiga was honest and forthright in his criticism, something that Kobayashi and other authors always appreciated. Even in his old age young writers had a tendency to look to him for unsparing advice.

By that time Shiga had become a somewhat intimidating sage-like presence, presiding benevolently over a large extended family. His later works, personal essays and stories centering on his grandchildren and the small creatures in his garden, are short but filled with a warm and gentle spirit. When he died of natural causes in a Tokyo hospital on 21 October 1971 at the age of eighty-eight, it seemed as if he had melted naturally back into nature, reflecting the perspective from which he had written throughout his career. As he wrote in one of his last essays, "Nairu no mizu no itteki," (1969; A drop of Nile River water), published two years before his death:

In the tens of millions of years since the human race came into being, countless people have been born, have lived, and have died. I was born as one such person and for now I am still alive. Yet speaking metaphorically I am but a drop in the leisurely flow of the eternal Nile; and just as I did not exist thousands of years ago, so shall I never be born again, no matter how many thousands of years may pass. . . . And that is fine with me.

(*Shiga Naoya zenshū* [*SNZ*], vol.7, p. 649)

Literary Approach

Shiga was a self-confident man who relied on his instinctive reactions to things and valued intuition over rational thought. He was confident he could recognize great art on the basis of his spontaneous response to its intrinsic "rhythm" alone, and challenged others to do so as well. As he wrote in a 1931 essay titled "Rizumu" (Rhythm):

However skillful its execution, however impressive its content, any work of art whose rhythm is weak strikes us as false, and therefore trivial. . . . Why is mannerism in art so bad? After all, if you repeat the same pattern over and over again, you are bound to get more skillful at it. The problem is that as your skill increases, your spiritual rhythm weakens. . . . This is why "skillful" works of art are generally disappointing.

(*SNZ*, vol. 7, pp. 8–9)

Shiga was determined not to let his own writing descend to the level of the "skillful." To ensure that his own prose was animated by the kind of vigorous rhythm he perceived in the sculpture of Auguste Rodin and the stories of Ihara Saikaku (1642–1693), for example, he labored long and hard over many of his pieces, often spending weeks on a single short story. Yet when the mood was right he could write very quickly—his novella *Reconciliation* was written in fifteen days, while some of his later stories were dashed off in an hour or so. Everything, however, was marked by that distinctive manner of writing known as the "Shiga style."

Shiga's impetus for writing was his desire to cure himself of the dark obsessions and frustrations that plagued him, which he initially blamed on his father's intransigence and Uchimura Kanzō's puritanical teachings. For Shiga, writing was a quest to work out his feelings directly and honestly, to seek truth in a way that might change the trajectory of his own life and at the same time be of value to his readers. He was confident that by "healing himself" he could help others as well. Consequently, Shiga's literature follows a clear pattern, which moves from what we might call the negative to the positive side of life's spectrum: from conflict to harmony, from ugliness to beauty, and from the unnatural to the natural. Once harmony, beauty, and naturalness had come to mark his daily existence, he could write only about an enlightened life.

Shiga operated on the premise that all good literature was at the deepest level autobiographical. Yet he was not concerned with the "facts" of his experience so much as its "texture." Consequently he accepted the validity of the images, events, and even characters that came to him spontaneously and naturally, whether while writing or in his daily life. Indeed, Shiga felt that such imaginative experiences were just as real as anything else, a perspective that gives his fiction an almost primitive feeling. Near the beginning of *Reconciliation*, for example, the "Shiga hero" (a term coined by William Sibley in his 1979 book of the same name) visits the family gravesite to ask his grandfather if he should visit his ailing grandmother despite having been banned from the house by his father:

I walked for a bit before Grandfather's grave. Before long he came back to life in my mind's eye. I told him I wanted to go see Grandmother that day, and asked for his advice. "Then by all means go and see her," Grandfather immediately replied. Though this conversation took place in my imagination, it was unusually clear and natural. There was that feeling of objective reality that dream encounters possess—I felt he was really standing there, alive again. I could even sense him reaching out to caress his aging wife. And although my heart clearly condemned Father, the Grandfather that same heart had called up wasn't critical of Father in the least.

I moved on to my mother's grave. Her image was less clear and lifelike. I put the same question to her that I had to Grandfather but she was so timid and indecisive I gave up and walked on.

I decided to go visit Grandmother.

(*SNZ*, vol. 2, pp. 325–326; cf. tr. pp. 177–178)

Alone among modern Japanese writers, Shiga was able to present this kind of "hallucinatory" experience in an entirely natural and forthright way. Yet the way the hero (who is obviously meant to be Shiga himself) perceives his own mental processes is clearly unusual. He says, for example, that he hates his father but that the grandfather whose image rises before him does not. This implies there is some "other self" within his heart (or mind—the distinction is not clear) that feels differently than he does. Shiga developed an entire literary style based on this view of human nature.

Another element of Shiga's approach to writing was that the longer he waited before turning his experiences into literature, the more symbolic his writing was liable to be. A novella like *Reconciliation*, for example, composed immediately after the healing of the rift with his father, is quite "factual," although the perspective it embodies is Shiga's alone. On the other hand, *A Dark Night's Passing*, sections of which were written more than two decades after the events they describe, is highly fictionalized: Shiga's paternal grandfather, for example, was hardly the seedy character who appears in the novel, nor was Shiga a child of incest. Yet as far as Shiga was concerned *Reconciliation* and *A Dark Night's Passing* were both autobiographical, for each honestly conveyed his deepest feelings in their most spontaneous and natural form. Somewhat paradoxically, therefore, Shiga was a novelist and short story writer who deplored the very idea of "fiction," which he associated with artificiality and authorial manipulation.

The Shiga Style

Shiga's distinctive style is difficult to describe to readers who are approaching his work in translation. The words most frequently used have been "pure," "powerful," "unadorned," "masculine," and "direct," but these alone cannot explain its effect or why it has proved so impossible to imitate. Some have compared it with the style of Ernest Hemingway, which can be characterized in similar terms, but the cultural and linguistic barrier separating the two writers limits the usefulness of the comparison. To appreciate Shiga's achievement more fully, therefore, we must briefly consider how his style works in Japanese.

The first thing a foreign student of Japanese notices when he or she picks up one of Shiga's works is how easy it is to read. The sentences are short, the language concrete. There is even something childish about the style, with simple phrases like "It was good" or "It was bad" popping up at crucial junctures. The focus is usually very narrow, and dominated by the perceptions of the protagonist. These perceptions, however, are remarkably autonomous, seeming to exist outside the protagonist's control. Take, for example, the graveside scene quoted above. Shiga's character does not "remember" his grandfather. Rather, he puts himself in a situation where the image of the dead man spontaneously appears in his mind. Once there, it acts on its own, surprising him with its opinions and feelings. Yet at the same time the character knows that the image comes from his own heart. He even comments how strange it is that, although he is quite sure he hates his father, the grandfather his heart has called up doesn't seem to hate him at all. In short, instead of consciously controlling his experience, the protagonist plays a passive role. His perceptions control him.

This principle underlies the Shiga style. Shiga's characters don't actively "think" or "feel" so much as having thoughts and feelings happen to them. This distinction usually cannot be communicated clearly in translation, since English lacks the vocabulary for describing autonomous psychological phenomena. The Japanese language, however, is particularly rich in this area. Most notably for our purposes, a whole range of mental states can be described through the use of the small but very important word *ki* (*chi* in Chinese), the same ideograph used in the names of some of the martial arts: aikido, tai chi, and *chi kung*, in which intuitive aspects of the participants' psychology are at least as important as physical training. In Japanese syntax, *ki* operates almost like an independent entity. When your *ki* "sinks," for example, you become depressed. If your *ki* "goes far away," you grow faint. A "long" *ki* signifies patience, a "short" *ki* impatience. When your *ki* "fastens" onto something, you notice it, and so on and so forth. Japanese people do not usually think of *ki* in this independent way: in functional

335

terms, these phrases work exactly like their English equivalents. But the role of *ki* in the Japanese language reflects a view of personality that readily accepts the normality of mental events occurring independently of a controlling self.

The Shiga style is constructed within this semantic-psychological space. The Shiga hero is dominated by his *ki*, which lives inside him like another self. It dictates his moods and thoughts and singles out the objects that grab his attention. When his *ki* turns inward, the hero plunges into a dark and unpleasant frame of mind. Obsessions and compulsions force him this way and that. He tries to escape by reasoning his way out, but his *ki* stubbornly refuses to let him do so. Willpower is also useless. Yet from time to time his *ki* releases its tyrannical grip and attaches itself to things in the outside world. Living creatures like animals, birds, and insects attract it. So do other phenomena which manifest the "rhythm" of life, like works of art and children. Certain powerful stimuli like the illness of a loved one can hold its attention for long periods of time. Finally, after an extended struggle, the pattern reverses itself and the *ki*'s focus shifts permanently outward, away from the hero's inner world. Once this occurs the hero is a transformed man, open and happy. Moreover, thanks to his *ki*'s ability to enter into things, he becomes peculiarly able to "merge" with his surroundings. Paradoxically, the very part of himself that once caused his painful self-centeredness—his *ki*—now serves to link him with the outside.

Shiga never conceptualized his own efforts in this manner. As far as he was concerned, he was just trying to convey the "rhythm" of his own experience with as much clarity and power as he could muster. He hoped the results would be beautiful, of course, like the works of Rodin, Saikaku, and the other artists he admired, but that beauty had to come from an inner source—it could not be a matter of technique. "Style" from his perspective was identical to "personality." Critics, too, spoke of the man and his style in the same breath. There

seemed to be no room for skepticism. Even Kobayashi Hideo (1902–1983), the greatest critic of his generation, admitted he was "awestruck" by Shiga's intuitive sense of what to include (and what to leave out) in describing a scene, concluding that the movement of Shiga's own *ki* was actually making the choices. Karatani Kōjin (b. 1941), who has inherited Kobayashi's mantle, has taken this line of analysis one step further. Does it even make sense, Karatani questions provocatively, to talk of "subjectivity" in Shiga's literature given the way that he and his characters are "subject" to their *ki*, which dominates their perception and judgment?

"Seibei's Gourds," "Han's Crime," and the Nature of the Artist

Two early stories, "Seibei to hyōtan" (1913; "Seibei's Gourds," 1960) and "Han no hanzai" (1913; "Han's Crime," 1956), touch upon Shiga's deep interest in the nature of artistic creation and its relationship to the unconscious rhythms of life. "Seibei's Gourds" tells of a twelve-year-old boy, Seibei, who is drawn to the gourds sold as decorative objects in many of the shops in his provincial hometown. Serious collectors prize gourds with unusual shapes, but Seibei prefers those which are even and symmetrical, and he devotes himself to tracking down and painstakingly preparing those that meet his standards. Then one day he comes across the perfect gourd, about five inches long with a seemingly commonplace shape. Instantly smitten, he refuses to let the gourd out of his sight, taking it with him to school where he polishes it under his desk during class. Caught in the act by his ethics teacher, a humorless man, his precious gourd is confiscated. After a home visit by the teacher, his infuriated father smashes the entire collection with a hammer. Seibei pales but says nothing. Not long afterward, he shifts his attentions to painting, and the story ends with the lines: "He no longer feels any bitterness either toward the teacher, or toward his father who smashed all his precious gourds to pieces. Yet gradually his father has begun to scold him for painting pictures" (*SNZ*, vol. 2, p. 61; tr. p. 89).

This brief, lighthearted story is beloved by many Japanese who may have first encountered it in their school textbooks. Yet, like Seibei's confiscated gourd (which is eventually sold to a collector for a small fortune) more is here than first meets the eye. What for example, explains Seibei's fascination with the gourds? We might note their resemblance to male genitalia, and see in their curved shape and dark recesses a further connection to the womb and its mysteries. These sexual connotations, however, are not the whole story. "Seibei's Gourds" is also a portrait of the artist as a very young man, who discovers a perfection and beauty within nature that includes, but is not limited to, the sexual principle. This intuitive appreciation carries him beyond the bounds of conventional society—represented by his moralistic teacher and repressive, boorish father—into the creative realm. For Seibei the gourds are linked to the powerful rhythm he is beginning to sense within himself, and his ability to extend this connection through his painting shows just how deeply felt, and how broad, it is.

"Seibei's Gourds" was published in January 1913, "Han's Crime" nine months later. In between, however, Shiga had suffered his train accident, which changed him markedly. "Han's Crime" was the first thing he wrote after leaving the hospital. It is a disturbing, claustrophobic story about a Chinese juggler who kills his wife during a stage act in which he hurls large knives in a tight pattern around her body. The story is set in the courtroom where the murder trial is being held, and its core consists of Han's interrogation by the trial judge. Uncharacteristically for Shiga, who disdained clever plots and surprise endings (the outcome of "Seibei's Gourds," for example, is given away in the story's opening lines), "Han's Crime" is tightly structured and concludes with the judge's dramatic verdict. Its real focus, however, is on the meaning of con-fession, the role of instinct, and the risks and joys involved in living a "natural" life.

Han's testimony is the opposite of what we normally expect from a man on trial: instead of proclaiming his innocence, or at least minimizing his guilt, he rebuts all evidence in his favor. Yes, he had entertained thoughts of killing his wife, who had conceived a child by another man and who was blocking his efforts toward living a "truer life." No, he had not thought it accidental when the knife struck her throat—he assumed he had done it on purpose. When he knelt in prayer the next moment it was a sham to fool the onlookers. Yet while preparing his plea the night before the trial it had suddenly dawned on him that he didn't know whether or not he had really intended to kill her. This realization, he says, made him intensely happy. "Because you had come to consider it an accident?" the judge asks. "No," Han answers, "because I no longer had the slightest idea as to whether it had been intentional or not. . . . In fact, I can plead neither 'guilty' nor 'not guilty.'" "(Then) do you not feel the slightest sorrow for your wife's death?" "None at all! Even when I hated my wife most bitterly in the past, I never could have imagined I would feel such happiness in talking about her death" (*SNZ*, vol. 2, pp. 90–91; tr. pp. 270–271). Strangely excited by Han's testimony, the judge without deliberation writes "Not Guilty" on the trial document.

While Seibei embodies the artist's sensitivity to the rhythms of nature and the self, Han epitomizes that zeal for truth at any price so essential to Shiga's autobiographical fiction. Like Shiga, Han once hoped Christianity would help him escape his personal labyrinth, but was disappointed. Thrown back on his own devices, he struggled to reason his way out, but failed. Finally at the crucial moment his instinct took over, guiding the knife on its fatal flight. Han does not realize this, however, until the night before the trial when he is preparing his defense, trying to organize and verbalize his thoughts and feelings in a manner that the judge, and he himself, can understand. Through this creative "literary" process he achieves his breakthrough and frees himself from his long nightmare. He also exercises a profound impact on the judge, the "reader," who is inspired by Han's hard-won epiphany. Thus, although "Han's Crime" is rightly considered one of Shiga's most fictional stories, it demonstrates the benefits of the confessional style of writing for author and reader alike.

Ōtsu Junkichi, *Reconciliation*, and the Return to Family

Unlike "Seibei's Gourds" and "Han's Crime," the novellas *Ōtsu Junkichi* (1912) and *Reconciliation* (1917) are closely based on actual events in Shiga's life. Together they form a literary record of Shiga's long feud with his father and the sequence of events that finally brought the two men back together, restoring peace to the family. There were natural reasons for the rift. Raised by his grandparents, Shiga worshiped his grandfather and was closer to his grandmother than to anyone else in the world. In a sense, therefore, he and his father were like siblings competing for parental love. Moreover, Shiga's stepmother, whom he called "Mother," was closer in age to him than to his father, another potential source of jealousy and frustration. Finally, Shiga's father was first dismayed and then, as the implications of having an author in the family became apparent, furious at his son's choice of profession. It was bad enough that Shiga showed no interest in supporting himself, but having complete strangers reading about private family matters—including their quarrel—was insupportable.

Ōtsu Junkichi, titled after the name of its hero and published in 1912, was based on events of five years earlier in 1907, when Shiga, in a welter of sexual frustration, had recklessly proposed to one of the family maids, only to have his plans vetoed by the entire family. Although Shiga blamed his father at the time, the novella makes it clear that his own erratic and volatile temperament was responsible. In fact it was Shiga's powerful evo-

cation of his state of mind that resonated with his new audience, who were struck by the direct and seemingly honest way he was able to communicate his feelings.

Chief among these feelings—the emotive coda as it were—is the dark, congested mood created by *ki* in its inward-turning mode. In Shiga's fiction this malaise can be triggered by the most trivial occurrence, like being made to wait for service in a bank. It can also, however, lead to despair or even violence, as in the case of the Chinese juggler Han, whose state of mind is described in terms quite similar to Junkichi's. Whereas Han achieves a personal breakthrough the night before his trial, however, Junkichi finds himself utterly stymied. Time and again he struggles to free himself, all the while convincing himself that his father is the ultimate cause of his affliction, the barrier blocking his way to a "truer life." Yet he is grappling with a phantom, for the roots of his problem lie within himself. Indeed, by the end of *Ōtsu Junkichi* it does not appear there is anything at all that can cure Junkichi's painful condition.

Reconciliation was published in 1917, five years after *Ōtsu Junkichi*, and ten years after the events that the earlier novella describes. Its hero is also an autobiographical novelist called Ōtsu Junkichi. Yet, whereas *Ōtsu* ends with Junkichi writhing in impotent frustration as the maid is whisked out of reach by his scheming father, *Reconciliation* concludes with a tearful reconciliation between the two men. In one sense, therefore, the latter work is a record of Junkichi's "cure." Moreover, just as the judge's verdict is really no more than a stamp of legitimacy on Han's personal breakthrough, so is the dramatic climax of *Reconciliation* merely the capstone of Junkichi's successful struggle to free himself from the malaise that had dominated his life. To appreciate the novella, therefore, it helps to look beyond the father-son relationship at the sequence of events that transformed Junkichi's (and by implication, Shiga's own) life.

Three events in particular stand out: the death of Junkichi's first child, the birth of his second, and the illness of his aging grandmother. *Reconciliation*'s literary success lies in Shiga's ability to evoke these intensely personal yet universal experiences. The description of the baby's illness and death is particularly memorable, albeit grueling reading. Until this point Junkichi has been a highly introspective character, but during the crisis his gaze, directed by his *ki*, never wavers as one procedure after another is carried out on the tiny body. In the end, eight people—Junkichi, his friends and neighbors and a local doctor—are working frantically trying to keep the baby alive, to no avail.

As *Reconciliation* progresses it becomes clear how much this painful experience has taught Junkichi. Gradually, he begins to break free of his self-centered view of things, on occasion even sympathizing with his father's position. Yet the enmity remains. A second child is born. In the absence of a doctor or midwife, Junkichi is forced to assist with the delivery, a breach of Japanese custom that allows him to witness the other pole of the life-death continuum. He finds the birth "beautiful." Buoyed by his turn of fortune and the presence of one of his closest friends, "M" (Mushakōji Saneatsu in real life), he feels things are finally looking up. Then, suddenly, his eighty-two-year-old grandmother falls ill. Breaking his father's ban, he goes to the family home to see her and is shocked by her weakened condition, which is described in the same unsparing language as the baby's death was. Soon, however, word comes that his father wants him out of the house. This is the scene that Junkichi has imagined leading to violence; yet in the end he is able to withdraw without provoking a confrontation. "I was exasperated," he reflects. "And I was angry too. Still, nothing had happened that I hadn't anticipated, so I was able to keep this exasperation from overwhelming me" (*SNZ*, vol. 2, p. 391; cf. tr. p. 221).

Shiga's use of the word "anticipate" connects to one of *Reconciliation*'s most striking features: the close relationship between Junkichi's struggle to write and his ongoing feud with his father. Shiga, it may be remembered, published virtually nothing in the four years

between his marriage and the reconciliation. He had promised the eminent novelist Natsume Sōseki that he would produce a long work about his feud with his father, which would be serialized in the mass-circulation *Asahi* newspaper. This was to be Shiga's big break—the work preceding his would be Sōseki's timeless masterpiece *Kokoro*—but it also presented a serious problem, since it meant that many of his father's friends and acquaintances (not to mention his father himself) would likely read it. Time and again he struggled to meet Sōseki's and his own expectations, only to fail. "Well then," Sōseki suggested to Shiga when he realized the seriousness of the problem. "Why not write a novel about being unable to write?"

Reconciliation is indeed a novella about being unable to write, strewn with references to works that Junkichi has been forced to leave unfinished. These apparently futile attempts, however, often have a positive influence on his personal life. In one planned novel begun shortly before his marriage, for example, Junkichi "anticipates" his own possible future by having a young man confront his father over his grandmother's deathbed. Junkichi intends to make the climax a bloody one, yet when he pictures the scene the two men suddenly throw themselves into each other's arms and weep violently. Junkichi is taken by surprise, and even cries himself. Yet he resists the temptation to plot the novel that way, reasoning that such things should not be planned in advance. Still he wonders if the same thing might not happen with his own father. "It was not inconceivable," he ponders, "that such an event might occur suddenly when our relationship was at its most wretched. Then again, it might not happen at all. Though I wouldn't know for certain until we reached that point, I sensed that something dwelt within both of us that could produce such an abrupt reversal." (*SNZ*, vol. 2, p. 368; cf. tr. p. 205)

This "you can't know till you get there" approach dominated Shiga's philosophy of life and art. Relationships, like stories, could not be plotted without sacrificing their integral rhythm and infecting the people involved. It is with a similar thought in mind that Junkichi makes his way to his father's study at the end of the novella. It is the anniversary of his mother's death, and her presence is very much felt, as is that of his dead child (on whose death anniversary the story began) and even that of his elder brother, who died before he was born. The priest has just left, so the whole family is still dressed in formal clothes, and when the reconciliation has been accomplished—rather too easily, some have complained—the house is awash in tears. Events follow with the stately inevitability of ritual: relatives are notified, the father takes Junkichi's young sisters to visit his home and see the new baby, and Junkichi arranges for a friend to paint his father's portrait as a symbolic gesture of respect. It is, in short, a most Confucian conclusion with all family members living and dead in their proper places and the prodigal son restored to the fold. Fittingly, then, the novella ends with a Chinese poem from the Sung dynasty which Junkichi's uncle, a Zen devotee, appends to his letter of congratulations on the reconciliation:

> From north, south, east, and west
> All fly home to roost
> Huddled together in the dead of night
> They gaze upon the thousand
>   snow-capped peaks

A Dark Night's Passing and the Return to Nature

Once the feud with his father was over, Shiga's writer's block disappeared. Exhilarated by the event, he dashed off *Reconciliation* in record time, and also wrote a number of short stories. Then he turned back to his bête noire, the long project he had originally promised the *Asahi* newspaper. He thought it a shame to throw away something on which he had labored so long and hard, yet he wondered how could he continue now that his feelings about his father—the focus of the narrative—had been so transformed. Over the next decade, he worked

to resolve this problem, publishing a rewritten portion here, a new chapter there, almost as if he were composing a linked chain of short stories. By 1928 all was complete except the final "Mount Daisen" section. By the time that was done in 1937 Shiga had been working on his magnum opus—now titled *A Dark Night's Passing*—for nearly twenty-five years, a span that made it more "fictional" and symbolic than anything else he had ever written. Indeed, by taking the "quest for harmony" theme of *Reconciliation* to a mythic level, Shiga turned *A Dark Night's Passing* into an epic for modern times.

As its title suggests, *A Dark Night's Passing* portrays the "Shiga hero"—here named Tokitō Kensaku—struggling to move from a state of spiritual darkness into a brighter world. It opens with Kensaku's recollections of his childhood: the death of his mother when he was six; the seedy grandfather who took him away from his family two months later; his attraction to the grandfather's young mistress, Oei; his father's inexplicable coldness; and, finally and most pathetically, his memory of the only time his mother showed she loved him, when he was balancing precariously on the roof of their home. After this brief introduction, the narrative voice shifts from the first to the third person and remains there until the novel's final lines. Yet the perspective is exclusively that of Kensaku, an even more tormented young man than Ōtsu Junkichi. For whereas Junkichi had a doting grandmother, a kind stepmother, and a bevy of lively young half-sisters on his side, Kensaku has no one except Oei—who has stayed on with him as a kind of housekeeper and surrogate mother after his grandfather's death—and an elder brother, Nobuyuki, whom he seldom sees. It is thus clear from the start that no joyous family reunion awaits Kensaku. If he is going to find a place to call home in this world, he will have to create it himself.

In the opening sections of *A Dark Night's Passing*, Kensaku, who like Junkichi has been influenced by puritanical Christian ideas regarding sex, seems to spend most of his time clumsily flirting with geishas and then agonizing about it afterward. Eventually he gives in and starts visiting prostitutes. As his state of mind grows more feverish, he begins harboring desires for Oei, who is twenty years older and the closest thing to a mother he has ever known. Realizing there is something unhealthy about this, and wanting to focus on his writing, he leaves Tokyo for the town of Onomichi on the island-studded Inland Sea, the spot where Shiga worked on the first drafts of what was to become *A Dark Night's Passing*. There Kensaku rents a small house on the slope overlooking the harbor. At first this works like a charm. His writing progresses and his spirits brighten. Before long, however, he is back where he began, his writing blocked and the daily monotony punctuated by nightly trips down the slope to the local brothel. Finally, during what he hopes will be a restorative boat trip around the islands, he comes up with the solution to his dilemma—he must marry Oei! Knowing that she will be startled (to say the least) by the idea, he writes to ask his brother Nobuyuki to broach the matter in his stead.

Nobuyuki's reply reveals the shameful secret of Kensaku's parentage: his real father is actually his detestable "grandfather," who took advantage of his daughter-in-law while his son was out of the country. Kensaku is shaken by the information. He spends much time contemplating the nature of sin and forgiveness and the vulnerability of a woman's lot; soon, however, he is back in Tokyo living with Oei as before. Then, in a scene that has inspired some and perplexed others, Kensaku's gloomy existence is suddenly brightened by the breast of one of the prostitutes he has been visiting:

When he reached out and held her round, heavy breast he was filled with an indefinable sense of comfort and satisfaction. It was as though he had touched something very precious. He let it rest on the palm of his hand, then shook it a little so that he could feel the full weight of it. There were no words to express the pleasure he experienced then. . . . It was for him somehow a symbol of all that was precious to him, of whatever it was that promised to fill the emptiness inside him.

(*SNZ*, vol. 5, p. 275; tr. p. 197)

The breast is far more than a sexual image. It could be likened, perhaps, to Seibei's perfect gourd, for its implications are wide-ranging and filled with a certain mystery. While it temporarily satisfies Kensaku's longing for maternal love, it also seems to manifest what Shiga perceived as the essence of life's riches in its perfect shape and weight. If Kensaku can somehow join himself to that fullness on a permanent basis, the image implies, then happiness will be his.

This hopeful atmosphere carries over into the second half of *A Dark Night's Passing*. When it opens, Kensaku is living in the beautiful old capital of Kyoto. Surrounded by its green hills and ancient art, he seems like a new man. He is able to marry the woman of his choice and they have a baby. When the infant falls ill and dies, however, his life begins to darken once again. Reverting to his self-centered mode of behavior, he neglects his equally bereaved wife. Then, while he is away on a trip, she is forcibly seduced by her cousin. He consciously attempts to forgive her. Yet the similarity between the circumstances of his own conception and this event make forgiveness impossible. Finally, after inadvertently knocking her down onto a train platform (a reflexive act that recalls the Chinese juggler Han's "guiltless" killing of his unfaithful wife, although Kensaku's wife here does not die), he decides to travel to Mount Daisen, a holy mountain overlooking the Sea of Japan, to try to cure his spiritual malady once and for all.

The "Mount Daisen" passages in *A Dark Night's Passing* are among the most famous in modern Japanese literature. In a simple but poetic style, they describe Kensaku's life on the mountain and the steps leading up to his final awakening. He lives in a small temple annex halfway up the slope. It is comfortable, but the food is bad and he grows progressively weaker. The Buddhist priests he meets are disappointingly profane. The several local people he befriends, though, strike him as almost holy in their purity, teaching him much about innocence and forgiveness. Most of the time, though, he spends alone. He particularly enjoys observing small birds and insects, and, when he writes to his wife, he encloses an essay describing a spider struggling with a beetle to show her his new frame of mind. One night he sets out to climb to the summit, but illness and physical exhaustion force him to stop partway. There, high on the slope, he undergoes the kind of loss of self we normally associate with a religious experience:

> He felt his exhaustion turn into a strange state of rapture. He could feel his mind and his body both gradually merging into this great nature that surrounded him. It was not nature that was visible to the eyes; rather, it was like a limitless body of air that wrapped itself around him, this tiny creature no larger than a poppy seed. . . .
>
> It was so still a night, even the night birds were silent. If there were lights in the village below, they were quite hidden by the mist that lay over the rooftops. And all that he could see above him were the stars and the outline of the mountains, curved like the back of some huge beast. He felt as if he had just taken a step on the road to eternity. Death held no threat for him.

(*SNZ*, vol. 2, pp. 578–579; tr. pp. 400–401)

Kensaku gently slips into sleep, and when he opens his eyes a new day is dawning. He notices everything—the plants and birds, the islands in the distance, the villages at the foot of the slope—as if for the first time. Then, as the sun rises over Mount Daisen, he sees the shadow of the mountain creeping toward him across the bay.

The rising sun, the sacred mountain, a mystical union with nature—no writer other than Shiga could have joined these three in this fashion without seeming pompous or sentimental. Given his open identification with his hero, moreover, Shiga was in effect proclaiming his own spiritual enlightenment. But Shiga's ability to communicate the dynamics of *ki*, that aspect of mind he saw as operating outside the reach of the conscious ego, was perfectly suited to the task of making Kensaku's union with "great nature" and its aftermath concrete and real, free of the self-congratulatory atmosphere that so often accompanies stories of enlightenment. Readers were inspired by these passages, not just when the book came out but later, after the debacle of the Pacific War, when it was hard to approach the future with any measure of self-confidence. The critic Akiyama Shun (b. 1930), for example, wrote that the second half of *A Dark Night's Passing* was the only piece of literature that really mattered to him during those years. Thus Shiga's portrait of a return to nature became a healing force for his countrymen and a touchstone for modern Japanese culture.

"At Kinosaki," "Night Fires," and the "Plotless" Story

Shiga was better at constructing short narratives than long ones. Parts of *A Dark Night's Passing* read more like short stories strung together than a cohesive novel; and the ending, in which the perspective shifts to Kensaku's wife as he hovers near death after his descent from the mountain, is weak. While Shiga had to labor over extended pieces, however, shorter ones were more like play for him, especially when they focused on nature and its creatures. In fact, although his most productive periods were relatively brief—from 1910 to 1913 and then again from 1917 until about 1929—Shiga wrote nature stories and sketches steadily throughout his life. This is not to say, however, that all are of a kind. "Kinosaki nite" (1917; "At Kinosaki," 1956), for example, is a structured story that reflects the shadow cast over Shiga's life by his near-fatal accident in 1913. "Takibi" (1920; "Night Fires," 1997), on the other hand, is an outwardly "plotless" work bathed in the kind of light that envelops the Mount Daisen sections of *A Dark Night's Passing*.

Given his antipathy toward plot, Shiga would not have been pleased to have "At Kinosaki" referred to as "structured." As far as he was concerned, this brief story was a factual record of his experiences while he was recuperating at a hot springs inn on the Sea of Japan. Yet as Stephen Kohl and others have pointed out, the deaths of the bee, the rat, and the lizard in this story follow a clear progression, which matches the hero's reactions to his own near-death experience. As the story opens, the hero appears to be in no physical pain—in fact he is enjoying "a pleasant feeling of quiet and repose" that he hasn't had in years. Still, his head is muddled, and he is strangely forgetful. He shows no interest in people but is drawn to a dead bee (a creature of the air) lying near his veranda, which strikes him as "lonely" but soothing. Then while on an afternoon stroll he sees a crowd tormenting a large rat (a creature of the earth), which is futilely struggling to get out of the river. Again the hero feels a kinship with the doomed animal. He reflects that after his accident he too had done everything he could to survive. Finally, while on an evening walk along a stream outside of town, he spies a small lizard (a creature of the deep) and idly tosses a stone in its general direction. To his surprise the stone strikes and kills the lizard, leaving the hero facing an animal he has inadvertently murdered. (The fact that lizards were the animals Shiga most hated during his youth adds a *Han's Crime*–like element to the story.) By chance, the lizard died. By chance, he survived. He knows he should be grateful, but the proper feeling doesn't come to him. "To be alive and to be dead were not two opposite extremes," he muses. "There did not seem to be much difference between them" (*SNZ*, vol. 2, p. 82; tr. p. 277). In the end we see him trudging down the slope in the dark, drawn by the lights of the town.

Life and death are brought together in quite different ways here and near the end of *A Dark Night's Passing*. In each story, the hero has his rational powers subverted by illness or accident, allowing new "irrational" forms of awareness to come to the fore. Kensaku's breakthrough, however, is the culmination of a long and arduous process, whereas the hero of "At Kinosaki" has the experience thrust upon him. His is not the joyous embrace of nature in all its dimensions. Rather, death alone is reaching out for him. At first he is attracted, but gradually the landscape around him grows more eerie, the creatures less appealing. He cannot help identifying with them, however, for like all Shiga's characters his *ki* attaches itself to whatever catches its attention. He is, as it were, being pulled down into the valley of death, and the story's final lines suggest that three years later he is still there.

A Dark Night's Passing and "At Kinosaki" both have clear trajectories, despite their great difference in length. The hero of *A Dark Night's Passing*, for example, is continually moving upward spatially (beginning in low-lying Tokyo) and backward in time, from a modern metropolis to one of the sites of Japan's ancient mountain religion. The hero of "At Kinosaki," by contrast, is heading in a downward direction, as is reflected in his final descent and the bee-rat-lizard sequence. In both instances, moreover, the trajectory is the main structural principle for the narrative. In other words, Shiga's hero either moves "up" toward a higher plane of consciousness (as in *A Dark Night's Passing* and *Reconciliation*) or "down" into a more desperate or gloomy frame of mind (as in *Ōtsu Junkichi* and "At Kinosaki"). In either case, writer and reader alike have a clear sense of direction as they move through the work: there is a thread holding the story together.

What happens, though, once enlightenment is attained? Almost by definition that condition implies not ups or downs, but a state of calm equilibrium. In the short story "Night Fires" Shiga undertakes to write his autobiographical fiction from such a standpoint. Shiga wrote the first half of "Night Fires" within days of the events described—a trip to the mountains he took with his wife shortly after their marriage—then completed the work five years later. It is, some readers have complained, a story in which nothing happens.

343

Shiga, his wife, and a close friend stroll in the mountains, take a boat ride on the lake, and build a bonfire. There are no accidents or quarrels, nor is there any strain between them and the young innkeeper who acts as their guide. The closest thing to drama is the innkeeper's story about his mother who "heard" him call when he was miles away struggling to make it home through deep snow. This anecdote, however, bears no obvious relationship to the rest of the narrative. In fact, on the surface there seems to be no thread of any kind holding the various pieces together.

Beneath the surface of "Night Fires," however, is quite literally a different story. Far from being a backdrop for human events, nature plays a vibrant, active role, while the human protagonists blend together in a kind of undifferentiated group identity. Like a chorus, they are shown thinking and feeling in unison, raising their voices in wonderment at the mysteries that surround them. Other boundaries are obliterated as well. Images of light and darkness reveal their essential oneness: the fires reflected on the water's surface; the stars in the water; the glowworms on the forest floor; and in the story's final image, the burning sticks from the bonfire thrown into the lake. "Red sparks scattered like powder as they hurtled through the night. Two identical flaming arcs, one above, one below, converging, meeting with a hiss on the water's face. Then total darkness" (*SNZ*, vol. 3, p. 5; tr. p. 61). Even the innkeeper's story serves to underscore the flimsiness of the "common sense" separation we assume to divide, in his case, the heart of a mother from the child she loves.

The thread that binds "Night Fires," in short, is taken from a cloth that is likely to be unfamiliar to us. It is made primarily of images, and has little to do with ideas, characterization, and dramatic development. Since it follows no linear pattern it can be broken off at virtually any point. Akutagawa Ryūnosuke was particularly enamored with this principle of composition. He called works like "Night Fires" "plotless stories," and said they evoked "the poetic spirit of East Asia." Yet Akutagawa was unable to write them himself. Instead, it took someone less analytical and more "intuitive" like Shiga Naoya to develop the form. Most of the stories Shiga managed to write after he finished *A Dark Night's Passing* were of the "plotless" variety. In them as in "Night Fires" the "Shiga hero" ceases to be the focus of the narrative—rather we see through him, as if he were transparent. In the process, the line between fiction and nonfiction, already so tenuous in Shiga's case, disappears altogether.

Selected Bibliography

PRIMARY WORKS

MAJOR WORKS

Ōtsu Junkichi. Chūō Kōron, 1912. Partial trans. by Ted Goossen in *Descant* (Toronto) 19, no. 4 (winter 1988).

"Seibei to hyōtan." *Yomiuri*, 1913. Trans. by Ivan Morris as "Seibei's Gourds." In *Modern Japanese Stories*. Edited by Ivan Morris. Tokyo and Rutledge, Vt.: Tuttle Press, 1962.

"Han no hanzai." *Shirakaba*, 1913. Trans. by Ivan Morris as "Han's Crime." In *Modern Japanese Literature*. Edited by Donald Keene. New York: Grove Press, 1956.

"Kinosaki nite." *Shirakaba*, 1917. Trans. by Edward Seidensticker as "At Kinosaki." In *Modern Japanese Literature*. Edited by Donald Keene. New York: Grove Press, 1956.

Wakai. Kuroshio, 1917. Trans. by Roy Starrs as *Reconciliation*. In his *An Artless Art: The Zen Aesthetic of Shiga Naoya*. Surrey, U.K.: Curzon Press, 1998.

"Takibi." *Kaizō*, 1920. Trans. by Ted Goossen as "Night Fires." In *The Oxford Book of Japanese Short Stories*. Edited by Theodore W. Goossen. Oxford: Oxford University Press, 1997.

An'ya kōro. Tokyo: Kaizō Press, 1937. Trans. by Edwin McClellan as *A Dark Night's Passing*. Tokyo: Kodansha International, 1976.

Shiga Naoya zenshū (*SNZ*). Tokyo: Iwanami Shoten, 1973. (Complete works of Shiga Naoya.)

OTHER SELECTED WORKS

"Abashiri made." *Shirakaba*, 1910. Trans. by Dunlop as "As Far as Abashiri," 1987. (A concise yet strangely touching account of an encounter with an overtaxed mother and her two children on a five-day train trip to Abashiri, probably to visit the father in the prison there.)

"Kamisori." *Shirakaba*, 1910. Trans. by Sibley as "The Razor," 1979. (The disquieting story of a fastidious barber pushed past the breaking point, who slits the throat of a particularly loathsome customer.)

"Nigotta atama" (A cobwebbed mind). *Shirakaba*, 1911. (As with "Han's Crime" and "The Razor," a portrait of a man driven to "unintentionally" kill someone. This time the victim is a dominant older woman, a relative of the protagonist's mother, with whom he is sexually involved.)

"Sobo no tame ni." *Shirakaba*, 1912. Trans. by Sibley as "For Grandmother," 1979. (A story focusing on Shiga's intense relationship with his grandmother, made particularly memorable by a disturbing dream sequence and the eerie figure of an albino mortician.)

"Haha no shi to atarashii haha" (Mother's death and my new mother). *Shuran*, 1912. (An account of the death of Shiga's mother when he was twelve and the introduction of her successor into the family some months later.)

"Kurōdiasu no nikki." *Shirakaba*, 1912. Trans. by Starr as "The Diary of Claudius," 1998. (A quirky version of *Hamlet* told from Claudius's point of view, in which he claims to be innocent of his brother's murder and tries to make peace with his nephew/stepson.)

"Ko o nusumu hanashi." *Shirakaba*, 1914. Trans. by Sibley as "The Kidnapping," 1979. (This story of a lonely writer who kidnaps a five-year-old girl provides another angle on the "Onomichi" section of *A Dark Night's Passing*.)

"Akinishi Kakita." *Shinshōsetsu*, 1917. Trans. by Dunlop as "Akinishi Kakita," 1987. (An amusing portrait of a dour but pure-hearted samurai who sends a bogus love letter to a beautiful young woman with unexpected results.)

"Kozō no kamisama." *Shirakaba*, 1920. Trans. by Dunlop as "The Shopboy's God," 1987. (An endearing story about a poor apprentice who is treated to a sushi meal by a shy nobleman. This is one of Shiga's most popular works.)

Aru otoko, sono ane no shi (A certain man and the death of his sister). *Osaka Mainichi Shinbun*, 1920. (A novella that covers much the same material as *Reconciliation* but from the perspective of the hero's younger brother. Shiga described *Reconciliation* as a fish freshly caught, this work as the same fish, dried.)

"Manazuru." *Chūō Kōron*, 1920. Trans. by Kohl as "Manazuru," 1977. (A charming story about two small brothers' trip to town, where the older boy is entranced by a heavily made-up female traveling performer.)

"Amagaeru." *Chūō Kōron*, 1924. Trans. by Dunlop as "Rain Frogs," 1987. (A story about a local sake brewer whose innocent young wife is seduced by a touring writer, leaving him in a strangely excited frame of mind.)

"Horibata no sumai." *Fuji*, 1925. Trans. by Fowler as "Dwelling by the Moat," 1977. (One of Shiga's most interesting nature stories, this tale raises the issues of guilt and forgiveness as these do (or do not) pertain to the animal kingdom.)

"Chijō." *Kaizō*, 1926. Trans. by Dunlop as "Infatuation," 1987. (One of several stories Shiga wrote about an affair he had while he was living in a place called Yamashina, and its impact on his marriage.)

"Kuniko." *Bungei Shunjū*, 1927. Trans. by Dunlop as "Kuniko," 1987. (Another of the so-called Yamashina cycle, this is a long story about a playwright's affair with an actress, and its tragic effect on his wife.)

"Hōnen mushi." *Shūkan Asahi*, 1929. (A beautiful essay-like story whose conclusion juxtaposes the fame of the writer with the brief lives of swarming insects.)

"Hai-iro no tsuki" (Harvest bugs). *Sekai*, 1946. Trans. by Kohl as "The Ashen Moon," 1977. (This slight essay describes Shiga's reaction to his encounter with a starving youth immediately after the end of World War II.)

"Yamabato." *Kokoro*, 1950. Trans. by Goossen as "Turtledoves," 1988. (A brief recounting of Shiga's affection for a pair of birds, one of which he ends up eating.)

"Asagao." *Kokoro*, 1954. Trans. by Goossen as "Morning-Glories," 1988. (A glimpse of Shiga's life in old age, this story includes another example of his close identification with nature, this time in the form of a kind of bee or "drone fly.")

"Shiroi sen" (White line). *Sekai*, 1956. (Shiga's final reminiscence about his mother. Since he was so young when she died his memories are indistinct, but he recalls the "white line" of her calf as she polished the floors.)

WORKS IN ENGLISH TRANSLATION

Dunlop, Lane. *The Paper Door and Other Stories by Shiga Naoya*. San Francisco: North Point Press, 1987. Reprint, New York: Columbia University Press, forthcoming. (Includes "As Far as Abashiri," "Akinishi Kakita," "The Shopboy's God," "Rain Frogs," "Infatuation," "Kuniko," and other stories.)

Fowler, Edward. "Death and Divine Indifference in 'Dwelling by the Moat.'" *Monumenta Nipponica* (Tokyo) 32, no. 2:225–234 (1977). (Issue includes Fowler's translation "Dwelling by the Moat.")

Goossen, Theodore, and Kin'ya Tsuruta, eds. *Nature and Identity in Canadian and Japanese Literature*. Toronto: University of Toronto and York University Joint Centre for Asia Pacific Studies, 1988. (Includes Goossen's translations "Turtledoves," "Morning-Glories," and other stories.)

Kohl, Stephen. "Shiga Naoya and the Literature of Experience." *Monumenta Nipponica* (Tokyo) 32, no. 2:211–224 (1977). (Issue also includes Kohl's translations "Manazuru" and "The Ashen Moon."]

Sibley, William. *The Shiga Hero.* Chicago: University of Chicago Press, 1979. (An interesting and exhaustive Freudian interpretation of the psychological development of Shiga's central character. Includes Sibley's translations "For Grandmother," "The Razor," "The Kidnapping," and other stories.)

Starrs, Roy. *An Artless Art: The Zen Aesthetic of Shiga Naoya: A Critical Study with Selected Translations.* Surrey, U.K.: Curzon Press Japan Library, 1998. (An interesting overview of Shiga's work, although not as current as its date of publication would suggest. Includes Starr's translations *Reconciliation*, "The Diary of Claudius," and other stories.)

FILMS BASED ON SHIGA'S WORKS

Akanishi Kakita. Directed by Itami Mansaku, 1936.

An'ya kōro. Directed by Toyoda Shirō, 1959.

SECONDARY WORKS

CRITICAL AND BIOGRAPHICAL STUDIES IN ENGLISH

Dunlop, Lane. *The Paper Door and Other Stories by Shiga Naoya.* San Francisco: North Point Press, 1987. Reprint, New York: Columbia University Press, forthcoming. (Includes "As Far as Abashiri," "Akinishi Kakita," "The Shopboy's God," "Rain Frogs," "Infatuation," "Kuniko," and other stories.)

Fowler, Edward. "Death and Divine Indifference in 'Dwelling by the Moat.' " *Monumenta Nipponica* (Tokyo) 32, no. 2:225–234 (1977). (Issue includes Fowler's translation "Dwelling by the Moat.")

———. "Shiga Naoya: The Hero as Sage." In his *The Rhetoric of Confession: "Shishōsetsu" in Early Twentieth-Century Japanese Fiction.* Berkeley: University of California Press, 1988.

Goossen, Ted. "Connecting Rhythms: Nature and Selfhood in Shiga Naoya's *Reconciliation* and *A Dark Night's Passing*." *Review of Japanese Culture and Society* 5:20–33 (December 1993).

Goossen, Theodore, and Kin'ya Tsuruta, eds. *Nature and Identity in Canadian and Japanese Literature.* Toronto: University of Toronto and York University Joint Centre for Asia Pacific Studies, 1988. (Includes Goossen's translations "Turtledoves," "Morning-Glories," and other stories.)

Hijiya-Kirschnereit, Irmela. *Rituals of Self-Revelation.* Cambridge, Mass.: Harvard University Press, 1996. (A broad and challenging look at modern Japanese autobiographical literature, with extensive mention made of Shiga and his approach.)

Karatani Kōjin. *Origins of Modern Japanese Literature.* Trans. by Brett de Bary. Chapel Hill, N.C.: Duke University Press, 1993. (Shiga features prominently in this sweeping overview by Japan's most provocative contemporary critic.)

Kohl, Stephen. "Han's Crime," "At Kinosaki," and "The Bonfire." In *Approaches to the Modern Japanese Short Story.* Edited by Thomas Swann and Kin'ya Tsuruta. Tokyo: Waseda University Press, 1982.

———. "Shiga Naoya and the Literature of Experience." *Monumenta Nipponica* (Tokyo) 32, no. 2:211–224 (1977). (Issue also includes Kohl's translations "Manazuru" and "The Ashen Moon."]

Mathy, Francis. *Shiga Naoya.* New York: Twayne, 1974. (A basic introduction to Shiga's life and work.)

Sibley, William. *The Shiga Hero.* Chicago: University of Chicago Press, 1979. (An interesting and exhaustive Freudian interpretation of the psychological development of Shiga's central character. Includes Sibley's translations "For Grandmother," "The Razor," "The Kidnapping," and other stories.)

Starrs, Roy. *An Artless Art: The Zen Aesthetic of Shiga Naoya: A Critical Study with Selected Translations.* Surrey, U.K.: Curzon Press Japan Library, 1998. (An interesting overview of Shiga's work, although not as current as its date of publication would suggest. Includes Starr's translations *Reconciliation*, "The Diary of Claudius," and other stories.)

Suzuki, Tomi. "Shaping Life, Shaping the Past: Shiga Naoya's Narratives of Recollection." In her *Narrating the Self: Fictions of Japanese Modernity.* Stanford, Calif.: Stanford University Press, 1996. Pp. 93–134. (A fascinating and up-to-date analysis of Shiga's work within a critical-historical framework.)

Ueda, Makoto. "Shiga Naoya." In his *Modern Japanese Writers and the Nature of Literature.* Stanford, Calif.: Stanford University Press, 1976. Pp. 85–110. (A clear and concise presentation of Shiga's views on art and literature.)

CRITICAL AND BIOGRAPHICAL STUDIES IN JAPANESE

Agawa Hiroyuki. *Shiga Naoya.* 2 vols. Tokyo: Iwanami Shoten, 1994. (An intimate look at Shiga's life and career by one of his most devoted followers, also a recognized author.)

Bungei Dokuhon: Shiga Naoya. Tokyo: Kawade Shobō, 1976. (A first-rate compilation with essays by Kobayashi Hideo and Karatani Kōjin.)

Honda Shūgo. *Shiga Naoya.* 2 vols. Tokyo: Iwanami Shoten, 1990. (A critical overview of Shiga's life and work.)

Kokubungaku 21, no. 4 (March 1976). (Special issue, "Shiga Naoya to Nihonjin.")

Nakamura Mitsuo. *Shiga Naoya ron.* Tokyo: Chikuma Shobō, 1966. (A fairly negative assessment by an eminent postwar critic who saw Japan's modern literature as lacking compared to that of the West.)

Shiga Naoya. 2 vols. Tokyo: Yūseidō, 1970. (A collection of classic critical essays from the journal *Nihon Bungaku Kenkyū Shiryō Sōsho.*)

Sudō, Matsuo. *Shiga Naoya no Shizen.* Tokyo: Meiji Shoin, 1979. (An examination of "nature" as it developed in Shiga's literature.)

Takahashi Hideo. *Shiga Naoya: Kindai to shinwa.*

Tokyo: Bungei Shunjūsha, 1981. (One of Japan's finest critics examines the mythic structure of Shiga's work, and analyzes its impact on modern Japanese culture.)

Yasuoka Shōtarō. *Shiga Naoya ron.* Tokyo: Bungei Shunjūsha, 1968. (A personal, often incisive treatment of Shiga's life and work by one of Japan's foremost postwar novelists.)

SŌSEKI

(NATSUME SŌSEKI)

1867–1916

JAY RUBIN

NATSUME SŌSEKI is a Japanese icon. Almost a century after his death, discoveries of new facts about his life excited journalistic interest, and programs about his life or new dramatizations of his works continued to appear on television. Some of Sōseki's earlier works are read by all Japanese as part of the standard school curriculum, while the more challenging later novels are an indispensable rite of passage for any serious reader. Even non-readers in Japan recognize Sōseki as the face on the thousand-yen bill they use everyday.

By issuing the new bill in 1984, the Japanese government intended to honor Sōseki as a special contributor to Japanese culture, but if he had been alive to witness this "honor," Sōseki himself probably would have protested that his image was being exploited. He viewed the motives of governments with deep distrust and spent the last five years of his life denying that he was a Doctor of Letters, the title that the Ministry of Education tried to designate him with in 1911.

Sōseki was, in other words, something of a curmudgeon, which can be seen in the pen name that he chose for himself. When he started writing for publication (not fiction, but a haiku critique in Chinese verse, under the tutelage of his friend, the haiku poet Masaoka Shiki) in 1889 at the age of 22, Natsume Kinnosuke

did what virtually all Japanese writers had been doing for centuries and continued to do into the early twentieth century: he chose a two-character "first" name with traditional literary associations. The haiku poet Bashō had done the same thing in 1681. (See the General Introduction for more on these traditional pen names.)

Born in 1867, when Confucian ideas of education were still predominant, the young Natsume Kinnosuke was deeply schooled in the classic literature of China, and it was in a well-known Chinese story that he found the label with which he wanted to identify himself. *Sō* (Chinese *shu*) means "to rinse the mouth out, to gargle," and *seki* (Chinese *shi*) means "stone." According to the story, a young man, wishing poetically to announce his intention to seclude himself in the countryside, told a friend, "I shall pillow my head on the stream and rinse my mouth out with stones." When the friend pointed out that what he really must have meant was "I shall pillow my head on a stone and rinse my mouth out in the stream," the would-be poet stubbornly insisted that he had not made a mistake: by pillowing his head on the stream, he meant he would be washing his ears, and by rinsing his mouth out with stones, he would be brushing his teeth.

The budding, young haiku poet was delighted by the stubbornness and eccentricity he saw in the story because they seemed to fit him so well. Sōseki wore the "Garglestone" label like a badge of honor even after he began producing the novels that established him as the single greatest modern Japanese writer and a truly original voice among those artists of the world who have most fully grasped the modern experience.

The same month that he chose his pen name (May 1889), Sōseki, a student at the elitist First Higher School, attended the inaugural meeting of a student organization called Dōtoku-kai (The Morals Society). The Society had been founded amid a wave of intense nationalism marked by the assassination of the Minister of Education, Mori Arinori, on 11 February for supposed offenses against the national gods, and by the founding of various societies dedicated to the preservation of the "national essence" *(kokusui)*. Sōseki had been swept up in the patriotic mood enough to join the Morals Society, but the speeches he heard at the meeting gave him second thoughts, and he took the initiative to give his own speech, in which he said, "The nation may well be important, but we cannot possibly concern ourselves with the nation from morning to night as though possessed by it . . . What a horror if we had to eat for the nation, wash our faces for the nation, go to the toilet for the nation!" *(Sōseki zenshū [SZ]*, vol. 16, pp. 612–613; tr. p. 313).

Like others of his time, Sōseki had youthful thoughts of making a life that would be of service to the nation, but he came eventually to realize that his personality quirks—even a touch of madness that he recognized—made him less suited to serving the nation than to serving his society (and perhaps mankind in general) by standing apart and offering his own critical assessment of life in the modern world. In the end, he became the writer most widely recognized as offering guidance in dealing with the great questions that all thinking young people face as they come to grips with their identity as mature members of society.

Histories of modern Japanese literature invariably assign Sōseki his own chapter while often treating most other writers in groups or movements, and they always label him an "antinaturalist," in opposition to the school that dominated the literary scene after the Russo-Japanese War of 1904–1905, the time when his career as a novelist began. Although he did in fact criticize certain naturalist writers, his own mature novels shared much thematically and stylistically with theirs. He clearly saw himself aligned with this new generation of writers who were questioning traditional values, and he spoke out in defense of naturalists when government agencies strove to diminish their impact.

Central to the literary project of the naturalists and of Sōseki—and what made them all appear deeply suspicious to members of the establishment—was their exploration of the self. Neither in the naturalists nor in Sōseki, however, is there to be found a simple affirmation of the independent self in opposition to family or nation. For, having found the self, the writers quickly realized that this modern entity brought with it the pain of isolation.

If these themes—rebellion, generational conflict, self-discovery, loneliness—sound somewhat adolescent, then perhaps the late Meiji period can be seen as a time of national adolescence. And if Sōseki was the writer who articulated these problems of his time with the greatest clarity and forcefulness, then perhaps he can be viewed as an artist of the stature of a Dostoyevsky, whose deep sensitivity to his age and nation yielded works that transcend both. Each new generation of Japanese readers rediscovers Sōseki. And Western readers who discover Sōseki find in him a modern intellect doing battle in familiar territory.

Childhood and Society

When he was born in Edo (later Tokyo) on 9 February 1867, Natsume Kinnosuke had already lost the chance to grow up in the warm and hugely complicated embrace of three prosperous families. The Natsume family had been of samurai stock a few generations before, but the family fortunes had probably improved thanks to their "descent" to mere townsman status. Kinnosuke's grandfather had come to the Shōgun's capital, Edo, where he was granted the right to clear overgrown land, and set himself up as a local administrator called *nanushi*. When, in 1852, he dropped dead, drunk, in one of the local restaurants that depended on his permission to do business, his thirty-six-year old son, Natsume Kohē Naokatsu, succeeded to the family headship—and never touched a drop of sake for the rest of his life. Kohē reinforced the family's wealth and prominence as chief representative of a union of twenty Edo *nanushi*. The Natsumes were referred to by locals with respect as "Genka," a term for the family home's imposing front entry (*genka=genkan*), which was decorated with symbols of their authority: a lance, a *sasumata* forked pole used to hold down criminals by the neck, and a *sodegarami* barbed pole used to snag the clothing of fleeing offenders. Perhaps because they were not samurai, however, the Natsume house does not appear on maps of the day.

Kohē had two daughters by his first wife, who died in 1853 at the age of 29. From this point, the record becomes convoluted and not always clear, but it is well worth tracing as an example of the kind of transactions that figured prominently (and, to some extent, still do) in Japanese family relations and in the life and works of Natsume Sōseki. (Ages are given here in the Western style: birthday to birthday.)

Kohē remarried in 1854 at the age of 36 (or possibly in 1855 at 37, though the earlier date is thought to be more likely). His new wife, Chie, aged 27, was the third daughter of a pawnshop owner/moneylender who had married into his wife's family and taken the name Fukuda. Chie, however, came to the Natsume family not as the daughter of her father, but as the adopted third daughter of her eldest half sister's husband, a successful charcoal dealer originally named Takahashi but who himself was officially adopted into the Fukuda family when he married Chie's half sister, Kaku. (Kaku was the daughter of their mother's first husband and had herself become a Fukuda through adoption.)

The adoption into the younger Fukuda family may have been a way to clean up Chie's complicated past. After a period of domestic service in the home of a domainal lord, Chie had married into the family of a pawnbroker like her own, but the strange relationship between her husband and his stepmother had prompted her to leave him and go to live with Hisa, her middle sister. Hisa had also retained the Fukuda name when she married and adopted her husband, whose original name had been Izubashi. The Izubashis were proprietors of a house of prostitution, which they lost to Hisa's father when they failed to pay off the money he had lent them against it. Hisa got both a business and a husband out of the deal. Chie was the only one of the three sisters not to adopt her husband but to take his surname. Through the three sisters, the Natsume, Izubashi, and Takahashi families grew so close they were said to be almost like one big family, children from one going to stay with others for days and weeks at a time.

Chie gave Natsume Kohē Naokatsu six children in addition to the two he had from his late wife. They were born between 1856 and 1867, but the fourth and fifth died in childhood (infancy in one case), and two others, both consumptives, died at the ages of thirty-one and twenty-eight, respectively, within a few months of each other in 1887. The sixth and last was Kinnosuke, the future Sōseki, born on a day designated by the astrological charts as Kanoe-saru or "Elder Brother of Metal." According to Taoist belief, people born on that day can be hugely successful, but one slip and they are likely to become great thieves. The best way to ward off the curse is to give the newborn a name having the character for "metal" *(kin)* in it, and so the Natsumes named their last child Kin, with the male "-nosuke" suffix attached. Given these measures to ward off ill fortune, Kinnosuke should have been well enough prepared to take his comfortable place in the big, prosperous Natsume-Izubashi-Takahashi clan, but too many years had gone by between the birth of Chie's first child and her last. Everything was different by that time.

351

The year after Kohē became family head in 1852, Commodore Matthew Perry arrived from America in a warship and demanded that Japan open its doors to the outside world. At a loss to deal with this unprecedented threat, the Tokugawa system of government that supported Kohē's authority began to crumble, slowly at first, but with accelerating speed as each month went by. The year Kohē probably married Chie, 1854, Perry was back and the Tokugawas acquiesced, leading to plots and counterplots between Tokugawa supporters and those loyal to the emperor, but relatively little bloodshed, despite the ubiquity of swords and swordsmen.

By the time Kinnosuke was born in February 1867, Chie was forty and Kohē forty-nine—in an era when those ages were much closer to the normal end of life, and certainly well past any respectable time to be having children. The day before Kinnosuke was born, a former ward of Kohē's by the name of Shiohara (Sōseki's spelling of the name, rather than "Shiobara") visited the house to ask about adopting him. Before that could be worked out, the infant was sent to the relative of a Natsume family maid to nurse but was brought home soon after by his sixteen-year-old half sister, Fusa. Sōseki himself tells the family story that she had seen him one night in a basket mixed in with the junk being sold in the stand run by his nurse's family. Fusa's compassion earned her nothing but a good scolding from Kohē. Milk was obtained thereafter from a cooperative neighbor lady. In the months following Sōseki's birth, political events continued to become more intense, culminating in the "restoration" of the emperor to power and the inauguration of an era of "enlightened rule" called Meiji in October 1868, when Sōseki was nearing two.

The restoration did little to reduce Natsume family authority in their area. The new government kept Kohē in place and gave him a position of local leadership in the city, renamed Tokyo, to replace the *nanushi* title he had held in Edo under the Tokugawa shogunate. He then renamed a nearby street Na-tsume Hill and the surrounding neighborhood Kikuichō, referring to the chrysanthemum (*kiku*) and well (*i*) motifs in the Natsume family crest. Both place names survive today in Tokyo's Shinjuku ward. The government also offered Kohē some free land nearby, but he passed it up for fear of the expense of fencing it in, a decision that later gave rise to sardonic family jokes about how they could have all been on easy street. One thing that did change, however, was Kohē's name. In 1872 the government decreed that all those with two names, such as Kohē Naokatsu, must henceforth use only one. At that time he decided in favor of his personal name, Naokatsu, rather than his "middle name," which was more an indication of rank than an individualized appellation.

The Natsumes seem to have kept the new baby for a few months before giving him up for adoption to the Shioharas. The infant was at least unconscious of how he was being traded around, but as he grew up in the family of his feuding adoptive parents, watching their marriage fall apart, he twice had the experience of being returned to the Natsume house, the second time permanently at the age of eight, when he learned that the old "grandparents" who lived there were actually his mother and father. Officially, however, Sōseki remained the adopted son of the Shioharas, and he went by the name of Shiohara Kinnosuke until the age of twenty, a legalistic oversight that caused his childhood friends some confusion and caused him some pain in later years. Sōseki recalled that he had been happy to be back with his real family, though his father was hard on him and unloving. His mother treated him warmly and occasionally took him to the theater, but she lived only six more years, dying just before Sōseki turned fourteen in 1881. A surviving photograph of her suggests the harshness and brevity of life in those days: though she died at fifty-four, she looks like a woman in her mid-seventies: it is small wonder the boy took her to be his grandmother.

Sōseki's novel *Michikusa* (1915; *Grass on the Wayside*, 1969) tells the painful story of the re-emergence in the mature Sōseki's life of his erstwhile adoptive father, who hoped to exploit their past relationship to squeeze some money out of him. Knowing full well that he is being exploited, the protagonist, Kenzō, decides to give him money for a while, but other relatives make their own demands on him as well, including his father-in-law:

They had briefly stretched out their hands, one man to give, and the other to take, then had immediately withdrawn them. Kenzō's wife stood on the side, watching the impersonal transaction and saying nothing.

(*SZ*, vol. 10, p. 229; tr. p. 121)

The scene is a grim poetic distillation of all the coldness and calculation that Sōseki had experienced in human relations, beginning from the time he was an infant.

The idealized model of relationships in Japan is one of intuitive sincerity and unquestioning devotion, of loyalty beyond intellect, but the ideal has been fashioned precisely because so much calculation goes on in daily life in Japan. A Japanese person is rarely free at any point in the day from the process of weighing and measuring of value in human relationships—the value of gifts, the percentage of that value which must be given back in return, the value of favors done, the degree of obligation or voluntariness behind that favor, the depth and duration of a bow, the respect level of a verb ending. The conflict between duty and human feeling *(giri-ninjō)* that comprised the ethical core of much Tokugawa-period drama was a dynamic of calculation, as often spelled out in long scenes parsing who owes what to whom, with human lives not infrequently the medium of exchange. There is no way to tell what melodramas of *giri* versus *ninjō* lay behind the human tangle of the Natsumes, the Izubashis, and the Takahashis with all their divorces, remarriages, adoptions, and half-siblings, but one thing is certain: the change in period label from "Tokugawa" to "Meiji" did nothing to modify the ingrained habits of calculation that remained vital in Japanese inter-

personal relations into the twenty-first century. Sōseki's novels deal with questions that transcend nationality, but they portray some of the darkest aspects of human exchange the world over by capturing this open secret of Japanese society. Sōseki wrote the following simple cry of the heart in early February 1915, for the last of his memoirs, *Garasudo no uchi* (1915; *Within My Glass Doors*, 1928):

Should I believe what others tell me, and interpret all their words and actions at face value? . . . I do not want to trust evil people, but neither do I want to harm those who are good . . . If there were an omniscient, omnipotent god in this world, I would kneel before that god and pray for it to release me from this anguish . . . But as things stand now, I can only be a fool deceived by others or a bundle of suspicions incapable of opening myself to anyone, filled with unease, unclarity, and unhappiness. How unfortunate is man if this is to continue his whole life long!

(*SZ*, vol. 12, pp. 598–600)

Whether or not Sōseki moved from this tortured honesty to a quasi-religious stance of *sokuten kyoshi* ("follow Heaven and abandon the self": apparently an original phrase of Sōseki's) in the final months of his life, as some of his "disciples" asserted, the body of works he left behind involved no such peaceful sidestepping of the issue of the self and its relation to others in society. He had been a member of the first generation of Japanese to learn from the West that the self was an entity of value beyond social categories—lord, vassal, father, son, husband, wife, mother, daughter—but to learn also that knowledge of the self, once attained, could never be given back. The stimulus of self-discovery was invariably accompanied by a shattering of the unconscious ties with the enfolding community that provide assurance of continuity and belonging, leaving in their place a painful awareness of transaction. Sōseki's early childhood probably sensitized him to this fact of life and so helped prepare him to be the one member of his generation who most effectively revealed the conflict between the independent self and the crushing mechanism of society.

Education of a Writer

Once he was settled again in the Natsume household, Sōseki lived what might be called a fairly "normal" life, but in his teens he developed a tendency to react to stress with physical ailments—most notably ulcers, the condition that eventually killed him. When Sōseki later talked about feeling anxiety in the pit of his stomach, he was speaking with deadly accuracy.

Whether he was sufficiently loved or not by his regained family, the young Sōseki was certainly given an elite education in keeping with his considerable intellectual talents and the family's social standing. (The family's financial standing was less firm: two of Sōseki's older brothers did things like stealing valuable swords and scrolls from the house and selling them to support their carousing.) The Chinese classics dominated his early studies, and he pursued the Chinese language and Chinese literature, which he loved, well into his teens. The increasing importance of Western culture, however, convinced him eventually that his future lay with English, which he made his major in his early twenties, entering the English Department of Tokyo Imperial University in 1890. In 1893 he was the second person to graduate with a major in English, continuing on in graduate school. He never "loved" English literature the way he loved Chinese, but he was by then committed to a scholarly career, and indeed he remained an academic until 1907, when he became a full-time writer at the age of forty. Including his first two years of part-time writing, Sōseki's career as a novelist lasted only twelve years following seventeen or more years as an academic, and even after he changed employers, Sōseki continued to think of himself as a scholar. The two careers were, for him, inseparable, much of the analytical activity—and the pain—of the first serving the creativity of the second.

The pain derived first of all from the lack of intuitive sense of mastery that is almost inevitable in learning a language after childhood. However artificial Japan's Chinese literary culture might have been (cut off as it was from spoken Chinese), it still allowed for immersion early enough in the lives of students so that they felt truly at home with its locutions. It is known from surviving manuscripts that Sōseki learned English well enough that he was able to write with a fluency and style unattainable by most Japanese even today, but he never overcame the sense that he had based his entire professional life on a language and literature that would never truly belong to him, and this caused him tremendous suffering. When he took his first job teaching English, he said in "Watakushi no kojinshugi" (1914; "My Individualism," 1992), a highly personal lecture he delivered to a young audience, "I felt like a fishmonger working in a pastry shop." He went on to say:

> Questionable as my language ability was, I knew enough to get along and managed to squeak by each day. Deep inside, however, I knew only emptiness. No, perhaps if it had been emptiness I could have resigned myself more completely, but there was something continually bothering me, some vague, disagreeable, half-formed thing that would not let me alone. . . .
>
> At the university I majored in English literature . . . For three years I studied, and, at the end, I still did not know what literature was. This was the root source of my agony.
>
> (*SZ*, vol. 16, pp. 589, 591–592; tr. pp. 292, 293–294).

The turning point for Sōseki came in London, where he was sent for two years (October 1900–December 1902) by the Ministry of Education for further study. Sōseki did not greet this rare opportunity to study abroad with enthusiasm. He was already thirty-three years old, in the fourth year of his fourth teaching position, living in Kumamoto at the far south end of Japan, and sending money from his salary each month to his half sister Fusa (his father's death in 1897 had relieved him of an even greater monthly burden; and the two free-spending elder brothers who had helped to dissipate the family's savings had died in 1887). He was the father of one daughter and due to have another child by a wife with suicidal tendencies that were exacerbated by pregnancy. (The first pregnancy had ended in a miscarriage. The marriage of the twenty-nine-year-old Sōseki to the nineteen-year-old Nakane Kyōko in 1896 had been an arranged one, following common practice at the time.) The allowance that the Ministry was offering to pay to support his wife and daughter in his absence was minuscule. As a teacher at one of the government's elite higher schools, though, he had little choice but to accept this order from the Ministry, with all its attendant hardships. He deposited his family with his in-laws in Tokyo and set sail for London in September 1900.

Once there, he mostly stayed locked in a series of gloomy lodgings, reading English literature. Eventually, as he says in his lecture on individualism, he realized that "No amount of reading was going to fill this emptiness in the pit of my stomach," and he determined to fashion for himself "a conception of what literature is, working from the ground up and relying on nothing but my own efforts." He would no longer be a mere imitator who "was boasting of borrowed clothes, preening with glued-on peacock feathers" when he regurgitated Western ideas to great applause in the Japanese academy. "It occurred to me now that I must become self-centered. I became absorbed in scientific studies, philosophical speculation, anything that would support this position."

Self-centeredness became for me a new beginning, I confess, and it helped me to find what I thought would be my life's work. I resolved to write books, to tell people that they need not imitate Westerners, that running blindly after others as they were doing would only cause them great anxiety . . . My anxiety disappeared without a trace. I looked out on London's gloom with a happy

heart . . . I would return to Japan with a strength I had not possessed when I left for England.

(*SZ*, vol. 16, pp. 592–596; tr. pp. 295–298).

Sōseki spent some potentially thrilling years in London, as the events surrounding the death of Queen Victoria and the beginning of a new age played themselves out, but his experience of discovery was almost entirely internal. He did go to watch the magnificent funeral cortege itself, perched on his landlord's shoulders to see over the heads of the tall crowd. He got out of the house occasionally to go to the theater, to learn how to ride a bicycle (a conscious attempt to find some relief from depression), and to visit the Tower of London (once) and the preserved home of Thomas Carlyle (1795–1881) (four times) (Carlyle's *Sartor Resartus* and *On Heroes, Hero Worship, and the Heroic in History* were widely read in Meiji Japan). But for the most part Sōseki stayed shut up in his room (or rooms—he was so dissatisfied with his living arrangements that he had no fewer than five different lodgings in his two years there), studying all the while. His gloomy recollections of the time suggest a degree of self-absorption bordering on madness, and in fact, Japanese acquaintances reported that he had indeed gone over the edge. Shortly after receiving the sad news that his haiku friend Masaoka Shiki had died, he left for Japan in December 1902 with hundreds of books and articles that would help him with his reassessment of literature from the ground up. As it happened, though, he wrote only one book "to tell people that they need not imitate Westerners," and that was his *Bungakuron* (1907; Theory of literature), which Sōseki referred to as the "deformed corpse" of his projected life's work as a scholar. (Sōseki's other book of criticism was an unedited collection of students' lecture notes.)

Back in Tokyo, Sōseki found his wife living in near-poverty and her once-prosperous and politically prominent father financially ruined by changes in the government. Now he had more people dependent on him than ever. He arranged to have a doctor certify him as suffering from nervous prostration so that he could leave his post in distant Kumamoto, and he took the two jobs offered to him in Tokyo beginning 1 April: teaching English twenty hours a week at the First Higher School and lecturing three hours a week at the Imperial University. To this combined income of ¥125 per month, he added ¥30 per month the following April by taking on three more hours a week of teaching at another university. The income was good but the family could never make ends meet, and the strain on his nerves was tremendous. His wife Kyōko became pregnant with their third child, but this did not prevent their relationship from deteriorating to the point where he sent her back to her parents for two months. A third daughter was born in November just after she returned to him.

Sōseki reworked the lectures that he delivered at the Imperial University in Tokyo, and published them as *Bungakuron*. This work presents a fine-grained analysis of the tools of literature that Sōseki brought to bear when the urging of friends and the expense of life in Tokyo convinced him to write fiction as a way to supplement his academic income. Here is where he worked out the psychological impact of colors that he consciously exploited in his fiction, as well as techniques involving painterly composition, angles, point of view, perspective, movement, stillness, and so forth. (See the translator's Afterword to *Sanshirō*.)

As Matsui Sakuko has observed in her detailed study, *Natsume Sōseki as a Critic of English Literature*, "Sōseki . . . discusses literature from the reader's standpoint . . . in terms of laws of psychology." (p. 120). The psychologist who had the greatest influence on Sōseki was William James (1842–1910), brother of novelist Henry, and the fountainhead of the theory of the "stream-of-consciousness" that influenced such western psychological novelists as Virginia Woolf and James Joyce. Under James's influence, Sōseki came to think of reading as a union of the reader's "succession of consciousness" *(ishiki no renzoku)* with the author's (*SZ*, vol. 19, pp. 312, 319).

If *Bungakuron* is a fair representation of Sōseki's lectures at the university, it is no wonder that students complained about his dry, "scientific" analyses after what must have been the rhapsodic presentations of his romantic predecessor, Lafcadio Hearn. The remarkable thing is that, in creating his own original fiction, Sōseki did not write novels like a professor. Or rather, it might be more accurate to say that he quickly became a good enough writer to exploit his academic discoveries without being obvious about them.

There was genuine passion driving Sōseki to write, which can be seen even in his theoretical statements on the function of the novel. The idea of a union of minds—of the reader's "succession of consciousness" with the author's—could not but appeal to a personality that had grown up with a strong sense of separateness:

Works of literature are, by their very nature, nonspecialist books. They are written to criticize or depict matters of common concern to all men. They bring people together, stripped naked, regardless of profession or class, and break down all such walls that separate us. Thus I believe them to be the most worthy and least harmful means for binding us together as human beings

("Dōraku to shokugyō" [1911; Pastime and profession], *SZ*, vol. 16, pp. 407–408).

Sōseki even coined his own term for this unifying function of literature, *kangenteki kanka*, which means something like "restorative influence," and which he explained as an experience beyond space and time in which the distinction between the reader and the writer breaks down entirely. ("Bungei no tetsugakuteki kiso" [1907; The philosophical foundations of the literary art], *SZ*, vol. 16, pp. 132–133, 136–137).

In spite of his highly intellectualized approach to writing, Sōseki was never mechanical about his craft, and he never stopped experimenting with his art. The result was a body of works that show thematic and technical consistency but also a continual process of growth and development.

Explosive Debut: *I Am a Cat*

Anyone who had read only the Sōseki novels featured in textbooks might be overwhelmed by the fact that there are so many studies of the author that use terms like "anguish" and "suffering" and "pain" in their titles. But it was above all his rich sense of humor to which Sōseki gave free rein in his early works. Sōseki's mother is often credited with having exposed him to the lively colloquial humor of the *yose* or variety theater, such that traces of the comic Rakugo storytellers' style can be noted in Sōseki's own comic writings. By the time he started writing, however, he had read widely and deeply in Sterne and Swift—had in fact written some substantial scholarly analyses of their works—and much of the crack-brained humor seen in his own works could as well be said to have English roots. The two are probably inseparable in Sōseki, and perhaps the most that can be said is that they both validated the tendency of his probing intellect to see absurdity in the world around him.

The part of the world that he first subjected to his penetrating wit was the one closest to him: his own academic life. He did this in a comic story that appeared in the New Year's 1905 issue of the magazine *Hototogisu*, which was published by some of the haiku-writing friends in whose company he had adopted the "Sōseki" pen-name sixteen years earlier. The title he gave it, "Wagahai wa neko de aru," is usually translated "I Am a Cat," but with its pompous four-syllable first-person pronoun and super-serious written-style verb carrying echoes of self-important politicians, it might better be represented as something like "Gentlemen, I Stand before You, a Cat." (Sōseki himself suggested use of the royal "we" [*SZ*, vol. 26, p. 284].) There is not much more to this plotless piece than the gag of having a scruffy stray introduce himself in such exaggerated terms, and many pages are devoted to his pratfalls in the human world, with only

puns and lively (but low-minded) jokes to carry the reader along. The joke-filled, Edo-flavored style was enough to arouse a demand for more, however, and Sōseki wrote a much longer sequel for the following month's issue, still not intending to turn it into anything like a novel. By the third installment, however—the first one to be printed with a chapter number—things were beginning to develop, and the comic portraits of the human beings observed by the cat were beginning to take on a genuinely satirical edge. Sōseki continued writing sequels for the magazine all that year and into the next until it emerged as a long, loosely plotted, ever-prolix and often funny critique of greed and affectation in Meiji society, the novel *Wagahai wa neko de aru* (1905–1906; *I Am a Cat*, 1972, 1979, 1986). Sōseki's language surged out in what seemed like an unstoppable—and is a virtually untranslatable—flow.

The nameless feline narrator lives in the home of a Sōseki-like higher school teacher of English, who himself is not given a name until chapter 3, where it is revealed to be "Kushami." This sounds like "Sneeze" but is written with characters suggesting "the agony of life in this world." Kushami tends to doze in his study and drool on his books. He disarms his wife's complaints about their tight finances by showing her a white hair he has yanked from his nostril while she is talking to him (the detailed description of this hair-pulling, in chapter 3, is hilarious and disgusting at the same time). Many jokes are made about Kushami's weak stomach and his lack of a doctoral degree, but some of the banter between Kushami and his wife can be downright creepy in retrospect. When he says he might still get a doctorate because "a certain Greek, Isocrates, produced major literary works at the age of ninety-four," she interrupts his further learned examples with, "Don't be silly. How can you possibly expect, with your stomach troubles, to live that long?" (*Nihon kindai bungaku taikei: Natsume Sōseki shū* [*NKBT*], vol. 24, p. 138; tr. pp. 185–186).

Much of the give-and-take between husband and wife is in the form of good-natured ribbing that gives an impression of intimacy and affection. He kids her about her short stature and the beginnings of a bald spot on the crown of her head caused by her matronly chignon. He makes no secret of the fact, however, that this was an arranged marriage, something qualitatively different from the love relationships that are discussed from time to time. Kushami is always telling his wife that she is an ignorant woman and he uses obscure Western references to put her down, but she invariably ends up making him look like a hollow, pretentious tyrant with less than complete confidence in his mastery of English, and her logic is always more sensible and down-to-earth than that of her husband. The farcical world of *I Am a Cat*, in other words, is merely the obverse side of one of Sōseki's most devastating portraits of human miscommunication and suffering, *Grass on the Wayside*, which covers the same anguished period in Sōseki's life, concentrating on the painful relationship of a husband and wife.

Unlike the protagonist of *Grass on the Wayside*, Kushami is constantly being visited by friends, most of them former students, and their silly conversations—some of them appealing set pieces derived from Greek legends or other tales that had caught Sōseki's fancy—comprise the bulk of the book, with the wife commenting now and then that their stories sound like pieces from the *yose* theater. The self-appointed intellectuals who drift through Kushami's house are a harmless and funny but sometimes pitiful lot, "boasting of borrowed clothes, preening with glued-on peacock feathers," as Sōseki described himself in his lecture on individualism, living in constant fear that someone might have read a book or learned a foreign word of which they are ignorant. Again, the farce has a potential darker side, as many of their airy theories touch upon death, suicide, murder, hanging, plague-carrying rats, the absurdity of belief in an omnipotent god, the ongoing Russo-Japanese War, recent literary developments (with mention of one "inscrutable" story by some fellow named Sōseki), the occult, the uncon-

scious, William James, psychosomatic illness, the increase (for better or worse) in women's independence under the new regime, and marital discord.

There is a long burlesque on the war in terms of rat hunting in chapter 5, written just after Japan's destruction of the Baltic Fleet in May 1905; and the jingoist euphoria of victory rampant when Sōseki was writing chapter 6 in September inspires in Kushami a bitter poem lambasting the indefinable, intangible "Japanese Spirit" *(Yamato-damashii)* that everyone in the country supposedly possesses, from Admiral Tōgō, destroyer of the Baltic fleet, down to the meanest swindler and murderer. Sōseki even hints at his own measures to dodge the military by writing his name with characters meaning "sent registration," which he had done—to Hokkaidō, whose citizens were exempt from the draft—at the age of twenty-five (*NKBT*, vol. 24, pp. 249, 506; tr., p. 190). He did not become a citizen of Tokyo again until September 1913.

Sōseki's antipathy for war hysteria came out in full force in a story he published in January 1906, the same month as the largely slapstick chapters 7 and 8 of *I Am a Cat* and four months after the end of the Russo-Japanese War, which had been fought from February 1904 to September 1905 over the question of which of those two imperial powers would dominate parts of Manchuria and Korea. The tone of the opening of "Shumi no iden" (1906, "The Heredity of Taste," 1974) is nothing short of ferocious:

Under the influence of the weather, even the gods run mad. A voice came shouting from within the clouds, "Slaughter men. Let loose the hungry dogs." This voice shook the sea of Japan into turbulence and rang as far as the ends of Manchuria. In immediate response to that voice, the Japanese and the Russians between them created a massive slaughter-house, two hundred miles long and two hundred miles wide, in the plains of Northern Manchuria.

(*SZ*, vol. 2, p. 185; tr. p. 117).

The panorama of war fills the rest of the page, increasing in fury and goriness. It turns out to be the fantasy of a bookworm who stumbles upon a huge crowd welcoming a general resembling Nogi Maresuke, "hero" of Port Arthur, and his troops back to Tokyo. The man is both touched and repulsed by the patriotic display, but finally he finds himself comically incapable of joining the crowd's heartfelt cries of "Banzai!" This sixty-page story combines an oddly distanced academic humor with vivid descriptions of the horrific sacrifices made by Japanese troops attacking Hill 203 overlooking Port Arthur, one of whom was the narrator's lovable best friend. It is one of the most gripping and, finally, enigmatic creations to have come from Sōseki's apparently indefatigable pen at this stage when he was writing *I Am a Cat* and what seems like a hundred other things all at once. He had obviously let the genie out of the bottle after all those years as an academic, and he could not stop himself.

The Sōseki whose name is written with the characters meaning "sent-registration" in *I Am a Cat* is supposedly the author of "Ichiya" (1905; One night), a dreamy piece that no one understands—including the author himself, and for good reason: the actual story called "Ichiya" is so crammed with colors, fragrances, sounds, and self-consciously "poetic" imagery that the main reaction to it was one of puzzlement. In it, two men, one with beard, one without, and a woman with sad eyes spend a night together, saying beautiful things and finally sinking into sleep and forgetfulness.

The satire of *I Am a Cat*, thus, covers a broad field, ranging from pretentious intellectuals to phony nationalism to Sōseki's own more fantastic writings. *I Am a Cat* also contains much ranting against the arrogance of the rich and powerful, a theme that resurfaced repeatedly and inevitably in Sōseki's more mature fiction as it probed the cold transactions of human relations. Kushami's rich neighbors, the Kanedas ("Moneyfield" or "It's Money"), who live in an ostentatiously large house and have "one of those *telephone* things I've heard so much about" (*NKBT*, vol. 24, p.

146; cf. tr. p. 201), use their wealth to buy the loyalties of the locals to spy on Kushami and generally make his life miserable. One can almost hear Kushami's indignation in Sōseki's own lecture on individualism given nine years later when he warned his wealthy young audience at the Peers' School to beware of crushing others' individuality through abuses of their power and money.

The closest thing to a plot in the novel traces the hopeless suit of one of Kushami's former students for the hand of the conceited daughter of the rich Kaneda family. When it comes to lambasting the rich, Sōseki routinely stoops to low humor. The mother's gigantic nose earns her the nickname Nosegirl *(Hanako)* and inspires endless tiresome nose jokes plus a lengthy disquisition on noses. Scholars, as useless as they are, always come off looking better than businessmen.

Sōseki's letters and his wife Kyōko's memoirs record the tremendous fun that Sōseki had writing *I Am a Cat*. When he read his new installments aloud, his young *Hototogisu* associates would roll over with laughter, and he derived joy from writing at all hours of the day and night. The more he wrote, the more he wanted to write, and the more he begrudged the hours he had to spend preparing his lectures. The summer vacation of 1905 was particularly frustrating in that regard. He wrote to several friends, expressing his desire to stop teaching and begin writing full-time. His frustration almost certainly played a part in the marked change in tone in the chapters of *I Am a Cat* that Sōseki wrote from the end of that year into the next, as the narrative moves away from the cat and his silly antics to focus on Kushami and his struggles to attain a measure of spiritual peace in a world full of unreliable humans. Chapter 9, which appeared in March 1906, is as bitter and intense and internalized as anything Sōseki ever wrote, so extreme in its negativity that the most scathing expressions are presented as those of an institutionalized lunatic, who writes to Kushami in the following vein:

Your closest friends might betray you. Your very parents may treat you with indifference. Even your own true love might cast you off. No man, naturally, can put his trust in wealth or worldly honors. Lands and peerages can vanish in the twinkling of an eye. The lifetime of scholarship treasured in your head will go moldy in the end. On what, then, do you intend to rely? What is there in this whole wide world on which you dare depend? God? God is but a clay figure fabricated by man in the depths of despair, a mere stinking corpse of congealed excrement evacuated from the bowels of men scared shitless.

(*NKBT,* vol. 24, p. 337; revised from tr. pp. 112–113).

Instead of ignoring this letter, as he has just done with a solicitation for yet another Russo-Japanese War victory celebration, Kushami finds himself moved to read it again and again. The cat tells us, "A man like my master, who has spent his whole life faking explanations for English words he doesn't know, naturally wants to wrench some meaning out of such a piece of mumbo-jumbo" (*NKBT,* vol. 24, pp. 338–339; revised from tr. p. 15).

The cat, who can read Kushami's thoughts *because* he is a cat (though "Don't ask me how"), goes on to trace a long internal debate that Kushami holds with himself, pitting Western positivism with its inevitable frustrations against the comforting Eastern passivism that he has been hearing about from his philosopher friend Yagi Dokusen, and which attracts him as the one promise of relief from the individualistic jungle of Japan's modern civilization. The more Dokusen opens his mouth, however, the more he reveals himself to be the Zen Buddhist charlatan that he is accused of being by Kushami's rational young friend Meitei, who blames Dokusen's mumbo-jumbo for having caused the above letter-writer's insanity. Kushami worries that his attraction to the madman's words may reveal some degree of madness in himself, and like the hypochondriac Daisuke of *Sore kara* (1909; *And Then,* 1978), one of Sōseki's greatest novels of psychological self-examination, he begins testing

his pulse and looking for signs of physical and mental illness. He begins to wonder if "human society is no more than a massing of lunatics," and the few sane people are the ones locked up in asylums, and he concludes, "I just don't understand anything anymore" (*NKBT,* vol. 24, pp. 361–362; tr. pp. 156–157). The strain of trying to understand makes him fall asleep. The cat's derision of his intellectual failings can do little to lighten this portrait of a depressive personality for whom sleep offers the only relief. Thus in chapter 9 of *I Am a Cat,* which begins with Kushami examining his pock-marked face in the mirror, and ends with his utter mental confusion, Sōseki has put the finishing touches on the portrait of the hero who appears again and again in his novels with different names—if far fewer jokes.

Sōseki published two more chapters to bring *I Am a Cat* to a close, one in April and the last one in August, between which he wrote one of his most memorable struggles between modern civilization and Eastern aestheticism, *Kusamakura* (1906; *The Three-Cornered World,* 1965). Indeed, he was writing with such intensity that the April installment of *I Am a Cat* appeared in the same issue of *Hototogisu* as the complete text of his short novel *Botchan* (1906; *Botchan,* 1972), and the two final chapters of *I Am a Cat* were among the longest and most energetic of the entire work. The family finances had improved enough by October 1906—aided perhaps by the death of his father-in-law in September— that Sōseki was able to quit his third job teaching at Meiji University. This was the month when the random visits of former students and other young Sōseki admirers reflected in *I Am a Cat* became formalized as the "Thursday Society" (*Mokuyōkai*), though Akutagawa Ryūnosuke, the most famous "disciple," did not join the group until 1915.

In chapter 10, which begins on the morning after Kushami's confusing mental struggle, Sōseki is clearly testing his ability to write in a straightforward realistic vein, as he describes the day's activities of Kushami, his wife, and three small daughters—the latter's cute antics viewed both in fond detail and in terms of what trouble they will be for Kushami when the day comes for him to marry them off. Chapter 11 is a hilarious experiment in story-telling, as one of Kushami's young friends tells the tantalizing story of his passionate determination to overcome old-fashioned masculine prejudices in his village against Western high culture by buying and then hiding and then finally *not* playing a violin.

In chapter 11, Kushami gives his gloomiest assessment yet of the curse of modern Japanese civilization, which, he says, is marked by the excessive growth of individualism, which in turn he blames, with wonderful illogic, for the upsurge in the number of detectives poking into everyone's private lives. His group agree that, a thousand years in the future, suicide will become the routine way to die and that divorce will be universal; already, people are so uninterested in each other that they do not bother reading each other's literature, a trend already well advanced in England as can be seen in the works of Henry James.

The final chapter portrays one last gathering of Kushami's group of friends, and is thus a summation of virtually all the issues that have been raised piecemeal in the course of this rambling writer's workshop. For, bound between covers, *I Am a Cat* is nothing so much as a compilation of first drafts, unruly pages that contain the seeds of everything that Sōseki would write in the ten years left to him. The closeted scholar Kushami himself, sometimes even with mustache and clouds of tobacco smoke, appears again and again in Sōseki's fiction, still torn between the painful transactions of modern society and the soothing calm of withdrawal and detachment. The problems of modern civilization and individualism and money form the backbone of virtually all of Sōseki's novels and much of his nonfiction. Even Sōseki's supposed ultimate solution to life's problems, *sokuten kyoshi* ("follow Heaven and abandon the self"), has its precursor here. When Kushami bemoans the "curse" of modern man's restless self-absorption, the philosopher Dokusen insists that

"the only cure lies in learning to forget the Self" (*NKBT*, vol. 24, p. 459; tr. pp. 318–319).

Other themes, however, would not be much pursued. Kushami's sharp critique of jingoism and the use of force became a central theme in *Botchan*, and *The Three-Cornered World* would end with a sad and angry farewell to a soldier leaving for the Russo-Japanese War, but Sōseki did not further develop war as a theme in his fiction and demonstrated no sensitivity to Japanese continental depredations.

While serializing his cat-story-turned-novel, it has been noted, Sōseki wrote several short stories and one short novel. The shorter pieces tended to be academic riffs on material such as the Arthurian legends or experiences Sōseki had had in London. "Rondon tō" (1905; "The Tower of London," 1992), for example, is a twenty-five-page rhapsody on English history presented as a series of visions experienced by a Sōseki-like narrator as he toured the tower. Full of personal and place names from ghastly historical events connected with the tower, it is saved from being a mere exercise in self-indulgent pedantry by Sōseki's ability to conjure up vivid images of murder and mayhem that seem to issue forth from some dark cavern of the psyche.

Botchan and *The Three-Cornered World*

The short comic novel *Botchan* appeared in the April 1906 issue of *Hototogisu* (along with chapter 10 of *I Am a Cat*) and won immediate fame for its portrait of a simple hero who emerges from a loveless childhood to fight a world dominated by liars and cheats. Whereas the narrator-cat of *I Am a Cat* is remarkable for his overblown first-person pronoun, *wagahai*, the twenty-three-year-old narrator of *Botchan* refers to himself with the simple, unpretentious, masculine "I," *ore*, and never reveals his name. In fact, he narrates from so deeply within his own thoughts that he rarely even has to call himself *ore*: he knows who he is. The reader bonds with him instantly.

Having lost his unloving parents and parted for life with his hostile brother, *ore* uses his share of their inheritance to pay for three years of schooling in math and science. He graduates near the bottom of his class, and for want of anything better to do accepts an offer to teach in a middle school in a town resembling Matsuyama on the island of Shikoku. Sōseki himself had taught in Matsuyama (his friend Shiki's hometown) in 1896 before he took the post in Kumamoto. While Sōseki's own stay was rather pleasant, *ore* encounters only liars, hypocrites and intellectual poseurs, and in the end he gains satisfaction by thrashing two of the biggest hypocrites at the school where he has been misunderstood and mistreated.

Ore accepts everything at face value. When he arrives to take up this new post, for example, and the principal of the school gives him a canned pep talk, telling him he will have to be a role model for the students, he immediately confesses his unworthiness and tries to give back his certificate of appointment. This endearing quality of *baka-shōjiki* or "foolish honesty" has won readers over ever since its first publication. According to Donald Keene, *Botchan* "has probably sold more copies than any other work of Japanese literature" (p. 315).

Although *ore* tells the reader that "My father never showed me the slightest affection" (*SZ*, vol. 2, p. 251; tr. p. 12) and provides other unpleasant details from his early life, the novel is saved from becoming a litany of misery, in part, by the love that is showered on *ore*—not by anyone in his family but by the kindly old maid, Kiyo. *Ore*, however, remains comically puzzled as to why Kiyo—or anyone else—would love him. (Perhaps not by coincidence, it was a family maid who whispered to the young Sōseki the true identity of his "grandparents," for which he was inordinately grateful.) In any case it is Kiyo who continues to call the adult *ore* "Botchan" or "Little Master" after her years of devoted service to the family. Sōseki no doubt hoped the book's title would also carry its pejorative connotation of foolish innocence, which emerges from the mouth of one of the hypocrites near the end.

Sōseki said in an interview, "To a point, Botchan is a character worth loving and sympathizing with, but I hope my readers will realize that he is a bit too simple and inexperienced to survive in today's complex society" (*SZ*, vol. 2, p. 446). For the most part, Sōseki's readers have *not* realized that; the book is enjoyed innocently by most readers, who encounter it in their youth: they cheer when *ore* beats up the bad guys at the end, never sensing the hollowness of his victory. Even as venerable a critic as Itō Sei seems to have been taken in. Donald Keene notes that Itō "pronounced Botchan to be 'typically Japanese' in his optimism, sympathy, innocence, and his lack of pettiness, arrogance, or slyness," although Keene distances himself from this view somewhat by calling it "an ideal" of sorts. Indeed, it is an ideal—or an idealization of the kind of simple honesty that most Japanese long for because it is so rarely attainable in undiluted form in Japanese—or any—society.

Botchan has no patience for the calculations and machinations that dominate his society, but he has no effective way to combat them. Of course, Japanese society is not full of the cartoonish villains who surround Botchan: they are exaggerated versions of the petty dishonesties that mark life in all societies around the world, and Botchan's thrashing of the chief villains at the end is a correspondingly cartoonish exaggeration of standing up for righteousness and simplicity. "Should I believe what others tell me, and interpret all their words and actions at face value?" Sōseki was still asking near the end of his life. In *Botchan* one can almost hear him saying, "If only we could!" and millions of Japanese readers have responded with nostalgia to the book's longing for childlike innocence.

Ruth Benedict took *Botchan* as an illustration of Japanese interpersonal relations when she did her documentary study of the Japanese psyche during World War II, *The Chrysanthemum and the Sword* (1946), noting Botchan's insistence on returning the pittance spent on him for some ice water by an associate he later believes to be plotting against him. "Such acute sensitivity about trifles, such painful vulnerability occurs in American records of adolescent gangs and in case-histories of neurotics. But this is Japanese virtue," she says, and she draws revealing parallels between Japanese emotional exchanges and American attitudes toward "financial transactions" (pp. 108, 112).

Benedict's analysis, however, rests on the assumption that Botchan equals Sōseki equals "typically Japanese," and although the Japanese majority view of Botchan's lovability seems to support her in this, it is important not to lose sight of the fact that Sōseki presents Botchan as a good deal less intelligent than his predecessor, the cat, who looks upon the human world with amusement. Botchan is not bright enough to be amused. Far from it: having been denied the love of his family, he is downright angry from beginning to end, much like a belligerent member of one of Benedict's adolescent gangs. Instead of laughing, he fumes, and the more he fumes, the more he talks about the need for violence, and the more he talks about violence, the more mention is made of the war that Japan is "presently" fighting against Russia (*NKBT*, vol. 25, p. 493, n. 28). The two come together in the next-to-last chapter as Botchan and his one ally plunge into a brawl that erupts during a celebration of Japan's great victory. Even Botchan can see the connection, as he and his friend are preparing to trounce the head rogue: "The only way to beat him was with brute strength. War, I thought, will always be present in the world. Even individuals resort to force to settle things in the end" (*SZ*, vol. 2, p. 387; tr. p. 159).

With the enacting of violence comes the kind of high-flown rhetoric so often used to justify it. Botchan and his pal speak of "justice," and they assure each other that they are going to carry out "divine retribution" (*tenchū*), the traditional language of Japanese assassins killing for a righteous cause (*SZ*, vol. 2, p. 391; tr. p. 391). Sōseki seems to have done almost too good a job at making his villains slimy and hypocritical. For most readers, his ironic commentary on war and violence is lost

in the rush of good feeling that accompanies the charge of the cavalry at the end.

The other truly memorable work that Sōseki wrote as a part-time novelist is *The Three-Cornered World*. Its title, *Kusamakura*, which literally means "grass pillow," is an epithet for travel that comes directly out of Japan's most conservative poetic tradition and alerts the reader to expect something old-fashioned. (Since such associations would be lost on a foreign reader, the translator has wisely chosen an evocative phrase from the text of the novel and provided it in context as an epigraph: "An artist is a person who lives in the triangle which remains after the angle which we may call common sense has been removed from this four-cornered world" [*SZ*, vol. 3, p. 34; tr. p. 48].) Elegantly stylized, there could hardly have been a work in starker contrast to something like Shimazaki Tōson's *Hakai* (March 1906; *The Broken Commandment*, 1974), the earnest, rather clumsily written study of outcaste suffering that had started Japan's naturalist revolution. In the midst of naturalism's cries for the unvarnished truth and condemnations of sheer stylistic polish, Sōseki struck a most discordant note when he told an interviewer that all he hoped to do in *The Three-Cornered World* was to leave the reader with an impression of beauty such as might be obtained from haiku.

But beauty does not exist in a vacuum in this novel. Depicted primarily as a kind of detached, "nonhuman" Eastern aestheticism that might have satisfied Kushami's Zen philosopher friend, scenes of beauty are consciously sought out as therapy for the ills of modern society, and each transcendent flight ends with the artist-protagonist's fall to earth—in one instance, quite literally on his rear end! Sōseki was well aware of the importance of *The Broken Commandment*, and he wrote to a friend in October 1906 expressing admiration for its utter seriousness: "Anyone who wants to make literature his life cannot be satisfied exclusively with beauty, but I want both at the same time. I want to frequent those detached regions of haiku, but I also want to write with the spiritual intensity of a hero of the Meiji Restoration, as though my very life were at stake," which is what he recognized in Tōson's novel and knew was missing from *The Three-Cornered World* (*SZ*, vol. 22, pp. 605–606).

The Professional Novelist: *Gubijinsō* and *The Miner*

By the time he wrote his letter contrasting his haiku novel with the new naturalism, Sōseki was indeed thinking seriously of making literature his life, despite lingering Confucian attitudes that looked upon novelists as entertainers closely tied to the world of the actor and the prostitute. He soon started to receive offers from several newspapers to join their staffs in various writing positions, but he turned them down until the Tokyo *Asahi Shinbun* offered to make him the highest-paid member of the staff as a full-time novelist. His salary would be ¥200 per month, which was ¥30 more than the editor-in-chief was receiving. He had been managing to take in ¥125–155 from his three teaching positions, which was vastly better than the ¥16 per month of an elementary school teacher or even the ¥50 middle-class average, but it was still a struggle for him and his wife Kyōko to make ends meet. What most attracted him, of course, was the time to write, free of academic chores. When he finally turned his back on the most prestigious university in the country in March 1907, the news caused an uproar. Sōseki himself wrote a statement for the *Asahi* in which he said that he did not understand why everyone should be so amazed. "If being a newspaperman *(shinbun'ya)* is a trade *(shōbai)*, then being a university man *(daigakuya)* is also a trade" (*SZ*, vol. 16, pp. 60–61), he insisted with the egalitarian spirit of his Edo townsman roots. And in a public lecture, he expressed his belief in the social validity of his profession with both humor and idealism:

My friends have all been laughing at me. They say I quit the university to spend my afternoons napping on the veranda. . . . Yes,

I nap in the afternoon—and in the morning and the evening, too . . . but I am not just sleeping, I'm lying there trying to think of something important. Unfortunately, I haven't come up with anything yet, but I am no *himajin* [man of leisure, lazy good-for-nothing]. . . . A *himajin* is someone who can contribute nothing to the world, who cannot provide an interpretation of how we ought to live and teach the common man the meaning of existence. . . . When an artist believes himself to be a *himajin*, he throws his calling out the window and offends Heaven. The artist must decide once and for all that he is no *himajin*.

(*SZ*, vol. 16, pp. 134–136).

If Sōseki thought he was going to "teach the common man the meaning of existence," then he still had a way to go before he could become more a novelist and less a professor. He learned his lesson quickly by writing two disastrous novels, *Gubijinsō*, (1907; The poppy) serialized in the *Asahi* from June to October 1907, and *Kōfu* (1908; *The Miner*, 1988) from January to April, 1908.

The Professor stands front and center in *Gubijinsō* in the guise of a character named Kōno, a philosopher who understands life and humankind and who knows how people "ought to live." It is above all this moral certitude that makes the novel unreadable today. The language is labored and ornate. The characters are painted in intense monochromes and act out a convoluted plot with conflicting loves and obligations, chance encounters, sly machinations, and dramatic confrontations. The novel was a hit even before it reached the newsstands, thanks in part to the success of Sōseki's earlier works and to curiosity about his highly publicized resignation from the university. One department store sold *Gubijinsō* robes, and a jewelry firm came out with *Gubijinsō* rings. Once the novel reached the pages of the newspaper, the enthusiasm spilled over into a warm public reception, if not universal critical acclaim. The shortcomings of the book were clear to Sōseki himself, again even before serialization. On 17 June 1907, he wrote to a friend that he was already finding his manuscript unpleasant to read, and by July he confessed that he wanted to kill off his heroine. A few years later he rejected another friend's suggestion that the novel be translated into German, saying that he would just as soon see the book go out of print in Japan, if it were not for the occasional royalty payment; still less did he want to compound the embarrassment by having Germans read the thing, too.

If the few brief mentions of *Gubijinsō* in his correspondence show Sōseki's dissatisfaction with that novel, *The Miner* demonstrates conclusively his absolute rejection of it. No two books from a single hand could have been more starkly different. Both novels begin with their central characters walking through the countryside, but there the similarity ends. In *The Miner*, the elaborate circumlocutions of the earlier novel have given way to a tough, telegraphic, colloquial prose—language that may suggest an unstoppable flow of thought but never invites the reader to linger over a well-turned phrase, as is so painfully true of *Gubijinsō*. And as different as the prose styles are the landscapes through which Sōseki's characters walk. The squarely-built aspiring diplomat Munechika and his tall, thin friend, the philosopher Kōno, who appear in the opening scene of *Gubijinsō*, are climbing the flanks of Mt. Hiei northeast of Kyoto, gazing at the peak towering above them, its very name reverberating with the rich history of Japan's traditional political and cultural center. Not only is the protagonist of *The Miner* walking through a nameless pine grove, the reader never gets to see what he looks like, so firmly is the narrative locked inside his brain (or his text), and he is identified only as "I" *(jibun)*. Far from being rich with historical associations, the landscape is almost phantasmagorical—dark and abstract. And from it, inexplicably, materializes a series of Bosch grotesques: the fat-lipped Chōzō with his protruding cheekbones and crooked, tobacco-stained teeth; the urinating tea-stand woman with her twisted mouth; men with suppurating eyes and sloping foreheads, pale

skin and wasted flesh; a bland, faceless bumpkin eternally swathed in his stinking red blanket; and a disturbingly bat-like boy who swoops down alone from the hills.

Ironically, *Gubijinsō*, with its roots firmly planted in nineteenth-century realism, was entirely fictional, whereas the abstractly modernist *Miner* was based in part on the experience of a young man who visited Sōseki in November 1907 for the express purpose of selling his "story" as material for a novel. The notes that Sōseki took at the time reveal that the young man worked for the notoriously polluting Ashio copper mine and carefully record the route he took to get there, but Sōseki has removed nearly all such identifiable labels from his narrative. Whereas it is possible to learn something about the scenery east of Kyoto or about wealthy Tokyo lifestyles from *Gubijinsō*, *The Miner* is worthless as travel literature, and it gives the reader hardly more than a glimpse of the life of the miners, for Sōseki has done everything he can to make the journey of his protagonist a psychological one. The story of a young man whose love life has fallen to pieces, *The Miner* simply shows the nineteen-year-old protagonist fleeing from Tokyo, being picked up by a procurer of cheap labor for a copper mine, then traveling toward—and finally burrowing into the depths of—the mine where he hopes to find oblivion.

Sōseki stripped away all the melodramatic elements from the young man's story, leaving only the bare bones of the journey and descent. He then turned this virtually nonexistent plot material into a novel by having the protagonist reflect at length on his every thought and perception, in terms both of what he noticed at the time and of what the experience means to him now as a mature adult. This prolix analysis of nonevents (such as a split-second interval of visual clarity that requires three pages of description and commentary) drove some readers to distraction. "You'd think Sōseki was some kind of antique dealer, the way he attaches a certificate of authenticity to everything in the novel," fumed one critic who had read about half the installments. (See the translator's Afterword for the preceding and following quotations.)

These remarks appeared in a March 1908 magazine symposium in which thirteen prominent writers and intellectuals gave their views on Sōseki. They saw him as an original stylist, a pioneer in humor, a writer attempting to transcend the real world, and a man "incapable of writing tragedy" whose works "are finally not modern fiction." Not one of the contributors had a good word for *The Miner*. After a year of spectacular popularity with *I Am a Cat*, *Botchan*, and *The Three-Cornered World* in 1906, Sōseki had disappointed the critics (if not the general public) with *Nowaki* (1907; The autumn wind) and *Gubijinsō* in 1907. He was not living up to his early promise, and *The Miner* seemed to confirm his decline.

Sōseki himself was aware of the difficulties many readers would have because he was not willing to give them a story. He did not want to investigate cause-and-effect relationships that link events, he told an interviewer, but rather to analyze the elements that compose events, each discreet from the other. Readers of *I Am a Cat* or "The Heredity of Taste" should not have found this disturbing, but the imagery of *The Miner* was too stark, the laughs too few and too intellectual, the analysis of psychological phenomena too nigglingly precise. *The Miner* remains Sōseki's least known novel, though subsequent commentators have loosely applied such terms as "stream-of-consciousness" and "avant garde" to a work closer to Samuel Beckett than to Tokugawa-period novels designed to "encourage virtue and chastise vice," as has been said of *Gubijinsō*.

In *The Miner*, the narrator's haphazard descent into the dark bowels of the earth parallels his descent into himself. The experience leads him to the conclusion that "there is nothing so unreliable as man" (*SZ*, vol. 5, p. 27; tr. p. 16), which seems to echo *I Am a Cat* ("In the whole wide world there's no creature more ready to cheat you than a human being" [*NKBT*, vol. 24, p. 56, tr. p. 38]) and *Botchan* ("There's nothing so unreliable as people" [*SZ*, vol. 2, p. 337; tr., p. 108]), but in this novel the

expression takes on a whole new meaning. When Botchan said "there's nothing so unreliable as people," he saw himself as the one honest man surrounded by liars and cheats. The self-righteous Dōya Sensei of "The Autumn Wind" defines "an ordinary human being" as someone who is "out to fool the world" (*SZ*, vol. 3, p. 353). By contrast, the narrator of *The Miner* reaches his conclusion on the unreliability of humans by observing himself: "Having witnessed the reeling, irregular activity of my fragmented soul, I must conclude from a thoroughly impartial view of the real me that there is nothing so unreliable as man." He supports his assertion by spelling out at great length what he calls "my theory of the non-existence of character." What we mistakenly call personality is "nothing but a bunch of memories," he insists. "In fact, there is no such thing as character, something fixed and final. The real thing is something that novelists don't know how to write about—or, if they tried, the end result would never be a novel" (*SZ*, vol. 5, pp. 27, 202, 27, 10; tr. pp. 16, 121, 16, 7), and the reader watches as the novel form disintegrates in *The Miner* along with any certitude regarding human character. *The Miner* is a bold, supremely modern work that will never have many readers but will stand as one of the foremost Japanese experiments in modern fiction. It was, in any case, a major breakthrough for Sōseki. Never again would an "ordinary human being" in his works be an evil "other." *The Miner* opened the way for him to become Japan's great modern tragic novelist even if, at the time, it contributed to a drastic decline in his popularity.

Serialized in ten installments between *The Miner* and Sōseki's next full-length novel (*Sanshirō* [1908; *Sanshirō*, 1977]) was one of Sōseki's most successful pieces of fantasy, "Yume jūya" (1908; "Ten Nights of Dream," 1974), a marvelously funny, creepy, and beautiful set of polished but enigmatic pieces presented without explanation as if they were actual dreams of the author. In one, a samurai struggles to achieve a state of Zen nothingness—and probably does, somewhere after the last line of the story. In another, a bored dreamer leaps over the railing of a huge ocean liner into the black empty sea, regretting as he falls that he did not stay aboard in spite of the ship's lack of destination or purpose. In the last and wildest piece, a character named Shōtarō stands on the edge of a cliff, knocking a gigantic herd of pigs over the edge one at a time before they can lick him; he tires and falls in the end, losing his panama hat in the bargain.

Sanshirō

If *The Miner* lost readers for Sōseki, his next novel, *Sanshirō*, brought them back again. Serialized after *The Miner*, from September through December 1908, it was instantly loved and remained so into the twenty-first century, attracting tourists to the campus of Tokyo University to see the pond that has been informally named for the twenty-three-year-old protagonist. Ogawa Sanshirō is a Kumamoto Higher School graduate who comes to Tokyo for the first time in his life to enter the university. His amazement at the uproar of the big city, his love for the modern, individualistic Mineko, whom he first sees by the university pond, his attraction to the quiet world behind the walls of the university, his problems with his comical friend Yojirō and the scientist Nonomiya are all sketched with a delicate, warmly humorous touch that qualifies *Sanshirō* as the first of Sōseki's mature novels. In *Sanshirō*, Sōseki returned to a third-person narrative in which he was able to stay close to his main character but occasionally comment on him from a distance as well, the stance he adopted in all but two of his remaining novels (and in both of those, the "I" narrator is a device for observing the central character).

Sanshirō himself might be seen as a Botchan without the anger, and all the other characters are memorable personalities who have risen above their early incarnations as caricatures in *I Am a Cat*, most notably Professor Hirota, one of the most appealing reincarnations of Kushami. Hirota has the Sōseki/Kushami mustache, he blows billows of "philosophical smoke," and like Sōseki/Kushami he is a teacher of English at the First Higher School. (The title "Professor" in the translation is something of a misnomer, but then Meiji "higher" schools were more like undergraduate liberal arts colleges than modern high schools.) Without Hirota's knowledge, Yojirō foments a movement to have him appointed to a university post to replace a foreign professor, a fiasco that comically inverts the student discontent with Sōseki as a replacement for Lafcadio Hearn.

The first real-world shock that Sanshirō experiences after leaving home in Kumamoto is delivered to him by a woman he meets on the train who maneuvers him into spending the night with her partway to Tokyo. He barely escapes with his purity intact and is just recovering from her branding him a coward when a stranger with a big mustache (who later turns out to be Hirota) delivers a shock to his national pride: "We can beat the Russians, we can become a first-class power, but it doesn't make any difference," he says coolly, and he calls Mt. Fuji, one of the most important symbols of the nation, "just a natural object."

> Sanshirō had never expected to meet anyone like this after the Russo-Japanese War. The man was almost not a Japanese, he felt.
>
> "But still," Sanshirō argued, "Japan will start developing from now on at least."
>
> "Japan is going to perish," the man replied coolly.
>
> Anyone who dared say such a thing in Kumamoto would have been taken out and thrashed, perhaps even arrested for treason.
>
> (SZ, vol. 5, pp. 291–292; tr. p. 15)

Sōseki gives Hirota and the novel depth and unity by investing him with a past that harkens back to the year when the twenty-two-year-old Sōseki himself spoke to the First Higher School's Morals Society against the excesses of nationalism. Hirota (and probably Sōseki, too) was part of a contingent from the school given rifles to shoulder as they stood on the curb to watch the passing of the funeral procession of Mori Arinori, the assassinated Minister of Education. Readers of *Sanshirō* will never know if, like Hirota, Sōseki saw a beautiful girl in the cortege who made a deep impression on him and became his unchanging, picture-like *mori no onna* ("girl in the Mori funeral procession" / "girl in the *mori* [forest]"), but Sōseki uses the historical event to pinpoint the year *before* Hirota was disillusioned by his mother's deathbed revelation of his real father's identity, when he presumably became the misanthrope he appears to be today. Thus, when Sanshirō loses Mineko to a more worldly young man and she is turned into a picture called "The Girl in the Forest," it can be assumed that this is the last year of Sanshirō's innocence. When the new year comes, he will almost certainly have an experience that will darken his life forever.

And Then

And then came Daisuke in *Sore kara (And Then)*. Sōseki wrote advertising copy for this novel explaining that it would be "and then" in three senses: "first, because *Sanshirō* was about a university student, and the new work would be about what 'then' happened; second, because Sanshirō was a simple man, but the new main character would be in a more advanced stage; and finally, because a strange fate was about to befall this character, but what 'then' followed would not be described" (from the translator's Afterword, p. 266). The major problem of *And Then*, which was serialized from June to August 1909, is how to deal with the protagonist, Daisuke, who was probably named in memory of one of Sōseki's dissolute elder brothers. He is so self-centered and so unwilling to *do* anything for most of the novel that you sometimes want to shake him and yell "Get a spine!" On the other hand, a great deal of what he thinks to himself and says to other people is so sharp and so right that you know he is expressing some of Sōseki's most deeply-held convictions.

Daisuke is less an heir of the Botchan-Sanshirō line than a refined version of Kushami-

Hirota. He is above all a mind—a modern, rational mind that has constructed a wall of philosophy between itself and the threat of social and emotional entanglements, only to be betrayed from within by uncontrollable irrational needs. The author gives the name "Michiyo" to the woman that Daisuke comes to realize his need for, but she is less a woman than a function of his psyche. The precision with which Sōseki portrays the workings of Daisuke's mind, however, and the intrinsic interest of Daisuke's analyses of his relationship to modern society, combine to make *And Then* one of the most important Japanese novels of the twentieth century.

Sōseki practically announces aloud with his bold opening sentence that the novel's major "action" will take place inside the protagonist's skull: "Someone clattered past the front gate—and then a huge wooden clog was dangling in space inside Daisuke's head" (*SZ*, vol. 6, p. 3; cf. tr. p. 1). So absorbed is Daisuke in his thoughts and feelings that at times he actually believes he is capable of sensing the layers of his own brain tissue. The father's bloody background as a samurai, the family's near-involvement in a major financial scandal, police surveillance of socialists, the struggles of a literary hack, an Englishman's garden party, a visit to an eel restaurant, Daisuke's banter with his houseboy, his endless mental and physical self-examination (in bed, in the bathroom, on the streetcar, in the smokey crush of Tokyo's middle-class housing)—all of these are elements of Daisuke's inner world. One of the most stunningly interior moments occurs when Daisuke mentally touches up a painting that fails to live up to his standards: "Soon, by controlling the colors that flew from his eyes, Daisuke was able to correct all the places that had displeased him" (*SZ*, vol. 6, p. 48).

The process by which Daisuke's realization of his need for Michiyo gradually works itself from the repressed corners to the conscious surface of his mind remains a major literary feat. Michiyo is, after all, a married woman, not someone he should be thinking of as a love object, and Daisuke himself had given his blessing to the match between Michiyo and his best friend. Equally striking is the flaming eruption of red that suggests at the end that Daisuke's confrontation with the real world is going to push him over the edge from obsession into madness.

This deep inward focus would be of some interest in any case, but what makes the novel truly fascinating is that Daisuke's misguided rationalizations for turning his back on the world are based on a devastatingly accurate analysis of the ills of modern society. One newspaper reviewer wrote at the time, "On page after page, we experience the excitement of encountering our own half-formed thoughts and feelings given clear expression." Daisuke's view of the stresses of Japan's modern civilization and individualism are not much different from Kushami's in *I Am a Cat*; indeed, they are close to Sōseki's own lecture, "Gendai Nihon no kaika" (1911; "The Civilization of Modern-Day Japan," 1992), to be discussed below, and to Sōseki's hopeless cry for human trust from his late memoirs quoted in the introduction to this article:

> Daisuke . . . believed that if people had faith in one another, there was no need to rely on gods. Gods acquired the right to exist only when they became necessary to deliver men from the anguish of mutual suspicion. Accordingly, he concluded that in those countries where gods existed, the people were liars. But he discovered that present-day Japan was a country having faith neither in gods nor men. He attributed it all to Japan's economic situation.
>
> (*SZ*, vol. 6, p. 155; tr. p. 115).

Religion was not a major theme in *And Then*, but it took a central position in Sōseki's next novel, *Mon* (1910; *Mon [The Gate]*, 1972).

Sōseki in Manchuria

And Then was still being serialized when an old school friend of Sōseki's with a high post in Manchuria invited him to "come have a look at what the Japanese are doing overseas." Newly wrested from Russian control, Manchuria was a great new money-making opportunity for thousands of Japanese with a little adventure in their hearts, and an increasingly common tourist destination for wealthy travelers curious to see this vast land now under Japanese dominion. Sōseki traveled around Manchuria and Korea from 6 September to 13 October 1909, serializing a column in the *Asahi* called "Man-Kan tokoro-dokoro" (Here and there in Manchuria and Korea) in 51 installments from October through December. If Sōseki seemed prescient in having *Sanshirō*'s Professor Hirota predict that someday Japan would "perish," he seems like nothing so much as an arrogant tourist in the record of his travels. His text routinely refers to Chinese as "Chinks" (*chan*) or "natives" *(dojin)*, describes them as "apathetic" or "cruel," complains about the "stink" and the "filth" of the country and the people, toward whom he adopts a consistently superior attitude (*SZ*, vol. 12, p. 235).

The friend who invited Sōseki was Nakamura Zekō, the president of the South Manchuria Railway, which had been ceded to Japan by Russia according to the terms of the Portsmouth Treaty following the Russo-Japanese War. Sōseki naturally associated only with high-placed Japanese, viewing Manchuria and Korea with the perceptions of a victor. Japan's puppet state of Manchukuo was not established for another twenty-three years, but already Japan was firmly in charge. Writing from Korea, Sōseki remarked in an 9 October postcard to one friend, "There are so many Japanese here, it's like being at home," and much of Sōseki's column was devoted to his meetings with the Japanese good old-boy network in Manchuria (*SZ*, vol. 23, p. 294).

Sōseki was back in Tokyo, and "Man-Kan tokoro-dokoro" had been appearing for less than a week when, on 26 October 1909, the legendary elder statesman Itō Hirobumi, Japan's resident general of Korea (whose authority had also been confirmed by the Portsmouth Treaty) was assassinated by a

Korean independence activist in the Manchurian city of Harbin. According to the critic Etō Jun, Sōseki's host, Nakamura Zekō, was close enough to Itō to end up with bullet holes in his coat and pants, and he helped carry Itō into the rail car where he died on a table half an hour later. Japan formally annexed Korea the following year. Sōseki, who had given *And Then*'s Daisuke a friend working in the resident general's office the year before (chapter 5), must have had a pretty good idea of "what the Japanese were doing overseas." For him, though, this was just a "pleasure trip" (*yūran*, *SZ*, vol. 12, p. 290). As strongly as he had written criticizing jingoism and depicting the horrible sacrifice of individual lives in the taking of a mountaintop vantage point, when he actually went to tour the famous strategic Hill 203 overlooking Port Arthur, where 59,000 Japanese, including both sons of General Nogi, had lost their lives in 155 days of fighting, he could only write "in admiration for the great determination of Japan's military men" (*SZ*, vol. 12, p. 285). Of course, it is unfair to fault the attitude of someone in 1909 with expectations from the year 2000, but it is hard not to be disappointed in Sōseki for having been so . . . ordinary.

Fortunately, the article does not represent Sōseki's entire attitude toward China, a country whose culture and literature he knew well and admired. In the entry for 15 March 1901, for example, the diary he kept in London says:

Why do Japanese hate so much to be taken for Chinese? The Chinese are a far more glorious people than the Japanese. They just happen, unfortunately, to have fallen upon hard times at the moment. . . . Think how much Japan has owed to China over the years! Westerners imagine they are flattering us when they say they like the Japanese but not the Chinese. Anyone cheered by such flattery would have to be silly and superficial enough to enjoy the lift it gives them to hear a helpful neighbor being slurred.

(*SZ*, vol. 19, p. 65).

Despite the title, "Man-Kan tokoro-dokoro" has nothing to say about Korea because the serialization broke off at the end of the year— before the account of Sōseki's "pleasure trip" was even half over. The explanation Sōseki offered readers in the 30 December installment was that it would be "strange" to serialize something from one year into the next, which was like no explanation at all. According to the critic Etō Jun, Sōseki had been looking for an excuse, however flimsy, to end the series since neither he nor—he was sure—his readers were interested in it anymore with all the excitement over the Itō assasination. It has been suggested, too, by the critic Ryū Kenki, that he was tired of writing pap that would please his host. He would have more interesting things to say about Manchuria in his fiction.

Mon (The Gate)

Although Daisuke was a far more intelligent and sophisticated character than Sanshirō, Sōseki thought of his story as sequentially linked with Sanshirō's, and he obviously thought of the next novel, *The Gate*, as the continuation of the story, the three forming a kind of trilogy. The hero of *The Gate*, Sōsuke (not to be confused with Sōseki), does not measure up to Daisuke intellectually any better than Sanshirō did. In fact, *The Gate* can be read as the story of what might have happened to an older Sanshirō who had taken his best friend's wife as Daisuke hoped to do. The hero of Sōseki's 1913 novel *Kōjin* (1913; *The Wayfarer*, 1967) sees the only answers to his modern anxiety as "To die, to go mad, or to enter religion" (*SZ*, vol. 8, p. 412; tr. p. 296). Sanshirō was still too innocent for such drama, and Sōseki himself was not ready to have his protagonist resort to death. Daisuke seemed headed for madness. Sōsuke will seek solace in religion. In fact, the *sō* in his name is part of the word for "religion."

Sōseki adopts a nearly-omniscient narrative perspective in *The Gate*, staying mostly with Sōsuke but occasionally providing glimpses of conversations or thoughts to which Sōsuke has no access. Because the narrator could tell the reader certain key information but chooses not to, the novel can be seen as flawed to a degree by authorial obfuscation. The narrator doles out hints about the "sinful" past of Sōsuke and his wife, but he never reveals exactly how Sōsuke took Oyone from his friend, Yasui. The novel simply shows Sōsuke and Oyone living their sad, quiet lives in their dark, little house beneath the cliff. The description of that life, however, has great power.

The opening description of Sōsuke trying to catch a few rays of sunlight on his cramped veranda makes it clear that this is a different world from Daisuke's. "The warm, clear autumn air carried the pleasant clip-clop of wooden clogs through the quiet neighborhood" (*SZ*, vol. 6, p. 347; cf. tr. p. 5). The surreal image of the "huge wooden clog . . . dangling in space inside Daisuke's head" has been transformed into an ordinary part of Sōsuke's commonsense world. Where Daisuke was a pampered rich boy, one of a series of "upperclass idlers" *(kōtō yūmin)* in Sōseki's fiction, Sōsuke is a self-described "flunkey" *(koshiben*, literally someone who carries a "boxed lunch at the waist" to his low-level position) who rides the crowded streetcar to work each day, has a dying tooth treated by his dentist, abandons any hope that he will ever be a success, and tries not to think too much about his past sins. Where Daisuke had the time to agonize over grand questions such as the relationship of Japan and the Western world, Sōsuke is a victim of the very texture of the impersonal crush of everyday urban life. Sōseki's choice of detail here is impeccable: he imbues the felt cushions on the street car, the advertisements, the shop windows and their contents, the sweet play of the landlord's many children (in contrast to Sōsuke's own childless home) with a resigned melancholy that tells the reader more about ordinary life in Meiji Tokyo than all of Daisuke's abstractions. Those early experiments at observing life in the Kushami household reach their full, sad flowering here. *The Gate* is a heartbreaking novel.

On a day-to-day basis, money is Sōsuke's biggest problem. An uncle cheated him out of most of his inheritance, and now he has to find a way to help his brother, Koroku, finish college. Sōseki is almost too careful in spelling out the details of Sōsuke and Oyone's finances, but he is just as careful to demonstrate the modulations in interpersonal relations based on calculation of financial advantage. Sōsuke's brother begins acting brotherly only when he needs Sōsuke's financial support.

Sōsuke's remark about his low status occurs in a passage that is ironic in several ways, both in the dramatic context of the novel and historically, as Sōseki brings to bear his recent experience in Manchuria and Korea. At one point, Sōsuke tells Oyone the "terrible news" that Prince Itō Hirobumi has been assassinated. She responds, " 'Terrible news,' you say, but judging from your voice, you're not particularly upset by it." Nothing in Sōseki's letters or diaries suggests that he was particularly upset by the assassination, either. His earlier references to Itō (in *I Am a Cat* and his diary) had usually been either mocking or outraged. The muted comic tone in *The Gate*, however, is not so much imposed by Sōseki the skeptic as drawn from his ordinary middle-class characters by Sōseki the novelist. That tone continues as the couple discusses the Itō matter a few days later with Sōsuke's brother, Koroku, but then it shifts suddenly at the end. Oyone remarks how terrible it must have been for Itō to have been murdered. Sōsuke responds:

"If it had been a flunky like me, it would be terrible, all right. But for someone like Itō, it was to his advantage to go to Harbin and be assassinated . . . . By being assassinated he stands a good chance of becoming a famous historical figure. He could never have achieved that just by dying." [In fact, Itō was a giant figure whose historical position had long been assured. His bearded visage graced the front of the thousand-yen bill from 1963 to 1984, when it was replaced by the mustachioed, high-collared image of Natsume Sōseki.]

"There's something in what you say."
Koroku seemed to accept his brother's logic,
at least in part, but finally he added, "But
still, Harbin . . . in fact, all of Manchuria is
a very unsettled place. I can't help feeling
that it's tremendously dangerous."

"That's because a lot of different people
are converging there."

At these words, Oyone's face took on a
strange expression as she looked at her husband. Sōsuke seemed to take note of this,
and quickly put an end to the conversation
by signalling her to clear the table.

(*SZ*, vol. 6, pp. 367–369; revised
from tr. pp. 21–23)

The reader does not know it yet, but Oyone
gives her husband a strange look because he
and she both know that one of the many people "converging" on Manchuria is Yasui, the
friend that Sōsuke betrayed some years ago, an
event that ruined all their lives. Manchuria
lurks in the background of the novel as a fact
of life for Japanese living through the early
years of the spreading empire, and a source of
danger. Sōsuke is shocked soon afterward to
hear that Yasui is back from Manchuria with a
fellow "adventurer" and will be visiting a
neighbor, and he decides to go to a temple in
nearby Kamakura to try Zen meditation.

Sōsuke's attempt to find religion is misdi-
rected from the start. He is willing to "take ten
or twenty days off from work" to give it a try,
but he quickly learns that the way of Zen is
difficult and often takes a lifetime (*SZ*, vol. 6,
p. 565; tr. p. 177). Like any Zen beginner, he
struggles with vagrant thoughts and physical
discomfort. He finds the Zen *kōan* he is given
to solve "totally irrelevant. It was as if he had
come for relief from a stomach-ache and had
been offered a difficult mathematics problem"
to think about (*SZ*, vol. 6, p. 577). He is motivated to keep trying not by inner need but out
of respect for the admirable young priest who
gives him instruction. Finally, he concludes it
has all been a waste of time. The narrator says
(in Edwin McClellan's beautiful translation):

He . . . looked at the great gate which would
never open for him. He was never meant to
pass through it. Nor was he meant to be
content until he was allowed to do so. He
was, then, one of those unfortunate beings
who must stand by the gate, unable to
move, and patiently wait for the day to end.

(*SZ*, vol. 6, pp. 598–599; cf. tr. pp. 204–205;
McClellan, *Two Japanese Novelists*, p. 45)

It is clear that Sōseki rejected religion as an
abdication of intellectual honesty. As he saw
it, with William James's help, all life was nothing other than the "succession of consciousness" (*SZ*, vol. 19, p. 312). For him, mind and
the external world were inseparable, and such
concepts as the transcendent or the absolute
were impossible to experience, mere delusions
(*mōsō*) or "hallucinations," to quote his English. As he put it in English, "Religion is after
all a matter of faith, not argument or reason."
Tearful Christian missionaries with their
claims of exclusive access to salvation he
found "pathetic," according to the critic Van
C. Gessel, and Buddhist claims of having experienced oneness with the universe were false
on the face of it because if all is one, there can
be no separate self present to perceive it (*SZ*,
vol. 21, pp. 46–48).

Sōseki himself, during a particularly severe
bout of mental suffering, had tried to achieve
satori or enlightenment at a Zen temple in
Kamakura for a few weeks over New Year's
1894–1895 at the age of 27. Like Sōsuke, he
was given the Zen *kōan* to solve: "What was
your original face before the birth of your
father and mother?"—a riddle that demands an
understanding of the immersion—indeed, the
loss—of the self in the oneness of the universe.
The idea is expressed in this poem entitled
"Original Face" (*honrai no menmoku*), in
which the great thirteenth-century Zen
thinker, Dōgen, defined his innermost self in
this utterly selfless way: "In the spring, cherry
blossoms, / in the summer the cuckoo. / In
autumn the moon, and in / winter the snow,
clear, cold" (Kawabata, pp. 6, 74). Sōseki, however, resorted to "mere intellect" when he gave

this answer to the *kōan:* "No phenomena independent of mind and no mind independent of phenomena" (*SZ*, vol. 21, pp. 12, 46). The priest treated his answer with contempt. Although Sōseki continued to have doubts about his own ability to attain enlightenment, he admired the serenity he recognized in some of the individual priests he met.

We saw how merciless Sōseki could be in satirizing Zen charlatanism in *I Am a Cat,* and in fact Sōseki continued to make fun of shaven-headed priests selling religion in some of the Chinese verse he wrote during the vaunted *sokuten kyoshi* period near the very end of his life: "The long tongue talks about Zen and gains nothing / The bald head peddles the Way—what does he desire?" (*SZ*, vol. 18, p. 415; Yiu, p. 193). Given Sōseki's consistent lack of religious faith, and his frequent reference (since *Cat*) to the "original face" *kōan* as a synonym for mumbo-jumbo, it was perhaps a foregone conclusion that Sōsuke would fail to find the peace he was hoping for in a Kamakura Buddhist temple. The remarkable thing about this section of *The Gate,* however, which is based very closely on Sōseki's own experience in Kamakura, is that the quest for faith is entirely Sōsuke's, not Sōseki's, and so it is presented in the novel as utterly serious, utterly respectful of the priests' sincerity, and finally tragic.

Self and Society

After Japan beat Russia in 1905, there was a distinctly new mood in the country. People were daring to say aloud that it was not so important to devote themselves completely to the nation anymore; they had been sacrificing themselves through high taxes and military service since the beginning of Meiji, and since they had brought the country to the point where it could beat a Caucasian nation, it was time to relax. Naturalist fiction, with its emphasis on the liberation of the individual, was gaining in popularity. In conservative minds, naturalism became confused with socialism, anarchism and individualism. All came from the West and all were equally "dan-

gerous thoughts." In response, when it came to power in 1908, the administration of Katsura Tarō, a former military man and powerful politician, embarked on a campaign to resuscitate the Confucian values of loyalty and filial piety through augmented programs of indoctrination and censorship.

Katsura's government staged a nationwide roundup of leftists beginning on 1 June 1910, and later tried twenty-six of the suspects in a secret trial on largely trumped-up charges of plotting to assassinate the emperor. They sentenced twenty-four of them to death. Twelve of the sentences were commuted to life imprisonment in a show of imperial magnanimity, and the final twelve were promptly executed in January 1911. The event came to be known as the High Treason Incident or the "Kōtoku Incident" after the name of the supposed ringleader, Kōtoku Shūsui, who was the most prominent leftist in the country and one of the twelve executed. (He is mentioned in the 1909 *And Then* in a passage making fun of the government's fear of leftists, before the leftist roundup and the executions that followed.)

During most of this rumor-filled, frightening period, Sōseki was in bed, recovering from a nearly fatal hemorrhaging of his stomach ulcers on 24 August 1910. Still, less than a month after the January 1911 execution, Sōseki treated the Katsura government to a shock that it was not prepared to handle. Without any reference to the Kōtoku Incident, and probably without any political intent in his own mind, Sōseki refused the Ministry of Education's conferral on him of the Doctor of Letters degree for his work as a scholar. He did this solely in defense of his personal integrity, but he made it a public act, publishing several essays and giving interviews on the matter, in which he said he resented the government's arrogance in ordering him to receive an "honor" without asking him if he wanted it. Sōseki refused to accept it, and the Ministry refused to take it back, the tug-of-war continuing in the press for many weeks. The government never did rescind the award, and Sōseki took great care thereafter, whenever he gave a talk or wrote anything, to be sure that any publicity announcing the event *not* use what he called the "mistaken" title. He did not want the false aura of authority attached to his name under any circumstances.

This uproar barely had time to quiet down when the Katsura government announced the formation of a kind of literary academy within the Ministry of Education to encourage the creation of "wholesome" literature embodying the Confucian values of loyalty and filial piety. When the news of the Committee on Literature came out on 18 May, Sōseki was ready with a three-part article for the newspaper. In it he said that the government had so far not only failed to encourage literature, it had *meddled* with it through censorship, and he warned that the government would use this "wholesome" label to meddle even more. Criticized in this way from the outside by Sōseki and others, and manipulated from within by more establishmentarian—but still antibureaucratic—writers such as Mori Ōgai (a holder of the Doctorate of Letters degree), the Committee on Literature self-destructed.

Three months later, in August 1911, Katsura was still in office and Sōseki was well enough to embark on a lecture tour with several *Asahi* colleagues at the request of the Ōsaka *Asahi Shinbun*. This involved a grueling schedule of touring and lecturing for seven days, at the end of which Sōseki vomited blood. He was unable to return to Tokyo until mid-September.

Sōseki's four talks revolved around the question of individual autonomy versus external coercion. This remained his focus whether he was discussing the position of the novelist in modern society, or criticizing the government's folly in attempting to impose outmoded moral concepts on an increasingly individualistic populace, or analyzing the tragic relationship of Japan to the Western world. This last theme was the central concept of the lecture "The Civilization of Modern-Day Japan," in which Sōseki comes out sounding a lot like Daisuke of *And Then* and Professor Hirota of *Sanshirō*.

Over the centuries, says Sōseki in this lecture, the dynamic process of civilization has led to progress in terms of an improved living standard, but not in terms of comfort for the human psyche. Progress brings with it heightened competition, which only tends to increase the "psychological pain" of existence for each individual. For the individual Japanese, it is even worse than for the modern Westerner because the country as a whole has lost its autonomy. Japan's civilization is motivated by the external pressure of the West, and this has its effect on the minutest details in the lives of individuals—matters as seemingly inconsequential as how to hold a knife and fork. The Japanese must endure not only the stress of competition but the additional psychological pain of keeping current with the latest developments that have been imported only half understood from the West. This is true in all fields, but it is especially evident in the case of the university professor, for whom "succumbing to a nervous breakdown is more or less to be expected." Scholars (who, he says, specialize in "making the comprehensible incomprehensible") symbolize the nervous strain that all Japanese must experience to some extent because their values are established for them elsewhere.

If the Westerners, whose mental and physical powers far surpass ours, took a hundred years to get where they are now, and we were able to reach that point in less than half that time . . . , then we could certainly boast of an astounding intellectual accomplishment, but we would also succumb to an incurable nervous breakdown; we would fall by the wayside gasping for breath. . . .

Assuming that my analysis is correct, we can only view Japan's future with pessimism. There seem to be fewer of us nowadays ridiculous enough to boast of Mt. Fuji to foreigners, but we do hear many people proclaiming that victory over Russia made Japan a first-class power. I suppose one can make such claims if one is an incurable optimist.

(*SZ*, vol. 16, pp. 427, 430–440; tr. pp. 269, 272–283)

Death Approaches: *The Wayfarer, Kokoro*

The shadow of death hangs heavy over the rest of Sōseki's career. Although he had recovered well enough from the lecture-tour ulcer attack to return to Tokyo in mid-September 1911, he had to undergo hemorrhoid surgery almost immediately and continued treatment for that malady through the following spring. There was another such operation in September 1912, followed by a period of deep depression for the whole first half of 1913. Sōseki had major ulcer flare-ups again in March–May 1913, September–October 1914, March–April 1915, and finally, the one from which he did not recover, 22 November 1916. Sōseki died on 9 December 1916. His last photographs show him looking a good fifteen or twenty years older than his actual age.

As if his own health problems (including diabetes initially misdiagnosed as rheumatism) were not bad enough, Sōseki had to endure the sudden death of his twenty-month-old fifth daughter, Hinako, in November 1911. He wrote what a terrible blow this was to him, as might be imagined from the unabashedly sentimental glimpses of fathers and children seen in *I Am a Cat* and *The Gate*. Ironically, the rich landlord's brood of happy children in *The Gate*, used as a contrast to Sōsuke's gloomy home, was clearly modeled on Sōseki's own; surviving Natsume family portraits show the girls with big butterfly bows in their hair as described in *The Gate*. Part of the novel that Sōseki · began immediately after Hinako's death, *Higan-sugi made* (1912; *To the Spring Equinox and Beyond*, 1985), reads like—and indeed was for Sōseki—a memorial to her. (Sōseki and Kyōko had six surviving children, four girls and two boys.)

On 25 March 1915, the day an ulcer attack hit him in Kyoto, Sōseki received a telegram that his sister Fusa, the one who had "rescued" him from a sidewalk stand as a baby, was near death from a stroke; she did not live out the month. The portrait of her in *Grass on the Wayside*, begun three months after her death, shows a crude and ignorant but good-hearted woman suffering terribly from asthma and mistreated by an unfaithful husband.

Sōseki increasingly sought relief from his many ills in painting and Chinese verse, steeping himself whenever possible in the kind of elegant, detached aestheticism he had described in *The Three-Cornered World* and which, along with Nō chanting, another hobby, had long been a source of pleasure for him. "How can the fellow . . . find the time for such nonsense?" he has his former self think about Nō chanting in *Grass on the Wayside* (*SZ*, vol. 10, pp. 8–9; tr. p. 6). His interest in the visual arts prompted him to do his own design for the first edition of *Kokoro* (1914; *Kokoro*, 1957) when it came out as the maiden commercial publication of a bookseller named Iwanami, now Japan's premier publisher. The distinctive orange and green design employing ancient Chinese characters has been used by Iwanami for each succeeding edition of Sōseki's complete works ever since.

Three of Sōseki's five remaining novels were seriously affected by his failing health and dwindling mental energy. Much of *To the Spring Equinox and Beyond*, serialized from January to April 1912 as a series of loosely connected episodes, is a meandering detective story that turns out to be a wild goose chase, its one most notable section being the "Rainy Day" chapter that Sōseki started writing on Hinako's birthday and finished on the hundredth-day anniversary of her death. Matsumoto, the "upperclass idler" in this novel, refuses guests on rainy days because of the painful association for him of such weather with the death of his tiny daughter. *The Wayfarer* was another novel that did not have a focus, and the serialization, which Sōseki had started in December 1912, was actually interrupted between April and September the following year after his medical problems flared up again. When it resumed, however, Sōseki threw away much of the inconclusive dramatic mechanism he had built up, narrowed the book's focus to a psychological study of the protagonist, and brought to completion a harrowing portrait of one of his most tortured "upperclass idlers," Ichirō, a professor, for whom there seemed to be no answer to the breakdown in human communication but faith, madness, or death. And finally, after being serialized in 188 tedious installments from May to December 1916, *Meian* (1916; *Light and Darkness*, 1971), remained far from finished upon Sōseki's death.

Two monumental deaths lay within the consciousness of the author of *The Wayfarer* and his readers, those of the Meiji emperor and his "loyal retainer," General Nogi Maresuke, who ripped open his belly to follow his lord in death. Indeed, the passing of the Meiji era was itself a kind of death that was reflected in Sōseki's work, given stunning confirmation by the grisly archaic rite of suicide performed by General Nogi and his wife on the night of the emperor's lavish funeral on 13 September. Sōseki began writing *The Wayfarer* two months after the funeral and suicides, but he did not refer to them directly in the book.

The lack of a firm anchor in its own time is part of what makes *The Wayfarer* Sōseki's grandest failure. Sōseki seems to have been searching for a way to dramatize the plight of his anguished hero without baldly plunging into Ichirō's mind and simply telling the reader, professorially, why he gets along so badly with his wife, his brother (the narrator, Jirō), and others close to him while he can manage meaningless social intercourse perfectly well. Once Sōseki was healthy enough to resume serialization in September 1913 after a five-month break, he seems to have tried for a while to pick up the pieces and then decided that all the dramatic complications and subplots of the novel's first three sections were not going to bring him any closer to Ichirō. At that point, he simply left the threads hanging and, instead, brought in a sympathetic friend, H, to observe Ichirō and write a long letter to his brother, complete with quotations from Ichirō about his inner torment. The last words from the first-person narrator, Jirō, are "The letter read as follows:" (*SZ*, vol. 8, p. 386; tr. p. 279). The rest of the book (sixty-three pages in the standard *zenshū* [Complete works]) is sur-

rounded by one set of quotation marks. (See especially the stunning translations found in Edwin McClellan's *Two Japanese Novelists*.)

One might regret that Sōseki never saw fit to rewrite *The Wayfarer* once he had worked the bugs out, but in a sense, he did, in his masterpiece *Kokoro*, which was serialized from April to August 1914. Here again is to be found the portrait of an anguished intellectual, viewed externally at first by an "I" narrator to arouse the readers' curiosity about him, and then from the inside. Where the letter revealing Ichirō in *The Wayfarer* is written by a friend and comprises less than 15 percent of the book, *Kokoro* presents a long letter (or "testament") by the man himself, and it occupies fully half the novel. And where Sōseki attempted to place Ichirō at the center of a drama involving several complex characters, he places Sensei at the center of the most important event of his time, the dramatic end of the Meiji era itself, simplifying the characterizations to such an extent that, rather than with names, they are identified only as *Sensei* ("teacher/master"), *Watakushi* ("I"), *Ojōsan* ("the young lady"), *Okusan* ("the wife"), K, and so forth—with one important exception to be discussed below. In using such names, Sōseki was developing another aspect of *The Wayfarer*, in which three of the most important characters are known only as Ichirō ("first son"), Jirō ("second son"), and H.

Echoes of many of the earlier novels are heard in the plot developments connected with money. Like Sōsuke of *The Gate*, Sensei was cheated of a substantial inheritance by an uncle. Early in the book, Sensei tries to warn the young narrator to make sure his inheritance is properly settled before his father dies. "I was a little shocked," writes the student, "to see Sensei being so intensely practical," and he assures Sensei that his relatives are good people, to which Sensei responds:

You seem to be under the impression that there is a special breed of bad humans. There is no such thing as a stereotype bad man in this world. Under normal conditions, everybody is more or less good, or, at least, ordinary. But tempt them, and they may suddenly change. That is what is so frightening about men.

When the student asks what kind of temptation Sensei has in mind, the older man laughs and says, "Money, of course. Give a gentleman money, and he will soon turn into a rogue." The student says, "Sensei's trite answer disappointed me" (*SZ*, vol. 9, pp. 77, 78–79, 82–83; tr. pp. 57–58, 60–61).

With these professedly "trite" remarks, Sōseki is echoing a major theme that has been seen in his works from the beginning. Money and its place in social intercourse were indeed of interest to Sōseki in and of themselves, but also as a metaphor for human transactions in general. The novel echoes *The Miner* when Sensei reveals his most disturbing insight about the unreliability of ordinary human beings after he has betrayed his friend K:

When I was cheated by my uncle, I felt very strongly the unreliableness of men. I learned to judge others harshly, but not myself. I thought that, in the midst of a corrupt world, I had managed to remain virtuous. Because of K, however, my self-confidence was shattered. With a shock, I realized that I was [just as human as] my uncle. I became as disgusted with myself as I had been with the rest of the world.

(*SZ*, vol. 9, pp. 288–289; tr. pp. 226–227)

After *The Miner*, there were to be no exceptions: "There is nothing so unreliable as man"—both other and self.

Sōseki originally intended *Kokoro* to be a series of interrelated short stories, but it emerged as his most perfectly formed novel. So unerringly does Sōseki home in on his subject, and so perfectly does he synchronize the events of the book with the end of the Meiji era that this simple drama of the fate of an egotistical "upperclass idler" emerges as the mythic embodiment of the fate of a nation, and stands as one of the world's great expressions of the modern predicament.

The deaths of the emperor and the general are seen not once but twice in the novel. This alone gives the events a sense of gravity and pervasiveness. They are seen first from the perspective of an ordinary family in the countryside (as in the passage on "I," a university student, and his family cited above), and second from the point of view of a sophisticated urban intellectual, the central character, Sensei. The contrast in their reactions is important, the country folks' being simple and emotional, Sensei's more complex—but still emotional.

For Sensei, the suicide of General Nogi—a man for whom he presumably would have had no sympathy—becomes a signal for his own long-delayed suicide. There is no single, clear reason why the suicide of Nogi should encourage Sensei to kill himself for having betrayed his friend K years before. Sensei certainly is not so loyal to the emperor or impressed by Nogi that he would follow his example. The key word for him is *junshi*, "to follow one's lord in death." "I had almost forgotten that there was such a word as '*junshi*,' " he writes in his testament. "It is not a word that one uses normally, and I suppose I had banished it to some remote corner of my memory" (*SZ*, vol. 9, p. 297; tr. p. 233). It takes him completely off guard, opening up wellsprings of feeling that he had assumed to have long since dried up, thanks to his education in "this modern age, so full of freedom, independence, and our own egotistical selves" (*SZ*, vol. 9, p. 41; tr. p. 29). His whole past comes back to him in a new way that takes priority over his devotion to his wife, for whom he has remained alive all these years. Rather than overcoming his self-centeredness with his wife, he transcends his ego by merging with his now-dead era, following it in death as surely as Nogi followed the emperor. This gives his death a heroic dimension, making it more than the snuffing out of one narrow egoist's life.

Sensei does, however, remain locked up inside himself, unable to confess his guilt to his wife, his determination to keep her "a pure, spotless thing" an ironic expression of the gulf that divides them (*SZ*, vol. 9, p. 288; tr. p. 226).

He fails to see, in other words, that she is an individual with a capacity for loneliness as great as his. She is, however, one of the few characters in the book to whom Sōseki has given a name, and with that name, Shizu, he hints at her fate. The wife of General Nogi, who followed her husband in death, was also named Shizu, with a feminine -ko ending. Where Shizuko died in keeping with traditional (or, rather, outmoded) norms, Shizu would have died in response to her husband's blindness to her individuality. Early on in the book, the narrator says, "To this day she does not know" about Sensei's suffering, implying that she is still alive. The last, resonant line of the book, however, addressed to the student-narrator, is, "So long as my wife is alive, I want you to keep everything I have told you a secret—even after I myself am dead" (*SZ*, vol. 9, pp. 34, 300; tr. pp. 24, 236). One does not know whether Sōseki meant the reader to take *Kokoro* as (1) a document published while Shizu was still alive and therefore a betrayal by the student of Sensei's final wish, (2) a document published after the death of Shizu, or (3) simply a privileged look into the mind of the student having no reference to the existence in the real world of a novel called *Kokoro*. Ruminating on these problems will no doubt keep scholars busy for many years to come. In any case, in *Kokoro*, Sōseki succeeded in painting a portrait of a man with an ego gone haywire and suggesting that his problems were the problems of an era—and of the human predicament transcending history. Echoing a key conversation in *The Wayfarer*, Sensei addresses the student near the end of his testament:

> Perhaps you will not understand clearly why I am about to die, any more than I can fully understand why General Nogi killed himself. You and I belong to different eras, and so we think differently. There is nothing we can do to bridge the gap between us. Of course, it may be more correct to say that we are different simply because we are two separate human beings.

> (*SZ*, vol. 9, p. 298; tr. p. 234)

"My Individualism"

Three months after he had succeeded so brilliantly in portraying the fatal potential of the ego in the modern world, Sōseki gave a talk in which he strongly urged his mostly student audience to live an individualistic lifestyle for the sake of their own personal happiness. He delivered "My Individualism" at Gakushūin, the Peers' School, which had been founded in 1877 for the education of Japan's new aristocracy, the former lower-ranking samurai who had effected the Meiji Restoration and wanted fancy titles to go with their new status. "Prince" Itō Hirobumi was one of those, and so was General Count Nogi Maresuke, who had been president of Gakushūin from 1907 until his dramatic death in 1912. If Sōseki did not see himself as forging into enemy territory to engage in single-handed combat, he was at least hoping to influence members of the coming generation of Japan's elite. He wanted these rich young men to have some appreciation for the individual human beings who would feel the impact of the power and money that someday would be theirs to wield.

His speech, then, was by no means an exhortation for his audience to go out and indulge their egos as they saw fit. After "confessing" to his audience that his discovery of self-centeredness in London played a key role in his life and urging his young audience to develop their own individual natures, Sōseki warned them that, as an ethical philosophy, individualism requires that the individual recognize the validity of others' egos. The individual must also strike a balance where patriotism is concerned, doing what he can for the sake of the nation but refusing to be swept up in nationalistic fervor. Because a person who makes his own ethical decisions may find himself cut off from communal support, "there lurks beneath the surface of his philosophy a loneliness unknown to others" (*SZ*, vol. 16, p. 609; tr. p. 309).

It is said there was a military man at Gakushūin who had come prepared to be outraged by Sōseki's advocacy of individualism but who left the hall pleased and relieved after Sōseki explained what he had meant by "my individualism" in contrast to the term that had been receiving so much attention of late. Individualism was not the antisocial stance that most Japanese assumed (and still assume) *kojinshugi* to be. And while Sōseki honestly warned his listeners of the loneliness experienced by the individual who stands apart from the group, he did not hesitate to affirm the importance to them of taking that step as he had done.

Grass on the Wayside

In *I Am a Cat*, the narrator says of his owner, Kushami, that he spends most of his time shut up in his study, napping. As the portrait is filled out, it becomes clear that, despite the comedy, Kushami's frequent naps are the defense mechanism of a depressive personality. The anonymous narrator of *Grass on the Wayside*, who observes the protagonist from an only slightly closer perspective than the cat views Kushami, tells us:

> Kenzō now was always exhausted when he came home. And because of his exhaustion—which was not entirely due to overwork, he was sure—he became more sedentary than ever. He took naps constantly. Sometimes he would even fall asleep while reading at his desk; he would then awaken with a start and get back to work with renewed desperation.

(*SZ*, vol. 10, p. 107; tr. pp. 202–203).

Kenzō is a self-portrait of Sōseki during one of the most depressed periods of his life, the time between his return from London in January 1903 and his first attempts at writing fiction late in 1904. The novel is by no means a factual chronicle, however, bringing in memories from childhood and events that actually occurred as late as 1910, and compressing them all into about a year. It is Sōseki's story—his extremely well-crafted fictional version—of how his childhood shaped his character and led to such relentless financial pressure on him that he almost had no choice but to become a writer.

More important than the degree of its adherence to fact, the narrative immediately establishes a critical distance between the narrator and Kenzō in the manner of Sōseki's 1910 novel *The Gate*. The narrative reveals thoughts that Kenzō himself does not know he has, and it often looks into the minds and observes the conversations of other characters—most notably Kenzō's wife, Osumi. Here, however, the reader is not tantalized with glimpses of melodramatic background events as in *The Gate*. Instead the drama of *Grass on the Wayside* remains entirely within the scope of everyday life. Focusing relentlessly as it does on a married couple who are just a hair's breadth away from saying nice things to each other and perhaps ending the impasse created by years of stubbornness and pride, the novel provides as much suspense as any adventure story. It achieves this suffocating tension by letting the reader know that both partners are essentially fond of each other and would like nothing better than to relate with kindness and love. Time after time they are on the verge of doing it: one partner makes a move that the other is not prepared to recognize, or a phrase is spoken more gently than usual, but the reply is as curt as ever. Each is so afraid of having his or her feelings hurt that the openings they give each other are subtle and fleeting; shells snap shut, and chances are lost forever. The intense psychological drama distinguishes this, Sōseki's only autobiographical novel, from less overtly fictional autobiographical works usually given the "I-novel" label. It is an authentic modern tragedy.

The core of the story involves the sudden reappearance in the scholar Kenzō's life of the man who was his adoptive father for eight years. This is of course based on Sōseki's own experience of having been officially adopted into the Shiohara family and returned to the Natsumes at age eight. Shiohara had once been a ward of the Natsumes, and the adop-

379

tion was seen as a favor to him from a superior. When he returned Sōseki, however, he insisted on keeping the boy in his own family register. Sōseki's father agreed to this at the time, but thirteen years later, Naokatsu had to pay Shiohara to have the nearly-twenty-one-year-old Sōseki returned to the family, at which time he legally became Natsume Kinnosuke. This signaled a change in Naokatsu's attitude as well. By this time, he had lost his two eldest sons, the playboys, to illness, the third son had no interest in education, and Sōseki, who was headed for the University, was obviously the only one he could depend on in his old age (he was already 70). Once Sōseki became a prominent figure, however, Shiohara came around looking for more money, demanding a large sum in March 1909, which led to ugly negotiations that lasted through the following January. Finally, Sōseki agreed to give him ¥100, in return for which he executed a document promising to end all contact with Sōseki, both financial and social. By this time, in real life, Sōseki and Kyōko had two more children—sons—and he had left his academic career far behind, but the novel climaxes with the birth of the third daughter in November 1903, and the nature of Kenzō's new writing is never made clear; one only knows that he enjoys it because it is not connected with his academic work.

The vehicle of human interchange in *Grass on the Wayside* is money. There is hardly a conversation in the book, hardly a scene involving two characters, that does not involve money in some way, and most of the time that way is exceedingly direct. Japanese society is shown here at its most brutally calculating. Money changes hands in return for the possession of human beings, for kindnesses rendered, for love spent, for care provided. There is even some of the contractual language quoted in the novel. In one scene, Kenzō and his wife are looking over a bundle of old documents that Kenzō's older brother has left with them concerning his adoptive father, here called Shimada. She reads aloud, "It says so here: 'In consideration of the fact that the said person

[i.e., Shimada], when a child and thus unable to earn a living, was for five years given shelter in our house. . . .' " The document specifies a lump sum and monthly payments of the kind that Sōseki's father had to make to get him back (*SZ*, vol. 10, pp. 96–98; tr. pp. 51–52).

Similar documents mark the end of the book as well. After Shimada has exacted moderate sums from Kenzō from time to time and made a fruitless attempt at re-adopting Kenzō, he gets bold and asks Kenzō directly for a large amount of money. Kenzō sends him out in anger but later agrees to negotiate with a go-between for a more reasonable sum, settling on ¥100.

At the end of the year, when all kinds of bills have to be paid (a standard motif of Tokugawa fiction), and when Kenzō has had to borrow money to make some of the payments that relatives ask of him, he has no cash to spare. He does have ten free days before the next term, however, and he knows from recent experience that he can get money from nonacademic writing. He picks up his pen:

He was menaced by the awareness that his health was steadily deteriorating. But he paid no heed, and worked furiously. It was as if he wanted to defy his own body, as if he wanted deliberately to abuse it for having failed him so badly. He thirsted for blood, and since others were not available for slaughter, he sucked his own blood and was satisfied.

(*SZ*, vol. 10, p. 312; tr. p. 166)

The money he earns by sucking his own blood is what he uses to pay Shimada. And so was born the novelist Natsume Sōseki, the novel seems to tell us—except that it did not happen quite that way. It makes a great story, though.

When the ¥100 is paid, Kenzō receives a formal letter: "In very old-fashioned language it stated that one hundred yen had been duly received and that the signer would henceforth avoid all contact with Kenzō. Kenzō could not recognize the handwriting, but Shimada's seal was unmistakable" (*SZ*, vol. 10, p. 315; tr. pp. 167–168). Shimada has also enclosed the document that he more or less forced Kenzō to write to him when the adoption was formally annulled. Kenzō's brother and brother-in-law are certain Shimada had Kenzō write this document when they parted so that he could one day sell it back to him, as he has now done for ¥100. They and Kenzō's wife are convinced that everything is now settled, but Kenzō knows better. Documents and formal agreements do not "settle" human emotions.

The novel ends on this note, with Kenzō still an embittered academic, the gulf between his wife and himself as wide as ever. For, unknown to her, unknown to anyone but the reader, all of this nasty business connected with the reappearance of Shimada in his life, has unleashed a stream of vivid memories from childhood and beyond. Kenzō likes to think that his superior education and his experience abroad have moved him far out of the sphere of his ignorant, old-fashioned family members, with their connections to the world of moneylenders and pawnshops from which Sōseki's own mother had come, but he realizes that, "Like his brother, whom he pitied, he had become a man of the past" (*SZ*, vol. 10, p. 114; tr. p. 61).

Grass on the Wayside is, in a sense, a historical novel, for Sōseki at this stage of his life had become a man of the past, as evidenced, too, in the memoirs *Within My Glass Doors* (1915). Large parts of *Grass on the Wayside* consist of frightening and pitiful scenes from childhood—the terror of a young boy whose parents are brawling, the disgust a child feels when he knows he is being used by one parent against the other, the loneliness when a child realizes he is nothing but a piece of furniture or an investment to the adults haggling over him, the horror of a little boy being pulled beneath the dark surface of a pond by a huge fish; other scenes recall the hysterical fits that Osumi experienced in the early days of their marriage, when Kenzō had to tie a string between them at night to prevent her from doing violence to herself and force water down her throat mouth-to-mouth. But even the "present" is past, as the narrator looks back on the days just after the turn of the century, when oil lamps were far more common in Tokyo houses than electric lights, few besides doctors and midwives had telephones in their homes, and "moving pictures" were a novelty. *Grass on the Wayside* is the most important product of Sōseki's reconsideration of his life, and the foremost product of his mature art.

Light and Darkness

If only Sōseki's career had ended with *Grass on the Wayside*! Some critics feel that, even unfinished, *Light and Darkness* (1916) is Sōseki's greatest work, and that it can be ranked as the greatest modern Japanese novel. In some ways, though, it seems to be another attempt by Sōseki to write what he failed to write in *The Wayfarer*—a fully fleshed-out drama played by a large cast of rounded characters having a complicated network of relationships. It seems much more like a novel from the nineteenth century European heyday of realistic fiction than anything else he ever wrote, and much of the praise heaped on the novel (more by academics than the general public) tends to be given in terms of how nearly it approximates that ideal. The trouble is that Sōseki was a twentieth-century writer, and he did much better with a modern minimalist razor than a rambling pen: *The Miner* rather than *Gubijinsō*; *Kokoro* rather than *The Wayfarer*; *Grass on the Wayside*—an amazingly economical novel for something that ranges so far in time and space—rather than *Light and Darkness*. What Sōseki discovered when he started sending off simultaneous fictional creations in 1905–1906, when he was writing the endlessly prolix *I Am a Cat* and the tight, tough *Botchan*, was that he was a word machine. He could write anything and keep it going for as long as he liked. His two great masterpieces, *Kokoro* and *Grass on the Wayside*, are works in which he reined himself in, simplified his language, concentrated on one or two central characters, and told a good story.

Kokoro's Sensei concluded that there was an unbridgeable gap between himself and his young friend, owing not merely to the difference in their ages but to the fact that they were two separate human beings. In *Light and Darkness*, which focuses on marriage, the apparent difference is one of sex, but the conclusion is again applicable to all human relationships: two separate human beings are as unlike as light and darkness, and while each is necessary to the other, the two can never become one.

Like *The Gate* and *Grass on the Wayside*, *Light and Darkness* remains firmly planted in the world of the everyday—almost too much so as the opening chapter starts with a doctor probing the hero's anus and provides a graphic description of the surgery he will need to fix his problem. As in *Grass on the Wayside*, Sōseki gives the narrator the ability to know more about his characters' minds than they themselves are aware of, and he exploits this near-omniscience to analyze their personalities in ever finer detail. There is no doubt that Sōseki had an extremely clear conception of his hero Tsuda's personality and that of his wife Onobu and of all the substantial cast of important characters. He also had an extremely clear idea of how he wanted them to fight each other on the battlefield of human relations (military terms make up a significant part of the narrator's vocabulary) as they struggle with the familiar Sōseki problems of money and the unreliability of human motives. The problem is that he can not seem to stop himself from telling the reader more than he or she would ever want to know about these matters.

There have been various theories, none of them convincing, on how *Light and Darkness*, with its den of egoists, might be an embodiment of *sokuten kyoshi*, Sōseki's supposed final philosophy of abandoning the self and following heaven. Sōseki himself never wrote anything explaining the phrase. He did, however, write the four characters themselves at least twice—and in his best handwriting, with a writing brush. Once, he drew them on a stiff square "poetry card" of the kind used for ornamental purposes. The other time he submitted the inscription to a publication called *Bunshō nikki* (A diary of style), which appeared about

twenty days before his death and featured a handsome reproduction of the brush-written phrase on the January title page. A different writer submitted a "motto" *(zayū no mei)* for each month. An anonymous editor explained Sōseki's motto this way:

> The characters meaning "Follow Heaven and Abandon the Self" are to be read *"Ten ni nottori, watakushi o saru."* "Heaven" means "nature." The phrase as a whole means "Follow nature and leave the self— the narrow subjectivity, which is to say, mere technique; always make your style as natural as possible, a sincere expression of your true feelings."

> (*SZ*, vol. 26, pp. 292, 537)

Sōseki probably meant more by the phrase than this, but not a great deal more. As far back as *I Am a Cat*, he had hinted that forgetting the self was a way to overcome the stress of the ego-centered life in modern society. He himself tried to do it in the last months of his life by writing Chinese verse in the afternoons after steeping himself in the unpleasant world of *Light and Darkness* in the mornings. *Sokuten kyoshi* was not as trivial as "Get a hobby to take your mind off your troubles." Perhaps it was Sōseki's final expression of his life-long desire for some reprieve from the strain of being Natsume/Shiohara Kinnosuke. Rather than Sōseki, Shiga Naoya was the one to write a novel of spiritual quest concluding with a *sokuten kyoshi*-like "loss of self," *An'ya Kōro* (1937; *A Dark Night's Passing*, 1976). (See the article on Shiga Naoya in this volume.)

Sōseki's death on 9 December 1916 was a major national event. Buddhist funeral services were presided over by one of the Zen priests from Kamakura who had been unable to help him attain enlightenment twenty-two years earlier. His ashes were buried in Zōshigaya cemetery, the fictive resting place of *Kokoro*'s K. Having "sucked his own blood" for twelve years to create some of Japan's great modern classics, Sōseki might have been bewildered—

or perhaps amused—to read a statement by the president of his alma mater—and later employer—Tokyo Imperial University: he lamented the fact that Sōseki had wasted his talents "writing novels for newspapers" when he could have had a brilliant career writing about Japan in English for foreigners.

Selected Bibliography

PRIMARY WORKS

ANNOTATED COLLECTIONS

Natsume Sōseki shū. Edited by Matsumura Tatsuo and Saitō Keiko et al. Vols. 24–27 of *Nihon kindai bungaku taikei.* 60 vols. Tokyo: Kadokawa Shoten, 1968–1974. Vol. 24: *Wagahai wa neko de aru.* (Abbreviated *NKBT* in citations. The present article draws extensively from this heavily annotated volume.)

Sōseki zenshū. 29 vols. Tokyo: Iwanami Shoten, 1993–1999. (Abbreviated *SZ* in citations. The standard edition of the complete works. This edition contains all Sōseki works cited. The detailed textual criticism and annotations in this edition have contributed enormously to the present article.)

FICTION AND NONFICTION

(Titles published during the same year are listed in order of publication. Tentative titles are given for untranslated works.)

Wagahai wa neko de aru. 1905–1906. Trans. by Aiko Itō and Graeme Wilson as *I Am a Cat.* 3 vols. Rutland, Vt., and Tokyo: Charles E. Tuttle Co., 1972, 1979, 1986.

"Rondon tō." 1905. Trans. and edited with introduction, commentary, and notes by Peter Milward and Kii Nakano as *The Tower of London.* Brighton, U.K.: In Print Publishing Ltd., 1992. (The heavily edited translation appears on pp. 23–59. Publication supported by the Soseki Museum, 80b The Chase, London SW 4 ONG, which was the last of Sōseki's lodgings in that city, from 20 July 1901 to 5 December 1902.)

"Koto no sorane." 1905. See "Yume jūya."

"Ichiya." 1905. One night.

"Shumi no iden." 1906. See "Yume jūya."

Botchan. 1906. Trans. by Alan Turney as *Botchan.* Tokyo: Kodansha International, 1972.

Kusamakura. 1906. Trans. by Alan Turney as *The Three-Cornered World.* London: Peter Owen, 1965.

Nowaki. 1907. The autumn wind.

"Bungei no tetsugakuteki kiso." 1907. The philosophical foundations of the literary art.

Bungakuron. 1907. Theory of literature.

Gubijinsō. 1907. The poppy.

Kōfu. 1908. Trans. by Jay Rubin as *The Miner.* Stanford, Calif.: Stanford University Press, 1988. (See the translator's Afterword for information and annotations on *The Miner* and "The poppy.")

"Yume jūya," 1908; "Koto no sorane," 1905; "Shumi no iden," 1906. Trans. by Aiko Itō and Graeme Wilson as *Ten Nights of Dream, Hearing Things, The Heredity of Taste.* Rutland, Vt., and Tokyo: Charles E. Tuttle Co., 1974.

Sanshirō. 1908. Trans. by Jay Rubin as *Sanshirō.* Seattle: The University of Washington Press, 1977.

Sore kara. 1909. Trans. by Norma Moore Field as *And Then.* Baton Rouge: Louisiana State University Press, 1978.

"Man-Kan tokoro-dokoro." 1909. Here and there in Manchuria and Korea.

Mon. 1910. Trans. by Francis Mathy as *Mon (The Gate).* London: Peter Owen, 1972.

"Dōraku to shokugyō." 1911. Pastime and profession.

"Gendai Nihon no kaika." 1911. Trans. by Jay Rubin as "The Civilization of Modern-Day Japan." In *Kokoro, a Novel, and Selected Essays.* Trans. by Edwin McClellan. Lanham: Madison Books, 1992. (See Preface, Forword to Essays, and annotations for background material and sources.)

Higan-sugi made. 1912. Trans. by Kingo Ochiai and Sanford Goldstein as *To the Spring Equinox and Beyond.* Rutland, Vt., and Tokyo: Charles E. Tuttle Co., 1985.

Kōjin. 1913. Trans. by Beongcheon Yu as *The Wayfarer.* Detroit: Wayne State University Press, 1967.

Kokoro. 1914. Trans. by Edwin McClellan as *Kokoro.* Chicago: Henry Regnery, 1957. Cited here from *Kokoro, a Novel, and Selected Essays.* Trans. by Edwin McClellan. Lanham: Madison Books, 1992.

"Watakushi no kojinshugi." 1914. Trans. by Jay Rubin as "My Individualism." In *Kokoro, a Novel, and Selected Essays.* Trans. by Edwin McClellan. Lanham: Madison Books, 1992. (See Preface, Forword to Essays, and annotations for background material and sources.)

Garasudo no uchi. 1915. Trans. by Matsuhara Iwao and E. T. Iglehart as *Within My Glass Doors.* Tokyo: Shinseidō, 1928.

Michikusa. 1915. Trans. by Edwin McClellan as *Grass on the Wayside.* Chicago: The University of Chicago Press, 1969.

Meian. 1916. Trans. by V. H. Viglielmo as *Light and Darkness.* London: Peter Owen, 1971.

SECONDARY WORKS

CRITICAL STUDIES IN ENGLISH

Benedict, Ruth. *The Chrysanthemum and the Sword: Patterns of Japanese Culture.* Boston: Houghton Mifflin Co., 1946. Reprinted, 1989.

Doi, Takeo. *The Psychological World of Natsume Sōseki.* Trans. by William Jefferson Tyler. Cambridge, Mass.: Harvard University Press, 1976.

Fujii, James A. *Complicit Fictions: The Subject in the Modern Japanese Prose Narrative.* Berkeley: University of California Press, 1993.

Gessel, Van C. *Three Modern Novelists: Sōseki, Tanizaki, Kawabata.* Tokyo: Kodansha International, 1993.

Hibbett, Howard. "Natsume Sōseki and the Psychological Novel." In *Tradition and Modernization in Japanese Culture.* Edited by Donald H. Shively. Princeton, N.J.: Princeton University Press, 1971. Pp. 305–346.

Iijima, Takehisa, and James M. Vardaman Jr., eds. *The World of Natsume Sōseki.* Tokyo: Kinseido Ltd., 1987.

Kawabata, Yasunari. *Japan the Beautiful and Myself.* Trans. by Edward G. Seidensticker. Tokyo: Kodansha International, 1969.

Keene, Donald. "Natsume Sōseki." In his *Dawn to the West: A History of Japanese Literature.* Vol. 3. New York: Columbia University Press, 1984. Reprinted, 1998. Pp. 305–354.

Lifton, Robert J., et al. *Six Lives, Six Deaths: Portraits from Modern Japan.* New Haven, Conn.: Yale University Press, 1979. (Contains a fascinating article on General Nogi.)

Lin, Lien-hsiang, ed. *A Symposium on Natsume Sōseki's "Kokoro."* Singapore: Department of Japanese Studies, National University of Singapore, 1994.

Matsui, Sakuko. *Natsume Sōseki As a Critic of English Literature.* Tokyo: The Centre for East Asian Cultural Studies, 1975.

Matsuo, Takayoshi. "A Note on the Political Thought of Natsume Sōseki in His Later Years." In *Japan in Crisis.* Edited by Bernard Silberman and H. D. Harootunian. Princeton, N.J.: Princeton University Press, 1974. Pp. 67–85.

McClellan, Edwin. *Two Japanese Novelists: Sōseki and Tōson.* Chicago: The University of Chicago Press, 1969.

———. "The Implications of Sōseki's *Kokoro.*" *Monumenta Nipponica* 14:356–370 (1958–1959).

Miyoshi, Masao. *Accomplices of Silence.* Berkeley: University of California Press, 1974.

Rubin, Jay. *Injurious to Public Morals: Writers and the Meiji State.* Seattle: University of Washington Press, 1984. (See annotations in this volume for sources on Sōseki's resignation from the University, his rejection of the Doctorate of Letters, and his critique of

the Committee on Literature, etc.)

Sakaki, Atsuko. *Recontextualizing Texts: Narrative Performance in Modern Japanese Fiction.* Cambridge, Mass.: Harvard University Press, 1999. (See esp. "The Debates on *Kokoro*: A Cornerstone," pp. 29–53.)

Yiu, Angela. *Chaos and Order in the Works of Natsume Sōseki.* Honolulu: University of Hawaii Press, 1998.

Yu, Beongcheon. *Natsume Sōseki.* New York: Twayne Publishers, 1969.

CRITICAL STUDIES IN JAPANESE

Ara Masahito, ed. *Sōseki bungaku zenshū bekkan: Sōseki kenkyū nenpyō.* Tokyo: Shūeisha, 1974. (This exhaustively detailed chronology is the major source for biographical information on Sōseki and his family. See esp. pp. 13–17 for names and birth and death dates of his immediate family members.)

Etō Jun. *Natsume Sōseki.* Tokyo: Keisō Shobō, 1965. (Breakthrough work, questioning the myth of *sokuten kyoshi.*)

———. *Sōseki to sono jidai.* 5 vols. Tokyo: Shinchōsha, 1970–1999. (See, esp., vol. 4, pp. 269–286 on Sōseki in Manchuria.)

Komiya Toyotaka. *Natsume Sōseki.* 3 vols. Tokyo: Iwanami Shoten, 1953.

Miyoshi Yukio et al., eds. *Kōza: Natsume Sōseki.* 5 vols. Tokyo: Yūhikaku, 1981.

Oka Yoshitake. "Nichiro sensō-go ni okeru atarashii sedai no seichō." 2 parts. *Shisō,* February 1967, pp. 137–149; March 1967, pp. 361–376.

Ryū Kenki. "Sōseki to Manshū." *Kokubungaku: Kaishaku to Kanshō* 63, no. 6:17–23 (June 1997).

Shimada Atsushi. "Sōseki no shisō." In *Nihon bungaku kenkyū shiryō sōsho: Natsume Sōseki.* Edited by Nihon bungaku kenkyū shiryō kankōkai. 3 vols. Tokyo: Yūseidō, 1970, 1982, 1985. Vol. 1, pp. 108–125.

Tamai Takayuki. "'Watakushi no kojinshugi' zengo." In *Nihon bungaku kenkyū shiryō sōsho: Natsume Sōseki.* Edited by Nihon bungaku kenkyū shiryō kankōkai. 3 vols. Tokyo: Yūseidō, 1970, 1982, 1985. Vol. 1, pp. 236–244.

———. *Natsume Sōseki ron.* Tokyo: Ōfūsha, 1976.

TANIZAKI JUN'ICHIRŌ
1886–1965

PHYLLIS I. LYONS

AT THE SAME moment Lafcadio Hearn was introducing Western readers to a new world he had fallen in love with, through such works as *A Japanese Miscellany: Strange Stories, Folklore Gleanings, and Studies Here & There* (1900), Tanizaki Jun'ichirō was a child growing up embedded in that very culture. Hearn was a foreigner; Tanizaki, a native son. And yet they had amazingly similar perspectives on what they observed and imagined. If Hearn can be faulted as an Orientalist for seeing Japan as mysterious, exotic, and aesthetically fascinating—so, too, can Tanizaki.

The first thing to know about Tanizaki is that he is one of the master storytellers in the modern Japanese literary tradition; the Japan he wrote about was a Japan he created. The second thing is that "desire"—emotional, intellectual, artistic and sexual—is his subject matter. His stories are filled with obsessions and fetishes, emotional abuse and mayhem; and also with tender yearnings, lyrical celebrations of beauty, and reverence for the elegance of tradition. Without psychological jargon (but with an early and deep study of Krafft-Ebing's nineteenth-century analyses of sexual pathologies) Tanizaki's imagination soared to the highest of ideals, even as many of his stories wallowed in cesspools of degradation. These phrases are not exaggerations: Tanizaki is known both for the charming perversity of his wicked imagination and for a rare appreciation and re-envisioning of the beauty of traditional images. He toyed with his characters and joyously invited all readers to join in his dedicated lifework of exploring the deepest levels of what makes human nature tick. What is most extraordinary about his stories, so many of which are about the pains of emotional and physical desire, is that for all their darkness, they are often richly comic. It was for the grandeur, wit, and unflinching honesty of his visions—in a long career that observed much of Japan's tumultuous modern history, and manifested itself in an enormous oeuvre encompassing long and short fiction, cultural commentary, plays, film scripts, and poetry—that he was reportedly the first Japanese writer to be considered for the Nobel Prize. Had he lived a few more years, he might well have won it.

The Life

Much of the standard narrative of Tanizaki's life comes from his own writings, although he was never considered an exponent of the "I-novel" *(shishōsetsu)* autobiographical mode of storytelling that dominated Japanese letters in the first half of the twentieth century. Regardless of literary currents, however, and the seemingly wide variation on what turn out to be relatively few grandly fundamental themes in Tanizaki's writing, he had a career-long fidelity to a world of self-created fantasy, fictions the writer imaginatively integrated into his own life. Major among the themes Japanese scholars identify are *akumashugi* (diabolism), *eien josei no tsuikyū* (pursuit of the eternal female), *josei sūhai* (Tanizaki glossed the term as "feminism," but a literal translation would be, "woman worship," with attendant masochism and assorted fetishisms), and *bosei shibo* (yearning for mother).

Standard descriptions of his life and work make his career appear to have had only one notable disjunction: in the middle of his life he became one of the most famous literary refugees in modern Japanese literature by semipermanently abandoning the modernizing Tokyo area of his birth and youth for the "more traditional" Kansai (Kyoto/Osaka/Kobe) region following the Great Kantō Earthquake of 1923. However, the habit of frequently changing residence had been deeply ingrained in Tanizaki's family life since his childhood; in a way, disruption in his life was the rule rather than the exception. And yet, despite domestic disruptions, the issues that occupied his late writing were the same ones that had vivified his earlier stories. Like repertory actors in the motion pictures that temporarily fascinated Tanizaki in the early 1920s, his characters changed costumes and dwelt in many fabulous settings, in many historical periods; but it was the same cast Tanizaki used to work out his profoundly perceptive understandings of human need and desire. Given his domestic instability, writing was his consistent anchor. For the nearly eighty years of his life, the one sure home he knew was the world of his own imagination.

Tanizaki was born on 24 July 1886, to an old and financially comfortable merchant family in the Nihonbashi section of Tokyo's traditional downtown *(shitamachi)*. The new nation itself was only eighteen years old at the time; pride in the still-vigorous old traditions of the "Edo world" (Edo was the pre-1868 name for Tokyo) strongly influenced Tanizaki's youth. Consciousness of himself as an "Edokko" (son of Edo) was the wellspring for his later interest in classical Japanese culture, and he continued to harken back to it in his writings until the end of his life. His grandfather, Kyūemon, who died when Tanizaki was two, was a strong personality and an energetic entrepreneur; he built a number of successful businesses, the best of which was a daily commodities newspaper that reported on activities of the rice exchange near the Tanizaki main house. Tanizaki's father, Kuragorō, was adopted into the family to be the husband of Kyūemon's third daughter, Seki. (Kuragorō's older brother was adopted as the first daughter's husband.) Aside from Kyūemon's oldest son, who inherited the main family headship when he died, Kyūemon's other sons were adopted out into other families, whereas the patriarch kept the three girls close to the family. Tanizaki's explanation of that family decision was that his grandfather was partial to the girls; he clearly idolized his successful grandfather, and cited him as the genetic source for his own tendency toward "feminism." (Subsequent scholarship has suggested that the Tanizaki family arrangements were a common merchant-family strategy to protect boys from the newly instituted military draft, a consideration Tanizaki never mentions.)

Tanizaki's father was as unsuccessful as his father-in-law was successful; every business project put into his hands died. He is reported to have adored his beautiful, pampered and high-strung wife; his failures created tension in the family as its financial situation became increasingly precarious. Tanizaki was the first surviving son (an older son had died soon after birth). As the precious heir, and the only child for over four years, the young Tanizaki was greatly pampered and sheltered. He seems to have been a sensitive child, by turns aggressive and expansive, nervous and shy. Such emotional tensions as the later births of six other children after his years as a privileged only child; the downward trajectory of family finances, occasioning the necessity for frequent moves to more cramped quarters (including, for a time, a return to the main house); and arguments between the parents and with Jun'ichirō over their financial state, which several times threatened the bright child's education, clearly affected him. From his failure to pass first grade (because he refused to be separated at school from his nursemaid), to his several bouts with *shinkei suijaku* (nervous prostration) in his early adult life, he periodically exhibited signs of a certain degree of emotional fragility; and many of the protagonists of his stories likewise reveal overwrought nervous systems. Not until his third marriage, in 1935, when he was nearly fifty years of age, did his life seem to settle down. That psychological stability undoubtedly contributed to the production of much of his most powerful writing in the final thirty years of his life.

In 1901 Tanizaki graduated from upper elementary school. Because of financial reverses, his father decided that that would be enough schooling for Jun'ichirō. However, the youth's intellectual brilliance was already evident. Tanizaki recalls in *Yōshō jidai* (1955–1959; *Childhood Years*, 1988) that one of his teachers joined with him in petitioning his uncle to help support him into Tokyo First Municipal Middle School. The following year, when family finances turned even worse, his teachers arranged a tutor-houseboy job with the family of a wealthy classmate. Scholars have made much of the insecurity, humiliation, and frustration Tanizaki felt at the time; however, they did not seem to interfere with his educational progress. In the middle of the second year, he took the qualifying exams for third year, and was skipped directly there. He began publishing poetry and essays in the school literary magazine, and by fourth year he was the editor. At the age of eighteen he graduated from First Middle and went on to study English law at the First Higher School in Tokyo. The next year he switched to the literature faculty where he continued writing. But in 1907 he was discovered to have formed a romantic attachment to one of the young maids in the household. He

was fired from his houseboy position, and moved into a dormitory. He graduated from First Higher in 1908.

Tanizaki entered the Japanese literature department of Tokyo Imperial University in 1908, but he increasingly showed an attraction to the life of a writer, which meant that he often did not attend class. According to his brother Seiji (later famous as a literary critic and scholar), he caused their mother a great deal of grief through the next several years over the irregularity of his habits. Despite his inconsistencies in the classroom, by 1910 he had become part of several lively literary and theater groups, and that year he published several well-regarded stories. This was a time of great ferment in the literary world; Tanizaki became well enough known in intellectual circles that when he could not pay his school fees in 1911, he did not resist his expulsion from the university.

Tanizaki's "Shisei" (1910; "The Tattooer," 1963) was singled out the same year for particular notice. Earlier in his own career the established writer, Nagai Kafū, had been much interested in French naturalism; by this time, however, he was one of the leaders of resistance to the increasingly inward-turned *shizenshugi* (Japanese "naturalism") sweeping the contemporary literary scene. Kafū recognized a decadent, romantic talent in the younger writer. In his now-famous 1911 appreciation, *Tanizaki Jun'ichirō-shi no sakuhin* (Tanizaki Jun'ichirō's work), Kafū noted three special qualities in the new work: a "mystical elegance born of physical fear" (*nikutaiteki kyōfu kara shōzuru shinmitsu yūgen*); a "total sense of the city" (*mattaku tokaiteki naru koto*); and a "perfection of writing style" (*bunshō no kanzen naru koto*). Kafū's astute assessment of Tanizaki's creativity and sensitivity to language presciently forecast Tanizaki's lifetime accomplishment.

The period from 1910 to 1923 was a particularly unstable one in Tanizaki's life. Some scholars focus on the "art for art's sake" *akumashugi* (diabolism) aspect of his writing, heralded by the 1912 novel, *Akuma* (The devil), and a number of Kabuki-like lurid plays and tales; some, on his infatuation with things Western, including living style, entertainment, and food; or on his fascination with the new motion picture industry; or on his series of detective/crime/wife-killing stories (Tanizaki is noted as one of the progenitors of the modern detective story form in Japan).

These, however, are not separate stages; they are all jumbled up together. In his personal life, Tanizaki himself drew attention (which scholarship has continued) to peculiarities in his living arrangements: in 1915 he married a reportedly conventional woman, Ishikawa Chiyo; their daughter (his only child), Ayuko, was born the next year. At the same time, he developed a relationship with his wife's younger sister, Seiko, who was a fledgling movie star (photographs always show her in a bathing costume for one of her parts), who lived with them and is taken to be the model for Naomi in the 1924 *Chijin no ai* (Love of a fool; translated as *Naomi*, 1985). In 1920 the famous "Odawara incident" occurred: Tanizaki's close friend, the poet Satō Haruo, began to feel pity and sympathy for the neglected Chiyo; the pity turned to deeper feelings, and Satō and Tanizaki began to arrange a trade—Tanizaki would divorce Chiyo, Satō would marry her, and then Tanizaki could marry Seiko. However, in 1921 Tanizaki changed his mind and reneged (some critics suggest that Seiko had other plans, and Tanizaki suddenly saw himself bereft of both women). The two writers exchanged denunciations and countercharges in print, and broke off relations (which they reopened in 1926); and then, in 1930, the plan was accomplished: Tanizaki divorced Chiyo, and she and Satō married and lived apparently happily ever after.

Meanwhile (we can say in retrospect), the solution to Tanizaki's decades of confusion was slowly forming, although at the time he could not have known it. In 1927, still a temporary refugee in the Kansai area after the great earthquake, and still married to Chiyo, Tanizaki happened to meet in Osaka a socially well-connected, married woman named Nezu

Matsuko. They met through her interest in the writings of Akutagawa Ryūnosuke, Tanizaki's friend and literary antagonist, who was touring in Osaka. Tanizaki's writing of the time reveals that his attention was powerfully drawn to the young woman. Eight years later, Tanizaki had finally achieved the life situation that served him happily until his death in 1965: he married Matsuko. Before this happened, Akutagawa committed suicide (later in 1927); Tanizaki divorced Chiyo and on 24 April 1931 married Furukawa Tomiko, a young woman barely half his age; and then he divorced Tomiko, having lived with her for less than two years. Matsuko, for her part, had had to divorce her husband, Nezu Seitarō, leaving their son with the Nezu family and only later retrieving the daughter, Emiko; she returned to her own family and resumed her maiden name, Morita, before she could finally marry Tanizaki (28 January 1935). The relationship seems to have ended the psychological wandering in Tanizaki's life, although he continued his pattern of frequent residence changes. Letters exchanged during their courtship indicate that Matsuko, though possessing the elegance of a well brought-up lady, had a luridness of imagination up to the challenge of Tanizaki's; he often acknowledged her as his muse. The relationship seemed to result in a rich intensification of Tanizaki's ability to create his special, liminal worlds. His works from the late 1920s and 1930s are sometimes characterized as a "return to tradition"; more symbolically, they show a successful integration of internal personal need and artistic creativity. Some of his finest stories come from this period, as well as his first "translation" into modern Japanese of the eleventh-century classic, *Genji monogatari* (1925–1933; tr. Waley, *Tale of Genji*, 1976), and a fictional chronicle of four sisters modeled on his wife and her sisters, *Sasameyuki* (1943–1948; tr. Seidensticker, *The Makioka Sisters*, 1957), that critics have called both "Tale of Genji."

The stability of Tanizaki's life seems to make it of less interest to scholars from this point on. There were minor happenings:

Tanizaki's daughter, Ayuko, married Satō Haruo's nephew in 1939; Tanizaki adopted his own youngest brother as his heir in 1938 and then disinherited him in 1939; Tanizaki legally adopted Matsuko's now-married daughter in 1947. But critical attention focuses more exclusively on his literary work.

Before and during World War II, Tanizaki had periodically run afoul of the authorities for the subject matter and manner of his writings. After the war, *Kagi* (1956; *The Key*, 1960) once more brought him similar unfriendly attention, at a time when D. H. Lawrence's *Lady Chatterley's Lover* was undergoing intense scrutiny in the Japanese courts. Tanizaki's stories, novels, and nonfiction writings (and two more redactions of *The Tale of Genji*) continued unabated until the end; but increasingly he was plagued by ill health. In 1958 a slight stroke impaired his writing hand; from then on, Tanizaki dictated his stories to a secretary. The first work to emerge in this fashion was "Yume no ukihashi" (1959; "The Bridge of Dreams," 1963), a masterly story with echoes of the aestheticism and perversity of both *The Tale of Genji* and his stories of the late 1920s and 1930s.

Tanizaki had long since begun to collect awards. In 1937 he was appointed to the Imperial Academy of Arts, and in 1941 to the Japanese Academy of Arts. After the war he was twice invited to lecture before the emperor; and in 1949 he was awarded the Imperial Order of Cultural Merit. In 1964 he was made an honorary member of the American Academy of Arts and Letters. He was being mentioned for the Nobel Prize in literature. After his death, a major annual literary prize was named in his honor.

On 30 July 1965, a week after his seventy-ninth (eightieth by Japanese count) birthday, Tanizaki died at his latest home in Yugawara, near Tokyo, of kidney and heart failure. He has two memorial sites: some of his remains are at Jiganji, the temple site of his family's burial plot in Tokyo; and the rest are at Hōnen'in, a temple in Kyoto. There, Tanizaki's ashes lie under a stone carved with the word *jaku*, which has a double meaning: in ordinary usage, "quietude"; in Buddhist terminology, "entering into enlightenment." The ashes of his wife and soulmate, Matsuko, were placed there, next to his, when she died in 1990.

Autobiography and Fiction: The "Plot Controversy"

Tanizaki grew up at a time when the Japanese language was undergoing a major transformation. His lifelong interest in language issues was undoubtedly influenced by what he experienced of the malleability of his native language, and the effects on Japanese of the languages of the outside world, particularly those of Europe, that came flooding into Japan at the end of the nineteenth century. His many experiments with dialect and orthography, his translations into Japanese of European writers, his several modern Japanese versions of the *Tale of Genji*, and his writings on language, including the 1934 *Bunshō tokuhon* (A manual of literary style), all attest to his deep-rooted fascination with the basic linguistic clay from which he constructed his stories.

A consideration in the "plot controversy" is the matter of the separability of the spoken and written languages in Japanese. The non-literate Japanese culture already had an ancient, rich oral tradition when it had the gruesome misfortune in the third century C.E. to encounter the writing system developed for the radically dissimilar Chinese language. Over a period of centuries, the Japanese wrestled Chinese writing into fitting their own linguistic needs; but from the beginning of "Japanese" writing in the eighth century, the record shows a concept of the discreteness of oral culture lying behind, and "speaking through," the written. Even today, scholars debate what degree of "orality" is still discernible even in much contemporary Japanese written expression. And yet, given twelve centuries of written literature, Japan also has a very deep sense of the singularity of its own textual history. In *Bunshō tokuhon*, Tanizaki argued that one still cannot read a Japanese text without hearing a voice speaking.

Late nineteenth- and early twentieth-century writers faced two additional story-telling issues: the forms of "modern" literary expression and the language with which expression is conveyed. The wide variety of native literary forms, both fictional and nonfictional, faced the competition of a complex and newly privileged Western form, the "novel," and the social and psychological concerns that it represented. For example, there was a new topic: the "I" subject, or "individual Self." It is not that Japanese never had "selves," but rather that the language had always embedded the individual in some societal matrix. The desire of writers to express new ideas required development of a new literary language; the accomplishments of the *genbun' itchi* (unification of speaking and writing) movement occurred largely between the 1880s and the early 1900s. (For a good discussion of the complex issues of Japanese language and literature reformation from the nineteenth century on, see Suzuki, *Narrating the Self.*)

Tanizaki inherited the old way of writing; he came to maturity in the time of reform; he helped expand the possibilities of the new writing; and he remained interested in the relation between traditional and modern styles of language. The "plot controversy" is a consequence of new literary concerns; it came to a head in the late 1920s, although its beginnings went back to the early years of the century. By this time, Western models (such as romanticism and naturalism) were domesticated, with opposing literary camps engaged in taking up strategic positions for control of the *bundan*, (literary establishment). (Suzuki has a good discussion of the larger context. What follows is a great simplification of Tanizaki's role in this very complex and foundational issue.)

European naturalism and romanticism—the first with an emphasis on the biological and sociological nature of the individual, the second with a privileging of individual creativity and social revolt—were seen as models for a new realism in fiction. Reactions against the language and situations that the increasingly introspective *shizenshugi* (Japanese naturalism) tended to produce, and a romantic emphasis on the author as the representative "Self," turned a number of writers toward a more aesthetically centered mode of expression. The names attached to some groups of writers give an idea of the direction of their romantic resistance, often built on European models: *tanbi-ha* (the "Aesthetes"), *taihai-ha* (the "Decadents"), and (the name given Tanizaki's version) *akumashugi* (diabolism). Especially as the protagonists of many stories started to bear significant (and recognizable) resemblence to the authors of those stories, theoretical positions in the *bundan* became increasingly polarized. By the early 1920s, the term *watakushi shōsetsu* (I-novel) began to be heard, first to designate stories told in the first person, and then to mean "stories to be identified with the author" (later commonly referred to in its homologous form, *shishōsetsu*). Such terms as "the true novel," "the novel of interior states," "the I-novel," "pure literature," and "popular fiction" governed the debates. Increasingly, the "I-novel" and "novel of interior states" came to be identified as "pure literature"; invented fictions were contrasted as "popular fiction."

Nagai Kafū had already noted several important characteristics of Tanizaki's writing. But now a fourth element came to be a conscious project as Tanizaki became enmeshed in the "I-novel" issue being fought out in the *bundan*: his deep commitment to the "fictionality" of fiction. The function of plot itself became a major fighting point. Tanizaki, the consummate storyteller, famously pledged his allegience in 1927: he took the position that structure was a defining quality of the novel form, and plot was the necessary manifestation of structure in the novel. While he knew that personal experience was the starting point for expression, his special literary gifts were in the service of plot construction, as Kafū had early recognized. In 1927, Akutagawa Ryūnosuke, celebrated for wonderfully inventive fictions, unwittingly opened a debate with Tanizaki. Akutagawa seemed to be going through a conversion experience: he suddenly espoused in print the discursive rather than the plotted story, for what he called the truest kind of writing. (His suicide three months later leaves the possibility that his judgments at the time were more "breakdown" than "conversion.") Tanizaki's stung response was in favor of creative fiction, in opposition to Akutagawa's lean toward the "storyless story" *(hanashi no nai shōsetsu)*. Tanizaki's rebuttal essays, subsequently collected as *Jōzetsu-roku* (1927; Record of garrulousness), became even firmer in defense of the art of fictions. In following years he wrote some pieces he identified as "popular fiction," and there are autobiographical elements in some of what he considered "authentic novels"; but in all his writing he passionately insisted on the priority of imaginative plot construction. Whatever he had to say about the human condition, he would say it as a marvelously powerful storyteller, and he believed that this was the highest literary calling.

The Stories

Tanizaki began his career with short stories, although he became equally a master of longer forms of fiction. Tanizaki's first several stories in 1910 caught critical attention, as well as the eye of government censors, who forced withdrawal of two of them, only the first of a kind of unwelcome attention that was to plague Tanizaki periodically even after the end of World War II and the U.S. Occupation.

"The Tattooer," one of these problem stories (and the one Nagai Kafū had admired), tells of an artist in premodern Tokyo who has patiently searched for the perfect canvas on which to inscribe the summation of his artistic imagination: the body of a beautiful young woman; he recognizes her by her foot as it protrudes from beneath the curtain of a palanquin. Many of the themes and motifs that color Tanizaki's writing for the next fifty years can already to be discerned here: the beautiful, cruel woman; the groveling, masochistic man;

the fetishes; the excitement of the senses. The story also points at what would become the writer's major mode of storytelling: the mystery story. Even with noncrime plots, Tanizaki was pre-eminently a writer of stories structured with secrets to be deciphered (or remain hidden) in the course of the narrative. For most of "The Tattooer," we do not know the design that has obsessed the tattooer and that seems to drain the life force from him as he works hour after hour transcribing it onto the body of the unconscious woman; only at the end of the story is it revealed, wickedly, on the back of what is clearly a newly minted dominatrix, brilliantly illuminated by the rising sun.

Many of the early stories are similarly structured: for example, "Dokutan" (1915; The German spy), an international mystery set in Japan during World War I; "Tojō" (1920; On the street), about a detective pursuing a wife-murdering husband; "Watakushi" (1921; "The Thief," 1963), about a petty thief in a college dormitory; "Hitofusa no kami" (1926; A lock of hair), the lurid story behind a bullet wound in a man's leg, received during the great earthquake; "Tomoda to Matsunaga no hanashi" (1926; The story of Tomoda and Matsunaga), the secret of two totally different (even in terms of body type) men who turn out to be the same man. But many of the later stories and novels, too, could be seen as mysteries, although conventionally they have not been called that: among them are *Quicksand*, *Some Prefer Nettles*, *The Makioka Sisters*, "The Bridge of Dreams," and *The Key*.

After settling into Kansai following the 1923 earthquake, Tanizaki wrote one successful novel, but then his career seemed to go on idle for a time. In 1927, however, it entered an extremely creative period. The intense pace of his personal life as he went through his three marriages was matched by his literary productivity. Between 1928 and 1934 (when he and Matsuko began living together), Tanizaki published some of his best-known and best-loved works: the novels *Quicksand* and *Some Prefer Nettles*, and a series of brilliant novellas and short stories, among them "Yoshino kuzu"

(1931; "Arrowroot," 1982), a geohistorical travel account that turns into the tale of a man searching for his mother, following in the tradition of the 1919 "Haha o kouru ki" ("Longing for Mother," 1980); *Bushūkō hiwa* (1931–1932; *The Secret History of the Lord of Musashi*, 1982), a cruelly humorous invented history of the childhood traumas and resulting sexual perversities of a fictional sixteenth-century warlord; "Mōmoku monogatari" (1931; "A Blind Man's Tale," 1963), an invented and perverse gloss on sixteenth-century historical figures; *Ashikari* (1932; *The Reed Cutter*, 1994), the atmospheric recollection of a fictional mother-obsessed man haunted by passions formed in the nineteenth century but evoking much earlier history; and "Shunkin-shō" (1933; "A Portrait of Shunkin," 1963), a mock-objective account of a man's historical research into the sadomasochistic relationship of two passionately connected (fictional) nineteenth-century traditional musicians.

Critics credit Tanizaki's move from the ugly, modernizing Tokyo largely destroyed by the earthquake to the quieter and gentler, more historic Kansai area as having revived his interest in Japanese classical culture. However, as is usually the case, there is more to the story than a change of address. There are multiple influences on what looked like stories harkening back to an older Japanese aesthetic; and "The Tattooer" shows that from the start, Tanizaki had been interested in the cultural transvestite possibilities of putting contemporary psychological explorations of obsession into premodern fancy dress. Nevertheless, the stories—which appeared just when the Japanese intellectual world was volubly discussing the pros and cons of a "return to Japan" *(Nihon e no kaiki)* in the context of militaristic nationalism as Japan geared up for war—without question do show an imaginative power turned to exploring fantasized relationships in what looks like a premodern Japanese world. Regardless of when they are set, they do evoke the "mystical elegance" Nagai Kafū had recognized twenty years earlier, sometimes produced by "physical fear" (although *The Secret History of the Lord of Musashi* is a parody of terror); and all of them beautifully create a complete sense of "place," if not "the city."

One later story is worthy of special mention. "The Bridge of Dreams" is the first of Tanizaki's late writings to require the help of a secretary because of the paralysis in his writing hand. One of his most masterful and slyly manipulative stories, it evokes some of the themes and atmosphere of *The Tale of Genji* in which Tanizaki was by this time so deeply steeped. It also ironically pushes a central Tanizaki theme, "yearning for mother," to its extreme: incest. It is witty and nasty; it is a mystery story whose secrets are barely disguised; and it is elegant and beautiful, a work of great maturity.

The Novels and Novellas

As Tanizaki began writing longer fiction, he also wrote some dramas, both modern and patterned after older Kabuki-like forms; few of them have ever been performed. His novels began appearing serially in the leading newspapers and journals of the day (such as *Chūō Kōron* and *Bungei Shunjū*), and a number of the earlier ones ended incomplete. But with *Naomi* (1924) he produced a story of lasting reputation. It is the first-person narrative of a bored, thirty-two-year-old engineer named Jōji, who decides that his life would be much spiced up if a sulky fifteen-year-old cafe waitress put herself into his Pygmalion-like hands. Critics point out the real-life echoes of Tanizaki's involvement with his aspiring movie starlet sister-in-law Seiko in the relationship of Jōji, the puppet master-turned-puppet, and the manipulative Naomi, whose name had attracted Jōji with its Western ring, and whose face seems to him reminiscent of Mary Pickford's. Without question, Tanizaki's own interest in things Western in the late 1910s and early 1920s has its part in this novel. But the tone of the narrative is highly ambiguous. Self-contempt and gleeful exhibitionism, critical distance and masturbatory delirium, calculation and obsession—all these are to be found in this story, as in many others. Critics often point to the Tanizaki in Jōji; but there is Tanizaki in Naomi as well, the Tanizaki who not long before had been toying with both his wife and his best friend in the "Odawara incident."

Without question, Naomi is a Tanizaki untrammeled by even rudimentary notions of limits. The gusto, amounting to gluttony, with which Tanizaki constructed, participated in, and manipulated audiences into consuming his creations is fully seen in this novel. At the same time, it can also be seen as a political allegory of a Japan seduced and abused by its lust for Western culture. Except, of course, that Tanizaki did not write political allegories; and the degree of ironic enjoyment the author seems to be deriving from his own storytelling is too palpable for a political allegory.

It is of course illusory to see the 1923 earthquake and subsequent move to Kansai as anything but a convenient marker between Tanizaki's earlier diabolistic and Western-turned writings and his "return to classical traditions." The themes and preoccupations of the 1930s writings were little different from those earlier and later, with "tradition" as the exoticism in place of "the West." Each of the short stories is constructed in Tanizaki's classic mystery-story mode, as are three novels planned, written, and serialized virtually simultaneously between 1928 and 1930. These novels show the range of themes and settings that Tanizaki was playing with as he adjusted to living in Kansai (or, we might also say, as he zeroed in on organizing his life around the woman he wanted). *Quicksand* began serialization first, in March 1928, and ended last, in April 1930; *Some Prefer Nettles* began in December 1928 and ended in June 1929; and *Kokubyaku* (Black and white) began and ended in 1929. There is a geographical migration in the three stories: *Kokubyaku* is set in Tokyo and Yokohama; *Some Prefer Nettles* is set in Kansai, but its characters are transplanted Kantō people; *Quicksand* is narrated by a woman from the Osaka area, to a male "adviser" whose written speech and observations indicate that he could be from Tokyo. Of the three, only *Some Prefer Nettles* places in the foreground the issues of "tradition/modernity" and "East/West." But what is happening in the background is what makes this novel, too, as much a mystery story as the others.

Kokubyaku is a professional writer's story about the world of professional writers. It toys with the relationships of autobiography, plot, real-life models, fictionality, and the author that were so involving Tanizaki and the *bundan* in the 1920s. It tells the story of a writer, Mizuno, who has written a murder story, using a particular fellow writer as the model for the victim in his story. Now, Mizuno fears that Kojima will be recognizable as the model; and if Kojima should chance to be murdered, Mizuno will be accused. He therefore spends much of the lengthy novel establishing an alibi for the time he suspects Kojima might be murdered. Kojima is of course murdered; and Mizuno's airtight alibi evaporates when the mysterious bondage mistress he had been hiding away with disappears, and he can't even find the house she had taken him to several times. He is of course suspected; and the novel ends with him on the brink of signing a confession to a murder he did not commit, out of terror that the police will otherwise torture him into a making a confession. (Again, while reiterating that Tanizaki was never overtly political, we must nevertheless recognize that in March 1928, the first of several major nationwide roundups of left-wing writers and activists took place with great publicity; and in 1933, as the military secured increasing control over civil authority in a Japan that had been at war on the continent since 1931, the Marxist writer Kobayashi Takiji was beaten to death while in police custody.) *Kokubyaku* is an extremely claustrophobic, obsessive, paranoiac novel, with glimpses of hallucinatory ecstasy provided through the disciplines of the Japanese sex professional, "Fraulein Hindenburg." But a short, convoluted passage midway through the novel presents a voice that sounds like Tanizaki's, telling us exactly what he is doing, and how he (and we) should enjoy it—that is, what his storytelling is all about:

Mizuno concocted a scene straight out of some European sexual adventure story, knowing it would provide the excitement his companion wanted. From that trunk he sprouted branches to which he attached leaves and added flowers, as he went into every minute detail. Nakazawa urged him on with absolute attention, from time to time licking his dry lips. The intensity of the listener communicated itself to the speaker, and Mizuno began to be pulled more and more into his own story, until he himself almost couldn't tell that it was a fiction. Each time his companion let out an envious groan, he grew more enraptured, and he was permeated with the joy he would have felt had he actually experienced the pleasures he described. He started to feel that it was actual sweet recollections he was caught up in.

(*Tanizaki Jun'ichirō zenshū* [1981–1983], vol. 11; p. 265)

Without being "autobiographical," how generously revelatory this passage is about what was Tanizaki's, but could be any author's, joy in imaginative creation!

Manji (1928–1930; *Quicksand,* 1993) is only barely more controlled, and it, too, is a darkly satirical obsession mystery story. The claustrophobic world it depicts is peopled by an intensely intertwined quartet: the narrator, Kakiuchi Sonoko, who is a married woman; Mitsuko, the young woman and fellow art student she falls in love with; Sonoko's husband, who eventually joins into a troilistic relationship with the two women; and Watanuki, the blackmailing boyfriend of Mitsuko. In a way, it can be seen as Tanizaki's gloss on the then-current "plot argument": by inverting—fictionalizing—the genders (and personalities) of the foursome in Tanizaki's contemporaneous marital imbroglio (himself, Satō Haruo, Chiyo, and the new element, Tomiko/Matsuko), he produces a story that is both autobiographical and fictional, and yet not "autobiographical fiction." From the beginning of the novel, it is clear that something catastrophic has happened; we know what it is by the end, but

rather than finding that all has been explained, we feel left with loose ends and questions. To write it, Tanizaki required linguistic assistance. He had begun serial publication using the standard (Tokyo-based) dialect of his other writings; but by the second installment he decided that it had to be told in the Osaka women's dialect of his narrator. Because this was not his natural voice, he hired several well-educated young graduates of a Kansai women's college to redo the narration into local speech after he produced the text.

Therefore, the story has a sly double exoticism: the lesbian theme and the Kansai woman's speech. And there is a hidden eroticism, too, because one can imagine the reactions of the young women of good family who have been "seduced" into "translating" the text into Osaka speech. Critics writing on this novel, though naming the love affair for what it is, somehow make little of the lesbianism in it. And this may be not out of prudishness or perplexity: the women's sexual relationship contains little (despite the elegant woman's speech) that distinguishes the relationship between these women from the ones Tanizaki created between a man and a woman. *Quicksand* is well liked by many readers, but the story seems to have more of an interest in exciting novelty than in emotional investment. (In the relatively liberal earlier 1920s, one entertainment Kansai had to offer tourists was the newly formed Takarazuka Women's Theater, with all-girl casts that inverted the centuries-old male-only traditions of Japanese theater.) The deliriously desiring Sonoko is in many ways akin to the obsessed men of *Naomi* and *Kokubyaku*; the seductive, manipulative, and amoral Mitsuko is rather like the Naomi and Fraulein Hindenburg Tanizaki had already released on his victim-men.

Tade kuu mushi (1928–1928; *Some Prefer Nettles,* 1955) is one of the best loved of all of Tanizaki's novels. It is serious and thoughtful, but also sly and witty. In its description of a married couple on the brink of divorce, it has an autobiographical aspect to it (Tanizaki was nearing the end of his first marriage); but it reaches deep into intrapsychic energies, even as it also offers a critique of Japanese modernity. It is of its time, but its concerns are archetypal. The translator of the novel, Edward Seidensticker, recognized its multilayered quality—personal, historical, sociological, and psychological—when he observed in his introduction that regardless of how much autobiography there might be in the story, Tanizaki is talking of much more than himself.

In *Some Prefer Nettles*, Shiba Kaname and his wife Misako are a relatively normal but unhappy couple in the late 1920s; their marriage is drifting toward divorce (not inconceivable for such a modern couple, the novel tells us), but they would like to accomplish it with the least pain and disruption for all involved, including their ten-year-old son, Hiroshi. Kaname is the decision-maker who will not make the decision; he is the instigator of the desire to be free. But by this time, Misako has a lover herself, seemingly with Kaname's tacit acquiescence. His cousin, Takanatsu, is the reality tester: he tells us that there is something bizarre about the non-movement in this seemingly dead relationship. Kaname frequents a brothel catering to foreigners, run by a blowzy Englishwoman, where he is one of the few Japanese allowed; his regular girl is an exotic Eurasian, Louise, whom he always vows never to see again, and always goes back to. The cast of characters is completed with the not-so-old "old man" (Misako's father) and Ohisa, his mistress (who is younger than Misako). The "old man" has taken up the hobby of being an Edo gentleman of leisure, and he is training his young mistress into the image of a woman of days gone by. In the course of the story, the thoroughly modern Kaname, who is described as a "woman worshiper," slowly gropes toward an attempt to define for himself what that means, as he begins to imagine the woman he wants to worship. Tokyo and Kansai, East and West, modern and traditional are all played off against each other in the clear light of intelligent people thinking intelligently about their lives. But hidden in the shadows is a much deeper, and well thought-out, drama of family

relationships. In rich and evocative images, instead of dry intellectualizations, Tanizaki sets about ordering the deep structure of the obsessions that vivify his writing. The subterranean story is of a man, Kaname (whose name itself means "pivot or key [to something]"), caught in a paralyzing incestuous dilemma: he cannot touch his wife because she is a "mother," and yet he needs to worship (as one would a mother, but not a prostitute) a woman to fulfill his imaginative needs. Ohisa offers a glimpse of a possible way out: she turns out to be a "pure" prostitute, a maternal non-mother.

After the completion of *Quicksand* in 1930, for the next several years Tanizaki turned to writing short stories and the Osaka-dialect novella *Neko to Shōzō to futari no onna* (1936; *A Cat, Shōzō and Two Women*, 1988; *A Cat, A Man, and Two Women*, 1990), an ironically comic story of a current wife and an ex-wife fighting over custody of the cat that the husband appears to care about more than he does for either of the two women. Though it is not an autobiographical *shishōsetsu*, it does echo Tanizaki's multiple romantic triangles of the previous several years (Satō Haruo, himself, and his recently divorced wife, Chiyo; himself, his even more newly ex-wife, Tomiko, and his new wife, Matsuko).

Tanizaki then began the long process of translating the *Tale of Genji*, not starting another major novel until 1942. *The Makioka Sisters* has a checkered textual history, because wartime censors kept interrupting its serial appearance; in fact, Tanizaki ended up publishing the first parts of this very long novel in book form as a private edition, in an unsuccessful attempt to avoid the authorities. With characters in part modeled on Tanizaki's wife, Matsuko, and her three sisters, it is loved by many readers for its leisurely, elegant, and nostalgic exploration of a golden world just about to face irrevocable change, that of an upper-middle-class family in 1939, just before World War II. The plot concerns the Herculean efforts of the more settled, married older sisters to get their passively resistant, "traditional," third sister married; but the beautifully evoked atmosphere that surrounds them is as much a part of the effect of the novel as the plot is. Discord, drama, and confusion come into the process with the intractability of the youngest sister, who gets into some nasty situations that affect the negotiations for her sister's marriage. The novel has been described in as disparate terms as an other worldly "picture scroll," like that of the *Tale of Genji*, on which Tanizaki was working at the time (Chiba Shunji, in *A Tanizaki Feast*; Fukuda and Hirayama); or on the other hand, from its very lack of reference to the contemporary political and military scene, as a reverse "political novel" (Chambers, also in *A Tanizaki Feast*).

In *Shōshō Shigemoto no haha* (1949–1950; *Captain Shigemoto's Mother*, 1993), Tanizaki made another major contribution to his collection of "yearning for mother" and "classical Japanese tradition" stories. As often happens in his fiction, the lead-in to the story is not its central focus: Heijū (an actual aristocrat, poet, and fabled lover, the subject of the tenth-century *Tale of Heijū*) is a lover of Shigemoto's mother; the story begins with him but is mostly about this lady, the son (Shigemoto) who is parted from her and spends his life yearning after her, and Shigemoto's father, an elderly man who has been duped into giving her away to another man, and spends the remainder of his life in paralyzing pain over his loss of her. It is an elegant evocation of the atmosphere of classical Japanese literature, because the narrator draws from real (and invented) sources; but its perversity and irony are fully twentieth-century, and the Tanizaki voice in the transparent storyteller is unmistakable.

Kagi (1956; *The Key*, 1969) is set in contemporary Kyoto. It is a wicked tale of a middle-aged man who experiences a failing of his sexual powers, and in order to whip up excitement, he periodically drugs and takes Polaroid photographs of his wife naked, with the assistance of his graduate student, who is engaged to the professor's daughter but gradually is drawn into an affair with the wife. By the end, the husband has died of a stroke, and the wife continues her confessional account alone. The story is told through the diaries of husband and wife, which they keep hidden from one another, but each has found the diary of the other and is reading it as marital life progresses. (He intentionally leaves the key to his hiding place out where she can see it to begin the process of unlocking each other's secrets.) How truthful are the diary entries, then, the story insinuates, if the wife might be creating a fiction to meet the needs of her husband? Does she love her husband, and sacrifice herself for him? Or was she (as she claims at the end) enticing him toward death for the fulfillment of her own needs? The novel casts such total suspicion on truth and pretense that even her self-demeaning confession is questionable. The brilliant trick of the story (unfortunately not transferred to the translation) is that the husband's and wife's diaries are represented in visually different Japanese orthographies (*katakana* and *hiragana*), rather as if one were in block type and the other in cursive script. Therefore, in addition to the intellectual exercise required of readers to follow all the hinted-at mysteries of the relationships, readers of the original Japanese must constantly readjust their visual bond to the text as they progress. The reward for dancing to Tanizaki's tune is that a wealth of extratextual associations come with the effort—issues of gender, generational age, and cultural traditions, to mention only a few. Nor do we miss the perverse poignancy of a seventy-year-old author with dangerous hypertension exploring failing energies, undiminished imagination, and the imminence of death. Only three years later Tanizaki had the first of the strokes that would affect his physical ability to write.

At long last, Tanizaki returned to Tokyo as the setting for *Fūten rōjin nikki* (1963; *Diary of a Mad Old Man*, 1965). It received the 1962 Mainichi Literary Prize, awarded in 1963. In some ways, it is Tanizaki's most cheerfully defiant piece of writing. At the age of seventy-seven, having already had a couple of strokes and beset by multiple other physical ills, Tanizaki wrote a comic novel about an old man, Utsugi, who has had a stroke; who has to control all appetites in order not to have another, fatal stroke; but who feels life is not worth living without the excitement of sexual imagination; and whose wonderfully perverse acting out of his need does indeed bring on a near-fatal and totally debilitating stroke—but not before he delivers one of the most magnificent self-affirmations imaginable. In a grand return to the beginning, Tanizaki uses foot fetishism as the device around which to assemble the plot, which is conveyed again through orthographically different scripts: the *katakana* of Utsugi's diary, and the *hiragana* of the last section, which contains a nurse's and doctor's reports and a daughter's notes. The old man worships his young daughter-in-law's feet; the family sees Satsuko as a saint to put up with the old man's nasty desires, but (we readers notice) she also seems to garner considerable material benefits from the old man for her compliance: Cardin scarves, a swimming pool. Here, too, the question is who is manipulating whom. Utsugi's concluding stroke is preceded by a stunning internal monologue on the imperishable, eternal persistence of sexual desire, and is brought on by the intensity of joyous energy the old man feels at acting out his fantasy. Utsugi has come up with a brilliant idea as he prepares his death arrangements. He had planned to order a Buddhist statue with Satsuko's face carved on it as his gravestone; but he hears by accident of an ancient memorial in Nara, the Buddha's Footprint Stone, and that decides him: he will have a tombstone carved in that shape—but with Satsuko's feet as the model! His overheated meditation on the implications produce a wildly comic—and profoundly human—rhapsody on need, desire, and the vitality of imagination, as he pictures his own cremated bones rattling around and groaning under the weight of Satsuko's footprint stone; but also anger that his needs place him in such a vulnerable, humiliating, suppliant position; and a recognition that his desire enacts as much revenge as adoration. The excitement of inking Satsuko's feet to create a template for the stone produces

the inevitable stroke, and the story ends like *The Key*, with the man's voice silenced.

Tanizaki's last major piece of fictionalized writing was *Daidokoro Taiheiki* (1962–1963; A kitchen *"Taiheiki"*). Invoking in its own title the ironically titled fourteenth-century war chronicle "Record of Great Peace," it is a comic, mock-heroic, autobiographically based account of domestic and class relations in the household of an elderly writer and his wife. Household members say that even at the time of his death he was already thinking ahead to his next project.

Essays, Translations, Films, Symposia

Tanizaki did not write very much nonfiction in the first twenty years of his career. *Jōzetsuroku* (mentioned above) columns he wrote in 1927 for the journal *Kaizō*, discussed the contemporary literary scene and the sociocultural atmosphere of the day. Its primary importance, however, is as the stage for Tanizaki's statement of commitment to "plot for the sake of storytelling" in his debate with Akutagawa Ryūnosuke.

In'ei raisan (1933; *In Praise of Shadows*, 1977) is taken by many to be Tanizaki's most extensive and direct statement of his aesthetic principles. As the title indicates, it is an essay about "shadows" and earthboundedness, which Tanizaki argues is the basis of Japanese aesthetics, in contrast to the upward soaring "light" of the West. There are many charmingly peculiar (dare we say, again, "perverse"?) ideas in the argument (the beauty of the traditional dim Japanese toilet with cedar-bough-filled urinal, where one can hear the mosquitoes buzzing, as against the garishness of the blindingly white porcelain-fixtured Western toilets, for example); a kind of reverse racism sneaks in, in a discussion of skin color (Japanese pale skin, even if paler than Western skin, is not as "white," and hence looks better under candlelight than electric light, and that's why shadows are so important in the Japanese aesthetic); women in the shadows receive special attention; and the East/West comparison is always lurking about. Readers who see no irony and take this essay literally might even imagine it proves orientalist stereotypes of the "Eastern sensibility." The translators do, however, cite a famous story about what the author reportedly thought of the essay: in competition to design a new house Tanizaki was planning to build, one architect reassured the writer that his familiarity with *In Praise of Shadows* would ensure that the house would be just what Tanizaki wanted. Tanizaki is reported to have responded, aghast, that no one could actually live in such a house! To be sure, the contrasts between light and shadows in Tanizaki's storytelling technique are important, accounting in part for its "mystery-story" quality: again and again, he shines a powerful spotlight on one part of the stage, so that we may miss what is creeping around elsewhere in the shadows. *In Praise of Shadows* is both profound and possibly a parody of the jingoism of 1930s "Japan-First" rhetoric. Whatever else the essay may say about Japanese culture, it does point to some of Tanizaki's deep-seated emotional values.

His work on translating *The Tale of Genji* into modern Japanese brought Tanizaki to think more deeply about the Japanese language itself and what he had come to understand after more than thirty years as a professional writer. The 1934 *Bunshō tokuhon* (A manual of literary style) is a study of the art of writing. Tanizaki's starting point was the paradoxical distinction and identity of spoken and written Japanese. He argued that even in a language like Japanese, which still had open access to classical grammatical forms, whereas its modern language was only recently developed in hard-fought intellectual debates, there was no fundamental difference between "practical" and "fine" writing: good practice of either required the same attention to such elements as sound, functionality, word choice, and tone. The written language, however, also had to take into account sentence style, appearance, and other proprieties. Tanizaki drew examples from modern

writers and classical writers both Japanese and foreign (Theodore Dreiser, Arthur Waley's then-recent translation of *The Tale of Genji*); discussed differences between "Chinese syntax" (*kanbun*) and "Japanese syntax" (*wabun*); proposed implications for the visual impressions produced by the two Japanese orthographies (*hiragana* and *katakana*) that he would exploit twenty years later in *The Key*. Above all, this man who loved complexity of plot in his stories called for "simplicity" in word choice and style. *Bunshō tokuhon* is a beautiful exploration by a working writer of his own idiosyncratic view of the genius of his mother tongue.

Starting in the 1920s, Tanizaki began exploringing psycho-geographical considerations in such essays as "Kansai no onna o kataru" (1929; Speaking of Kansai women) and "Tokyo o omou" (1934; Thinking of Tokyo). In 1955–1956, he once more returned to his own early experience of Tokyo. *Childhood Years: A Memoir* is a nostalgic retrospective of both the author's life and the vanished world that had formed him. Like such earlier reflections as "Jōtarō" (1914; Jōtarō), and "Itansha no kanashimi" (1917; The sorrows of a heretic) that have provided critics with much material taken as autobiographical, *Childhood Years* looks back some sixty years at Tanizaki's childhood and early youth; it also vividly evokes the traditional environment of the "old Tokyo" in which he grew up. It is moving, entertaining and informative; exactly how much is "recollection" and how much is "re-creation" (Tanizaki's brother Seiji attests to Jun'ichiro's prodigious memory, but the work was, after all, written sixty and more years after the facts) is irrelevant to the way the work has been read: it gives a beautifully "total sense of place" of a nineteenth-century culture long past, and a fundamental source for the standard "story of Tanizaki."

Translation is important in Tanizaki's career in several ways: his reading and translating of English into Japanese; his translations of *The Tale of Genji* from classical to modern Japanese; and translations of his writing into English and other European languages. His fairly extensive readings of such American and European fin de siècle "decadents" as Edgar Allan Poe, Oscar Wilde, and Charles Baudelaire clearly added to his baroque imagination, already fed by childhood experience of Kabuki and Edo-influenced melodramas and adventure stories. There is some indication that he had assistance in doing his translations into Japanese of such stories as Thomas Hardy's "Barbara of the House of Grebe" and (from English translation) Stendhal's "L'abbesse de Castro"; but, as letters he wrote in English indicate, his personal command of the language was sufficient for such exercises.

The Tale of Genji is a complicated matter. As perhaps the most important literary masterpiece in nine hundred years of Japanese cultural history, it has rather the status of an icon: to be approached carefully, if at all. Motoori Norinaga had done some of the first scholarly work on it, in the eighteenth century. But the language had changed so much even by then that it was difficult to read, and even harder to understand; by the time it was "rediscovered" in the early twentieth century, the task of making it accessible to contemporary audiences was monumental. Nevertheless, in the twentieth century it was brought into modern Japanese by four different writers drawing on continuing *Genji* scholarship (including the two translations into English) and adopting different translation strategies: by the poetess Yosano Akiko (1912), three versions by Tanizaki (1939, 1951–1954, 1959), the novelist Enchi Fumiko (1972–1973); and the writer and cultural commentator Setouchi Jakuchō (1998). Of them, perhaps only Setouchi's ten-volume version has achieved the status of a best-seller (as of 2000, over two million copies had been sold). She has said that although Tanizaki, the only male translator among the four, beautifully reproduced in modern Japanese the ambiguity of "speaker, spoken-to, and spoken of" potential in the classical syntax, and the transparency between interior and exterior discourse, he had in effect made a modern text almost as difficult to decipher as the original, which is why the task of render-

ing a modern *Genji* has continued. But the years Tanizaki spent working and reworking his text clearly further enhanced and refined his appreciation of the possibilities of the Japanese language, and his own imagination. Few people read his translation these days, and there is little scholarly work on it; but it does occupy four volumes of the latest edition of Tanizaki's complete works.

A good number of Tanizaki's major novels and short stories and some of his essays have been translated into English as well as several European languages. Some of those translations began to appear during his lifetime, but such central works as *Quicksand, Childhood Years,* and *Captain Shigemoto's Mother* have only recently joined the extensive list available.

Though Tanizaki's "return to tradition" has been seen as a post-earthquake, early 1930s phenomenon, most of his *shinkabuki* (new Kabuki) playwriting of the 1910s and 1920s—and, ironically, even his avant-garde involvement in the nascent Japanese film industry in 1920–1921—remind us that his entire upbringing and much of his education—as well as much of Japanese intellectual life—were steeped in traditional culture. He worked on four films as writer, co-writer or codirector. One of them, *Jasei no in* (1921; The lust of the white serpent), was drawn from the same eighteenth-century collection of ghost tales by Ueda Akinari, *Ugetsu monogatari* (*Ugetsu Monogatari: Tales of Moonlight and Rain,* 1974), used by the film director Mizoguchi Kenji in his classic 1953 film, *Ugetsu.* Tanizaki's brief but intense participation in the film industry (including several essays on film he wrote at the time) brought even his family into its fold: his sister-in-law was the piquant lead actress in his *Amachua kurabu* (1920; Amateur club); his five-year-old daughter, Ayuko, had a part in it; and the Tanizaki home in Odawara was used as a set.

More than twenty of Tanizaki's works have been filmed commercially in Japan, some by such well-known directors as Mizoguchi Kenji, Kinugasa Teinosuke, and Ichikawa Kon. None of the versions he saw in his lifetime pleased him; apparently, as with his short-lived experience of trying to write film scripts, his own imagination was richer than film could deliver, especially given the intrusion of directors' (or film companies') visions. Nothing but the total control of a writer would serve him.

Already in Tanizaki's lifetime, major literary and intellectual journals were dedicating special issues to his work. One of the important early special issues was *Bungei*'s 1956 *Tanizaki Jun'ichirō dokuhon* (A Tanizaki Jun'ichirō reader). The Asahi Shinbunsha, in cooperation with Tanizaki's long-time publisher, Chūō Kōronsha, published the catalog of a major retrospective celebrating Tanizaki's hundredth birthday in 1986, *Tanizaki Jun'ichirō: Hito to bungaku ten* (An exhibit. Tanizaki Jun'ichirō: The man and the works). In 1995, an international conference took place in Venice that brought together Tanizaki specialists from around the world. The proceedings of that conference, which included some relatively little-studied but interesting aspects of Tanizaki's work, have been published in English as *A Tanizaki Feast*. The proceedings of a conference accompanying an exhibit at the Kanagawa Kindai Bungakkan in 1998 have been edited by Kōno Taeko as *Ika ni shite Tanizaki Jun'ichirō o yomu ka* (1999; How should we read Tanizaki?).

The Tanizaki Museum in Ashiya, outside Kobe (situated in one of Tanizaki's many homes, "Ishōan"), survived the 1995 Hanshin great earthquake without significant damage. Perhaps now the mad old man's bones are resting easier.

Selected Bibliography

PRIMARY WORKS

COLLECTED WORKS

Tanizaki Jun'ichirō zenshū. 30 vols. Tokyo: Chūō Kōronsha, 1957–1959; 28 vols. Tokyo: Chūō Kōronsha, 1966–1970; 30 vols. Tokyo: Chūō Kōronsha, 1981–1983. (Critical studies and translations are generally based on these editions of Tanizaki's complete works.)

STORY COLLECTIONS IN ENGLISH

Būshūkō hiwa (1931–1932); *Yoshino kuzu* (1931). Trans. by Anthony H. Chambers as *The Secret History of the Lord of Musashi and Arrowroot.* New York: Alfred A. Knopf, 1982.

Ashikari (1932); *Shōshō Shigemoto no haha* (1949–1950). Trans. by Anthony H. Chambers as *The Reed Cutter and Captain Shigemoto's Mother: Two Novellas.* New York: Alfred A. Knopf, 1993.

Neko to Shōzō to futari onna (1936). Trans. by Paul McCarthy as *A Cat, a Man, and Two Women.* New York: Kodansha International, 1990. (Also contains "The Little Kingdom" ["Chiisana ōkoku," 1918] and "Professor Rado" ["Rado sensei," 1925 and "Zoku Rado sensei," 1928].)

Seven Japanese Tales. Trans. by Howard Hibbett. New York: Alfred A. Knopf, 1963. (Contains "A Portrait of Shunkin" ["Shunkinshō," 1933]; "Terror" ["Kyōfu," 1913]; "The Bridge of Dreams" ["Yume no ukihashi," 1959]; "The Tattooer" ["Shisei," 1910]; "The Thief" ["Watakushi," 1921]; "Aguri" ["Aoi hana," 1922]; "A Blind Man's Tale" ["Mōmoku monogatari," 1931].)

NOVELS AND STORIES

"Yanagi-yu no jiken" (1918). Trans. by Phyllis I. Lyons as "The Incident at the Willow Bath House." In *Studies in Modern Japanese Literature: Essays and Translations in Honor of Edwin McClellan.* Edited by Dennis Washburn and Alan Tansman. Ann Arbor: Center for Japanese Studies, University of Michigan, 1997. Pp. 321–339.

"Haha o kouru ki" (1919). Trans. by Edward Fowler as "Longing for Mother." *Monumenta Nipponica* 35, no. 4:467–483 (winter 1980).

Chijin no ai (1924). Trans. by Anthony H. Chambers as *Naomi.* New York: Alfred A. Knopf, 1985.

Tade kuu mushi (1928–1929). Trans. by Edward Seidensticker as *Some Prefer Nettles.* New York: Alfred A. Knopf, 1955.

Manji (1928–1930). Trans. by Howard Hibbett as *Quicksand.* New York: Alfred A. Knopf, 1994.

Neko to Shōzō to futari onna (1936). Trans. by Matsui Sakuko as *A Cat, Shōzō and Two Women.* New South Wales, Australia: Wild Peony, 1988.

Sasameyuki (1943–1948). Trans. by Edward Seidensticker as *The Makioka Sisters.* New York: Alfred A. Knopf, 1957.

Kagi (1956). Trans. by Howard Hibbett as *The Key.* New York: Alfred A. Knopf, 1960.

Fūten rōjin nikki (1963). Trans. by Howard Hibbett as *Diary of a Mad Old Man.* New York: Alfred A. Knopf, 1965.

ESSAYS

In'ei raisan (1933). Trans. by Thomas I. Harper and Edward Seidensticker as *In Praise of Shadows.* New Haven, Conn.: Leete's Island Books, 1977.

Yōshō jidai (1955–1956). Trans. by Paul McCarthy as *Childhood Years: A Memoir*. New York: Kodansha International, 1988.

SECONDARY WORKS

CRITICAL AND BIOGRAPHICAL STUDIES

Ara Masahito, ed. *Tanizaki Jun'ichirō kenkyū*. Tokyo: Yagi Shoten, 1972.

Boscaro, Adriana, and Anthony Hood Chambers, eds. *A Tanizaki Feast: The International Symposium in Venice*. Ann Arbor: Center for Japanese Studies, University of Michigan, 1998.

Chambers, Anthony H. *The Secret Window: Ideal Worlds in Tanizaki's Fiction*. Cambridge, Mass.: Council on East Asian Studies, Harvard University, 1994.

Chiba Shunji. *Kanshō Nihon gendai bungaku, 8: Tanizaki Jun'ichirō*. Tokyo: Kadokawa Shoten, 1982.

———, ed. *Tanizaki Jun'ichirō: Monogatari no hōhō*. Nihon bungaku kenkyū shiryō shinshū. Tokyo: Yūseidō, 1990.

Fukuda Kiyoto and Hirayama Jōji, eds. *Tanizaki Jun'ichirō: Hito to sakuhin*. Tokyo: Shimizu Shoin, 1966.

Gessel, Van. *Three Modern Novelists: Sōseki, Tanizaki, Kawabata*. New York: Kodansha International, 1993.

Hata Kōhei. *Kami to gangu to no aida: Shōwa shonen no Tanizaki Jun'ichirō*. Tokyo: Rokkō Shuppan, 1977.

Ito, Ken K. *Visions of Desire: Tanizaki's Fictional Worlds*. Stanford, Calif.: Stanford University Press, 1991.

Itō Sei. *Tanizaki Jun'ichirō no bungaku*. Tokyo: Chūō Kōronsha, 1970.

Kōno Taeko. *Tanizaki bungaku to kōtei no yokubō*. Tokyo: Bungei Shunjūsha, 1976.

———, ed. *Ikanishite Tanizaki Jun'ichirō o yomu ka*. Tokyo: Chūō Kōronsha, 1999.

Lippit, Noriko Mizuta. *Reality and Fiction in Modern Japanese Literature*. White Plains, N.Y.: M. E. Sharpe, 1980.

Noguchi Takehiko. *Tanizaki Jun'ichirō ron*. Tokyo: Chūō Kōronsha, 1973.

———, ed. *Tanizaki Jun'ichirō: Shinpojiumu Nihon gendai bungaku 16*. Tokyo: Gakuseisha, 1976.

Nomura Shōgo. *Denki Tanizaki Jun'ichirō*. Tokyo: Rokkō Shuppan, 1972.

Pollack, David. *Reading Against Culture: Ideology and Narrative in the Japanese Novel*. Ithaca, N.Y.: Cornell University Press, 1992.

Rubin, Jay. *Injurious to Public Morals: Writers and the Meiji State*. Seattle: University of Washington Press, 1984.

Saeki Shōichi. *Monogatari geijutsu ron: Tanizaki, Akutagawa, Mishima*. Tokyo: Kōdansha, 1979.

Sakaki, Atsuko. *Recontextualizing Texts: Narrative Performance in Modern Japanese Fiction*. Cambridge, Mass.: Harvard University Asia Center, 1999.

Seidensticker, Edward. "Tanizaki Jun'ichirō, 1886–1965." *Monumenta Nipponica* 21, nos. 3–4:249–265 (1966).

Shinchō Nihon bungaku arubamu, 7: Tanizaki Jun'ichirō. Tokyo: Shinchōsha, 1985.

Suzuki, Tomi. *Narrating the Self: Fictions of Japanese Modernity*. Stanford, Calif.: Stanford University Press, 1996.

"Tanizaki Jun'ichirō dokuhon." Special issue of *Bungei* (March 1956).

"*Tanizaki Jun'ichirō: Hito to bungaku*" ten. Tokyo: Asahi Shinbunsha, 1986.

Ueno Chizuko, Ogura Chikako, and Tomioka Taeko. *Danryū bungakuron*. Tokyo: Chikuma Shobō, 1992.

TŌSON

(SHIMAZAKI TŌSON)
1872–1943

MARVIN MARCUS

THE LONG AND productive career of Shimazaki Tōson, whose lifetime essentially spans the prewar history of modern Japan, placed him at the very center of the Tokyo literary establishment—the so-called *bundan*—where he figured as a dominant presence. Together with Mori Ōgai (1862–1922) and Natsume Sōseki (1867–1916), Tōson played a key role in laying the foundation for a modern literary sensibility in Japan. His writing, however, presents certain challenges to those expecting major literary careers to be synonymous with brilliant innovation and creative breakthrough. Despite having emerged on the literary scene as a pioneering modernist, first in poetry and then fiction, Tōson went on to cultivate a style of autobiographical narrative that elevated the notion of authorial sincerity and authenticity as a criterion of serious literature. The bold strokes of his early career, which earned the author a secure niche in the *bundan*, gave way to a literature of self that foregrounded the author as struggling youth, beleaguered family member, tortured soul, spiritual seeker, and—finally—literary patriarch. Tōson's elite stature found concrete expression in a remarkable succession of books, written for diverse readerships, that established the author's repertoire of "life stories" as a fixed commodity on the literary marketplace.

A writer who sought to minimize the distance between life and art, and who brilliantly marketed the life in collaboration with his publishers, Shimazaki Tōson has attracted both high praise and a substantial amount of criticism. The collected works, which include several classics of *kindai bungaku*—Japan's prewar literature—provide an unobstructed view of the literary and cultural crosscurrents that shaped the age. Most important, Tōson is one of a handful of early modern writers whose careers have come to be regarded as emblematic of *kindai no seishin*—the spirit of modern Japan in the prewar period. *Kindai* may be defined simply as "modern" or "modern age," but in the context of literary history the term has come to possess rich layers of meaning. The transformational *kindai* epoch holds a particular fascination for Japanese, and the lives of its representative writers have been "read" inseparably from their literary texts.

For Shimazaki Tōson, personal experience was to serve as the touchstone for much of his writing. His collected works constitute an elaborate autobiographical tapestry, woven of episodes and incidents drawn from his life. Owing to the strong current of personalism that characterized *kindai bungaku*, the work of certain authors came to be interpreted as unadulterated expressions of self. To put it the other way around, Tōson's literary texts have long served as source material for endless biographies and appreciations. This seemingly naive approach has not gone unchallenged, but the Tōson biography merits more than routine attention as an introduction to the author's lifework.

Early Life and Education

Born on 25 March 1872—the dawn of the Meiji period (1868–1912)—Shimazaki Haruki (Tōson is a pen name) was the eighth and youngest child of a family that held the hereditary post of village head *(shōya)* in Magome, a small town in the mountains of present-day Nagano Prefecture and a way station along the Nakasendō, the road connecting the shogunal capital of Edo and the imperial capital of Kyoto. A Shimazaki ancestor had in fact founded the village in the sixteenth century, and the family-run inn was the official lodging for dignitaries traveling along this major thoroughfare.

As a boy raised in the rural gentry class and reared within the *ie*, the traditional family network, young Haruki lived in relative comfort. His father, Masaki, was a rather remote figure, an ardent nativist who longed for the end of shogunal rule and the restoration of the emperor. With the creation of a modern Japanese state in the 1870s, however, Shimazaki family fortunes began to decline. In 1881 Masaki sent two of his sons, Haruki and his older brother Tomoya, to Tokyo. Having displayed a penchant for book learning, Haruki had earned a special place in his father's affections. But a new world beckoned, and the Shimazaki brothers joined the wave of migration that brought countless provincial youth, who faced dim prospects in the rural backwaters, into the very heart of a rapidly modernizing Japan.

Once in Tokyo, Haruki did not return home for decades. But the story of his youth—the idyllic rural upbringing, the coming of age in the great urban center—appeared prominently in his subsequent writings. Equally significant

was the story of his ongoing relationship with the extended family, the *ie*, an institution that underwent dramatic change in the modern era. For a while, Haruki lived with his married older sister Takase Sono (1856–1920), a complex and troubled woman who figured prominently in the Shimazaki family saga. When she and her husband left Tokyo, Haruki moved into the home of Yoshimura Tadamichi, an old acquaintance of the Shimazakis. The Yoshimuras became surrogate parents, and the years spent in their Tokyo home served as the setting for numerous literary reminiscences that evoke a happy boyhood. In the meantime, Haruki's father struggled to hold the family together in rural Magome, but he descended into madness and died in 1886 in pathetic circumstances. His citified son, however, had long since grown estranged from his embarrassingly awkward and boorish father.

Higher education served as the gateway to a literary career for Shimazaki Haruki and many of his youthful contemporaries. Intent upon learning English, which was the passport to Western culture and learning, Haruki entered a Presbyterian school, Meiji Gakuin, in 1887. The school, whose faculty included native English speakers, introduced Haruki to Christianity, and so it was that the earnest fifteen-year-old studied the tenets of the faith and was duly baptized. Although not much drawn to religious observance, Haruki was moved by Christian humanism and the transforming power of confession and redemption. He was equally drawn to the masterworks of English literature.

Following his literary baptism in Shakespeare, Byron, and Wordsworth, and some attempts at translating literary biography, Haruki graduated from Meiji Gakuin, albeit at the bottom of his class. Still undecided as to his future, the budding romantic worked for a time as a store clerk in Yokohama. In the meantime he submitted occasional pieces for the *Jogaku Zasshi* (Journal of women's studies). The editor, Iwamoto Yoshiharu (1863–1943), was impressed with the young man, who by then had adopted the pen name

Tōson. In his capacity as headmaster of Meiji Jogakkō, a private girls' school affiliated with Meiji Gakuin, Iwamoto extended to the fledgling writer an offer to teach English at the school. He accepted, and in the course of his first year on the faculty he joined a group of young writers in Iwamoto's sphere who in 1892 had founded *Bungakkai* (World of literature), a short-lived but very influential literary coterie. Tōson's affiliation with this bohemian cadre of romantics marks the starting point of what would be a half century spent at the center of the Japanese literary world.

The Young Romantic

As a teacher at Meiji Jogakkō, Tōson fell in love with one of his students, Satō Sukeko. She happened to be engaged already, and the ill-starred relationship became the source of much torment. At his wits' end, the young teacher resigned his position and fled Tokyo for an extended period of vagabonding and soul-searching in Kansai, the Kyoto-Osaka region to the west of Tokyo. This would be the first of several flights from the scene of personal difficulty, each of which would figure in numerous literary retellings.

Returning from Kansai, Tōson rejoined the Meiji Jogakkō faculty and renewed his ties with the *Bungakkai* coterie. Family difficulties required that he take on the burden of caring for his mother. Sukeko by this time had married, only to die of complications from pregnancy. Distraught, Tōson once again resigned his teaching post and left Tokyo, accepting a position in the northern city of Sendai. It was during his year in Sendai (1896–1897) that he produced his first book of poetry, *Wakanashū* (1897; Collection of seedlings). This volume of strikingly modern verse placed Tōson on the literary map.

Returning to Tokyo from Sendai, the young romantic continued publishing collections of verse. At the same time he immersed himself in the Western prose of authors such as Tolstoy, Dostoevsky, Rousseau, Ruskin, and Maupassant, all read in English. In 1899 his mentor Iwamoto arranged a marriage with Hata Fuyuko, the daughter of a wealthy Hokkaido merchant, and shortly thereafter the couple left Tokyo for Komoro, a remote castle town located on the scenic Chikuma River, where Tōson had accepted yet another rural teaching post at the local academy.

In the course of the five-year stay in Komoro (1899–1905), Tōson gradually abandoned poetry in favor of prose, a not uncommon pattern among late-Meiji writers. Trying his hand at short fiction, he also experimented with a form of literary "sketching" known as *shaseibun*. Tōson's impressive collection of Komoro sketches, heavily weighted toward lyrical description and detailed observation, would be incorporated into subsequent work.

Three daughters were born to the couple, who had to learn to live in straitened circumstances. Determined to make a go of it as a writer of fiction, Tōson set to work on a major novel, to be entitled *Hakai* (1906; *The Broken Commandment*, 1974). Having borrowed money from his in-laws, he resigned the teaching post and devoted himself to the project. In 1905 the family returned to Tokyo, where Tōson struggled to complete his novel. The family was reduced to privation, and the three Shimazaki daughters died, one by one, in the course of a year. Tōson would go on to recount the sad tale of a father's literary ambition and the tragic toll it exacted.

In the meantime, the publication of *The Broken Commandment* in 1906 propelled the young author into the forefront of the Tokyo *bundan*. It also established his reputation for uncompromising dedication to literary pursuits.

Naturalism

The Broken Commandment, which concerns a tormented young man who must come to terms with his true identity through the purging powers of confession, enjoyed instant and widespread acclaim. Although clearly fictional, the novel helped inspire an important *bundan* movement—*shizenshugi* ("naturalism"). Loosely modeled on the literary realism of the French writer Émile Zola, this Japanese naturalism sought to elevate authenticity and sincerity as hallmarks of serious literature. With the further impetus provided by Tōson's colleague Tayama Katai (1871–1930), the movement came to promote confessional accounts based on the author's personal experience. Naturalism enjoyed a rather brief heyday as a formal coterie—roughly 1906 to 1912. But its credo of literary self-representation would have lasting consequences, with Tōson playing a key role as Japan's quintessential "personalist" writer.

With the rise to prominence of naturalism, Tōson embarked on a series of autobiographical novels and short stories that retold episodes concerning his relationship with family and friends. In keeping with journalistic practices that had taken hold in the *bundan*, he published the longer novels initially in newspaper installments. He also contributed hundreds of essays across the spectrum of contemporary arts and culture, which appeared in numerous periodicals. Gradually, the author's life and opinions became a staple of the Japanese reading diet, thanks to the vigorous literary journalism that kept his name in print.

As Tōson's *bundan* reputation waxed, the Shimazaki family also grew. Three sons—Kusuo, Keiji, and Ōsuke—were born between 1905 and 1908. But the birth of daughter Ryūko in 1910 gave rise to complications that took the life of his wife Fuyuko. Her untimely death placed the author, now in his prime, in the midst of a new domestic crisis that would have serious repercussions. A niece, Komako, the seventeen-year-old daughter of his brother Hirosuke, was pressed into service to help with domestic chores and care of the four young children. The widower gradually became intimate with his niece, managing to keep the affair secret until her pregnancy precipitated yet another crisis. Once again, Tōson's response was to flee the scene. Arranging for the foster care of his children, he sailed for France in April 1913, a self-imposed exile that would last for three years.

Tōson's naturalist credo, coupled with the rising tide of *bundan* personalism, had estab-lished the literary vehicle for his ongoing self-reflection. And so, as with earlier episodes of escape and relocation, the sojourn in France would generate an outpouring of literary personalia—a writer's personal reflections and reminiscences about aspects of his or her life—over a period of decades.

Middle and Later Years

Having maintained his authorial ties in absentia, Shimazaki Tōson reentered the *bundan* with a vengeance upon his return from France. The literary marketplace under the new emperor Taishō (1912–1926) expanded dramatically, and Tōson was quick to capitalize on new developments. He aligned himself with an emergent "pure literature" *(junbungaku)* coterie—authors who stood in opposition to the burgeoning market for cheap literary entertainment. Despite the contentious literary terrain, Tōson remained a fixture among diverse readerships, including young people and women. And throughout, the autobiographical agenda would predominate. In 1917, for instance, Tōson embarked on a series of writings for young people *(dōwa bungaku)* that systematically retold episodes from his youth and from more recent adventures, including the stay in France. He also resumed the fictionalized reminiscence of his Tokyo schooldays.

The Shimazaki family troubles, however, remained unresolved, as Tōson resumed his relationship with his niece Komako. Finally, intent on making a clean break, he opted for a literary exposé: a confessional novel that would disclose the entire sordid affair in daily newspaper serialization. What resulted was *Shinsei* (1919; New life), a *bundan* bombshell that sparked much controversy regarding the alleged "purity" of such accounts and the matter of Tōson's moral culpability. In the final analysis, the *Shinsei* scandal only enhanced the author's status as literary celebrity. He published nearly forty books during the 1920s, not including a twelve-volume edition of his collected works. This period witnessed a dramatic expansion of literary commerce in Japan, with well-known writers finally in a position to command impressive royalties.

Family crises, which had long served as a defining Tōson theme, gradually gave way to stability and a hopeful middle age. As the family nest began to empty, Tōson became engaged to Katō Shizuko, a woman twenty-four years his junior. Having weathered long years of turmoil and discord, the author was poised to reinvent himself once again.

Return to the Countryside

The 1920s witnessed Tōson's reconnection with his ancestral home in Magome, his *furusato.* Intent upon restoring a Shimazaki family presence in the village, Tōson paid a visit to Magome, bought parcels of land and real estate with his royalty windfalls, and installed his eldest son, Kusuo, there as an agricultural student. In the process he found himself immersed in village life for the first time in over forty years, an experience that would prove transformative.

Tōson made frequent visits to Magome. Anxious to retrace his family's lineage, the documentary record of which had been destroyed in a fire in 1895, the author embarked on an ambitious literary project: an account of Japan's entry into the modern era as told through the life of his father. Research on what would become Tōson's acknowledged masterpiece, *Yoake mae* (1935; *Before the Dawn*, 1987), began in 1927. Like Mori Ōgai, who late in life abandoned fiction in favor of historical and biographical writing, Tōson dedicated himself to the task of fleshing out the record of a man who had died some forty years earlier and a family with which he had a difficult and troubled relationship.

Before the Dawn is a monumental work. The monthly serialization, which spanned six years, was an all-consuming labor. Its completion in October 1935 was a major *bundan* event, occasioning a round of literary prizes, commemorative events, special journal issues, a play, a film script, and the publication of a massive eleven-volume edition of Tōson's works. In effect publication of *Before the Dawn* signaled the spiritual rebirth of Shimazaki Tōson and positioned him at the forefront of the Japanese literary world. In November 1935 the author was selected as first chairman of the newly formed Japan PEN (poets, playwrights, essayists, editors, and novelists) Club, and in July of the following year he embarked on a long journey to Buenos Aires as the Japanese delegate to the annual conclave of the International PEN Club. From Argentina, Tōson traveled to the United States and Europe before returning to Japan in January 1937. As with the earlier sojourn in France, this second overseas trip served both as an outlet for journalistic reportage and as material for a travel memoir, entitled *Junrei* (1940; Pilgrimage).

As Japan entered into open hostilities with China in 1937, Shimazaki Tōson enjoyed a privileged position within the *bundan.* The nation was now filled with patriotic endeavor, with writers and intellectuals expected to accommodate themselves to the new order. While not overtly sympathetic with the militarist regime, Tōson contributed to the chauvinist agenda in his declining years. Following a prolonged period of ill health, the author began work on two final projects. First, following a sixteen-year hiatus he returned to youth-oriented autobiography with the publication of *Chikaramochi* (1940; Ricecakes for stamina), an episodic memoir personally addressed to Japan's young people. He also conceived of a sequel to *Before the Dawn*, entitled *Tōhō no mon* (1943; Gate of the east). Intent on tracing the Shimazaki family chronology to the 1920s, he pursued extensive research for several years. Serialization began in January 1943. But on 21 August of that year, while at his desk working on the third chapter of his book, Tōson suffered a cerebral hemorrhage. He died the following day, at the age of seventy-one.

Poetry

Donald Keene, arguably the foremost scholarly Western interpreter of Japanese literature, has designated Shimazaki Tōson as the creator of modern Japanese poetry and the purest lyrical poet of modern Japan. Like many of his contemporaries, Tōson began as a poet, only to reinvent himself as a writer of fiction *(shōsetsu)*. But the lyrical voice would characterize much of his prose writing as well.

Tōson's emergence as a poet in the 1890s reflects his tutelage in the British Romantics as a student at Meiji Gakuin. Wordsworth, Byron, and Shelley served as models for a new lyricism of the self, which would challenge the orthodoxy of a native poetic tradition epitomized by the fourteen-hundred-year-old *waka* form, with its fixed prosody of thirty-one syllables. Initially experimenting with verse translation, Tōson began in 1892 to publish his own poetry in the "new style" of free verse known as *shintaishi*. In 1897, during the period of teaching in Sendai, he came out with *Wakanashū*, a collection of intensely lyrical verse that was greeted with considerable acclaim. The following verses from "Pillow of Grass" are representative:

> I am like the morning cloud
> That brought rain the night before;
> Or I am like the evening rain
> That tomorrow will be a floating cloud.
> Like leaves that have fallen
> I was carried by the wind;
> And with the clouds of the morning
> Came over the river at night.
> Perhaps here, in Miyagi Plain,
> In this ancient wilderness without a path
> I shall cease to wander,
> And find some rest.
>
> (*TZ*, vol. 1, p. 17; tr. McClellan, 1969, pp. 76–77)

Having established himself as a promising young poet, Tōson went on to publish three more collections, each marked by romantic wanderlust and expressions of youthful anguish. Some have commented on the narrow emotional range of this poetry, pointing to its uninspired adaptation of the Western romantic model. But the work is not merely derivative.

Powerfully drawn to Japan's own classical tradition, Tōson often invokes the spirit of Bashō (1644–1694) and of Saigyō (1118–1190), revered poets who had come to epitomize the spiritual journey and the quest for personal enlightenment through poetry. In other words, Tōson and his contemporaries were subject to a very complex calculus of influences and inspirations, both native and foreign.

Drawn to the broader horizons of prose fiction, Tōson essentially abandoned poetry following the publication of *Rakubaishū* (1901; Fallen plum blossom collection). But he remains identified with one particular poem, "Song on Traveling the Chikuma River," written in rural Komoro, at the site of the ruined castle. The first and last stanzas are as follows:

> By the old castle of Komoro
> In white clouds, a wanderer laments.
> The green chickweed has not sprouted,
> The grass has not yet laid its carpet;
> The silver coverlet on the hills around
> Melting in the sun, the light snow flows.
>
> . . . .
>
> Ah, what does the old castle tell?
> What do the waves on the banks reply?
> Think calmly of the world that has
>   passed,
> A hundred years are as yesterday.
> The willows along the Chikuma River
>   are misted,
> The spring is shallow, the water has
>   flowed.
> All alone I walk around the rocks
> And bind fast my sorrow to these banks.
>
> (*TZ*, vol. 1, p. 237; tr. Keene, 1956, pp. 201–202)

Tōson's *shintaishi* verse became a model of romantic expressivism. It had a galvanizing effect on the Meiji *bundan*, paving the way for the work of gifted poets such as Kitahara Hakushū (1885–1942) and Hagiwara Sakutarō (1886–1942). His four verse collections earned a niche in the emerging canon of *kindai* literature, and the poetic persona has long endured.

Fiction

Having devoted the first decade of his literary career to poetry, Tōson spent roughly the next two decades as a writer of *shōsetsu*—prose fiction. During this period he produced five long works. The first, and the best known, *The Broken Commandment*, is the only one not obviously autobiographical. This was followed by *Haru* (1908; Spring), *Ie* (1911; *The Family*, 1976), *Sakura no mi no jukusuru toki* (1919; When the cherries ripen), and *Shinsei* (New life). These novels form the core of Tōson's naturalist writings, which relate events and episodes in the life of the author and his circle of family, friends, and literary acquaintances. Tōson also wrote a number of shorter autobiographical accounts, some of them among his most affecting work.

Taken together, Shimazaki Tōson's naturalist fiction forms a major current of *kindai* literature. Like Sōseki, with whom he has been productively compared, Tōson utilized the medium of *shinbun shōsetsu*—"book-length" fiction originally published in daily newspaper serialization. But unlike Sōseki, he created a literary world defined by the borders of memory and personal experience.

The Broken Commandment

"*Rengeji de wa geshuku wo kaneta*"—with this famously laconic opening line ("The Rengeji Temple took in boarders") Tōson begins the story of Segawa Ushimatsu, a young schoolteacher undergoing a crisis of identity. Ushimatsu is an *eta* (literally, "full of filth"), a member of the Japanese pariah caste identified with ritually impure occupations such as leather tanning and animal slaughter. Despite being indistinguishable physically from other Japanese, members of this group, more commonly known as *burakumin* ("township dwellers"), had for centuries been subject to segregation and discrimination. And even though accorded a measure of equality with the advent of Meiji social reformism, the group remained the target of even more systematic maltreatment under their politically correct

designation as *shinheimin* ("new commoners"). In short, Tōson had chosen to confront one of Japan's cultural taboos.

As its title suggests, *The Broken Commandment* has to do with transgression and liberation. Thanks to his father's scrupulous concern for his son's future, Ushimatsu has succeeded in concealing his true identity and in gaining a teaching post in the rural town of Iiyama. Details of the school and the town itself are skillfully drawn, and the novel affords a compelling view of small-town life at the turn of the century. The portrayal of the inner workings of the school and its staff, who range from sympathetic fellow teachers to crass, scheming administrators, enhances the work's impressive realism. Indeed, *The Broken Commandment* has long served as a documentary source for *kindai* cultural history.

The plot, however, hinges on the complex subjectivity of the anguished protagonist and the painstaking process whereby he finally violates his father's admonition—and dying request—never to divulge the secret of his *eta* identity, lest he forfeit all chance of success and advancement.

> One thing more [his father] added: that the only way—the only hope—for any *eta* who wanted to raise himself in the world was to conceal the secret of his birth. "No matter who you meet, no matter what happens to you, never reveal it! Forget this commandment just once, in a moment of anger or misery, and from that moment the world will have rejected you forever." Such had been his father's teaching.
>
> It was as simple as that. *Tell no one:* that was the whole commandment.
>
> (*TZ*, vol. 2, pp. 9–10; tr. Strong, pp. 9–10)

While raising quite sensitive social concerns, the novel stops short of overt political engagement and instead focuses on the emotional state of its protagonist, who is burdened with conflict, remorse, and guilt. The conflict pits the father, the voice of traditional authority, against the repressed "true self," the inner voice yearning for expression. Ushimatsu understands that he must unburden himself through a confessional "coming out," but he remains incapable of taking the initiative. Much like Utsumi Bunzō, the ineffectual protagonist of Futabatei Shimei's landmark novel *Ukigumo* (1889; *Drifting Clouds*, 1967), Ushimatsu is plagued by indecision. But unlike Bunzō, who is left without a lifeline, Ushimatsu is not alone. He has the inspiring example of Inoko Rentarō, a fellow *eta* who had revealed his own identity in a moving literary confession before becoming involved in promoting *eta* rights.

The first section of *The Broken Commandment* portrays the emotional gridlock of its protagonist, which is relieved only by occasional bursts of lyrical prose inspired by the author's intimate familiarity with the local landscape:

Patches of mist formed over the opposite bank of the Chikuma River; already the peaks of the Kosha range had faded into the darkness, and only the fields stood out in the dying light from the sun as it sank beneath a russet sky, hidden by the mountains. Dusk enfolded the woods and clusters of farmhouses beyond. If only one could enjoy the beauty of such a scene to the full, free of care and mental suffering, what a time of bliss youth would be! The more painful Ushimatsu's inward conflict, the deeper his sense of such beauty, of external nature as a living force permeating his very being.

(*TZ*, vol. 2, p. 51; tr. Strong, p. 45)

Ushimatsu is the victim of *hanmon* (youthful anguish), a chronic affliction of many *kindai* literary protagonists. But with the death of his father—a cowherd fatally gored by a rogue bull—events take a dramatic turn. As suspicions are raised regarding his actual identity, Ushimatsu learns that a local politician, a reprehensible character named Takayanagi, has secretly married an *eta* woman in order to get hold of her wealthy father's money. And in the meantime, he makes the acquaintance of Rentarō, who is promoting Takayanagi's rival for election to the Diet. Circumstances are closing in on Ushimatsu, all but compelling him to confess once and for all. But he remains indecisive, and his guilt drives him to the brink.

It is only when Inoko is murdered following an appearance in Iiyama that Ushimatsu is at long last transformed. Having tragically missed the opportunity to make his confession to Inoko, whose Christ-like role is evident, he awakens to his true nature in a burst of inspiration:

For the first time Ushimatsu realized the corrosive effect on his character, on the natural self that he had been born with, of the perpetual obsession with concealment. . . . What good did it do, the endless agonizing? *I am an eta.* Why should he not declare the truth, openly and boldly, to all the world? Suddenly a new courage was within his grasp. The man he had been till now was dead. . . . Ushimatsu sensed the approach of a new dawn.

(*TZ*, vol. 2, pp. 259–261; tr. Strong, pp. 217–219)

Rather incongruously, the young teacher's spiritual rebirth is enacted in front of his class as an exercise in abject self-abasement and contrition, as he prostrates himself on the wooden floor and begs for forgiveness from his astonished students. And the novel ends even more incongruously as Ushimatsu is miraculously rescued from the dubious fate that would await a "confessed" *eta*. The deus ex machina solution is twofold: first, the "reborn" protagonist receives an offer from a wealthy local *eta* to join him in a cattle-ranching venture in Texas; and second, the protagonist marries Oshio, the girl he has secretly fallen in love with but has despaired of ever being able to win over. In other words, what had been a compelling tale ends on a painfully contrived note.

However, *The Broken Commandment* has withstood the test of time as a bona fide literary landmark, a "classic" of *kindai bungaku* almost from its inception. Much has been made of the author's debt to Dostoevsky—in particular, the figure of Raskolnikov from

Crime and Punishment—and his use of Christian theology and symbolism. Equally significant is Tōson's crafting of an unadorned literary style that reinforces the work's realism and its penetrating psychological narrative.

Despite imperfections that it shared with other pioneering works of late-Meiji literature, *The Broken Commandment* pointed to new directions that others would follow. Some have lamented the fact that a literature of genuine social engagement was not one such outcome. Rather, in the hands of Tayama Katai, the act of literary confession would be identified not with a fictional protagonist but with the author himself. This development, closely associated with the naturalist school, was to have profound meaning for Shimazaki Tōson.

Haru

Under the aegis of the naturalist movement that he had himself helped inspire, Tōson essentially abandoned creative fiction in favor of "artless" subjectivity and the painstaking inventory of one's personal sphere *(shinpen)*. He went on to chronicle the travails of young adulthood, over which anxiety, insecurity, and indecision reigned. His second novel, *Haru* (Spring), establishes the narrative pattern for subsequent works. Spanning the years of Tōson's affiliation with the *Bungakkai* coterie, 1893 to 1896, the plot centers on the comings and goings of the group's five mainstays. In the style of a *roman à clef*, where each character is understood to represent some actual figure, the author casts himself as Kishimoto Sutekichi, a name he used in subsequent works as well. The group's charismatic leader, Kitamura Tōkoku (1868–1894), is cast as Aoki Shin'ichi, a poet and ardent *bungaku seinen* ("literary youth") burdened with a wife and children and a host of domestic troubles.

Commencing with Kishimoto's return from his Kansai travels, *Haru* presents a series of seemingly random scenes featuring the *Bungakkai* regulars, who engage in earnest discussions of love, the meaning of life, and the ills that afflict modern Japan. They are a mutual commiseration society, and Aoki, who rails against the arid conventionalism of the age, is their informal spokesman.

The novel's dramatic interest, however, centers on Kishimoto's miserable love life. Having fled Tokyo in the wake of his unfulfilled longing for Katsuko, who had been his student, Kishimoto is once again tied up in romantic knots. He escapes to the countryside, returns, and escapes again. In the meantime Aoki commits suicide, although the motive remains vague. Then Katsuko marries, and before long she too dies. And as if this were not enough, Kishimoto has to assume unexpected burdens owing to the imprisonment of his older brother, accused of fraudulent business dealings. Unhinged by the mounting crises, Kishimoto attempts suicide, but even this ends in failure. Finally resolving to start anew, he accepts a teaching post in the northern city of Sendai. "He could hear the melancholy sound of the rain outside. He leaned his head against the window and dreamed hopefully of all that the future might hold for him. He was utterly exhausted. He thought: 'I do want to live—even I'" (*TZ*, vol. 3, p. 245; tr. McClellan, 1969, p. 100).

As a historical document, *Haru* provides an "insider account" of a major *kindai* literary coterie. Adhering close to the naturalist agenda, which valorized authenticity of spirit and mood over mere plot contrivance, the novel brings to life the world of the *bungaku seinen*—the Meiji literary youth who loom so large in the saga of a modernizing Japan. But Tōson's aesthetics of authenticity, the holy grail of *shizenshugi* ("naturalism"), yielded a highly fragmented, episodic narrative that would have limited appeal beyond the *bundan*.

Ie

This long and brooding novel, whose Japanese title, *Ie*, means both "house" in the physical sense and family, has been cited by some critics as the masterwork of Japanese naturalist fiction. In it, Tōson sought to elaborate upon his conflicted relationship with family. In so doing, he created a case study, in effect, of the difficulties encountered when the traditionally dominant system of patriarchal kinship confronted the forces of modernization in the *kindai* period.

As with Tōson's other autobiographical writing, *The Family* encompasses a discrete phase of the author's life, 1898 to 1910. In terms of literary chronology, it begins where *Haru* left off. This tale of family dysfunction and personal crisis was written in the wake of his wife's death in May 1910, which left the middle-aged author as the only parent of four young children. For a writer committed to testing the fault lines of the "personal sphere," this was an apt occasion to explore the stifling quality of one's own family life and its relentless intrusions. As such, it is the "perfect" naturalist novel, whose generous supply of dirty linen was aired in full view of the nation's newspaper readers in its initial serialization.

As with *Haru*, *The Family* is marked by a pastiche of episode and incident rather than sustained plot. Domestic scenes predominate, with considerable care lavished on capturing the look and feel of interior space. This time casting himself as Koizumi Sankichi, Tōson projects an attitude of clinical detachment as he presents his "anatomy" of two parallel family spheres—his own Shimazaki clan (named Koizumi in the novel) and the Takase clan (named Hashimoto in the novel), into which his elder sister Sono had married. In its alternation of scenes from the two familial perspectives, the novel gradually reveals the bleak consequences of a system that entitles incompetent family heads to maintain their authority.

A keen observer of the deterioration of these once-proud families, Sankichi is himself embroiled in familial conflict, as he remains incapable of reaching out to his own wife, Oyuki:

The house somehow came to seem empty. There were times now when the two would sit down to a meal in silence, not looking at each other. It hurt Oyuki to see her husband so silent and hard. And now there were so many times when she simply did not know

what this difficult husband of hers would say next. One minute he would look at Ofusa, their little daughter, and say lovingly: "She has cheeks just like my mother's." Then the next minute an exchange such as this would ensue: "Are you sure Ofusa is my child?"

"Don't be silly. Whose child can she be if she isn't yours?" There was nothing that hurt Oyuki more than this kind of senseless talk.

Or he would suddenly ask: "What ever made you marry me in the first place?"

"How do you expect me to answer a question like that?"

"I don't know. Perhaps I should go off on a trip. I feel in the mood for it."

> (*TZ*, vol. 4, pp. 100–101;
> tr. McClellan, 1969, p. 120)

Sankichi's daughters die, as does his favorite nephew Shōta. His wife has an affair, yet the marriage somehow survives. The family persists, like some chronically diseased organism, as its members lead lives that are troubled, disconnected, and ultimately meaningless.

Although its social critique is muted since the author scrupulously targets the personal sphere, *The Family* has been applauded for its penetrating view of a bankrupt and anachronistic institution. A melancholy portrayal of failed relationships and sterile marriages, the novel is not an attempt to curry favor with a readership wishing to be entertained. As for the Shimazaki clan, Tōson duly assumed the family headship abdicated by his older brother. Later in life he would go on to don the mantle of cultural patriarch.

Sakura no mi no jukusuru toki

Begun in 1913, written for the most part in France, and completed following the return to Japan, Tōson's fourth novel *Sakura no mi no jukusuru toki* (When the cherries ripen) revisits the author's youth—specifically, the five years (1888–1893) that immediately precede the period depicted in *Haru*. These years span his enrollment as a student at Meiji Gakuin and departure for the extended trip to the Kansai.

This "prequel" to the 1908 novel begins in the mode of Proustian reminiscence, with a preface in which the Tōson narrator finds himself transported back to the halcyon days of youth by the scent of cherry blossoms. Indeed, much of the novel, centering once again on the Kishimoto protagonist, involves the recollection of earlier days—the happy years spent in the home of the Tanabes, his Tokyo foster family; incidents at boarding school; and occasional reminders of his father, who died not long after coming to Tokyo for a visit.

As with *Haru*, much of the action takes place in and around schools. Young Kishimoto discovers the glories of English literature, which he consumes voraciously. He is dazzled by Wordsworth and tries his hand at writing. He begins making the acquaintance of literary people. Graduation day, however, is a bittersweet occasion, giving rise to a surge of nostalgic longing.

[Kishimoto] noticed that tiny cherries had fallen here and there on the road outside the gate . . . He picked up one or two, then remembered long-ago days in his village in the mountains when he had gathered nettletree nuts and fallen jay feathers. Without realizing what he was doing, he pressed to his face the cherries he had gathered and sniffed the fairy-tale fragrance. It occurred to him that this was the symbol of the happiness of his younger days.

(*TZ*, vol. 5, p. 512; tr. Keene, 1984, vol. 1, p. 267)

Unsure about what to do with his life, Kishimoto works for the Tanabes in their store in Yokohama. He begins writing for a literary journal, through which he befriends a group of fellow *bungaku seinen*—the nascent *Bungakkai* coterie. Thanks to the journal's editor, who takes him on as a protégé, Kishimoto is employed as an English teacher at a Christian school for young women. It is here that he falls

in love with Katsuko. Their ill-starred affair yields unrelenting frustration and anxiety. The young man finds solace not through the church, which he ultimately abandons, but through the example of the poet-sage Bashō. Bestirring himself to thoughts of spiritualized wandering in the Bashō style, he quits his job, bids farewell to his friends, and sets out on foot for Kyoto.

Read together with *Haru*, this account of a decade in the life of Kishimoto Sutekichi stands as an elegy to the spirit of Meiji youth. The novel's palpable poignancy and its heavily nostalgic flavor may reflect the point of view of the author "exiled" in France. As with *Haru*, its companion volume, the novel's accumulated accounts of mid-Meiji schooling—dorm life, libraries, prayer meetings in the school chapel, and encounters with students and teachers (including a number of foreigners)—contribute to its value as cultural history.

Shinsei and *Arashi*

A confessional novel, *Shinsei* (New life) is one of Tōson's best known and least admired works. It can be seen as the author's attempt to bestow on himself that which he had granted to the protagonist of *The Broken Commandment*—namely, the "new life" of the novel's title. Invoking the *shizenshugi* ("naturalism") notion of confession as the apex of artistic purity, the author exposes through a public medium the skeleton in his closet. The sin in question is the extended affair with his niece, begun almost a decade earlier in the wake of his wife's death in 1910.

Published in two volumes that span some six years in the author's life, *Shinsei* begins with the gradual revelation of the fact that the protagonist—once again, Kishimoto Sutekichi—is sleeping with his niece Setsuko, some twenty years his junior. Setsuko reveals that she is pregnant, whereupon Kishimoto struggles with the unsavory prospect of humiliation and censure. Essentially indifferent to the fate that might befall the niece, he falls prey to personal anxiety and torment. And rather than face up to his brother Yoshio, the girl's father, Kishimoto opts for a strategic retreat from the scene: he escapes Japan on a steamship and travels to France, where he remains in self-imposed exile for three years.

The stay in France, which had already yielded a harvest of literary reportage and reminiscence, gives rise to some of the novel's high points. Tōson's undeniable gift as literary impressionist is brought to bear in his depiction of Parisian street scenes, pastoral views of the French countryside, and encounters with Japanese expatriates. But for his protagonist, life overseas is marked by isolation, introversion, and bouts of self-pity:

> When he got back to his room he was quite exhausted by the long walk under the fresh young leaves. He had seen so many streets that day. He went to the window and stood there, utterly forlorn. Far away in the sky were fluffy white clouds like those he remembered seeing from the mountains of Shinshū. Blown about by the early spring breeze, they changed their shape endlessly. He watched them alone, with no one beside him to share his thoughts . . . I have become homesick, he thought disgustedly. He felt the strain of exile so acutely then that he could have thrown himself onto the bare wooden floor and wept.

> (*TZ*, vol. 7, pp. 144–145; tr. McClellan, p. 132)

The first half of *Shinsei* ends as Kishimoto bestirs himself and returns to Japan. The second half details the unhappy consequences of his resuming the affair with niece Setsuko. Kishimoto erects an elaborate rationalization of the illicit relationship, compromising his familial role. Having run out of excuses, he finally resolves to end the subterfuge by openly confessing the affair—in the form of a novel to be entitled *Shinsei*. Once again, literary confession comes to the rescue of a tormented soul, albeit at the cost of shattered family ties.

Shinsei was an heir to the dominant traits of *kindai* fiction that emerged in the 1880s and became established during the heyday of *shizenshugi* ("naturalism"). With its revisitation of chronic ineffectuality and pained introspection, and the Zen-like conundrum that females represent for bedeviled males, the novel fits squarely in the lineage established by *The Broken Commandment* and *Haru*. But its transparently self-serving agenda did not go unnoticed by fellow writers, who expressed outrage at what they regarded as Tōson's shameless hypocrisy and moral bankruptcy.

Besides raising questions regarding the author's integrity, *Shinsei* was open to criticism for its excessive length, weak characterization, and dyspeptic plot. Yet at the same time it sold very well and enhanced Tōson's reputation in certain quarters as a standard bearer of the elitist pure-literature camp. This, however, was to be his last attempt at writing novels in the naturalist style.

Arashi (1927; Tempest) was the author's fifth and final collection of short fiction. Its nine stories constitute a mosaic of family portraits that carry forward the lineage of reminiscence begun with *The Family*. Hailed by critics as a masterpiece of so-called state-of-mind fiction (*shinkyō shōsetsu*), *Arashi* features, in its title story, an earnest account of a father's relationship with his four children, the eldest of whom are about to leave home and pursue their own lives. Essentially a sequel to *Shinsei*, the story presents dramatized encounters between the father and his growing children, combined with personal reflections on the trials and tribulations of raising children after the loss of a spouse.

Perhaps the most moving story in the *Arashi* collection concerns sister Sono. Entitled "Aru onna no shōgai" (The life of a certain woman), it recounts the final stages of Sono's madness and the deterioration of her own family. Harking back to the sister's finely wrought characterization in *The Family*, this account also foreshadows the moving portrayal of the father's madness in *Before the Dawn*. Indeed, some of Tōson's finest writing reflects an abiding concern for the insanity that plagued the family.

Taken together, Tōson's autobiographical fiction stands as a valiant, albeit flawed, attempt to convey the textures and moods of one's social universe. For better or worse, it helped establish the primacy of the personal voice in modern Japanese literature.

Literary Personalia

Shimazaki Tōson's essential indifference to the more creative possibilities of fiction can be variously interpreted. One factor, however, that reinforced his autobiographical agenda concerns prevailing practices of literary publishing, which vigorously promoted personal narratives by well-known writers. The new market for literary personalia—accounts of writers "thinking out loud"; reflecting on the passing scene; reminiscing about their youth, travels, hobbies, pets—essentially coincided with the author's *bundan* debut. Tōson was immediately drawn to this new horizon of literary self-reference, and his work in three specific areas—personal essay, travel narrative, and youth reminiscence—is noteworthy.

Between 1909 and 1936 Toson published six volumes of *kansōbun*, literary impressions. The hundreds of essays, sketches, and personal ephemera that fill these volumes, originally printed in periodical form for diverse readerships and collected into book form at regular intervals, cover a range of topics, themes, and issues. For the women's magazines he held forth on the rights of women, the awakening of feminist consciousness, notable woman writers, and domestic economy. For the burgeoning youth readership he submitted stories and fables, reminiscences, and travel accounts. For the literary journals he wrote widely on current trends in the arts, both domestic and foreign. He reviewed books, plays, and art exhibits and contributed all manner of literary gossip and opinion.

Taken together, Tōson's essays and impressions constitute a literary miscellany par excellence, and in microcosm they encompass the journalistic orientation that had taken hold in the *bundan*. While lacking intellectual sparkle, the author's observations are conveyed in a comfortable, chatty style that became a narrative signature. In a sense, then, they are an extension of the larger personalism that is the hallmark of his literature.

The time-honored genre of travel writing—*kikōbun*—which had achieved prominence during the shogunal epoch (1192–1867), flourished in the *kindai* period, when ordinary Japanese could enjoy relatively unrestricted travel. Thus Tōson was by no means alone in taking to the road and writing about it. Commencing with the romantic wanderlust of the early poetry, Tōson's literature freely draws upon episodes of travel and extended stays both at home and abroad. Such writing provided an especially congenial outlet for the author's unique autobiographical agenda.

Once again, literary journalism plays a significant role here, since much of Tōson's travel writing originated as "on-the-road" reportage dispatched to Japan's daily newspapers. The three years spent in France proved especially productive in this regard. But for the most part, the author writes of his experiences in a distinctive mode of literary reminiscence. Tōson is most affecting when engaged in the mode of lyrical sketching that he had mastered while teaching in rural Komoro. In fact, his accumulated impressions of Komoro and its environs, published in 1912 as *Chikumagawa no suketchi* (*Chikuma River Sketches*, 1991), is a masterful example of this genre of pictorial-realist narrative. The following sketch, entitled "In the Pine Forest," is representative:

Our feet make no sound on ground spread deep with fallen pine needles. The remaining daylight filtering through the pine trees seems harsh to our eyes. There is only a bit of yellow remaining in the western sky and not a single bird calls out.

We go out of one pine grove directly into another. Moonlight shines in among the trees and the grove seems smoky from the evening mists that fill it, giving a grayish cast to the spaces between the slender trunks. The distance fades into darkness, the tree trunks are black. We are surrounded by a deep, lonely peacefulness.

(*TZ*, vol. 5, p. 91; tr. Naff, 1991, p. 68)

Whether recounting his youthful vagabonding in the Kansai or the years spent in a Parisian pension, the Tōson narrator remains a detached observer of the scene, prone to introspection and bouts of lyrical melancholy. Travel represented at least the possibility of discovery and spiritual rebirth, as evidenced by the frequent homage to Saigyō and Bashō, celebrated literary travelers who inspired a deepening connection to his literary heritage. And the day-to-day experiences, however mundane, became a repertoire of episode and incident available for subsequent use. The stay in France, for instance, forms the core of *Shinsei* and also generated a set of essays and reminiscences that variously recount the exotic ocean voyages, life in Paris, French arts and culture, and the stay in rural Limoges. The same pattern of travel reportage followed by personal reminiscence applied in the case of Tōson's world tour of 1936–1937.

Travel also served as a source of moral edification, lessons learned along life's journey. This didacticism is especially prominent in the case of the writings for young people, which form a remarkable part of Tōson's autobiographical project. Eager to enter the burgeoning market for youth-oriented literature (*dōwa bungaku*) upon his return from France, Tōson produced the first of what would be four collections of children's stories (*dōwa*), written over three decades, each drawing upon the familiar repertoire of personal reminiscence. He began with *Osanaki mono ni* (1917; For young people), a recounting of the sojourn in France in some eighty brief episodes. Here the author establishes his narrative model: a mixture of personal incidents and moralizing fables, related by an affectionate "Dad" (*Tōsan*) to his own children gathered at his side.

With the second *dōwa* collection, entitled *Furusato* (1920; Village home), the reminiscing father returns to his childhood in Magome, spinning tales of kindly village folk and friendly woodland creatures that evoke homespun virtues—frugality, simplicity, harmony with nature—and traditionalist esprit. What emerges is an idyllic realm of timeless value, a mythic spiritual homeland that would stand as a bulwark against the encroaching modernization of Japanese society and culture. The scene shifts with the next collection, *Osanamonogatari* (1924; Youthful tales). In this sequel to "Village home," the paternal narrator retells his experiences in Tokyo as a young lad who had left his village home.

Following long years spent on the *Before the Dawn* project, Tōson returned to youth-oriented autobiography very late in life, with a final *dōwa* collection entitled *Chikaramochi* (1940; Ricecakes for stamina). This unique work presents, in a series of chronologically ordered episodes, a synopsis of the nearly fifty years of personal narrative. The didactic agenda is conspicuous. Beginning with childhood reminiscence and ending with accounts of the stay in Komoro, the work incorporates hometown moralism, accounts of exemplary characters who have taught important lessons, and the general wisdom acquired by one who has experienced life's journey (*jinsei no tabi*). The patriarchal narrator, revisiting many tales told in earlier works, calls attention to his own childlike spirit (*kodomo no kokoro*) as he constructs this final version of the Tōson saga, presented to the nation's youth for their edification.

Here, once again, the author has eschewed creative storytelling in favor of the unalloyed personalism that was his literary trademark. In fact, Tōson spoke of his *dōwa* writing in almost missionary terms, expressing the wish that this writing would survive as his literary legacy. In the case of *Chikaramochi*, written at a time of war, the task of autobiographical retrospection is placed in the service of contributing to the strengthening of the nation's moral and spiritual fiber.

Yoake mae

Shimazaki Tōson's undisputed masterpiece, *Yoake mae* (Before the Dawn), is typically spoken of as a culmination, a return to family and native roots following years of troubled wandering, a redemptive process of self-discovery achieved through telling the story of Japan's own coming of age in the modern era. This is a monumental work of historical novelization, which consumed fully a decade of research and writing. Most simply put, it traces events in the life of the Shimazaki family, centering on Tōson's father Masaki (renamed Aoyama Hanzō), from the year of Commodore Perry's arrival in Japan (1853) until Masaki's death in 1886.

Tōson's meticulous research, largely conducted in Magome during the 1920s, enabled him to reconstruct the world of his father, a man he knew only through disjointed childhood recollections. Hanzō first appears in *Before the Dawn* as a young intellectual, imperial loyalist, and ardent adherent of the nativist scholar Hirata Atsutane (1776–1843). From his rural outpost in Magome, Hanzō struggles to make sense of the radical changes set in motion by the arrival of foreigners on Japanese soil.

Lavishly interspersed with historical detail, Book One recounts the final years of the Tokugawa shogunate from the vantage point of the small post town nestled in the mountains of Shinshū. Tōson adopts Hanzō's point of view and through it brilliantly evokes the look and feel of nineteenth-century village life. Exquisitely sensitive to the encroachment of Western civilization and the many evils it represents, Hanzō is increasingly drawn to a xenophobic embrace of nativist values. But the pace of change appears relentless.

Book Two commences with the Meiji Restoration of 1868, which witnessed the birth of a new, modern nation of Japan and the gradual demise of the traditional order. The Aoyama family has grown, and a correspondingly large share of the novel details events in the lives of Hanzō's children. Much of the action concerns Okume (modeled on his sister Sono), a disturbed young woman prone to suicidal impulses; and Wasuke (modeled on the author), a bright young lad who is the apple of his father's eye.

But Hanzō continues to dominate the tale, which begins to take on dark tones early in Book Two. The death of his own father is a portentous event, signaling the final demise of the Tokugawa age. He soon falls prey to disorientation and delusion:

> Hanzō began to grow restless. At times he held to the thought of contenting himself in the role of village sage, bringing learning to the untutored children of the farmers. At other times he would realize that this was no time to remain hidden away in the mountains, simply observing the fate of a defunct post station. These impulses were in constant conflict within him.

(*TZ*, vol. 12, p. 325; tr. Naff, 1987, p. 607)

Obsessed with the threat posed by Japan's rampant Westernization, the quixotic Hanzō travels to Tokyo in 1874, intent on being heard. Learning of a planned imperial procession, he inscribes a poem of remonstration on a fan—a traditional gesture of protest—then joins the gathered throng and rushes at the imperial carriage, throwing the fan inside. The assembled crowd is aghast as the half-crazed supplicant is seized by the police.

As recounted in *Before the Dawn*, the final decade of Hanzō's life is marked by a steady retreat into a private world of old books, anxieties, and fugitive dreams. Returning to Magome following the ill-fated trip to Tokyo, Hanzō secludes himself in the house and devotes himself to the education of his children. Painfully aware of the irreversibility of Japan's modernization, he sends his two youngest sons to Tokyo for their schooling. Their absence, however, provokes pangs of loneliness and longing: "He could feel his children everywhere. In his study, sitting on the cushions. In the breast of his kimono, in his sleeves" (*TZ*, vol. 12, p. 448; tr. Naff, 1987, p. 701).

In 1884 the reclusive Hanzō rouses himself and travels to Tokyo to visit his sons. But the arrival on the scene of the awkward, rustic father hardly proves a cause for rejoicing: "To Wasuke the mere presence in this city of a person like Hanzō constituted an uncomfortable dissonance. . . . He could only think of his father as someone back in the Kiso mountains, as if he wanted him to remain there forever. . . . In the end Hanzō gave up with a sigh. Was this the child he had come all the way to Tokyo to see?" (*TZ*, vol. 12, p. 478; tr. Naff, 1987, p. 721).

And so with the accelerating pace of Meiji modernization, Hanzō grows increasingly ineffectual in his role as family head: "The foundations of the house of Aoyama in Magome were crumbling. . . . It was no longer possible to conceal the fact that this family, with traditions and distinguished lineage going back to the late sixteenth century, was being rocked by storms beyond its ability to weather" (*TZ*, vol. 12, p. 456; tr. Naff, 1987, p. 706). Loneliness and isolation give way to delusion and paranoia. Discovered one day in the village temple preparing to set it ablaze, Hanzō is placed in a cell. Here he lives out his remaining days, a madman horribly reduced to an animal existence. His death comes as a welcome release from unspeakable torment.

Through his incarnation as Aoyama Hanzō, Tōson's father Shimazaki Masaki is portrayed as a small man caught up in, and ultimately destroyed by, the great eddying currents of historical change. His favorite son, rescued as it were from a foundering ship, would become a survivor. As a writer he would embrace the modern and achieve success and acclaim, not infrequently at the expense of others. In this sense, *Before the Dawn* can be read as a form of spiritual autobiography. Through this redemptive act of literary reconstruction, Tōson erected a fitting memorial to his father and to an extraordinary chapter of Japanese history.

The Tōson Legacy

As a founding father of modern Japanese literature, Shimazaki Tōson has enjoyed canonical status from the very inception of *kindai bungaku*—modern (Japanese) literature—as an academic discipline. And while his image may not grace any of the nation's banknotes—a status reserved for Natsume Sōseki, who presides over the thousand-yen note—Tōson has never ceased to figure as a cultural icon. Despite its curiously understated style and lack of novelistic interest, his work is widely recognized for its faithful documentation of *kindai* society and culture. Thus Tōson's status reveals much about the role of literature in the construction of a Japanese national identity.

In short, Tōson has figured prominently in what can be called the mythology of *kindai* Japan, a cultural project that deployed certain key writers as witnesses, oracles, fonts of essential wisdom. The enduring appeal of what may be termed the Tōson saga concerns the manner in which the life, painstakingly rendered into a mosaic of personal narratives, is seen as recapitulating the course of *kindai* cultural history itself. Critics have pointed out the archetypal quality of Tōson's themes: the romantic quest for identity and individuality, the anxieties and perplexities of youth, the constraints of family and duty, the return to traditional values and nativist roots. The man, in his elaborate literary transmutation, came to stand for his age. Having borne personal witness to the coming of age of modern Japan, Tōson died on the very cusp of changes that would totally transform the nation in the wake of its crushing defeat in World War II.

The standard literary histories rank Shimazaki Tōson together with Sōseki and Mori Ōgai as figures of sufficient gravity and authority to merit the quasi-official designation of *bungō*—great writer. Detractors, on the other hand, point to the distinctly unimpressive oeuvre redeemed only by a handful of major works (*The Broken Commandment*, *The Family*, and *Before the Dawn*) and by a practiced, if at times sentimental, lyricism that brings life to an otherwise barren narrative landscape. The lofty reputation, they argue, is an artifact of an outmoded *kindai* canon, which reflects the elitism of the *bundan* and its endemic insiderism.

The Japanese literary canon in fact came under attack in the later decades of the twentieth century, a development reflecting the ongoing transformation of Japanese society and culture. Hence the notion of a "Tōson legacy" is indeed problematic. To be sure, the "greatest hits" remain readily available in inexpensive editions, and his name still figures in the literary catechism taught in the nation's schools. But the author has not aged well. The agenda of sincerity and authenticity has little to attract contemporary readers, who are put off by domestic tedium, pained introspection, the insistent paternalism, the cultural chauvinism, and the heavy-handed didacticism. Most ironically, this famously personal writer appears curiously impersonal in his literary guise.

Yet there is another side to the story. Tōson's traditionalism, which taps into the richly emotive concept of *furusato*, or provincial roots, strongly resonates with a trend of nativist thinking whose theme is Japanese uniqueness. Indeed, the traditionalist idyll lives on in Magome, the Shimazaki ancestral village, which has been converted into a sort of national *furusato* theme park, attracting literary pilgrims and day-tripping tourists from far and wide. This and many other "living museums" that dot the landscape attest to a dominant strain of nostalgia among modern-day Japanese. As a literary incarnation of the *kindai* esprit, Shimazaki Tōson—the amalgam of man, work, and legend—may be said to have earned his place in the sun.

Selected Bibliography

PRIMARY WORKS

MAJOR FICTION

Hakai. Tokyo: Uedaya, 1906. Trans. by Kenneth Strong as *The Broken Commandment*. Tokyo: University of Tokyo Press, 1974.

Haru. Tokyo: Uedaya, 1908.

Ie. Tokyo: Uedaya, 1911. Trans. by Cecilia Segawa Seigle as *The Family*. Tokyo: University of Tokyo Press, 1976.

Sakura no mi no jukusuru toki. Tokyo: Shun'yōdō, 1919.

Shinsei. Tokyo: Shun'yōdō, 1919.

Arashi. Tokyo: Shinchōsha, 1927. (Collection of short autobiographical fictions.)

WRITINGS FOR YOUNG PEOPLE

Osanaki mono ni. Tokyo: Jitsugyō no Nihonsha, 1917.

Furusato. Tokyo: Jitsugyō no Nihonsha, 1920.

Osanamonogatari. Tokyo: Kenkyūsha, 1924.

Chikaramochi. Tokyo: Kenkyūsha, 1940.

OTHER MAJOR WORKS

Wakanashū. Tokyo: Shun'yōdō, 1897.

Chikumagawa no suketchi. Tokyo: Sakuma Shobō, 1912. Trans. by William E. Naff as *Chikuma River Sketches*. Honolulu: University of Hawaii Press, 1991.

Yoake mae. Tokyo: Shinchōsha, 1935. Trans. by William E. Naff as *Before the Dawn*. Honolulu: University of Hawaii Press, 1987. (Contains an excellent introductory essay.)

Junrei. Tokyo: Iwanami Shoten, 1940. (Collection of travel narratives originally serialized in 1937.)

Tōson Zenshū. 19 vols. Tokyo: Chikuma Shobō, 1966–1971. (The standard edition of the collected works. Abbreviated as *TZ*, with volume and page numbers, in citations.)

SECONDARY WORKS

CRITICAL AND BIOGRAPHICAL STUDIES

Bourdaghs, Michael. "Shimazaki Tōson's *Hakai* and Its Bodies." In *New Directions in the Study of Meiji Japan*. Edited by Helen Hardacre with Adam Kern. Leiden and New York: Brill, 1997. Pp. 161–188.

Fujii, James A. *Complicit Fictions: The Subject in the Modern Japanese Prose Narrative*. Berkeley: University of California Press, 1993. (See esp. pp. 1–102.)

Itō Kazuo. *Shimazaki Tōson jiten*. Tokyo: Meiji Shoin, 1972.

Keene, Donald. *Dawn to the West: Japanese Literature of the Modern Era*. 2 vols. New York: Holt, 1984. (See vol. 1, pp. 254–271, for discussion of Tōson's prose works, and vol. 2, pp. 204–215, for discussion of his poetry.)

———, ed. *Modern Japanese Literature: An Anthology*. New York: Grove Press, 1956.

Kobayashi Ichirō. *Shimazaki Tōson kenkyū*. Tokyo: Kyōiku Shuppan Sentā, 1986.

Lewell, John. *Modern Japanese Novelists: A Biographical Dictionary*. Tokyo and New York: Kodansha International, 1993. (See the essay "Shimazaki Tōson," pp. 385–398.)

Marcus, Marvin. "Versions of Self in the Writings of Tōson Shimazaki." *The Japan Foundation Newsletter* 27, no. 2:15–20 (January 2000).

McClellan, Edwin. *Two Japanese Novelists: Sōseki and Tōson*. Chicago: University of Chicago Press, 1969.

———. "Tōson and the Autobiographical Novel." In *Tradition and Modernization in Japanese Culture*. Edited by Donald H. Shively. Princeton, N.J.: Princeton University Press, 1971. Pp. 347–378.

Miyoshi Yukio. *Shimazaki Tōson ron*. Tokyo: Chikuma Shobō, 1984.

Walker, Janet A. *The Japanese Novel of the Meiji Period and the Ideal of Individualism*. Princeton, N.J.: Princeton University Press, 1979.

ACKNOWLEDGMENTS

AKUTAGAWA RYŪNOSUKE. Excerpts from "The Martyr" from *Rashomon and Other Stories*, translated by Takashi Kojima. Copyright 1952 by Liveright Publishing Corporation. Reprinted with the permission of Liveright Publishing Corporation. Excerpt from "A Fool's Life" from *The Essential Akutagawa*, edited by Seiji Lippit. Copyright © 1999. Reprinted with the permission of Marsilio Publishers Corp. Excerpt from *Kappa*, translated by Geoffrey Bownas (Tokyo: Tuttle, 1971). Copyright © 1971. Reprinted with the permission of Peter Owen Ltd.

SAKAGUCHI ANGO. Excerpts from "Discourse on Decadence," translated by Seiji M. Lippitt, from *Review of Japanese Culture and Society* (October 1986). Reprinted with the permission of The Center for Inter-Cultural Studies and Education, Josai University, Tokyo.

ATOMIC BOMB WRITERS. Tōge Sankichi, "Eyes," and excerpt from "When Will That Day Come?" translated by Richard Minear, from *Hiroshima: Three Witnesses*. Copyright © 1990 by Princeton University Press. Reprinted with the permission of the publishers.

DAZAI OSAMU. Excerpts from "One Hundred Views of Mt. Fuji" from *Self Portraits: Tales from the Life of Japan's Greatest Decadent Romantic Osamu Dazai*, translated by Ralph McCarthy. Copyright © 1991. Reprinted with the permission of Kodansha International, Ltd.

FUTABATEI SHIMEI. This essay by Dennis Washburn has been revised from sections of his *The Dilemma of the Modern in Japanese Fiction*. Copyright © 1995 by Yale University. Reprinted with the permission of Yale University Press.

HIGUCHI ICHIYŌ. Excerpts from "Child's Play," and "Troubled Waters" from *In the Shade of Spring Leaves: The Life and Writings of Higuchi Ichiyo, A Woman of Letters in Meiji Japan*, edited and translated by Robert Danly. Copyright © 1981 by Robert Danly. Reprinted with the permission of W. W. Norton & Company, Inc.

KAWABATA YASUNARI. Excerpts from "Nature," translated by Michael Emmerich in *First Snow on Fuji*. Copyright © 1999 by Michael Emmerich. Excerpts from "The Dancing Girl of Izu" from *The Dancing Girl of Izu and Other Stories*, translated by J. Martin Holman. Copyright © 1998 by J. Martin Holman. Both reprinted with the permission of Counterpoint Press, a member of Perseus Books, L.L.C.

KŌNO TAEKO. Excerpts from "Toddler-Hunting" and "Snow" from *Toddler-Hunting & Other Stories*, translated by Lucy North. Copyright © 1961 by Kōno Taeko. Reprinted with the permission of New Directions Publishing Corporation.

NISHIWAKI JUNZABURŌ. Excerpt from "A Fragrant Stoker"; excerpts from "Profanus"; excerpts from "No Traveller Returns"; excerpt from "Eterunitasu"; excerpts from "The Extinction of Poetry"; excerpt from "The Song of Choricos"; "Weather"; and "The Sun" from Hosea Hirata, *The Poetry and Poetics of Nishiwaki Junzaburō: Modernism in Translation*. Copyright © 1993 by Princeton University Press. Reprinted with the permission of the publishers. "Tenki," "Taiyo," and excerpts from "Shitsurakuen" from *Teihon, Nishiwaki Junzaburō zenshū*. Copyright © 1981. Reprinted with the permission of Chikuma Shobo Publishing Co. Ltd. Excerpts from "Paradis Perdu" from *Nishiwaki Junzaburō zenshū*, edited by Kagita Yukinobu et al. Copyright © 1983. Reprinted with the permission of Chikuma Shobo Publishing Co. Ltd. Bashō, *karumi*, from Ueda Makoto, *Bashō and His Interpreters: Selected Hokku with Commentary*. Copyright © 1991 by the Board of Trustees of the Leland Stanford Junior University. Reprinted with the permission of the publishers, Stanford University Press.

ŌE KENZABURŌ. Excerpt from "Japan, the Ambiguous, and Myself" (Nobel Prize acceptance speech, 1994) from *Japan, the Ambiguous, and Myself: The Nobel Prize Speech and Other Lectures*. Copyright © 1994 by The Nobel Foundation. Reprinted with the permission of Kodansha International, Ltd.

MORI ŌGAI. Excerpt from "The Dancing Girl," translated by Richard Bowring, from *Mori Ōgai: Youth and Other Stories*, edited by J. Thomas Rimer. Copyright © 1994 by the University of Hawaii Press. Excerpts from "Daydreams" and "Casuistica" from Marvin Marcus, *Paragons of the Ordinary: The Biographical Literature of Mori Ōgai*. Copyright © 1993 by the

University of Hawaii Press. All reprinted with the permission of the publishers.

SHIGA NAOYA. Excerpts from "Reconciliation," translated by Roy Starrs, from *An Artless Art: The Zen Aesthetic of Shiga Naoya*. Copyright © 1998 by Roy Starrs. Reprinted with the permission of Curzon Press, Ltd. Excerpts from *A Dark Night's Passing*, translated by Edwin McClellan. Copyright © 1976. Reprinted with the permission of Kodansha International, Ltd.

NATSUME SŌSEKI. Excerpts from *Grass on the Wayside*, translated by Edwin McClellan. Copyright © 1969. Reprinted with the permission of The University of Chicago Press. Excerpts from "My Individualism," translated by Jay Rubin, in *Kokoro: A Novel, and Selected Essays*, translated by Edwin McClellen. Copyright © 1992. Reprinted with the permission of Madison Books, Inc. Excerpts from *I Am a Cat*, 3 volumes, translated by Aiko Ito and Graeme Wilson. Reprinted with the permission of Charles E. Tuttle Co., Inc. of Boston, Massachusetts and Tokyo, Japan. Excerpts from "The Civilization of Modern-day Japan," and "Kokoro" translated by Jay Rubin, in *Kokoro: A Novel, and Selected Essays*, translated by Edwin McClellan. Copyright © 1992. Reprinted with the permission of Madison Books, Inc.

SHIMAZAKI TŌSON. "I am like the morning cloud" and excerpt from "The Family" from Edwin McClellan, *Two Japanese Novelists: Sōseki and Tōson*. Copyright © 1969. Reprinted with the permission of The University of Chicago Press. Excerpts from *The Broken Commandment*, translated by Kenneth Strong. Copyright © 1974. Reprinted with the permission of the University of Tokyo Press. Excerpt from "In the Pine Forest" from *Chikuma River Sketches*, translated by William Naff. Copyright © 1991 by University of Hawaii Press. Reprinted with the permission of the publishers.

CONTRIBUTORS

Davinder L. Bhowmik. Assistant Professor of Japanese literature at the University of Washington. Her publications include the translation of "Ukuma Junsa," in *Southern Exposure: Modern Japanese Literature from Okinawa.* KŌNO TAEKO

Christopher Bolton. Assistant Professor of Japanese at the University of California, Riverside. His doctoral dissertation was titled "Science and Fiction in the Work of Abe Kōbō." ABE KŌBŌ

Charles Cabell. Assistant Professor of Japanese culture in the Department of Foreign Languages and Literatures at the University of Montana. He received his Ph.D. from the Department of East Asian Languages and Civilizations at Harvard University in 1999. His dissertation, "Maiden Dreams: Kawabata Yasunari's Beautiful Japanese Empire, 1930–1945," explored the relationship of Japanese culture and empire. KAWABATA YASUNARI

Joel Cohn. Associate Professor of Japanese at the University of Hawaii at Manoa. He is the author of *Studies in the Comic Spirit in Modern Japanese Fiction.* DAZAI OSAMU

James Dorsey. Assistant Professor of Japanese at Dartmouth College. He is finishing a manuscript on the critic Kobayashi Hideo and coediting a book of translations and essays on Sakaguchi Ango. SAKAGUCHI ANGO

Matthew Fraleigh. Ph.D. candidate in the Department of East Asian Languages and Civilizations at Harvard University. His primary area of research is literature of the late Tokugawa and early Meiji period, specifically Ryūhoku and his contemporaries. NARUSHIMA RYŪHOKU

Ted Goossen. Professor at York University. SHIGA NAOYA

Howard Hibbett Professor at Harvard University. AKUTAGAWA RYŪNOSUKE

Hosea Hirata. Associate Professor of Japanese at Tufts University. He is the author of *The Poetry and Poetics of Nishiwaki Junzaburō: Modernism in Translation.* NISHIWAKI JUNZABURŌ

Charles Shirō Inouye. Associate Professor of Japanese and Dean of the Colleges at Tufts University. He is the author of *Japanese Gothic Tales by Izumi Kyōka* and *The Similitude of Blossoms—A Critical Biography of Izumi Kyōka, Japanese Novelist and Playwright.* IZUMI KYŌKA

Phyllis I. Lyons. Associate Professor of Japanese Language and Literature at Northwestern University. Among her publications are *The*

Saga of Dazai Osamu: A Critical Study with Translations, which won the 1983 Friendship Fund Japanese Literary Translation Award. She is currently writing a book on Tanizaki Jun'ichirō. TANIZAKI JUN'ICHIRŌ

Marvin Marcus. Associate Professor of Japanese at Washington University in St. Louis. His publications include *Paragons of the Ordinary: The Biographical Literature of Mori Ōgai* and "The Writer Speaks: Late Meiji Reflections on Literature and Life," in *The Distant Isle*. MORI ŌGAI and SHIMAZAKI TŌSON

Lucy North. Received her Ph.D. from Harvard University in 2000. She has translated a collection of stories by Kōno Taeko, *Toddler-Hunting and Other Stories*. ENCHI FUMIKO

Jay Rubin. Professor of Japanese literature at Harvard University. He has published work on prewar literary censorship and on Natsume Sōseki and Murakami Haruki, in addition to several translations of works by both authors. MURAKAMI HARUKI and NATSUME SŌSEKI

Atsuko Sakaki. Associate Professor in the Department of East Asian Studies at the University of Toronto. Her publications include *Recontextualizing Texts: Narrative Performance in Modern Japanese Fiction* and *The Woman with the Flying Head and Other Stories by Kurahashi Yumiko*. KURAHASHI YUMIKO

Ann Sherif. Professor at Oberlin College and the author of *Mirrors: The Fiction and Essays of Koda Aya*. She has translated fiction by Koda Aya, Yoshimoto Banana, and other Japanese authors. HIGUCHI ICHIYŌ

Stephen Snyder. Professor of Japanese literature at the University of Colorado, Boulder. He is the author of *Fictions of Desire: Narrative Form in the Novels of Nagai Kafū* and coeditor of *Ōe and Beyond: Fiction in Contemporary Japan*. He has also translated works by Ōe Kenzaburō, Murakami Ryu, and Yoshimura Akira. NAGAI KAFŪ

Karen Thornber. Ph.D. candidate in the Department of East Asian Languages and Civilizations at Harvard University. ATOMIC BOMB WRITERS

Dennis Washburn. Professor of Japanese and Comparative Literature at Dartmouth College. He is the author of *The Dilemma of the Modern in Japanese Fiction*, coeditor of *Word and Image in Japanese Cinema*, and translator of Ōoka Shōhei's *The Shade of Blossoms* and Yokomitsu Riichi's *Shanghai*. FUTABATEI SHIMEI, MISHIMA YUKIO and ŌE KENZABURŌ

Eve Zimmerman. Assistant Professor of Modern Japanese Literature at Wellesley College. Her recent translation, *The Cape and Other Stories from the Japanese Ghetto*, was published by Stone Bridge Press in 1999. NAKAGAMI KENJI

INDEX

T

ISBN 0-684-80598-7

90000